Healthcare Information Technology Exam Guide for CHTS and CAHIMS Certifications

Healthcare Information Technology Exam Guide for CHTS and CAHIMS Certifications

Kathleen A. McCormick, Ph.D.
Brian Gugerty, DNS, R.N.
John E. Mattison, M.D.

New York   Chicago   San Francisco
Athens   London   Madrid   Mexico City
Milan   New Delhi   Singapore   Sydney   Toronto

Library of Congress Cataloging-in-Publication Data

Names: McCormick, Kathleen Ann, author. | Gugerty, Brian, author. | Mattison, John E., author.
Title: Healthcare information technology exam guide for CHTS and CAHIMS certifications / Kathleen A. McCormick, Ph.D., Brian Gugerty, DNS, R.N., John E. Mattison, M.D.
Other titles: Healthcare information technology exam guide for CompTIA healthcare IT technician and HIT Pro certifications
Description: Second edition. | New York : McGraw-Hill Education, [2017] | Revision of: Healthcare information technology exam guide for CompTIA healthcare IT technician and HIT Pro certifications / Dr. Kathleen Ann Mccormick, Dr. Brian Gugerty. 2013.
Identifiers: LCCN 2017032761 | ISBN 9781259836978
Subjects: LCSH: Health services administration—Information technology—Examinations—Study guides. | Medical informatics—Examinations—Study guides. | Electronic data processing personnel—Certification—Study guides. | Computer technicians—Certification—Study guides. | BISAC: COMPUTERS / Certification Guides / General.
Classification: LCC RA971.6 .M29 2017 | DDC 362.10285—dc23 LC record available at https://lccn.loc.gov/2017032761

McGraw-Hill Education books are available at special quantity discounts to use as premiums and sales promotions, or for use in corporate training programs. To contact a representative, please visit the Contact Us pages at www.mhprofessional.com.

Healthcare Information Technology Exam Guide for CHTS and CAHIMS Certifications

This book was written by John E. Mattison in his private capacity. No official support or endorsement by Kaiser Permanente is intended or should be inferred.

Brian Gugerty's chapter authoring contributions and editorial work contained in this book do not represent the official position of the Centers for Disease Control and Prevention.

Sheila A. Ochylski's chapter authoring contributions and editorial work contained in this book do not represent the official position of the Veterans Health Administration.

HL7®, HEALTH LEVEL SEVEN®, CARE CONNECTED BY HL7®, CCD®, CDA®, FHIR®, and GREENCDA™ are trademarks owned by Health Level Seven International. HL7®, HEALTH LEVEL SEVEN®, CARE CONNECTED BY HL7®, CCD®, CDA®, and FHIR® are registered with the United States Patent and Trademark Office.

1 2 3 4 5 6 7 8 9   LCR   21 20 19 18 17

ISBN: Book p/n 978-1-259-83693-0 and CD p/n 978-1-259-83694-7
of set 978-1-259-83697-8

MHID: Book p/n 1-259-83693-2 and CD p/n 1-259-83694-0
of set 1-259-83697-5

Sponsoring Editor Timothy Green	**Acquisitions Coordinator** Claire Yee	**Indexer** Jack Lewis	**Illustration** Cenveo Publisher Services
Editorial Supervisor Janet Walden	**Copy Editor** William McManus	**Production Supervisor** Pamela Pelton	**Art Director, Cover** Jeff Weeks
Project Editor Howie Severson, Fortuitous Publishing	**Proofreader** Paul Tyler	**Composition** Cenveo® Publisher Services	

Information has been obtained by McGraw-Hill Education from sources believed to be reliable. However, because of the possibility of human or mechanical error by our sources, McGraw-Hill Education, or others, McGraw-Hill Education does not guarantee the accuracy, adequacy, or completeness of any information and is not responsible for any errors or omissions or the results obtained from the use of such information.

This book is dedicated to our families, since books are "family affairs." We express gratitude for our family members' support, encouragement, and patience while we took evenings and weekends away from them to write the book and coordinate the chapters.

The growing McCormick Family now includes a Kate, Anina, Prunella, and Christine, in addition to Francis, Sr., Francis, Jr., Ellen, Simon, and Christopher. I am forever grateful to this family throughout the years that were spent on developing this book.

Brian Gugerty dedicates the book to Kathleen Bartley, his wife, Sean, Ryan, and Dylan, his sons, and to the memory of Helen M. Gugerty, R.N., and Leo J. Gugerty.

John dedicates the book to Mindy, his wife, Shawn, Michelle, and Heidi, his children, and his parents Jim and Joanne, who inspired us all toward kindness and service to others.

The book is also dedicated to the HIT professionals, clinical informaticians, and STEM professionals in healthcare organizations, HIT-focused companies, government agencies, and professional associations that the authors have been privileged to work with, learn from, and be inspired by.

ABOUT THE LEAD AUTHORS

Kathleen A. McCormick, Ph.D., R.N., FACMI, FAAN, FHIMSS, is an author, senior practitioner, and consultant in healthcare informatics, genomics, and bioinformatics. She has authored or co-authored more than eight books and hundreds of publications, including the McGraw-Hill title *Essentials of Nursing Informatics*, now in its sixth edition. Dr. McCormick has a B.S. and M.S. in nursing and an M.S. and Ph.D. in physiology, and has been involved in informatics since 1978. As a tenured scientist at the National Institutes of Health, Dr. McCormick retired as a 06 Captain in the U.S. Public Health Service. Following her retirement, she worked for 16 years in the healthcare IT industry as a vice president and chief senior scientist/executive contractor for SRA (now CSRA), SAIC, and Leidos. Since 2013, Dr. McCormick has been a lecturer, author, and consultant. Her fellowships in informatics include the College of Medical Informatics through AMIA, the American Academy of Nursing, and the Healthcare Information and Management Systems Society (HIMSS). Dr. McCormick is an elected fellow of the prestigious National Academy of Sciences, National Academy of Medicine (formerly the Institute of Medicine).

Brian Gugerty, DNS, R.N., is a Senior Service Fellow at the CDC's National Center for Health Statistics/Division of Health Care Statistics, where he advises Center leadership on healthcare data standards and policy issues regarding interoperability. As the founder and former CEO of GiC Informatics, he developed innovative approaches to assist physicians and clinicians to effectively and efficiently use EHRs during the critical EHR "go-live" period and then optimize EHR use on an ongoing basis. Dr. Gugerty has been in the clinical informatics field for 27 years. His experience includes teaching, clinical informatics research, clinical software development, and consulting to healthcare organizations. Dr. Gugerty has authored or co-authored more than 40 articles and book chapters on the theory, practice, and future of clinical informatics and is a frequent presenter of these topics.

John E. Mattison, M.D., is Chief Medical Information Officer and Assistant Medical Director for Kaiser Permanente, SCAL. Dr. Mattison focuses on transforming care delivery with information technology, through convergence of exponential technologies and data liquidity. He led the design and implementation of the largest integrated electronic health record in the United States, and is the founder of the international XML standard for health record interoperability known as CDA, CCD, and CCDA. He has led various national innovation programs including virtual care, sponsored or led numerous digital health projects implemented at scale, is senior advisor to the Tricorder X-Prize, and mentors many digital health startups. Dr. Mattison chairs the eHealth Workgroup of the Global Alliance for Genomics and Health (GA4GH) and is a board member of Open mHealth, the NIH-funded "Policy and Ethics in Precision Medicine," the Simms-Mann Foundation, BioCOM, Big Data Advisory Board, and IOT Advisory Board. He teaches at multiple universities, including Exponential Medicine at Singularity University, UCSD, Stanford, USC, and UCLA. Dr. Mattison has published widely on IOT, global genomics, policy, privacy, security, international research collaboration models, interoperability, mobile health, community health, mindfulness and resilience, and healthcare transformation. He has published in *Nature*, *JAMIA*, and *JAMA*, has been quoted in *Wall Street Journal*, *Forbes*, *Fast Company*, *Modern Healthcare*, *Modern Physician*, *Mobile Health News*, and *Sloan Management Review*, and has authored chapters for four books. Dr. Mattison keynotes and hosts many national and international conferences and frequently consults globally. He is an active participant on several global initiatives to bring Internet services to underserved communities to provide access to both jobs and healthcare. His contributions to healthcare have been recognized by various national awards. His current work focuses on leveraging a Motivational Formulary®™ with motivicons®™ across the Healthcare Plecosystem®™ to restore ancient wisdom, mindfulness, and resilience while creating a "Behavioral Symphony of Wellness."®™

A recent keynote video featuring Dr. Mattison is available for viewing at https://exponential.singularityu.org/medicine/innovation-at-scale-virtues-of-plecosystem-approach-with-john-mattison/.

About the Foreword Author

John D. Halamka, M.D., M.S., is the International Healthcare Innovation Professor at Harvard Medical School, Chief Information Officer of the Beth Israel Deaconess System, and a practicing emergency physician. He strives to improve healthcare quality, safety, and efficiency for patients, providers, and payers throughout the world using information technology. He has written five books, several hundred articles, and the popular Geekdoctor blog. He is also an organic farmer in Sherborn, Massachusetts, overseeing 15 acres of agriculture, animals, and cider/mead making.

About the Section Editors

Part I: Healthcare and Information Technology in the United States

J. Marc Overhage, M.D., Ph.D., is a general internist who earned a doctorate in biophysics and completed a fellowship in medical informatics. During his 25-year tenure at Regenstrief Institute and Indiana University, Dr. Overhage practiced medicine, served as the Sam Regenstrief Professor of Medical Informatics, and studied a variety of informatics topics including clinical decision support, the impact of healthcare IT on providers, and health information exchange. During that time, along with his colleagues, he developed the Indiana Network for Patient Care and studied the role of health information exchange on public and population health. Subsequently, he founded and served as CEO of the Indiana Health Information Exchange before becoming the Chief Medical

Informatics Officer for Siemens Healthcare and now Cerner Corporation. Dr. Overhage is a Master of the American College of Physicians, a fellow of the American College of Medical Informatics, and a fellow of the National Academy of Medicine.

Part II: Fundamentals of Healthcare Information Science

Andre Kushniruk, M.Sc., Ph.D., is a professor in health informatics and Director of the School of Health Information Science at the University of Victoria in Canada. He is also an adjunct professor at Aalborg University in Denmark and an honorary professor at the University of Hong Kong. He is a fellow of the American College of Medical Informatics and a fellow of the Canadian Academy of Health Sciences. Dr. Kushniruk conducts research in a number of areas including usability engineering, electronic health records, evaluation of the effects of information technology, human-computer interaction in healthcare and other domains, and cognitive science. He has published widely in the area of health informatics, with over 200 peer-reviewed publications, and his work is known internationally. Dr. Kushniruk has advised on a variety of key national and international committees and projects. He focuses on developing new methods for the evaluation of healthcare IT and studying human-computer interaction in healthcare. Dr. Kushniruk holds undergraduate degrees in psychology and biology, as well as an M.Sc. in computer science and a Ph.D. in cognitive psychology from McGill University.

Part III: Healthcare Information Standards and Regulation

Donald T. Mon, Ph.D., is a senior director in the Digital Health Policy and Standards (DHPS) department at Research Triangle Institute (RTI), where he leads the standards and interoperability practice. In this capacity, he represents RTI in key national and international standards development activities and directs RTI's business development and project implementation related to data, functional, and interoperability standards. Dr. Mon has served as board chair of Health Level Seven International (HL7), co-chair of the HL7 EHR Work Group, president of the Public Health Data Standards Consortium, and subject-matter expert in the U.S. Technical Advisory Group (the U.S. representative to ISO Technical Committee 215–Health Informatics). Dr. Mon has more than 35 years of experience in health information management (HIM), healthcare IT, and informatics. Prior to joining RTI, Dr. Mon was vice president of practice leadership at the American Health Information Management Association (AHIMA), where he led the implementation of AHIMA's top strategic national and international initiatives. He has developed IT strategic and business process reengineering plans, and helped design, develop, and maintain large-scale databases and information systems for the Biological Sciences Division/Pritzker School of Medicine at the University of Chicago, Catholic Healthcare West, University of Illinois at Chicago, Premier, Inc., Oracle Corporation, Rush University Medical Center, and Schwab Rehabilitation Hospital.

Part IV: Implementing, Managing, and Maintaining Healthcare IT

Michael J. Beller, M.D., M.M.M., is a vice president and physician executive working in Cerner Corporation's Investor Owned/Federal Organization. He currently serves as the lead physician for the Cerner/Leidos partnership implementing a new electronic health record for the Military Health System. Prior to joining Cerner in 2001, Dr. Beller was a Family Medicine Residency Director for Intermountain Healthcare in Provo, Utah. He has published articles on computerized physician order entry, quality improvement, and management and has presented to audiences around the country on CPOE and quality of care. He received his medical degree from Creighton University and a master's in medical management from Tulane University.

Part V: Optimizing Healthcare IT

Lead author **John E. Mattison**, M.D., CMIO.

Part VI: Making It All Secure: Healthcare IT Privacy, Security, and Confidentiality

Lori Reed-Fourquet, M.C.S., is a principal at e-HealthSign, LLC, consulting in health informatics. She is the convener for ISO TC215, WG4 on Health Information Security, Privacy, and Patient Safety. She is also a member of the IT Infrastructure Planning and Technical committees; IHE Quality, Research, and Public Health Planning and Technical committees; and the HL7 Security and HL7 Public Health and Emergency Response committees. Ms. Reed-Fourquet has been working in medical and health informatics for more than 20 years, serving in numerous leadership capacities creating successful collaborations involving diverse healthcare communities in competing markets. She was part of the contracting teams to the Office of the National Coordinator for Health Information Technology (ONC) and the Security and Privacy and the Standards Harmonization initiatives as part of the U.S. efforts to advance nationwide interoperable healthcare IT. She serves as a technical assessor for the American National Standards Institute (ANSI), the ONC Approved Accreditor for the Permanent Certification Program for Health Information Technology (HIT). She holds a master's of computer science degree from Rensselaer Polytechnic Institute.

About the Contributors

Chris Apgar, CISSP, CEO, and president of Apgar & Associates, LLC, is a nationally recognized information security, privacy, HIPAA, and electronic health information exchange expert. He has more than 17 years of experience assisting healthcare organizations comply with HIPAA, HITECH, and other privacy and security regulations. Mr. Apgar also has assisted healthcare, utilities, and financial organizations implement privacy and security safeguards to protect against organizational harm and harm to consumers. Mr. Apgar is also a nationally known speaker and author. Mr. Apgar has been a Certified Information Systems Security Professional since 2002 and he is a senior member of the Information Systems Security Association. His education includes a bachelor of science degree in psychology and an associate of science degree in accounting. Mr. Apgar served on the Work Group for Electronic Data Interchange board of directors for eight years and is the chair of the Oregon Prescription Drug Monitoring Program Advisory Commission.

Dixie B. Baker, Ph.D., M.S., M.S., FHIMSS, is a Senior Partner at healthcare consulting firm Martin, Blanck & Associates, where she provides consulting services in the areas of healthcare IT, EHR technology, privacy and security technology, and the sharing and protection of genomic and clinical data. Dr. Baker was one of the original members of the Health IT Standards Committee (HITSC) when it was formed in 2009, and served the full two terms allowed by law. Dr. Baker chaired the HITSC Security Workgroup throughout her tenure, and led the Nationwide Health Information Network (NwHIN) Power Team that developed metrics for assessing the readiness of technology specifications to become national standards. Dr. Baker co-chairs the Security Working Group of the Global Alliance for Genomics and Health, a worldwide coalition to facilitate the sharing of genomic and clinical data to accelerate the discovery and translation of biomedical knowledge. She is a member of the Advisory Council for Health Level Seven International (HL7), and the Academy of Medicine's DIGITizE Action Collaborative, which is developing standards for integrating genomic data into EHRs. She also serves on the Scientific Advisory Board of the European Genome-Phenome Archive (EGA) of the European Bioinformatics Institute (EBI), and on the Institutional Review Board for Genetic Alliance. Dr. Baker is a fellow of the Healthcare Information and Management Systems Society (HIMSS). In 2013, HealthcareInfoSecurity.com named Dr. Baker one of its inaugural "Top 10 Influencers in Health Information Security" and in 2017, Health Data Management named her one of the top 75 Most Powerful Women in Healthcare IT. Dr. Baker holds a Ph.D. in special education and an M.S. in computer science from the University of Southern California,

as well as M.S. and B.S. degrees from Florida State University and The Ohio State University, respectively.

Kimberly Baldwin-Stried Reich, M.B.S., M.J., PBCI, RHIA, CPHQ, FAHIMA, is a credentialed healthcare information management, quality management, case management, and healthcare compliance professional with more than 25 years of experience in a variety of healthcare settings. Ms. Baldwin-Stried Reich holds a master's of business from the Lake Forest Graduate School of management, a master's of jurisprudence in health law and policy from the Loyola School of Law-Beazley Institute for Health Law and Policy in Chicago, and a post-baccalaureate certificate in clinical informatics (PBCI) from the Johns Hopkins School of Medicine. Ms. Baldwin-Stried Reich is the first Registered Health Information Administrator (RHIA) to successfully complete the Johns Hopkins program and is a 2011 recipient of the AHIMA e-HIM Triumph Award. Ms. Baldwin-Stried Reich is currently employed as a compliance and case management professional for Lake County Physicians' Association in Waukegan, Illinois. She is the lead author of *E-Discovery and Electronic Records* (AHIMA Press).

Elizabeth Borycki, R.N., HBScN, M.N., Ph.D., is the Director of the Social Dimensions of Health program and the Director of the Health and Society program in the Office of Interdisciplinary Studies at the University of Victoria in Victoria, British Columbia, Canada. She is a professor in the School of Health Information Science at the University of Victoria. Her research interests include clinical informatics, health information systems safety, patient safety, human factors, and educating health professionals about EHRs and health services research. Dr. Borycki has authored or co-authored over 150 articles, book chapters, and books. She has served as Academic Representative for Canada for Canada's Health Informatics Association (2007–2013) and as Vice President representing North America on the board of directors for the International Medical Informatics Association (IMIA; 2010–2013). Dr. Borycki founded the IMIA working group focusing on health informatics for patient safety and is currently the Scientific Program Committee Co-Chair for Medinfo 2017. Dr. Borycki returned to the board of directors of IMIA in August 2016 as Vice President, Special Affairs. She received her Ph.D. from the Department of Health Policy, Management, and Evaluation at the University of Toronto, a master's degree in geriatrics and community health nursing from the University of Manitoba, and an honors bachelor's of science in nursing degree from Lakehead University.

Jane Brokel, Ph.D., R.N., FNI, is currently an adjunct assistant professor for the University of Iowa College of Nursing and a nurse for Heartland Home Care, Inc. She has taught nursing, research, and informatics courses the past six years. She serves on the executive committee and advisory council for the state of Iowa Health Information Network to represent nursing's perspective in developing health information exchange. Dr. Brokel is the current president of NANDA International, Inc., an international nursing organization defining nursing knowledge, and has published on the experiences and findings with patient-centered workflows, clinical decision support knowledge development, and measuring patient-desired outcomes. She has more than 35 years of experience in various nursing roles, which includes 20 years using databases and healthcare information technologies.

Brian Dixon, Ph.D., M.P.A., FHIMSS, is an associate professor at the Indiana University Richard M. Fairbanks School of Public Health and a research scientist at the Regenstrief Institute Center for Biomedical Informatics in Indianapolis, Indiana. Dr. Dixon's research focuses on applying informatics methods and tools to improve population health in clinical and public health organizations. His work leverages clinical and administrative data in electronic health records to improve population outcomes, better understand threats to public health as well as care delivery processes, examine public health business processes, and make population surveillance more efficient. Dr. Dixon's research also involves the design, implementation, and evaluation of information infrastructures as well as data quality in support of continuous use of electronic data. Dr. Dixon also teaches courses on informatics and health information exchange to future leaders in clinical and public health. Before joining the faculty at Indiana University, Dr. Dixon managed informatics research and development projects for Regenstrief and the Indiana Health Information Exchange.

Floyd P. Eisenberg, M.D., M.P.H., FACP, is president of iParsimony, LLC, serving organizations and clinical system vendors interested in repurposing data for measurement, clinical decision support, reporting, and research. Dr. Eisenberg received his M.D. degree from Penn State University, followed by a residency in internal medicine at Abington Memorial Hospital in Abington, Pennsylvania, and a fellowship in infectious diseases at Temple University.

His experience includes ten years of clinical practice in Norristown, Pennsylvania; network quality improvement activities at Independence Blue Cross; and EHR development at Siemens Medical Solutions Health Services. He led the initial efforts to develop healthcare standards to express quality measurement directly from EHRs at National Quality Forum and subsequently as an independent consultant. Dr. Eisenberg is currently working on harmonization standards for clinical decision support and measurement as well as collaborating with the HIMSS Immunization Integration Program for EHRs. He is a member of the Health IT Standards Committee (HITSC) of the Office of the National Coordinator for Health Information Technology (ONC), and a co-chair of the HL7 Clinical Quality Information Workgroup.

Alistair Erskine, M.D., is Chief Informatics Officer at the Geisinger Health System. He is responsible for sequencing innovative technologies, harmonizing data across the enterprise, and aligning healthcare systems to optimize patient experience. Dr. Erskine heads the Division of Informatics, which engages staff in the design and configuration of Geisinger's clinical information systems and evolves Geisinger's facilities to take advantage of ultramodern technologies. Dr. Erskine oversees Geisinger's Unified Data Architecture, a hedged data management environment powered by big data and traditional relational database systems to ensure that data collected as a byproduct of clinical and research investigation are accessible for new discovery and appropriate secondary use. Dr Erskine is the Program Director of Geisinger's ACGME-accredited Clinical Informatics Fellowship program and participates on

several clinical informatics research grants (e.g., PCORI, NIH). Prior to Geisinger, Dr. Erskine was appointed Associate Dean of Medical Informatics at Virginia Commonwealth University and was a member of the board for the 650-physician Medical College of Physicians practice plan. Dr. Erskine trained at Brown University and Virginia Commonwealth University Health System and is triple board-certified in internal medicine, clinical informatics, and pediatrics. He is currently engaged in a two-year program with MIT Sloan School of Management and is on faculty at The Ohio State University in the department of biomedical informatics.

Cheryl A. Fisher, Ed.D., R.N.–BC, is currently the program director for Professional Development for Nursing and Patient Care Services at the National Institutes of Health Clinical Center, in Bethesda, Maryland. She received her doctorate in instructional technology from Towson University and has a postgraduate certificate in nursing informatics from the University of Maryland and a postgraduate certificate in nursing education. Dr. Fisher is responsible for all the central nursing education at the NIH Clinical Center and is actively working to reconceptualize courses utilizing technology to increase accessibility of all educational offerings. She is an adjunct professor for the University of Maryland and teaches graduate courses in nursing informatics. Dr. Fisher is also board certified in nursing informatics.

Amy Lorraine Flick, PMP, is a Principal Owner and Project Leadership Practice Lead at DPT. DPT stands for "Driving Performance Together" and is a business performance consulting firm based in Grand Rapids, Michigan, specializing in customer relationship management (CRM), business process management, and project leadership. Ms. Flick is a graduate of the University of Notre Dame, receiving a bachelor's of business administration with a marketing concentration. Her career in healthcare began in 1992 at Parke-Davis Pharmaceutical in field sales for Michigan and Northern Indiana providers, pharmacies, and hospitals. Building upon her sales experiences in primary care, hospitals, and neurology, Ms. Flick performed key training, project, technology, and leadership roles in pharmaceuticals, healthcare benefits, and for a nationally recognized not-for-profit health system in Michigan. Ms. Flick earned the Project Management Professional (PMP) certification in 2005. In 2008, she joined DPT as a Senior Consultant, and her focus became working with senior leaders in for-profit and not-for-profit organizations to create, grow, improve, and innovate business performance. Ms. Flick became a Principal Owner of DPT in 2011, achieving a longtime personal goal for entrepreneurship. Amy specializes in the design and organization of work to align with strategic plan objectives, governance model design, vendor partner relationship management advisory, project portfolio design and implementation, and operational area assessment and advisory supporting due diligence work for mergers and acquisitions.

Lisa A. Gallagher, BSEE, CISM, CPHIMS, FHIMSS, has over 30 years of professional experience in systems engineering, hardware design, and software development, as well as healthcare privacy, security, and public policy. Ms. Gallagher is currently Managing Director in PwC's Healthcare Industries Advisory Cybersecurity and Privacy practice. She most recently served as Vice President, Technology Solutions for the Healthcare Information and Management Systems Society (HIMSS). Ms. Gallagher is currently a co-chair of the ONC Health IT Standards Committee (HITSC) to the HHS Office of the National Coordinator for Health IT (ONC) in a data security expert role.

Diane Hibbs, D.O., FACOOG, is a physician executive with Cerner Corporation. In this role, she is responsible for improving physician satisfaction with and usage of technologies to influence and enhance patient care. Prior to her current role, she served as a physician informaticist with Banner Health. Clinically trained as an OB/GYN, she continues to be an end user of an EMR as a part-time OB hospitalist.

Julie Hollberg, M.D., is the Chief Medical Information Officer for Emory Healthcare and Assistant Professor, Division of Hospital Medicine, Department of Medicine at Emory University School of Medicine. In her current role, Dr. Hollberg is responsible for providing medical direction and governance for the system's electronic medical record and related clinical applications. Her focus is on increasing the usability of EMR systems for clinicians and using information technology to improve the quality and safety of patient care.

Liz Johnson, M.S.N, FAAN, FCHIME, FHIMSS, CHCIO, R.N.–BC, is the nationally recognized and award-winning Chief Information Officer, Acute Care Hospitals & Applied Clinical Informatics for Tenet Healthcare. Ms. Johnson provides the strategic vision and tactical planning for all clinical, patient management, imaging, productivity, and supply chain systems used across Tenet's acute-care hospitals nationwide. As a pioneer in nursing and nurse informatics, Ms. Johnson led the most aggressive and successful EHR implementation effort in the nation. Due to her leadership, Tenet Healthcare is now a national model of healthcare reform, using quantifiable data to transform clinical practice to enhance care delivery and improve patient outcomes through the use of EHR systems. Ms. Johnson is also honored to serve in various elected, assigned, and philanthropic positions at the national level, including appointment to the Health IT Standards Committee (HITSC) of the Office of the National Coordinator (ONC); appointment to the Health Level 7 International (HL7) board of directors; and election by the College of Health Information Management Executives (CHIME) to the board of directors and as CHIME Board Chair. Ms. Johnson has been recognized in the industry as one of "The Most Powerful Women in Healthcare IT" and as one of "50 Top Healthcare Information Technology Experts" for being a guiding light in the industry and advancing the important work of healthcare IT.

Bipin Karunakaran, M.S., M.B.A., is the Vice President of Enterprise Data Management at Geisinger Health Systems. He is responsible for the build and implementation of major data processing, aggregation, and reporting systems, including the big data system at Geisinger. He is also responsible for advanced analytics systems used to process millions of clinical notes to extract key diagnosis using Natural Language Processing (NLP) and predictive modeling, helping providers make better informed care decisions. Mr. Karunakaran was the principal developer for Microsoft's first version of the digital media encoder on the Web. He led the team at the Walt Disney Company responsible for the first companywide implementation of big data. Mr. Karunakaran has held board seats as a technical advisor for two major startups. He received his M.S. in computer science and engineering from University of Washington, Seattle, and his M.B.A. from the UCLA Anderson School of Business, Los Angeles.

J. Michael Kramer, M.D., M.B.A., is a senior vice president and the chief quality officer with Spectrum Health. As chief quality officer, Dr. Kramer is the leader for Spectrum Health's Quality Outcomes and Electronic Medical Records teams. He is actively engaged in advancing the quality, safety, and analytics strategy of all Spectrum Health's inpatient, outpatient, and insurance businesses. In his CMIO roles, Dr. Kramer has been a national leader in designing methodologies for implementing and optimizing systems that assist clinicians in achieving high-quality care and evidence-based outcomes. Dr. Kramer brings to his role as CQO more than 20 years of information systems experience. He previously taught applied clinical informatics at the University of Michigan. Dr. Kramer is currently highly engaged in implementing MACRA and supporting the integrated care model across Spectrum Health's 180 practice locations and 9 hospitals using five different electronic medical records.

Philip J. Kroth, M.D., M.S., is an associate professor at the University of New Mexico (UNM) School of Medicine. He is also the director of the Biomedical Informatics Research, Training and Scholarship unit at the UNM Health Sciences Library and Informatics Center and Section Chief of Clinical Informatics in the UNM Department of Internal Medicine. Before joining UNM in 2004, Dr. Kroth received his B.S. in computer engineering from the Rochester Institute of Technology in 1987, his M.D. degree from the Medical College of Ohio in 1995, and completed his residency in internal medicine at the State University of New York at Buffalo in 1999. He completed a research fellowship in biomedical informatics at the Regenstrief Institute at the Indiana University Medical Center, where he also earned an M.S. in clinical research in 2003. At UNM, in addition to practicing as a general internist, Dr. Kroth directs a post-doctoral research fellowship in biomedical informatics as well as the new clinical informatics fellowship for physicians. Dr. Kroth is board certified in both internal medicine and clinical informatics.

Roman Mateyko has worked in the telecommunications industry in both management and engineering roles in the private and public sector. After moving to Victoria in 1988, he joined the Government of British Columbia where he worked in engineering, service management, contract management, planning, and strategy. During his tenure as a Network Planning Manager, he was responsible for the planning and engineering of the Provincial Learning Network, which connected 2,000 schools to SPAN/BC, the province's data network. He is currently Executive Director, Architecture and Planning Administrator's Office of the CIO in the Ministry of Labour, Citizens' Services. Before joining government, Mr. Mateyko worked in the cellular industry and for a common carrier. His experience includes negotiations, contract management, service management,

engineering, planning, implementation, and operations of large-scale physical and logical networks. Mr. Mateyko has a bachelor of applied science in electrical engineering from the University of Toronto, is a professional engineer, a member of the IEEE, and is currently an adjunct assistant professor at the University of Victoria.

Mac McMillan is co-founder and CEO of CynergisTek, Inc., a top-ranked information security and privacy consulting firm focused on the healthcare IT industry. He is a member of CHIME's AEHIS Advisory Board, recognized as a HIMSS fellow, and former chair of the HIMSS Privacy & Security Policy Task Force. Mr. McMillan brings nearly 40 years of combined intelligence, security countermeasures, and consulting experience from positions within the government and private sector and has worked in the healthcare industry since his retirement from the federal government in 2000. Mr. McMillan is a thought leader in compliance, security, and privacy issues in healthcare, contributing to several industry trade publications and blogs. He was recognized in *Becker's Hospital Review*'s lists of influential healthcare IT leaders by both its writers and readers in 2015, and was named one of the top 10 health information security influencers of 2013 by *HealthInfoSecurity*. Mr. McMillan served as Director of Security for two separate defense agencies, and sat on numerous interagency intelligence and security countermeasures committees while serving in the U.S. government. He holds a master of arts degree in national security and strategic studies from the U.S. Naval War College and a bachelor of science degree in education from Texas A&M University. He is a graduate of the Senior Officials in National Security program at the John F.

Kennedy School of Government at Harvard University and a 1993/4 Excellence in Government Fellow.

John Moehrke is a standards architect focused on healthcare information exchange interoperability, security, and privacy. He is co-chair of the HL7 Security Workgroup, a member of the FHIR Management Group, and part of the core founding members of HL7 FHIR. Mr. Moehrke is an active member in the United States' national initiatives to create a Nationwide Healthcare Information Network for both the Exchange architecture and the Direct Project. He participates in DICOM, HL7, ISO, and IHE. He has been active in healthcare standardization since 1999, during which time he has authored various standards, profiles, and white papers. Mr. Moehrke has become a well-known security and privacy expert in the standards organizations and government regulations. Mr. Moehrke graduated from the Milwaukee School of Engineering with a bachelor of science degree in computer science and engineering. Mr. Moehrke has an internationally read blog at https://healthcaresecprivacy.blogspot.com/.

Alex Mu-Hsing Kuo, Ph.D., is a full-time associate professor at the School of Health Information Science at the University of Victoria in British Columbia, Canada. He has been a visiting scholar at the Electronic Commerce Resource Centre (ECRC) at Georgia Tech, and at the Center for Expanded Data Annotation and Retrieval (CEDAR) at the Stanford University School of Medicine. Dr. Kuo is the chair of the IEEE Big Data Education Track as well as the study group leader of Metadata Standard for Big Data Management at the IEEE Big Data Initiative (BDI). With over 20 years of programming and data analysis practical and research experience, Dr. Kuo has written over 150 peer-reviewed publications. His research interests include cloud computing and big data application to healthcare, health data interoperability, health database and data warehousing, data mining application in healthcare, e-health, and clinical decision support systems.

Sean Murphy, FACHE, CPHIMS, CISSP-ISSMP, CIPT, HCISP, is a vice president and Chief Information Security Officer at Premera Blue Cross, Seattle, Washington. As a healthcare information security expert with over 20 years of experience, Mr. Murphy has had success at all levels of healthcare. Prior to his current career in healthcare information security, Mr. Murphy was a lieutenant colonel in the U.S. Air Force Medical Service Corps. His proudest professional military accomplishment was his service as senior mentor to the Afghan National Police Surgeon General's Office in support of Operation Enduring Freedom. He has master's degrees in business administration (advanced IT concentration) from the University of South Florida and in health services administration from Central Michigan University. He is also an adjunct professor at Saint Leo University, a fellow of the American College of Healthcare Executives, and is board-certified by the Healthcare Information Management Systems Society. Mr. Murphy is also a Certified Information Systems Security Professional and Information Systems Security Management Professional.

Donald Nichols, Ph.D., is a principal scientist in the Research on Healthcare Value, Equity, and the Lifespan (REHVEAL) program at RTI International in Washington, DC, and the program director for RTI's Health Equity Analytics and Solutions Program. Throughout his 15 years as an academic and social policy researcher, Dr. Nichols has gained experience working on projects involving program evaluations, demonstration designs, payment methodologies, performance measures, and economic modeling. His research includes evaluations of the Maryland Multi-payer Patient Centered Medical Home (PCMH) demonstration and the Centers for Medicare and Medicaid Services' implementation of the Multi-Payer Advanced Primary Care Practice (MAPCP) demonstration. Dr. Nichols was previously on the faculty of Washington University in the Department of Economics where he taught courses in health economics and econometrics. He completed his doctoral work in economics at Stanford University where he was the recipient of the National Science Foundation and Ford Foundation fellowships.

Sheila A. Ochylski, DNP, R.N., is the Chief Nursing Informatics Officer for the Veterans Health Administration, where she provides leadership and strategic direction to enhance care and improve health outcomes for veterans through the use of Health Information Technology. Dr. Ochylski brings with her over 30 years of executive-level experience. Her background includes emergency room and intensive care nursing followed by 20 years as a business owner/nurse entrepreneur operating a large private duty staffing company. Recently Dr. Ochylski served as a nurse leader/executive director of transformation of one of the nation's largest Catholic health systems. As Executive Director of Transformation, Dr. Ochylski led a team tasked with coordinating the implementation of new Electronic Health Record systems to over 90 hospitals across five different platforms.

Gila Pyke, BCompSc software engineering, is the president of Cognaissance and senior consultant specializing in privacy, security, and risk management, as well as interoperability standards in the healthcare IT domain. She has been working in IT since 1994, and fell in love with healthcare IT in 1999 and has never looked back. She has been instrumental in the successful implementation and management of risks in healthcare IT projects in the United States, Canada, France, Belgium, Austria, and Saudi Arabia. In all of her work as an implementer, consultant, and chair of standards development committees such as IHE ITI, Ms. Pyke insists that a high-communication, personalized approach to helping stakeholders manage risk is always the most successful.

Joyce Sensmeier, M.S., R.N.–BC, CPHIMS, FHIMSS, FAAN, is the vice president of informatics at HIMSS. In her current role, she is responsible for the areas of clinical informatics, standards, interoperability, privacy, and security. Ms. Sensmeier became board certified in Nursing Informatics in 1996, earned the Certified Professional in Healthcare Information and Management Systems in 2002, and achieved HIMSS fellowship status in 2005. Ms. Sensmeier is president of IHE USA and previously served as the standards implementation technical manager for the Healthcare Information Technology Standards Panel (HITSP). Ms. Sensmeier was recognized in 2010 as a fellow of the American Academy of Nursing, the highest honor in the field of nursing. She is also co-founder and ex-officio chair of the Alliance for Nursing Informatics.

Dennis M. Seymour, CISSP, HCISPP, ITILv3, is a consultant for Blue Cross Blue Shield of Michigan leading the information security training and awareness program. Prior to his current role, he was the chief security architect for Ellumen, Inc. He has more than 22 years of healthcare-specific security experience, including 15 years of experience at the enterprise level for the Department of Veterans Affairs, Veterans Health Administration, in the positions of technical security advisor and information security officer, with the responsibilities of policy development, system controls assessment and certification, and medical device security policy development and compliance with HIPAA, NIST, FISMA, and other requirements. Mr. Seymour has served as the chairperson of the Healthcare Information and Management Systems Society (HIMSS) Privacy and Security Steering Committee and has been a member of the HIMSS Medical Device Security Task Force, Mobile Security Work Group, and Risk Assessment Work Group. In 2010 Mr. Seymour was a finalist for the International Information Systems Security Certification Consortium [(ISC)²] U.S. Government Information Security Leadership Award (GISLA) in the contractor division.

Omid Shabestari is a medical doctor and Ph.D. in health informatics. He received his medical degree from Tehran University of Medical Sciences in 1999 and his Ph.D. in health informatics from City University of London in 2010. Since 1994, Dr. Shabestari has served as a digital health consultant with executive responsibilities for both public and private sectors in several

countries. His experience includes eight years as CMIO and also supporting a variety of digital health initiatives at organizations such as the National Health Service (NHS), Pfizer, and Cancer Care Ontario. In addition, he has held academic positions as assistant professor of health informatics at the University of Victoria and the University of Toronto in Canada teaching relevant courses and supervising graduate students since 2012. Dr. Shabestari collaborates with several scientific journals and granting agencies as a scientific reviewer. He is very passionate about converting health data into meaningful information by different diagnostic and predictive analytics models and using them at the point of care to improve healthcare delivery. He currently serves as the director of healthcare analytics at Carilion Clinic and is a member of the Health Management Academy in the United States.

Allison Viola, M.B.A., RHIA, is a Director, Health IT with Kaiser Permanente, where she identifies, develops, and recommends strategic policy positions on healthcare IT issues and advises senior executives across all the regions, functions, programs, and entities on the adoption and implementation of positions related to standards, architecture, clinical models, information privacy, and information exchange. She reviews and assesses new healthcare IT standards and technologies, and new applications of technologies in healthcare for possible use, development, and/or influence by Kaiser. Prior to Kaiser Permanente, Ms. Viola has worked in managing large healthcare IT system life-cycle implementations, data mapping, and support; policy and strategy; and security solutions such as biometrics and public key infrastructure analysis. She also currently serves on DC's

Health Information Exchange Finance Sustainability Subcommittee. Ms. Viola holds an M.B.A. in finance from George Washington University, a B.S. in health information management with certification as a Registered Health Information Administrator from Temple University, and a B.S. in business administration with a marketing concentration from Bloomsburg University.

Axel Wirth, CPHIMS, CISSP, HCISPP, is a Healthcare Solutions Architect providing strategic vision and technical leadership within Symantec's Healthcare Vertical, serving in a consultative role to healthcare providers, industry partners, and healthcare technology professionals. Drawing from over 30 years of international experience in the medical device, healthcare IT, and cybersecurity industries, Mr. Wirth supports healthcare organizations in their efforts to solve critical compliance, security, and privacy challenges. Mr. Wirth actively contributes to industry organizations and is a frequent speaker at conferences, forums, and webcasts. He is leading the IHE PCD Cybersecurity working group and is an active participant in the Medical Device Innovation, Safety and Security Consortium (MDISS). In addition, he supports several government healthcare security initiatives and collaborates with security thought leaders across the industry. Mr. Wirth holds a B.S. in electrical engineering from the University of Applied Sciences in Düsseldorf, Germany, and an M.S. in engineering management from The Gordon Institute of Tufts University.

About the Instructor Resource Contributors

Juliana J. Brixey, Ph.D., M.P.H., R.N., earned her doctoral degree from The University of Texas Health Science Center at Houston, School of Health Information Sciences (School of Biomedical Informatics, SBMI) in 2006. Dr. Brixey is an associate professor at the University of Texas Health Science Center at Houston. She holds a joint appoint with SBMI and School of Nursing. Dr. Brixey is Director of the UTHealth Center for Interprofessional Collaboration. Her research interests include interruptions in workflow, patient safety, user-centered design, and the use of social media for online education. She has a strong commitment to excellence in education. This is demonstrated by her contributions to the development of educational materials in health informatics. Dr. Brixey is an active leader in professional informatics and nursing organizations.

Jack E. Brixey holds an M.S. in biomedical informatics as well as B.S. degrees in Biology and Medical Technology. He is certified by the American Society of Medical Technology (MTASCP). Following retirement as a researcher in the chemical industry, Mr. Brixey began a third career as a health informatics consultant. In this role, he has co-authored two teaching guides for health informatics textbooks. He volunteers his time for special projects identified by the American Medical Informatics Pioneers in Nursing Informatics History Project.

Prior to retirement, Mr. Brixey worked more than 35 years in chemical research, engineering, and medical laboratory science. Projects spanned from the production of ultra-high purity chemicals for the Atomic Energy Commission to the development of high-capacity energy sources for aerospace use. In healthcare, Mr. Brixey has extensive experience working in medical laboratories for the military, veterans', and civilian hospitals.

Vanessa Buckley holds an M.Ed. and M.S. in biomedical informatics from UTHealth School of Biomedical Informatics (SBMI). Currently an instructor at UTHealth School of Nursing, Ms. Buckley has over 20 years' experience assisting in grant-funded research projects and running complex data analysis for imaging studies in the field of neuropsychology. This research focuses on patients diagnosed with schizophrenia, behavioral disorders, and addictions, and veterans with mild traumatic brain injuries. Ms. Buckley's additional professional experience includes serving as a teaching assistant at the University of St. Thomas, a graduate assistant at Texas Woman's University, and a tutor at Ross Elementary to students with intellectual disabilities.

CONTENTS AT A GLANCE

CONTENTS

FOREWORD

Every year, I travel a few hundred thousand miles helping governments craft healthcare IT strategy. The culture in each country is different but the problems are the same all over the world. This book is an invaluable reference for understanding what has come before and what trends are likely to shape the future.

The authors are a who's who of the advisors and consultants who shaped thousands of pages of federal regulations across the past two U.S. presidential administrations. As the chair of the Bush-era Healthcare Information Technology Standards Panel and the co-chair of the Obama-era Healthcare Information Technology Standards Committee, I worked side by side with these authors and I can say with confidence that they have an inside view of the "sausage being made."

Part I of this book covers healthcare information technology in the United States, but the concepts it relates from the past two decades of policy apply globally. The United States spends 17 percent of its gross domestic product on healthcare and yet does not lead the world in quality, safety, or efficiency. The United States must move from a fee-for-service reimbursement to value-based purchasing—paying for outcomes and quality—if it is to bend the cost curve. The IT tools necessary to keep people healthy are quite different from those needed to document episodes of care when they are sick. Part I provides valuable insights into the care coordination tools needed in the future to reduce cost and improve quality. Although the Obama administration's Meaningful Use program has had mixed results, public health reporting of immunizations, syndromic surveillance, and reportable lab results has been implemented successfully at a national scale. You'll learn how that was achieved in Chapters 1–4.

In Part II, you'll learn about the major issues shaping health information science. Today's hot trends include team-based communication, mobile computing, analytics, and cloud computing. In 2017 and beyond, I believe that the role of IT leaders will fundamentally change from choosing and integrating the best technology to managing complex projects successfully and ensuring a highly usable result. All of these issues are discussed in Chapters 5–12.

Part III focuses on standards and regulation. An old joke notes "the great thing about healthcare IT standards is that there are so many of them." Creating standards is complex and involves harmonization of multiple stakeholders with a near infinite number of use cases. What is the difference between harmonization and compromise? Harmony means that everyone is happy with the consensus. Compromise means that everyone is equally unhappy with the consensus. Since standards are adopted by consensus, achieving harmony means that standards include a little bit of everyone's wish list. The danger is that a consensus approach to designing a duck could produce a platypus—it's supposed to be a bird with feathers but turns out to be a mammal with hair. You'll hear from experts about the Meaningful Use standards and how we attempted to balance the needs of the many with a relatively low burden for developers, then wrote it into regulation.

Part IV focuses on the day-to-day operations of healthcare IT organizations. I've been a CIO for 20 years, and during that time, we've evolved from products that had to be self-developed to highly reliable commodity services available at reasonable cost. Keeping IT running flawlessly while also introducing continuous improvement/change takes hands-on management and a thick skin. You'll hear from leaders in the trenches in Chapters 18–22.

Part V focuses on innovation. I sometimes describe introducing new technologies into mission-critical production systems as changing the wings on a 747 while it's flying. The world of big data, precision medicine, genomics, and telehealth requires us to break old paradigms of architecture and functionality while not interrupting existing care processes and revenue cycles. There are risks, but risks can be mitigated with appropriate planning. You'll learn how in Chapters 23 and 24.

Part VI focuses on security. Today, as CIO, I spend 25 percent of my time on security-related matters. The new threats are no longer bored college students. We're dealing with state-sponsored cyberterrorism, hacktivism, and organized crime. I describe healthcare IT security as a cold war. The faster the good guys innovate, the faster the bad guys innovate. We're asked to share more data with more stakeholders for more purposes but never spill a single byte. It's an impossible task. You'll hear from the experts who created many of the regulations and best practices we're using today to keep information private.

I hope you enjoy this book as much as I have and that it finds a place of importance on your bookshelf. Regardless of the political and economic divisiveness we'll encounter in the world over the next few years, we know that healthcare IT automation is a universal priority in every society to optimize existing resources and keep our aging societies as healthy as possible. Be well!

John Halamka, M.D., M.S.
International Healthcare Innovation Professor at Harvard Medical School
Chief Information Officer of the Beth Israel Deaconess System
and a practicing emergency physician

ACKNOWLEDGMENTS

The first acknowledgment goes to a welcomed coauthor, Dr. John E. Mattison, who guided us in the outline for the book, recommended new authors, and joined us authoring chapters. The next acknowledgment goes to the section editors of this book, who worked on the chapters while also leading healthcare informatics projects nationally, developing national policies, leading industries, serving as Chief Medical Informatics Officers (CMIOs), and working in academic institutions. Dr. Marc Overhage, Dr. Andre Kushniruk, Dr. Don Mon, Dr. Michael Beller, Dr. John E. Mattison, and Lori Reed-Fourquet spent time shaping the outlines and the chapters to ensure that they responded to the vision of providing one healthcare information technology book that you can use not only to prepare for the CAHIMS and CHTS exams but also as a valuable reference in your IT career. The next round of thanks goes to the contributors, who were equally stressed during this very intensive time in healthcare IT to work over and above their work schedules to get this book delivered and out to the community.

Behind all of us was a team from McGraw-Hill Education that is matched by no other in the dedication and commitment to pursuing what the healthcare information technology domain requires at this time. This team includes the leadership of Tim Green, executive editor, International and Professional Group; Claire Yee, editorial coordinator; and the legal department, which we challenged with dozens of individual contracts. Tim provided special leadership in creating a book that provides a vision in a creative way that is responsive to the CAHIMS and CHTS exams.

When production started, we were joined by a team of specialists: Howie Severson, project manager for copyediting and page proofs; Bill McManus, copy editor; Janet Walden, editorial supervisor from McGraw-Hill Education; and Paul Tyler, references editor and proofreader. What a dedicated team to maintaining quality, readability, and format.

Finally, the book's online learning center can be attributed to the dedicated team working with Amy Stonebraker, acquisitions editor, and Claire Yee. Joining that team were Juliana Brixey, Jack Brixey, and Vanessa Buckley, who developed the online teaching outlines, test bank of questions, and PowerPoint slides.

Additional Resources for Instructors

Whether used as a self-study guide or a classroom text, this book is designed to prepare readers for the AHIMA CHTS and HIMSS CAHIMS, as well as the field of healthcare information technology.

For those using this book in a classroom, please visit this book's Online Learning Center:

http://highered.mheducation.com/sites/1259836975/

The Online Learning Center provides instructor support materials in a format that follows the organization of this book. On this site you will find the following:

- An instructors' manual that contains learning objectives, classroom preparation notes, instructor tips, and a lecture outline for each chapter
- Engaging PowerPoint slides on the lecture topics
- Full color artwork from the book
- Test bank files that allow you to generate a wide array of paper- or network-based tests

Please contact your McGraw-Hill sales representative for more information.

PART I

Healthcare and Information Technology in the United States

CHAPTER 1

Healthcare Information Technology: Definitions, Stakeholders, and Major Themes

Kathleen A. McCormick, J. Marc Overhage,
John E. Mattison, Brian Gugerty

In this chapter, you will learn how to
- Define the complex evolution of the computer network environment in healthcare information technology (HIT)
- Explain the fast uptake of HIT in the continuum of healthcare
- Describe how the increase in volume of HIT has expanded the capabilities to measure the value of healthcare
- Describe the need to prepare an adequate workforce aware of the unique HIT environment
- Define the roles of HIMSS and AHIMA in support of HIT credentialing, education, and training

This chapter provides an overview of some of the updated content in this second edition as well as new content pertaining to the rapid advances in healthcare information technology (HIT). These rapid advances will be briefly mentioned in this introductory chapter and further defined in later chapters. The evolution of HIT has occurred from simple systems to much more complex computer network environments.[1] With this expansion, the technology has become a component of the entire continuum of care, which results in silos of information and data on individuals and communities of people. The need for integrated networks, standards, and security/cybersecurity has intensified as these systems are more commonly being used to increase the volume of HIT and monitor the value of healthcare.

The new generation of healthcare IT personnel must have adequate knowledge and skills to participate in the workforce delivering services and technology. Achieving certification is the best way for these technology and healthcare professionals to demonstrate proficiency with a standard body of knowledge endorsed by professional healthcare organizations. Two types of certification are the focus of this second edition. The first, Certified Associate in Healthcare Information and Management Systems (CAHIMS), is awarded by the Healthcare Information Management Systems Society (HIMSS). CAHIMS is a professional certification for emerging professionals who may not have a lot of experience in healthcare IT but seek a career in the field. The other is the Certified Healthcare Technology Specialist (CHTS) series from the American Health Information Management Association (AHIMA). This series originated with the Office of the National Coordinator for Health Information Technology (ONC) HIT Pro categories of exams and covers six IT roles for people in health information management. Both certifications will be described in more detail later in this chapter.

The Explosion of Healthcare Information Technology

During the past decade, the following factors have contributed to massive expansion in healthcare IT:

- A huge increase in the number of connected networks and network-enabled devices (commonly called the Internet of things [IoT])
- Access to healthcare through mobile devices, patient portals, and cloud services
- Critical cybersecurity threats
- Integration of healthcare networks
- The volume of genomics data
- The need to analyze big data

With this expansion in HIT, the healthcare informatics community has also come to realize that data standards are required to truly achieve interoperability and to mine the data for quality, efficiencies, effectiveness, and cost. In addition, the consumer has embraced direct-to-consumer genomics, mobile devices, portals, and the Internet. Consumers now demand secure and easy access to their healthcare information via healthcare apps on their mobile devices and via the Web on their home computers. When the authors defined the necessary components to understand healthcare IT in the first edition of this book, the enterprise architecture was fairly simple, consisting of a boundary, a network, a data center containing servers located in a defined, secure area, and desktop computers within a closed network. Contrast that to the time of writing of this second edition, and the architecture now contains mobile devices connected from any location, cloud services, and credentialed people accessing data in federated database infrastructures operated by business associates and other types of third-party providers. The hardware configurations that underlie the architectures for healthcare IT, the networks that support healthcare IT connections, and the services that provide diverse applications have become much more complex.

This contrast is depicted in Figure 1-1. The section on the left portrays the simpler healthcare information system that was developed 20 years ago and discussed in the first edition of this book. This second edition describes the current, more complex system depicted on the right. This highlights the rapidly evolving complexity of the computer network environment in which healthcare IT operates. Services are increasingly delivered through the Internet. Electronic health records (EHRs), for example, which historically were core applications running in a healthcare system's data center, are frequently delivered as hosted services today. In addition, the rapidly expanding number of network-capable devices—whether mobile devices for accessing applications, communication devices, medical monitoring devices, or consumer devices such as fitness monitors and network-enabled scales—adds to the complexity and the requirements for various forms of federation and authentication. The regulatory framework for device manufacturers and importers comes from the Food and Drug Administration (FDA). The complexity of designing these systems becomes even greater when the corresponding requirements of privacy, confidentiality, security, and cybersecurity of systems and devices are taken into consideration.

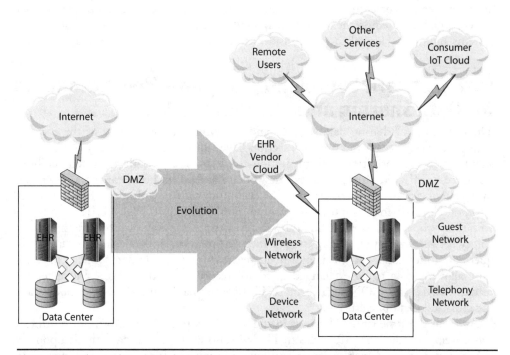

Figure 1-1 The evolving complexity of the healthcare information systems (DMZ = demilitarized zone, a network security layer)

This complexity has resulted in challenges of interoperability and interconnectedness mediated via a number of new resources. Through cloud services, mobile wireless devices, and the Internet of things, everything can be connected, requires nearly continuous updating, and requires a new understanding of how we defend, protect, and secure this new complex environment. Mobile devices now outperform the supercomputers of only 20 years ago. In this all-connected healthcare environment, the functionality is amazing, but the possibility of glitches, bugs, and exploitation from cybercriminals or mischief-makers is challenging and even formidable. Twenty years ago a handful of system administrators and software engineers managed the entire enterprise infrastructure, but now management is highly distributed across many interdependent networks. Keeping thousands of computers, tens of thousands of applications, and billions of records of all sorts properly functioning and secure in this new type of enterprise requires new healthcare IT skills.

In addition to the availability of more devices, healthcare professionals have more access to the Internet and cloud services from healthcare facilities and consumers have more access to healthcare information via the Internet (e.g., healthcare information on the Internet, mobile devices, and patient portals). The Internet was designed for universal open access and maximal participation. Security was not a priority when developing the Internet, but has since become the top priority. Migration from a low-security infrastructure to a high-security infrastructure is progressing slowly and painfully because of the conflicts between the competing objectives of "open" and "secure." Those conflicts will require decades of ongoing negotiation and new skills in how to implement a balanced approach. The complexity of designing these systems becomes even greater when the corresponding requirements of privacy, confidentiality, security, and cybersecurity of systems and devices are taken into consideration.

New Network Complexity Requires New Standards for Data Sharing and Interoperability

The challenges of sharing data securely and achieving interoperability of the complex enterprises described in the previous section have led to the development of new open standards for authorization and integration. In 2014, Fast Healthcare Interoperability Resources (FHIR) was introduced as a new open standard for healthcare data, developed by Health Level Seven International (HL7), a nonprofit organization. FHIR is based upon developer-friendly application programming interfaces (APIs). FHIR provides for RESTful web service access (RESTful web services are one way of providing interoperability between computer systems on the Internet) to granular data elements that can be queried for individual patient data or in aggregate for population data while at the same time allowing data to be exchanged in health records in both human- and machine-readable XML and JSON data formats. FHIR also enables multiple data models and vocabularies used in healthcare.

At about the same time FHIR was introduced, an application platform for healthcare was developed called SMART Health IT. It is also an open standard (built upon the OAuth standard), and enables developers to create applications seamlessly within an EHR or on a data warehouse. This framework allows clinical care and technical IT support users in healthcare to more seamlessly draw upon the entire library of applications being used in clinical care, mobile applications, research, and public health.

SMART Health IT can be used in conjunction with the data models of FHIR to support the diverse use cases and third-party application services, to express medications, problem lists, laboratory data, and even genomic data. Currently, SMART libraries are available for HTML5/JavaScript, iOS, and Python. The libraries comprise a gallery of applications not restricted to a single EHR platform. In addition, the technology can host multiple commercial (typically requiring payment) and open source (free) applications.

System interoperability must be capable of data sharing, interoperability of data elements, and compliance with vocabulary, terminology, and messaging standards. Without common standards, boutique terms used in clinical practice have to be mapped and harmonized to national and international standards in order to measure value, monitor quality, determine if outcomes have been met, and assure safety of care. We continue to suffer from more terminology standards than warranted by the variety of use cases. Every "harmonization" effort suffers from some degree of semantic degradation, and hence a smaller set of terminologies is highly desirable.

Having surpassed the 25th anniversary of the launch of the Human Genome Project, the United States is embarking on a new journey called the Precision Medicine Initiative (PMI), a major component of which is the *All of Us* Research Program, the goal of which is to enroll 1 million Americans in a study of their genetic and genomic information with patient healthcare and lifestyle data using the EHR and mobile applications and sensors.[2, 3] A genetics analysis of one patient is estimated to produce about 1 terabyte of data in a single encounter.[4] That is considered *big data*, a topic explored in detail in Chapter 23. The influences of genetics and genomics across the continuum of care begin in preconception/prenatal care and continue through diagnosis and screening of disease, and monitoring therapeutic decisions of disease and recurrence.[5] New evidence guidelines that predict the uptake, metabolism, and excretion of drugs are known for at least 36 common medications at the time of writing.[6] Roadmaps, workflow pathways, and algorithms are being developed to include these new types of data into the EHR.[7, 8] Together with telehealth utilization, these innovations will be discussed more broadly in this book. The role of social media and the personal health record will also be discussed in this second edition.

The organization of the book has changed in this edition so that more pages could be dedicated to these new advances in healthcare IT. In subsequent chapters, these concepts will be defined and the major themes will be expanded. A new Glossary defines the important terms used in this edition. The major stakeholders in healthcare IT are defined in a new appendix based upon the Standard Occupational Classification (SOC) codes for the United States. Please see Appendix C for how to access this content.

The Role of HIT in the Continuum of Healthcare

The continuum of healthcare today goes from conception to death. Depending on the circumstances, most healthcare in the United States begins either prior to conception (fertility counseling, genetic screening, etc.) or upon discovery of pregnancy. Often, prenatal care includes genetic and genomic studies of the parents and the fetus. This starts the healthcare record for many individuals today. A person born in the United States typically is delivered in a hospital and then becomes a consumer of ambulatory care. Unless emergency room visits are required, a healthy child or adolescent sees healthcare providers only for vaccinations, school and camp physicals, and regular check-ups. More recently, a nurse practitioner or pharmacist in a retail clinic or pharmacy might also see the child or adolescent. Telehealth may be available if online consultation is required for services not rendered by the nurse practitioner. When hospitalized, consumers (whether children, adolescents, or adults) become patients in community health practices in small, medium, or large healthcare facilities. As the consumer advances in age and develops chronic or acute healthcare conditions, they may be seen in specialized laboratory settings, diagnostic and treatment settings, or in a day hospital. With advancing age, a consumer may develop more serious chronic and acute healthcare conditions and require hospitalization, followed by rehabilitation in a center or as an outpatient. Advancing further, some consumers may require care for functional disabilities (that is, the inability to engage in activities of daily living [ADLs] such as walking, dressing, eating, or toileting themselves). This may require healthcare workers (and robots) to provide care in their home, or it may require assisted living, skilled nursing care, or nursing home care. In the late stages of life, hospice care may be appropriate, which focuses attitudes and resources on dying with dignity, quality, and comfort.

In each of these areas in the continuum, the expanding role of healthcare IT has driven the use of technology in all environments (ambulatory, inpatient, long-term care, and even home to the consumers themselves). There are four transformative catalysts in present-day healthcare throughout the United States that are driving changes in the way healthcare IT supports the health of the public:

- A focus on population health with services and the use of mobile technologies to support wellness and disease prevention
- Self-management for those with chronic disease and transitioning of resources and services from acute care to community and home care
- A person-centric focus in care delivery and services for consumer empowerment
- Healthcare system reform using EHRs and other technologies that extend across all levels of services and care settings, including the person's home

The Increasing Volume and Shift to Value of Healthcare IT

The Health Information Technology Economic and Clinical Health (HITECH) Act of 2009 and its funding focused on increasing the volume of EHRs in hospitals and ambulatory care. Provisions of the HITECH Act incentivized the measurement of value and the adoption of Meaningful Use (MU). Currently the measurement of value is focused on MACRA and MIPS. These concepts will be described in the following sections.

Increasing the Volume of EHRs

As of 2011, the adoption of comprehensive EHRs in U.S. hospitals was only 8.7 percent according to a report of the results of a 2012 Robert Wood Johnson Foundation survey.[9] Basic EHR adoption was 18 percent, and those reporting use of any EHR was 26.6 percent. Adoption of the EHR was a key objective of the HITECH Act, and that objective is increasingly being met. In a more current briefing from May 2016, the ONC describes a huge increase in the adoption of the EHR by non-federal acute-care hospitals from 2008 to 2015 (based on data from the American Hospital Association). In 2015, nearly all reported hospitals (96 percent) possessed a certified EHR technology (compared to 72 percent in 2011, the first year certification began), and 84 percent of hospitals adopted at least a basic EHR system (compared to 9.4 percent in 2008).[10] The certification of EHR systems began in 2011 to recognize EHRs that meet technological capability, functionality, and security requirements adopted by the Department of Health and Human Services (HHS). (Notably, the report identifies two subtypes of hospitals that still had basic EHR adoption of 55 percent or less in 2015: children's hospitals and psychiatric hospitals.[10]) Of those that have adopted EHRs, they are moving to optimization and updates of the systems, measuring value from the systems, and securing the infrastructure.

NOTE   Also with the enactment of the HITECH Act in 2009, cybersecurity became a priority moving forward with the anticipated increase in the number of electronic health records to secure. One of the issues is that HIPAA currently does not include security risk analysis that covers personal health information (PHI) cybersecurity in medical devices, even though many devices include PHI. The issues that revolve around cybersecurity will be further discussed and described in Chapters 30 and 31.

The previously mentioned Robert Wood Johnson Foundation study also reported that the percentage of office-based physicians in 2011 who had a basic EHR was 33.9 percent, and 57.0 percent for any type of EHR.[9] As of 2015, according to an ONC report, 87 percent of office-based physicians have adopted any EHR, and 78 percent have adopted a certified EHR. Over half, or 54 percent of office-based physicians, have adopted a basic EHR.[11] While this represents a significant doubling of office-based physicians using an EHR, survey results indicate that a majority of offices with fewer than five physicians are still struggling to adopt an EHR.

Measuring the Value of Healthcare

Concurrent with this second edition, reimbursement changes are pushing for wider value-based care with Comprehensive Primary Care (CPC and CPC+), and the Medicare Access and Chip Reauthorization Act (MACRA) of 2015 rewards healthcare providers for providing quality care. The MACRA quality program proposes two paths for reimbursement based upon quality: the Merit-based Incentive Payment System (MIPS) and the Alternative Payment Models (APMs). These will be further discussed in Chapters 3 and 16.

The concept of value-based healthcare that is dependent upon an interoperable healthcare IT system became evident in the recent passage (December 2016) of the 21st Century Cures Act, the previously mentioned *All of Us* Research Program of the Precision Medicine Initiative,[3] and in bipartisan statements of the U.S. executive and legislative branches of government. The 21st Century Cures Act ("Cures Act") provides $4.8 billion of new funding for advances in PMI research into variations of disease ($1.5 billion), the Cancer Moonshot to speed cancer research ($1.8 billion), and investments in the BRAIN initiative to study brain diseases, including Alzheimer's ($1.5 billion).[12] In addition, the Cures Act incentivizes the FDA to utilize flexible approaches in reviewing medical devices that represent breakthrough technologies, and adds $500 million regulatory modernization of the development of new drugs and devices. The Cures Act will also ensure EHRs are interoperable for seamless patient care.

As this second edition goes to press, Donald J. Trump has recently become the 45th President of the United States and has appointed Dr. Tom Price as the new HHS secretary. Both have strongly advocated repealing the Affordable Care Act (ACA). It is unquestionable that the ACA regulatory burden and format may change and take a new vision for care delivery and measuring the value of healthcare. Indications are that there will not be a diminution of efforts to build infrastructure for interoperability, to improve quality monitoring, and to deliver more cost-effective and efficient healthcare embracing the new technologies and science of genetics and genomics.

A draft white paper on patient-generated health data (PGHD) policy prepared by Accenture was recently released by the ONC.[13] With the increase in consumer technologies, including mobile applications and wearables, the white paper addresses the prospects and challenges for clinicians and researchers going forward through 2024.

The increase in the volume and complexity of healthcare IT requires personnel who demonstrate a standard of knowledge that distinguishes them from others in this competitive HIT workplace environment. By becoming certified in healthcare IT, you demonstrate that you have mastered the knowledge and gained the skills and tools to work in this healthcare environment. In addition, you become more valued in this competitive and expanding marketplace, thus expanding your career opportunities.[14]

Preparing a Critical Mass of Certified Healthcare IT Technicians and Professionals

The new and evolving complex healthcare information technology environment requires building a new type of HIT workforce.[15] To help meet the growing demand for HIT professionals, the ONC facilitated the enactment in 2009 of the HITECH Act, which funded nearly $33 billion between 2011 and 2016 to subsidize adoption of HIT in the United States.[16] Part of this money funded the Health IT Workforce Development Program, the goal of which was to train a new workforce of skilled HIT professionals who are able to help providers implement electronic health records and achieve meaningful use of EHR systems.

Employment of healthcare IT professionals is expected to increase by 20 percent through 2018, according to the Bureau of Labor Statistics. The U.S. government estimates that we will need more than 50,000 healthcare IT workers to help medical providers with electronic medical records—a number expected only to grow as the American population ages. A more recent Bureau of Labor Statistics report has identified that there were 188,600 jobs available in 2014 for medical records and health information technicians. This includes the category of employees who need a postsecondary certificate to enter the healthcare information technician job, and some may need an associate's degree. The job outlook for this category has been updated for 2014 through 2024, with an estimated 15 percent growth (much faster than the average of all other job categories). Between 2014 and 2024, the expected increase in the number of jobs over the current number of jobs is 29,000.[17]

The Bureau of Labor Statistics currently has ten categories of computer and information technology occupations (excluding management): computer and information research scientists; computer network architects; computer programmers; computer support specialists; computer systems analysts; database administrators; information security analysts; network and computer systems administrators; software developers; and web developers. According to the Bureau's 2015 *Occupational Outlook Handbook* (OOH), the median annual salaries for 2015 for these occupations range from $51,470 for computer support specialists (typically requiring an associate's degree) to $110,620 for computer and information research scientists (requiring a doctoral or professional degree). The median salary for computer and IT occupations requiring a bachelor's degree range from $77,810 for network and computer systems administrators to $100,690 for software developers.[18]

The 2015 OOH reports for the category of computer and information systems managers (which includes chief medical information officers and chief nursing information officers) a median wage of $131,600 per year. The growth in this category is expected to be 15 percent from 2014 to 2024. The Bureau estimates an increase of 53,700 new jobs during this same timeframe.[19] This category also includes project managers who plan, coordinate, and direct the computer-related activities.

The 27th Annual HIMSS Leadership Survey reflects the opinions of IT professionals in U.S. healthcare provider organizations regarding the use of IT in their organizations.[20] This study puts a finger on the pulse of healthcare IT annually and is reported at the Annual HIMSS meeting. This study covers a wide array of topics crucial to healthcare IT leaders, including IT priorities, issues driving and challenging technology adoption, IT security, as well as IT staffing and budgeting plans. Based on the feedback of 282 healthcare IT professionals, nearly three-quarters of the participants in the 2016 survey reported that their focus will be on clinical integration (73.8 percent), primary care provider efficiency (72.3 percent), mandated quality metrics improvement (68.4 percent), and care coordination (67.4 percent). This compares to previous HIMSS Annual Leadership Surveys, which indicated that federal mandates, including meeting Stage One, Two, and future versions of Meaningful Use requirements and a conversion to ICD-10, would be the issues driving their efforts in the years ahead.

Since there is no category of nursing informatics in the Bureau of Labor Statistics, HIMSS conducts a survey of compensation for nursing informatics certifications. In 2014, a nurse with an informatics certification made an average of $121,830 annually, compared to $106,537 for comparable registered nurses without certification.[21]

The Roles of HIMSS and AHIMA in Support of Healthcare Information Credentialing, Education, and Training

As indicated in the chapter introduction, the professional organizations currently certifying in HIT are HIMSS (CAHIMS certification) and AHIMA (CHTS series). The AHIMA CHTS certifications support the continuation of the previously described ONC objective to prepare a critical mass of healthcare IT technicians and professionals. (Until very recently, CompTIA also offered HIT certification through its Healthcare IT Technician certification exam, but it has retired this certification as of February 28, 2017, and does not plan to renew or replace it.[22])

Healthcare Information and Management Systems Society (HIMSS)

HIMSS is a global, cause-based, not-for-profit organization with more than 50,000 members focused on better health through information technology (IT). HIMSS conducts surveys of its members, including CIOs and other executive leaders, and the results of these surveys serve today as the primary source for understanding the evolving roles, responsibilities, and professional background of informatics professionals. HIMSS has offered certification to members since 2002 when it established the Certified Professional in Healthcare Information and Management Systems (CPHIMS). A more recent certification, Certified Associate in Healthcare Information and Management Systems (CAHIMS), focuses on emerging professionals who may not have experience with HIT.

The CAHIMS exam is focused on leadership, technology environment, analysis, and privacy and security.[23] The content of the exam is meant to demonstrate professional knowledge in healthcare information and management systems. It provides the person obtaining the certification a solid foundation upon which to strengthen their abilities, acquire more experience, and advance their career path.

In addition to certification, HIMSS offers broad educational programs, resources, and training in healthcare IT in a variety of formats. These include conference sessions, virtual events that provide access to a series of digital educational programs including webinars. HIMSS has regional chapter-sponsored courses that provide credits that can be applied for CPHIMS/CAHIMS certification.

American Health Information Management Association (AHIMA)

Since March 2013, AHIMA has been administering the exams for healthcare IT previously available from the ONC. AHIMA is the member association for health information management (HIM) professionals and offers certification of coders and health professionals for information management. AHIMA focuses on roles specific to HIM fields, including privacy and security, diagnosis and treatment coding, electronic health records, reimbursement, regulatory compliance, healthcare information technology, and information governance.

AHIMA serves 103,000 HIM professionals. In addition to HIM professionals, AHIMA members also include companies and consultants, individuals, and academic institutions with a focus on HIM programs. The AHIMA certification exams focus on individuals trained through short-duration, nondegree healthcare IT workforce development programs, as well as on members of the workforce with relevant experience and various types of training and academic preparation. The U.S. Department of Veterans Affairs (VA) has approved all AHIMA certification exams for reimbursement for active-duty military and veterans. Pearson VUE offers the AHIMA exams in multiple locations throughout the country. AHIMA offers a variety of education and training programs for certification, through conferences and webinars.

The AHIMA CHTS series includes the following six exams: Clinician/Practitioner Consultant (CHTS-CP); Implementation Manager (CHTS-IM); Implementation Support Specialist (CHTS-IS); Technical/Software Support Staff (CHTS-TS); Trainer (CHTS-TR); and Practice Workflow and Information Management Redesign Specialist (CHTS-PW).[24]

The next six sections are taken from the AHIMA web site: https://my.ahima.org/certification/getcertified.[24]

Certified Healthcare Technology Specialist-CP Exam (CHTS-CP)

The Clinician/Practitioner Consultant Examination conveys the background and experience of a licensed clinical and professional or public health professional. Workers in this role will:

- Suggest solutions for health IT implementation problems in clinical and public health settings.
- Address workflow and data collection issues from a clinical perspective, including quality measurement and improvement.
- Assist in selection of vendors and software.
- Advocate for users' needs, acting as a liaison between users, IT staff, and vendors.

Certified Healthcare Technology Specialist-IM Exam (CHTS-IM)

Implementation Manager Examination demonstrates a candidate's ability to provide on-site management of mobile adoption support teams throughout the implementation process of health IT systems. Prior to training, workers will have experience in health, IT environments, and administrative or managerial positions. Workers in this role will:

- Apply project management and change management principles to create implementation project plans to achieve the project goals.
- Interact with office/hospital personnel to ensure open communication with the support team.
- Lead implementation teams consisting of workers in the roles described above.

- Manage vendor relations, providing feedback to health IT vendors for product improvement.

- Apply project management and change management principles to create implementation project plans to achieve the project goals.

- Interact with office/hospital personnel to ensure open communication with the support team.

- Lead implementation teams consisting of workers in the roles described above.

- Manage vendor relations, providing feedback to health IT vendors for product improvement.

Certified Healthcare Technology Specialist-IS Exam (CHTS-IS)

Implementation Support Specialist Examination tests a candidate's ability to provide on-site user support throughout the health IT system implementation process. Previous background in this role includes information technology or information management. Workers in this role will:

- Execute implementation project plans, by installing hardware (as needed) and configuring software to meet practice needs.

- Incorporate usability principles into design and implementation.

- Test the software against performance specifications.

- Interact with the vendors as needed to rectify problems that occur during the deployment process.

Certified Healthcare Technology Specialist-TS Exam (CHTS-TS)

Technical/Software Support Staff Examination assesses a candidate's ability to maintain systems in clinical and public health settings, including patching and upgrading software. Candidate backgrounds include information technology or information management. Workers in this role will:

- Interact with end users to diagnose IT problems and implement solutions.

- Document IT problems and evaluate the effectiveness of problem resolution.

- Support systems security and standards.

Certified Healthcare Technology Specialist-TR Exam (CHTS-TR)

Trainer Examination conveys the ability to design and deliver training programs to employees in clinical and public health settings. Previous background includes experience as a health professional or health information management specialist. Experience as a trainer is desired. Workers in this role will:

- Be able to use a range of health IT applications, preferably at an expert level.
- Communicate both health and IT concepts as appropriate.
- Assess training needs and competencies of learners.
- Design lesson plans, structuring active learning experiences for users.

Certified Healthcare Technology Specialist-PW Exam (CHTS-PW)

This Exam portrays the skills needed to reorganize a provider's work to effectively use health IT to improve health care. Candidates may have backgrounds in health care or information technology, but are not licensed clinical professionals.

Workers in this role assist in reorganizing the work of a provider to take full advantage of the features of health IT in pursuit of meaningful use of health IT to improve health and care. Individuals in this role may have backgrounds in health care (for example, as a practice administrator) or in information technology, but are not licensed clinical professionals. Workers in this role will:

- Conduct user requirements analysis to facilitate workflow design.
- Integrate information technology functions into workflow.
- Document health information exchange needs.
- Design processes and information flows that accommodate quality improvement and reporting.
- Work with provider personnel to implement revised workflows.
- Evaluate process workflows to validate or improve practice's systems.

Chapter Review

This chapter described the evolution that has occurred in the HIT computer network environment in the past few years. This evolution has resulted in a much more complex environment that presents technical challenges in several areas that are mentioned in this chapter and described in depth in this new, second edition. Among the challenges introduced in this chapter are the need to navigate new and updated data standards intended to help the United States achieve interoperability in healthcare; actually achieving interoperability among the wave of new consumer health apps and devices; and improving security and cybersecurity in systems and devices to match the greater complexity of today's network environment. The emerging IoT, more service-oriented architectures, and cloud services also present challenges in this new environment. This chapter also defined the workforce that needs to be prepared to meet these challenges. Finally, this chapter defined the roles of the major organizations that certify individuals for working in HIT.

Questions

To test your comprehension of the chapter, answer the following questions and then check your answers against the list of correct answers at the end of the chapter.

1. What has incentivized the uptake of healthcare information technology in the United States?

    A. FDA regulations for drug manufacturing

    B. The insistence of the U.S. population on identity management and quality

    C. The financial incentives in the HITECH Act

    D. The inability of paper-based charts to accommodate the volume of healthcare information

2. What is the Bureau of Labor Statistics estimated growth in the number of healthcare IT workers through 2018?

    A. The growth is expected to increase by 20 percent through 2018.

    B. There is no growth expectations for healthcare IT workers.

    C. The growth is expected to increase by 50 percent through 2018.

    D. A decrease is expected because there is currently a surplus of healthcare IT workers.

3. In recent years, what has added to the complexity in understanding healthcare information technology?

    A. The challenge of maintaining privacy, confidentiality, and security in the widely expanding complex architecture

    B. Greater access to healthcare data from multiple groups, including patients

    C. The increase in mobile computing and the use of clouds for storage

    D. All of the above

4. What innovations are driving new roadmaps, workflows, and algorithms in the delivery of healthcare?

    A. Mobile health alone

    B. Mobile devices, genetics, genomics, telehealth

    C. Ever-increasing delivery of services via the Internet, including EHRs as hosted services

    D. None of the above

5. Which U.S. government agency provides the regulatory framework for device manufacturers and importers?

    A. NIST

    B. FDA

    C. AHRQ

    D. NIH

6. What aspect of HIPAA security risk analysis covers cybersecurity for medical devices?

   A. HIPAA currently does not include security risk analysis that covers PHI cybersecurity in medical devices.

   B. HIPAA covers cybersecurity in the FDA regulations for medical devices.

   C. The FTC covers the HIPAA regulations for cybersecurity for medical devices.

   D. HHS covers cybersecurity for medical devices in its OCR regulations.

7. In what year did cybersecurity become a priority concern for healthcare organizations?

   A. Cybersecurity has not become an issue for information technology for healthcare organizations.

   B. Cybersecurity became a priority concern for healthcare organizations in 2011.

   C. Cybersecurity became a priority concern for healthcare organizations in 2009.

   D. Cybersecurity became a priority concern for healthcare organizations in 2015.

8. What event has led to the surge in cybersecurity threats to healthcare organizations?

   A. The HITECH Act of 2009

   B. The passage of HIPAA

   C. The coordination of regulations from the FDA

   D. The FTC changes in telehealth

Answers

1. **C.** The financial incentives in the HITECH Act have incentivized the uptake of healthcare information technology in the United States.

2. **A.** Employment of healthcare IT professionals is expected to increase by 20 percent through 2018, according to the Bureau of Labor Statistics.

3. **D.** Understanding healthcare IT has become more complex in recent years because of the challenge of maintaining privacy, confidentiality, and security in the widely expanding complex architecture; healthcare data has become more accessible to multiple groups, including patients; and mobile computing and the use of clouds for storage have increased.

4. **B.** Mobile devices, genetics, genomics, and telehealth are driving new roadmaps, workflows, and algorithms in the delivery of care.

5. **B.** The FDA is the U.S. government agency that provides the regulatory framework for device manufacturers and importers.

6. A. HIPAA currently does not include security risk analysis that covers PHI cybersecurity in medical devices. However, many devices include personal health information.

7. C. Cybersecurity became a priority concern for healthcare organization in 2009 with passage of the HITECH Act.

8. A. The HITECH Act of 2009 is the event that has led to the surge in cybersecurity threats to healthcare organizations.

References

1. Donaldson, S. E., Siegel, S. G., Williams, C. K., & Aslam, A. (2015). *Enterprise cybersecurity: How to build a successful cyberdefense program against advanced threats.* Apress.

2. Collins F. S., & Varmus, H. (2015). A new initiative on precision medicine. *New England Journal of Medicine, 372*(9), 793–795.

3. National Institutes of Health. (2017). *All of Us Research Program: Precision Medicine Initiative.* Accessed on January 24, 2017, from https://www.nih.gov/research-training/allofus-research-program.

4. Savage, N. (2014). Bioinformatics: Big data versus the big C. *Nature, 509*(7502), S66–S67.

5. McCormick, K. A., & Calzone, K. A. (2015). Big data initiatives: Genomics and information technology for personalized health. In V. K. Saba & K. A. McCormick (Eds.), *Essentials of nursing informatics, sixth edition* (pp. 707–725). McGraw-Hill.

6. Relling, M. V., & Evans, W. E. (2015). Pharmacogenomics in the clinic. *Nature, 526*(7573), 343–350.

7. Hoffman, J. M., Haidar, C. E., Wilkinson, M. R., Crew, K. R., Baker, D. K., Kornegay, N. M., & Relling, M. V. (2014). PG4KDS: A model for the clinical implementation of pre-emptive pharmacogenetics. *American Journal of Medical Genetics Part C: Seminars in Medical Genetics, 166C*(1), 4555.

8. DIGITizE: Displaying and integrating genetic information through the EHR. Accessed on October 14, 2016, from www.nationalacademies.org/hmd/Activities/Research/GenomicBasedResearch/Innovation-Collaboratives/EHR.aspx.

9. Robert Wood Johnson Foundation, Mathematica Policy Research, Harvard School of Public Health. (2012). *Health Information technology in the United States: Driving toward delivery systems change.* Accessed on January 25, 2017, from www.rwjf.org/content/dam/farm/reports/reports/2012/rwjf72707.

10. Henry, J., Pylypchuk, Y., Searcy, T., & Patel, V. (2016). *Adoption of electronic health record systems among U.S. non-federal acute care hospitals: 2008–2015.* ONC Data Brief 35. Accessed on January 24, 2017, from https://dashboard.healthit.gov/evaluations/data-briefs/non-federal-acute-care-hospital-ehr-adoption-2008-2015.php.

11. Office of the National Coordinator for Health Information Technology. (2016). *Office-based physician electronic health record adoption.* Accessed on January 25, 2017, from https://dashboard.healthit.gov/quickstats/pages/physician-ehr-adoption-trends.php.

12. U.S. House of Representatives Committee on Energy and Commerce. (2016). *The 21st Century Cures Act fact sheet.* Accessed on January 26, 2017, from https://energycommerce.house.gov/sites/republicans.energycommerce.house .gov/files/documents/114/analysis/20161128%20Cures%20Fact%20Sheet.pdf.

13. Accenture. (2016). *Conceptualizing a data infrastructure for the capture, use, and sharing of patient-generated health data in care delivery and research through 2024.* Accessed on January 25, 2017, from https://www.healthit.gov/sites/default/files/ Draft_White_Paper_PGHD_Policy_Framework.pdf.

14. McCormick, K. A., Gugerty., B, & Sensmeier, J. (2017). A comparison of professional informatics-related competencies and certifications. *Online Journal of Nursing Informatics, 21*(1). Available at www.himss.org/library/online-journal-nursing-informatics-volume-21-winter-2017.

15. Perlin, J. B., Baker, D. B., Brailer, D. J., Fridsma, D. B., Frisse, M. E., Halamka, J. D., ... Tang, P. C. (2016). *Information technology interoperability and use for better care and evidence.* Vital Directions for Health and Health Care Series. Discussion Paper, National Academy of Medicine. Accessed on October 12, 2016, from https://nam.edu/wp-content/uploads/2016/09/Information-Technology-Interoperability-and-Use-for-Better-Care-and-Evidence.pdf.

16. Office of the National Coordinator for Health Information Technology. (2011–2015). *Federal health information technology strategic plan.* Accessed on December 21, 2016, from https://www.healthit.gov/sites/default/files/utility/ final-federal-health-it-strategic-plan-0911.pdf.

17. Bureau of Labor Statistics, U.S. Department of Labor. (2015). Medical records and health information technician. *Occupational outlook handbook, 2015.* Accessed on June 14, 2016, from www.bls.gov/ooh/Healthcare/Medical-records-and-health-information-technicians.htm.

18. Bureau of Labor Statistics, U.S. Department of Labor. (2015). Computer and information technology occupations. *Occupational outlook handbook, 2015.* Accessed on June 15, 2016, from www.bls.gov/ooh/computer-and-information-technology/home.htm.

19. Bureau of Labor Statistics, U.S. Department of Labor. (2015). Computer and information systems managers. *Occupational outlook handbook, 2015.* Accessed on June 15, 2016, from www.bls.gov/ooh/management/computer-and-information-systems-managers.htm.

20. HIMSS. (2016). *27th annual HIMSS leadership survey.* Accessed on January 26, 2017, from www.himss.org/27th-annual-leadership-survey/full-report.

21. HIMSS. (2014). *Nursing informatics workforce survey salary resource guide.* Accessed on June 15, 2016, from www.himss.org/2014-nursing-informatics-workforce-survey-salary-resource-guide.

22. CompTIA®. *CompTIA Healthcare IT Technician retirement.* Accessed on June 15, 2016, from https://certification.comptia.org/certifications/healthcare-it-technician.

23. HIMSS CAHIMS certification. Accessed on June 15, 2016, from www.himss.org/health-it-certification/cahims.

24. AHIMA certification exam portal. Accessed on January 23, 2017, from https://my.ahima.org/certification/getcertified.

U.S. Healthcare Systems Overview

Philip J. Kroth

In this chapter, you will learn how to

- Define major types of organizations through which healthcare is delivered in the United States
- Identify the venues in which healthcare is delivered
- Describe training and experience healthcare professionals require
- Delineate the types of healthcare
- Identify organizations that regulate healthcare
- Discuss the major healthcare system changes that are occurring or will occur in the foreseeable future

This chapter is designed to provide a brief and high-level overview of how the U.S. health-care system is structured and major changes that are occurring or will occur in the foreseeable future. Its target reader is a healthcare information technology (HIT) professional who is relatively new to working in the healthcare system. The chapter is by no means meant to be comprehensive. There are many other sources that you can look to for more information. These sources are referenced by topic throughout the chapter. The chapter is organized to allow you to use it either as an introductory primer on the healthcare system in general or as a reference or glossary. When using it as a reference or glossary, you may jump directly to topics of interest as you traverse other parts of the book. This chapter includes six major sections, with subsections as appropriate. The table of contents and the chapter outline will help you to quickly find sections of interest.

U.S. Healthcare Delivery Organizations and Management Structures

The U.S. healthcare system comprises many and very different healthcare delivery organizations with varied management structures. Many of these organizations provide the same or similar services but are targeted toward different populations and have different funding streams. Some are not-for-profit while others are for-profit. Some are public entities while others are corporate entities with public or private ownership. Most are in a state of transition as political, economic, and regulatory pressures seek to remake the patchwork quilt of services that has characterized the U.S. healthcare system.

Private Medical Practices

Private medical practices are perhaps what most Americans think of when they think about the healthcare system. These are privately owned and operated, ambulatory (outpatient) practices where a group of healthcare providers (most commonly physicians) are in a business partnership to provide medical care to members of a given community. These are also known as group practices. A solo practice is an ambulatory practice that has only one physician. A group practice may offer only one medical specialty, such as family medicine. Group practices may also be owned by larger healthcare organizations such as a hospital where the physicians are paid as hospital employees. A practice that includes many medical specialties, such as general internal medicine, ophthalmology, and pediatrics, is called a *multispecialty* practice. Many practices also have clinicians other than physicians to consult with patients, such as physician assistants (PAs) and nurse practitioners (NPs). These "midlevel" providers can assess and treat patients, write prescriptions, and order tests. In most states, midlevel providers must be under the supervision of a licensed physician. Group practices also employ non-medically trained staff to perform billing, collections, accounting, office management, payroll, and, increasingly, IT functions. As of 2012, approximately two-thirds of U.S. physicians worked in group practices.[1]

The overhead required to operate group practices is increasing substantially. Government regulations in the form of increasingly complex billing requirements, quality reporting requirements, and electronic health record (EHR) systems requirements are combining to make it more difficult to start and continue operating small medical practices. Because of these factors, the number of physicians who become employees of larger healthcare organizations is likely to continue to increase. In fact, a recent survey of physicians reported that 21 percent of physicians are now employees of hospital systems.[2]

Health Maintenance Organizations (HMOs)

HMOs were created by the 1973 HMO Act. HMOs require covered patients to use the physicians and services approved by the HMOs (see Chapter 3 for details of HMO payment models). In the early years of managed care, HMOs typically had freestanding clinical facilities that provided "one-stop shopping" for patients. Primary care physicians, pharmacists, X-ray technicians, physical therapists, and some medical specialists were all employed by the HMO and worked in its facilities. This kind of organization is also known as a "staff-model" HMO because all of its healthcare providers are employees.

HMOs focus on defined populations of patients with presumably known medical risks and set premium levels using claims histories and patient population actuarial data. The concept is that the financial risk for covering the target population that had been previously borne solely by the insurance companies could be shared with the healthcare providers. Healthcare providers are therefore incentivized to improve the efficiency of care delivery and reduce costs.

Independent Practice Associations (IPAs)

Independent practice associations were also created by the 1973 HMO Act but, unlike HMOs, do not have the freestanding clinical facilities with "one-stop shopping" for its patients. IPAs can be thought of as HMOs without walls. IPA managed care organizations contract with existing physician practices and other healthcare providers to provide care to their members. Each IPA often requires participating providers to care only for its members.

Preferred Provider Organizations (PPOs)

Preferred provider organizations are similar to HMOs but with the significant exception that physicians and other healthcare providers (hospitals, pharmacies, etc.) do not share financial risk as with HMOs. Also, patients are not required to use physicians on the PPO's approved provider list; they may use any provider but must pay higher copayments and/or deductibles if they use unapproved providers.

PPOs contract with physicians and other healthcare providers for individual services and then resell these services to employers and other insurance companies. PPOs profit by leveraging large economies of scale and purchasing power to negotiate payment rates with physicians and hospitals. Physicians and hospitals benefit from a predictable flow of patients, allowing a certain amount of reliable financial stability (e.g., the ability to predict the coming year's patient volumes).

Hospitals

Hospitals are facilities that provide acute care where the average length of stay is generally less than 30 days. Hospitals may be not-for-profit or for-profit, may be sponsored by religious organizations or governments, and may have specially designated purposes. As of January 2016, the following list summarizes the 5,627 hospitals in the United States:[3]

- Nongovernment not-for-profit community hospitals (2,870)
- Investor-owned (for-profit) community hospitals (1,053)
- State and local government community hospitals (1,003)
- Federal government hospitals, including VA hospitals (213)
- Nonfederal psychiatric hospitals (403)
- Other, e.g., prison hospitals, college infirmaries, nonfederal long term care hospitals (85)

Of these, approximately 5 percent (or approximately 400) are teaching hospitals that are affiliated with U.S. medical schools.[4] Teaching hospitals provide the venue for essential training of medical students and residents. Teaching hospitals and hospitals not formally affiliated with a medical school also provide educational venues for nurses, pharmacists, dentists, therapists of all kinds, as well as a host of other medical professionals. Despite the fact that they compose only 7 percent of U.S. hospitals, teaching hospitals provide 25 percent of all Medicaid hospitalizations, 35 percent of all hospital charity care, and 61 percent of all pediatric intensive care unit beds.[4]

Public hospitals can be sponsored by city, county, state, and federal agencies to provide acute healthcare to the poor and provide healthcare services that are typically expensive but not profitable. Trauma centers, burn units, psychiatric emergency services, and alcohol detoxification centers are examples of essential community services that are not profitable and usually require some kind of supplemental operational funding.

Private hospitals can be not-for-profit or for-profit. The Presbyterian and Catholic health systems in the United States are examples of not-for-profit hospital systems. For-profit hospitals often focus on types of specialty care that are fairly well reimbursed by insurance companies and therefore profitable. See the upcoming "Specialty Hospitals" section for more details.

Academic Health Centers

Academic health centers are usually portions of major universities where a hospital or hospitals are co-located with medical, nursing, pharmacy, dentistry, and many other medical training programs, along with a significant medical research infrastructure. The co-location of medical research, medical training, and university hospitals and their associated infrastructures provides synergies that drive the advancement of medical science and innovation in healthcare services in general. Academic health center hospitals and other facilities also provide a significant amount of specialized and charity care.

Specialty Hospitals

Specialty hospitals are healthcare centers that focus on particular diseases or services. They can be either not-for-profit or for-profit. "Heart hospitals" are an excellent example of specialty hospitals. Heart hospitals focus on cardiac care and are often owned by large cardiology group practices. They focus on streamlining the care of acute and chronic cardiac conditions by incorporating all the testing and treatment facilities for cardiac care under one roof. For example, heart hospitals have the facilities for procedures such as emergency heart catheterization to treat patients who experience acute myocardial infarctions (heart attacks). They also have many types of cardiac diagnostic equipment and services, including ultrasonography, exercise treadmill testing, cardiac imaging, and so forth. By leveraging economies of scale provided by high cardiac patient volumes as well as the relatively high reimbursement for cardiac procedures, these kinds of hospitals are usually quite profitable. Other types of for-profit specialty hospitals include cancer care centers, orthopedic hospitals, and plastic surgery centers.

Not-for-profit specialty hospitals include psychiatric hospitals that provide inpatient psychiatric care. While there are for-profit inpatient treatment centers specializing in the treatment of addiction to alcohol and other substances, many of these facilities are not-for-profit and receive government funding to offset their high costs, often-meager insurance company reimbursement, and high percentages of charity care for uninsured patients.

Public Health Departments

Public health departments are administrated at the city, county, state, and federal levels. They are government organizations that focus on the health of populations rather than individuals. The World Health Organization (WHO) defines public health as follows: "The science and art of promoting health, preventing disease, and prolonging life through the organized efforts of society."[5] To accomplish their mission, public health departments focus on prevention of disease and attempt to mitigate factors in society that foster disease in populations.

The National Association of County and City Health Officials (NACCHO) produced a report based on a survey it conducted of local health departments in 2013. The report puts activities of health departments into four categories (you are urged to review the report for more information):[6]

- Programs and services
- Emergency preparedness and response
- Assessment, planning, and improvement
- Public health policy

Just a very few examples of local health department activities include public vaccination programs and enforcement of food safety standards at restaurants and other facilities that prepare and handle food. They monitor for communicable disease outbreaks and foster public health education on healthy eating choices. They also advocate and attempt to influence politicians and geographic area planning experts to ensure adequate distributions of parks and walking and biking areas to encourage physical activity.

Public health departments have demonstrated their value repeatedly. Despite a history of significant accomplishments and the enormous savings incurred by promoting prevention over treatment, public health departments at all levels of government continually struggle for funding. Their budgets are often at the mercy of the whim of elected officials and state and local budget mandates. See Chapter 4 for a more detailed discussion of public health and public health departments.

Other Healthcare Organizations

There are many other healthcare organizations that provide health services to various communities in the United States and abroad. The U.S. Department of Defense provides healthcare to its 9.4 million service members all over the globe with 55 hospitals, 245 dental facilities, and 373 medical clinics.[7] The Indian Health Service (IHS), a division of the U.S. Department of Health and Human Services (HSS), focuses on providing care to Native Americans. The U.S. Department of Veterans Affairs (VA) provides healthcare to veterans of the U.S. Armed Forces. There are many other healthcare organizations as well, but discussion of all of them is well beyond the scope of this chapter. Suffice it to say that the U.S. healthcare system is made up of a patchwork of many organizations that focus on different patient populations and organizational missions.

Healthcare Venues

There are many different types of venues through which healthcare is delivered in the United States. The following are brief descriptions of some of the major venues.

Ambulatory Care Centers

Ambulatory care centers are also known as outpatient care centers. Ambulatory care centers of medical group practices have long been the mainstay for primary care services where most patients go to see their primary care and specialty physicians for routine care. However, as medical technology has advanced and as managed care has pressured hospitals to discharge patients faster, many kinds of healthcare that were previously provided on an inpatient basis are now provided in outpatient centers to save money and improve outcomes. For example, many kinds of surgery that previously required at least a night's stay in the hospital are now routinely performed in ambulatory surgery centers. Examples includes simple hernia repairs, some orthopedic procedures done through an arthroscope (a device that allows joint surgery to be performed with only one or two 1 cm incisions), and a variety of plastic surgery procedures. This allows patients to return home the same day as their surgeries were performed. This saves the cost of an overnight stay in the hospital and allows patients to recuperate at home.

Hospital Ambulatory Care Centers

To capitalize on the move from inpatient to outpatient care, many hospitals established ambulatory care centers to maintain their revenue as well as to leverage the use of their facilities by the patients who use these centers. Hospitals hire physicians as employees not only to generate revenue from outpatient care but also to funnel patients into their more traditional inpatient and ancillary services such as laboratories, X-ray services, and other diagnostic services. Often, such ancillary services are major sources of a hospital's income compared with the income generated in the ambulatory care centers themselves.

Urgent Care Centers

Because of physician shortages in many areas, overcrowded emergency departments, and other factors, urgent care centers have become a popular alternative for patients seeking care for urgent but non-life-threatening medical issues. These centers are commonly established in convenient locations such as strip malls, with free parking and other amenities. Urgent care centers typically offer evening and weekend hours as well, to provide services during the times it is most difficult to be seen by a primary care physician. Many insurance plans encourage the use of urgent care centers over the much more expensive emergency departments. Urgent care centers are owned and operated by physician groups, insurance companies, and hospital systems. Hospital systems can leverage their ancillary services to make additional profit by funneling business from urgent care centers to these services.

Retail Clinics

A more recent development in the ambulatory care business is retail clinics. These are often located in pharmacies, supermarkets, airports, shopping centers, and "big box" stores such as Target and Walmart. They are most often staffed by midlevel providers (i.e., physician assistants and nurse practitioners) and are designed to handle simple medical conditions such as sore throats and ear aches, routine vaccinations, and physicals for school, sports, camp, and employment. According to a recent RAND Corporation study, there are over 2,000 retail clinics in the United States and 40 percent of the clinics' visits are for low-acuity healthcare needs for which patients would otherwise see their own doctor.[8] However, 60 percent of the visits are for issues for which patients would likely not seek help from their doctor. The study suggests that the increased convenience of these clinics is actually increasing healthcare costs despite the use of lower-level providers.

Similar to retail clinics, many pharmacies now offer vaccinations given by specially trained pharmacists. Patients can receive routine vacations in the store without a prescription and often without cost as the pharmacy charges the patient's insurance and waives the copay. Pharmacies sometimes offer in-store discounts as part of the service. Some retail pharmacy chains offer retail clinics as well.

Acute Care

Acute care is defined as care that is of an emergent or life-threatening nature that cannot be provided in an outpatient setting. Most acute care settings are in hospitals. The following are a few examples.

Emergency Departments

Emergency care is provided in hospital emergency departments (EDs). Aside from providing immediate and life-sustaining treatment to those who need it, EDs essentially triage patients into three groups: 1) those requiring hospitalization and further acute care (e.g., a patient with a gunshot wound requiring surgery); 2) those who can be appropriately treated in the ED and then sent home (e.g., suturing a minor wound); and 3) those who do not need emergency care and are referred to follow up with appropriate practitioners in the ambulatory setting (e.g., a patient with a toothache).

By law, EDs accept all patients regardless of their ability to pay. Because of this, many uninsured patients attempt to use the ED as their source for primary care or present with medical conditions that could have been easily prevented had they sought treatment earlier in an ambulatory setting. These factors contribute significantly to the overcrowding conditions in EDs.

In an attempt to cope with overcrowding, EDs have developed "fast track" or streamlined processes of care for illnesses that often require less than 24 hours of treatment, such as an asthma exacerbation or chest pain that is unlikely to be due to a cardiac condition. Fast tracks are often administered by midlevel providers and follow strict protocols so that patients can be treated and discharged in a timely and safe manner. In addition to taking these measures to cope with overcrowding, EDs often now have several specialized teams to deal with certain emergent diagnoses that require urgent intervention. For example, stroke teams and cardiology teams work with the ED to ensure that patients who have strokes or myocardial infarctions (heart attacks) are seen and treated by an appropriate specialty team within a prescribed time frame. The deployment of such teams has shown significant improvement in both acute stroke and cardiac care.

Trauma Centers

Trauma centers are accredited hospital programs that treat acute trauma in all its forms. Trauma centers are accredited based on their capabilities of both facilities and personnel, with Level-1 being the most highly capable. Upon receiving notice that a trauma patient is expected, an interdisciplinary trauma team is assembled to evaluate and treat the patient, often before the patient even arrives in the ED (such as by air ambulance). Trauma centers focus on a seamless transition for the patient from rapid evaluation in the ED, to surgery in the operating room, to post-operative care in the trauma ICU, through to discharge and follow-up care. Trauma centers maintain patient registries and track outcomes so the system can continuously be evaluated and improved. Because trauma centers require a great deal of very expensive equipment and personnel, many states have only one Level-1 trauma center and require government subsidies to keep it solvent.

Burn Centers

Similar to trauma centers, burn centers involve an interdisciplinary team in the hospital to manage burn patients' care from the moment they arrive in the ED through to post-discharge care and rehabilitation. Also like trauma centers, burn centers are expensive and therefore often require supplemental funding to operate.

Long-term Care Facilities

The Centers for Disease Control and Prevention (CDC) describes long-term care facilities (LTCFs) as "[n]ursing homes, skilled nursing facilities, and assisted living facilities... [that] provide a variety of services, both medical and personal care, to people who are unable to manage independently in the community."[9]

Skilled Nursing Facilities

A skilled nursing facility (SNF) that is certified under Medicare or Medicaid is defined as "an institution (or a distinct part of an institution) which is primarily engaged in providing skilled nursing care and related services...."[10] SNFs have 24-hour nursing care supervised by registered nurses (RNs) or licensed practical nurses (LPNs). Although patients of any age can use SNF services, most are elderly with multiple, chronic medical conditions requiring 24-hour nursing care.

Assisted Living Facilities

Although there is no universally accepted definition of assisted living, the National Center for Assisted Living provides the following: "In general, assisted living combines housing, personal care services, and nursing and health care in an environment that promotes maximum independence, privacy, and choice for people too frail to live alone but too healthy to require 24-hour nursing care."[11] In short, assisted living facilities (ALFs) are designed for patients who require long-term care but not around-the-clock nursing care as with SNFs. Services typically include "24-hour assistance with scheduled and unscheduled needs, social and recreational activities, three congregate meals per day plus snacks, laundry service, housekeeping, transportation, assistance with activities of daily living…and the provision and/or coordination of a range of other services that promote quality of life."[11]

Home Care/Visiting Nursing Services

Home care is care provided in the home for patients who require long-term care. It can be full time, part time, or 24 hours per day. Often provided through a home healthcare agency, different healthcare personnel can be deployed for different patient needs. For example, a home health aide can assist the patient with activities of daily living (e.g., bathing, dressing, meal preparation, and eating) while a registered nurse can be dispatched on a regular or as-needed basis to assess the patient's healthcare status (e.g., draw blood for routine lab testing, measure blood pressure and vital signs, assess the adequacy of pain control, medication setup and administration, and education). Home care agencies also can provide home-based physical therapy, occupational therapy, and respite care that provides occasional periods of home care so the patient's family caregivers or other caregivers can have a break from providing 24-hour-a-day care.

Community/Population Care

Community or population care focuses on the health of communities and populations rather than individuals. Organizations that focus on community health may be funded by government or private charities and vary widely in the populations they focus on and in their missions. The following provide only a few examples.

Federally Qualified Health Centers

Federally Qualified Health Centers (FQHCs) are healthcare organizations that receive enhanced reimbursement from Medicare and Medicaid if they meet a number of requirements, which include targeting an underserved population, charging a sliding-scale fee based on income, providing comprehensive services, having an ongoing quality assessment program, and having a board of directors.[12] Some examples of FQHCs are Community Health Centers that focus on underserved populations, Migrant Health Centers that focus on workers who move frequently, and Health Care for the Homeless Centers that focus on homeless adults and children.

Hospice/Palliative Care

Hospice care may be provided in an inpatient unit specially designed for palliative care or at home. Hospice or palliative care is often another service provided by home care agencies. Hospice care is most commonly provided in the home with support of hospice caregivers, family, and/or friends. Palliative care focuses on managing pain, nausea, or other discomfort associated with terminal disease. Hospice care is instituted when the patient's physician believes the patient has a life expectancy of less than six months and the patient does not desire further curative treatment. Patients with end-stage cancer often enter hospice care when further cancer treatment is not likely to yield any benefits and the patient wishes to be kept comfortable at home until death.

Types of Healthcare

There are many kinds of healthcare in the United States, many of which may occur in one or more of the aforementioned healthcare venues. A comprehensive review of all types of healthcare is beyond the scope of this chapter. We provide some salient examples here.

Primary Care

The vast majority of medical care occurs in primary care settings, also known as general medical care or personal healthcare. Primary care is where most patients first seek help for general medical problems. Primary care physicians (PCPs) are generally trained as family medicine physicians, general internal medicine physicians, or pediatricians.

General Medical Care

Primary care physicians deal with virtually every medical condition. The PCP's role is to manage the whole patient by diagnosing and treating illnesses as well as referring patients to specialists when there is a particular need, such as surgery or other specialty care. It is also the role of the PCP to coordinate care among all specialists the patient may be seeing, to ensure the best possible overall care.

Preventive Medicine

While many patients go to their PCP when they are sick or injured, PCPs also work with patients to try to prevent illnesses. For example, a PCP may recommend the use of seatbelts, check a patient's blood pressure, recommend that a patient quit smoking, or order a screening mammogram.

Medical Screening   *Medical screening* refers to performing tests on patients who have no signs or symptoms of a disease. The goal is to identify treatable diseases in the very early stages in order to start treatment as quickly as possible and avoid disease progression or complications. For example, all newborn infants are screened for rare metabolic diseases shortly after birth and all women are screened for breast cancer with mammograms beginning at age 50. Most patients are not aware that screening tests are not 100 percent accurate. Tests can be positive when no disease exists (false positive) and negative when disease does exist (false negative). Because screening tests are performed on large populations of patients, they are designed to be inexpensive and generally to favor false-positive results over false-negatives. Patients with positive screening tests generally are referred for "gold standard testing" that is much closer to 100 percent accurate. For example, a patient whose mammogram screens positive for a mass usually goes for further imaging and often a biopsy of the suspected tumor to confirm that the screening test is indeed positive. There are several breast conditions that mimic a tumor but are completely benign. However, because missing an actual cancer would be catastrophic for the patient, screening mammograms are recommended to ensure that as few cancers as possible are missed, despite the many false-positive results that will occur and end up causing unneeded biopsies.

Anticipatory Guidance Pediatricians give advice to parents based on the child's age and risk factors. This is called *anticipatory guidance*. As an example, when parents bring in a newborn baby for his or her two-week checkup, the pediatrician often recommends that the parents lower the temperature on their home's hot water heater to prevent accidentally scalding the baby. When the baby begins to crawl, the pediatrician typically recommends storing all home chemicals in unreachable locations or in child-safe cabinets. A family medicine physician may give anticipatory guidance to an 18-year-old patient by recommending, for example, to wear their seatbelt and refrain from using their phone when driving.

Behavioral Health

Behavioral health is provided in both inpatient (e.g., psychiatric hospital) and outpatient (e.g., behavioral health clinic) environments and focuses on psychiatric illnesses. Psychologists (usually doctoral-level providers who deliver talk therapy and behavioral therapy), psychiatrists (physicians who prescribe psychiatric medications), and social workers (who provide counseling and help with social issues) work in these venues, often as part of an interdisciplinary team.

Specialty Care

The American Board of Medical Specialties identifies 24 medical specialties (such as Surgery, Internal Medicine, and Pediatrics) and over 130 subspecialties (such as Addiction Psychiatry, Pain Medicine, Pediatric Emergency Medicine, and, notably, Clinical Informatics) for which it currently offers board certification.[13] Specialists generally have broader areas of practice than subspecialists. As technology and the science of medicine continue to advance, even more subspecialties are likely to be created as knowledge in the fields increases. Generally, patients are referred to medical specialists and subspecialists by PCPs. However, specialists and subspecialists also make referrals, and often patients self-refer.

Emergency Care

Emergent medical issues are those that are immediately life-threatening (e.g., a heart attack, stroke, or severe burns) or require immediate attention (e.g., a severe skin laceration or small fracture). Most hospitals have emergency departments, including specialty hospitals (e.g., psychiatric emergency rooms in psychiatric hospitals, cardiac emergency rooms in heart hospitals, etc.). There are also pediatric EDs with board-certified physicians in pediatric emergency medicine who specialize in the emergency treatment of children. Patients without insurance or the ability to pay for medical services often resort to using the ED for nonemergent medical issues, such as for minor infections or uncomplicated urinary tract infections. This is a serious national problem because the cost of treating routine medical issues in the emergent setting is often many times higher than the cost of treatment in the primary care setting.

Urgent Care

Urgent care is the care of non-life-threatening but still emergent medical issues such as uncomplicated urinary tract infections, mild to moderate asthma exacerbations, and ear infections. Urgent care is usually available during regular business hours and after hours. Some urgent care centers may be open 24 hours per day. Because of the high cost of treating non-life-threatening emergencies in the emergency department, most insurance companies provide coverage for urgent care in its many forms.

Acute Care vs. Chronic Care

Acute care refers to the diagnosis and treatment of early or presenting stages of a disease or illness whose treatment is usually limited to a defined period of time. Presenting symptoms of acute illnesses often appear suddenly and can be severe. Pneumonia is an example of a disease that may require acute care as a patient becomes feverish and short of breath, requiring oxygen or even mechanical ventilation. Pneumonia is treated with antibiotics and usually resolves within a week or two.

Chronic care refers to the diagnosis and treatment of illnesses that can span years or decades of life. Chronic diseases usually have symptoms that often present very gradually and that are not severe. Diabetes is an example of a chronic illness that requires chronic care. Patients require education about diabetes so they can manage their blood sugar level with a wide range of medications and dietary modifications. Patients with diabetes require ongoing diabetic prescriptions and routine screenings for retinal, kidney, and heart diseases, to name a few. Patients often live for more than half a century with chronic diseases that require chronic care.

Patient Education

Patient education takes place in virtually all healthcare venues. Critical to the successful treatment of most diseases is patient understanding of their disease and treatment requirements. This is especially true for chronic diseases such as diabetes. Diabetics benefit greatly from improved lifestyle (diabetic diet and regular exercise) and knowledge of how to control blood glucose level (how to use a glucometer to measure blood glucose, how to use and dose insulin, etc.). Education is a significant component of the treatment of addiction, as patients who better understand the disease are more likely to maintain sobriety. Most hospitals have patient education departments to provide patient education to both inpatients and outpatients. Many group practices and specialty centers have full-time patient educators as well as certified diabetic educators in primary care clinics, ostomy nurses in surgical clinics, and so on.

Integrative Medicine

Integrative medicine is a relatively new term that describes healthcare where the same provider offers both complementary and mainstream medicine in a coordinated manner.

An example of integrative medicine would be a physician prescribing both antihistamine drugs and treatment with an acupuncturist to treat seasonal allergies.

Complementary medicine is when a patient adds nonmainstream treatments to those prescribed by their physician. Complementary medicine is very popular in the United States. In 2012, data from the National Health Interview Survey (NHIS) indicated that 33 percent of adults and 12 percent of children used at least one complementary health approach, with dietary supplements being the most commonly used complementary medicine.[14]

Alternative medicine is the use of nonmainstream treatments in place of conventional medicine, usually without the supervision of a physician.[15] An example would be forgoing chemotherapy for a cancer in favor of using only herbal supplements.

Telehealth

According to the Center for Connected Health Policy, "Telehealth encompasses a broad variety of technologies and tactics to deliver virtual medical, health, and education services. Telehealth is not a specific service, but a collection of means to enhance care and education delivery."[16] Telehealth is practiced by a wide variety of primary care and specialist physicians using a variety of technologies to connect patients to physicians who otherwise could not see each other in person. Just a few examples include tele-dermatology, where images of skin rashes are sent for diagnosis by dermatologists; tele-radiology, where X-ray images are sent for interpretation by radiologists; and tele-psychiatry, where psychiatrists interview and treat patients at a distance. Some retail clinics such as Walgreens are also beginning to use telehealth so they don't have to maintain full-time onsite clinicians at all locations.

Healthcare Professions

There are myriad types of healthcare professionals. This section focuses on a few of the most common types of healthcare professionals and how they are trained and certified to practice.

Certification and Accreditation

Most healthcare professions have both certifying and accrediting bodies. Individuals receive certification indicating they possess the necessary education, training, and experience to practice in their specialty. Certification of individuals often requires passing a board exam that is maintained and administered by a board of experts. Training programs receive accreditation indicating that the design and operation of the training program meets the standards of the profession. Most certifying and accrediting bodies are independent, nonprofit organizations formed by professional organizations to ensure impartiality and limit any potential or perceived conflicts of interest. Some examples of the training and certification requirements of various healthcare professionals follow.

Physicians

Becoming a physician in the United States requires completion of the following educational sequence:

1. Undergraduate degree with premed required coursework in biology, chemistry, and math (4 years).

2. Medical degree from an Association of American Medical Colleges (AAMC) accredited medical school (4 years).

3. Accreditation Council for Graduate Medical Education (ACGME) accredited residency training program (3–6 years).

4. American Board of Medical Specialties (ABMS) certification in the specialty of the physician's residency by passing a board exam.

5. Optional ACGME accredited fellowship for subspecialization, which can be in one or more subspecialties (1–4 years).

6. Optional certification in the subspecialty of the physician's fellowship(s) by passing a board exam.

7. Maintenance of Certification (MOC) that includes ongoing required educational programs and recertification exams in each of the specialties and subspecialties in which a physician is certified (various educational activities and recertification board exam usually every 10 years). Many physicians maintain several specialty and subspecialty certifications.

As previously mentioned in the "Specialty Care" section, ABMS identifies 24 medical specialties and over 130 subspecialties for which it currently offers board exams.[13] The U.S. Bureau of Labor Statistics reported a total of 708,300 physicians and surgeons practicing in the United States in 2014.[17]

Nurses

A registered nurse (RN) can be trained in a two-year associate degree program at a community college or a junior college, a two- to three-year diploma program offered through a hospital, or a four- to five-year bachelor's of science degree program at a university or college. Nurses with a bachelor's degree can undertake advanced studies in several clinical areas to develop the needed competence for teaching, supervision, or advanced practice. Advanced practice RNs take on various advanced practice roles such as nurse practitioners, clinical nurse specialists, nurse anesthetists, or nurse midwives. There are also master's degree and doctoral programs for nurses who wish to specialize. In 2015, the American Nurses Association (ANA) estimated there were 3.4 million registered nurses in the United States.[18] RNs must pass the National Council Licensure Examination for RNs (NCLEX-RN) to be licensed in the United States or Canada.[19]

Licensed practical nurses (LPNs) work under the direct supervision of an RN or physician. LPNs train for one year at state-approved technical/vocational schools or community/junior colleges. Like RNs, LPNs must pass an examination for licensure.

In 2014, there were a total of 719,900 LPNs and licensed vocational nurses (LVNs) in the United States.[20]

Pharmacists

Pharmacists must complete six years of training in a pharmacy school accredited by the American Council for Pharmacy Education that awards a PharmD degree. After graduation, pharmacists must pass a state-licensing exam and complete an internship with a licensed pharmacist before practicing. Some pharmacy schools also offer master's and PhD degrees that allow pharmacists to specialize in one or more of eight specialty areas.

Dentists

Similar to physicians, dental school applicants require a bachelor's degree. Dental students must complete four years at a dental school accredited by the Commission on Dental Accreditation (CODA). Passing a board exam given by the Joint Commission on National Dental Examinations (JCNDE), which administers the certification tests for dentists, is also required. There are nine recognized dental subspecialties for which a dentist must complete a dental residency to earn a subspecialty credential. In 2014, there was a total of 151,500 dentists practicing in the United States.[21]

Allied Health Personnel

Allied health personnel represent a varied and complex array of healthcare disciplines and support, complement, or supplement the professional functions of physicians. There are over 80 allied health professions. A few examples include laboratory technologists and technicians, therapeutic science practitioners (e.g., physical and occupational therapists), and speech language pathologists. There is a variety of training programs, and many states have licensing requirements. Approximately 60 percent of all healthcare providers are allied health personnel.[22]

Healthcare Reform and Quality

As rapidly as care delivery is changing, the ways in which care is paid for and how the quality is measured are changing faster. These changes will lead to significant adaptations in the organizations of care delivery systems, the ways in which healthcare providers interact, and the process of care itself.

Costs—U.S. Expenditures Overall Compared to Other Countries

According to the World Bank, the United States spent 17.1 percent of its gross domestic product (GDP) on healthcare in 2014, which represents $9,403 annually per capita. This was up from 13.1 percent in 1995 and is the highest percentage of GDP that any major Western country spends on healthcare.[23] Despite its highest of costs, the United States ranks only 37th on WHO's ranked country list of overall health system performance. The United States' ranking is between 36th-ranked Costa Rica and 38th-ranked Slovenia.[24] The extremely high costs coupled with the relatively low quality of care delivered is the motivation for multiple government programs to either reduce costs or improve healthcare quality in the United States.

Affordable Care Act (ACA)

The Affordable Care Act (ACA), also known as "Obamacare," was signed into law by President Obama on March 23, 2010. It is the federal government's most comprehensive attempt to control the costs of healthcare and improve its quality. Most of the law has been implemented over the last six years. Some provisions will not go into effect until 2018. Examples of some of the law's major provisions include[25]

- Requiring all Americans to have some basic form of health insurance or pay a federal tax penalty
- Creating health insurance exchanges through which uninsured Americans can buy coverage in an arena where there is competition between insurance companies
- Providing subsidies for the purchase of coverage through state exchanges to Americans who have the least ability to pay
- Allowing young adults to continue coverage on their parents' health insurance up to the age of 26
- Ending preexisting condition exclusions (barring insurance companies from refusing to insure an applicant due to an existing medical condition)
- Ending lifetime limits on insurance coverage
- Providing preventative care at no cost
- Removing insurance company barriers to emergency services

HITECH Meaningful Use Provision

On February 17, 2009, President Obama signed into law the Health Information Technology for Economic and Clinical Health (HITECH) Act as part of the American Recovery and Reinvestment Act (ARRA). The HITECH Act "provides HHS [Health and Human Services] with the authority to establish programs to improve health care quality, safety, and efficiency through the promotion of health IT, including electronic health records and private and secure electronic health information exchange."[26] Part of HITECH was intended to incentivize the adoption of the "meaningful use" of electronic health records (EHRs) by physicians, physician groups, and hospitals by paying them a bonus if and when they reached 1 of 3 progressive stages of "meaningful use." Each stage requires that physicians and healthcare organizations meet a defined set of objectives that make up each level. The complexity of the objectives increases with each stage. The program accelerated the adoption of EHRs, but by the end of November 2014, only 25.2 percent of physicians and 43.1 percent of hospitals had met stage 2 requirements.[27, 28]

Medicare Access and CHIP Reauthorization Act of 2015

On April 16, 2015, President Obama signed into law the Medicare Access and CHIP Reauthorization Act of 2015 (MACRA). The law extended funding for Medicaid's Children's Health Insurance Program (CHIP) for two years and created a schedule that predictably specifies the inflation rate for Medicare physician reimbursements rather than having Congress address physician reimbursement annually.[29] MACRA is designed to help move Medicare reimbursement from the current, volume-based system (i.e., fee-for-service, where more services alone result in more payments) to a value-based system (i.e., value-based care, where providers are rewarded, or penalized, for the quality of patient outcomes). The clear goal is to incentivize quality of care over volume of care. MACRA combined three previous quality-reporting programs (including the Meaningful Use program) into one unified reporting system. Under MACRA, physicians may choose participation in one of the two MACRA payment systems described next.[30]

Merit-based Incentive Payment System (MIPS)

MIPS allows individual physicians or physician groups to collect and report various quality metrics for reporting to CMS. The metrics essentially score physicians on the following:

- Quality of care (30 percent of score)
- Resource use (30 percent of score)
- Clinical practice improvement activities (15 percent of score)
- Meaningful use of certified EHR technology (25 percent of score)

The score will determine whether a physician or physician group will receive a financial bonus or penalty based on the amount of their Medicare reimbursement at the end of each year.[31]

Alternate Payment Models (APMs)

Those who choose to participate in the APMs program will not be subject to MIPS adjustments. Physicians choosing APMs will receive an annual incentive payment based on 5 percent of the previous year's performance in the new payment model.[32] See Chapter 3 for additional details.

Healthcare Regulatory and Research Organizations

Healthcare is a highly regulated industry with multiple government and private organizations involved in oversight of multiple aspects of the industry. In addition, healthcare delivery and medical research are tightly intertwined, adding complexity that has to be taken into account.

Regulation

There are numerous health regulatory agencies, and they exist at multiple levels of government. What follows are some of the regulatory bodies most relevant to healthcare in general and to health information technology in particular.

Centers for Medicare and Medicaid Services (CMS)

CMS is part of the federal government under the Secretary for Health and Human Services that administers Medicare (federal health insurance for Americans 65 and older and others with certain medical conditions) and Medicaid (federally subsidized, state-administered healthcare for low-income individuals). The estimated CMS budget for the 2016 fiscal year is $970.8 billion.[33]

Because CMS is a very large source of healthcare funding, it exerts regulatory authority over the healthcare providers it reimburses for care. In addition, because CMS pays for such a large portion of healthcare in the United States, many other public healthcare agencies, and even private insurance companies, often follow many of CMS's regulations. The Affordable Care Act, for example, is administered primarily through CMS. The MACRA and Meaningful Use programs are also administered by CMS. Although in the case of HIT, the Office of the National Coordinator for Health Information Technology (ONC) sets the regulations for meaningful use and EHR certification standards, while CMS enforces these by administering the financial aspects of the regulations.

Office of the National Coordinator for Health Information Technology (ONC)

The ONC is responsible for setting policies and standards for, as well as promoting the use of, HIT in the United States. According to its website:

> The Office of the National Coordinator for Health Information Technology (ONC) is at the forefront of the administration's health IT efforts and is a resource to the entire health system to support the adoption of health information technology and the promotion of nationwide health information exchange to improve healthcare. ONC is organizationally located within the Office of the Secretary for the U.S. Department of Health and Human Services (HHS). ONC is the principal federal entity charged with coordination of nationwide efforts to implement and use the most advanced health information technology and the electronic exchange of health information. The position of National Coordinator was created in 2004, through an Executive Order, and legislatively mandated in the Health Information Technology for Economic and Clinical Health Act (HITECH Act) of 2009.[34]

There is a great deal of information about the ONC's activities, programs, and standards on its website, www.healthit.gov.

U.S. Food and Drug Administration (FDA)

The FDA "is responsible for protecting the public health by assuring the safety, efficacy, and security of human and veterinary drugs, biological products, medical devices, our nation's food supply, cosmetics, and products that emit radiation."[35] With over 16,700 full-time employees, the 2017 FDA budget proposal is $5.1 billion. Notably, even though the adoption of HIT has been shown to hold the potential to affect patients' health in a seriously negative manner,[36, 37] the FDA does not regulate HIT as medical devices. HIT is primarily regulated by the ONC and the CMS.

The U.S. Centers for Disease Control and Prevention (CDC)

While not a regulatory agency of the government, the CDC "keeps America secure by controlling disease outbreaks; making sure food and water are safe; helping people to avoid leading causes of death such as heart disease, cancer, stroke, and diabetes; and working globally to reduce threats to the nation's health."[38] The CDC employs more than 14,000 people in 11 facilities. The CDC's budget for fiscal year 2016 is $7 billion. The CDC also aggregates various health data sets from healthcare organizations around the country and throughout the world.

The CDC's Emerging Infections Program (EIP) is a network of state and local health departments, academic institutions, and others that submit data on infectious diseases to contribute to a CDC database used to monitor invasive bacterial disease. A few examples of the data sets the CDC collects and maintains are as follows:[39]

- **Active Bacterial Core surveillance (ABCs)** Active population-based laboratory surveillance for invasive bacterial disease, including groups A and B *streptococcus*, *Haemophilus influenza*, *Neisseria meningitidis*, *Streptococcus pneumoniae*, and methicillin-resistant *Staphylococcus aureus* (MRSA).

- **FoodNet** An active population-based laboratory surveillance database used to monitor the incidence of foodborne diseases. Surveillance is conducted for seven bacterial and two parasitic pathogens.

- **Healthcare-Associated Infections–Community Interface (HAIC) projects** Active population-based surveillance for *Clostridium difficile* and other healthcare-associated infections caused by bacteria such as MRSA, *Candida*, and multidrug-resistant gram-negative bacteria.

The Joint Commission (JC)

The Joint Commission is an independent, not-for-profit organization that is the accrediting body for most hospitals, ambulatory care centers, behavioral health centers, home healthcare, and other healthcare organizations in the United States. To maintain accreditation, healthcare organizations must undergo an onsite survey visit every three years. The survey focuses on structural, process, and outcome measures elements during the onsite visits. Structural elements evaluate the adequacy and safety of the physical facilities (e.g., whether the facilities are adequate to prevent patient falls). Process elements evaluate various clinical, administrative, and work processes (e.g., what fall-prevention processes are in place, such as asking patients who check into an ambulatory clinic if they feel steady on their feet). Outcome measure elements focus on various patient outcome metrics (e.g., what the rate of patient falls in the hospital is and whether the rate is increasing or decreasing). While the JC does not evaluate HIT specifically, many of the elements it evaluates require appropriate HIT deployment. JC accreditation is a requirement to receive reimbursement from Medicare and Medicaid.

Research

The last 50 years have seen remarkable growth of scientifically rigorous research in medicine, dentistry, nursing, and other health professions. This has fostered the move toward evidence-based medicine through which the practice of medicine is driven by scientific evidence, rather than just clinical impression, tradition, and anecdotal reports. There are essentially four types of research:

- **Basic science or "bench" research**   Biochemists, physiologists, biologists, pharmacologists, and other scientists work on the myriad of biochemical processes that occur in disease and in health. Experiments are performed on animals, in petri dishes, or in test tubes.

- **Clinical research**   Research performed on groups of humans. An example of clinical research is testing which of two drugs works better for controlling high blood pressure.

- **Population or epidemiological research**   Research on how disease impacts populations and how the social determinants of health interact with disease in populations. An example of population research is how the children in Flint, Michigan, have been (and will be) affected by their water system's lead poisoning.

- **Health services research**   Studies the operation and outcomes of the healthcare system itself and ways to improve quality and reduce costs. An example of health services research is a study to determine the impact on cost or quality of the installation of an EHR system in a clinic.

Biomedical research is funded from a variety of sources. Most researchers at universities write applications for grants to fund their research, and the funders award grants to those researchers who they believe are working on appropriate and meaningful scientific problems and who are the best qualified to do the work. According to a 2015 analysis, total biomedical research funding in the United States was $117 billion in 2012 (4.5 percent of total U.S. healthcare expenditures).[40] However, the annual rate of growth of biomedical research spending declined from 6 percent per year (1994–2004) to 0.8 percent (2004–2012).[40] Although the United States is still the leader in dollars spent, the U.S. leadership role has been declining in recent years. The major sources of U.S. biomedical research funding are described next.

National Institutes of Health (NIH)

NIH is the primary federal funding source for biomedical research. NIH is composed of 29 individual institutes and centers. The total NIH budget for fiscal year 2016 is $31.3 billion. A complete list of all the institutes and centers, along with their functional statements and organizational charts, is available online.[41]

One of the NIH institutes, the National Library of Medicine (NLM), is the primary federal funder of biomedical informatics and health IT research. Among many other services, NLM maintains a curated index of most of the world's biomedical literature, accessible via its search engine, PubMed.[42]

Agency for Healthcare Research and Quality (AHRQ)

AHRQ is a relatively small government agency within HHS with an annual budget of just under $480 million.[43] However, it has an important mission to produce evidence to make healthcare safer, higher quality, more accessible, equitable, and affordable, and to work within the U.S. Department of Health and Human Services and with other partners to make sure that the evidence is understood and used.[44] In alignment with its mission, the AHRQ funds health services research as well as a substantial HIT portfolio that evaluates the effectiveness of HIT to improve the quality of healthcare and reduce its costs. The AHRQ also maintains over 11,000 evidence-based clinical practice guidelines that have met the AHRQ's evaluation criteria. These have been collected in a database, organized by searchable topics, and made available online to healthcare professionals and the general public at the AHRQ's National Guideline Clearinghouse (www.guideline.gov).

Others

There are many other sources of biomedical research funding in the United States, including other government agencies, charitable foundations, and private industry.

Chapter Review

This chapter provided a high-level overview of how the U.S. healthcare system is structured and major changes to expect. The structures are complex, in part due to the nature of the task, but also due to funding and regulatory intricacies. Even the terminologies, abbreviations, and implicit assumptions can be daunting to master, and it is safe to say that no one understands all aspects of healthcare deeply. Given the complexity and rapid rate of change in this area, no overview will be complete or fully up to date and the details will continue to change, but the basic concepts and characteristics should continue to hold true at least for multiple years. This change means that health IT systems need to be adaptable and to anticipate that the environment in which they are used will continue to evolve, adding yet another dimension to an already challenging field.

Questions

To test your comprehension of the chapter, answer the following questions and then check your answers against the list of correct answers at the end of the chapter.

1. Which of the following describes academic health centers?
   A. Any healthcare venue where research is performed
   B. Usually a portion of a major university where hospital(s) are co-located with schools such as medicine, nursing, and pharmacy
   C. Limited to one institution per state
   D. Required to conduct federally funded research or lose their accreditation

2. Which of the following does *not* characterize urgent care centers?

   A. Usually open during late evening and weekend hours

   B. Located in convenient locations in the community such as in shopping centers and malls

   C. Designed for patients who need immediate but not life-threatening care

   D. Owned only by public health agencies

3. Which of the following is not true about emergency departments?

   A. Can refuse treatment to patients who are unable to pay

   B. Are designed to provide immediate and life-sustaining treatment to patients who are seriously ill or injured

   C. Are often overcrowded because many underserved patients use the emergency department as their source for primary care medical issues

   D. Treat heart attacks, strokes, and traumatic injuries (e.g., people in serious traffic accidents)

4. Which of the following is true of hospice care?

   A. Focuses on managing patients' pain, nausea, and any other discomforts associated with a terminal illness (i.e., when the patient is believed to have less than six months to live)

   B. Can be provided to patients who are still receiving active treatment for their disease (e.g., chemotherapy)

   C. Is only provided in the inpatient setting

   D. Is only provided by hospitals

5. Which of the following is *not* a provision of the Affordable Care Act (ACA):

   A. Requires all Americans to have a basic form of health insurance or pay a federal tax penalty

   B. Allows a young adult to continue coverage on their parents' health insurance up to the age of 26

   C. Requires all Americans to see only physicians assigned to them by the federal government

   D. Ends preexisting condition exclusions so that insurance companies cannot refuse to insure an applicant due to an existing medical condition

6. Which of the following does *not* accurately describe the Office of the National Coordinator for Health Information Technology?

   A. Is responsible for setting policies and standards for, as well as promoting the use of, health IT in the United States

   B. Charges fines to physicians or hospitals that do not comply with its health IT regulations

C. Is also known as "the Office of the National Coordinator" or "the ONC"

D. Is organizationally located within the Office of the Secretary for the U.S. Department of Health and Human Services (HHS)

7. Which of the following is a true statement about medical screening?

   A. Performs tests on patients who have no signs or symptoms of a disease with the goal to identify treatable diseases in the very early stages in order to start treatment as quickly as possible and avoid disease progression or complications

   B. Cannot have "false positive" or "false negative" results

   C. Is performed when a physician is fairly certain a patient has a particular disease

   D. Is typically performed on patients suspected of having a disease in order to help the physician make an accurate diagnosis and begin treatment in a timely and cost-effective manner

8. Which of the following does *not* accurately describe Federally Qualified Health Centers (FQHCs)?

   A. Healthcare organizations that receive enhanced reimbursement from Medicare and Medicaid if they meet a number of requirements

   B. Include such examples as Community Health Centers that focus on underserved populations, Migrant Health Centers that focus on workers who move frequently, and Health Care for the Homeless Centers that focus on homeless adults and children

   C. Target underserved populations, charge a sliding-scale fee based on income, and have ongoing quality assessment programs

   D. Any health center that receives reimbursement from Medicare or Medicaid

Answers

1. **B.** It is a hospital or health system that has a formalized relationship with a university. Academic health centers usually support the training of many of the health professions, support and conduct research, and offer care not widely available in the regions they serve.

2. **D.** Urgent care centers are somewhat similar to emergency departments in that they provide care outside of the usual hours that ambulatory care providers are available, but urgent care centers are not designed to provide care for complex or life-threatening illnesses. In addition to offering longer hours, they tend to be located for convenient access. Pharmacies, health systems, private medical practices, and others can own and operate urgent care centers.

3. **A.** All emergency departments must treat patients regardless of their ability to pay.

4. **A.** Hospice care is provided in a variety of settings, including at home. The care is focused on palliative care, including the patient's spiritual and emotional needs, and is not intended to cure or treat the patient's illness.

5. C. The ACA includes many provisions but attempts to preserve patient choice of insurance plan and providers within the insurance plan's provision.

6. B. While the ONC defines many of the technological criteria and coordinates across federal and nonfederal partners, the Center for Medicare and Medicaid Services, as the largest payer of healthcare in the United States, has created incentives for providers to adopt (and penalties for providers who do not adopt) HIT under the Meaningful Use program of the ACA, and will continue to do so under MACRA.

7. A. As part of preventive care, medical screening is one of the few healthcare activities targeted at healthy individuals rather than those with a disease.

8. D. FQHCs are established by a very specific federal program. There are many health centers that share many characteristics with FQHCs but do not meet all of the program requirements and, therefore, are not FQHCs.

References

1. Centers for Disease Control and Prevention (CDC). (2012). *National ambulatory medical care survey: 2012 state and national summary tables.* Accessed on August 21, 2016, from www.cdc.gov/nchs/data/ahcd/namcs_summary/2012_namcs_web_tables.pdf.

2. Punke, H. (2014, July 14). 8 statistics on physician employment. *Becker's Hospital Review.* Accessed on August 2016, 2016, from www.beckershospitalreview.com/hospital-physician-relationships/8-statistics-on-physician-employment.html.

3. American Hospital Association. (2016). *Fast facts on US hospitals.* Accessed on February 18, 2016, from www.aha.org/research/rc/stat-studies/101207fastfacts.pdf.

4. Association of American Medical Colleges. (2016, Sept. 25). *Why teaching hospitals are important to all Americans.* Accessed on December 8, 2016, from https://news.aamc.org/for-the-media/article/teaching-hospitals-important-americans/.

5. World Health Organization. (1998). *Health promotion glossary.* Accessed on August 22, 2016, from www.who.int/healthpromotion/about/HPR%20Glossary%201998.pdf.

6. National Association of County and City Health Officials. (2014). *2013 national profile of local health departments.* Accessed on August 21, 2016, from http://archived.naccho.org/topics/infrastructure/profile/upload/2013-National-Profile-of-Local-Health-Departments-report.pdf.

7. Tricare. (2015). *Tricare facts and figures.* Accessed on August 21, 2016, from www.tricare.mil/About/Facts.

8. Ashwood, J. S., Gaynor, M., Setodji, C. M., Reid, R. O., Weber, E., & Mehrotra, A. (2016). Retail clinic visits for low-acuity conditions increase utilization and spending. *Health Affairs, 35,* 449–455.

9. CDC. (2015). *Nursing homes and assisted living (long-term care facilities [LTCFs]).* Accessed on August 21, 2016, from www.cdc.gov/longtermcare/.

10. Long Term Care Education.com. (n.d.). *Skilled care facilities.* Accessed on August 21, 2016, from www.ltce.com/learn/skilledcare.php.

11. National Center for Assisted Living. (2001). *The assisted living sourcebook.* Accessed on August 21, 2016, from www.ahcancal.org/research_data/trends_statistics/Documents/Assisted_Living_Sourcebook_2001.pdf.

12. U.S. Department of Health and Human Services (HSS), Health Resources and Services Administration. (n.d.). *What are federally qualified health centers (FQHCs)?* Accessed on September 12, 2016, from www.hrsa.gov/healthit/toolbox/RuralHealthITtoolbox/Introduction/qualified.html.

13. American Board of Medical Specialties. (n.d.). *Specialty and subspecialty certificates.* Accessed on March 28, 2016, from www.abms.org/member-boards/specialty-subspecialty-certificates/.

14. National Center for Complementary and Integrative Health (NCCIH). (2015). *What complementary and integrative approaches do Americans use? Key findings from the 2012 national health interview survey.* Accessed on May 13, 2016, from https://nccih.nih.gov/research/statistics/NHIS/2012/key-findings.

15. NCCIH. (2016). *Complementary, alternative, or integrative health: What's in a name?* Accessed on May 13, 2016, from https://nccih.nih.gov/health/integrative-health.

16. Center for Connected Health Policy. (n.d.). *What is telehealth?* Accessed on August 23, 2016, from http://cchpca.org/what-is-telehealth.

17. U.S. Department of Labor, Bureau of Labor Statistics. (2016). Physicians and surgeons. *Occupational outlook handbook, 2016–2017.* Accessed on August 24, 2016, from www.bls.gov/ooh/healthcare/physicians-and-surgeons.htm#tab-1.

18. McMenamin, P. (2015). *ANA: Voice of 3.4 million nurses and growing.* Accessed on September 8, 2016, from www.ananursespace.org/blogs/peter-mcmenamin/2015/06/29/ana?ssopc=1.

19. Bureau of Labor Statistics. (2016). How to become a Registered Nurse. Accessed on January 26, 2017 from https://www.bls.gov/ooh/healthcare/registered-nurses.htm#tab-4.

20. Bureau of Labor Statistics. (2016). Licensed practical and licensed vocational nurses. *Occupational outlook handbook, 2016–2017.* Accessed on May 8, 2016, from www.bls.gov/ooh/healthcare/licensed-practical-and-licensed-vocational-nurses.htm.

21. Bureau of Labor Statistics. (2016). Dentists. *Occupational outlook handbook, 2016–2017.* Accessed on May 11, 2016, from www.bls.gov/ooh/healthcare/dentists.htm#tab-1.

22. ExploreHealthCareers.org. (2016). *Allied health professions overview.* Accessed on May 11, 2016, from http://explorehealthcareers.org/en/Field/1/Allied_Health_Professions.aspx.

23. The World Bank. (n.d.). *Health expenditure, total (% of GDP).* Accessed on August 25, 2016, from http://data.worldbank.org/indicator/SH.XPD.TOTL.ZS.

24. Tandon, A., Murray, C. J. L., Lauer, J. A., & Evans, D. B. (2001). *Measuring overall health system performance for 191 countries* (GPE discussion paper series: no. 30). World Health Organization. Accessed on August 2016, 2016, from www.who.int/healthinfo/paper30.pdf.

25. HHS. (n.d.). *About the law.* Accessed on April 3, 2016, from www.hhs.gov/healthcare/about-the-law/index.html.

26. Office of the National Coordinator for Health Information Technology (ONC). (n.d.). *Health IT legislation and regulations.* Accessed on August 25, 2016, from www.healthit.gov/policy-researchers-implementers/health-it-legislation.

27. Healthcare Information and Management Systems Society. (2015, Jan. 16). *CMS and ONC provide MU data update to Health IT Policy Committee.* Accessed on March 9, 2016, from www.himss.org/News/NewsDetail .aspx?ItemNumber=37995.

28. ONC. (2015, Jan. 13). *Data analytics update.* Health IT Policy Committee meeting. Accessed on March 9, 2016, from www.healthit.gov/facas/sites/faca/files/HITPC_Data_Analytics_update_2015-01-13_v3.pptx.

29. Fabian, J. (2015). Obama signs $200 billion "doc fix" bill. *The Hill*, April 16. Accessed on December 16, 2016, from http://thehill.com/homenews/administration/239165-obama-signs-200b-doc-fix-bill.

30. Centers for Medicare and Medicaid Services (CMS). (n.d.). *MACRA: Delivery system reform, Medicare payment reform.* Accessed on March 8, 2016, from www .cms.gov/Medicare/Quality-Initiatives-Patient-Assessment-Instruments/Value-Based-Programs/MACRA-MIPS-and-APMs/MACRA-MIPS-and-APMs.html.

31. Conway, P., Gronniger, T., Pham, H., Goodrich, K., Bassano, A., Sharp, J. P., … MacHarris, M. (2015, Sept. 28). MACRA: New opportunities for Medicare providers through innovative payment systems (updated). *Health Affairs Blog.* Accessed on March 8, 2016, from http://healthaffairs.org/blog/2015/09/28/macra-new-opportunities-for-medicare-providers-through-innovative-payment-systems-3/.

32. CMS. (2016). *Quality Payment Program.* Accessed on December 16, 2016, from https://qpp.cms.gov/.

33. CMS. (2016). *HHS FY2016 budget in brief: CMS budget overview.* Accessed on December 16, 2016 from https://www.hhs.gov/about/budget/budget-in-brief/cms/.

34. ONC. (n.d.). *About ONC.* Accessed on March 8, 2016, from www.healthit.gov/newsroom/about-onc.

35. U.S. Food and Drug Administration. (n.d.). *What we do.* Accessed on August 26, 2016, from www.fda.gov/AboutFDA/WhatWeDo/default.htm.

36. Han, Y. Y., Carcillo J. A., Venkataraman, S.T., Clark, R. S., Watson, R. S., Nguyen, T. C., … Orr, R. A (2005). Unexpected increased mortality after implementation of a commercially sold computerized physician order entry system. *Pediatrics, 116*, 1506–1512.

37. Sittig, D. F., Ash, J. S., Zhang, J., Osheroff, J. A., & Shabot, M. M. (2006). Lessons from "unexpected increased mortality after implementation of a commercially sold computerized physician order entry system." *Pediatrics, 118*, 797–801.

38. CDC. (n.d.). *Fast facts about CDC.* Accessed on August 26, 2016, from www.cdc.gov/about/facts/cdcfastfacts/cdcfacts.html.

39. CDC. (n.d.). *Emerging infections programs.* Accessed on August 26, 2016, from www.cdc.gov/ncezid/dpei/eip/index.html.

40. Moses, H., III, Matheson, D. H., Cairns-Smith, S., George, B. P., Palisch, C., & Dorsey, E. R. (2015). The anatomy of medical research: US and international comparisons. *JAMA, 313*, 174–189.

41. National Institutes of Health. (n.d.). *Organization charts/functional statements.* Accessed on August 16, 2016, from https://oma.od.nih.gov/DMS/Pages/ Organizational-Changes-Org-Chart-Function.aspx.

42. U.S. National Library of Medicine. (n.d.). *About the National Library of Medicine.* Accessed on August 26, 2016, from www.nlm.nih.gov/about/index.html.

43. DHS, Agency for Healthcare Research and Quality (AHRQ). (2015). *Fiscal year 2016 justification of estimates for appropriations committees.* Accessed on August 26, 2016, from www.ahrq.gov/sites/default/files/wysiwyg/cpi/about/ mission/budget/2016/cj2016.pdf.

44. DHS, AHRQ. (n.d.). *About AHRQ.* Accessed on May 24, 2016, from www.ahrq .gov/cpi/about/index.html.

An Overview of How Healthcare Is Paid For in the United States

Donald Nichols*

In this chapter, you will learn how to

- Explain how Americans pay for the healthcare they receive
- Describe how health insurance plays a central role in healthcare payment
- Understand what Medicare, Medicaid, and commercial health insurance programs are and how they are similar and how they are distinct
- Describe the five major types of insurance products
- Explain how healthcare reform is likely to affect the organization of and payment for healthcare in the future

Healthcare is different from most other goods and services purchased in the United States in that the purchase of healthcare services involves, in almost all cases, the participation of a third party: the health insurance firm. While there are mechanisms to provide (and to pay for) care to those who lack health insurance—so-called funds for charity or uncompensated care—the care for the vast majority of Americans is paid for by the government (through the Medicare and Medicaid programs) or by private health insurance, which is almost always tied to employment. To understand how healthcare is paid for in the United States, it is necessary first to understand how insurance operates in the United States.

*This chapter updates Chapter 2, by Cary Sennett and Donald Nichols, in *Healthcare Information Technology Exam Guide for CompTIA* Healthcare IT Technician & HIT Pro™ Certifications* (McGraw-Hill Education, 2013). The author acknowledges the contributions of Cary Sennett in the first edition.

The Nature of Health Insurance

In theory, the objective of health insurance is to pool risk. Illness—particularly catastrophic illness that could bankrupt a family—is (fortunately) rare. Insurance is a vehicle that allows individuals to pay (for example, annually) a relatively small amount to an insurance pool, which covers the costs (of necessary services) for those individuals who are unfortunate enough to need care. It is important to note that insurance works only when there is broad participation and, in particular, only when individuals who are at low risk for illness participate (to counterbalance those who are at high risk for illness). The cost of insurance—the insurance *premium*—is set based on predicted expenses (the so-called actuarially fair value, to which administrative costs are added) for all individuals in the covered population; if only high-risk/high-cost individuals participate in the insurance pool, the cost of insurance is likely to be perceived as prohibitive (and, in fact, the primary objective of insurance—to pool risk—is lost).

Initially, health insurance in the United States was designed to protect against potentially catastrophic expense, in particular, the cost of hospitalization or other care that was not routine. Over time, though, insurance has evolved from a risk-mitigation strategy to a prepayment strategy; that is, more and more, health insurance in the United States is designed to cover not only unexpected and potentially catastrophic healthcare needs but predictable healthcare needs (for example, preventive services).

For example, many economists—including the author—argue that using insurance as a prepayment vehicle is not only inefficient (the economists' term) but wasteful. If an individual expects to have a service (for example, a woman expects to have a mammogram), bundling it into insurance means that the price of insurance rises by the expected cost of the mammogram *in addition to* the administrative fee that is loaded on by the insurance administrator. Using insurance to prepay for the mammogram simply adds that administrative cost. That said, the coverage by insurance of routine (preventive) services is now almost universal. Despite the theoretical argument that coverage for preventive care is not a goal of insurance, the marketplace appears to have spoken: the role of insurance has evolved from pure risk mitigation to include prepayment. The market for healthcare purchasing is complex; arguments about the proper role of insurance require consideration that is beyond the scope of this chapter.

The Structure of Health Insurance

Health insurance establishes rules for paying for healthcare, but at the end of the day, the dollars that are disbursed through health insurance systems come from other sources. It is important to take a brief look at who pays for what.

To begin with, Americans purchase (or, in some cases, receive as an entitlement) health insurance; when they do, they pay an annual premium, which typically depends on their family structure (whether they are purchasing insurance for themselves or for their family) and the nature of the insurance they are purchasing. When they use that insurance (to purchase or, more accurately, to obtain reimbursement for healthcare services that are covered by that insurance), they may also face costs (which depend on the nature of the insurance), in particular, a deductible and a copayment. The insurance *deductible* is a sum (that is tied to the structure of the insurance policy and hence to its price) that the insured must pay for healthcare services before the insurer pays; in other words, it is a way of maintaining the original objective of insurance (to protect against very high costs). A deductible typically must be met on an annual basis so that insurance covers nothing until it is met, but once it is met, it need not be paid again in that year. In addition to the deductible, there is typically a *copayment*: the consumer's share of the cost for every service that is reimbursable. Again, copayment levels vary across insurance contracts and clearly tie to price; the higher the copayment, the higher the consumer's share of the cost of the service and (importantly) the more likely it is that the consumer will forego a high-cost service (or substitute a lower-cost service for that high-cost one). So, the purpose of a copayment is less to transfer payment (cost) from the insurer to the insured than it is to increase the sensitivity of the insured to the cost of service and—through that—reduce demand for services (and especially reduce demand for high-cost services).

Insurance in the United States

With the preceding brief overview of the nature and structure of insurance complete, we turn our attention to the insurance market in the United States.

There are three primary mechanisms through which Americans currently receive health insurance:

- **Commercial (private) health insurance**, which in the vast majority of cases is provided through an employer (employer-sponsored health insurance) but which can be purchased on an individual basis (typically at significantly higher cost). In 2015, the majority of Americans—approximately 214 million—were covered by private/commercial insurance programs,[1] with the vast majority of those (about 178 million, or 83 percent) through employer-sponsored health insurance.

- **The federally sponsored Medicare program**, which provides an insurance benefit to the elderly (Americans 65 and older), as well as to those who are disabled and those with end-stage renal disease (ESRD). In 2015, Medicare insured approximately 51.9 million Americans.

- **The Medicaid program**, which is administered by the states but funded by both the state and federal governments and which provides an insurance benefit to the economically disadvantaged as well as to certain categories of women (especially pregnant women) and children (through Medicaid or through a similar program called the State Children's Health Insurance Program [SCHIP], or now simply the Children's Health Insurance Program [CHIP]). In 2015, these programs insured approximately 62.4 million Americans.

In addition, nearly 14.9 million Americans received health insurance/healthcare through the military healthcare system (including Tricare and programs offered by the U.S. Department of Veterans Affairs).

A significant number of Americans do not have health insurance. A major objective of the Patient Protection and Affordable Care Act (PPACA or ACA)—President Obama's landmark health-reform legislation—is to significantly reduce the number of Americans without health insurance, primarily through expansion of Medicaid but also through the application of an insurance "mandate" that increased participation of low-risk individuals who formerly opt out of the insurance market. In 2009, shortly before the ACA was signed into law, there were 50.7 million Americans without health insurance.[2] By 2015, this number had decreased by 43 percent to 29 million.

ACA includes a requirement that individuals who do not have health insurance provided through their employer or another source (e.g., Medicare or Medicaid) purchase health insurance (or pay a penalty that the Supreme Court of the United States has recently declared "a tax"): the so-called individual mandate. Subsidies are provided to those who are least able to afford that insurance. A policy goal of that "mandate" clearly is to reduce the number of individuals who are uninsured (and thereby to increase their access to care), but it is also to increase the size of the insurance risk pool (so that risk is spread across a larger group) and therefore to reduce the cost of insurance to the individual by bringing into the insurance pool low-risk individuals who historically have opted out of the insurance system. (By bringing that group in, average risk—and hence the actuarially fair value, or price—declines.)

Insurance Products

It is necessary, before going into more detail about how publicly and privately funded insurance programs pay for care, to point out that there is a range of insurance "products" that differ significantly in ways that affect payment. Although there is more variation (and arguably more innovation) across products in the commercial/private market, this product variation appears in both Medicare and Medicaid. To summarize, five major types of products are prevalent in the United States:

- **Traditional "open access"/fee-for-service (FFS) products**, which allow those individuals who are insured to obtain care anywhere they choose and reimburse providers on the basis of charges.

- **Preferred Provider Organizations (PPOs)/"tiered networks,"** which allow individuals to receive care from a network of "preferred providers"—typically hospitals and physicians with whom discounts have been negotiated. PPO agreements may (or may not) permit individuals to obtain care outside of the preferred provider network—at significantly higher cost to the individual seeking care (through a higher copayment).

- **Health Maintenance Organizations (HMOs)**, which significantly restrict access to care for insured individuals to a (typically relatively small) network of providers; which provide a range of value-added services, including care-management services intended to improve quality and reduce cost by supporting patient self-management, preventive care, and coordinated care; and which often reimburse providers not on a fee-for-service basis but on a capitated (per-member per-month) basis to create incentives among providers for fiscally responsible care.

- **Point of Service (POS) plans**, which allow individuals to choose (at the point of service) whether to seek care under the PPO or under the HMO. POS plans typically offer more choice than HMOs but require that a patient have a primary care physician (who serves as the "point of service contact"), so they typically offer less choice than a PPO.

- **Health Savings Accounts (HSAs), High-Deductible Health Plans (HDHPs), Consumer-Directed Health Plans (CDHPs)**, and other products that transfer much more of the financial risk to the consumer. This is a heterogeneous and rapidly evolving portfolio of offerings that currently constitutes a small share of the insurance market but that may become more important as insurers seek ways to make consumers more sensitive to the cost of the healthcare services they purchase.

Each of the main structures of insurance programs in the United States will be described in the following sections.

Commercial (Private) Insurance in the United States

As noted, the majority of Americans receive health insurance through their (or a family member's) employer; health insurance as a benefit of employment has been the predominant form for several decades. Employer-sponsored health insurance has its roots in the wage and price controls that were in place during World War II and in favorable treatment under the tax code: employers offered richer health insurance benefits to attract and retain employees when wages were controlled and have added to the value of that benefit because the dollars that are set aside for health insurance benefits are effectively tax-free income to employees.

Employer-sponsored health insurance can follow either of two distinct (although, for employees and their families, often indistinguishable) paths: employers may purchase health insurance from an entity that pools risk and administers the health insurance program, or the employer may self-insure (that is, bear the risk itself) and hire (typically a health insurance firm to serve as) a third-party administrator (TPA) of its health insurance program. The TPA administers not only the basic mechanics of the insurance program (such as enrollment, payment of claims to providers, or reimbursement of payments made by consumers) but also a wide array of programs designed to improve health and/or manage cost (ranging from efforts to select and guide consumers to high-quality, cost-effective providers to programs intended to support consumer efforts to manage their own health and illness—so-called care, or disease, management programs). Many large firms elect to self-insure; smaller firms (which are not able to pool risk over a large population) will more often purchase insurance (although as the cost of healthcare and therefore the actuarially fair price of health insurance rises, many firms with fewer than 50 employees are electing not to offer health insurance).

In either case, the health insurance benefit is typically structured as described earlier in the section "Insurance Products": employees have a choice as to whether to purchase insurance (which is heavily subsidized, as a benefit, by the employer, but the employee still pays, on average, between 15 percent and 25 percent of the premium), and employees often (but do not always) have a choice among insurance providers and/or insurance plans.

Commercial insurance plans/products will differ with respect to the extent to which they offer choice among providers, with respect to the nature and extent to which there are programs available to support employee or employer health-related goals, and (based on those) with respect to their premium, deductible, and copayment costs. Most employer-sponsored plans cover "major medical" (hospital and ambulatory service providers); coverage of prescription drugs is common but not universal.

Commercial products are as briefly described earlier in the section "Insurance Products." The near majority (about 48 percent) of workers were enrolled in PPOs in 2016,[3] 15 percent were in HMOs, 9 percent were in POS plans, and 29 percent were in higher-risk plans (HSAs, HDHPs, CDHPs, and the like). Only about 1 percent of workers were enrolled in conventional open-access plans.

The distribution of workers across insurance products reflects what has been, over the past decade or more, a corporate priority of the first order: to control healthcare costs. That only 1 percent of workers purchase health insurance that provides open access undoubtedly reflects both employers' unwillingness to offer such open-access plans and the cost differentials that employees who choose them face. The preponderance of PPOs reflects the trade-off between choice and cost, which has been the conundrum; while PPOs offer significant choice among providers, there may be strong financial incentives to seek care in the PPO network so that choice is effectively constrained.

In the same way, the rapid growth of consumer-directed and high-deductible health plans—the penetration of which grew by more than 600 percent between 2006 and 2016 to nearly 30 percent—reflects employers' interest in creating pressure for cost control, not by restricting access but by creating an incentive for employees and their families to purchase health services wisely. It seems very likely that this trend will continue—as will innovations in payment beyond discounted fee-for-service plans; current trends are discussed in the earlier section "Insurance Products."

Medicare

Medicare is the insurance program for Americans older than 64; it covers, as well, Americans who are disabled (receiving Social Security Disability Insurance for 24 months), including those disabled by Lou Gehrig's Disease and those with end-stage renal disease, which oftentimes requires dialysis.

Medicare pays for healthcare in two ways. The majority (nearly 70 percent) of beneficiaries choose to enroll in traditional Medicare, which reimburses for care on a fee-for-service basis.[4] The remainder enroll in Medicare Advantage (managed healthcare; so-called Medicare Part C) plans, which collect premiums from Medicare (on a risk-adjusted capitated basis; that is, they are paid a per-member per-month [PMPM] fee by Medicare and pay physicians, hospitals, and others providers on an FFS or PMPM basis for care of the beneficiaries that they manage with that premium).

Medicare FFS operates through three distinct benefit programs:

- **Medicare Part A** Hospital insurance and covers inpatient and, in some cases, convalescent care in skilled nursing facilities. In the past, Medicare paid hospitals based on charges for every service provided. With rapid cost inflation,

Medicare introduced a fixed-priced "episode-based" payment system using diagnosis-related groups (DRGs) in the 1980s and updated to Medicare Severity diagnosis-related groups (MS-DRGs) in October 2007. MS-DRGs are severity and case-mix adjusted, and most MS-DRGs account for complications. MS-DRG rates are updated regularly to assure that payment reflects changes in cost (as may, for example, follow the introduction of new technology related to the Health Information Technology for Economic and Clinical Health [HITECH] Act). MS-DRGs are intended to capture the bundle of services typically provided to patients with specific conditions/receiving specific procedures/ with specific predictable needs—for example, patients with pneumonia or who have a stroke or who have a joint replacement procedure. Paying the hospital a fixed fee for the bundle of services typically provided to such patients creates an incentive for hospitals to improve efficiency (and, in particular, to reduce the use of unnecessary, marginally valuable, or unnecessarily high-cost services). Because MS-DRGs are set at the average cost for patients of a given type, hospitals will lose money on some patients (who have above-average service needs) but will make money on others (who have below-average service needs). For hospitals with reasonable volumes, the expectation is that (on average) MS-DRG prices are fair.

- **Medicare Part B**   Major medical; that is, it pays for covered services that are not included under Part A (or medications, covered in the next bullet). In general, it covers ambulatory services (including physician services) and durable medical equipment (a major expense in the Medicare population).

  Medicare pays physicians and other qualified providers on an FFS basis, where fees are set (a Medicare fee schedule) based on a resource-based relative value scale (RBRVS). The RBRVS is an effort to estimate the resources required to deliver a given service (described by a code called a *current procedural terminology* [CPT] code; CPT codes in most cases define the billable service). These are defined in Chapter 13. Medicare's fee for a given service—the price it pays providers—is the product of the relative value units (RVUs) associated with that service (the CPT code for that service) and a "conversion factor," which effectively assigns a dollar value to an RVU. The RBRVS is updated annually by an RBRVS update committee (the RUC) that is composed of 29 physicians—through a process that is often contentious because adjustments to the RBRVS are effectively a zero-sum game (an increase in the value of one service means that another service must be reduced in value).

- **Medicare Part D**   Covers medications; it was introduced as part of the Medicare Modernization Act of 2006. Medicare beneficiaries are eligible to obtain Part D benefits through stand-alone prescription drug plans (PDPs) or bundled with the Part C benefit (through a Medicare Advantage managed care plan). Unlike Part A and Part B (which provide standard benefits to all beneficiaries), PDPs (and MA PDPs) are able to offer a wide variety of pharmacy benefits—more or less inclusive, more or less generous, at different price points—

to offer Medicare enrollees many options. Exceptions include medications administered in an ambulatory setting; for example, chemotherapy administered intravenously to a patient with cancer in a physician's office or day hospital is reimbursed under Part B, at 106 percent of the average sales price. In some cases, there has been concern that the number of options is overwhelming and that beneficiaries cannot understand what plan might be best suited for them.

Medicaid

Medicaid is a public insurance program available to low-income Americans including children, pregnant women, parents, seniors, and individuals with disabilities. It is jointly funded by federal and state governments but fully administered by states. The federal government provides a percentage (known as the federal medical assistance percentage [FMAP]) of the funding of each state's Medicaid budget. FMAPs vary across states and are determined by criteria such as a state's per-capita income. By law the minimum FMAP is 50 percent (a one-to-one match), and the maximum is 83 percent. In 2016, Mississippi has the highest FMAP at 74.17 percent. Thus, for every $1 contributed by Mississippi to Medicaid, the federal government contributes $2.87.[5]

While there are minimum federal standards to which states must adhere in their eligibility rules and covered services, states have some liberty in the designs of their Medicaid programs through the use of waivers. Mandatory populations include children under age 6 below 133 percent of the federal poverty level (FPL), older children below 100 percent FPL, pregnant women below 133 percent FPL, and elderly and disabled Social Security Disability Insurance (SSDI) and Supplemental Security Income (SSI) beneficiaries below 74 percent FPL. However, the ACA permits states to opt into expanding their Medicaid eligibility to all citizens below 138 percent FPL including working parents and childless adults. Mandatory benefits include inpatient and outpatient hospital services, physician services, nursing facility services, and home health services. Many states use waivers to expand their covered populations (e.g., have higher FPL thresholds) and covered services (e.g., prescription drugs, clinic services, and hospice services). In 2001, only about 40 percent of Medicaid expenditures were spent on mandatory services for mandatory populations.[6]

Like Medicare, Medicaid reimburses for care through two payment mechanisms: FFS and managed-care arrangements. Some states are also adopting integrated-care delivery models. Working within federal guidelines and approval, states design their reimbursement methodology. When determining their reimbursement rates for FFS, states may base them upon the costs of providing the services, the reimbursement rate of commercial payers in the private market, and/or a percentage of the reimbursement rate of Medicare. The reimbursement rate of Medicaid is typically significantly lower than that of commercial payers and Medicare.

States can make managed care enrollment voluntary or can seek a waiver from the Centers for Medicare and Medicaid Services (CMS) to require enrollment in a Managed Care Organization (MCO). Currently, most states have waivers to implement mandatory managed care in parts of their states or for certain categories of beneficiaries or to implement statewide mandatory managed-care enrollment as part of a demonstration.[7] Thus, the national Medicaid MCO enrollment rate is significantly higher than that of Medicare. Some states have managed-care enrollments rates that are 100 percent (Hawaii and Tennessee), and in other states the Medicaid population is covered under different delivery systems.[8]

Medicaid's Role in Long-Term Care

Because of its inclusion of low-income elderly, its coverage of nursing home care and home healthcare, and the unpopularity of long-term care (LTC) insurance, Medicaid is a major player in the financing of long-term care. Fifty-one percent of all long-term care is funded through Medicaid.[9] In 2014, 25 percent of Medicaid expenditures purchased long-term care.[10] The quick growth in the percentage of Medicaid dollars spent on LTC has led to legislative attempts to contain the growth, such as the development of an LTC prospective payment system based on MS-DRGs (vs. the previous fixed rates), certificate-of-need laws for the construction of nursing homes, and regulations on the "spending down" of wealth by the elderly to qualify for Medicaid.

Children's Health Insurance Program (CHIP)

Title XXI of the Balanced Budget Act of 1997 established the Children's Health Insurance Program (CHIP), formerly known as State Children's Health Insurance Program (SCHIP). This program is designed to provide health insurance for children from low-income households that earn too much to qualify for traditional Medicaid. Like Medicaid, CHIP is administered by states but funded jointly by federal and state governments. States receive an enhanced federal medical assistance percentage (eFMAP) to fund CHIP. The CHIP eFMAP is typically higher than the Medicaid FMAP (see Use Case 3-1). States that cover children with greater than 300 percent FPL receive their FMAP only for CHIP federal matching. However, unlike traditional Medicaid, federal dollars for CHIP are capped. Thus, each state is allocated part of this amount and must supply matching funds according to its FMAP.

Use Case 3-1: FMAP and eFMAP Rates

As mentioned in the text, Medicaid and CHIP are jointly funded by the federal and state governments. For both programs, the federal government provides a percentage of the funds. The percentages vary across states. FMAP is the federal government's contribution percentage toward a state's Medicaid program, and eFMAP is the contribution percentage toward a state's CHIP program. While the FMAP and eFMAP are not equal, there is a mathematical relationship between the two. A state's eFMAP is never less than its FMAP. The amount of additional percentage points of the eFMAP is equal to 30 percent of the difference between a state's FMAP and 100 percent. Furthermore, for years between 2016 and 2019, the ACA provides an additional 23 percentage points of eFMAP. This provision in the ACA also increases

(continued)

the maximum eFMAP from 85 percent to 100 percent. The following equation more clearly demonstrates the ACA-augmented relationship between the two rates:

$$eFMAP = min[FMAP + 0.30 \times (100\% - FMAP) + 23\%, 100\%]$$

State's FMAP	FMAP + 0.30 × (100% − FMAP) + 23%	eFMAP
50%	50% + 0.30 × (100% − 50%) + 23% = 50% + 0.30 × 50% + 23% = 50% + 15% + 23% = 88%	88%
60%	60% + 0.30 × (100% − 60%) + 23% = 95%	95%
80%	80% + 0.30 × (100% − 80%) + 23% = 109%	100%[*]

[*]Recall that the maximum eFMAP is 100%.

For individuals who were eligible for Medicaid prior to the ACA's Medicaid expansion, the FMAP of a state is determined by a comparison between the state's per capita income and the nation's per capita income using the formula in the following table. However, this FMAP must be at least 50 percent and less than 83 percent. For individuals who are newly eligible for Medicaid due to the ACA Medicaid expansion, the FMAP from 2014 through 2016 is 100 percent and will decrease each year thereafter until it reaches 90 percent in 2020.

State Per Capita Income	$1 - 0.45 \times \dfrac{\text{state per capita income}^2}{\text{national per capita income}^2}$	FMAP
$38,263	$1 - 0.45 \times \dfrac{\$38{,}263^2}{\$40{,}584^2}$ $= 1 - 0.45 \times 0.8889$ $= 1 - 0.40$ $= 0.60$	60%
$27,056	$1 - 0.45 \times \dfrac{\$27{,}056^2}{\$40{,}584^2} = 0.80$	80%
$44,867	$1 - 0.45 \times \dfrac{\$44{,}867^2}{\$40{,}584^2} = 0.45$	50%

Uncompensated Care

Although healthcare providers are compensated for the majority of their services through commercial insurance, public insurance, or private payments, they do not receive payments for a significant portion of their services. This care is known as uncompensated care. There are two sources of uncompensated care: charity care and bad debt.

Charity care is care for which the provider never expected compensation because the patient was determined to be unable to pay. Bad debt is defined as services for which the provider expected reimbursement due to the insurance and/or financial status of the patient. Inability to collect the funds may result from an inability to collect copayments and/or deductibles from insured patients, or to collect full payment from uninsured patients whose financial situation does not officially qualify them for charity care. Eligibility for charity care usually depends on factors such as individual and family income, assets, employment status, and the availability of alternative sources of funds.

Given the existence of the Emergency Medical Treatment and Labor Act, which mandates all emergency rooms to provide stabilizing care to patients with emergency conditions regardless of their ability to pay, and state laws such as New Jersey's N.J.S.A. 26:2H-18.64, which makes it illegal for any hospital to "deny any admission or appropriate service to a patient on the basis of that patient's ability to pay or source of payment," uncompensated care is an expected part of the healthcare system. Coughlin et al. estimate that uncompensated care in the United States totaled $84.9 billion in 2013. Hospitals bear the bulk of these losses (60 percent), while physicians and clinics evenly split the remaining portion.[11] The AHA estimates that between 1990 and 2014, uncompensated care as a percentage of all hospital expenses has ranged between 5.3 and 6.2 percent.[12]

Hospitals typically do not write off the costs associated with uncompensated care. Rather, federal and state direct service programs reimburse hospitals via state and local tax appropriations and/or cost-shifting to private payers. This means that uncompensated care is a problem that extends beyond providers and nonpaying patients.

One strategy that hospitals and physicians have tried to use to recover losses associated with uncompensated care (as well as to make up shortfalls when Medicaid payment rates fall below the providers' actual cost) is to raise prices to private payers. While providers do not have the ability to set prices unilaterally, they generally have more opportunity to negotiate with private payers than with Medicare and Medicaid. This "cost-shifting" raises insurance premiums, which ultimately is transmitted back to the employers who pay the largest portion of those premiums. This has an impact on their costs (therefore their profitability)—and is a force that can discourage smaller employers from offering health insurance. It also drives them to shift costs directly to their employees—through higher premiums, higher deductibles, and higher copayments. Cost-shifting is a serious concern, in a setting in which providers may be seeking to increase the revenue they derive from private payers, as public payers (Medicare and Medicaid) seek to reduce their costs. Shifting costs from Medicare to the private sector may preserve the Medicare Trust Fund—but it does not improve the efficiency of the healthcare system in the United States.

While cost-shifting is a significant concern, providers have other sources to cover the expenses related to the majority of their uncompensated care. In 2013, federal, state, and local governments did not fund 38 percent of the uncompensated care.[11] The largest sources of funding for uncompensated care are Disproportionate Share Hospital payments/adjustments through the Medicare and Medicaid programs. Hospitals that treat a large number of Medicaid, low-income, and uninsured individuals receive these payments, which help to preserve Medicare and Medicaid patients' access to care.

Trends in Payment/Payment Reform

Intense pressure on all payers—employers, the states, and the Medicare Trust Fund—has driven innovations in payment. These innovations have moved at a somewhat different pace across those three sectors. In general, the private sector has more aggressively sought change than have governments (both state and federal), but changes in the way the government pays for care (and, especially, changes in the way Medicare pays for care) have much more impact, given the scale of public programs.

The ACA established the Center for Medicare and Medicaid Innovation (CMMI), also called the CMS Innovation Center, to test innovative healthcare delivery and payment models. One CMMI initiative is the State Innovation Models (SIM) Initiative in which states receive funds to implement various enabling strategies to transform the healthcare systems within their states. Each of the participating 6 SIM Round One Model Test states and 11 SIM Round Two Model Test states are supporting alternative payment models as part of their SIM initiatives.

The Medicare Access and CHIP Reauthorization Act (MACRA) is another mechanism through which the government incentivizes the implementation of alternative payment models. Passed in 2015, MACRA provides bonus Medicare payments to providers who have significant participation (measured by healthcare dollars or patient count) in alternative payment models.

While there have been a number of innovations in payment over the years, alternative payment models can be grouped into three major categories:

- Pay-for-performance (P4P)/provider incentive programs
- Episode-based, or bundled, payment
- Payment reform coupled to delivery system innovation

Pay-for-Performance (P4P)/Provider Incentive Programs

Pay-for-performance programs are incremental innovations off of a fee-for-service payment platform. The idea of P4P is simple: the payer (private or public) offers providers additional payment for achieving performance targets, which are designed to improve quality but also achieve long-term reductions in cost. There are, for example, many short-term or physiologic health outcomes—hemoglobin A1c in patients with diabetes or cholesterol in patients with (or at high risk for) coronary artery (heart) disease—for which a strong logical case (and, in some cases, a data-driven empirical case) can be made that investing in care to achieve better outcomes will lead to improved health and lower total cost over time. By creating an incentive for providers to achieve health-related outcome targets, health can be improved (and costs controlled).

The introduction of P4P programs had to wait for the development and diffusion of quality metrics that could support the setting of performance targets. That was led by the Joint Commission and the National Committee for Quality Assurance (NCQA) through the development and deployment of a set of standard metrics for hospitals (ORYX) and health plans (the Healthcare Effectiveness Data and Information Set [HEDIS]). HEDIS metrics—which include statistics that address clinical quality, member satisfaction, and utilization (and will likely include measures of efficiency in the future)—permitted employers (and their employees) to select health plans (initially HMOs, but over time PPOs as well) based on both price and quality ("value") rather than on price alone. But they also permitted the setting of performance targets, which strategy has diffused, over time, both to the interface with providers and to the public sector. So, for example, P4P has diffused rapidly into FFS arrangements with physicians and hospitals in the private sector.[13] The Centers for Medicare and Medicaid Services has introduced quality payment differentials to hospitals based on hospital scorecards and has begun to introduce quality incentives to physicians through the Physician Quality Reporting System (PQRS; initially, the Physician Quality Reporting Initiative [PQRI]). That said, the performance of P4P programs (for achieving real improvements in value) has been described as "lackluster."[14] So, policymakers—in both the public and private sectors—have sought more powerful payment reforms.

Episode-Based, or Bundled, Payment

Many would argue that any payment innovation that begins with FFS—that is, a system that intrinsically motivates the delivery of more, and more intensive, care—will not achieve the results necessary to create a sustainable, high-performing healthcare system in the United States.[14] As a result, there have been innovations that begin with a radically different approach to payment—one that creates incentives that are in the opposite direction of FFS (and hence drives intrinsically toward lower cost).

Such approaches "fix price." That is, they are designed to provide a fixed fee that will cover all services (defined in some way) rather than reward the provider for each service independently. The first—and arguably strongest—such payment innovation is capitation, which is payment of a fixed amount on a per-member per-month basis for all services a member may require.

Capitation was prevalent in the early 1990s, with the introduction of HMO-style managed care. And capitation continues to be prevalent, at the point at which employers (and/or governments) pay health plans.

But capitation did not work well at the physician level—for many, many reasons. Physicians, especially in the early 1990s, were inexperienced with (and lacked the tools they needed to manage) the clinical risk that accompanied the financial risk inherent in capitation, and physicians have limited control over costs (for example, once a patient is hospitalized). So—although we may see and are, in fact, seeing capitation of providers reemerge (see the section "The Accountable-Care Organization")—there have been efforts to create payment strategies that are more discrete (and clinically manageable) than capitation.

Important among those are episode-based, or bundled, payments. The notion of a bundled payment is to offer a fixed fee—not for all services that a patient may require in a month (or over a year) but for the set of services a patient typically requires when they have a particular condition or procedure. To the extent that care is predictable for (for example) patients who are having elective surgery, or even for patients with conditions like diabetes, it should be possible to predict the needs (and therefore the costs) for patients during the course of a specific episode of care.

This is not a new idea; in fact, as discussed previously, it is the foundation of Medicare's DRG system for paying for hospital care, and it is the basis for which Medicare pays for outpatient dialysis for patients with ESRD. But what has emerged is broadening the scope of payment bundles and extending the "bundle" from the inpatient (or facility) stay (alone) to an interval that includes both pre- and post-hospital care. By setting a fixed fee for a bundle that includes, in particular, post-discharge events, the provider bears risk for the costs that would follow an adverse outcome (such as a complication requiring significant ambulatory care or even a rehospitalization). So, the bundled payment creates a potentially strong incentive to optimize pre-hospital care (so that the patient is well prepared and the hospital stay can be minimized), to optimize care over the inpatient stay itself (so that the patient is not discharged prematurely and does not develop a complication or return to the hospital), and to optimize the post-discharge interval (so that gains achieved in the hospital are maintained and the discharge plan carefully executed).

There is considerable interest in, and innovation regarding, bundled payment. In the private sector, some provider organizations (notably, Geisinger Health System in Danville, Pennsylvania) have moved proactively to offer fixed-price bundles to payers (through their ProvenCare program).[15] There are private-sector pilots underway in many parts of the country to evaluate bundled payment strategies that may be more realistic in markets in which provider organizations have not achieved the level of integration that Geisinger has; notable pilots include those led by PROMETHEUS Payment in five sites across the country and those led by the Integrated Healthcare Association (IHA) in California. That said, bundled payment remains, as of 2016, the exception and not the rule in the private sector.

Medicare has tested bundled payment strategies in two large demonstrations: one in the 1990s (the Medicare Participating Heart Bypass Center Demonstration)[16] and one that began in 2009 (the Acute Care Episode Demonstration).[17] In addition, CMMI is currently implementing the Bundled Payment for Care Improvement initiative,[18] which offers organizations the opportunity to test a broad range of approaches to bundled payment. Furthermore, several states are supporting episode of care models with their SIM Initiative funding. Finally, Section 2704 of the ACA establishes a demonstration project for Medicaid programs in up to eight states to evaluate bundled payments. So, the expectation is that there will be, in the public sector, testing and evaluation of bundled payment approaches, but it may be some time before they have moved into the mainstream.

Payment Reform Coupled to Delivery System Innovation

A primary objective of payment reform (including P4P and bundled payment) is to drive changes in the processes through which care is delivered—to increase coordination, eliminate redundancy, and thereby enhance quality and eliminate waste. That transformation of the care-delivery system will almost certainly require some restructuring of it. So, I expect—and in fact have seen—changes in the structure of the healthcare marketplace, where payment reform is underway.

On the other hand, there has been innovation in the delivery system, driven by the primary interest providers have in improving the quality and efficiency of care. The risk in such innovation is that it will in fact improve efficiency—so that providers that operate in an FFS environment will (as a consequence) see their revenue and profits fall.[19]

As a result, there is a clear need to link delivery system innovation to payment reform. There are two important delivery system innovations that are now linked to payment reform:

- The patient-centered medical home (PCMH)
- The accountable-care organization (ACO)

The Patient-Centered Medical Home (PCMH)   The PCMH is a "health care setting that facilitates partnerships between individual patients, and their personal physicians, and when appropriate, the patient's family, with the goal of providing comprehensive primary care for children, youth and adults."[20] Originally conceived and advanced by the medical societies representing the primary care disciplines (the American Academy of Pediatrics, the American Academy of Family Physicians, the American College of Physicians, and the American Osteopathic Association),[21] the concept has been embraced widely—at least among those who pay for healthcare.

The detailed requirements that describe a PCMH can be found elsewhere;[22, 23] what is important for the purposes of this discussion is that the providers must invest (significantly) in the infrastructure (including the HIT infrastructure) required to achieve the functionality, which is the PCMH. The rate at which the PCMH concept diffused was limited by the lack of a return on that investment. In response, many private payers have begun to offer a per-member per-month fee to practices that are certified PCMHs, which recognizes the additional capabilities (to improve care and reduce cost) that are expected in practices that achieve that recognition. That (patient management) fee is in addition to the FFS payment the practice earns when it sees a patient; the expectation is that a patient (or "case") management fee will be more than recovered through reductions in expenditures for other healthcare services (such as inpatient hospital stays).

Medicare tested the PCMH through two demonstrations: the Multi-Payer Advanced Primary Care Practice (MAPCP) Demonstration and the Federally Qualified Health Center (FQHC) Advanced Primary Care Practice (APCP) Demonstration. In addition, CMMI tested the PCMH model through a Comprehensive Primary Care (CPC) initiative that provides for multipayer support of primary care practices to support their efforts to offer more effective and coordinated primary care. Building upon CPC, CMMI is testing another multipayer PCMH-based model known as Comprehensive Primary Care Initiative Plus (CPC+). Finally, PCMHs are being evaluated at the state level (for example, in addition to the eight MAPCP states, a multipayer initiative in Maryland).[24] The PCMH model is one of the most popular healthcare delivery models that SIM Model Test states are supporting in their initiatives. Given this level of interest in the PCMH model, one can expect that, at least in the short run, payment of a PMPM management fee to qualified PCMHs will be more prevalent and a more important part of the revenue stream for primary care practices.

The Accountable-Care Organization   The system for delivering healthcare in the United States is poorly organized, with weak relationships among the many providers and sites at which patients receive care. As a result, care is poorly coordinated and often redundant, patient outcomes suffer, and precious resources are wasted.

Many believe that solving this problem requires the creation of strong incentives and the infrastructure needed to drive care coordination and integration across providers. This has led to the articulation of the concept of an accountable-care organization (ACO). While ACOs are defined in different ways, what is common to all definitions—and is at the core of the concept—is that it is a delivery system entity that is prepared to accept accountability for the clinical and financial outcomes of the patients to whom it delivers care.

ACOs are emerging in both the public and private sectors.[25] There are two especially important innovations that link ACOs to changes in Medicare payment, described next. However, it should also be noted that CMS is taking its experience from these two initial ACOs to implement the Next Generation ACO Model in 2017.

- **Medicare Shared Savings Program (MSSP)**   A payment innovation linked to the operations of ACOs.[26] The program was mandated by the ACA (though participation is voluntary), regulations describing the program were released in late 2011, and delivery systems began participating in 2012. Participation requires the creation of an entity that includes primary care physicians (and typically includes hospitals). As of January 2016 there were 433 MSSP ACOs.[27] Each ACO is paid on a discounted FFS basis (and providers that are part of the ACO are paid by the ACO according to agreements that operate within the ACO) but Medicare shares "savings" that are derived from the ACO's efforts to deliver high-quality, coordinated, cost-effective care. "Savings" are calculated as the difference between what spending would have been (for those Medicare enrollees for whom the ACO is responsible) and what spending actually was, adjusted for factors that are beyond the control of the ACO. The ACO's share of savings depends on a number of factors, including (very importantly) how the ACO performs on a set of quality metrics designed to assure that savings are not generated by withholding (or "stinting") on care.

  The MSSP ACO is, then, a delivery system innovation tightly linked to a change in the way care is paid for. In its current form, it builds off of an FFS payment model; it is, in some ways, "simply" a P4P program with strong incentives to achieve financial as well as quality performance targets, and it operates to create incentives across provider types (in particular, to align incentives for hospitals and physicians). It is important to note that, in the best case, ACO revenue will be less than pure FFS revenue. (The ACO incentive is to reduce Medicare's cost relative to projected FFS cost in a given year; to the extent that it does, it receives some share—up to 50 percent—of that difference. But that will always be less than it would have received had there been no ACO.) So, the ACO is able to succeed economically only if it can reduce production cost more than it reduces billings. This has proven to be a challenge for many organizations.

- **Pioneer ACO Program (Pioneer)**[28]   An alternative to the MSSP. Unlike the MSSP (which is not a pilot or demonstration; any organization that qualifies can participate), Pioneer is a pilot run out of CMMI; 32 organizations were originally selected in 2011 on a competitive basis (9 Pioneer ACOs remained in 2016) to operate as ACOs in a payment environment that creates much greater opportunities for shared savings (but also much greater downside risk in the event that savings are not realized) but also intentionally moved toward a "population-based payment model" (that is, a per-member per-month payment; previously called *capitation*) that creates even more powerful incentives for cost control. Like the MSSP, there are strong protections to assure quality; in addition, there are incentives to encourage Medicare Pioneer ACOs to develop performance-based payment arrangements with other payers.

  The Pioneer program represents an important opportunity to allow healthcare organizations that have developed advanced care management/care coordination infrastructure to capture the financial gains associated with the effective use of that infrastructure. The Pioneer program sends a signal that CMS understands that there is a need to consider a move away from FFS Medicare, if Medicare is to achieve its triple aim of better care, better health, and lower cost.

Chapter Review

This chapter described the complex systems through which healthcare is paid in the United States. In particular, it described how insurance works and how costs are shared by the ultimate payers of care (the federal and state governments, employers, and individual Americans themselves), and it expanded on the main structures of programs. The chapter defined the major payers and the types of insurance products offered. Finally, the chapter discussed changes in the way care is paid for and delivered as part of healthcare reform or that may be accelerated by healthcare reform in the future.

Questions

To test your comprehension of the chapter, answer the following questions and then check your answers against the list of correct answers at the end of the chapter.

1. Which of the following is true?
    A. Individuals pay a relatively small percentage of the annual cost of their insurance.
    B. Individuals pay a copayment that is a relatively small percentage of the cost of most services they use.
    C. Individuals with private health insurance—particularly those with employer-sponsored health insurance—pay (and are likely to pay in the future) a larger share of the cost associated with their healthcare than individuals with Medicare or Medicaid.
    D. All of the above.

2. Which of the following are *not* insurance products commonly offered in the United States?

   A. Traditional/open-access health insurance plans

   B. Preferred Provider Organizations (PPOs) and Health Maintenance Organizations (HMOs)

   C. Independent Practice Associations (IPAs) and Patient-Centered Medical Homes (PCMHs)

   D. Consumer-Directed Health Plans (CDHPs) and Health Savings Accounts (HSAs)

3. Which of the following is true of the Medicare program?

   A. All Americans older than 64 must participate.

   B. The distribution of its beneficiaries across insurance products is very different from private insurance.

   C. It has, since its inception, covered hospital care, ambulatory care, and prescription drugs.

   D. All of the above.

4. In general, how does Medicare pay physicians?

   A. Based on what physicians charge

   B. Based on fees that are negotiated with physicians

   C. Based on a fee schedule that is based on the resources required to deliver different services

   D. On a capitated (per-member per-month [PMPM]) basis

5. In general, how does Medicare pay hospitals?

   A. Based on what hospitals charge for each service they provide

   B. Based on fees that are negotiated with hospitals for each service they provide

   C. Through a shared savings program that rewards hospitals for saving money

   D. Through a "bundled payment" system that offers a fixed price for all hospital services delivered during a hospital stay

6. Which of the following is true?

   A. Accountable-care organizations (ACOs) are delivery system entities that are emerging in response to financial incentives to reduce the cost and improve the quality of healthcare.

   B. Patient-centered medical homes (PCMHs) are nursing homes that are designed to assist patients to make the transition from hospital care to home care.

      C. The Medicare Shared Savings Program (MSSP) is a way that Medicare beneficiaries can share in savings that derive from their efforts to take better care of themselves.

      D. Bundled payment programs are an exciting innovation, but to date there is very little experience with them.

7. Which of the following is true of the insurance mandate in the Affordable Care Act?

      A. It will mean that the federal government and the states will no longer need to provide Medicaid.

      B. One of its goals was to increase the efficiency of insurance by bringing more (and lower-risk) Americans into the insurance risk pool.

      C. It is unconstitutional, because the federal government cannot require Americans to buy anything (even health insurance).

      D. It does not support delivery system innovations such as ACOs.

8. Given the ACA supplement, what is the minimum FMAP that will qualify a state for the maximum eFMAP?

      A. 83%

      B. 67.14%

      C. 85%

      D. 100%

Answers

  1. D. Individuals with private insurance typically pay less than 25 percent of their annual premium, and Medicare and Medicaid enrollees pay less than that. Similarly, copayments—though rising and often perceived as high—are typically far less than the cost of the service provided. As costs (and therefore insurance premiums) rise, insurance products are evolving to shift costs to individuals, both to reduce the employer (or public) contribution to care and to create an incentive for individuals to use care wisely.

  2. C. IPAs are groups of individual physicians and medical practices that provide services to managed-care organizations. PCMHs are medical practices that have put in place the infrastructure needed to coordinate care. IPAs and PCMHs will often contract with managed-care organizations (in particular, PPOs and HMOs), but they do so to provide care (not to provide insurance).

  3. B. Traditional (open-access, FFS) care dominates Medicare. That is very rare in the private sector. The distribution of its beneficiaries across insurance products is very different from private insurance.

4. **C.** Physicians are paid based on the Medicare fee schedule, which in turn is based on a resource-based relative value scale (RBRVS).

5. **D.** Medicare has paid hospitals for more than two decades using diagnosis-related groups (DRGs) that cover hospital—but not physician—services provided during a hospital stay. Increasingly, hospital reimbursement can be enhanced (or threatened) by quality performance. The Medicare Shared Savings Program (MSSP) is a voluntary program that gives hospitals (through establishing accountable-care organizations) the opportunity to improve profitability by generating savings (but only if they reduce their own production costs as well).

6. **A.** PCMHs are primary care practices, with infrastructure designed to coordinate care (primarily ambulatory care, although transitions from hospital to home are important as well); they are not nursing homes. The MSSP is a program that permits providers (and, in particular, ACOs)—not patients/beneficiaries—to share savings with the Medicare program. There is considerable experience with bundled payments already—through hospital DRGs and through Medicare and private-sector pilots and demonstrations from the 1990s and early twenty-first century.

7. **B.** The Affordable Care Act intended to increase the efficiency of insurance by bringing more (and lower-risk) Americans into the insurance risk pool.

8. **B.** Between 2016 and 2019 the maximum allowed eFMAP is 100 percent; thus, to find the answer, the following algebra equation must be solved for x:

$$x + 0.30 \times (100\% - x) + 23\% = 100\%$$

References

1. U.S. Census Bureau. (2016). *Coverage numbers and rates by type of health insurance: 2013 to 2015 (Table 1).* Accessed on October 11, 2016, from www2.census.gov/programs-surveys/demo/tables/p60/257/table1.pdf.

2. DeNavas-Wall, C., Proctor, B. D., & Smith, J. (2010). *Income, poverty, and health insurance coverage in the United States: 2009.* Accessed on October 11, 2016, from www.census.gov/prod/2010pubs/p60-238.pdf.

3. Kaiser Family Foundation (KFF). (2016, Sept. 14). *2016 employer health benefits survey.* Accessed on October 11, 2016, from http://kff.org/report-section/ehbs-2016-summary-of-findings/.

4. KFF. (2016, May 11). *Medicare advantage.* Accessed on October 11, 2016, from http://kff.org/medicare/fact-sheet/medicare-advantage/.

5. KFF. (2016). *Federal medical assistance percentage (FMAP) for Medicaid and multiplier.* Accessed on October 16, 2016, from http://kff.org/medicaid/state-indicator/federal-matching-rate-and-multiplier/?currentTimeframe=1&sortModel=%7B%22colId%22:%22FMAP%20Percentage%22,%22sort%22:%22desc%22%7D.

 6. Henry Kaiser Foundation Medicaid overview. (n.d.). Accessed on September 8, 2012, from www.kff.org/medicaid/upload/Medicaid-An-Overview-of-Spending-on.pdf. [However, this page is no longer available to access].

 7. Paradise, J., & Musumeci, M. (2016, June 9). *CMS's final rule of Medicaid managed care: A summary of major provisions.* Accessed on October 18, 2016, from http://kff.org/medicaid/issue-brief/cmss-final-rule-on-medicaid-managed-care-a-summary-of-major-provisions/.

 8. KFF. (2016). *Share of Medicaid population covered under different delivery systems.* Accessed on October 18, 2016, from kff.org/medicaid/state-indicator/share-of-medicaid-population-covered-under-different-delivery-systems/?currentTimeframe=0&sortModel={"colId":"Location","sort":"asc"}.

 9. Reaves, E. L., & Musumeci, M. (2015, Dec. 15). *Medicaid and long-term services and supports: A primer.* Accessed on October 11, 2016, from http://kff.org/medicaid/report/medicaid-and-long-term-services-and-supports-a-primer/.

10. KFF. (2015). *Distribution of Medicaid spending by service.* Accessed on October 11, 2016, from http://kff.org/medicaid/state-indicator/distribution-of-medicaid-spending-by-service/?dataView=1&currentTimeframe=0&sortModel=%7B%22colId%22:%22Location%22,%22sort%22:%22asc%22%7D.

11. Coughlin, T. A., Holahan, J., Caswell, K., & McGrath, M. (2014). *Uncompensated care for uninsured in 2013: A detailed examination.* Accessed on October 11, 2016, from https://kaiserfamilyfoundation.files.wordpress.com/2014/05/8596-uncompensated-care-for-the-uninsured-in-2013.pdf.

12. American Hospital Association. (2016, January). *Uncompensated hospital care cost fact sheet.* Accessed on October 11, 2016, from www.aha.org/content/16/uncompensatedcarefactsheet.pdf.

13. Schneider, E., Hussey, P. S., & Schnyer, C. (2011). *Payment reform: Analysis of models and performance measurement implications.* Technical Report. RAND Corporation.

14. Rosenthal, M. B., Landon, B. E., Norman, S. L. T., Frank, R. G., & Epstein, A. M. (2006). Pay for performance in commercial HMOs. *New England Journal of Medicine, 355,* 1895–1902.

15. Geisinger. (n.d.). *ProvenCare by Geisinger ensures quality care comes standard.* Accessed on October 18, 2016, from www.geisinger.org/sites/provencare/.

16. Cromwell, J., Dayhoff, D. A., McCall, N. T., Subramanian, S., Freitas, R. C., Hart, R. J., … Stason, W. (1998). *Medicare participating heart bypass demonstration, executive summary.* Final Report. Waltham, MA: Health Economics Research.

17. CMS Innovation Center. (n.d.). *Medicare Acute Care Episode (ACE) demonstration.* Accessed on October 18, 2016, from https://innovation.cms.gov/initiatives/ACE/.

PART I

18. CMS Innovation Center. (n.d.). *Bundled payments for care improvement (BPCI) initiative: General information.* Accessed on October 18, 2016, from https://innovation.cms.gov/initiatives/bundled-payments/index.html.

19. Pham, H. H., Ginsburg, P. B., McKenzie, K., & Milstein, A. (2007). Redesigning care delivery in response to a high-performance network: The Virginia Mason Medical Center. *HealthAffairs, 26*(4), 532–544. Accessed on October 18, 2016, from http://content.healthaffairs.org/content/26/4/w532.full.pdf+html.

20. Patient-Centered Primary Care Collaborative (PCPCC). (n.d.). *Defining the medical home.* Accessed on October 18, 2016, from www.pcpcc.org/about/medical-home.

21. Sia, C., Tonniges, T. F., Osterhus, E., & Taba, S. (2004). History of the medical home concept. *Pediatrics, 113*(5), 1473–1478.

22. U.S. Department of Health and Human Services (HHS), Agency for Healthcare Research and Quality (AHRQ). (n.d.). *Defining the PCMH.* Accessed on October 18, 2016, from https://pcmh.ahrq.gov/page/defining-pcmh.

23. HHS, AHRQ. (n.d.). *PCMH citations collection.* Accessed on October 18, 2016, from https://pcmh.ahrq.gov/citations-search?search_api_views_fulltext=PCMH.

24. Maryland Health Care Commission. (n.d.) *Maryland Multi-Payor Patient Centered Medical Home Program.* Accessed on October 18, 2016, from http://mhcc.maryland.gov/pcmh.

25. Mostashari, F., & Colbert, J. (2014, May 12). *How community health centers are taking on accountable care for the most vulnerable.* Accessed on October 18, 2016, from www.brookings.edu/blog/up-front/2014/05/12/how-community-health-centers-are-taking-on-accountable-care-for-the-most-vulnerable/.

26. CMS. (n.d.). *Medicare Shared Saving Program.* Accessed on October 18, 2016, from www.cms.gov/Medicare/Medicare-Fee-for-Service-Payment/sharedsavingsprogram/index.html.

27. CMS. (2016, April). *Fast facts: All Medicare Shared Savings Program (Shared Savings Program) ACOs.* Accessed on October 11, 2016, from www.cms.gov/Medicare/Medicare-Fee-for-Service-Payment/sharedsavingsprogram/Downloads/All-Starts-MSSP-ACO.pdf.

28. CMS Innovation Center. (n.d.). *Pioneer ACO model.* Accessed on October 18, 2016, from https://innovation.cms.gov/initiatives/Pioneer-ACO-Model/index.html.

Healthcare Information Technology in Public Health, Emergency Preparedness, and Surveillance

J. Marc Overhage, Brian E. Dixon

In this chapter, you will learn how to

- Define population health and explain how it differs from healthcare delivery
- Describe the role of public health in managing illness outbreaks, epidemics, and pandemics
- Identify and explain issues that affect the use of data for population health
- Apply health data definitions and standards, as well as privacy and confidentiality issues, in typical public health scenarios
- Identify when public health departments can receive identifiable health information to perform public health functions without patient authorization
- Recognize and explain how population health and clinical care needs complement each other

Most people think about healthcare as being focused on the diagnosis and treatment of disease, while others perceive it to also include prevention of disease and maintenance of health and well-being. Furthermore, the notion of healthcare, especially the delivery of healthcare, is often targeted toward an individual patient. Doctors, nurses, and other healthcare professionals are often concerned with preventing, diagnosing, or treating a disease in the patient who is sitting in an exam room or lying in a hospital bed. Another, and equally important, aspect of healthcare is population health, which is focused on the prevention, diagnosis, and treatment of diseases for an entire population of people rather than one individual at a time. Evolving models of healthcare delivery, such as team-based care and accountable care (see Chapters 1 and 2 for additional discussion), are focused on managing specific populations of patients, namely those who are regular consumers of healthcare at those clinics or hospitals. However, the notion of population health dates back several hundred years and is strongly associated with governmental public health departments.

Public health is concerned with preventing disease, prolonging life, and promoting health for populations. Public health departments work to prevent epidemics and spread of disease, protect against environmental hazards, prevent injuries, promote and encourage healthy behaviors, respond to disasters and assist communities in recovery, and assure the quality and accessibility of health services. These activities are generally focused on geographic populations, or the entire group of people living in a city, county, state, or nation. In the United States, local (often county) health departments provide "on the ground" services, including vaccination against communicable diseases, primary care and dental care to the uninsured population, and nutrition programs for people with diabetes or for low-income populations. The work by local health departments is supported by state health departments, who in turn are supported by the U.S. Centers for Disease Control and Prevention (CDC), which in turn is part of the World Health Organization (WHO). Countries other than the United States typically have governmental ministries of health that provide these services and collaborate with the CDC through the WHO.

Accomplishing the core functions of essential public health services requires public health departments to monitor the health status of the population, investigate population health problems and hazards, mobilize community partners to address health problems, develop policies and plans, educate the public about health issues, and undertake various assurance activities.[1] Some essential differences between clinical care and public health are depicted in Table 4-1.

Many different people and organizations have a stake in public health, including public health practitioners (primarily those who work in public health departments in the United States), governments, employers, community groups, private payers, and, ultimately, all of us as individuals, since our health is, in part, determined by the health of others around us. Research shows that medical care and genetic factors are only responsible for about a third of a person's health and well-being.[2] Environmental and social factors, as well as behavioral choices people make, are larger determinants of health outcomes. Recent research provides evidence that a person's ZIP code may predict health outcomes better than knowing about the person's family history of disease or their past medical conditions.[3]

Table 4-1 Differences Between Clinical Care and Public Health Perspectives		Clinical Care	Public Health
	Scale	Individual	Population
	Focus	Disease	Prevention
	Approach	Treatment	Health promotion
	Scale	1 at a time	Millions at a time

TIP   Public health departments may provide individual patient care, but their core functions are typically focused on populations and not on individual patients.

Despite these differences, clinical care and public health interact in many ways. For example, clinical-care providers administer many immunizations that prevent communicable diseases, while public health professionals identify outbreaks of disease that may influence a provider's choice of treatment for a patient presenting with specific symptoms. For example, a patient with fever and cough might be managed differently during an influenza outbreak than in other circumstances.[4]

The American Recovery and Reinvestment Act (ARRA), passed in 2009, and the Prevention and Public Health Fund, passed in 2010 as part of the Affordable Care Act (ACA), will dramatically alter the perspective on population health in the United States over the coming years. Both pieces of legislation provide significant support for initiatives focused on improving the population's health. The ARRA, through the Health Information Technology for Economic and Clinical Health (HITECH) Act, provides funding designed to stimulate the adoption and "meaningful use" (which is being incorporated into the Advancing Care Information dimension of the Medicare Access and CHIP Reauthorization Act of 2015 [MACRA]) of electronic health records (EHRs) to advance the ability of health care providers to measure the quality of care provided to populations as well as subpopulations (e.g., patients with diabetes, patients who had a stroke, etc.) and promote health information exchange (HIE), in which clinical care and public health departments can electronically share data and information about population health (see Chapter 14). The ACA, through the Prevention and Public Health Fund, provides for expanded and sustained national investment in disease prevention, wellness promotion, and public health activities. The ACA also advances the concept of accountable-care organizations (ACOs), which are provider-led organizations focused on managing the health of a population and incented to do so through new compensation models. Together these initiatives provide an opportunity to improve population health by using healthcare IT. These initiatives also create an opportunity for clinical care, ACOs, and public health departments to work together to interconnect healthcare IT systems in a way that supports optimal healthcare delivery and outcomes for populations.

Public Health Reporting

To be able to improve a population's health, you have to be able to measure it. While a care provider might use a laboratory test and a thermometer to measure the health of an individual, measuring the health of a population requires different tools such as surveys, electronic surveillance, and statistical analysis methods. This is not as easy to do as it might sound. For example, we currently use more than 190 separate sources of data to track our progress against our national health goals as described in Healthy People 2020.[5] Take something as seemingly simple as knowing how many people in a population have diabetes (the number of people with a condition divided by the number of people in the population at a single point in time is called the *population prevalence*) and whether this number is growing or shrinking (the number of people to get the condition over some period of time divided by the number of people in the population is called the *incidence*).

The traditional approach to measuring prevalence and incidence has been to carry out carefully constructed surveys of the populations. The CDC, for example, conducts a number of such surveys. Another approach is case reporting, sometimes referred to as *active surveillance* since it requires action on the provider's part, in which care providers report selected data about patients who meet specified criteria for having notifiable conditions (conditions that public health departments require providers or laboratories to report under law) to public health departments that aggregate the data and track it to identify trends in conditions or procedures of interest. For example, most local health departments collect data on individuals who test positive for Lyme disease, hepatitis C, and tuberculosis (or TB). These diseases can create significant harm to both the health system with respect to cost and individuals with respect to disability and death. New cases of disease are tracked so that epidemiologists at the health department can measure the number of new cases and compare the rate of current cases to historical ones to identify if and when an outbreak may be occurring. In addition, disease investigators at health departments, often public health nurses, can contact patients with these diseases and work with community organizations (e.g., schools, day care facilities, employers) to prevent the further spread of these diseases to the people who live or work with the individuals who are sick.

Gathering information on notifiable conditions is challenging. A major challenge is that reporting disease information to departments requires busy clinic staff to fill out additional paperwork and submit it to local public health authorities. Even when providers are motivated to report about patients who have relevant conditions, they are often unaware of which conditions are reportable, don't think about reporting while in the midst of providing care, have difficulty remembering how to report, and so on. In addition, these reports require considerable time and expense for public health departments to manage. Some reports, such as birth certificates, also require validation or certification by a health professional.

TIP Many of the case definitions provided by public health departments to guide providers on which cases to report require a diagnostic laboratory test as part of the case definition.

The use of healthcare IT in clinical care has created new opportunities for improving public health reporting. Structured and coded data captured in healthcare IT systems can be used to facilitate or automate reporting. A laboratory information system, for example, can be configured to automatically generate a report via a standards-based electronic message to departments when a result indicates a reportable condition. Similarly, information systems that receive electronic laboratory reports, or electronic messages sent by lab information systems, can be configured to automatically recognize positive test results for notifiable conditions.[6] This approach to reporting, often referred to as *passive surveillance* because it does not require action on the provider's part, has been shown to be faster and to identify more cases than manual reporting;[7] however, the reports may be missing some of the data elements that public health departments need because the healthcare

IT system doesn't have the data. A laboratory system, for example, will not contain data about whether the patient received treatment for a specific infection and so can't include this data in a report. Therefore, many states require both laboratories and providers to report information for notifiable conditions; these are referred to as "dual" reporting laws.

Traditionally, public health has focused on tracking conditions diagnosed by care providers, but after the anthrax exposures in 2001, interest increased in tracking potential diseases to identify natural or human-initiated outbreaks as soon as possible. This led to using data obtained prior to a diagnosis, which is an approach referred to as *syndromic surveillance* (Figure 4-1).

Syndromic surveillance refers to an approach in which evidence of an increasing number of patients with a specific set of symptoms or findings (called a *syndrome*) is tracked with the expectation that a developing pattern of disease will be found earlier than if public health departments waited until providers identified a diagnosis causing these symptoms. This approach might prove particularly important in cases in which an unusual underlying cause might not be recognized for days or weeks. The figure illustrates that, after an exposure, the number of patients with symptoms will climb over time and then, usually, decline. The number of patients diagnosed with the condition will follow a similar pattern but will typically lag behind the appearance of symptoms by several days. While a variety of data such as rates of absenteeism and purchase of specific over-the-counter drugs have been used in attempts to identify disease outbreaks, using this type of data is not syndromic surveillance. Syndromic surveillance is limited to the use of data collected about patients as part of their care before a diagnosis has been established.

 TIP While it is sometimes possible for healthcare IT systems to determine which data are reportable to public health departments, it may not be easy. Determining whether a test result is positive (usually indicating the presence of a disease or condition), for example, can be difficult for the healthcare IT system, and in some cases it is a negative result to a test that would indicate that it should be reported.

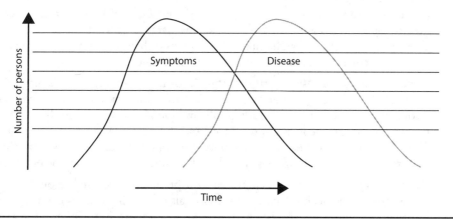

Figure 4-1 Syndromic surveillance

Registries

In addition to surveillance activities in which public health departments gather data on emerging infections and track disease prevalence, many health departments also maintain population health *registries*. A registry is a special type of database used to collect information on a population, usually focused on a single disease, a group of related diseases, or a specific grouping of environmental contaminants. The data within registries are collected from many different sources, including insurance claims transactions, patient self-reported questionnaires or surveys, and medical record chart reviews. In addition to public health departments, other entities create and maintain registries, including research organizations, medical societies such as the American College of Cardiology, and health systems and ACOs that desire to capture additional data beyond what are in their EHR system.

Registries enable public health departments, health systems, and other organizations that use them to longitudinally follow a population over time and examine trends (e.g., Are there more people with diabetes now than ten years ago?) with respect to both care delivery (e.g., Are people with diabetes receiving annual foot exams?) and outcomes (e.g., Do individuals with high blood pressure die sooner than those with normal blood pressure?). Information from registries can be used to estimate survival rates and risks for specific diseases; to measure quality of care indicators; to evaluate short- and long-term effects of environmental exposures; and to test epidemiological hypotheses. Registries are therefore used not only in public health but also by researchers, providers (who want to look at populations they care for), and payers (who want to look at populations they insure).

The following are some common types of registries created and maintained by public health departments:

- **Immunization registry** Almost every state in the United State has an immunization registry that captures information on individuals who receive a vaccine, including information about the vaccine given, the provider who administered the vaccine, and the patient who received the vaccine. Just over half of U.S. states require at least one type of healthcare provider to report immunizations to the registry.[8] These registries enable health departments to identify populations who are protected against vaccine-preventable diseases. The registries further provide forecasting reports to help healthcare providers, especially pediatricians, identify when a patient is due for a vaccine.

- **Cancer registry** These registries capture information on individuals diagnosed with cancer. Hospitals typically capture the information about patients who have a confirmed case of cancer, including information about the person diagnosed, the type of cancer, the location of cancer, and the treatment given to the patient. The data captured by hospitals are reported to state-level cancer registries, which then report final case information to the CDC and other national-level registries.

- **Birth registry** State health departments further require that all live births be reported to the health department. Hospitals or birthing centers capture information about the baby, the mother, and the father. This includes information about birth defects as well as other reportable conditions. The registries support both the issuance of birth certificates, which serve as legal identity documents, and surveillance of trends with respect to birth rates, infant mortality, and identification of diseases passed from mother to child.

- **Death registry** These registries capture the date of death and the cause of death from certified death certificates submitted by county coroners and funeral directors. The registries support epidemiological work to understand the causes of death and the risk factors associated with comorbidity. (Comorbidity is a medical condition that exists simultaneously with and usually independently of another medical condition.)

 TIP Be sure that you can provide a good definition of a registry.

One component of the "meaningful use" program that incentivizes adoption of healthcare IT systems is a requirement for providers to identify and report information to specialized registries. Here are some examples of specialized registries:

- **Statewide trauma registry** Many states require that hospital-based emergency departments report cases of injury (e.g., injuries to the head or neck, insect bites, burns) to a registry maintained by the state public health department. These registries are used to identify causes of injury and death as well as the severity of injuries and costs of care associated with treating injuries from motor vehicle accidents, poisonings, fires, and so on.

- **Birth defects registry** State health departments also collect information about children to promote fetal health, prevent birth defects, and improve the quality of life for individuals living with birth defects. Data are reported on infants and young children for disorders such as autism, Down syndrome, and fetal alcohol syndrome. The registries are used to plan services for children with special health or education needs and provide resources to families.

- **Physician Quality Reporting System (PQRS)** This is a qualified clinical data registry sponsored by the Centers for Medicare and Medicaid Services that captures information regarding the quality of care delivered by outpatient clinicians. The registry is used to examine trends in the quality of care clinicians provide to their patients, helping to ensure that patients get the right care at the right time.

 NOTE Many public health departments operate laboratories that perform specialized testing related to disease of particular public health interest. Some of this testing overlaps with tests performed in hospital laboratories, but some tests are highly specialized. You might want to incorporate data from these laboratories into a care provider's healthcare IT system. Ideally, the test results from these laboratories would be available in a format such as the HL7 Clinical Document Architecture (CDA) using a coding system such as LOINC, which would allow them to be incorporated into healthcare IT systems.

Health Alerts

Based on their population perspective, departments will periodically have information about emerging disease outbreaks or trends that they need to communicate to healthcare providers. Examples include suggestions for providers to perform specific diagnostic testing based on patterns that public health departments are seeing in symptoms being reported. For instance, a foodborne outbreak of salmonella may prompt the health department to ask providers to test all patients they see with symptoms of diarrhea or vomiting. This allows the health department to identify the specific type of salmonella organism and track who has been affected by the outbreak. Another example might be to alert providers to specific treatment suggestions based on patterns observed across a community. For instance, awareness by the health department of drug-resistant organisms in populations treated for common diseases like skin infections may suggest that providers should consider alternative antibiotics than those to which the organisms are resistant. Most of the time, these messages or recommendations are not specific to individual patients but rather relevant to populations or groups of patients.

Public health departments maintain a system called the Health Alert Network (HAN)[9] that primarily supports alerting between public health departments. In addition to publication and outreach through postings in relevant settings (for example, emergency departments), today public health departments may use a variety of mechanisms to reach individual providers, including mail, facsimile, or e-mail. In addition, there may be benefits to creating reminders within healthcare IT systems that providers use while caring for patients in order to alert them under specific conditions. This is sometimes referred to as *public health decision support*. This might be particularly helpful when public health departments suggest structured data that would be helpful to collect for patients who meet specified criteria or when it would be helpful for providers to order a specific kind of diagnostic test to provide more information on the cause of disease. While some demonstrations of this type of capability have been carried out,[10] only limited healthcare IT systems have the ability to incorporate these types of alerts. Alerts from public health departments are not always well received by providers, because the alerts are sometimes perceived as not being relevant to their practice; other reasons that the alerts may be unwanted are limitations to scalability and targeting and alert fatigue.

Privacy and Security

Preserving the privacy and confidentiality of patients is critical. Public health departments often provide both clinical care and public health services, and these two different functions have different privacy and security implications. When providing clinical care, public health departments are considered covered entities under the Health Insurance Portability and Accountability Act (HIPAA) and are subject to the same rules and requirements as other care providers. When providing public health services, different rules and requirements apply.

To enable public health departments to monitor the population's health, HIPAA provides exceptions for covered entities, including care providers, to disclose protected health information to public health departments without patient authorization when the data are required or permitted by federal, state, or tribal statutes. These exceptions include the prevention and control of diseases, injuries, or disabilities; vital events such as deaths and births; issues to support public health surveillance; epidemiological investigations and interventions; and information sent to a foreign government agency that is collaborating with a public health department (to investigate a disease outbreak, for example). There are also exceptions for the disclosure of data about people at risk for contracting or spreading a disease; workers' compensation and workplace medical surveillance; health oversight; instances of child abuse and neglect; domestic violence; neglect of the elderly or incapacitated; and data on adverse events, for product tracking, to facilitate product recalls or replacement and post-marketing surveillance reporting to pharmaceutical or device manufacturers. In cases of domestic violence, HIPAA additionally requires the covered entity to either seek agreement of the victim or make a determination that reporting is necessary to prevent serious harm to the individual or other potential victims.

TIP   Public health departments are *not* covered entities under HIPAA. In some cases, parts of their activities such as direct provision of clinical care are subject to the same privacy and security rules.

In certain limited cases such as disease surveillance, a limited data set might suffice, and covered entities might be more comfortable reporting data in this fashion. In other cases, aggregated data such as a count of the number of influenza cases seen in an emergency department in a 24-hour period might suffice. Aggregated data better protect patient confidentiality than a limited data set but can be difficult to validate and can make it much more difficult to obtain additional details about a case should they be needed. Approaches have been developed that rely on assigning an arbitrary identifier that allows the provider to link to the individual patient's data to overcome some of these limitations.

TIP   While HIPAA grants broad exceptions that allow covered entities to disclose protected health information to public health departments, covered entities are frequently cautious and seek clear assurances that they are allowed to make these disclosures. This is particularly true when the disclosures involve conditions or data that might not traditionally have been perceived as relevant to public health.

Scope of Data

Public health functions may require almost any of the types of data that are required for clinical care, including diagnoses, laboratory results, radiographic results, medications, and vital signs. The scope of data that public health departments might require is significantly driven by performing syndromic surveillance and the need to investigate outbreaks. In addition to these ubiquitous types of data, public health applications often benefit from geographic location data. Such data are often useful in tracking the spread of disease but are available only in limited form (usually restricted to knowing the patient's home address) in most traditional healthcare IT systems. Geolocation data are increasingly available through devices such as patients' mobile phones, but these data are not yet routinely captured in healthcare IT systems.

 TIP Healthcare IT systems used by providers often identify providers by using one or more IDs, and the messages they typically exchange don't include details such as name or phone number. If these messages are repurposed for use by public health departments, the specific provider information will often need to be added to the message.

Clinical Information Standards

In general, uses of healthcare IT for public health rely on the same clinical data standards as other uses of healthcare IT. The same terminology standards, including LOINC, ICD-10, and RxNORM, are applicable. In some cases, population health applications have driven the development of relevant standards such as CVX, a code set used to identify the vaccines administered and reported to immunization registries.[11] Another example is the International Classification of Disease (ICD), which was first developed, and continues to be maintained, by the WHO to standardize how countries report causes of death. Similarly, population health uses common, shared message format standards, including HL7. As for other applications of healthcare IT, public health has some unique use cases for which there are specific implementation guides that specify details appropriate to them that are different than for other use cases. Examples of use cases for which there are implementation guides specific to public health include reporting vaccinations and reportable conditions.

Public health is also unique in its use of *value sets*, which are subsets of terms drawn from a standardized vocabulary that apply to a given use case.[12] A good example is the Reportable Conditions Mapping Table (RCMT). The RCMT is a value set published by CDC that includes the specific LOINC and SNOMED CT terms that represent reportable conditions that providers report to public health departments. The RCMT includes, for example, the various kinds of lab tests for Lyme disease along with the SNOMED CT terms assigned to various genetic variants of the microorganisms that cause Lyme disease. The CDC publishes a variety of value sets for public health use cases, including terms used by providers for reporting to cancer registries, terms associated with healthcare-acquired infections, and terms for use when reporting to immunization registries.

Because departments often receive data from multiple care providers, they may have to match patients across those providers in order to avoid double counting when estimating the incidence or prevalence of conditions. They would typically employ the same approaches to patient matching as providers use in a master patient index within or between care providers.

Trends and What to Expect in the Future

Looking forward, there are a number of ways that healthcare IT is likely to evolve to better support public health. For example, you can expect that even more information will flow from providers to public health departments to meet compliance with the meaningful use and evolving Advancing Care Information programs incentivizing adoption of EHR systems. Consequently, as public health departments become more aware of emerging disease trends, more information about community health will flow to providers in the context of care, such as enabling EHR systems to access a patient's lifelong vaccination history and provide decision support about missing vaccinations. Similarly, the evolving need for collaboration between members of a patient's care team will increasingly necessitate public health department communication electronically with clinical-care providers about population health events.

Methods for monitoring population health are undergoing a transformation as well. They are transforming from field-based and descriptive to clinical, analytical, and experimental. Whereas previously public health professionals would physically gather data from patients, hospitals, and clinics via paper chart review, increasingly public health departments seek access to new data sources, including EHR systems but also newer sources including social media, mobile phone applications, and over-the-counter medication sales data. For example, some health departments are using Yelp! restaurant review data to identify and track disease outbreaks,[13] while other health agencies are using Twitter to identify seasonal flu outbreaks.[14] This evolution underway in public health will require increased access to data about individuals in the population as well as additional data about the environment in which they live and the system in which they receive healthcare. In 2015, the Robert Wood Johnson Foundation initiated a call to create a Culture in Health where clinical and public health departments could work together to address the social determinants of health. While there are some communities experimenting with combining data on social determinants, including education, criminal activity, and poverty, with data from EHR systems to better understand the underlying causes of disease and disability,[15] the capacity for doing this is absent in many communities. Together, through the creation of interoperable networks of healthcare IT systems, it may one day be possible to more fully understand and intervene to improve the social, behavioral, and environmental determinants of health in addition to the genetic and health system causes of disease and poor health.

Chapter Review

Public health and clinical care are complementary processes. The types of data required to manage both are the same, but the context and purpose of data use are different. Whereas public health focuses on monitoring and intervening in the health of populations, clinical care focuses on caring for one patient at a time. Data generated by providers in the course of clinical care, such as diagnoses, medication prescribed, immunizations administered, and laboratory test results, can be very useful for public health use cases, and HIPAA provides specific exemptions that allow covered entities to share specific types of data with public health departments. Data transmission and coding standards are essentially the same for public health applications, though there are specific implementation guides tailored to accommodate aggregated data across a population rather than data on a single patient. Public health departments use data primarily to measure the prevalence and incidence of diseases in populations. Laboratory results generated by public health departments may be available to incorporate into healthcare IT and used by clinical-care providers, and you can expect that additional summary data and suggested clinical actions generated by public health departments will be pushed into providers' healthcare IT systems in the future.

Questions

To test your comprehension of the chapter, answer the following questions and then check your answers against the list of correct answers at the end of the chapter.

1. Which types of information systems are relevant to public health informatics?

    A. Immunization registries

    B. Cancer registries

    C. Electronic medical records

    D. All of the above

2. Who is responsible for creating and implementing regulations relevant to public health?

    A. Multiple agencies in federal, state, and local governments as well as some territories

    B. The Office of the National Coordinator for Health Information Technology (ONC)

    C. The Office of the Assistant Secretary for Planning and Evaluation (ASPE) in the Department of Health and Human Services (HHS)

    D. The Centers for Disease Control and Prevention (CDC)

3. In the United States, responsibility for collecting and sharing data on population health is distributed at what organizational level(s)?

    A. Federal (e.g., CDC)

    B. State and territorial

    C. Local (e.g., county and city health departments)

    D. Federal, state, and local

4. Which of the following activities are designed to simplify data collection and public health department reporting for clinical practitioners?

    A. The efforts of the ONC and CMS under ACA and MACRA to stimulate adoption of electronic medical records and health information exchange

    B. HIPAA rules that prohibit sharing data for public health purposes so no activities are allowed

    C. Neither of the above

    D. Both of the above

5. Which of the following is true regarding clinical information standards that have been adopted to facilitate sharing of data between clinical-care providers and public health departments?

   A. LOINC codes for clinical observations and the HL7 Clinical Document Architecture have been adopted.

   B. The United States has yet to adopt clinical information standards to facilitate sharing between clinical-care providers and public health departments.

   C. All standards being developed are for acute care hospital environments.

   D. All of the above.

6. Why do clinicians often fail to report disease cases to public health departments?

   A. Clinicians must take time to fill out paperwork for which they are not reimbursed, and are unaware that certain diseases need to be reported to health authorities.

   B. Electronic medical record systems are not connected to the Internet, preventing transmission.

   C. There are no requirements to report diseases to public health agencies.

   D. All of the above.

7. In syndromic surveillance, public health departments capture which type(s) of data from healthcare providers electronically?

   A. Diagnostic codes representing the diseases affecting patients seen by the providers

   B. Symptoms or prediagnostic data representing reasons why the patient visited the providers

   C. Laboratory results representing confirmed diseases in patients who visit the providers

   D. Statistical data from hospitals on the number of patients who come in with signs of the flu

Answers

1. **D.** Understanding and improving the public's health depends on interoperability between clinical information systems such as electronic medical records, public health laboratory information systems, and public health-related registries.

2. **A.** The essential governmental role in public health is guided and implemented by a variety of federal, state/territorial, and local regulations and laws as well as federal, state/territorial, and local governmental public health departments.

3. **D.** Responsibility for data collection and sharing in public health is shared by federal, state, and local health departments.

4. A. By providing subsidies, guidelines, and other incentives for adoption of EMRs and implementation of health information exchange (HIE), the federal government through CMS and the ONC is making it easier for clinical providers to adopt healthcare IT based on clinical information standards that will facilitate reporting data for public health purposes.

5. A. Several standards for terminologies (e.g., LOINC) and transport (e.g., HL7 CDA) have been adopted to facilitate exchange of information between clinical-care providers and public health departments.

6. A. Clinicians are not always trained to know which diseases need to be reported, and there are few incentives for clinicians to report disease cases other than satisfaction in knowing they are contributing to the common good.

7. B. Syndromic surveillance focuses on prediagnostic data, sometimes referred to as "chief complaints," to provide preclinical diagnoses of specific diseases to inform monitoring of overall trends.

References

1. Centers for Disease Control and Prevention (CDC). (2013). The public health system and the 10 essential public health services. In *National Public Health Performance Standards*. Accessed on June 10, 2016, from www.cdc.gov/nphpsp/essentialServices.html.

2. Braveman, P., & Gottlieb, L. (2014). The social determinants of health: It's time to consider the causes of the causes. *Public Health Reports, 129*(Suppl 2), 19–31.

3. Cooper, R. A., Cooper, M. A., McGinley, E. L., Fan, X., & Rosenthal, J. T. (2012). Poverty, wealth, and health care utilization: A geographic assessment. *Journal of Urban Health, 89*(5), 828–847.

4. Gibson, J. D., Richards, J., Srinivasan, A., & Block, D. E. (2015). Public health practice applications. In V. K. Saba & K. A. McCormick (Eds.), *Essentials of nursing informatics, sixth edition*. McGraw-Hill.

5. CDC. (2011). *Healthy people 2020.* Accessed on August 8, 2016, from www.cdc.gov/nchs/healthy_people/hp2020.htm.

6. Dixon, B. E., Grannis, S. J., & Revere, D. (2013). Measuring the impact of a health information exchange intervention on provider-based notifiable disease reporting using mixed methods: A study protocol. *BMC Medical Informatics and Decision Making, 13*(1), 121.

7. Dixon, B. E., Siegel, J. A., Oemig, T. V., & Grannis, S. J. (2013). Electronic health information quality challenges and interventions to improve public health surveillance data and practice. *Public Health Reports, 128*(6), 546–553.

8. Martin, D. W., Lowery, N. E., Brand, B., Gold, R., & Horlick, G. (2015). Immunization information systems: A decade of progress in law and policy. *Journal of Public Health Management and Practice, 21*(3), 296–303.

   9. CDC. (2016). *Health Alert Network (HAN).* Accessed on August 8, 2016, from http://emergency.cdc.gov/han/.

10. Dixon, B. E., Gamache, R. E., & Grannis, S. J. (2013). Towards public health decision support: A systematic review of bidirectional communication approaches. *Journal of the American Medical Informatics Association, 20*(3), 577–583.

11. CDC. (2016). *IIS: Current HL7 standard code set CVX—vaccines administered.* Accessed on August 8, 2016, from www2a.cdc.gov/vaccines/iis/iisstandards/ vaccines.asp?rpt=cvx.

12. Alyea, J. M., Dixon, B. E., Bowie, J., & Kanter, A. S. (2016). Standardizing health-care data across an enterprise. In B. E. Dixon (Ed.), *Health information exchange: Navigating and managing a network of health information systems* (pp. 137–148). Academic Press.

13. Schomberg, J. P., Haimson, O. L., Hayes, G. R., & Anton-Culver, H. (2016, March 29). Supplementing public health inspection via social media. *PLOS ONE, 11*(3), e0152117.

14. Signorini, A., Segre, A. M., & Polgreen, P. M. (2011). The use of Twitter to track levels of disease activity and public concern in the U.S. during the influenza A H1N1 pandemic. *PLOS ONE, 6*(5), e19467.

15. Comer, K. F., Grannis, S., Dixon, B. E., Bodenhamer, D. J., & Wiehe, S. E. (2011). Incorporating geospatial capacity within clinical data systems to address social determinants of health. *Public Health Reports, 126*(Suppl 3), 54–61.

PART II

Fundamentals of Healthcare Information Science

CHAPTER 5

Computer Hardware and Architecture for Healthcare IT

Omid Shabestari

In this chapter, you will learn how to

- Identify computer hardware used in healthcare
- Define basic IT terms and concepts
- Recognize computer system components
- Identify different types of computers used in healthcare
- Discern trends in hardware requirements in healthcare
- Manage computer assets
- Troubleshoot common, healthcare computer user challenges

Technologies used in healthcare have evolved rapidly over the past several decades. Early computer applications in healthcare were typically stand-alone and focused on very specific and somewhat isolated health-related functions. The advent of modern computing, including introduction of transistors and integrated circuit (IC) technology, has led to major advances that have supported today's generation of health information systems, including the emergence of electronic health records, patient billing systems, and decision support systems. Advances in microprocessors, local area networks, and databases characterized important trends in the 1970s and 1980s, and computing was transformed with the advent of personal computers.

This chapter will describe how essential technologies in healthcare depend on the appropriate hardware components being connected in a way that allows for their effective implementation and interconnection. In addition, advances in web-based computing and the advent of mobile health applications and cloud computing have continued to shape healthcare, and new trends are emerging constantly. Specialized software and hardware also continue to be developed and advanced in areas ranging from medical imaging to patient monitoring. An understanding of healthcare IT hardware and architectures and trends in these areas is important for putting healthcare IT into context. One of the most major advances in healthcare IT has been the widespread deployment of electronic medical records (EMRs) in physician offices and clinics and electronic health records (EHRs) that can interconnect patient data from multiple health information systems and run in large hospital and regional environments.

Computer Hardware

An important perspective for considering the many advances in healthcare IT comes from considering a computer as a system, where you can classify its hardware components in three groups: input devices, output devices, and system components.

Input Devices

Input devices include any component that allows entry of data into a computer system. Some of the traditional input devices include the keyboard and the mouse. Although the standard forms of keyboard and mouse are still commonly used in healthcare, concerns have been raised that they may be sources for spreading infections in healthcare settings, similar to concerns about the sanitary condition of doorknobs and elevator keys.[1] As a result, the National Health System in the UK decided to replace the conventional keyboard and mouse with infection prevention devices. These devices have a sealing surface that prevents contamination from going between keys (see Figure 5-1). They do not have any raised or recessed surface for bacteria to hide. They also have flash indicators that inform end users to clean them on a preset frequency. They can be cleaned with hospital-grade antibacterial wipes and sprays and can even be rinsed under a faucet.

Figure 5-1   Infection prevention keyboard

Another device that is commonly used in healthcare systems is the digital pen and signature pad. These devices are commonly used in graphical activities in healthcare such as getting patient consent and marking significant areas on X-rays or other types of graphs. Advances in handwriting recognition software now allow users to enter text into EMRs and EHRs using a digital pen.

Speech input, discussed below, is extensively used in hospital operating rooms, and other innovative methods for providing input to computer systems abound in this complex environment as well. Besides the infection prevention keyboard, which is commonly used in operating rooms, a touchless mouse based on infrared proximity sensing has been evaluated and has shown promise.[2] A touchless gesture solution for surgeons to view images while performing surgery is provided by the Microsoft Kinect; it is used as an input device to picture archiving and communication system (PACS) stations in operating rooms.[3] A similar navigation system is used for dental surgery.[4]

Barcode scanners are another type of input device that are increasingly used in hospitals and healthcare settings. A barcode scanner (also known as a barcode reader) is a device that can read and write printed bar codes to a computer. In healthcare they are used to read bar codes on medication labels and read patient identification codes (which may be printed on patient wrist bracelets) to ensure that the right medications are given to the right patient.

Speech input has also become an important mode for providing input to healthcare computing systems. For example, a number of EHR vendors provide healthcare professionals (e.g., physicians) with speech recognition capabilities that allow the health professional to dictate patient information directly to the system, or in some cases to operate complex surgical equipment using verbal commands when one's hands are not available to use a keyboard.

Another example of a touchless control system is the infrared tracking device that monitors the point of gaze of the user on the screen. This device was traditionally used in human-computer interaction labs for user interface optimization. It has also been used for medical training, such as to evaluate timely attention to the details among training surgeons during an operation in a virtual reality environment.[5] In addition, many of the new medical devices can be connected directly to computers for medical imaging, EKG analysis, EEG analysis, automated medical lab analysis, and barcode scanning.

A range of digital imaging is used in the medical industry and leads to the creation of digital input to healthcare computer systems. This can range from scanned copies of birth records to results of clinical investigations and lists of medications. All-in-one devices are commonly used as they can serve as a printer, photo copier, scanner, and fax machine. A range of devices are now commonly used for document imaging, including flatbed scanners, handheld scanners, photocopiers, and smartphone apps.

A scanned image can be saved, stored, and input into computer systems in several formats, including

- **Tagged Image File Format (TIFF)**   Data tags can be indexed and are searchable.
- **Portable Document Format (PDF)**   Text and images can be stored within a single file, data tags can be indexed and are searchable, and bookmarks and hyperlinks can be added.
- **Joint Photographic Experts Group (JPEG)**   Natively viewable in a web browser.
- **Graphics Interchange Format (GIF)**   Natively viewable in a web browser (like JPEG), but is best used to store images with large areas of the same color (because it has a limited color palette).

The resolution of a document is measured by the number of pixels per inch (PPI) of a scanned document. Different rates of compression are used to reduce storage space of scanned documents. Some healthcare systems use document management software which can be integrated with EMRs and EHRs.

Output Devices

Output devices are the interfaces that extend the results of the system processing to other systems or end users. Some of the traditional output devices include monitors and printers. In many clinical settings, large-size digital TVs are used for communication with patients. For example, information such as a listing of the next scheduled patient, using initials or some other way to mask patient identity, and patient education content can be delivered via these TVs in the waiting room. High-resolution graphical outputs can now be made available across hospital settings—for example, large-screen monitors used in operating room environments, allowing for rapid signal detection and color calibration. The quality of stored documents can be measured in terms of dots per inch (DPI). For example, 72 DPI may be sufficient for displaying on a computer monitor, whereas 600 DPI might be needed for print quality. The color depth affects how many shades of color are available, with 48-bit color depth being superior to 24-bit color depth. Clinical desktop display monitors have also evolved to allow for high-resolution display of imaging at an increasingly lower cost throughout the hospital setting.

System Components

This section will describe the main system components of a computer: the central processing unit, motherboard, random access memory, and storage components. It will start with the connectors that serve to join the input and output devices to the system components. System components used to be "the parts inside the box" of the computer. In many cases that still applies but it's not always the case, and we'll see that some storage components are "outside the box."

Connectors

Computers use different type of connectors for input and output devices (peripherals). Traditionally, each type of device had its own dedicated port on computers. Some equipment connects to a computer via a serial port (often referred to as an RS-232 port) or a PS/2 port. Most modern peripherals plug into a Universal Serial Bus (USB) port, shown in Figure 5-2. USB 3.0 and the emerging USB 3.1 provide faster input and output speeds. An eSATA port is another type of fast connector usually for external storage drives.

Up to 127 USB devices can be plugged into a USB port by using USB hubs, which offer additional USB ports. Smaller USB devices such as flash drives draw their power from the USB port, whereas other USB devices such as large-capacity hard disks or EKG devices have their own external power supply. Table 5-1 lists the three USB standards.

Most of the latest computer systems do not have traditional serial or PS/2 ports. A modern computer may have many USB ports but not have a serial port, while specific medical equipment may require a serial port connection. A USB-to-serial adapter may be used in this situation. Adapters are available for all types of connections.

Some of the more advanced medical devices connect indirectly to computers via wireless connections such as Wi-Fi or Bluetooth technologies. Rivaling USB, some systems have an IEEE 1394 (often referred to as FireWire) port. Devices such as video cameras and hard disks can connect to FireWire ports. Up to 63 devices can be daisy-chained together on a single FireWire bus for transfer speeds of either 400 MBps or 800 MBps (FireWire 400 and FireWire 800, respectively).

NOTE Bus is a general term for a communication mechanism that transfers data between components within a computer or between computers. The term bus applies to hardware components like wire and optical fiber as well as software, including communication protocols.

Figure 5-2
A USB port and an eSATA port on a laptop (photo courtesy of NotebookCheck © 2016)

Table 5-1	Standard	Maximum Throughput
USB Standards	USB 1.0	12 Mbps (megabits per second)
	USB 2.0	480 Mbps
	USB 3.0	5 Gbps (gigabits per second)

Traditionally, audio and video devices had separate ports with RGB ports for video and specific ports for audio in and audio out. The recent trend is to use High-Definition Multimedia Interface (HDMI) and mini-HDMI ports for transferring uncompressed video data and compressed or uncompressed digital audio data. Computer cameras are either built-in or connect via USB ports.

 TIP Wi-Fi and Bluetooth are wireless technologies and therefore are susceptible to environmental conditions, such as electrical storms and other forms of electromagnetic interference.

Central Processing Unit

The *processing unit* is the component of the system responsible for performing calculations and other types of data processing. In general, processing units are grouped in two categories: central processing unit (CPU) and graphical processing unit (GPU). CPUs are responsible for the processing of data. They are also often referred to as microprocessors. GPUs are specifically responsible for rendering graphics. The speed of a CPU is typically measured in gigahertz (GHz, or billions of operations per second) or millions of instructions per second (MIPS). More power is drawn from a faster CPU, which will also generate more heat. A CPU chip may be multicore, meaning it may contain several separate CPUs (such as four, which is known as quad core). The CPUs used in portable devices are specially designed to operate with low energy consumption to increase the battery life of those devices.

Motherboards

The motherboard of a computer is a thin printed circuit board (PCB) that contains the main components of a computer, including the CPU, memory, and connectors and slots for input and output (I/O) devices. The board contains a socket for housing the CPU (along with fans next to the socket to cool the computer as the CPU generates heat) as well as a socket for a read-only memory (ROM) chip that contains the startup instructions for the computer (known as the BIOS, or basic input/output system). The board is considered the "mother" of all components, as its name indicates.

The components on the motherboard are connected by what is known as a bus. Slots in the bus allow new hardware components to be connected to the computer, allowing the CPU to communicate with peripheral devices. There may be different types of bus slots for graphics cards and additional slots to connect hardware, which are known as Peripheral Component Interconnect (PCI) slots. A computer may have a single PCI slot and several PCI Express (PCIe) slots, which use lanes for data throughput.

PCIe slots come in a variety of types, such as ×1 (with one lane and a data throughput of 250 megabytes per second [MBps] unidirectionally and 500 MBps bidirectionally), X8, and X16 (which has a maximum bidirectional throughput of 8 gigabytes per second [GBps]). The type of operating system that can be installed on a computer depends on the internal bandwidth of the motherboard. Also, one or more expansion slots may be contained on the motherboard.

Random Access Memory

Processing units require an environment for processing information. This environment is provided by random access memory (RAM). RAM is electronic memory where the operating system (OS), application software, and any documents you are actively working on exist so they can be rapidly accessed by the device's CPU (as required during data processing). Newer operating systems require a higher amount of RAM to operate. In addition, a higher amount of RAM allows more programs to run concurrently. Sufficient RAM is needed to run modern operating systems and healthcare applications. In a Windows-based system, you can find out how much RAM the computer has by clicking the Start menu, right-clicking Computer, choosing Properties, and looking for Installed Memory (RAM). Data stored in RAM requires electricity.

TIP 32-bit computers cannot address more than 4GB of RAM.

Storage Components

Storage components are capable of maintaining the data permanently (i.e., after the computer is turned off). They can reside inside computer systems, be connected via USB ports, or be shared across the network. Using the storage space shared in the network will allow roaming profiles. This feature enables the network users to have access to their personal space (documents, desktop, downloads, and favorites) from any computer in the network.

Internal hard disk devices (HDDs) mostly use Serial Advanced Technology Attachment (SATA) hard drives instead of Integrated Drive Electronics (IDE) connectors. More advanced computers may also use solid-state drive (SSD) technology, meaning there are no moving parts, unlike traditional hard disks. No moving parts means less wear and tear, noise, power draw, and heat, and often means faster data access times, which comes at a price premium. High-end workstations and servers might use Small Computer Systems Interface (SCSI) hard disks. Table 5-2 summarizes the three disk technologies.

Additional storage can be achieved by locally plugged-in external hard disk storage, including USB flash drives (often called thumb drives). Handheld medical devices, such as smartphones, digital cameras, portable media players, and tablets, often have a small amount of internal data storage capacity that can be transferred to a computer via direct USB connection or computer network. Some equipment may allow use of removable storage media such as Secure Digital (SD) cards. Use of memory sticks and SD cards may be prohibited in some hospital contexts because of security concerns (i.e., because the device is small, it may be stolen, lost, or misplaced).

Standard	Throughput	Description
IDE	Up to 133 MBps	Used by older desktops and laptops, with either a 40- or 80-wire data cable and Molex power connector. Motherboards in the past often had both a primary and secondary IDE pin connector. Each allowed up to two IDE devices, where one device was designated as the master and the other as the slave.
SATA	Up to 750 MBps (SATA 3.0), 3 Gbps (eSATA)	Common in today's computers. Uses a seven-wire data cable and a SATA power connector. The number of SATA connectors depends on the motherboard. Some computers have an eSATA port for external SATA drive connectivity.
SCSI	Up to 640 MBps	Many SCSI standards have been developed over the decades; Ultra640 is one of the newest. A SCSI card or host bus adapter (HBA) is required and may be built into the motherboard's chipset. Newer SCSI standards allow up to 16 SCSI devices on a single SCSI bus. Both ends of the SCSI bus must be terminated, and each SCSI device requires a unique SCSI ID.

Table 5-2 Hard Disk Standards

Data can be stored on CDs, DVDs, and Blu-ray optical discs. A writable drive is needed for writing to, or burning data to, these storage devices. Bootable DVDs may contain operating system installations (and may be used to restart a computer whose operating system may have been corrupted). Table 5-3 compares the three standards in terms of their storage capacity.

Backup tapes are also used for data storage, typically for archiving large amounts of digitally recorded data, and are used as long-term backup because hard drives may fail over time. The device that reads or writes to the tape is known as a tape drive. There are a number of tape standards. Up to 800GB of data can be stored on a single Digital Linear Tape (DLT). New tape storage technology has been developed with new magnetic tape technological advances potentially allowing tape capacity of 185TB. In backing up health data, most backups involve an archive bit, which is cleared when a file is backed up (except in a differential backup) and is turned back on only if a change is made to the file (indicating need for a backup), as shown in Figure 5-3. Types of backup are also listed in Table 5-4.

Table 5-3 Optical Disc Standards	Type of Media	Capacity
	CD	Up to 999MB
	DVD	4.7GB (up to 17GB if dual layer)
	Blu-ray	25GB (up to 50GB if dual layer)

	Backup Type	Description
Table 5-4 Common Backup Types	Daily (full)	Backs up all files in the specified location and clears the archive bit. Takes the longest to back up but is the quickest to restore.
	Differential	Backs up only files that have changed since the *previous full backup* (files with the archive bit turned on) and does not clear the archive bit.
	Incremental	Backs up only files that have changed since the *previous incremental or full backup* (files with the archive bit turned on) and clears the archive bit. Takes the least amount of time to back up but the longest to restore.

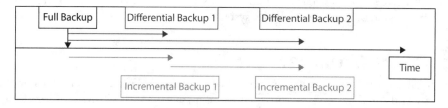

Figure 5-3   How the different types of backups work

The backup of health data is essential, and onsite backup of data can be done using tape, CD/DVD, and other media. The backup of data offsite might involve transferring data to an offsite secure location using physical media.

TIP   Full and incremental backups clear the archive bit. Differential backups do not clear the archive bit.

Cloud Computing, ASPs, and Client-Server EMR Systems

Increasingly, data from health applications is being stored over the Internet using application server providers (ASPs), which are companies that offer providers or health-care organizations storage and access to data and software services over the Internet that would otherwise have to be located on their own local computers. Some electronic medical record (EMR) vendors provide storage of patient data accessible to EMR and EHR systems remotely over the Internet. A trend in this direction is *cloud computing*, where services (storage, programs, and applications) may be hosted over the Internet, from servers at remote locations. Using this approach, all that is needed to run applications or store data on the cloud is a web browser and a connection to the Internet via an Internet service provider (ISP). Advantages of cloud computing include potential reduction in data backup costs and difficulty (if the data does not need to be stored locally, local server hardware does not need to be set up and maintained). However, in healthcare settings, careful consideration must be given to how well the stored data is kept private and confidential and the degree to which the data transmitted or stored using cloud computing is secure from being intercepted or stolen (which requires strong encryption of any personal health data).

In contrast, client-server EHR systems require locating an EHR server onsite, which assigns the responsibility of running the system to the local IT staff. This approach involves connecting one or more client workstations to the computer running the EMR system (on the onsite EMR server). The advantage is faster access speeds than cloud-based EMR systems and more local control over EMR data. In addition, added functionality could be created using application programming interfaces (APIs). Historically, another way of connecting an EMR system to end users is to use dumb terminals, which consist of a screen and keyboard that connect users to a remote computer system such as a mainframe system running the EMR system.

Hardware Management

Even if a healthcare organization uses cloud computing, ASPs, and other forms of offsite hardware and software services, some hardware management is always required for even a small operation. In medium and large healthcare organizations, there are often dedicated HIT staff assigned to the function of hardware management. As this section will describe, hardware management encompasses a wide variety of tasks as well as new types of hardware for healthcare uses.

Operating Systems and Hardware Drivers

Computer hardware requires a specialized type of software called an operating system for loading other applications. Computers normally come with a preinstalled OS, such as Microsoft Windows or Apple macOS. If you want to upgrade a computer's OS or install a different OS, you have to make sure that your OS supports the hardware. Microsoft publishes a list of hardware that will work with each version of its Windows operating systems; this list is called the Windows Compatible Products List.

The files that support interaction of the OS with different hardware modules are called *drivers*. When a new hardware device (e.g., a printer) is added to a computer system, a compatible software driver must be installed in the operating system so that the hardware device can communicate with the OS. Although most operating systems support generic drivers, installing the specialized drivers will allow use of all the features provided in the hardware. The exception is monitors, which usually use generic drivers. In many cases, the computer's operating system will detect new hardware and automatically download and install the right driver, but this is not always the case, such as when the computer doesn't have an Internet connection. When manually installing a driver, be sure to install the right driver; for example, a 64-bit installation for Windows Server requires a 64-bit driver.

Networking Hardware

Computers in isolation are not very functional and in almost all use cases require connection to a network via a wired or wireless connection, or both, as presented in Table 5-5. Historically, computers used to be connected to remote networks via dial-up modem devices, but today they typically rely on shared network devices such as routers for these connections. Network hardware includes

- Routers, which are devices that forward data packets between computer networks
- Switches, which connect devices together on a computer network
- Bridges, which connect multiple network segments
- Hubs, for connecting multiple Ethernet devices
- Repeaters, which receive signals and retransmit them with a stronger signal

Networks can be physically arranged in different topologies such as star and ring configurations. In addition, there are a number of different types of transmission media for networks, ranging from copper wire to optical fiber as well as wireless transmission of data across a network. Some complex networks are heterogeneous, consisting of a network of networks. The Internet itself can be considered to be such a network as it connects a huge number of nodes, which in turn may be networked.

From a hardware perspective, many computer networks use network cables and switches to interconnect devices, while others use wireless technologies. Ethernet switches are used to connect computers to Ethernet networks and may have 24 RJ-45 ports that would allow 24 devices to be plugged in, with additional high-speed ports to allow for more devices to be interconnected on a local area network (LAN). Routers can be wired and wireless, and are plugged into switches for connection to other networks, including the Internet. A Windows computer network consists of Windows client operating systems and domain controllers (DCs), which are Windows servers that include Active Directory (AD), a directory service that is used to manage user account information, passwords, groups, and computer accounts.

Network Standard	Maximum Throughput	Description
Ethernet (IEEE 802.3)	Up to 25 GB/s	A set of standards specifying the physical layer and data link layer's media access control (MAC) of wired Ethernet implementations.
RJ-45 port allowing a network cable to be plugged in	Up to 10 Gbps	Wired networking; offers the best speed and security.
Wi-Fi 802.11b/g/n	Up to 200 Mbps	Wireless; 802.11b speed is 12 Mbps, 802.11g speed is 54 Mbps, and 802.11n speed is up to 200 Mbps. Maximum range is typically in the 100-foot range.
Bluetooth	Up to 2 Mbps	Wireless; maximum range is typically in the 30-foot range.

Table 5-5   Common Network Transmission Standards

Portable Computers

Healthcare is a distributed service. There is a high demand for having computing resources available at the point of care, such as the hospital bedside or outside the hospital during homecare or emergency services. Traditionally, Computers on Wheels (COWs) have been used in hospitals where durability and full-sized input devices are often required. COWs allow computers (which could include both desktop and tablet computers) and associated hardware and software technologies (e.g., barcode scanners, EHR access, etc.) to be packaged in a single mobile cart that can be moved from room to room in a hospital (see Figure 5-4). COWs are designed to work in a wireless environment and can have batteries connected to the bottom of them to allow for lengthy usage time.

Thin clients are increasingly used in healthcare settings. These computers are lightweight systems that are designed to connect to the central server from remote locations and run the applications on the server (i.e., most of the processing is done on the server computer instead of the client computer). The operating system of the thin clients is usually installed into a read-only computer chip (firmware) rather than hard disk. This helps them to be resistant to computer viruses, malware, and accidental damage by their users. Smartphones, which are in fact computers plus phones, and tablet computers, which are increasingly the thin client of choice, are rapidly being adopted in healthcare settings. Some organizations strictly limit the use of cell phones on the network whereas others are more accepting, even going so far as to encourage endusers to "bring your own device" (BYOD) and supporting the connection of those devices to the healthcare organization's network.

Figure 5-4
Computer on
Wheels

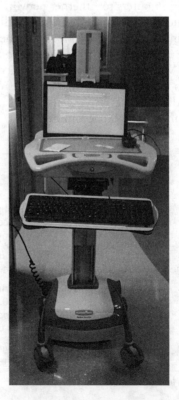

Wearable Computers

These devices attach to or are worn by patients or healthcare providers and contain sensors for continuous measurement of different health indicators. Some examples of these devices are insulin pumps that can transfer data via USB ports or Bluetooth connectivity, and activity-monitoring devices such as Fitbits. Wearable computers are also worn by healthcare providers, such as Google Glass.[6] Wearable computers mostly interact with other portable devices such as smartphones.

Server Computers

A server is a computer program that provides services to other computer programs (known as "clients" of the server in client-server architectures) and to end users. Servers are usually connected to a network (or the Internet), where computers (or people) can request their services. There are a number of different types of servers. For example, file servers store and share files on a network, database servers provide access to databases over a network, print servers are connected to printers and carry out print jobs, and application servers host particular applications (such as an EHR system) that can be accessed by multiple users or other programs over a network.

Servers are typically designed to be able to work on a 24/7 basis with no downtime. This continuous service requires a high level of resilience and fault tolerance. Some of the features that facilitate this requirement are power supplies with multiple input sources that switch the power source in real time in case of a power loss. Other ways of ensuring continuous uptime include using error-correcting code (ECC) RAM that can detect and correct the most common kinds of internal data corruption, using a redundant array of independent disks (RAID) system to provide data mirroring and fault tolerance, and using hot-plug hard disks that can prevent data loss resulting from hard disk failures. RAID systems are available at seven levels, numbered from zero to six, providing different levels of data mirroring and fault tolerance. In addition, software solutions such as clustering provide mirrored systems and prevent a complete system failure from affecting services. In the event of a power outage, it is imperative that the server shut down gracefully to prevent potential file corruption or damage to hardware components. An uninterruptable power supply (UPS) solves this problem; it has a bank of batteries and several electrical outlets. UPSs are designed in different sizes to serve single or multiple servers.

Trends in Meeting Hardware Requirements

Current trends in HIT and health informatics have affected hardware requirements in a number of ways. First, the demand for storage space is increasing exponentially. Consistent with this trend is the need to store large amounts of genomic information, as that information is beginning to be collected from patients. In addition, the large amounts of data collected by wearable devices (that provide continuous health monitoring) and digital high-resolution medical imaging contribute to this increasing demand. The second pressing demand is more processing power required for advanced analytics and predictive modeling. The solutions to these increasing demands can be categorized in two ways: scaling up hardware (aka vertical scaling) and scaling out hardware (aka horizontal scaling).

Scaling Up Hardware

With this approach, you increase the resources in the same machine. Some server machines have extra capacity to add additional processors, memory, or storage space, but this capacity may be limited. The solution that has the least limitations is to use blade servers. These machines have a modular design, enabling you to add multiple motherboards containing both CPU and RAM to them, but from the operating system point of view, they all appear to be a single machine. Some of the high-end supercomputer blade systems have specially designed racks. Scaling up of the storage space is limited to the number of bays available for adding new hard disks. This solution is relatively limited, and in most cases scale-out solutions provide better flexibility.

Scaling Out Hardware

With this approach, you extend the availability of resources outside of a single system. The most common application is for data storage, which has two primary categories:

- **Network-attached storage (NAS) solutions**   These specialized devices can be accessed via a computer network, use standard network connection protocols, and can be mapped as a network drive. This technology has highly penetrated the small and medium-sized networks and you can even buy a reasonably priced unit for using in your home network.

- **Storage area network (SAN) solutions**   These larger solutions normally use fast Fibre Channel connections and SCSI protocols and can be introduced as a shared local drive among several clustered servers.

Both NAS and SAN solutions can bundle several hard disks and present them as a single unit. Some software solutions, such as database systems, do not accept NAS drives as a local drive and do not use them for storing live databases, whereas SAN solutions can be used for any kind of server-based storage requirement.

A third, increasingly popular category of solutions for scaling out hardware in the healthcare industry is cloud computing, particularly the Infrastructure as a Service (IaaS) model in which the cloud services provider hosts the hardware. They could be located in a variety of geographical regions, which has caused some concern about moving data to them in healthcare because of data privacy legislation such as HIPAA. Some of the cloud venders have tried to address this concern by providing dedicated private cloud environments with a defined location of the systems. Cloud computing solutions are very suitable for EHR systems, especially in small businesses such as primary care offices. They are also useful for interaction with patients and provide them the opportunity to contribute to their electronic health records. An example of such a solution is Microsoft HealthVault.[7]

Virtualization solutions such as Microsoft Hyper-V and Citrix XenServer applications are another way of scaling out. These applications allow running multiple operating systems concurrently on a single machine and share hardware resources.

Computer Asset Management

Healthcare IT technicians are frequent users of IT asset tracking and auditing software. This class of software has evolved quickly as the number of devices serviced by the IT department has grown rapidly in recent years. The software can now scan workstations and other devices such as printers, routers, and switches across the healthcare enterprise connected over the LAN or virtual private network (VPN). The scan provides details about hardware and software installed in all workstations and improves system maintenance.

Classifying Different Server Types, Environments, Features, and Limitations

Servers are powerful computers fulfilling one or more specific roles. Networking operating systems (NOSs) such as Red Hat Enterprise Linux and Windows Server 2012 can be installed on regular desktop computers, or even laptops, though proper server-class hardware tends to give the best results because it has more RAM, storage capacity, and faster CPUs than a desktop or laptop computer. Depending on how the server will be used, more RAM than normal might be required. For example, a locally hosted EMR application server serving hundreds of users needs more RAM (and processing power, and most likely disk space) than a locally hosted file server serving a few dozen users. Servers often duplicate power supplies and disk systems to make the server highly available. In the event of a power outage, it is imperative the server shut down gracefully to prevent potential file corruption or damage to hardware components. As previously mentioned, an uninterruptable power supply (UPS) solves this problem; it has a bank of batteries and several electrical outlets to allow critical devices to be plugged in. It is also common for servers to have multiple network interface cards (NICs) as well as USB, FireWire, and eSATA ports.

Modern network appliances may have a NOS preinstalled and preconfigured to serve a specific function. Many organizations run NOSs as virtual machines using virtualization software such as VMware, Citrix XEN, or Microsoft Hyper-V, which allows more than one virtual server to run on a single physical computer at the same time.

The configuration of the NOS and the software installed really determines the server role:

- **File server**   Serves folders and files to network users. The NOS controls access to this resource. Management and backup of these files is performed centrally on the server.

- **Print server**   Serves printers to network users. Print jobs are spooled first to the print server and then de-spooled to the physical print device. The NOS controls access to the printers.

- **Database server**   Allows network users to access one or more databases that contain tables, which contain records. The NOS may authenticate users, but the database software has its own security model.

- **Application server**   Hosts a specific application, such as an EMR system, for multiple-user network access. In a client/server EMR environment, this server would be the responsibility of local IT staff. ASPs, or cloud computing providers, host application servers for their clients, so the servers are their responsibility.

Server software requires the correct NOS, version, and updates. For example, an EMR system designed to run on Windows Server 2008 may not run on Windows Server 2012, and most likely will not run on Red Hat Linux Enterprise Server. Server software will sometimes require other software to be installed and configured in a specific manner. These issues are irrelevant if your EMR system is hosted by an ASP, which assumes this responsibility.

Server disk storage may physically exist inside the server or the server might access disk storage on a SAN (or a combination of both may be used). A SAN hosts high-speed, high-capacity disks that are centrally managed on a storage network that various servers can access. Users access the server, for example, to update a patient's electronic record in an EHR system, and the server writes that data to disks stored on the SAN. Storing an echocardiogram in an EHR, for example, takes more space than storing medical documents, since an echocardiogram would be stored as video content. The NOS, and often the server-based application software, can restrict how much space is consumed by users, how large stored data can be, and how long data is retained before it must be archived.

The Role of the Desktop Support Technician

Most medium-to-large-sized healthcare organizations bundle the responsibilities for computer asset management with basic technical support for the many end users who use the systems into the role of desktop support technician. Desktop support technicians are responsible for many tasks including issues pertaining to hardware, devices, operating systems, application software, and basic network problems. In a healthcare organization, a desktop support technician sets up, maintains, and troubleshoots end-user devices in healthcare clinical and business environments. This person must have good communication skills, a professional demeanor, and the ability to liaise effectively between people in Information Services (IS) and a diverse group of end users. Typical responsibilities for the desktop support role include new equipment setup, imaging and deployment, application troubleshooting, trouble ticket management, documentation of technical procedures, and research of new products for improved clinical and business processes.

The Desktop Technician and the EHR/EMR Environment   One common task of a desktop support technician is setting up a basic PC workstation within an EHR/EMR environment. A workstation requires either room temperature or slightly cooler to operate properly. As introduced earlier, thin client workstations are computers with limited configuration flexibility and processing power; these are useful when the EMR/EHR client software will be run on the server side. Often the thin client OS is installed into computer chips (firmware) rather than being installed on a hard disk. Care must taken to ensure fans and vents are not obstructed; otherwise, the system will overheat or, in modern systems, simply shut down. Once all hardware components are plugged in (including the power supply and network cable), if the machine does not have a prein-stalled OS, you can manually install the OS or use a mechanism such as disk imaging to apply an OS image captured from a reference system.

The way in which the EMR system is accessed will determine the type of hardware and software you need. There are three distinct methods by which a workstation accesses an EMR system:

- Application software installed on the workstation communicates with the EMR system over specific network channels (ports); these ports must be allowed to travel through firewalls.

- A web browser, and possibly web browser plug-ins such as a PDF viewer, can be used to access an EMR. Web browsers use standard port numbers (80 and 443) that most firewalls allow.

- A remote-access client such as Windows Remote Desktop (formerly called Terminal Services) can be used to access an EMR. The user launches and interacts with the EMR system locally, but all processing occurs on the EMR application server. Windows Remote Desktop Protocol (RDP) uses port 3389.

The Desktop Technician and Troubleshooting   Another common task of a desktop support technician is troubleshooting and solving common PC problems. Sometimes software or hardware fails. Files become corrupt, cables become disconnected, or software updates need to be applied—quite a variety of problematic sources. The following is a general troubleshooting methodology tailored to evaluate and solve common PC problems:

1. *Identify the problem.* If providing telephone support, be careful; make sure you and your client understand each other's terminology (try to avoid too much computer jargon, though!). Ask for specific error codes and error messages. Can you duplicate the problem? What is the scope: a single station, a single printer, or everybody on the network?

2. *Determine probable cause, and test possible solutions.* First, reboot the computer. This solves many inexplicable computer problems. Then test the easy stuff! Is the power cable disconnected? Does the printer toner or printer ink ribbon need to be changed? Is the keyboard layout changed to a different language? Does the station have a valid IP address? Does the logged-in user have the proper permissions? The list is endless. If you determine the issue should be escalated to a different technician, then do that.

3. *Ensure the problem is solved.* Sometimes fixing one thing breaks something else. Thoroughly test your fix and have the user test the fix; until you both agree the problem is solved, it is not.

4. *Document your solution.* Most organizations have a knowledge base used by technicians and help desk staff to document the problem and solution. This knowledge base can be searched in the future when the same problem occurs.

Some hardware has a relatively limited lifespan, especially hard disks. It is only a matter of when the hard disks will fail, so data backups, discussed earlier in this chapter, are of paramount importance.

Peripherals such as mice, keyboards, scanners, printers, and so on may have problems with their power supplies or data connection cables. For USB devices, make sure the cable is plugged in snugly. Remember that the OS may detect the hardware you've plugged in, but it may not have a driver so that you can use the hardware. Visit the vendor website for the most up-to-date driver for your hardware.

Software vendors occasionally release patches and updates for their software. A patch corrects a problem of some kind. An update may also correct problems, but it can also add functionality. A hotfix addresses a very specific problematic issue, and sometimes the hotfix is not made downloadable to the public; you might receive an e-mail from the vendor with a link to the hotfix in response to your request. Over time, patches, updates, and hotfixes can be built into a service pack (SP). The Windows OS has built-in automatic updating capabilities. If your update settings are grayed out, it means your machine is configured via Group Policy settings on an Active Directory domain controller and the system administrator has revoked your access to change these settings.

There is often a complex interaction between healthcare IT (e.g., EMRs and EHRs) and medical devices (e.g., infusion pumps, barcode scanners, and patient monitors). If you suspect that a medical device is malfunctioning, you can take a number of practical steps before escalating the problem, including checking whether the power is on, checking the network connection, checking that all I/O devices are functioning correctly (if not, the most common issue is that a device driver is not enabled or is out of date), checking whether the device is interfacing correctly with other systems and software (such as EMRs), and, if necessary, checking all configuration settings.

Escalation of Issues to HIT Specialists   The desktop support technician is usually backed up by a less general specialist in the IT department who takes over "second-level" or "third-level" support issues. These are issues that usually require more focused expertise to resolve. For example, with healthcare software such as EMR software, a number of problems can occur and may be reported by clinicians, such as storage or retrieval of incorrect patient data, data from the wrong patient appearing in a record, incomplete data, and delays in updating data in patient records and systems. It is important to locate and isolate affected modules or fields, determine the type of file or data affected, and escalate the problem to the proper support level (e.g., hospital IT management, or a vendor in the case of serious problems that can't be rectified locally).

Due to the increase in wireless transmissions of patient data in healthcare settings, it is important to ensure patient and health data is being transmitted properly and without error. The responsibilities for this important job lie with the network analyst. A network analyst has end users complete system performance surveys (where lengthy access and response times are sometimes reported), checks access point placements, and uses advanced healthcare network monitoring software (which is increasingly being adopted in hospitals and healthcare settings) to troubleshoot a variety of problems and suboptimal conditions among other duties. Server load and utilization is checked to ensure proper and efficient access to information across a healthcare setting by the network analyst. Load and utilization can also be analyzed using network-monitoring software to analyze throughput, rate of transmission, and errors in transmission of data over time. This data provides useful reporting to management that can alert the organization to potentially serious issues in data transmission.

Beyond the functions provided by the desktop support technician and their second- and third-level specialists in the HIT department, HIT management and leadership develops and manages policy to ensure availability of the critical HIT resources under their control. One example of this is development of fail-safe downtime procedures to ensure continued functioning of the healthcare institution in the case of a major healthcare IT system failure or electrical blackout. Chapter 20 provides many more examples of these types of HIT management and leadership responsibilities.

Chapter Review

This chapter introduced common computing hardware components that the HIT professional must understand to support computing devices in a healthcare environment. Gone are the days when only a few elite people had the skills and knowledge to work with medical equipment and software. Web-based EMR systems hosted locally or by an ASP (private versus public cloud) have become the norm, along with using handheld wireless devices to access these systems. From the smallest rural medical practice up to the largest hospitals and research facilities, all are now demanding a standard of competence from their IT support staff; this is the purpose of HIT certification.

Questions

To test your comprehension of the chapter, answer the following questions and then check your answers against the list of correct answers at the end of the chapter.

1. Which piece of hardware allows multiple network devices to be plugged in?
   A. Router
   B. NIC
   C. Switch
   D. Domain controller

2. EMR systems can be hosted by which third-party entity?
   A. ISP
   B. NIC
   C. SAN
   D. ASP

3. A user clicks an icon on their desktop and then types https://intranet.acme.us/emr to launch an EMR application. This user is using a thin client workstation. Which term best describes the type of EMR client station?
   A. Web browser client
   B. Terminal Services client
   C. Remote Desktop client
   D. ASP client

4. Which of the following provides the fastest data transfer rate?

 A. USB 3.0

 B. FireWire 800

 C. IDE

 D. SATA 3.0

5. You are asked to convert a patient paper chart to an EMR. What type of hardware should you use?

 A. Printer

 B. NIC

 C. Scanner

 D. USB keyboard

6. Which type of backup clears the archive bit? (Choose all that apply.)

 A. Daily

 B. Differential

 C. Incremental

 D. Full

7. You are an IT technician for a small rural medical clinic. The attending physician asks for the fastest type of external hard disk storage available for her state-of-the-art laptop. What should you recommend?

 A. eSATA

 B. IDE

 C. USB 2.0

 D. FireWire 400

8. After troubleshooting a software application problem, you discover that the vendor has a link on its website to download a script file that solves the problem. When you click the link, instead of downloading the script file, you are asked to provide your e-mail address so that you can be sent the script file. What term best describes this script file?

 A. Service pack

 B. Hotfix

 C. Update

 D. Patch

Answers

1. **C.** Network devices plug into a switch so that they can communicate. Routers interconnect different networks; network devices do not plug directly into a router. Network interface cards (NICs) allow devices to communicate on a network. Domain controllers are Windows servers that can service domain user logon requests; they hold a copy of the Active Directory database that replicates to other domain controllers.

2. **D.** An application service provider (ASP) provides application services to its clients. The hardware and software installation, configuration, and maintenance are the responsibility of the ASP, not the client; the client pays a fee to use the service, such as an EMR system. An Internet service provider (ISP) is a company that provides subscribers or other users access to the Internet. A NIC allows connectivity to a network. A storage area network (SAN) is a specialized high-speed storage network used by servers.

3. **A.** HTTPS is a web browser protocol. Even though some applications other than web browsers can use HTTPS, a web browser client is the best answer. Remote Desktop (formerly Terminal Services) clients do not normally use HTTPS; they normally use Remote Desktop Protocol (RDP). ASP client is a possible answer, but web browser client is the best answer.

4. **D.** SATA 3.0 is rated at 750 MBps (6 Gbps), USB 3.0 at 625 MBps (5 Gbps), FireWire 800 at 100 MBps (800 Mbps), and IDE at 133 MBps.

5. **C.** Scanners can digitize physical paper documents such as patient charts. Printers do the opposite; they take digital data and print onto a physical medium such as paper. NICs allow connectivity to a network. A USB keyboard plugs into a USB computer port (older keyboards have a different plug that plugs into a computer PS/2 keyboard port).

6. **A, C, D.** Only differential backups do not clear the archive bit. The archive bit is a file attribute that determines whether a file must be backed up. Changes to a file turn on the archive bit, which means the file must be backed up, but unlike incremental and full backups, which clear the archive bit, performing a differential backup does not clear the archive bit, meaning the file will be backed up again during the next backup regardless of whether it has changed.

7. **A.** eSATA (3 Gbps), USB 2.0 (480 Mbps), and FireWire 400 (400 Mbps) are external disk interfaces; IDE is only internal.

8. **B.** Hotfixes are solutions to very specific problems and are not normally publicly available for download like service packs, updates, and patches typically are. Many vendors will send you an e-mail message with details on how to obtain the hotfix.

References

1. Neely, A. N., & Sittig, D. F. (2002). Basic microbiologic and infection control information to reduce the potential transmission of pathogens to patients via computer hardware. *Journal of the American Medical Informatics Association, 9*(5), 500–508.

2. Microsoft. (2011). *Touchless interaction in medical imaging.* Accessed on September 2, 2016, from http://research.microsoft.com/en-us/projects/touchlessinteractionmedical/.

3. Ryu, Y.S., Koh, D.H., Ryu, D., Um, D. (2011). Usability Evaluation of Touchless Mouse Based on Infrared Proximity Sensing. *Journal of Usability Studies, 7*(1), 31–39.

4. Dargar, S., Kennedy, R., Lai, W., Arikatla, V., & De, S. (2015). Towards immersive virtual reality (iVR): A route to surgical expertise. *Journal of Computational Surgery, 2*(2).

5. Rosa, G., M., & Elizondo, M.L. (2014). Use of a gesture user interface as a touchless image navigation system in dental surgery: Case series report. *Imaging Sci Dent. 44*(2): 155–160.

6. Zemke, B. (2015). *How Google Glass will transform healthcare.* Accessed on September 29, 2016, from http://extremenetworks.com/how-google-glass-will-transform-healthcare/.

7. HealthVault. (2016). *What Is HealthVault?* Accessed on September 29, 2016, from https://www.healthvault.com/.

6

Programming and Programming Languages for Healthcare IT

Alex Mu-Hsing Kuo, Andre Kushniruk

In this chapter, you will learn how to
- Explain the importance of programming for healthcare information technology
- Describe operating systems and their functions
- Identify the differences between interpreted and compiled programming languages
- Use object-oriented programming languages
- Apply web markup and scripting languages
- Understand simple HTML and XML statements

In the world of computers, a *program* is a sequence of instructions or machine codes telling the computer how to perform specific tasks. Machine code is the computer's primitive language and consists of sequences of binary 1s and 0s that the computer processor (e.g., made by Intel or AMD) understands. To simplify the process of programming, a wide variety of higher-level programming languages have been developed. A programming language can be defined as a set of notations designed for writing programs to communicate instructions to a computer. Many programming languages are in existence today, such as BASIC, Perl, Fortran, COBOL, C, C++, and Java. An understanding of healthcare information technology requires knowledge about programming and programming languages that can be used for implementing healthcare information systems (HISs).

As this chapter will illustrate, a range of different programming languages have been used to create software in healthcare. They generally fall into one of two categories: interpreted languages (e.g., Basic and Perl) or compiled languages (e.g., Fortran and COBOL). With a compiled language, a computer program (or set of programs) called

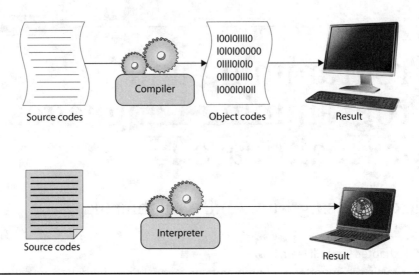

Figure 6-1 Compiler vs. interpreter working process

a compiler transforms the language source codes into machine-specific instructions (a binary form known as *object code*) before being saved as an executable file. With interpreted languages, the code is saved in the same format that it was created in. Next, an interpreter immediately translates the high-level instruction into an intermediate form, which the interpreter then executes. The interpreter analyzes and executes each line of source code in succession, without looking at the entire program (see Figure 6-1). Basically, interpreting code is slower than running the compiled code because the interpreter must analyze each statement in the program each time it is executed and then perform the desired action. Nevertheless, the compiled code simply performs the entire program, which is more efficient and has higher performance.

Languages and Virtual Machines

Modern computer systems consist of a number of layers, starting with the underlying hardware layer (the hardware that the computer software runs on), moving up to layers dealing with operating systems, and finally moving up to layers dealing with running application software (e.g., applications written for business or healthcare). The evolution of computer systems can be characterized by the invention of many languages, which were developed over time to specifically make programming and human interactions with computers easier. Initially computer systems were programmed in machine language (1s and 0s, as mentioned earlier in this section). Programming at the machine level was tedious and difficult, and as a result, assembly languages appeared early in the evolution of computer systems. Assembly languages use symbolic instructions, such as "Load a register with a value from memory location A," which in a specific assembly language might look like "LOAD R0 A." The limitations of assembly languages are that they require knowledge of a computer's specific architecture, such as the central processing unit (CPU) registers or memory locations, and will run only on specific types of computers (IBM mainframe, Mac, PC, etc.). To make interacting with computers simpler, operating systems began to evolve that would take care of low-level functions of running computer software so that programmers could focus on the task they want to carry out, rather than worrying about how to interact with underlying hardware and lower levels of hardware and software.

Operating Systems

Operating systems have evolved to make writing programs and running computer systems easier by handling lower-level computer functions instead of operating at the machine or assembly language level. Essentially, an operating system creates a virtual layer or machine, where functions or operations are simulated with software rather than actually existing in the hardware. The functions of an operating system are as follows:

- **Process management** A process is an individual program or operation, such as a word processing application being run on a PC. Each process needs resources to run to completion (e.g., CPU time, memory, files, and input/output devices), and the operating system manages this.

- **Memory management** For a program to be executed, it has to be mapped to memory addresses and loaded into computer memory; this is also handled by the operating system.

- **Storage management** The operating system provides a uniform and logical view of the storage of information in files and maps files onto physical media.

- **Protection and security** The operating system controls access to processes and access by users to computer resources.

- **Distributed system management and processing** Network operating systems allow for the sharing of files and resources across an entire network.

There are many types of operating systems, with Microsoft Windows being one operating system that has been used extensively for HISs. Hospitals and healthcare organizations have widely adopted Microsoft operating systems, initially running Microsoft DOS and now Microsoft Windows. Apple's Mac OS X (recently rebranded macOS) has also become widely used in HIT. In addition, open source operating systems are common; these operating systems have been made available in source-code format rather than compiled binary code. Linux and Unix are examples of this type of operating system. The C language was created in conjunction with the development of the Unix operating system, and it allowed for an efficient and modular approach to the development of that operating system. The C language itself also became a widely used type of programming language, as will be described in the next section.

Recently, mobile health applications are popping up all over. Health professionals are incorporating them into their healthcare practices and management to be more effective and efficient. Patients are using them to monitor specific aspects of their health, fill in gaps in their medical care, and take more responsibility for their well-being. These mobile health applications are usually installed in mobile devices running mobile operating systems (MOSs). An MOS allows smartphones, tablets, and other mobile devices to run applications and programs. Examples of mobile device operating systems include Apple's iOS, Google's Android, Microsoft's Windows 10 Mobile, Linux Foundation's Tizen, BlackBerry 10 (based on the QNX OS), and Firefox OS.

In healthcare, the issue of the interoperability of systems is critical. If operating systems and applications are not interoperable, electronic data cannot be exchanged. Although the cross-platform exchange of data between systems such as Windows and macOS has improved, it's important to carefully consider the ability of different hardware and software to seamlessly exchange health data.

The C Language

C is a general-purpose compiled language initially developed by Dennis Ritchie between 1969 and 1973 at Bell Labs. It was designed to provide language constructs that map efficiently to machine instructions, and to require minimal runtime support.[1]

To edit a C program, the very first thing you need is a text editor to edit the C source codes. Several text editors are available for editing a C program, such as Adobe Dreamweaver, Microsoft WordPad, Microsoft Notepad, and TextPad (from Helios Software Solutions). Among them, TextPad (www.textpad.com) is a powerful, general-purpose editor for Microsoft Windows that can edit plain-text files. It is very easy to use, with all the features that a power C programmer requires. The second tool you will need is a C compiler that you can use to compile the program. Examples are GNU Compiler Collection (GCC), MinGW compiler, and Code::Blocks for Windows.

Now, we will use a very simple example to explain how to edit and run the following C program. We use TextPad to edit the program.

```
#include <stdio.h>
  main()
  {
    printf("Hello World!\n");
    printf("This is my first C program.");
  }
```

At the very beginning of the C program is the syntax *#include <stdio.h>*. This links the standard input/output (I/O) library to the program so that the program can interact with the screen, keyboard, and file system of the computer. In C, libraries are files of already-compiled code, which you can merge with your program at compilation time. Each library comes with a number of *associated header files* (.h), which make the functions easier to use.

The second line of the program is *main()*. Every C program must contain a function called *main()*. It is the start point of the program execution. The *main()* function declares the start of the function, while the two curly brackets (lines 3 and 6) after *main()* show the start and finish of the function. Curly brackets in C are used to group statements into

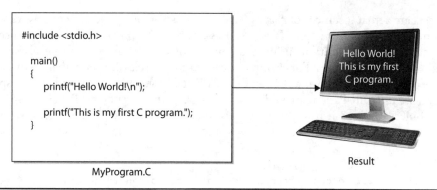

```
#include <stdio.h>

main()
{
    printf("Hello World!\n");

    printf("This is my first C program.");
}
```

MyProgram.C

Hello World!
This is my first
C program.

Result

Figure 6-2   A simple C program printing two lines of text

a function or in the body of a loop. Such a grouping is known as a *compound statement* or a *block*.

The most common type of instruction in C is a *statement*, which is the smallest independent unit in the language. You write statements in order to convey to the compiler that you want to perform a task. Statements in C are terminated by a semicolon. C-language syntax is case sensitive. Most C programs are in lowercase letters. For example, the fourth line in this program, *printf("Hello World!\n");*, will print the words "Hello World!" on the screen. The text to be printed is enclosed in double quotes. The \n at the end of the text tells the program to print a newline as part of the output. Line 5, *printf("This is my first C program.");*, is used to write out the text "This is my first C program." on the screen.

After finishing the source code editing, we save it as MyProgram.c (with .c as the file extension). Now, we are able to use a C compiler (e.g., GCC) to compile the program. For example, the compilation command on Unix is *cc o "MyProgram MyProgram.c."* At this point, if there are errors in the program, the compiler will show the error information on the screen. We should then correct these errors in the program and recompile the program. If there are no more errors in it, the compiler will return no error messages and will create an object file called *MyProgram* (in Unix, the default object filename is *a.out*). Then, we can execute the object file to see the output, as shown in Figure 6-2.

The C++ Language

Since the C programming language was developed, new approaches to programming have appeared. One of the most significant advances has been the concept of object-oriented programming. C++ is an object-oriented programming language developed as an extension to the C language by Bjarne Stroustrup at Bell Labs in 1983. It is now one of the most popular programming languages and is implemented on a wide variety of hardware and operating system platforms. Object-oriented programming is focused around the concept of *objects*, which represent things around you. An object can be a person, place, or thing. For example, an object can be used to represent a patient.

PART II

Objects are actual instances of classes (e.g., the class Patient). The Patient class can have a number of attributes (e.g., Name, Address, Patient Number, etc.), which objects of that class have. In addition, using the concept of classes, objects can be classified or organized into hierarchies. For example, a Patient may be classified as either an In-Patient (if the patient is in the hospital) or an Out-Patient (if the patient is outside the hospital). In-Patient and Out-Patient are said to be *subclasses* of the parent class Patient. C++ added these object-oriented features to its syntax with the ability to define classes, such as a Patient class, which for the Patient class would look something like this:

```
Class Patient
{
   // Here would go the statements defining the class in detail
   // could specify attributes like Name, Address, Patient Number
   // could also specify the operations that could be done on Patient objects
}
```

The C++ syntax and program development processes are very similar to those of the C language. You can use any text editor to edit a C++ program file. If you are on a Unix machine, you would save the file with the filename *xxx.C* (make sure it ends with .C, not .c—it is case sensitive!), while if you are on a Windows operating system, you would save the file with file extension *.cpp*. For example, you could use TextPad to edit a C++ program called *MyProgram.C* (Figure 6-3).

In the program, the first line, *// my first program in C++*, is a comment line, as indicated by the beginning two slashes (*//*). Comment lines do not affect the behavior of the program. You can use comments to include short explanations or definitions within the program to help the reader understand the programming logic.

The second line beginning with a hash (#), *#include <iostream>*, is a directive for the preprocessor. It is not a regular code line with expressions (which are combinations of symbols adhering to C++ programming rules of expression), but instead contains instructions for the compiler's preprocessor. In this case, the directive *#include <iostream>* tells the preprocessor to include the *iostream* standard file. This specific file includes the declarations of the basic standard I/O library in C++, and it is included because its functionality is going to be used later in the program.

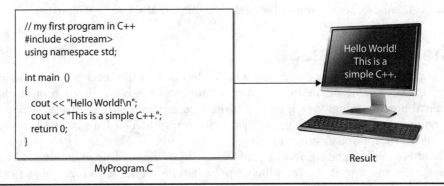

```
// my first program in C++
#include <iostream>
using namespace std;

int main ()
{
  cout << "Hello World!\n";
  cout << "This is a simple C++.";
  return 0;
}
```

MyProgram.C

Result

Figure 6-3 A simple C++ program printing out two lines of text

The third line, *using namespace std;*, includes all parts of the namespace in C++. Creating a namespace in C++ is useful to organize a set of related algorithms, function objects, program utilities, and other collections of code that can logically be grouped together. Thereby this sets apart a portion of code for more effective programming, referencing across the program, and code understandability across programmers, among other uses. The namespace *std* includes all standard C++ libraries. The *iostream* library we mentioned earlier is part of the *std* namespace. Therefore, when we use the *std* namespace, we don't need to include the extended name of the *iostream* file.

The fourth line, *int main ()*, is the point at which the C++ program starts its execution, independently of its location within the source code. It does not matter whether there are other functions with other names defined before or after it. The *main()* function is always the first one to be executed in any C++ program. For that same reason, it is essential that all C++ programs have a *main()* function. Similar to C, the two curly brackets (lines 5 and 9) after *main()* show the start and finish of the function.

The sixth and seventh lines, *cout << "Hello World!\n";* and *cout << "This is a simple C++.";*, will write out the words "Hello World!" and "This is a simple C++." on the screen, respectively. The *cout* is the name of the standard output stream in C++. It is declared in the *iostream* standard file within the *std* namespace.

The eighth line, *return 0;*, is a return statement that causes the *main()* function to finish. A return code of *0* for the *main()* function is generally interpreted to mean the program worked as expected without any errors during its execution. This is the most usual way to end a C++ console program.

Next, we will use a compiler (e.g., GCC for a Unix machine) to compile the program. At the Unix prompt, we type the following command:

```
g++ MyProgram.C o MyProgram
```

Then, a file called *MyProgram* is located in the same directory containing *MyProgram.C*. To run the program, we simply type *MyProgram* at the Unix prompt. Two lines of words will display on the screen, as shown in Figure 6-3.

There are several advantages to using C++, as follows:[2]

* C++ is a third-generation language that allows programmers to express their ideas at a high level as compared to low-level assembly languages.

* C++ also allows a programmer to get down into the low-level workings and fine-tune as necessary. For example, it allows the programmer strict control over memory management.

* C++ is a language with international standards. After years of development, the C++ programming language standard was ratified in 1998 as ISO/IEC 14882:1998. The standard was amended by the 2003 technical corrigendum, ISO/IEC 14882:2003. The current standard extending C++ with new features was ratified and published by ISO in 2014 as ISO/IEC 14882:2014. Code written in C++ that conforms to the international standards can be easily integrated with preexisting codes and allows programmers to reuse common functions. This will dramatically reduce program development time.

✳ Since C++ is an object-oriented language, this makes programming easier and allows easy reuse of code or parts of code through inheritance.

✳ As mentioned at the beginning of this section, C++ is a very widely used programming language. Many tools and study resources are available for C++ program development.

The Java Language

Java is an object-oriented programming language originally created by Sun Microsystems (subsequently acquired by Oracle). The language syntax is very similar to C or C++, but Java has a simpler object model and fewer low-level facilities.[3] To design a Java program, all source code is first edited in plain-text files with .java as the file extension. The programmer can use any text editor (e.g., Adobe Dreamweaver, Microsoft WordPad or Notepad, or TextPad) to edit the code. These source files are then compiled into .class files by a Java compiler. The .class file contains *bytecodes*, which are the machine language of the Java Virtual Machine (Java VM or JVM). Then, the just-in-time code generator converts the bytecode into the native machine code, which is at the same programming level. Because the JVM is available on many different operating systems, the same .class files are capable of running on different operating systems, such as Microsoft Windows, macOS, or Linux (see Figure 6-4).[4] In other words, the same Java application is able to run on multiple platforms through the JVM.

To run a Java program, you need two tools: the Java Development Kit (JDK) SE and a text editor. In the example of Figure 6-5, we use TextPad to edit the source code (*HelloWorld.java*). The Java programming language *compiler* (*Javac*) can translate

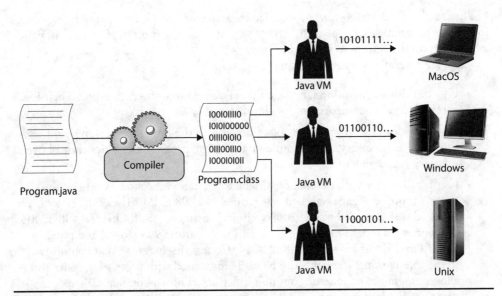

Figure 6-4   An overview of the Java programming process

(by pressing CTRL-1) the source codes into bytecodes (*HelloWorld.class*) that the Java Virtual Machine can understand. Then, the Java application *launcher tool* uses the JVM to run (press CTRL-2) the program. It will then display the greeting "Hello Java World!"

In conclusion, using Java as a system development tool has the following benefits:[5]

- **Object oriented**   Java programs can be easily extended because Java is an object-oriented programming language.

- **Platform independent**   When a Java program is compiled into platform-independent bytecode, rather than compiled into platform-specific code such as C or C++, the bytecode can be distributed over the Web and interpreted by the JVM on whichever platform it is being run.

- **Architecture neutral**   The Java compiler generates an architecture-neutral object file format, which makes the compiled code executable on any processors that have the Java runtime system.

- **Portable**   The architecture-neutral and implementation-independent characteristics of Java make it very portable.

- **High performance**   With the use of just-in-time compilers, Java enables high performance.

- **Multithreaded**   With Java's multithreaded feature, it is possible to write programs that can do many tasks simultaneously. This design feature allows developers to construct interactive applications that run very smoothly.

- **Distributed and dynamic**   Java is designed for a distributed environment on the Internet and is considered to be more dynamic than C or C++. Also, Java programs can carry an extensive amount of runtime information that can be used to verify and resolve accesses to objects at runtime.

- **Easy to learn**   Java is designed to be easy to learn. If you understand the basic concept of object-oriented programming (OOP), then you can easily master Java.

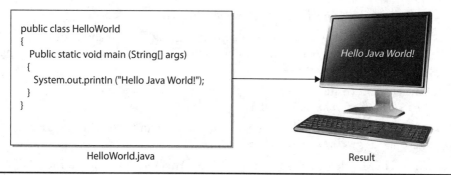

```
public class HelloWorld
{
    Public static void main (String[] args)
    {
        System.out.println ("Hello Java World!");
    }
}
```

HelloWorld.java   Result

Figure 6-5   A simple Java program printing "Hello Java World!"

Hypertext Markup Language (HTML)

HTML is a markup language for describing web pages, not a programming language like Java or C++. Markup tags (also called *elements*) are the major components in an HTML document (usually called a *page*). They are keywords (tag names) surrounded by angle brackets, as in <html>. HTML tags normally appear in pairs like <html>...</html>. *Tags* and *elements* are often used to describe the same thing. Additionally, the tag names are not case sensitive.

An HTML page can be considered a document tree that could contain four main parts, as follows:[6]

- **Doctype (optional)**   The first tag to appear in the source code of a web page is the *doctype* declaration. The <!doctype> is not an HTML tag. It is an optional part that provides the web browser with information (a declaration) about what kind of document it is and what HTML version is used in the page so that the browser can display the document correctly.

- **HTML**   Immediately after the <!doctype> comes the <html> element. It is the root element of the document tree, and everything that follows is a descendant of that root element.

- **Head (optional)**   The <head> tag is used for text and tags that do not show up directly on the page. It is a container for all the head elements. Elements inside <head> can include scripts, instruct the browser where to find style sheets, provide meta information, and more.

- **Body**   The <body> tag is used for text and tags that are shown directly on the page. This is where the page shows the contents. Everything that you can see in the browser window is contained inside this element, including paragraphs, lists, links, images, tables, and more.

An HTML element is everything from the start tag to the end tag. There are rules for editing HTML elements.[6]

- HTML elements normally come in pairs like <h1> and </h1>.
- An element starts with a start, or opening, tag (e.g., <h1>) and ends with an end, or closing, tag (e.g., </h1>). The end tag is written like the start tag, with a forward slash before the tag name.
- The element content is everything between the start and end tags (e.g., <h1>*Introduction to HTML*</h1>).
- Some HTML elements have empty content. An empty element is closed in the start tag, as in
 ("
</br>").
- Most HTML elements can have attributes. Attributes provide additional information about HTML elements. Similar to elements, there are several rules for editing attributes.[6]
    - Attributes are always specified in the start tag.
    - Attributes come in name and value pairs, as in name="value".

To understand the HTML document structure and how different elements or attributes work, it's useful to consider a simple web page with typical content features, as shown in Figure 6-6. In this example, the author uses the HTML5 doctype for the document. The <title> tag shown in the browser toolbar defines the page title as "Alex's Home Page." It is required in all HTML/XHTML documents.

The text between <body> and </body> is the visible page content. Here, the text "Introduction to HTML" between <h1> and </h1> is displayed as a heading. The text "Edited by Alex Kuo" between <p> and </p> is displayed as a paragraph, and the tag <font> specifies the font size (4), font face (verdana), and color (red) of the text. Size, face, and color are attribute names of this tag, while 4, verdana, and red are values for each attribute, respectively.

The <a> tag creates a link to another document by using the href attribute. In this example, the hyperlink text is "Visit W3Schools," and the URL for the link is http:// www.w3schools.com/.

In real application, you would use a text editor to edit an HTML document and save it as *xxx.html* (*.html* is the file extension of an HTML document). Then, you would use

```
<!DOCTYPE html>
<html>
  <head>
    <title> Alex's Home Page</title>
  </head>
  <body>
     <h l> Introduction to HTML</h1>
     <p> <font size = "4" face="verdana" color= "red"> Edited by Alex Kuo </font></p>
     <a href="http://www.w3schools.com/">Visit W3Schools</a>
  </body>
</html>
```

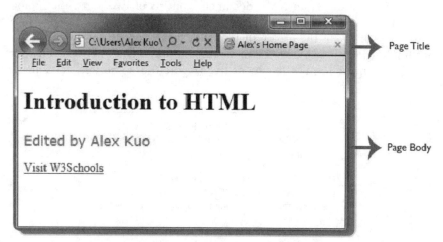

Figure 6-6   A simple HTML document and the corresponding web page

a web browser (e.g., Microsoft Internet Explorer, Google Chrome, or Firefox) to read the HTML document and display it as a web page. The browser does not display the HTML tags but uses the tags to interpret the content of the page.

Web-based HTML content can be enhanced with multimedia on a variety of software platforms. For example, Adobe Flash is an animation program/platform that can be used to enhance web pages with video, animation, and interactivity. It can be used to stream audio and video, and flash animations have been used for broadcasts, games, and advertising. Flash content can be displayed on computer systems using Adobe Flash Player, which is a freely available plug-in for web browsers.

Extensible Markup Language (XML)

XML is a markup language much like HTML. However, it is different from HTML, which was designed to display data with a focus on how data looks. XML was created to structure, store, and transport data. So, an XML document is nothing more than a plain-text document. Any software that can handle plain text can also handle XML.[6]

The tags used in HTML are predefined. However, XML tags are designed to be self-descriptive and not predefined. Document authors must define their own tags. For example, the tags in Figure 6-7 are not predefined in any XML standard. These tags are defined by the author.

It is also important to understand that XML is not a replacement for HTML. The main objective of XML is to simplify data sharing and transport (data interoperability). In the real world, one of the most time-consuming challenges for computer system developers is to exchange data between incompatible systems over the Internet because computer systems and databases contain data in incompatible formats. XML data is stored in plain-text format. This provides a software- and hardware-independent way of storing data. Also, exchanging data as XML greatly reduces this complexity, since the data can be read by different, incompatible applications as well as by humans.

As shown in Figure 6-7, an XML document consists of two parts: the prolog (also called the *XML declaration*) and instances (also called *XML elements*). The first line in an XML document always is the prolog that defines the version (in this example, 1.0) and the encoding used (ISO-8859-1 = Latin-1/West European character set). The elements in an XML document form a document tree (Figure 6-8). The tree starts at the root

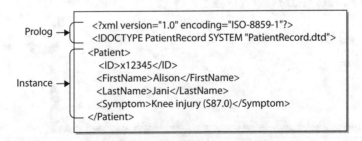

Figure 6-7 A simple XML document with author-defined, self-descriptive tags

(<bookstore>) and branches (<book>) to the lowest level of the tree. All elements can have subelements (child elements, such as <title>, <author>, etc.).

There are two types of XML documents: well-formed XML and valid XML. A *well-formed* XML document has XML syntax as follows:

- The document must have a root element (e.g., <bookstore>).

- All elements in the document must have a start tag and a closing tag (e.g., <book> ... </book>).

- Tags are case sensitive (e.g., <BOOKSTORE> ≠ <bookstore>).

- Elements must be properly nested (<bookstore> <book> ...</bookstore></book> is not a correct XML structure).

- XML attribute values must be quoted (e.g., <book category="COOKING">).

A *valid* XML document is a well-formed XML document that also conforms to the rules of a document type definition (DTD) or schema. Therefore, a valid XML must be a well-formed document. However, it may not be true that a well-formed XML is a valid document (Figure 6-9).

There are several benefits to using XML.[67]

- XML is a W3C Recommendation (which is considered a Web standard), endorsed by software industry market leaders.

- XML tags are designed to be self-descriptive and not predefined. New tags can be created as they are needed.

- Tags, attributes, and elements provide context information that can be used to interpret the meaning of content. For example, <price>30.00</price> represents a book's price as $30, thus opening up new possibilities for highly efficient search engines, intelligent data mining, agents, and so on. This is a major advantage

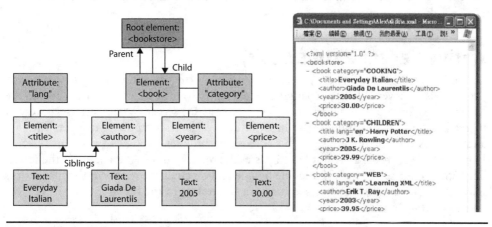

Figure 6-8 An XML tree structure

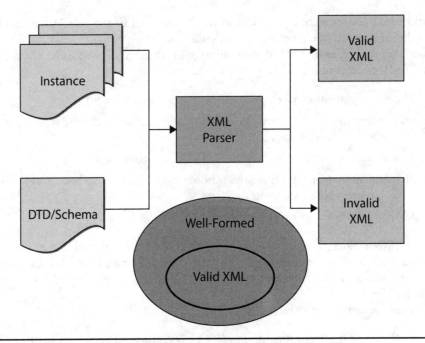

Figure 6-9 Two types of XML document

over HTML or plain text, where context information is difficult or impossible to evaluate.

- XML supports multiple data formats and can easily map existing data structures such as relational databases to XML. This is very beneficial to data interoperability.
- Information coded in XML is easy to read and understand and can be processed easily by computers.

Active Server Pages (ASP)

Active Server Pages (ASP) is a powerful tool for making dynamic and interactive web pages. It is a server-side script language developed by Microsoft that runs inside the Microsoft Windows Internet Information Services (IIS) server. When you use a browser to read an HTML document, the browser at the client computer interprets the tags and displays the document as a web page on the browser. However, when an Internet Explorer browser reads an ASP file, IIS passes the request to the ASP engine at the server. The ASP engine reads the ASP file line by line and executes the scripts in the file. Scripts may access any data or databases and return the results to the browser as plain HTML (see Figure 6-10).

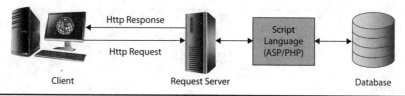

Figure 6-10 An ASP working process

An ASP file can contain text, HTML, XML, and scripts, and it has the file extension *.asp*. The ASP commands are surrounded by the symbols <% and %>. Similar to C, C++, Java, HTML, and XML editing, you use a text editor to edit an ASP file and save it as *xxx.asp*. For example, in Figure 6-11, the *<% response.write …%>* command in the *ASPtest.asp* file is used to output the text "Hello ASP. I like you." to the browser.

Figure 6-12 shows a more complex ASP file that accesses a Microsoft Access database and converts the data stored in a Student table to an XML document.

There are several benefits to using ASP, as follows:[6]

- ASP can be used to dynamically edit, change, or add any content on a web page.
- ASP customizes a web page to make it more useful for individual users.
- ASP responds to user queries or data submitted from HTML forms.
- Programmers can easily use ASP to access any data or databases and return the results to a browser.
- ASP provides good application security (since ASP code cannot be viewed from the browser).
- ASP can minimize network traffic because the scripts are run on the server side.
- Compared with CGI and Perl, ASP is easier to learn.

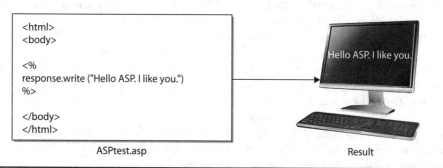

Figure 6-11 A simple ASP file and the corresponding result in a browser

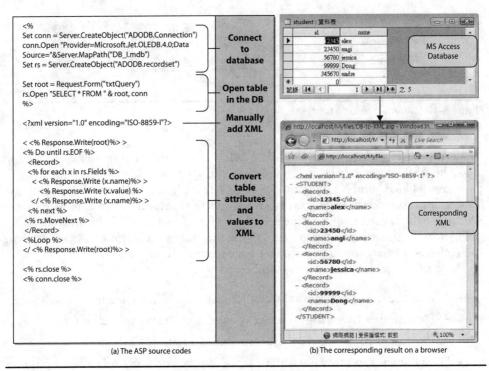

(a) The ASP source codes   (b) The corresponding result on a browser

Figure 6-12   A more complex ASP file to convert database data to an XML document

PHP: Hypertext Preprocessor (PHP)

PHP: Hypertext Preprocessor (PHP) is also a server-side scripting language where scripts are executed on the server and returned to the browser as plain HTML, like ASP. PHP runs efficiently on different platforms (Windows, Linux, Unix, etc.) and is compatible with almost all servers used today (Apache, IIS, etc.). It supports many databases, such as MySQL, Informix, Oracle, Sybase, Solid, PostgreSQL, Generic ODBC, and more.[8]

A PHP document has a file extension of *.php* and can contain text, HTML tags, and scripts. A script always starts with *<?php* and ends with *?>*. The script can be placed anywhere in the PHP document. Each code line in it must end with a semicolon, which is a separator and is used to distinguish one set of instructions from another. For example, in Figure 6-13, the *<?php echo "Hello PHP. I love you."; ?>* command will output the text "Hello PHP. I love you." to the browser.

In Figure 6-14 (a), the PHP script accesses a Microsoft Access database and converts the data stored in a Student table to an XML document shown in Figure 6-14 (b), which is the same database and result shown in Figure 6-12 (b).

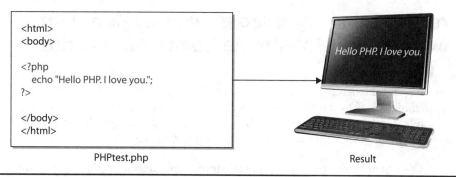

```
<html>
<body>

<?php
   echo "Hello PHP. I love you.";
?>

</body>
</html>
```

PHPtest.php   Result

Figure 6-13   A simple PHP file and the corresponding result in a browser

There are several benefits to using PHP, as follows:[6]

- PHP is open source software that can be downloaded and used freely.
- PHP runs efficiently on different platforms and supports many databases (e.g., MySQL, Informix, Oracle, Sybase, Solid, PostgreSQL, and Generic ODBC).
- PHP is compatible with almost all servers used today (e.g., Apache, IIS, etc.).
- PHP is easy to learn and runs efficiently on the server side.

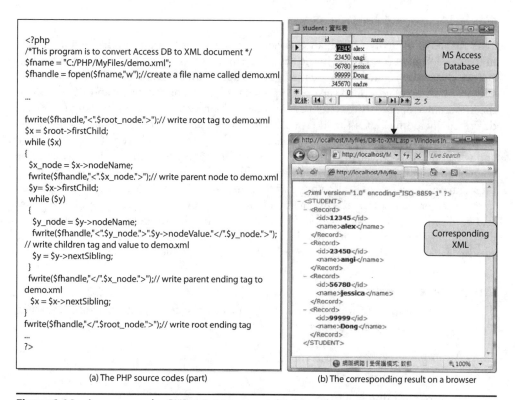

(a) The PHP source codes (part)   (b) The corresponding result on a browser

Figure 6-14   A more complex PHP script to convert database data to an XML document

Programming Languages and Development Environments for Mobile Health Application Development

There are several languages that can be used to develop mobile health applications. These tools include Java, Objective-C, C++, Swift, Python, and HTML5. The language chosen for mobile development depends on the mobile operating system device used. Here are development languages for two major mobile operating systems:

- **iOS** Swift is the main language for developing mobile applications running on Apple iOS. Xcode is an integrated development environment (IDE) containing a suite of software development tools for developing mobile applications for iOS. Swift is a multi-paradigm, compiled programming language for iOS, OS X, and watchOS applications that builds on the best of C and Objective-C (a hybrid of C). The iOS SDK is Apple's software development kit to develop mobile applications for iOS.

- **Android** The official language for Android development is Java. It is possible to develop C and C++ apps using the Android Native Development Kit (NDK), but Google doesn't promote that practice.

Chapter Review

This chapter provided you with an overview of a number of languages that are often used in the development of software in the healthcare industry. For details on any one of the languages, the reader is referred to the many books and manuals available. The chapter began with a discussion of compiled versus interpreted programming languages and also discussed the importance of operating systems. A number of high-level programming languages were described, including C, C++, and Java. Although not a programming language, the Hypertext Markup Language (HTML) is integral to understanding how web applications work and was also discussed, along with XML for structuring, storing, and transferring data. The chapter also discussed Active Server Pages (ASP), a powerful tool for making dynamic and interactive web pages, and PHP, a popular scripting language. All of the languages described in this chapter are used in creating many different types of HIT applications, and their use and application in healthcare will continue to grow. Finally, programming languages and development environments for mobile health application development is described for the two main mobile device operating systems of iOS and Android.

Questions

To test your comprehension of the chapter, answer the following questions and then check your answers against the list of correct answers at the end of the chapter.

1. A compiler is a _____.

   A. set of machine codes

   B. programming language

   C. program that transforms language source codes into machine-specific instructions

   D. sequences of binary 1s and 0s

2. Apple iOS or Google Android is a _____.

   A. webpage design language

   B. wording system

   C. compiling language

   D. mobile device operating system

3. You can use _____ to edit a C program.

   A. Microsoft Word

   B. TextPad

   C. Microsoft PowerPoint

   D. Microsoft Excel

4. C++ is _____.

   A. an object-oriented programming language

   B. a first-generation language

   C. a markup language

   D. by Sun Microsystems

5. In Java, _____.

   A. the syntax is not similar to C++

   B. bytecodes are the machine language of the Java Virtual Machine

   C. the same program cannot run on different machines

   D. you use Microsoft Word to edit the source program

6. HTML is a _____.

   A. markup language

   B. general-purpose programming language

   C. machine language

   D. network protocol

7. Which of the following statements is correct?

   A. XML was designed to display data with a focus on how the data appears.

   B. The tags used in XML are predefined.

   C. XML tags are designed to be self-descriptive and not predefined.

   D. A well-formed XML document is also a valid XML document.

8. What is the purpose of PHP: Hypertext Preprocessor (PHP)?

  A. It was designed to protect data security.

  B. It defines an XML structure.

  C. It cannot run efficiently on different computer platforms.

  D. It is a server-side scripting language where the scripts are executed on the server and returned to the browser as plain HTML.

Answers

1. **C.** A compiler is a program that transforms language source codes into machine-specific instructions. The code is then saved as an executable computer-readable file.

2. **D.** Apple iOS and Google Android are mobile device operating systems.

3. **B.** You can use TextPad to edit a C program. Adobe Dreamweaver, Microsoft WordPad, and Microsoft Notepad are other text editors that can be used to edit C programs.

4. **A.** C++ is an object-oriented programming language that is currently one of the most popular programming languages and is implemented on a wide variety of hardware and operating system platforms.

5. **B.** In Java, bytecodes are the machine language of the Java Virtual Machine.

6. **A.** HTML is a markup language for describing web pages. HTML is not a programming language like Java or C++.

7. **C.** XML tags are designed to be self-descriptive and not predefined. Document authors must define their own tags.

8. **D.** PHP: Hypertext Preprocessor (PHP) is a server-side scripting language where the scripts are executed on the server and returned to the browser as plain HTML.

References

1. King, K. N. (2008). *C programming: A modern approach, second edition.* Norton.

2. Overland, B. (2011). *C++ without fear: A beginner's guide that makes you feel smart, second edition.* Prentice Hall.

3. Core Java Tutorial. Overview of Java. Accessed on January 22, 2017, from https://sites.google.com/site/alljavadevelopers/j2se-turorial.

4. Tutorialspoint.com. (n.d.). Java: Overview. In *Java tutorial.* Accessed on August 18, 2016, from www.tutorialspoint.com/java/java_overview.htm.

5. Java Programming. Features of Java. Accessed on January 22, 2017, from http://www.sitesbay.com/java/features-of-java.

6. W3Schools.com. Accessed on August 19, 2016, from www.w3schools.com.

7. Fawcett, J., Ayers, D., & Quin, R. E. (2012). *Beginning XML, fifth edition*. Wrox.

8. Gilmore, W. J. (2012). *Beginning PHP and MySQL: From novice to professional, fourth edition*. Apress.

PART II

Databases, Data Warehousing, Data Mining, and Cloud Computing for Healthcare

Alex Mu-Hsing Kuo

In this chapter, you will learn how to
- Explain what a database is and why it is important in healthcare information technology
- Explain what data warehousing and data mining are
- Develop and manage a web-based database application, a data warehouse system, or a data mining project
- Identify how cloud computing can be used for large-scale database management purposes
- Identify and explain issues for developing database applications, data warehouse systems, clouds, or data mining projects in healthcare

Healthcare Databases

Healthcare is the most data-intensive industry in the world.[1,2] Patient information stored in health information technology (HIT), including electronic health records (EHRs), can be used by healthcare professionals for patient care, for treatment advice, and for surveillance of a patient's health status; it can be used by healthcare researchers in assessing clinical treatment, procedures, and effectiveness of medications; and it can be used by administrative personnel in cost accounting and by managers for planning. The challenge for a traditional HIT is how to make data useful for clinicians and empower them with the tools to make informed decisions and deliver more responsive patient services.

A healthcare database is a collection of related patient health data organized to facilitate its efficient storage, querying, and modification to meet the healthcare professional's needs.[3] Nowadays, many healthcare environments have applied database technologies to improve work efficiency and reduce healthcare costs. The following are some important database application areas in healthcare:[3, 4]

- **Solo practice**   General practitioners (GPs) find that most of their needs for HIT are focused on patient data management, schedule keeping, and billing. The data management functions of modern databases allow GPs to easily maintain and retrieve patient health information and reduce paperwork as well as documentation errors.

- **Group practice**   The operation of a group practice where several healthcare professionals cooperate in providing care creates many problems regarding access to medical records. Data for the record are generated at multiple sites, but the entire record should be complete and legible whenever and wherever it is retrieved. Databases that store large volumes of data over long periods of time from patients (and from other clinical sources) provide support to healthcare teams for accessing and analyzing patient data during the process of providing patient care.

- **Clinical research**   Databases are usually involved in the study of medications, devices, diagnostic products, or treatment regimens (including information about the safety and effectiveness of drugs intended for human use). The data in these databases may be used to inform decision making for the prevention, treatment, and diagnosis of disease. When studies become moderate to large in terms of their populations and observation period, a database approach becomes essential.

- **Service reimbursement**   Perhaps the largest databases in use that are related to healthcare are those associated with reimbursement for health services. Requirements for inquiry and audit are generating the need for more complete medical encounter information. This leads the healthcare providers who handle reimbursement accounting to consider database technologies.

- **Health surveillance**   This refers to the collection and analysis of health data about clinical syndromes that have a significant impact on public health. Data from databases can be used to detect or anticipate disease outbreaks. Then, governments can drive decisions about health policy and health education. Surveillance databases serve an important role as collections of disease reports as well as patient behavior.

- **Healthcare education**   Databases are also used for healthcare education. Such databases contain medical student and laboratory data so that students can receive appropriate assignments, be matched to the patient population, and have their progress tracked.

- **Electronic health records (EHRs)**   Databases are at the core of EHRs, which are designed to allow users (e.g., physicians, nurses, and other health professionals) to store and retrieve patient data electronically. Data available to users in the EHR are stored in and retrieved from databases.

Database Basics

Before database systems were developed, data were stored in traditional electronic files. Traditional file-processing systems have several drawbacks such as program-data dependency, duplication of data, limited data sharing, lengthy development times, and excessive program maintenance.[1] Database technologies have evolved since the 1960s to ease increasing difficulties in maintaining complex traditional information systems with a large amount of diverse data and with many concurrent end users. Over the past few decades, there has been an increase in the number of database applications in business, industry, healthcare, education, government, and the military.

A database model (database schema) is the structure or format of a database, described in a formal language supported by the database management system (DBMS). Within the database model, the data dictionary provides a description of all data elements stored in a database, including the names of data, data types, display format, internal storage format, and validation rules. The data dictionary itself can therefore be considered "data about data" or metadata. Several different database models have been used in DBMSs: the hierarchical model, the network model, the relational model, and the object-oriented model have been proposed since the concept of a DBMS was first created.[1] Among them, the relational database model is the most commonly adopted model today and is widely used in the healthcare industry. Thus the remainder of this chapter will focus on the relational database model.

The relational database model is a collection of *relations* that refer to the various tables in the database. The *table* is the basic data structure of the relational model. A table includes three components:

- **Name**   Used to uniquely identify a table
- **Column (also called attribute/field)**   A set of data values with particular data types (e.g., CHAR, NUMBER, DATE, etc.)
- **Row (also called instance/tuple/record)**   A set of related data, in which every row has the same structure

In a table, the *primary key* (PK) is a column (or combination of columns) that is used to uniquely identify a record in a table (e.g., an employee number in an employee database). The *foreign key* (FK) identifies a column in one table that refers to a column (usually a PK) in another table. For example, in Figure 7-1, the table's name is EMPLOYEES and it has many columns and rows (this is a database table for a hospital employee database). The first three columns record, respectively, the employee's ID (EMPLOYEE_ID), first name (FIRST_NAME), and last name (LAST_NAME), and the subsequent columns record other important details about the employee. For example, in Figure 7-1, reading across the rows from the top down, you can see that the first employee has the EMPLOYEE_ID of 100, has the FIRST_NAME Steven, and has the LAST_NAME King. The second row describes the information for EMPLOYEE_ID 101. The columns represent the fields (or attributes) of each employee record. A healthcare database consists of data stored in many such tables (that are linked together through foreign keys).

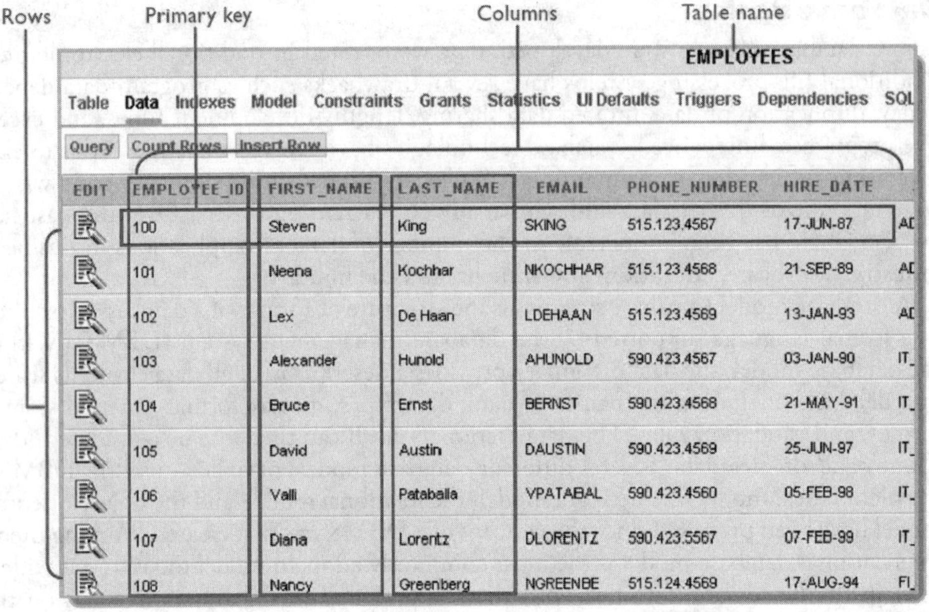

Figure 7-1 A relational database table structure

A relational database management system (RDBMS) is a set of software programs that control the organization, storage, management, and retrieval of data in a database. Structured Query Language (SQL) is a nonprocedural programming language that enables a user to manage a (relational) database. Using SQL statements, the user can query tables to display data, create objects, modify objects, and perform administrative tasks. SQL statements are divided into three categories:

- **Data Definition Language (DDL) statements** These statements create, alter, and drop database objects.
- **Data Manipulation Language (DML) statements** These statements query, insert, update, and delete data in tables.
- **Data Control Language (DCL) statements** These statements commit or roll back the processing of transactions.

For example, the following DML statement retrieves all employee_id, first_name, last_name, job_id, and salary data from the EMPLOYEES table in Figure 7-1:

```
SELECT employee_id, first_name, last_name, job_id, salary
FROM Employees;
```

Database Application Development Process

A healthcare database application design process usually includes four stages (Figure 7-2):

- **Stage 1** Analyze the business scenario and extract business rules.
- **Stage 2** Design an entity relationship diagram (ERD) based on the business rules extracted from stage 1.
- **Stage 3** Select a database model (e.g., Oracle DB) and create a physical database (tables, views, functions, etc).
- **Stage 4** Choose a development tool (e.g., Oracle APEX) to implement the application.

Analyzing the Business Scenario and Extracting Business Rules

Business rules describe the operations, definitions, and constraints that are intended to embody the business structure or to control or influence the behavior of an organization.

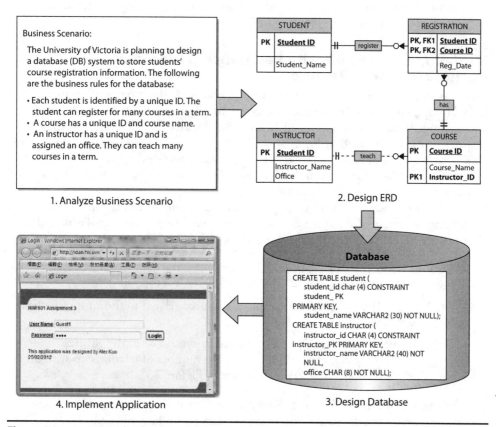

1. Analyze Business Scenario

2. Design ERD

3. Design Database

4. Implement Application

Figure 7-2 A generic database application design process

Many database system developers believe that clear business rules are very important in database modeling because they govern how data are stored and processed. To model a database, the system analyst needs to do the following:[1]

- Identify and understand those rules that govern patient's health data.
- Represent those rules so that they can be unambiguously understood by system developers.
- Ensure the rules are consistent (a rule must not contradict other rules).

For example, the Island Medical Program at the University of Victoria (UVic) is planning to design a database (DB) system to store each medical student's course registration information. The following are some business rules for the database:

- Each medical student is identified by a unique ID. The student can register for many courses in a term.
- A course has a unique ID and course name.
- An instructor has a unique ID and is assigned an office. They can teach many courses in a term.

Modeling Database: Entity Relationship Diagram Design and Normalization

The next step is to model the database. Data modeling is the process of creating a data model by applying formal data model descriptions using data modeling techniques. Several techniques have been developed in the past decades for the design of data models, such as the entity relationship model (ERM), IDEF-1X, object-relational mapping, object role model, and relational model. For database model design, the ERM is the most commonly used tool for communications between database system analysts, programmers, and end users during the analysis phase.

The ERM produces a type of conceptual schema or semantic data model that is used to organize a relational database and its requirements in a top-down fashion (for an example, see Figure 7-3). It contains three major elements:

- **Entities** A person, place, or object about which the data are collected (the boxes in Figure 7-3 labeled STUDENT, INSTRUCTOR, etc.).
- **Attributes** Type of information that is captured related to the entity (the fields inside each box in Figure 7-3).
- **Relationships** The associations and connections between the entities. Depending on the cardinality and modality, a number of relationship symbols are introduced (the lines connecting the boxes in Figure 7-3).

When people design an ERM, they usually use an ERD to serve as a blueprint for database programmers to follow the business rules to build a physical database. This is very similar in building construction. An architect designs a building blueprint, and

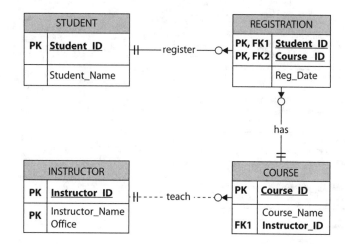

Figure 7-3
The ERD for UVic course registration system

workers follow the information contained in it to erect the structure. For example, based on the business rules extracted in the previous section, I used Microsoft Office Visio 2007 to construct the ERD shown in Figure 7-3.

Creating a Physical Database Using Structured Query Language

After creating the ERD, programmers are able to create a physical database based on the blueprint. Physical database design requires several decisions that will affect the integrity and performance of the database system. The information needed for this process includes the following:

- **Table/column name**   Usually uses a singular noun or noun phrase, and the name should be specific to the organization (e.g., a university DB uses STUDENT for the table name and uses student_id for the column name in the table to store the student's ID number)

- **Data format**   Defines the data type (e.g., NUMBER, CHAR, DATE, etc.) for each column to minimize storage space and maximize data integrity

- **Constraints**   Specify the number of instances (e.g., an instructor can teach a maximum of five courses) or value range (e.g., a course score is between 0 and 100) for one column

- **Default value**   Is the value a column will assume (e.g., default value for score is 0) if a user does not provide data

Then, database programmers use SQL to create a physical database with several tables. For example, the four CREATE TABLE statements shown in Figure 7-4 create four tables according to the ERD in Figure 7-3.

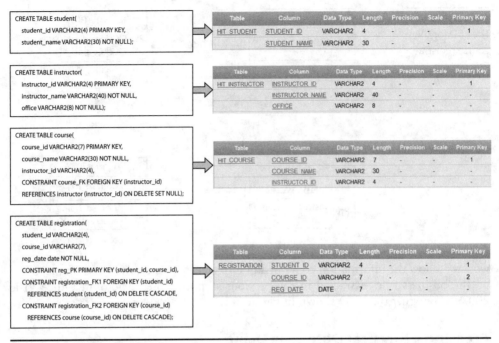

Figure 7-4 Four CREATE TABLE statements

Implementing a Healthcare Database Application

The last stage for the database application development is to choose a tool to implement the application. For example, in developing a web-based healthcare database application, there are several available tools for this purpose, such as PHP: *Hypertext Preprocessor* (PHP), Active Server Pages (ASP)/ASP.NET, Process and Experiment Automation Real-time Language (PEARL), Oracle Application Express (APEX), Java, and C++. Among them, Oracle Application Express is a free, rapid web application development tool for an Oracle database (Oracle is one of the most widely used DBMSs in healthcare today). Using only a web browser and limited programming experience, a database application designer can develop and deploy professional applications that are both fast and secure. For example, using APEX, a page is the basic building block of an application. When you build an application in Application Builder, the APEX interface, you create pages that contain user interface elements, such as tabs, lists, buttons, items, and regions. Then, you add controls to a page on the page definition. For example, based on the tables created in stage 3, I developed a simple web-based database application for health informatics course registration using APEX, as shown in Figure 7-5. In this application, readers can use any Internet browser (e.g., Internet Explorer, Firefox, Chrome) to log into the application (http://db2.his.uvic.ca:8080/apex/f?p=132 ; use username=guest and password=guest). The home page will show all the students' registration information. The user also can click the tabs at the top of the page to view or edit student profiles, instructor information, and course descriptions.

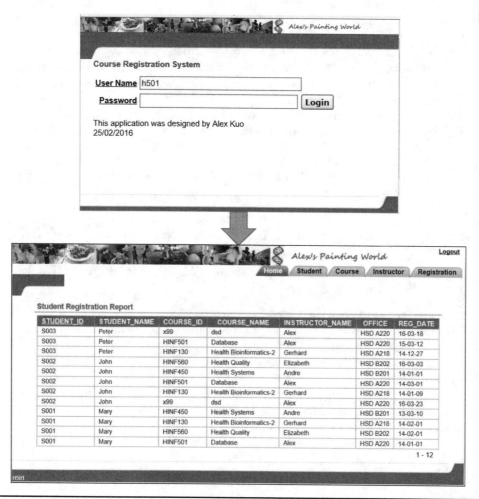

Figure 7-5 A simple APEX application for online course registration

Use Case 7-1: A Web-Based Healthcare Database Application

Background

Take the Pressure Down (TPD) is a joint initiative of the Heart and Stroke Foundation (HSF) and Beacon Community Services in BC, Canada. The program consists of free community clinics providing blood pressure monitoring, risk assessments, and education about hypertension. Readings from TPD sessions can help doctors and clinicians to monitor a patient's blood pressure when they are not visiting the doctor's office or clinic. Previously, TPD volunteers used a paper-based form to record patient's blood pressure, demographic, lifestyle, and health history data. There were three main drawbacks to using this method: paper-based forms required large physical storage; collected data were not available for further review and analysis; and patients/researchers could not access the data at anytime and from anywhere. For these reasons, the TPD research team decided to develop a web-based database system to manage the data, while allowing both patients and physicians to review and monitor blood pressure readings online. The new system requirements include

- First-line nurses/volunteers are able to enter data online, and researchers can access data and perform online analysis anytime, anywhere, and via any device.
- Patients and physicians can review blood pressure history through the Internet, including via a mobile app.
- The system is scalable to contain 34 million records to accommodate the development of a (Canada) national database.
- The system is able to export data into an XML/Excel format for further data interoperability with other systems.

System Implementation and Functions

The system uses Oracle Database 11*g* Express Edition (XE) as the backend database and the APEX 4.2 Application Builder user interface development tool. Take Blood Pressure Down (TBPD) is the application program/system that was built to enable TPD to be accessed and interacted with by community members.

There are four types of users in the system: administrator users can access all system resources, including user accounts and stored data; nurse/volunteer users can input patient data and view/modify the data if the person has the patient's permission; physician/researcher users can view all patient data; and patient users can only review his/her own blood pressure history.

The system functions can be represented by the following four usage scenarios:[5]

- **Scenario 1** Dave Fisher is an HSF volunteer to take blood pressure readings and provide recommendations for people. Dave uses the system online registration function to create a volunteer account:

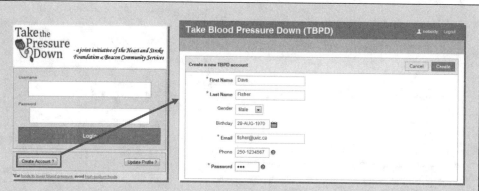

- **Scenario 2**   Abdul Rauf is a sedentary, middle-aged (DOB 1970) father of two, who often eats fast food as a result of his employer's frequent last-minute requests that he work overtime. As a consequence of his fast-paced and demanding work environment, he has little time for exercise. Having recently learned that heart disease and stroke are strongly related to high blood pressure, Abdul has decided that he should get his blood pressure assessed when he has time. After completing his weekly shopping, Abdul notices the HSF mobile kiosk at Bay Centre advertising a free service to help with blood pressure reduction through self-monitoring. He speaks to Dave Fisher, who is volunteering at the kiosk, and decides to get a blood pressure assessment. Dave registers Abdul to the system as a new patient and then records Abdul's blood pressure and related health information including demographic, lifestyle, and health condition data. Dave also helps him download the mobile TPD app:

(continued)

Since the systolic reading (142) falls in Stage 1 hypertension range, the system prompts alert information to recommend that Abdul see his family doctor:

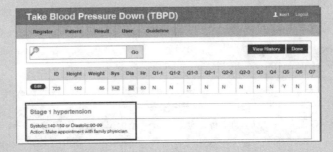

- **Scenario 3** Abdul visits his family doctor, who makes several recommendations to help lower his blood pressure and advises him to continue participating in the TPD program, which he does for the next nine months. Abdul uses his iPhone to review his blood pressure history:

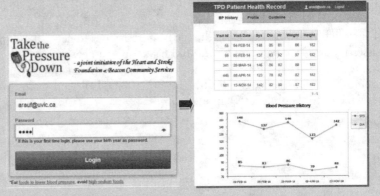

- **Scenario 4** Dr. Jeff Li, the manager of HSF BC, provides regular reports that will be used both to assess the success of engagement with the public and to provide blood pressure status for the local population. Dr. Li starts and interacts with the TPD application by selecting appropriate parameters to generate statistical charts that would assist in identifying trends that would enable him to gauge the success of the intervention/project; for example, the average patient's systolic pressure by area, as shown in the following image (a). The data can be exported into an Excel format for advanced data analysis, as shown in image (b).

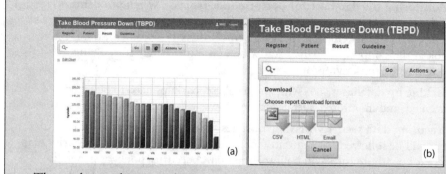

The reader can log in to the system at http://db3.his.uvic.ca:8080/apex/f?p=500 as a volunteer (Email: Dfisher@uvic.cav, Password: 123) to enter patient data; as a doctor (Email: Tom@uvic.ca, Password: 123) to view patient records; or as a researcher (Email: JeffLI@uvic.ca, Password: 123) to analyze patient data. Also, the reader can log in to the TPD Personal Health Record system at http://db3.his.uvic.ca:8080/apex/f?p=501 (Email: clee@uvic.ca, Password: 123) to review the blood pressure history as well as exam/test reports for another patient (Christina Lee).

Database Administration and Security

When developing databases, database administration is an important topic that needs to be taken into account in order to ensure that critical health data are managed efficiently and effectively. Another key concept when developing databases for storing and using sensitive health data is security.

Database Administration

Database administration refers to a set of functions for logical and physical database design and for dealing with management issues, such as ensuring database performance, data security and privacy, data backup and recovery, and database availability.[1] A database administrator (DBA) must have a sound understanding of current hardware and software (e.g., operating systems [OSs] and networking) architectures, security/privacy policies, and data processing procedures to ensure enough disk space is always available, backups are performed regularly, indexes are maintained and optimized, and database statistics are up to date.

The main database administration tasks are as follows:[4]

- **Managing database memory**   One of the most important aspects of managing a database is to make sure that there is always enough disk space. As the data size grows, the DBA needs to evaluate whether to allocate more memory to the database.

- **Managing users**   The task includes creating/dropping user accounts, locking and unlocking user accounts, resetting account passwords, granting administrative privileges, and assigning quotas.

- **Monitoring the database for performance issues**   When problems occur within a system, it is important to perform an accurate and timely diagnosis before making any changes to the system. If there is a problem, the DBA may look at the symptoms, analyze statistics, and immediately start changing the system to fix those symptoms.

- **Backing up databases**   As with any database, backups need to be scheduled, executed, and monitored. Details of the process will be discussed in the next section.

- **Executing data security/privacy policies**   Security policies define the rules that will be followed to maintain security in a database system. A security plan details how those rules will be implemented. A security policy is generally included within a security plan. To maintain database security, a DBA follows the organization security plan to grant privileges to enable the user to connect to the database, to run queries and make updates, and to create schema objects.

Database Security

Database security refers to protecting the data against accidental or intentional loss, destruction, misuse, or disclosure to unwanted parties. Some common data security issues include the following:

- **Theft and fraud**   This occurs when any person uses another person's means of access to view, alter, or destroy data. In some cases, the thief can access a computer room to steal database hardware.

- **Data breaches**   A data breach is the intentional or unintentional release of confidential data (e.g., patient's health records) to unauthorized third parties.

- **Loss of data integrity**   Data integrity is imposed within a database at its design stage through the use of standard rules and procedures and is maintained through the use of error checking and validation routines. When data integrity is compromised, data will be invalid or corrupted.

- **Loss of availability**   Loss of availability means that data, applications, or networks are unavailable to users and may lead to severe operational difficulties of an organization.

To protect data, database security management must establish administrative policies and procedures, create physical protection plans, institute backup and recovery strategies, and apply hardware or software technologies. Security countermeasures can be categorized into technical and nontechnical methods,[1, 6] as described in the following sections. Database backup and recovery is another fundamental best practice in database security management and will also be described below.

Technical Data Security Methods

Technical data security methods include the following:

- **Integrity controls**   Data are kept consistent and correct by means of controls that a database administrator puts on the database. This may involve limiting values a column may hold, constraining the actions that can be performed on the data, or triggering the execution of certain procedures to track access to data (e.g., recording which user has done what and has accessed which data). The tracking or auditing of who accesses patient data (and for what purposes) is especially important given the sensitivity of personal health data.

- **Authentication**   This refers to a way of identifying a user (a person or a software program) by having the user provide a valid ID and password before the access is granted. The process of authentication is based on each user having a unique set of criteria for gaining access.

- **Authorization**   This refers to verifying that the user has authority to access a database object (e.g., table, procedure, or function) before allowing the user to access it. In other words, this determines which actions an authenticated principal is authorized to perform on the database. The tasks required to control authorization are also referred to as *access management*. As an example of how authentication and authorization work together to provide database security, a user called Alex wants to log in to the www.CyberHealth.com server to use the EHR system that can be accessed from that site. In this example, authentication is the mechanism whereby the system running at www.CyberHealth.com should securely identify the user Alex. The authentication must provide answers to the following questions:

  - Who is the user Alex?

  - Is the user Alex really who he represents himself to be?

To answer these questions, the server depends on some unique bits of information known only to Alex. It may be as simple as a password or public key authentication or as complicated as a Kerberos-based system. If the authenticating system can verify that the shared secret was presented correctly, then the user Alex is considered authenticated. What's next? The server running at www.CyberHealth.com must determine what level of access Alex should have. For example, is Alex authorized to view a specific patient's data? Is Alex authorized to modify the patient's data? Is Alex authorized to delete the patient's data? In this example, the server uses a combination of authentication and authorization to secure the system. The system ensures that the user claiming to be Alex is really Alex and thus prevents unauthorized users from gaining access to secured resources running on the EHR system at the www.CyberHealth.com server.

- **User-defined procedures**   User-defined procedures or interfaces allow system designers to define their own security procedures in addition to the authorization rules.

- **Data encryption**   This refers to mathematical calculations and algorithmic schemes that transform plain text into cybertext; in other words, text is converted into a form that is not readable to unauthorized parties. Using encryption, a key specifies the particular transformation of plain text into cybertext, or vice versa, during decryption. The following are two common encryption methods for data protection:

- **Secret-key encryption (aka symmetric-key cryptography)**   This refers to a class of algorithms for cryptography that use trivially related, often identical, cryptographic keys for both decryption and encryption. Examples of popular and well-respected symmetric algorithms include AES, Blowfish, CAST5, RC4, TDES, and IDEA.

- **Public-key encryption (aka asymmetric-key cryptography)**   In public-key cryptography, a user has a pair of cryptographic keys: a public key and a private key. The private key is kept secret, while the public key may be widely distributed. Incoming messages would have been encrypted with the recipient's public key and can be decrypted only with the recipient's corresponding private key. Examples of popular and well-respected public-key algorithms include RSA, ElGamal, Knapsack, ECC, and Diffie-Hellman.

- **Firewall**   This refers to an integrated collection of security measures designed to prevent unauthorized electronic access to a networked computer system. It is also a device or set of devices configured to permit, deny, encrypt, decrypt, or proxy all computer traffic between different security domains based upon a set of rules and other criteria.

- **Intrusion detection system (IDS)**   This refers to software and/or hardware designed to detect unwanted attempts at accessing, manipulating, and/or disabling of computer systems, mainly through a network, such as the Internet.

- **Data masking**   This refers to the process of obscuring (masking) specific data within a database table or column to ensure that data security is maintained and sensitive customer information is not leaked outside of the authorized environment. Common methods of data masking include encryption, masking (e.g., numbers for letters), substitution (e.g., all male names = Alex), nulling (e.g., ####), or shuffling (e.g., zipcode12345 = 51432).

Nontechnical Data Security Methods
Nontechnical data security methods include the following:

- **Personnel controls**   This refers to exerting control over who can interact with a resource. The resource can be database data, an application, or hardware. Activities such as monitoring to ensure that personnel are following established security practices can be carried out. Standard job controls, such as separating duties so no one employee has responsibility for an entire system or keeping system developers from having access to production systems, should also be enforced (particularly in healthcare, where the data stored can be considered to be sensitive).

- **Physical access controls**   These limit access to particular computer rooms in buildings and are usually part of controlling physical access. Sensitive equipment (hardware and peripherals) must be placed in secure areas (e.g., locked to a desk or cabinet). Also, an alarm system can deter a brute-force break-in.

- **Maintenance controls**   The healthcare organization should review external maintenance agreements for all hardware (e.g., server, networks) and software (e.g., source codes) that the database system is using to ensure system performance and data quality.

- **Data privacy controls**   Breaches of confidential data (e.g., patient health data) could result in loss of user trust in the organization and could lead to legal action being taken against the healthcare organization. Information privacy legislation plays a critical role in protecting user data privacy. For example, the U.S. Health Insurance Portability and Accountability Act (HIPAA) is a federal law enacted to ensure that the freedom of patients to choose healthcare insurers and providers will not come at the expense of the privacy of their medical records.[7]

Database Backup and Recovery

Database backup and recovery are mechanisms for restoring databases quickly and accurately after loss or damage. A DBMS should provide four basic facilities for the backup and recovery of a database:[1]

- Backup facilities that provide periodic backup copies of the database (backup data should be kept offsite at safe locations)

- Journalizing facilities that maintain an audit trail of transactions and database changes

- A checkpoint facility by which the DBMS periodically suspends all processing and synchronizes its files and journals to establish a recovery point

- A recovery manager that allows the DBMS to restore its original condition if needed

Much more about security can be found in Part VI of this book.

Data Warehouses for Healthcare

The need to analyze large amounts of health data is becoming increasingly important to managers, healthcare organizations, and healthcare researchers. In response to this, new ways of organizing health data have been developed to help health professionals and managers query health data. As a consequence, in recent years the concept of a data warehouse has emerged in healthcare.

What Is a Data Warehouse?

Healthcare is information dependent and cannot be provided efficiently without data regarding the patient's past and current conditions. Patient health records provide the who, what, when, where, and how of patient care, and they are the resources needed for further decision support and knowledge discovery. Unfortunately, in the real world, clinical data come from many different sources, such as patient visits, test results, laboratory reports, diagnoses, therapy, medication, and procedures. These data are usually stored in distributed and heterogeneous databases. For example, a patient's registration data may be stored in a Microsoft Access database, a laboratory report may be stored in a Sybase database, diagnosis information in an IBM Informix database, and medication information in an Oracle database. Healthcare professionals need to integrate the data from several transaction information systems (databases) to provide quality treatment and patient care. However, heterogeneous data and distributed data repositories make clinical decisions difficult (Figure 7-6). A data warehouse (DW) integrates (extracts, transforms, and loads [ETL]) data from several transaction information systems into a staging area. It is believed that a DW can provide healthcare professionals with clinical intelligence that enables them to better understand problems, discover opportunities, and measure performance.[8]

Bill Inmon defined the data warehouse as "a subject-oriented, integrated, non-volatile and time-variant collection of data in support of management's decisions."[9] In other words, a data warehouse is a repository of an organization's electronically stored data designed to facilitate reporting and analysis. This classic definition of a data warehouse focuses on data storage. However, the means to retrieve and analyze data; to extract, transform, and load data; and to manage the dictionary data are also considered essential components of a data warehousing system.

The Differences Between a DW and OLTP

Online transaction processing (OLTP) refers to a set of programs that help users manage transaction-oriented applications in industries, such as banking, airlines, supermarkets, and manufacturing. These transaction-oriented applications include data entry and retrieval transactions. Data warehouses are different from OLTP based on the following five aspects.

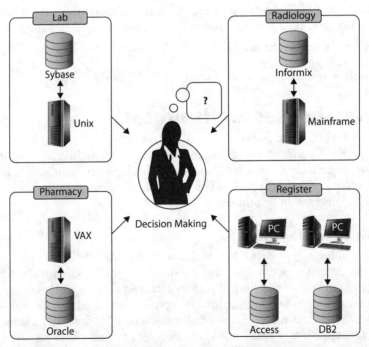

Figure 7-6 Heterogeneous data and distributed data repositories make clinical decision making difficult.

Design Objectives

- OLTP is a software system that facilitates and manages transaction-oriented applications, typically for data entry and retrieval transaction processing.
- A DW is a decision-making-oriented repository. It is mainly used for decision analysis, with strong interoperability between different computer systems.

Data Types

- OLTP contains department detail, short-period data, snapshot, and/or ongoing status of business.
- A DW consists of an enterprise-level, integrated, time-variant, and nonvolatile collection of data. Data often originates from a variety of sources. It may include five types of data (Figure 7-7): current operational data, legacy data, lightly digested data, heavily digested data, and metadata.

Functionalities

- OLTP provides online query, modify, insert, and delete functions. Efficiency and steadiness are major goals for OLTP.
- DW is subject-oriented and supports a variety of decision analysis functions as well as strategic operational functions.

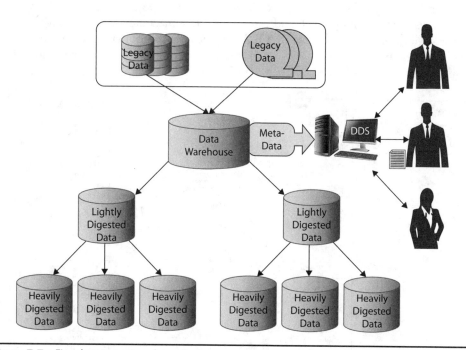

Figure 7-7   Five data types in a data warehouse

Data Structures

- OLTP usually contains many relational tables and is highly normalized.

- A DW uses a star schema to store data. The star schema consists of a few "fact tables" (possibly only one, justifying the name) referencing any number of "dimension tables." The fact table holds the main data while the smaller dimension tables describe each value of a dimension and can be joined to fact tables as needed (Figure 7-8).

Analytical Capabilities

- OLTP helps users control and run fundamental business tasks. It possesses limited analytical capabilities.

- A DW enables users to analyze different dimensions of multidimensional data. For example, it provides time series and trend analysis views.

Data Warehouse Models

Data warehousing supports a variety of decision analysis functions as well as strategic operational functions. Data often originate from a variety of sources (different types of databases), formats, and types, and are generally consolidated, transformed, and loaded into one or more instances of a DBMS to facilitate a broad range of analytical applications. A data warehouse may consist of a single large enterprise-wide database to which users and administrators connect directly, or it may incorporate several smaller systems, called *data marts*, each of which addresses a specific subject area within the overall warehouse. Online analytical processing (OLAP) is the core component of data warehousing and analytics. It gives users the ability to interrogate data by intuitively navigating from summary data to detail data.

Figure 7-8
A star schema
data structure

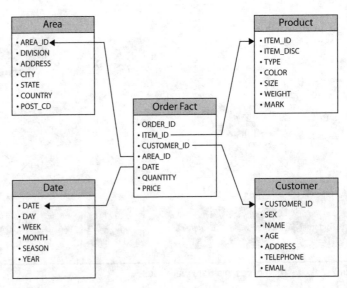

In real applications, you can use four aspects—functionalities, storage location, topology, and data status—to categorize a data warehouse model, as described in the following sections.

Categorized by Functionalities (Enterprise DW vs. Department DW)

- An enterprise DW (also called EDW, Figure 7-9) supports a variety of decision-analysis functions as well as strategic operational functions.
- A department DW (also called a data mart, a subset of EDW) is usually oriented to a specific purpose or major data subject that may be distributed to support businesses and contains analytical data designed to focus on specific business functions for a specific community within an organization.

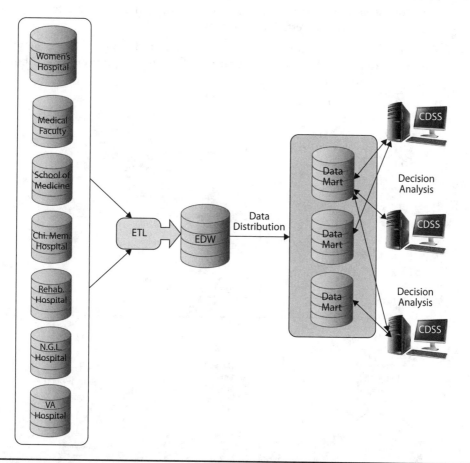

Figure 7-9 Enterprise DW vs. department DW (data mart) model. (CDSS refers to clinical decision support system)

Categorized by Storage Location (Centralized DW vs. Distributed DW)

- A centralized DW consists of a single large enterprise-wide database. Data often originate from a variety of sources and are loaded into one or more instances of a DBMS to facilitate a broad range of analytical applications. The main benefit of this model is that data are more consistent and easy to maintain. However, the major concern of this model is that it has high development and maintenance costs (based on the data level and security level).
- A distributed DW (Figure 7-10) usually consists of several department DWs (data marts). This model is suitable for companies doing distributed business operations.

Categorized by Topology (Physical DW vs. Virtual DW)

- A physical DW stores all aggregate data in a physical storage location. The DW consists of five types of data: current operational data, legacy data, lightly digested data, heavily digested data, and metadata.
- A virtual DW does not store data in a physical storage location. This model is a virtual (conceptual) DW that uses an intranet/Internet to connect all distributed databases (Figure 7-11).

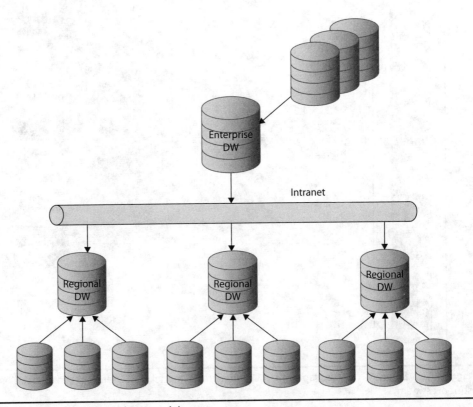

Figure 7-10 A distributed DW model

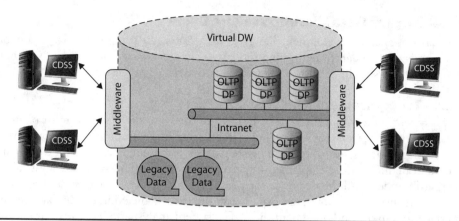

Figure 7-11   A virtual DW model

Categorized by Data Status (Dynamic DW vs. Static DW)

- A dynamic DW consists of a snapshot DW and a longitudinal DW (Figure 7-12). It can be applied to an organization that needs both short-term tactical analysis and long-term strategic analysis. This model requires high development and maintenance costs. Therefore, it is seldom used in real applications.

- A static DW is an EDW or a data mart that consists of a nonvolatile (static) collection of data.

Figure 7-12
A dynamic DW
model

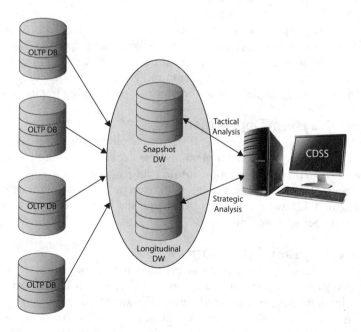

A Healthcare Data Warehouse Life Cycle

The classical system development life cycle (SDLC) is not suitable for data warehouse development.[9] The data warehousing industry is in agreement that the data warehouse life-cycle model should consist of the following five major phases.[10, 11, 12]

Phase 1: Requirement Analysis

All IT systems of any kind need to be built to suit user needs. A system must be usable. If the system is not used, there is no point in building it. To become a real organizational asset leveraged throughout healthcare systems, user requirements must be carefully analyzed and defined before implementing a data warehouse. The system analyst talks to the user to understand the details of the processes, the business, the data, and the issues; arrange site visits to get firsthand experience; discuss the meaning of the data, the user interface, and so on; and document them. The system analyst also lists the nonfunctional requirements such as performance and security.

Phase 2: System Design

Key activities in this phase are to determine the data warehouse model; design the extraction, transformation, and loading system; and draw the front-end applications. Tasks typically include cataloging the source system, defining key performance indicators (KPIs) and other critical business metrics, mapping decision-making processes underlying information needs, and designing the logical and physical schema.

Phase 3: Prototype Development

This phase builds the three parts that are designed in the previous phase: the data stores, the ETL system (including data quality system and metadata), and the front-end applications. With some caution and consideration, these three parts can be built in parallel. The most important consideration when building in parallel is to define accurate interfaces between the parts. The primary objective of prototype development is to constrain, and in some cases reframe, end-user requirements by showing opinion leaders and heavyweight analysts in the end-user communities precisely what they had asked for in the requirement analysis phase or in the previous prototyping iteration.

Phase 4: System Deployment

Deployment typically involves two separate deployments: the deployment of a prototype into a production-test environment and the deployment of a stress-tested, performance-tested production configuration into an actual production environment. Once a user-approved DW is ready, the development team puts all the components in the production boxes (the ETL system, the data stores, and the front-end applications) and deploys the system for actual production use.

Phase 5: System Operation

This phase involves the day-to-day maintenance of the data warehouse. The operations team continues to administer the data warehouse and to support the users. There are basically three types of support: helping new and existing users using the system, administering new users and their access rights, and solving errors or problems that happen when using the data warehouse. Users will also have enhancement requests: to add more data to the data warehouse (or change existing data), to add a feature to the front-end applications, or to create new reports or new data structures. In such cases, the development team may include these requests in the next release.

Data Mining in Healthcare

As the amount of stored health data increases exponentially, it's increasingly recognized that such data can be analyzed or "mined" to uncover new and important patterns. This section explores the role of data mining in identifying and revealing important patterns or trends in health data.

What Is Data Mining?

Data mining (DM) is different from OLAP that focuses on the interactive analysis of data and typically provides extensive capabilities for visualizing the data and generating summary statistics.[13] Data mining is "an integral part of knowledge discovery in database (KDD), which is the overall process of converting raw data into useful information."[14] In other words, it is the process of automatically discovering useful information in large data repositories (e.g., data warehouses). The data mining process consists of four major transformation phases,[15] as shown in Figure 7-13.

1. **Problem definition phase**   A healthcare data mining project starts with an understanding of the healthcare problems. Data mining experts, business experts (healthcare setting managers), and domain experts (healthcare professionals) work closely together to define the project objectives and the requirements from a healthcare quality improvement perspective. The project objective is then translated into a data mining problem definition. In the problem definition phase, data mining data and tools are not yet required.

2. **Data preprocessing phase**   The original or "raw" data provided for data mining often need certain levels of preprocessing before the data can be input to a data mining algorithm. The purpose of preprocessing is to transform the raw data

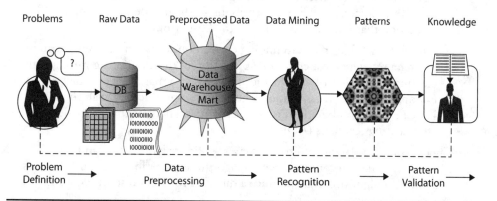

Figure 7-13   A generic process of data mining

into an appropriate format for subsequent analysis. The tasks involved in data preprocessing include fusing data from multiple sources (files, spreadsheets, or database tables), cleaning data, integrating data, and transforming data.

Real-world data tend to be incomplete (lacking attribute values or certain attributes of interest or containing only aggregate data), noisy (containing errors or outlier values that deviate from the expected), and inconsistent (e.g., containing discrepancies in the department codes used to categorize items). Data cleaning routines attempt to fill in missing values (e.g., fill in the most probable values), smooth out noise (e.g., apply binning, regression, and clustering algorithms to remove noisy data), and correct inconsistencies in the data (e.g., correct a patient's age that might be listed as −25 or 154).

Data integration involves merging data from multiple sources inside/outside heterogeneous databases, data cubes, or flat files into a coherent data store (e.g., data warehouse) for further data mining processing. This task usually encounters many interoperability issues. Kuo et al.[16] described several interoperability issues and approaches to deal with the issues.

For example, data from multiple data resources may need to be transformed into forms appropriate for mining, such as transforming patient gender from male/female data to M/F or 1/0, normalizing data values from −100~100 to 1.0~1.0, or categorizing age ranges from 0~130 to youth/middle-age/senior.

3. **Pattern recognition phase** This phase involves choosing the proper data mining algorithm to discover the patterns. Basically, these algorithms can be divided into four types:

- **Clustering** This refers to the task of discovering groups and structures in the data that are in some way or another similar, without using known structures in the data.

- **Classification** This refers to the task of generalizing a known structure to apply to new data. In other words, it predicts one or more discrete variables, based on the other attributes in the data set.

- **Regression** This refers to predicting one or more continuous variables, such as profit or loss, based on other attributes in the data set. It attempts to find a function that models the data with the least error.

- **Association** This refers to finding correlations between different attributes in a data set. The most common application of this kind of algorithm is for creating association rules, which can be used in a market basket analysis. For example, the Apriori association algorithm can produce association rules that indicate what combinations of medications and patient characteristics lead to adverse drug reactions (ADRs).[17]

Choosing the best algorithm to use for a specific analytical task can be a challenge. While you can use different algorithms to perform the same business task, another algorithm may produce a different result, and some algorithms can give more than one type of result.

4. **Pattern validation phase**   Pattern (rule) validation is the process of assessing how well the mining models perform against real data. It is important that the mining team validates the discovered patterns before deploying them into a production environment. There are several approaches for validating the patterns.[18] The following are some examples:

- **Using statistical validity to determine whether there are problems in the data or in the model**   A number of statistical methods can be used to evaluate the data mining model quality or pattern accuracy, such as cross-validation and receiver operating characteristic (ROC) curves.

- **Separating the data into training and testing sets to test the accuracy of patterns**   It is common for the data mining algorithms to find patterns in the training set that are not present in the general data set. To deal with the so-called over-fitting issue, the validation uses a test data set that the data mining algorithm was not trained on. The learned patterns are applied to the data set, and the resulting output is compared to the desired output.

- **Asking domain experts to review the results of the data mining to determine whether the discovered patterns have meaning in the targeted business scenario**   In a health data mining project, physicians and healthcare domain experts will be involved in the validation process to interpret the accuracy of the patterns.

Applications of Data Mining in Healthcare

In recent years, data mining has received considerable attention as a tool that can be applied to healthcare research and management. To perform descriptive and predictive analysis, data mining employs various analysis methods, which include clustering, classification, regression, and association analysis (as discussed in the previous section), to discover interesting patterns in the given data set that serve as the basis for estimating future trends. For example, Kuo et al. proposed an association analysis algorithm for the detection of adverse drug reactions in healthcare data.[17] The Apriori algorithm was used to perform association analysis on the characteristics of patients, the drugs they were taking, their primary diagnosis, co-morbid conditions, and the ADRs or adverse events (AEs) they experienced. This analysis produced association rules that indicate what combinations of medications and patient characteristics lead to ADRs. Cheng et al. proposed the use of classification algorithms to help in the early detection of heart disease, a major public health concern all over the world.[19] Balasubramanian and Umarani identified the risk factors associated with high levels of fluoride content in water, using data mining algorithms to find meaningful hidden patterns to support meaningful decision making about this real-world health hazard.[20] The Concaro et al. study[21] focused on the care delivery flow of diabetes mellitus and applied a data mining algorithm for the extraction of temporal association rules on sequences of events. The method exploited the integration of different healthcare information sources and was used to evaluate the pertinence of care delivery flow for specific pathologies in order to refine inappropriate practices that lead to unsatisfactory outcomes.

In research of data mining applied to cancer detection and treatment, Luk et al.[22] used Artificial Neural Network (ANN) and Classification And Regression Tree (CART) algorithms to distinguish tumor from non-tumor liver tissues. Eventually, they revealed that these classification algorithms were suitable for applying the building of a tissue classification model based on the hidden pattern in the proteomic data set. In addition, ANN and CART algorithms generated good predictive abilities for differentiating between tumor and non-tumor tissues for liver cancer. Cao et al. proposed the use of data mining as a tool to aid in monitoring trends in clinical trials of cancer vaccines. By using data mining and visualization, medical experts could find patterns and anomalies better than just looking at a set of tabulated data.[23] Many other real data mining applications in healthcare have been described.[24] Kalish has also described many real-world examples of how data mining has helped to reduce healthcare cost.[25]

Despite the benefits of applying data mining to healthcare quality improvement, Shillabeer and Roddick[26] have indicated several inherent conflicts between traditional applications of data mining and applications in medicine. Perhaps the most challenging issues for the application of this technology to healthcare are data security and privacy. Therefore, an organization must formulate clear policies regarding the privacy and security of patient health records before embarking on data mining, and it must enforce those policies with its partner-stakeholders and agencies.

Cloud Computing in Healthcare

Cloud computing is becoming a major trend in business and computing and is becoming an important topic in healthcare IT. Cloud computing can be defined as a model for enabling convenient, on-demand network access to a shared pool of configurable computing resources that can be rapidly accessed with minimal management effort or service-provider interaction.[5] Cloud computing differs from traditional approaches in a number of ways. Cloud computing can provide a wide range of computing resources on demand anywhere and anytime. The approach eliminates up-front costs and infrastructure development by cloud users (as services and infrastructure can be hosted over the Internet) and it allows users to pay for use of only those computing resources they need and on a short-term basis as needed.[27] As the reader may be able to tell by this overview paragraph about cloud computing, cloud computing is much more than data storage. However, cloud computing does have major data storage capability and is used more and more by database administrators as important scalable data storage and ready access components of an overall DBMS. Hence the introduction and discussion to cloud computing's inclusion in this chapter, in addition to several other chapters in this book where this major phenomenon could reside as well.

Cloud Computing Models

Cloud computing includes three major models:

- **Software as a Service (SaaS)** Healthcare applications (e.g., EHRs) can be hosted by a cloud service provider and made available to customers (e.g., physicians) over a network (typically the Internet). The EHR application can be provided to the user through a thin client interface (e.g., a browser). In healthcare, several vendors are offering applications using the SaaS model. Examples of SaaS in other areas include Google Apps, Oracle On Demand, Salesforce.com, and Microsoft Azure SQL Database.

- **Platform as a Service (PaaS)**   Development tools such as operating systems and development frameworks can also be hosted in the cloud and accessed remotely through a browser. Using this approach, developers can build applications without installing software tools on their computer, making the process of development easier.

- **Infrastructure as a Service (IaaS)**   IaaS provides hardware assets that can be accessed remotely. For example, the cloud can provide storage, hardware, servers, and networking components. The cloud service provider has the responsibility for housing, running, and maintaining the services and the client typically pays on a per-use basis.

Cloud Computing Deployment Models

There are three main models for deploying cloud computing:

- **Private cloud**   A proprietary network or data center supplies hosted services to specific users. Here the infrastructure on the cloud is operated and controlled exclusively for a specific organization and is not made public.

- **Public cloud**   The cloud services (applications and storage) are made available for public use and the cloud is owned by an organization that sells cloud services.

- **Hybrid cloud**   This kind of cloud combines multiple clouds that can be private or public. For example, an organization may provide and manage some resources within its own data center but rely on other services provided externally.

Examples of Cloud Computing in Healthcare

Medical record services are now beginning to be offered "in the cloud," such as through Microsoft HealthVault and Amazon Web Services (AWS). AWS hosts a collection of healthcare IT offerings, including healthcare data storage applications and web-based health records services; for example, AWS can be used to build personal health record (PHR) offerings. In the pharmaceutical industry, companies are beginning to streamline business operations using cloud-based software. In the government sector, the U.S. Department of Health and Human Services (HHS) Office of the National Coordinator for Health IT (ONC) has selected a cloud computing and project management system to manage the selection and implementation of EHR systems. In Europe, consortia have used cloud computing services for supporting remote monitoring, diagnosing, and assisting of patients outside of a hospital setting.[28]

Pros and Cons of Cloud Computing in Healthcare

Although cloud computing promises to provide more flexibility, less expense, and more security to end users, its application in healthcare has both strengths and weaknesses.

A significant strength to cloud computing is its scalability for data storage. Data storage for even a medium-sized database application in healthcare can be tricky to plan for given the changing and sometimes unpredictable nature of clinical practice. For example, if a HIT application adds patient genotype functionality to its existing patient phenotype capability, its data storage needs may rise significantly. A cloud computing highly scalable data storage solution to challenges like these is very attractive to DBAs. Another strength includes the fact that hardware and server issues (in terms of cost and complexity of maintaining technology) that exist for locally installed legacy systems are largely eliminated with cloud computing. Smaller hospital and medical practices that typically don't have internal IT staff to maintain and service in-house infrastructure may find this alternative attractive. Furthermore, the pay as you go model can be attractive to physicians and many healthcare organizations.

Several limitations and considerations need to be taken into account before deciding on a cloud-based solution in healthcare. First, there may be lack of familiarity and experience with cloud computing, requiring, among other things, substantial training for HIT staff. Second, insufficient evidence currently exists to show the cloud approach is suitable for more than only a few healthcare applications. Although the approach has been successfully applied in other domains, differences particular to healthcare may make it too difficult to implement more widely at the current time, including the need to ensure the security and privacy of health data stored or accessed using a cloud-based approach. State/province, federal/national, or even international legal data jurisdiction concerns are being raised. Questions about potential performance unpredictability, including data transfer bottlenecks and unknown impacts on the increasing importance of data interoperability in healthcare, are also being raised.

Cloud computing and its use in healthcare is evolving rapidly. Given the many advantages of cloud computing, the current disadvantages or areas of concern are likely to be resolved, mitigated, or substantially eliminated.

Chapter Review

Healthcare is the most data-intensive industry in the world today. Health information systems can be used by healthcare professionals to improve healthcare services and reduce costs. The challenge for HIT is how to make data useful for clinicians and empower them with the tools to make informed decisions and deliver more responsive patient services.

In this chapter, the requirements for databases in healthcare and the basics of relational databases, database models, database administration, and security were discussed. The steps involved in developing healthcare databases were described and illustrated, including a use case of a web-based healthcare database application. Two important and emerging database applications, health data warehousing and data mining, were also described and discussed.

A data warehouse (DW) integrates data from several transaction information systems (databases) into a staging area. DWs can provide healthcare professionals with clinical intelligence that will enable them to better understand clinical problems, discover opportunities, and measure the performance of healthcare systems.

Data mining (DM) is the process of automatically discovering useful information from large data repositories (e.g., data warehouses). In recent years, data mining has received considerable attention as a tool that can be applied in healthcare research and management.

Cloud computing is a model for enabling convenient, on-demand network access to a shared pool of configurable computing resources that can be accessed with minimal management effort or service-provider interaction. One of the configurable and scalable resources of cloud computing is its large and relatively affordable data storage capability. Given HIT's increasing need for data storage, this is an attractive attribute for HIT managers.

A case study was also used to help you learn about the concepts of databases, data warehouses, and data mining in healthcare.

Questions

To test your comprehension of the chapter, answer the following questions and then check your answers against the list of correct answers at the end of the chapter.

1. What is a database model?

    A. A file processing system

    B. The structure of a database

    C. A set of mathematic algorithms

    D. A database management system (DBMS)

2. In the relational database model, _____.

    A. a table name is used to uniquely identify a column

    B. the primary key is used to identify a column in one table that refers to a column in another table

    C. tables are the basic unit of data storage

    D. Data Control Language (DCL) statements can commit or roll back the processing of transactions

3. What is a database management system (DBMS)?

    A. A set of software programs to control the organization, storage, management, and retrieval of data in a database

    B. A nonprocedural programming language

    C. A data security mechanism

    D. A set of Data Definition Language (DDL) statements

4. What is the most commonly used tool for modeling a database?

   A. Entity relationship diagram

   B. IDEF-1X

   C. Object role model

   D. Spiral developing model

5. Which of the following statements is correct?

   A. Authorization is a way of identifying a user before access is granted.

   B. A database administrator puts integrity controls on the database to ensure that data are kept consistent and correct.

   C. Data breaches mean that data, applications, or networks are unavailable to database users.

   D. Data security is not important in the database system design.

6. A distributed data warehouse _____.

   A. stores all aggregated data in a single physical storage location

   B. is also called online analytical processing (OLAP)

   C. usually consists of several department data marts

   D. consists of snapshot and longitudinal databases

7. What is *not* the reason for creating a data mart?

   A. Lowering cost

   B. Providing more business functions

   C. Improving end-user response time

   D. Creating a collective view for a group of users

8. Which of the following is considered a potential negative issue with cloud computing in healthcare?

   A. The high cost of setting up cloud computing

   B. Lack of easy accessibility to data resources

   C. Privacy and confidentiality of health data stored on a cloud

   D. Need for advanced technical knowledge

Answers

1. **B.** A database model is the structure of a database.

2. **C.** In the relational database model, tables are the basic unit of data storage.

3. **A.** A database management system (DBMS) is a set of software programs to control the organization, storage, management, and retrieval of data in a database.

4. A. The most commonly used tool for data modeling database is an entity relationship model (ERM).

5. B. Integrity controls keep the data consistent and correct by means of controls that a database administrator puts on the database.

6. C. A distributed data warehouse usually consists of several department data marts.

7. B. Creating a data mart is not for providing more business functions.

8. C. The confidentiality and privacy of data must be considered when using a cloud-based solution for healthcare applications involving the storage of health data.

References

1. Hoffer, J. A., Prescott, M. B., & McFadden, F. R. (2005). *Modern database management, seventh edition.* Pearson.

2. Hey, T., & Tansley, S. (Eds.). (2010). *The fourth paradigm: Data-intensive scientific discovery.* Microsoft Research.

3. Collen, M. F. (2011). *Computer medical databases: The first six decades (1950–2010).* Springer-Verlag London.

4. Murray, C., et al. (2014). *Oracle Database Express Edition 2 day DBA, 11g Release 2 (11.2).* Oracle. Accessed on July 15, 2016, from http://docs.oracle.com/cd/E17781_01/server.112/e18804/toc.htm.

5. Kuo, M. H. (2015). Implementation of a cloud-based blood pressure data management system. *Studies in Health Technology and Informatics, 210,* 882–886.

6. Wiederhold, G. (1981). Database technology in healthcare. *Journal of Medical Systems, 5,* 175–196.

7. Health Insurance Portability and Accountability Act (HIPAA). (1996). Privacy and security rules. Accessed from https://www.hhs.gov/hipaa/index.html,

8. Akhtar, M. U., Dunn, K., & Smith, J. W. (2005). Commercial clinical data warehouses: From wave of the past to the state of the art. *Journal of Healthcare Information Management, 12,* 20–26.

9. Inmon, W. H. (2005). *Building the data warehouse, fourth edition.* John Wiley & Sons.

10. WhereScape Software. (2003). *Understanding the data warehouse lifecycle model, revision 2.* Accessed on July 12, 2016, from www.bossconsulting.com/oracle_dba/white_papers/DW%20in%20oracle/DW_model_lifecycle.pdf.

11. Kimball, R., Ross, M., Thornthwaite, W., Mundy, J., & Becker, B. (2008). *The data warehouse lifecycle toolkit, second edition.* John Wiley & Sons.

12. Rainardi, V. (2011). *Building a data warehouse with examples in SQL Server.* Apress.

13. BARC. (2010). *What is OLAP? An analysis of what the often misused OLAP term is supposed to mean.* Accessed on January 28, 2017, from http://barc-research.com/research/business-intelligence/.

14. Tan, P. N., Steinbach, M., & Kumar, V. (2005). *Introduction to data mining.* Addison-Wesley.

15. Fayyad, U., Piatetsky-Shapiro, G., & Smyth, R. (1996). The KDD process for extracting useful knowledge from volumes of data. *Communications of the ACM, 39,* 27–34.

16. Kuo, M. H., Kushniruk, A. W., & Borycki, E. M. (2011). A comparison of national health data interoperability approaches in Taiwan, Denmark and Canada. *Electronic Healthcare, 10,* 14–25.

17. Kuo, M. H., Kushniruk, A. W., Borycki, E. M., & Greig, D. (2009). Application of the Apriori algorithm for adverse drug reaction detection. *Studies in Health Technology and Informatics, 148,* 95–101.

18. *Richesson, R. L. (2012). Clinical research informatics.* Springer.

19. Cheng, T. H., Wei, C. P., & Tseng, V. S. (2006). Feature selection for medical data mining: Comparisons of expert judgment and automatic approaches. *Proceedings of the 19th IEEE Symposium on Computer-Based Medical Systems*, IEEE Computer Society, Washington, DC, June 22–23 (pp. 165–170).

20. Balasubramanian, T., & Umarani, R. (2012). Clustering as a data mining technique in health hazards of high levels of fluoride in potable water. *International Journal of Advanced Computer Sciences and Applications, 392,* 166–171.

21. Concaro, S., Sacchi, L., Cerra, C., & Bellazzi, R. (2009). Mining administrative and clinical diabetes data with temporal association rules. *Studies in Health Technology and Informatics, 150,* 574–578.

22. Luk, J. M., Lam, B. Y., Lee, N. P., Ho, D. W., Sham, P. C., Chen, L. … Fan, S. T. (2007). Artificial neural networks and decision tree model analysis of liver cancer proteomes. *Biochemical and Biophysical Research Communications, 361,* 68–73.

23. Cao, X., Maloney, K. B., & Brusic, V. (2008). Data mining of cancer vaccine trials: A bird's-eye view. *Immunome Research, 4,* 7.

24. Canlas Jr., R. D. (2009). *Data mining in healthcare: Current applications and issues.* Carnegie Mellon University.

25. Kalish, B. M. (2012). Digging for dollars: Data mining is an evolving tactic that can help reduce health care costs. *Employee Benefit Adviser, 10,* 36.

26. Shillabeer, A., & Roddick, J. (2007). Establishing a lineage for medical knowledge discovery. *ACM International Conference Proceeding Series, 70,* 29–37.

27. Mell, P., & Grance, T. (2010). The NIST definition of cloud computing. *Communications of the ACM, 53*(6), 50.

28. IBM. (2010). *European Union consortium launches advanced cloud computing project with hospital and smart power grid provider.* Accessed on July 29, 2016, from www-03.ibm.com/press/us/en/pressrelease/33067.wss.

PART II

Networks and Networking in Healthcare

Roman Mateyko

In this chapter, you will learn how to
- Explain how telecommunications networks are evolving with the advent of the Internet
- Describe key data networking concepts
- Describe the functions a data network performs using the OSI model of communications
- Describe how data flows in a wired or wireless network
- Describe HL7 and its use in transmitting healthcare data

This chapter is a brief tour through the topic of data networks and their use in healthcare. The topic of data networks is broad, deep, and constantly evolving. Many books have been written about data networks, so the best that a single chapter on the topic can do is give you an appreciation of key concepts, components, and approaches associated with data networks.

Telecommunications and Healthcare

The topic of data networks falls under the more general area of data communications. Data communications has roots in both telecommunications and computer science. Telecommunications is a broad topic area with relevance to healthcare. Doctors, nurses, and patients have been using telephones and telephone networks to talk to each other since the beginning of telephone service. Ambulances have used radio networks to communicate to hospitals to inform them of the state of patients in their care. Television networks have been used to inform citizens about the status of epidemics. The Internet and wireless networks of tomorrow have the potential to radically change the way healthcare is delivered.

From Voice to Data Networks and the Global Internet

For most of the past century, telecommunication was characterized by the emergence of special-purpose networks. First came the telegraph, which used a series of dots and dashes to communicate. Then came the voice network, which for most of the twentieth century was the truly global network. It consisted of end devices—telephones—that were attached by wire to a central office switch. Telephone systems were owned and operated by telephone companies. The voice network was engineered to transport voice conversations. Then came radio networks, which eliminated the need to run wire, made it possible to broadcast information to the masses, and made it possible to communicate with an ambulance rushing a patient to a hospital. Radio networks were then followed by television broadcast networks, which added the dimension of moving images to sound transmission. These networks had television sets as end devices connected to a cable head end. In the last third of the twentieth century, data networks emerged. Some were public, and some were private. They were controlled by enterprises, academic institutions, governments, and common carriers, and these networks transported data. Finally, cellular networks appeared. They made it possible for subscribers to place a voice call to anybody, anywhere and anytime, and then to check their e-mail on handheld devices such as the iPhone. Each of these networks had a specific function, but they presented a challenge to the providers of those networks in that they were independent networks, created especially for the traffic they carried and costly to manage on an individual basis.

The holy grail of the telecommunications industry has been the integration of these different networks into one. This has been attempted a number of times in the context of new technologies such as the Integrated Services Digital Network (ISDN) in the 1980s and then the Broadband Integrated Services Digital Network (BISDN) in the early 1990s; neither succeeded in totality. But then the Internet emerged to become the global network. Technological advances in the last 20 years have made it possible to carry data, voice, and video traffic over the Internet and over networks based on Internet technologies. It looks like the Internet will be the single network that carries it all.

Today different networks exist in the typical hospital setting: voice networks, pager networks, Wi-Fi networks, hardwired local area networks (LANs), ambulance radio networks, Bluetooth body monitoring networks, the Internet, and cellular networks. Each network has to be considered individually when it comes to planning, implementing, and operating, and these networks have to interoperate, which is sometimes a technical challenge. Healthcare will benefit greatly when the business needs that these separate networks fulfill can be accomplished using the Internet.

A single chapter cannot do the topic of data networks justice. However, since convergence will one day mean that Internet-type networks will carry all types of traffic (data, voice, and image) and interconnect all types of devices, then the focus of this chapter on Internet-type networks will give you the fundamentals you need to understand communications in the healthcare setting.

Data Communications Concepts

This section deals with the fundamental communications concepts that are key to understanding why healthcare networks are built the way they are and how they work.

Connectivity: The Geometrical Nature of Networks

Data networks make it possible for people or machines to communicate with each other, and these networks do it in the most efficient way possible. This efficiency is achieved by using technology and by making intelligent trade-offs.

Figure 8-1 shows how the number of connections increases as the number of endpoints of a network grows. The relationship is geometric ($\sim n^2/2$). What this tells you is that it takes a lot of connections to make sure that many people or things can talk to each other in a network. And if you think about it, the maximum number of simultaneous conversations that you can have is $n/2$. (If you have an odd number of end points, then it is $(n - 1)/2$, which means in the case of an even number of connections that $n^2/2 - n$ connections are dormant.) If you were to use copper wires to connect these endpoints, you would be wasting a lot of copper, and that was what happened in the early days of telephony until innovations such as the switchboard and telephone switch were invented.

Figure 8-2 shows what happens when humans apply technology. The many connections are replaced with N connections into a box or piece of technology that magically ensures each end node can talk to any other end node. At one point in time, in voice networks, the stuff in the box was a set of relays and gears that connected one telephone to another, and the box was called a *mechanical central office switch*. Today the stuff is a special-purpose computer built of silicon chips running a software program called a *router*, or *switch*, that routes messages from one end node to another or to a network of these devices, also called the Internet, that routes messages globally. The efficiency that the technology in the box provides is traded off against the possibility that if too many messages are being sent through this box or combinations of boxes, some of them will

Figure 8-1
The connectivity problem

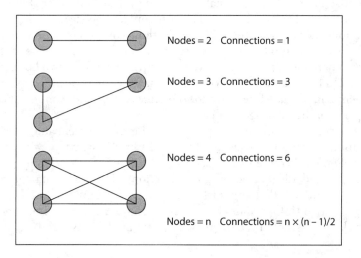

Nodes = 2   Connections = 1

Nodes = 3   Connections = 3

Nodes = 4   Connections = 6

Nodes = n   Connections = n × (n − 1)/2

Figure 8-2
Technology
applied to the
connectivity
problem

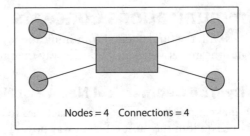

Nodes = 4   Connections = 4

be dropped; thus, the system has limited capacity, and that limited capacity is usually statistical in nature.

Exercise 8-1: Plotting Connectivity

Plot the equation n × (n − 1)/2 in a spreadsheet to see how the number of connections increases and compare the two approaches.

1. In column A of the spreadsheet, put the numbers 1–25.

2. In column B, put the equation n × (n − 1)/2.

3. In column C, put the equation n/2. Chart these to see the relationship. You can either ignore the odd numbers or use the equation (n − 1)/2.

Communication Models

Data networks originated as the need for computers to exchange information arose. In the case of the early Internet, universities needed to interconnect their computers to share research data. In the case of private data networks built by corporations and health-care organizations in the latter part of the past century, these organizations needed a way to interconnect computers and users to computers supplied to them by computer manufacturers such as International Business Machines (IBM) and Digital Equipment Corporation (DEC). These computer manufacturers developed their own data network technologies and sold them alongside their computers. The problem occurred when information had to be shared across two or more data networks that were based on different computer manufacturers' technology. For example, two hospitals, each having data networks based on different computer manufacturers' technology, needing to exchange patient data would either have to somehow custom interconnect their networks or have to perform the exchange manually.

The computer community recognized this as a problem and developed two models of computer communications to solve it: the Open Systems Interconnect (OSI) seven-layer model (also called the *OSI stack*) and the Internet five-layer model. Both models define a set of standards that describe the functions of modern data communication systems. The OSI model, though widely accepted as a product of the International Standards Organization (ISO) standardization process, was never fully implemented because of the popular emergence of the Internet. The OSI model is used today in a theoretical way and

Figure 8-3
Comparison of
OSI and Internet
communications
models

OSI Layer	Internet Layer
Application	Application
Presentation	
Session	
Transport	Transport
Network	Network
Data Link	Data Link
Physical	Physical

is part of jargon used by network professionals. The Internet model is implemented by the global Internet and by networks based on Internet technologies.[1] Figure 8-3 shows the two models side by side.

In both models, data in digital form (binary 1s and 0s) sent from an application residing in a transmitting device is passed down from the topmost layer—the application layer, which is the layer that interacts with a human—and is then encapsulated with control information from the layer below it until it reaches the physical layer where the binary 1s and 0s are turned into a physical representation—a pulse of light or electricity. Other than the physical layer, the functions of the other six layers are implemented in software. This process is then performed in reverse in a receiving device until it gets to the human at the application layer at the other end. In the model, the layer below performs a service to the layer above it. Each layer in the transmitter is said to have a virtual connection with each layer in the receiver, other than the physical layer, which has a physical connection. What follows is a brief description of each layer.

Physical Layer

Layer 1, or the physical layer, is responsible for converting the logical 1s and 0s coming from layer 2 into some type of physical signal such as a burst of electrons (voltages) or photons (light pulses).

Data Link Layer

Layer 2, or the data link layer, is responsible for controlling when a device should transmit (also known as *media access*), delimiting the message boundaries of the continuous string of 1s and 0s coming from layer 1 into packets, and ensuring that the transmission is error free by detecting and sometimes correcting errors.

Network Layer

Layer 3, or the network layer, is responsible for routing messages along the best route possible by building routing tables and assigning network addresses to devices attached to the network.

Transport Layer

Layer 4, or the transport layer, is responsible for error checking; flow control; sequencing packets; establishing, maintaining, and terminating conversations; and packetizing larger messages into smaller messages.

Session Layer

Layer 5, or the session layer, is responsible for initiating, managing, and terminating a communication session; initiating any adjunct services such as logging onto devices, file transfer, or security; and recovering from transport layer interruptions.

Presentation Layer

Layer 6, or the presentation layer, is responsible for displaying, formatting, and editing inputs and outputs (from the application layer). This layer makes it possible to display the same data on different terminal types. This layer may also be responsible for encryption.

Application Layer

Layer 7, or the application layer, is the interface between the human using the network and the network. A suite of applications exist at this layer such as HTTP (also called the Web), e-mail, the Domain Name System (DNS), and File Transfer Protocol (FTP).

Communications Protocols

Communications protocols define messages, message formats, and the rules for exchanging those messages between computers and communication devices. Imagine two computers communicating with each other, and associated with each computer is the seven-layer OSI model. As mentioned, each layer in one computer communicates virtually with each layer in the other computer according to a communications protocol. Transmission control protocol/Internet protocol (TCP/IP) is the prime example of a communication protocol for modern computer and communication devices. It is the fundamental communication protocol of the Internet. It can also be used as a protocol in a private network such as an intranet.

Figure 8-4 shows the message format of a generic protocol data unit (PDU). A PDU is associated with a communications protocol. The information in the PDU is represented

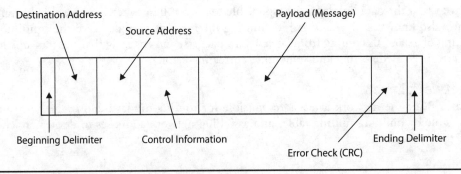

Figure 8-4   Generic PDU

by 1s and 0s. Other than the physical layer, each layer in the OSI model has a PDU associated with it.

NOTE   Network professionals commonly call the data link PDU a *frame* and the network PDU a *packet*.

Each portion of the PDU is called a *field* and has a specific role. The two delimiters at each end of the PDU tell the system where the PDU starts and stops. Delimiters are analogous to capital letters and periods in a sentence. The destination address tells the system where the PDU is going, and the source address tells the system where the PDU has come from. The control information field carries in it codes that tell the system what to do. For example, one of those codes could signify that a transmitter wants to start a conversation with a receiver in a similar way that the alert tone on a cellular phone alerts a caller to an incoming call. The payload carries the message that is being transmitted. In the OSI model, payload is usually the PDU from the layer above it. Examples of the types of messages that could be transmitted in the payload at the application layer in a healthcare setting include information about a patient's medication, a transmission of a medical image, or real-time data coming from a patient-monitoring device such as a heart rate monitor. The payload could also contain HL7 information as described later in this chapter. Finally, the error check field is a type of quality control on the frame. The transmitter performs an algorithm that mathematically relates the information in the transmitted PDU to the error check field. The receiver performs that algorithm on the received PDU and then checks to see whether the value it calculated is the same as that sent in the error check field. If it is not, the same PDU is said to be in error, and some type of error correction is invoked such as retransmitting the PDU. A cyclic redundancy check (CRC), the specific error check depicted in Figure 8-4, is one such type of error check, whereby PDU has a short check value attached that is checked by the receiving system.

Data and Signals

In computer systems, information and data are represented as 1s and 0s; this is a logical representation. This is also true of all the layers of the OSI model except for the physical layer. At the physical layer, the logical 1s and 0s become something that is real or physical, such as a burst of electrons or photons. The presence or absence of these bursts can signify a 1 or a 0. A chart of the amplitude or power of these bursts over time is referred to as a *signal*.

Figure 8-5 shows two signal types. The first is a sine wave, and the second is a pulse signal; 1s and 0s can be encoded in sine waves by varying amplitude, frequency, and phase. In pulse signals, a 1 can be represented by the presence or absence of a pulse.

Information is transmitted through a network when these signals representing 1s and 0s travel through wires, fibers, and by radio propagation; each is considered a different transmission media. Each type of media has its own physical characteristics that affect those signals. Two such key characteristics are susceptibility to noise and maximum capacity, also called *bandwidth*.

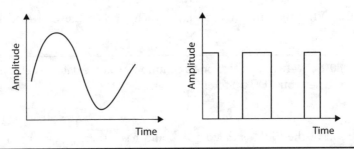

Figure 8-5 Examples of signals

Susceptibility to noise relates to how easily external signals not associated with the transmitted signal can get induced into the media and thus distort the transmitted signal. This distortion leads to errors. In the case of the pulse signal, there may be a spike of noise that causes an empty spot where there is no signal to look like a pulse. The receiver then interprets that noise burst as a 1, which is not what the receiver sent and is therefore an error. Maximum capacity relates to how much information transmission media can carry. For example, fiber-optic media can carry much more information than can copper media, and a coaxial cable can carry more information than a 26-gauge telephone cable.

Digitization

Digitization is the process of representing something like an image or sound using discrete samples and then being able to reconstruct it with a certain level of fidelity. Sampling of music and then storing those samples as binary digits on a plastic disc is how music is distributed using CDs. A similar thing is done with medical imaging associated with picture archival and communication systems. Binary digits or 1s and 0s are the same things that data networks transport. Given that images and voice signals can be sampled, those samples can be carried by data networks. This is how the Internet will become the single network carrying data, voice, and video traffic.

Throughput

A measure of how much data can be moved through a network successfully is called *throughput*. Throughput is measured in bits per second (bps). Usually people will use the term *bandwidth* and state it in terms of bits per second. In data networks, throughput can be affected by many things; one of those is the capacity of the transmission medium that places an upper limit on throughput. Another is the latency through the network. Latency is often the result of how digital signals are transmitted and processed by hardware and software in devices that make up the network. For example, as a packet encounters a router in its path across the network, it is read into the receive buffer of a router, analyzed, and put out onto the transmit buffer of that router. Every time this happens, a small delay is added to the packet's journey. For a given amount of information transmitted, the longer it takes to transmit that information because of all these delays, the lower the throughput.

Addressing in Data Networks

If one device, the transmitter, wants to send information to another device, the receiver, it must know where to send that information. That means the receiver must have some type of identifier that distinguishes it from other, possibly similar receivers on the network. That identifier is usually called an *address*. In TCP/IP networks there are four types of addresses to consider.

MAC Addresses

Media Access Control (MAC) addresses exist at the data link layer. They are usually depicted as six groups of two hexadecimal numbers and are 48 bits long; see Figure 8-6. They exist in hardware, are assigned by device manufacturers, and are therefore fixed. They are also referred to as *Ethernet addresses* since they are what appear in the source address and destination address fields of Ethernet PDUs.

IP Addresses

IP addresses exist at the network layer. They are depicted as four groups of up to three decimal numbers separated by dots and are 32 bits long; see Figure 8-6. They exist in the software configuration of a network device and are either assigned manually by an administrator or assigned through a process called Dynamic Host Configuration Protocol (DHCP). These addresses are also broken down into the network part and host part, the delineation depending on the class of address.

Currently IP version 4 addresses exist in the global Internet. IP version 6 addresses are now being introduced and should supplant IP version 4 addresses in time. IP version 6 addresses contain 128 bits and therefore have a much greater address space than their IP version 4 counterparts. The world's adoption of IP version 6 addresses will become critical because the IP version 4 address space is just about exhausted.

IP addresses are sometimes associated with subnet masks; see Figure 8-6. Subnet masks are a pattern of 1s and 0s that subdivide a range of IP addresses for routing and administrative purposes.

IP addresses are assigned to organizations by the Internet Corporation for Assigned Names and Numbers (ICANN).

IP addresses can be either dynamically assigned (i.e., each time a client logs in, a different IP address gets assigned) or static (i.e., a client has a fixed or constant IP address assigned by a network administrator). Servers using DHCP grant IP addresses to clients dynamically and for a limited time interval. DHCP is used to obtain configuration information, includ-

Figure 8-6
Sample network addresses

Address Type	Example
Data Link (Ethernet)	07-13-54-ac-76-cc
Network Layer (IP Address)	143.56.98.101
Subnet Mask	255.255.255.192
Port Address	80 (Web Browsers)
Hostname (Web)	www.somename.com

ing an IP address. Two advantages of dynamic IP addressing are that there are fewer risks for security (because a new IP address is generated for each login), and that network configuration is automatic so it does not require an administrator. However, static IP addressing can be a more reliable way to ensure secure access to files stored on an organization's network computers.

Transport Control Protocol (Layer 4) Port Addresses

Port addresses exist in layer 4 of the TCP/IP communications model. These port addresses are 16 bits long, and each port address is uniquely associated with an application. Port addresses 0 through 1023 are considered well-known ports, and the remaining port addresses are available for dynamic assignment. For example, web browsers use port address 80, and mail applications use port address 25. When an application is transmitting a message, it identifies to the TCP software which source port address it is sending from and which destination port address it is sending to. The TCP software then puts these in the source and destination fields of the layer 4 PDU it builds.[1]

Hostname

Hostname addresses exist at the application layer. They are usually depicted as a group of letters separated by dots. The letters usually form meaningful words such as www.google .com; see Figure 8-6. Hostnames reside in software in the host and also in Domain Name System servers. DNSs are databases that relate IP addresses to hostnames for the purpose of address resolution. DNSs form a domain name system; somewhat like the white pages, they relate human-friendly names to computer-understandable names, which are the addresses. ICANN manages the Internet domain system and authorizes private companies to assign domain names.

Address Resolution

Address resolution occurs at various levels when a sender is transmitting a message to a receiver. For example, when a user clicks a link in a web browser (the sender), a browser request message is sent to a web server (the receiver). That request is eventually placed into a packet at layer 3; however, that packet needs a destination IP address. That IP address is supplied by resolving that hostname through the Domain Name System to an associated IP address. That IP address is then placed in the destination field of the IP packet and sent into the network. At the other end, as that packet emerges on the LAN to which the web server (the receiver) is attached, the packet is placed in a data link frame, which needs a MAC destination address in order for it to arrive successfully. This MAC address is resolved to the IP address through the Address Resolution Protocol (ARP).

To determine which MAC address is associated with the destination IP address, the device sends a broadcast message to the LAN with the destination IP address in its payload. All the devices on the LAN receive that message, but only the device whose IP address matches replies. This reply has the MAC address of the replying device embedded in it. This MAC address is then used as the destination address for the data link frame, which transports the web request to the server.

End devices have caches that store these address resolutions temporarily. For example, a workstation will have a DNS cache and an ARP cache.

The World Wide Web as an Example of a Network Application

The World Wide Web (WWW) is one of the most popular network applications in use today and is increasingly used for transmitting healthcare data. It is an example of a client-server architecture where the client is a web browser such as Firefox and the server is a web server running a program such as Apache. The presentation and descriptive markup language that is used to generate web pages is HyperText Markup Language (HTML). The protocol used by the client to request a web page and by the server to respond to that request is HyperText Transfer Protocol (HTTP). The addressing mechanism that is used to locate a web page is called a *universal resource locator* (URL).

HTTP is a textual protocol that defines the rules and format for message exchange. For example, HTTP defines a request command that is used to request information from a server. The PDU for this command has a request line, a request header, and a request body. HTTP is an application protocol using the underlying services of TCP. When a link is clicked in a browser, it opens a TCP session with the host identified in the URL and sends that request via port 80 of the TCP PDU. The URL identifies the protocol (HTTP, FTP, or HTTPS) in use, the network location (host and port), and the path name to the data object on the server. The server then responds with an HTTP response. The PDU for a response is composed of a response status field, a response header, and the response body that contains the web page the client requested.[2]

PANs, LANs, MANs, and WANs

Data networks can be categorized according to physical extent, anywhere from centimeters to kilometers. The range of a given data network often dictates the type of underlying technology used and the design of the communications protocol that is needed. The way TCP/IP networks are designed is that the network and transport layers of TCP/IP are abstracted from the lower layers. Thus, TCP/IP rides on top of the two lowest layers and provides an end-to-end service for devices attached to the network.

PANs

Personal area networks (PANs) span the human body and the area near the human body. The communications technologies used here are typically Wi-Fi and Bluetooth, which are wireless technologies. The technology used includes network interface cards (NICs), which provide wireless interfaces for devices such as laptops, heart rate monitors, and tablets. The management of these networks usually falls to a healthcare unit in the organization whose staff members evaluate, select, purchase, deploy, and provide operational support for these devices.

LANs

Local area networks (LANs) span rooms or buildings. Wireless transmission and wired transmission are used. The communications technologies employed are typically Wi-Fi and Ethernet, also known as IEEE 802.3. The equipment includes NICs, hubs, switches, wireless access points, and file and print servers. Here again, the deployment model is usually local, with the organization's staff evaluating, selecting, purchasing, deploying, and providing operational support for these devices.

MANs

Metropolitan area networks (MANs) are on the order of city blocks and urban areas. Again, wireless and wired technologies are used. Examples for physical transport technologies include 26-gauge copper telephone wire, cable plant, short-haul fiber optic, point-to-point microwave, and cellular networks. The communications technologies include Ethernet, ADSL, LTE, and WiMAX. Small ISPs, local carriers, and regional carriers tend to provide services at this level. Organizational staff manages contracts and service levels with suppliers of these services and interconnects their managed network infrastructure (PANs and LANs) to these networks.

WANs

Wide area networks (WANS) are on the order of large cities, provinces and states, and countries. Wireless and wired technologies are used as transport. Examples of transport technologies include point-to-point long-haul microwave, long-haul fiber systems, and satellites. Communications technologies include wide-area Ethernet over fiber, wavelength division multiplexing (WDM), and legacy carrier technologies such as Asynchronous Transfer Mode (ATM), Optical Carrier (OC), and Time Division Multiplexing (TDM). Regional and national carriers operate at this level. Organizational staff manages contracts and service levels with suppliers of this service and interconnects their managed network infrastructure to these networks.

The foregoing categories of networks can create a context for the reader to think about how healthcare information is communicated in the healthcare system. For example, monitoring devices on a patient can be continuously sending data via a PAN that connects to a device in the LAN. As the patient moves through a hospital, those monitoring devices connect and reconnect to various LANs that exist in that hospital. The application that analyzes that data may be running on a server located across the city from the hospital, and thus the data are gathered and then sent via a MAN to that server to be processed. The analysis of that real-time patient data may trigger a need for the patient to undergo a diagnosis by a specialist who is located in another city. That specialist and the patient would use a WAN to set up and use a video-conferencing system to perform that diagnosis.

How a Network Works

This section will describe how a typical TCP/IP network works. It will discuss application and network architectures and describe the components used to implement those architectures and the protocols used. It will also describe two examples of data transfer: one device communicating with another device on the same LAN and one device communicating with another device on another LAN across a WAN.[1]

Application Architectures

Two fundamental application architectures exist on a network: peer to peer and client server. In a peer-to-peer architecture, all devices on a network are equal and can perform the same function; there is no master. A peer-to-peer model works well when there are a limited number of users and has the advantage of being simple but the disadvantage of not being scalable. Also, the traffic pattern on peer-to-peer networks is random because any device may be talking to any other device. An example of a peer-to-peer application is instant messaging (IM). The first example presented in this section (see Figure 8-7) will follow the data flow between two workstations (W1 and W2) exchanging an IM message on LAN1.

In client-server architecture, there are many clients and one server. That server performs a set of centralized functions for those clients. An example of client-server architecture is the Web. A web server has multiple web browsers, or clients, sending requests to it for web pages. It acts like a file server in that it is a central store of web pages. The client and server do not need to be on the same LAN; they just need to be connected to the network, as shown in Figure 8-7. A client-server model has the advantage of being able to scale and provide greater control but the disadvantage of unnecessary overhead for small scale. The second example presented in this section (also shown in Figure 8-7) will follow the data flow from a web browser to a web server. Here workstation W1, which is the client and is running a web browser, sends HTTP requests to server S2, the server, through LAN1 and across the WAN and then through to LAN2.

Network Architectures and Implementations

Network architectures vary according to the needs of the network. Networks used for healthcare purposes are different from networks used for business purposes. The architecture associated with Figure 8-7 is a simplified version of a WAN architecture, which is one that you may find in a healthcare setting.

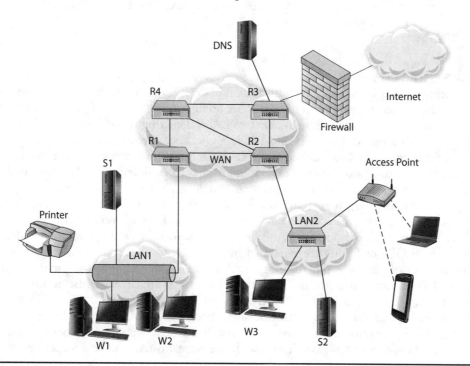

Figure 8-7   How a network works

Wide Area Network

The network in Figure 8-7 shows an implementation of a typical network architecture. There is a WAN that interconnects two LANs (LAN1 and LAN2) and then interconnects both to the Internet. A MAN or backbone network could serve the same function as the WAN in the diagram except that it would have a different geographic scope and use different technology. The WAN in Figure 8-7 consists of routers interconnected with communication circuits. Routers move messages (PDUs) according to a set of instructions that each has, called a *routing table*. Routing tables are dynamically built using routing protocols. These routing protocols are software programs that optimize the path that messages take by analyzing changes occurring in the network such as addition or deletion of networks or circuits, the utilization of circuits, and latency across circuits. Common routing protocols include Routing Internet Protocol (RIP) and Open Shortest Path First (OSPF). Routers are said to implement layers 1 to 3 of the OSI stack.

There are two more connections pictured in Figure 8-7, one to the Internet and one to a domain name server. Most modern networks connect to the Internet, and they usually do this using a special routing protocol called Border Gateway Protocol, whose job it is to make the rest of the Internet aware of the existence of the network by advertising its IP addresses. A firewall is also positioned between the Internet and the network. The firewall protects the network by filtering out unwanted traffic. The job of the domain name server is to resolve hostnames to IP addresses for this network.

 NOTE Domain name servers are part of a globally interconnected hierarchical network that stores and distributes all hostname and IP address pairs.

Local Area Network

The purpose of a LAN is to interconnect a set of devices that are within physical proximity. A LAN makes it possible for users to share resources such as print, file, and fax servers. Attached to the WAN in Figure 8-7 are two LANs depicting two different architectures. LAN1 shows a bus architecture, and LAN2 shows a star architecture. These are physical architectures. The bus architecture of LAN1 is rarely used today. This architecture is implemented using a single coax cable that attaches to each device. LAN2, the physical star, where wires spread out from a central switch to all devices, is the way most LAN topologies are implemented today. Also attached to router R2, via the central switch, is a wireless access point, which shows how a wireless network could overlay a wired network.

From a network perspective, LANs are seen as broadcast domains where broadcasts of layer 2 PDUs or frames are generated by one device wanting to communicate with another device on the LAN. Although LAN1 and LAN2 differ at the physical layer, they function similarly at the data link layer. Broadcasts are characteristic of most LAN protocols and in particular of the widely adopted Ethernet protocol (802.3), which uses Carrier Sense Multiple Access with Collision Detection (CSMA/CD). In Ethernet, several devices are connected to a common infrastructure such as a shared coaxial cable or the backplane of a hub or switch. If one device wants to transmit to another device, it

PART II

enters the MAC address of that device in a frame and then transmits that frame bit by bit onto the communications medium. All devices receive that broadcast frame, but only the device to which it is addressed recognizes it and then "reads" it in; other devices on the LAN ignore the broadcast. Because the transmitter is transmitting the frame, it also listens for any corrupted transmissions. If it detects one, it stops its own transmission and assumes another transmitter tried to transmit at the same time, which caused the collision. If there are no collisions, the receiver takes the frame and passes it up the OSI stack until it gets to the application layer where the message is delivered to the application. If there is a collision, each device that was trying to transmit simultaneously waits a different amount of time, the duration of which is determined randomly, and then retries its transmission.

Attachments to the LAN include end devices such as workstations, printers, servers, hubs, switches, and routers. To participate in the LAN, each device needs a network interface card and, in the case of a wired LAN, a cable attaching it to a hub or switch. End devices such as workstations and servers implement the complete OSI stack. They also run application layer software, which in the example is instant messaging client software. Alternatively, a user at W1 may be sending messages to a web server such as the server S2 in LAN2. Both these are done at the application layer. Those messages, however, are sent down the stack to each layer and to the physical layer where pulses of electricity or light emanate from the interface across the network, and then the inverse process occurs at W2 or at the server. In contrast, devices such as routers are said to communicate at the bottom three layers of the OSI stack. For example, W3 and the server will be communicating to the switch at layer 2 and below.

LANs provide the same function in a healthcare setting except in addition to workstations, servers, and printers, there could be health-specific devices, such as patient monitors, infusion pumps, and ventilators, attached to the LAN. Note that healthcare LANs need to be more robust and secure than most other types of LANs. They must be robust because missing patient data, especially real-time monitoring data, can affect patient safety. They must be secure because of the privacy requirements associated with patient data.[3]

 TIP A service-level agreement (SLA) is a contract between an Information Technology (IT) service provider and a customer (for example, a hospital) that specifies what services the IT provider will furnish and almost always contains specific measures of the services to be provided. SLAs are commonly used for network service providers or ISPs, and contain such measures as percentage of time services will be available and how many simultaneous users can be served. Information Services (IS) departments in healthcare and other industries have adapted the SLA idea for internal, department-to-department agreements. An internal SLA specifies what the IS department's responsibilities are, primarily around implementing, maintaining, and communicating the status of the IT services. In an internal SLA, the receiving department is also responsible for notifying the IS department (in a manner that is timely, complete, and accurate) of service failures or issues, and then assisting the IS department in the resolution of these failures or issues.

Device Configuration

Before an end device can start communicating, it must be configured. This configuration can happen either manually or automatically. The manual method involves having a network administrator configure the device or provide information for the user to do so. The automatic method involves using the Dynamic Host Configuration Protocol (DHCP). In either case, the following minimal information is configured on an end device: its IP address, a subnet mask, the IP address of its DNS server, and the IP address of the LAN gateway. In Figure 8-7, routers R1 and R2 are also called *gateway routers* because they are the gateway out of the LAN onto the bigger network. The address of the DNS server is needed to decode the hostname into an IP address. The subnet mask is used by the device to discern whether the destination address of a PDU it is sending resides on the local LAN. If not, then the PDU is forwarded to the gateway. The combination of IP address and subnet makes it possible for the device to determine whether it should be sending information to the gateway on the LAN for which it has the IP address.

NOTE The end device already knows its MAC address because it is assigned by the equipment manufacturer and exists in hardware.

Device Configuration in an End-to-End Network

The application layers of two devices that are communicating across a network are abstracted from that network. The complexity of the underlying network is hidden from them. The sending application and device usually determine the location of the destination application and device based on resolving a hostname to an IP address. Knowing that IP address and the port to which the application wants to connect (destination port address), the sending device software sets up a circuit that connects it virtually to the destination device. Then the reverse occurs, and a bidirectional communication channel is established between the two applications at both ends of the network. Neither device knows there may be LANs, WANs, switches, and routers in the path. Furthermore, TCP ensures a reliable transmission by having the transmitter resend PDUs that the receiver detects are in error. This mode of communication is also known as *connection-oriented communications*.

NOTE You should understand that this is a highly simplified explanation of the mechanism of transmission and error recovery; much detail has been omitted.

Ping is a useful network administration utility that can be used to check whether a host can be reached on an Internet Protocol (IP) network. It can also be used to assess how long it takes for messages to be sent from an originating host computer to a computer receiving the messages. Another useful TCP/IP utility is traceroute (known as tracert in Windows), a command-line tool that can be used to find the route of packets of information moving through a network to reach a host. By tracing the path of messages, traceroute/tracert can be used to test and troubleshoot problems in networking.

Use Case 8-1: A Device Communicating with Another Device on the Same LAN

In this example, device W1 will be sending an instant message to device W2 (see Figure 8-7). Let's assume that W1 has already resolved W2's IP address through a previous DNS request. (Note that W1 would have used the DNS's IP address that is stored in its configuration to reach the DNS to resolve W2's IP address.) Upon creation of the message by the user, the IM software tells the TCP layer which destination port address to use. The destination port field, source port field, and other fields of the TCP PDU, including the payload where the IM message resides, are filled in. The TCP PDU is then moved to the network layer where it is encapsulated with layer 3 information such as W2's IP address as the destination address and W1's IP address as the source address. Layer 3 checks the destination address against the gateway address and the subnet mask and determines that the IP address is on LAN1. This layer 3 PDU is then handed down to layer 2 and encapsulated with layer 2 information. The software searches for W2's IP address in its ARP cache; if it finds it, it places W2's MAC address in the destination field. If not, it does an ARP request as described in the previous section and places W2's MAC address in the destination field. Finally, it places its own MAC address in the source field.

The data link then broadcasts the layer 2 PDU to all devices attached to the LAN and, assuming there is no collision, W2's layer 2 software recognizes its MAC address and stores W1's PDU in its input buffer. The other devices on the LAN disregard this PDU since the destination MAC address does not match their MAC address. W2's data link then discards the layer 2 information and sends the layer 3 PDU up to the network layer. Similarly, W2's layer 3 software passes the layer 4 PDU up to layer 4. Layer 4 checks to see whether there were any errors and, if not, inspects the destination port address and passes the payload to the IM software, which passes it onto the user at the application layer.

Use Case 8-2: A Device Communicating with Another Device on Another LAN Across a WAN

In this example, W1 will be sending an HTTP request to the web server S2 on LAN2 (see Figure 8-7). The user on W1 enters a URL with S2's domain name in it. Let's assume W1 has made a similar HTTP request previously and holds S2's hostname and IP address in its DNS cache. The HTTP request is formed and sent to W1's layer 4 with the destination port of 80. The layer 4 PDU is formed and placed in the layer 3 PDU's payload along with S2's IP address as the destination address. Layer 3 then uses the subnet mask to compare the PDU's destination address with

(continued)

the gateway IP address stored in its configuration. It determines that the PDU's destination address is not on the local LAN. Knowing this, the software places the PDU in a layer 2 frame, which has the gateway's (R1) MAC address set as the destination address. (If W1 didn't have the gateway MAC address in its cache, it would issue an ARP request to determine it.) W1's data link layer then transmits the layer 2 PDU, which finds its way to the gateway router R1.

The software in R1 removes the layer 3 PDU from the layer 2 PDU payload and discards the rest of the layer 2 PDU. Whereas layer 2 is responsible for ensuring that one device can communicate to another device on a LAN, layer 3 is responsible for determining the best path a given PDU will take to traverse the network. Referring to Figure 8-7, a PDU starting out on R1 can take any number of paths to get to LAN2: R1-R4-R3-R2, R1-R2, or R1-R4-R2. Unlike what happens at layer 2, routers do not broadcast PDUs at layer 3; they route PDUs, and they do this based on information they have stored in routing tables. Thus, R1 processes the layer 3 PDU by inspecting its destination IP address, matching it with a routing table entry, and determining which of the many paths it should take.

When that determination is made, R1 puts the layer 3 PDU back in a layer 2 PDU payload and sends it on one of the two ports associated with the three paths leaving R1. Let's assume that path R1-R2 is the path chosen. The PDU then moves along the path from R1 to R2, which could be a WAN circuit such as a fiber-optic channel. It arrives at R2, and R2 repeats the process of discarding the layer 2 information and looking at the destination address of the PDU. According to its routing table, the destination address is on the router port associated with LAN2.

Router R2 then creates a layer 2 PDU with a destination MAC address equal to that of S2's MAC address based on an ARP table lookup using the IP address in the PDU. The layer 3 PDU is placed into the payload of the layer 2 PDU. The layer 2 PDU is then broadcast on LAN2 and received by S2 since it is addressed to S2. S2 then moves the PDU up to the application layer where the web server responds.

 NOTE The network layer packet or layer 3 PDU that is created at the source is never modified as it moves across the network. In contrast, layer 2 PDUs are created and destroyed.

Exercise 8-2: Checking Configuration Information

Query your device for configuration information and relate it to the previous section.

1. If you are running a Windows operating system, open the Command Prompt window (press WINDOWS KEY-R, type **cmd**, and press ENTER) and enter the command **IPCONFIG /ALL** at the command prompt.

2. Look at the information displayed and pick out the configuration information for your workstation.

3. What are its IP address, subnet mask, gateway address, MAC address, and DNS address? Some clients have other interface information; what is it?

TIP Many small medical office practices still connect to the Internet via an Internet modem. Some Internet modems connect via an Ethernet network cable, but most now connect via Universal Serial Bus (USB). The Internet modem cable plugs into a router via the WAN or Internet jack. After connecting the cable, the HIT technician should turn the modem off and back on to allow the router to recognize it.

Wireless Networks

The term *wireless networks* can be used in many contexts. For example, you could consider a satellite network a wireless network. However, this chapter is about data networks in healthcare and the wireless networks that are dramatically changing how healthcare is done and that give patients, nurses, and doctors the ability to move around in the work setting. These are Bluetooth, Wi-Fi, and cellular networks. Since the healthcare IT practitioner will likely manage Wi-Fi networks, the focus of this chapter will be primarily on Wi-Fi networks.

The first thing to consider about wireless networks such as Wi-Fi is that they use the electromagnetic spectrum (radio waves) as a medium of transmission, and this medium places limitations on the bandwidth available for transmission. In a given space and at a given frequency band, only one signal can be transmitted; two would interfere with each other. Whereas running these signals in separate cables that are properly shielded will not lead to these signals interfering with each other, radio spectrum is shared, limited, and subject to interference.

The second thing to consider about wireless networks is that they are wireless; they have no cable, there are no connectors, and there are no ports to attach to. That means a user doesn't have to plug into anything or call anybody to provision a port on a network for them; they can connect to the network just by turning their wireless interface card on. This makes it possible for clinicians, doctors, and nurses to move from patient to patient, or from room to room, maintaining a connection with the network. A network can be created in a building almost instantaneously without needing to run cables. But this also means anybody else can connect to the wireless network as well, and if the wireless network extends to the parking lot of the hospital, they don't even have to gain access to the building. Anybody with an air interface can listen to the radio transmission and read what is being transmitted in plain text. This is especially critical in the healthcare setting where the types of data being transported include primarily patient data, care data, diagnosis data, and treatment data. These types of data have to be kept private. For this reason, wireless networks have to be secured using various techniques such as encrypted transmission.[3]

The third thing to consider about wireless networks is that in the healthcare setting their utility is very evident. They make it possible for doctors to be more productive.

For example, when visiting multiple patients on their rounds, doctors have access to clinical information systems; they don't have to head back and forth to some tethered terminal to get their records. And when a doctor leaves the hospital and realizes she forgot to do something like order pharmaceuticals for a patient, she can pull over in her car, turn on her smartphone, and place that order remotely.[3]

Wireless Applications and Issues in a Healthcare Setting

Wireless networks enable a number of healthcare applications, including biomedical devices, voice communications, real-time location-based services, guest access, and clinical access. Each of these applications provides benefits to the healthcare systems; however, some create new considerations.

Patients who need to use monitoring devices are no longer tethered by cables; instead, these devices communicate wirelessly and thus enable those patients to be mobile. Patients can have a heart monitor put on in the hospital and then go home, all while having their hearts continuously monitored. The foregoing is a benefit for the patient; however, a new concern is introduced. Unlike the cable, where the possibility of having an interruption in the transmission of data is unlikely, a patient leaving a hospital and going home will traverse any number of networks: an 802.11 network in the hospital, a cellular network in the car, and then a Wi-Fi network attached to the Internet at home. As handoffs to each of the different networks occur, the biomedical system has to deal with possible data interruptions and synchronization problems.[3]

Wireless technologies increase health practitioner productivity by enhancing voice communications. They make it possible to immediately contact a doctor through the use of cellular phones or voice-enabled smartphones. They determine the availability of staff through presence technology. They facilitate collaboration through conferencing technologies. However, wireless technologies, which are in the unlicensed band, are susceptible to interference and need to coexist seamlessly with legacy systems such as high-quality voice and nurse call systems.

Wireless technologies enable real-time location services for hospitals. By using 802.11-configured devices or RFID tags, hospitals can locate things such as lost heart rate monitors or staff members who are urgently needed and not responding to their cellular phones.[3]

Guest access (the provision of Internet connectivity to patients or to a patient's associates) makes it possible to connect at a time when it is especially critical to have access to the Internet. Guest access also brings with it a number of considerations: authentication, resource control, logging, and control of access infrastructure.

WLAN Topology

Figure 8-8 shows the typical topology of a WLAN. It is similar to a typical LAN topology except the transmission medium is radio spectrum. It consists of an access point (AP), a radio spectrum, and the wireless NICs that are terminated in end devices. The AP functions as a repeater and a distribution point connecting the end devices via radio spectrum to the wired network. As a repeater, the AP repeats frames sent by end devices to their

Figure 8-8
WLAN network

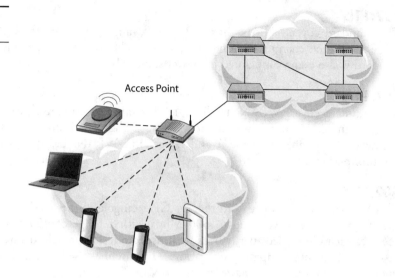

destination. Most of the time, the traffic pattern has a star shape moving from the end device through the AP onto the wired network to some destination. Distribution is done via antennas that are attached to the AP. The two basic types of Wi-Fi antenna are omni-directional and directional. An omnidirectional antenna has a donut-like radiation pattern. A directional antenna's radiation pattern is focused in one direction. With the right combination of antennas on multiple APs, a consistent coverage pattern can be arranged.[1]

802.11 Standards

The 802.11 set of standards define how wireless LANs are to be implemented, their modulation techniques, and their protocols. These standards work in the 2.5 GHz band and in the 5 GHz band (which is also called the instrument, scientific, and medical [ISM] band and is an unlicensed band in most countries). Within each band are channels that make it possible to isolate the transmission of multiple APs in the same space. The 2.4 GHz band is shared with devices such as microwave ovens, cordless telephones, and Bluetooth, and therefore 802.11b and 802.11g devices that operate in the 2.4 GHz band suffer from interference. These standards use direct-sequence spread spectrum (DSSS) and orthogonal frequency-division multiplexing (OFDM) modulation techniques. The media access control mechanism is Carrier Sense Multiple Access with Collision Avoidance (CSMA/CA). Here, rather than sending out a message and sensing if a collision occurred, the transmitter waits for a signal from the AP that it is clear to send a signal before it sends the message.[4]

802.11a

This standard covers wireless WLANs in the 5 GHz range. There are eight channels in this frequency range, and each channel runs at 54 Mbps. NICs can be located a maximum of 300 feet from the AP. This is a legacy standard and is being supplanted by newer standards.

802.11b

This standard covers WLANs in the 2.4 GHz range. There are three channels in this range, with each channel running at 11 Mbps. The maximum range is 450 feet. This standard is also being supplanted by newer standards.

802.11g

This standard covers WLANs in the 2.4 GHz range. There are three channels in this range, with each channel running at 54 Mbps. The maximum range is 300 feet. It is backward compatible with the A and B versions. WLANs based on this standard are commonplace today.

802.11n

This standard covers WLANs in the 2.4 GHz range and the 5 GHz range. The speed the WLAN can achieve is up to 600 Mbps with a range of 450 feet. This standard achieves such high speeds partly because it uses a novel approach to antenna design that takes advantage of multipath propagation. The antennas used in this standard are called *multiple-input multiple-output antennas* (MIMO).

 TIP Wireless site surveys are one approach to use when planning and designing a wireless network. Required wireless coverage ranges, data rates, network capacity, and other factors are taken into account during a site visit. Testing for RF interference, analysis of building floor plans, and other techniques lead to optimum placement of wireless access points.

Security

Unlike wired networks where network access is physical (you need to plug a cable into a port and that port is in a room that has a door that may be locked), wireless networks can be accessed by anyone who is within range of the wireless signal. Therefore, wireless networks need to be secured, especially if they happen to be carrying sensitive patient data. There are different ways of securing wireless networks, and some are more or less secure than others.

Not broadcasting the service set identifier (SSID) is a less secure way of securing a wireless network. To get on the network, the user needs to know the SSID. When the user enters it, upon getting prompted by the system, the user sends it to the AP. What makes it less secure is that the SSID is stored in plain text, which means anybody sniffing the WLAN can get the SSID. Another less secure way of securing the LAN is MAC filtering. When MAC filtering is used, only a specified set of MAC addresses are given access to the network. The reason it is less secure is that a hacker sniffing frames on a wireless network can read a MAC address and then use that MAC address to gain entry into the network.

Wired Equivalent Privacy (WEP) was the original security mechanism associated with 802.11. It required the user to manually enter a key, which would be used to encrypt transmitted data. Manual key entry limits scale and exposes WLANs to security breaches (keys being stored on sticky notes). Thus, WEP was replaced by Wi-Fi Protected Access (WPA) and then WPA2 (also known as 802.11i). 802.11i uses the Advanced Encryption Standard (AES) and is considered a more secure way of securing wireless LANs.[4, 5]

Other security measures that can be considered for healthcare networks include the following:[3, 5]

- Antenna and signal gain design that limits the WLAN footprint to the true usage perimeter.
- Policies preventing attachment of wireless devices to the enterprise network.
- Avoiding meaningful names for the WLAN SSID since this provides readily accessible information to hackers.
- Implementing intrusion detection methods on the WLAN. For example, the issuance of multiple incorrect SSID frames could trigger an event.
- Recognizing that the WLAN will always be a less secure network and then treating it as such by isolating it from the core network and placing appropriate safeguards, such as firewalls, between it and the core network.

Bluetooth

Also known as 802.15, Bluetooth covers data exchange over very short distances in the ISM band (2.4 GHz to 2.48 GHz). It supports fixed and mobile devices and is used in PANs. Bluetooth uses a modulation scheme called *frequency-hopping spread spectrum* (FHSS). Depending on which version of Bluetooth is being used, the data rate varies from 1 Mbps to 3 Mbps. The protocol used is a master-slave protocol where a master can control up to seven slaves. Examples of devices that use Bluetooth are laptops, wireless phones, iPhones, and GPS. Bluetooth can be used to transmit short-range health sensor data.[1]

WAP, WML, and HTML5

Wireless Application Protocol (WAP) is a standard that describes how browsers and servers communicate with each other over a wireless mobile network and defines an environment for application development. This standard includes a layered architecture similar to the OSI stack where the bottom layer, Wireless Datagram Protocol (WDP), is an adaptation layer to different wireless network technologies. The four layers above the WDP layer are then consistent for all communication devices and provide for interoperability. Figure 8-9 shows these layers. The Wireless Session Protocol (WSP) is analogous to a stripped-down version of HTTP. The Wireless Application Environment (WAE) originally included the Wireless Markup Language (WML), again analogous to HTML and based on Extensible Markup Language (XML).[6]

HTML5, the newest version of the Web's markup language, has as some of its design objectives to support the development of cross-platform mobile applications, to run in low-power and small form factor devices such as iPhones and iPads, and to support multimedia applications found on these devices.

PART II

Figure 8-9
WAP protocol
suite[6]

WAE	Wireless Application Environment
WSP	Wireless Session Protocol
WTP	Wireless Transport Protocol
WTLS	Wireless Transport Layer Security
WDP	Wireless Datagram Protocol
Wireless Data Network Infrastructure	

Cellular

Cellular networks provide users with the ultimate ability to be untethered anywhere, and it is possible that one day they will become the ultimate access method for telecommunications. Long Term Evolution (LTE) is the newest cellular network standard and has gained global acceptance. The designers of LTE had the following objectives in mind: take advantage of emergent digital signal processing techniques and modulation techniques, and use an IP transport fabric. The upload peak rate of LTE is approximately 75 Mbps, and the download peak rate is 300 Mbps. The multiplexing techniques used are frequency division duplexing and time division duplexing. Voice can be carried on the LTE networks using Voice over IP technologies, but there are also hybrid methods available to carry voice. LTE has a low data transfer latency of 5 milliseconds. LTE can support cell sizes that range from 10 meters up to 100 kilometers. There is backward compatibility with previous cellular systems.[7]

Sample Network

This section introduces a typical network, one that contains components found in most networks today. Each component and its function in the network will be described. A diagram of this network is shown in Figure 8-10.

Purpose of a Network

Since networks are expensive to equip, deploy, and maintain, they should have a value proposition. Fundamentally, networks connect things. The sample network shown in Figure 8-10 connects different departments of a hospital to a data center, the Internet, and a cloud service. A pharmacy and a gift shop are connected to applications in a data center. A surgical ward is connected to the network. In the clinic, a server, a terminal, and a phone are connected to applications in the data center. Lastly, a wireless access point in the emergency ward connects patients and members of families of patients to a wireless network. In today's modern healthcare setting, this type of connectivity is expected by doctors, staff, the administration, patients, their families, and members of the public.

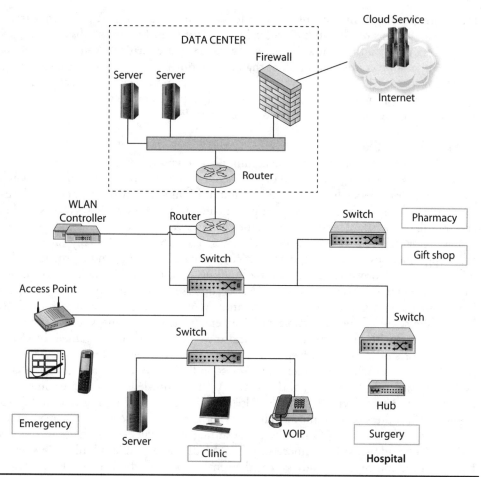

Figure 8-10   Sample (typical) network diagram

Components of the Sample Network

The following components are depicted in Figure 8-10: an Ethernet hub, network switches, routers, access points, a WLAN controller, and a firewall. Servers, tablets, smartphones, terminals, and VoIP phones are also shown in the diagram but will not be discussed since the focus of this chapter is on network components—not the end devices that attach to them. Servers do participate in the network via their network interface cards and also if they are running software that implements network components such as firewalls and routers.

Ethernet Hubs

The purpose of an Ethernet hub, also commonly known as a hub (and will be referred to as a hub going forward), is to distribute information (packets) from all devices and to all devices connected to it. A hub is said to work in broadcast mode, meaning it copies the information sent into one of its ports to all of the other ports. A hub also acts as a repeater and cleans up the physical digital signal sent to it. Ethernet hubs are equipped with RJ-45 ports and use the Ethernet standard. They are relatively simple devices and require little or no configuration other than connecting power and RJ-45 cables. At one time hubs were used extensively to connect network components; however, as the relative cost of network switches fell, hubs were eventually replaced by network switches, which could perform the same role but had more functionality.

Network Switches

The purpose of a network switch, also commonly known as a switch, is to forward traffic destined from a device connected to one of its ports to one or more ports of that switch. The term *switch* is generally used in telecommunications and networking and could exist in a number of different contexts; examples include telephone switches, ATM switches, and multilayer switches. This section focuses on layer 2 virtual LAN (VLAN) switches.

Layer 2 switches operate at the data link layer. These switches generally carry out the following functions: forwarding data traffic, filtering data traffic, and segmenting data traffic. A switch forwards data traffic by building up a forwarding table, also called a MAC address table. This table associates MAC addresses with switch ports. As a data link frame enters a port on the switch, its destination MAC address is read and compared to a list of addresses in a forwarding table, and if an entry exists, the frame is copied out to the port associated with this entry. If no entry exists in the table, then the frame is broadcast to all the ports of the switch except the port that the frame entered on. This broadcast should result in an acknowledgment from a responding device whose address is the same as the destination MAC address of the frame. As the acknowledgment frame comes back from the responding device, its source address will be read by the ingress port and stored in the MAC address table of the switch along with the ingress port ID. The next time a frame is sent using that MAC address, a forwarding entry will exist in the MAC address table and a broadcast will be unnecessary. The MAC address table is built up by having ports read the source MAC addresses as they enter a port on the switch. This process is most intense when the switch is initialized. Once the forwarding table is complete, the communications across the switch become more efficient.

A switch segments data traffic using VLANs. VLAN membership can be defined in different ways, including switch ports, MAC addresses, and IP addresses. Thus a specific set of switch ports can be associated with a specific VLAN. This capability can be aligned with corporate domains in an enterprise allocating VLANs to departments such as accounting, admissions, or pharmacy. The effect of VLAN functionality is that frames entering a particular port assigned to a particular VLAN will only be broadcast on other ports that are members of that VLAN. Data traffic will not move across VLANs (unless the VLANs are connected by a router). This segmentation makes the collision domain smaller, makes the communication more efficient, and helps security. Furthermore, much of the layer 2 switch functionality is provisioned in hardware rather than software, making a switch a high-performing network component.

A switch has different forwarding techniques to deal with the possibility of frames having errors or being malformed; two of these techniques are store and forward and cut-through switching. In the store-and-forward configuration, complete frames are read into the switch and verified for integrity before being forwarded. With this technique, frames with errors are not forwarded and do not waste the switch's resources. With cut-through switching, the frame is forwarded once the destination address is received and read. With this method, latency across the switch is reduced, but it is possible to forward a frame in error.[8]

VLANs can be extended beyond a single switch. This is achieved using the 802.1Q protocol, which adds a label to the Ethernet frame. Thus, two switches can communicate over a common trunk by passing Ethernet frames with labels identifying the VLANs that exist on both switches. Layer 2 switches configured with 802.1Q on a port can be connected to a router that has an interface configured for 802.1Q, thus terminating multiple VLANs logically in the router. The router can then route traffic between these VLANs. This replaces multiple physical LAN connections into the router.

Layer 2 switches can be provisioned in different ways: desktop, chassis, and rack. They can have redundant systems such as CPU cards and power supplies. Depending on the speed of the interfaces, the associated ports can have either copper or fiber-optic interfaces. Switches can also be provisioned with Power over Ethernet (PoE), which provides power to end devices such as VoIP phones. Depending upon the sophistication of the Layer 2 switch, it can be either unmanaged or managed. Switch management is usually implemented through some type of command-line interface or by using the Simple Network Management Protocol (SNMP). Some configuration parameters that can be set include

- MAC filtering
- Spanning Tree Protocol (STP)
- Shortest Path Bridging (SPB)
- Simple Network Management Protocol
- Port mirroring
- Trunking[8]

Routers

The purpose of a router is to forward data packets to networks it is connected to and to interconnect and terminate LANs. Routers are also fundamental building blocks of the Internet. Routers come in all shapes and sizes: home routers that terminate ISP connections; large sophisticated enterprise routers; access, distribution, and core routers; and routers that act as firewalls. They are located in various parts of the network: at home, in small offices, in offices of global enterprises, and at the interface between large peer network providers. The routers shown in Figure 8-10 could be customer premises equipment (CPE) belonging to service providers or access routers that form part of an enterprise's WAN. This section focuses on access routers.[9]

Routers work at layer 3, the network layer—they collectively move packets from a source to a destination in the network. To do this, routers execute two functions. The first is the creation of a routing table that contains information on routes that packets can take through the network. This routing table is made up of static routes, typically configured by network administrators, and dynamic routes, the result of distributed algorithms called routing protocols that routers execute. Dynamic routing algorithms are generally classified into two categories: distance vector and link state. Examples of routing algorithms include Routing Information Protocol (RIP), Open Shortest Path First (OSPF), Enhanced Interior Gateway Routing Protocol (EIGRP), and Border Gateway Protocol (BGP).[9]

The second function that routers execute is forwarding packets. They do this by comparing the network address part of the destination IP address of the transiting IP packet to the list of network addresses in the routing table. When a match is found, routers forward the packet to the next hop destination. If no match is found, they forward the packet to a default route. In many cases the default route is the Internet. A router's performance is tied to how quickly it can perform these two functions.[9]

Routers connect LANs together. In the case of the sample network, Figure 8-10, the router is connecting multiple VLANs together. When routers connect to LANs, they terminate the LANs' collision domains. The networks that routers connect to can have different physical media (e.g. copper and fiber). Routers have other functions as well, such as network address translation (NAT), port forwarding, and firewall functions.

Network Address Translation

Network address translation (NAT) is a method of mapping one IP address space into another by modifying network address information in IP packet headers while they move through a router.[10] The NAT function provides two benefits to networks. It helps with security by hiding a network behind one address and helps alleviate the problem of IPv4 address exhaustion. Usually a public routable address on the outside of the network will be mapped to a private address space on the inside of the network.

NAT works by swapping the source address (usually a private address) of an internal host with a public external IP address in the transmitting packet. This is done for all packets that come from internal hosts: their respective private source addresses are swapped for the external publicly routed IP addresses. Then the unique combination of internal private address and port is associated with a specific port in the transmitting packet and tracked in a translation table. Different port numbers are chosen for packets sourced from different hosts. When the packets exit the network, they all have the same source address (the publicly routable address) but different port numbers that are tracked in a translation table. When the receiving host answers, it does so using the publicly routable source address as a destination address and uses the tracked port number. When the packet arrives at the NAT device, it uses the translation table to find the private address and port pair.[11]

There are problems with the NAT process for which workarounds are needed. For example, one can browse external web sites from the internal network but can't browse internal web sites from the external network. Port forwarding can deal with this situation and is described next. Note that the foregoing discussion on NAT has been simplified; NAT is a complex topic.[11]

Port Forwarding

Port forwarding comes into play when NAT is used in a network. Because NAT effectively hides an internal network made up of many devices using many IP addresses (usually private IP addresses) and only exposes one public IP address, it's impossible for an external request to be made on a service residing in an internal host in that network. Port forwarding maps the port (usually a well-known port such as port 80) with the internal IP address as the request traverses the network gateway (router). The request can then find the server in the internal network.[12]

Port forwarding is configured by having a network administrator reserve a port number on the router for the specific application/server that will need to be communicated with on the internal network. External clients/hosts wishing to access the application/server will need to be given this port number and the public gateway address of the router. Usually that port is then assigned to be used by the application/server only. Situations in which port forwarding is required include when remote users require access to e-mail servers, access to HTTP servers, or FTP access to an internal server from the Internet.[13]

Router Configuration

Routers can be configured from a console port, using a remote access program such as Telnet or via management systems. Most routers are configured using a command-line interface that is unique to the manufacturer. As stated previously, routers can be sophisticated devices, which means there are many things that could be configured on the router. The key configuration options are security parameters, hostname, login credentials, routing protocols and their parameters, interface configuration such as IP addresses and address ranges, network management, access control lists, and policies.

Wireless Access Points and WLAN Controllers

The purpose of this section is to discuss the use of WLAN controllers in the network, (wireless LANs and their standards have been covered in previous sections of this chapter). WLAN controllers make it possible to manage large numbers of WLAN access points—a situation that faces healthcare organizations, particularly if they have many branch locations and wish to extend WLAN services. Furthermore, users such as resident and visiting physicians, patients, and patient family members are becoming more reliant on mobile devices such as smartphones, tablets, and laptops. Healthcare organizations are also taking advantage of the benefits of networked but untethered devices such as mobile e-infusion pumps and glucose meters. The expectation is becoming greater to be able to communicate anywhere and anytime, creating the need for a reliable and smoothly functioning WLAN.[14]

When WLANs first started appearing, access points were installed in offices connected to the local Ethernet. This was manageable as long as there was a small number of these locations. Network administrators managed these access points individually and were able to make software upgrades, maintain the access points, and deal with security issues. However, as the number of access points increased, a need arose to provision central management. A solution to this is the centralized WAN controller where management, data, and control functions are concentrated on a single device.[15]

A characteristic of this centralized management architecture is that traffic travels from the access point to the controller and back again. In this architecture the controller has the intelligence and the access point has little or no intelligence. This provides advantages such as the ability to roam between access points, the deployment of security profiles to end devices, policy enforcement services, and scalability. As with any centralized architecture, this introduces a single point of failure as well as the possibility of congestion since traffic has to flow to and from a single point. Having said that, adding computer and power redundancy to centralized controller systems alleviates some of these concerns.[15, 16]

Another type of controller architecture is the distributed model using a hybrid approach—data stays at the edge instead of flowing back to a central point and some functions get centralized but the access points have more intelligence to manage local functions. Enterprises have a choice of approaches, either controller based or controller-less based. A controller-less approach means less cost (no central infrastructure required), no single point of failure, and possibly a simpler deployment environment depending on the size of the enterprise.[16]

Firewalls

The purpose of a firewall is to protect an enterprise's internal network by limiting access to that network from the external network. Usually the firewall is protecting the internal network from the public Internet, but it could also be protecting internal networks from each other. As with other security components, firewalls align with the enterprise's security policies. Firewalls fall under the topic of security and have broad scope, which is why they will be treated briefly in this section.[17]

Firewall functionality can be implemented in different ways: as standalone devices, as an application running on a server, virtual machines, and on other network devices such as routers (access control lists can be defined on routers to do basic packet filtering).[17] Firewall functionality can also be combined in different ways. Two basic firewalls types are described next.

Network Layer or Packet Filter Firewalls

Network layer, also called packet filter firewalls, are basic firewalls that operate on TCP/IP packets. They either forward or filter packets based on rules associated with header information such as source and destination IP address, port numbers, or protocol types. Access control lists implement the rules. These firewalls further subdivide into stateless and stateful firewalls. Stateless firewalls work on a single packet at a time and do not retain information about that packet, whereas stateful firewalls "remember" characteristics about a session, which makes them better at detecting anomalies in packets that are part of that session.[18]

Application Layer Proxy Firewalls

Application layer firewalls operate at the application level of the Internet communications model. As proxies they are placed between the client and server in a client-server connection. They inspect the packets in depth and look for anomalies associated with application process flow and for improper content such as worms and Trojans.[17, 18]

Firewall Configuration

Firewalls are configured by defining rules. An example of a basic rule is the "implicit deny," which by default prevents any packet from traversing a router unless an explicit rule is created to allow certain packets to get through. Another example is denying packets that have source addresses that exist on the internal network.[17]

The diagram in Figure 8-10 shows a firewall facing the Internet, protecting the internal network from threats coming from the Internet. In networks composed of many geographically dispersed networks and where mobile devices are being used, firewalls may be positioned at multiple locations to protect the edge of the network. In this circumstance, enterprises can take advantage of firewall management systems that provide consistent policies to multiple firewalls.

Cabling

The devices in Figure 8-10 will be interconnected using either copper or fiber media. The devices will likely be located in a data center or a wiring closet and will be interconnected using some type of structured cabling approach. Lower speed equipment will be connected using copper media, and higher speed equipment will be connected using fiber media. Patch panels will be used to organize cable runs, and patch cords will be used to make final connections.

The copper media used will typically be Category 5, 5e, 6, and 6a unshielded twisted pair (UTP) cable and patch cords terminated in RJ-45 connectors. The fiber media will likely be single-mode fiber cables and patch cords.

Use Case 8-3: Network Troubleshooting Scenario

Scenario

Bob had just finished installing all the equipment and cables for his data center upgrade in which he was moving from a physical network to a virtual local area network—see Figure 8-11. It meant that instead of connecting the clinic, pharmacy, and emergency LANs individually to separate ports on the router, he could connect them into a single switch, which then interconnected into one port on the router. VLANs gave him the flexibility he needed in the future to make changes.

Bob needed to verify that everything was working, so the first thing he did was to Telnet to Router B to check the MAC table. He expected to see the MAC table filled with MAC addresses associated with all the devices in VLANs 100, 200, and 300.

He was able to ping from Router B to Switch A. Switch A's MAC table was filled with the entries he expected to also see in Router B. What was wrong and how could Bob fix it?

(*continued*)

Resolution

Bob needed to check his router settings. He saw a complete MAC table on the switch, and with 802.1Q trunking on between Router B and Switch A, he should have seen all the MAC table entries in the router's MAC table. He did not have 802.1Q turned on in the router for the interface that was connected to Switch A. Once he configured the router properly the switch could understand the frames and build the MAC table.

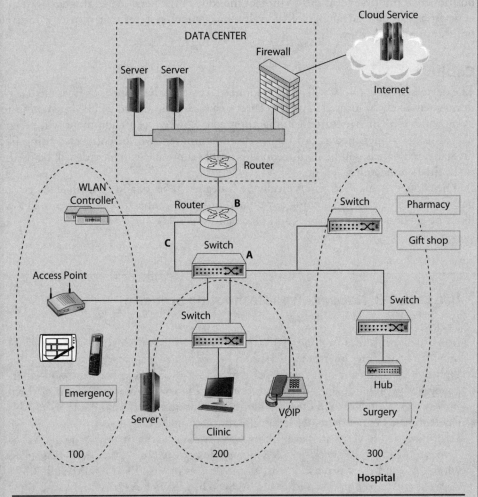

Figure 8-11 Sample (typical) network diagram for Use Case 8-3

Transmission of Healthcare Data (HL7)

This final section of the chapter describes HL7, which is both a standards organization and a standard. The "L7" in HL7 refers to layer or level 7 of the OSI stack and relates to the healthcare applications that reside at the application layer.

According to www.hl7.org, "Founded in 1987, Health Level Seven International (HL7) is a not-for-profit, ANSI-accredited standards developing organization dedicated to providing a comprehensive framework and related standards for the exchange, integration, sharing, and retrieval of electronic health information that supports clinical practice and the management, delivery and evaluation of health services. HL7 is supported by more than 1,600 members from over 50 countries, including 500+ corporate members representing healthcare providers, government stakeholders, payers, pharmaceutical companies, vendors/suppliers, and consulting firms."[19]

HL7 is a framework for exchanging data in healthcare and was a response to the costs associated with writing interfaces for the growing number of healthcare applications. Since the nature of healthcare applications is that they are unique, each interface is therefore different. That means for a given application, a developer needs to write an interface for every other application that the application will interface with. With HL7, a developer just needs to follow the standard for message exchange and knows that the application will interface with any other application that follows the HL7 standard.

There are two versions of the HL7 standard in existence today: HL7 v2 and HL7 v3. HL7 version 3 is an improvement over HL7 v2 since the people who defined it had the advantage of seeing what worked and didn't work for HL7 v2. They also had the advantage of incorporating innovations in computing methodologies, best practices, and technological innovation such as XML in the intervening time between the HL7 v2 release and the start of HL7 v3's development. Having said that, the majority of HL7 implementations today are according to HL7 v2, and there are two reasons for this. The first is that HL7 v2 was around for ten years, and it captured the initial investments in application development at that time. Second, one of the objectives of HL7 v2 was to have high adoption rates, and to do that, the designers purposely left about 20 percent of the standard flexible. Furthermore, HL7 v2 was focused on clinical interfaces and applications, whereas HL7 v3 is focused on medical informatics.[20]

Many of the functions and business processes in healthcare lend themselves to automation. This includes exchanging data between various suborganizations and systems within hospitals, between various political entities such as governments, and for use in health informatics. HL7 tries to standardize what are essentially unique healthcare models for hospitals, clinics, and labs. The value of HL7 comes from the network effect; the more people who use it, the greater its value becomes; and the greater its value becomes, the more people who use it. As the number of applications that use HL7 increases, the motivation to adopt it increases for those applications that have not yet adopted it.[20]

HL7 v2

Development on HL7 v2 began in 1987. Its design reflects the healthcare information concerns of the time, which were admissions, discharges, transfers, orders, and reports.

HL7 v2 is also a flexible standard, meaning it can be added to over time, and this is why a key design principle of HL7 v2 is its backward compatibility.

The key HL7 v2 design concepts are message syntax, segment structure, fields, delimiters, data types, and vocabulary. In HL7 v2, messages are triggered by events. There are different message types, and each message is composed of segments. Each segment has a three-character identifier that comes first, followed by fields, which contain components and subcomponents. Delimiters separate these components and subcomponents. An example of a message type is the ORM message. ORM stands for an order message. Examples of delimiters include the field separator (|) and the component separator (^). Each segment has a definition table.[21]

The patient identifier (PID) segment is a very common segment across message types. It has a number of components, such as PID-5 (patient name) and PID-7 (date/time of birth). For example, a patient name would be represented as |john^doe|. Another example of a segment is the AL1 (allergy) segment, which contains patient allergy information, including codes for allergy type and severity. The BLG segment contains information about billing, such as the charge type, when to charge, and the reason for the charge. The IN1 (insurance) segment contains information about insurance policy coverage, for example, insurance plan and company ID. The MSH (message header) segment is included in every HL7 message and contains the source of the message, its purpose, and its destination. The OBR (observation request) segment contains information about exams, diagnostic studies, and observations and assessments specific to a result or order. As a final example, the SCH (schedule activity information) segment contains information about scheduled appointments. The Z segment is a special segment that enables developers to create their own segments, thereby allowing flexibility for "local" extensions to HL7 v2.

Segments contain fields. An example of a field within a segment is the Healthcare Provider Type Code field, which contains information to identify what type of provider cared for a patient. This field can be contained in an HL7 message within various segments, for example, the BLG segment. HL7 recommends using the Health Care Provider Taxonomy values—derived from another standard, ANSI ASC X12—in this field. For example, 207PS0010X is the code for Sports Medicine; an emergency physician with special knowledge in sports medicine.

Data types are another HL7 v2 design concept. Data types define the values, formats, and vocabulary that fields, components, and subcomponents can have. Data types are also categorized as simple and complex. Simple data types contain a single value, whereas complex data types may contain more than one, and each of those can be a different data type. An example of a simple data type is DT, or date. Its format is YYYY[MM[DD]]. An example of a complex data type is SAD, or street address, which includes the house number and street.[21]

HL7 v3

Development on HL7 v3 started in 1992 with an aim to improve upon HL7 v2. The development team had at its disposal the accumulated knowledge learned from the many existing implementations of HL7 v2 and was able to apply new IT best practices.

It addressed the need for the following: a consistent application data model, formal methodologies to model data elements and messages, well-defined application and user roles, and precision in the standard.[20]

A key goal of the HL7 v3 development work was to create a more rigorous standard than HL7 v2, one that would lend itself to vendor conformance testing. HL7 v2 made vendor conformance testing difficult because there were a lot of HL7 v2 variants. These variants resulted from the flexible design of HL7 v2, which made it possible to have optional data elements and segments. This left it up to implementers to ensure conformance.

HL7 v3 combines object orientation and a Reference Information Model (RIM) to create HL7 v3 messages. This results in a standard that is extensible, is current, can be conformance tested, is abstracted from technology, and covers healthcare exhaustively. At the top of the RIM backbone, there are three main classes:[21]

- Act, which refers to something that has happened or will happen
- Role, which is a position, job, or competency
- Entity, which is something that is living or nonliving

The meaning of each class is determined by structural attributes. These three are linked using the association classes ActRelationship, Participation, and Rolelink. As in HL7 v2, there are data types defined such as name and addresses. Figure 8-12 shows an example of patient identifier coding in HL7 v2 and HL7 v3. The purpose of this

```
HL7 v2
PID|||000-00-1111||Doe^John^H^^^^ 121 smith Dr.^^Someroad
Somestate^xx^00012||(999)555-5555|(666)666-6666|||||AC00000000|| CR
HL7 v3
    <patient>
        <patient>
            <id root="1.23.456.7.899876.5432" extension="12345"/>
            <patient_Person>
                <id root="1.23.456.7.899876.5432" extension="12345"
assigningAuthorityName="xx" validTime="2012-06-21"/>
                <nm xsi:type="dt:PN" use="L">
                    <family/>
                    <given>John</given>
                    <given>Doe</given>
                </nm>
            </patient_Person>
        </patient>
    </patient>
```

Figure 8-12   Comparison of HL7 v2 and v3 coding

example is to convey the structural difference in how the information is coded; it is not necessarily an accurate depiction. Note that HL7 v3 has adopted the XML style.

Advances in networking hardware and software discussed in this chapter, HL7, and other health data standards such as ANSI ASC X12 in the past three decades have enabled vast increases of volume of healthcare network transmissions. Despite this progress, ever increasing volume creates the potential for problems. For HL7 messages, problems may include incomplete data transmission, data being transmitted in wrong segments, deactivated threads or nodes, missing or incomplete patient data in key segments, data out of order and potentially misread, and scrambled or timed-out messages (for example, due to fax or network failure), all potentially leading to medical error. In healthcare, network administrators must be keenly aware of the potential for such issues.

HL7 FHIR

Fast Healthcare Interoperability Resources (FHIR), pronounced "fire," is a relatively new, emerging specification for exchanging healthcare information electronically. In early implementations, FHIR is building on and working with HL7 v3 implementations. FHIR uses many approaches and standards that are used in network computing broadly across industries, such as XML and JSON formats, and is implemented using REST and/ or service-based architecture.[22] This exciting development represents an opportunity for the healthcare industry to leverage existing and already widely adopted interoperability standards and, importantly, the many experienced people who have used these standards in other industries.

EHR Outbound Communication

Electronic health record (EHR) systems frequently need to interoperate with one of many other systems within a healthcare organization, and also with systems outside of the organization. In the vast majority of cases in the United States, this is accomplished by system-to-system software interfaces that comply with HL7 standards.

Let's see how this works with a billing example. Some EHR systems have a billing module that interacts directly with other modules, such as the ADT (admission, discharge, transfer) module. If a healthcare entity uses that billing module within its EHR system, no interface from the EHR system to the billing module is required. Quite a few billing systems, independent of a healthcare entity's EHR system, predate the current EHR system, and the billing departments have often prevailed over the IT department to maintain the independent billing system. Some of these billing systems are subsystems or modules of practice management systems. In some cases, a particular EHR system does not have a billing module. When an independent billing system is preferred or required, an interface between the EHR system and billing system is required. HL7 handles EHR-to-billing-system outbound communication with the BLG segment. In many cases the technical management of these interfaces is managed by a third system known as an interface engine.

Chapter Review

Internet and wireless technologies are changing how telecommunications services work and are provided in healthcare. The Internet holds the promise of converging voice, video, and data traffic onto a single network. Wireless technologies promise to extend connectivity to people anywhere and at any time. These changes are also motivating healthcare innovations as telecommunications is applied to problems in clinical settings, making it possible for clinical staff to work with greater flexibility and sometimes do things they couldn't do previously.

This chapter focused on TCP/IP networks since they will likely be the transport networks of the future. Concepts necessary to the understanding of how TCP/IP networks work were introduced: connectivity, communications models, communications protocols, throughput, addressing, applications, and PANs, LANs, MANs, and WANs. To understand how networks work, it is useful to know how data flows. The chapter covered two examples of data transfer: transfer between two workstations on the same LAN and data transfer between a workstation and server on a different LAN. Wireless networks offer the benefits of mobility to clinicians, which makes the provision of services to patients more efficient and effective. The predominant wireless LAN technologies and standards were covered.

The "Sample Network" section built on the foundations of the previous sections and described key components of networks such as hubs, switches, and routers. Methods of managing networks, such as network address translation, port forwarding, and router configuration, were discussed. Key tools such as wireless access points and WLAN controllers, firewalls, and cabling techniques for networks were covered. Finally, the HL7 standards (and the standard development organization by the same name) were introduced. This important set of standards, including its existing v2 and v3 main forms and its emerging FHIR standard, governs much of what is transmitted on healthcare computer networks.

Questions

To test your comprehension of the chapter, answer the following questions and then check your answers against the list of correct answers at the end of the chapter.

1. How many connections would be needed to fully connect six people?

   A. 6

   B. 15

   C. 12

   D. 18

2. A PDU has what basic structure?

   A. A beginning delimiter and ending delimiter with a payload between these two delimiters

   B. A beginning delimiter and ending delimiter, source address and destination address fields, a control field, a payload field, and an error check field

    C. Source address and destination address fields and a payload

    D. A control field and a payload

3. Which layer of the OSI model is responsible for determining the best route through a network?

    A. Network layer

    B. Physical layer

    C. Session layer

    D. None of the above

4. With a client-server architecture, _____.

    A. one or more clients request the services of one server

    B. each device is a client and a server

    C. one or more servers request the services of clients

    D. it is better to work at a small scale since there is little overhead

5. While a network layer PDU traverses the network, _____.

    A. its destination MAC address never changes

    B. the source IP address is matched to the last gateway it passes

    C. its destination IP address is changed to that of the first router it encounters

    D. its source and destination addresses do not change

6. What is different about wireless networks versus wired networks?

    A. A wireless network is constrained to a 1-meter radius versus a wired network that can span rooms or city blocks.

    B. The OSI stack is different for a wireless network versus a wired network.

    C. Wired networks use radio waves to communicate.

    D. Wireless networks use radio waves to communicate.

7. An Ethernet hub _____.

    A. is a repeater that cleans up the digital signal

    B. is another term for a network switch

    C. replaced switches as a network element

    D. cannot be used to distribute a digital communication

8. HL7 v2 _____.

    A. is no longer used

    B. has the majority of implementations because vendors discounted prices greatly

    C. is exhaustive and rigorous because it has an RIM

    D. has the majority of implementations because adoption was a design goal and the developers purposely made it flexible in order to get that adoption

Answers

1. **B.** n × (n − 1)/2 = 6 × (6 − 1)/2 = 15 connections would be needed to fully connect six people.

2. **B.** There are seven basic fields: a beginning delimiter and ending delimiter, source address and destination address fields, a control field, a payload field, and an error check field.

3. **A.** The network layer is responsible for routing and therefore figuring out the best path through the network.

4. **A.** Client-server architecture by definition is many-to-one since the resources are centralized in the server.

5. **D.** While a network layer PDU traverses the network, its source and destination addresses do not change, which is how the end-to-end capability of TCP/IP is guaranteed.

6. **D.** Wired networks use wires, and wireless networks depend on radio waves.

7. **A.** An Ethernet hub is a repeater that cleans up the digital signal. It serves some of the same purposes as network switches but should not be confused with network switches, which perform the same role but have more functionality.

8. **D.** HL7 v2 has the majority of implementations because adoption was a design goal and the developers purposely made it flexible in order to get that adoption. Another factor is that it was the first and only standard for ten years until HL7 v3 was written.

References

1. FitzGerald, J., & Dennis, A. (2009). *Business data communications and networking, tenth edition.* John Wiley & Sons.

2. Schulzrinne, H. (1996). World Wide Web: Whence, wither, what next? *IEEE Network Magazine, 10*(2), 10–17.

3. Cisco. (2010). *Cisco Medical-Grade Network (MGN) 2.0: Wireless architectures.* Accessed on January 29, 2017, from www.cisco.com/c/en/us/solutions/enterprise/design-zone-industry-solutions/index.html..

4. Hiertz, G., Denteener, D., Stibor, L., Zang, Y., Costa, X. P., & Walke, B. (2010). The IEEE 802.11 universe. *IEEE Communications Magazine, 48*(1), 62–70.

5. Bragg, R., et al. (2004). *Network security: The complete reference.* McGraw-Hill/Osborne.

6. Danielyan, E. (2003). WAP: Broken promises or wrong expectations? *Internet Protocol Journal, 6*(2). Accessed on June 16, 2016, from www.cisco.com/c/en/us/about/press/internet-protocol-journal/back-issues/table-contents-24/wap.html.

7. Parkvall, S., Furuskar, A., & Dahlman, E. (2011). Evolution of LTE toward IMT-Advanced. *IEEE Communications Magazine, 49*(2), 84–91.

8. "Network switch." *Wikipedia*, April 11, 2016. Accessed on June 16, 2016, from https://en.wikipedia.org/wiki/Network_switch.

9. "Router (computing)." *Wikipedia*, May 30, 2016. Accessed on June 16, 2016, from https://en.wikipedia.org/wiki/Router_(computing).

10. Javvin Technologies. (2005). *Network protocols handbook, second edition* (p. 27). Javvin Technologies.

11. "Network address translation." *Wikipedia*, June 9, 2016. Accessed on June 16, 2016, from https://en.wikipedia.org/wiki/Network_address_translation.

12. "Definition of: port forwarding." *PC Magazine*, October 11, 2008. Accessed on June 16, 2016, from www.pcmag.com/encyclopedia/term/49509/port-forwarding.

13. "Port forwarding." *Wikipedia*, March 25, 2016. Accessed on June 16, 2016, from www.wikivisually.com/wiki/Port_forwarding.

14. Savage, M. (2016). Upgrading the network in healthcare: Two approaches. *Network Computing*. Accessed on June 16, 2016, from www.networkcomputing .com/cloud-infrastructure/upgrading-network-healthcare-two-approaches/ 732001772.

15. Cisco. (2016). *Cisco wireless controllers at a glance.* Brochure. Accessed on June 16, 2016, from www.cisco.com/c/dam/en/us/products/collateral/interfaces-modules/ services-modules/at_a_glance_c45-652653.pdf.

16. Chubirka, M. (2013). Evolution of the WLAN controller. *Network Computing*. Accessed on June 16, 2016, from www.networkcomputing.com/networking/ evolution-wlan-controller/1123406767.

17. Harris, S. (2013). *CISSP all-in-one exam guide, sixth edition* (pp. 628–651). McGraw-Hill Education.

18. "Firewall (computing)." *Wikipedia,* June 12, 2016. Accessed on June 16, 2016, from https://en.wikipedia.org/wiki/Firewall_(computing).

19. Health Level Seven International. (n.d.). *About HL7.* Accessed on January 29, 2017, from www.hl7.org/about/index.cfm?ref=nav.

20. Corepoint Health. (n.d.). *The HL7 evolution: Comparing HL7 versions 2 and 3.* Accessed on January 29, 2017, from www.slideshare.net/Corepoint/comparing-hl7-v3-with-hl7-v2.

21. Benson, T. (2010). *Principles of health interoperability HL7 and SNOMED.* Health Informatics series. Springer.

22. HL7. (2015). *FHIR overview.* Accessed on July 1, 2016, from https://www.hl7.org/ fhir/overview.html.

Systems Analysis and Design in Healthcare

Andre Kushniruk, Elizabeth Borycki

In this chapter, you will learn how to

- Describe the importance of good systems analysis and design for healthcare information technology
- Implement systems design and analysis principles and methods
- Utilize the systems development life cycle (SDLC)
- Apply traditional approaches to systems analysis and design
- Employ object-oriented approaches to systems analysis and design
- Describe trends in systems analysis and design in healthcare

Increased information demands are leading to the development of more advanced healthcare information systems (HISs) and healthcare information technology. This chapter introduces the main concepts and techniques of modern systems design and analysis as applied to HISs. At the core of successful system development in healthcare is good systems analysis and design. This involves the selection and use of appropriate methods of analysis for assessing the information needs of a healthcare organization. System design involves specifying in detail how the components of systems will work together to provide useful functionality. As you will see, this needs to be based on an in-depth understanding of healthcare problems and the needs of healthcare professionals.

This chapter aims to describe the role and importance of systems analysis and design in rapidly changing healthcare environments. Approaches to systems analysis and design will be described, including traditional structured approaches to systems development and modeling of system requirements and design. Additionally, newer approaches such as object-oriented (OO) systems analysis and design as well as Agile system development will be described. Different design and implementation strategies and methodologies will be described, with an emphasis on understanding their advantages and disadvantages as they relate to healthcare. The reasons for the success and failures of HISs will be discussed, along with consideration of designs that might have helped to avoid failures.

Approaches to system design will also be discussed in the context of a variety of healthcare information systems, ranging from electronic health record (EHR) systems to decision support systems. It has become increasingly clear that engineering information systems in healthcare is complex and requires the careful and informed application of appropriate methods and approaches to developing information systems. In this chapter, we will discuss the need for improving the development of information systems, and we will provide you with the background for understanding the complexity of HIT. We will also introduce a range of methods that can be used for improved systems analysis and design.

Systems Analysis and Design in HIT

A system can be defined as a collection of interrelated components (subsystems) that work together as a whole to achieve an outcome.[1] There are many types of systems, ranging from biological systems to political systems. A health information system is a collection of interrelated components or subsystems that input and process data to produce an output that is needed for healthcare tasks. For example, EHR systems have been designed to support physicians' use of information in dealing with patients.[2] An EHR system might consist of the following subsystems: patient scheduling, medications, documentation, laboratory information, and diagnostic imaging. As shown in Figure 9-1, these subsystems could be broken down further into subsystems (e.g., the medication subsystem could be broken down into a computerized physician order entry [CPOE] subsystem and a medication administration record [MAR] subsystem). In addition, computer systems contain both manual and automated processes, which is an essential consideration, where some parts of the system involve manual activities (such as the entry of patient data by a clinician into a system using a keyboard) and some parts are automated or internal to the system (such as the automated application of decision rules for the detection of adverse drug interactions).

Figure 9-1
Subsystems of an electronic health record system

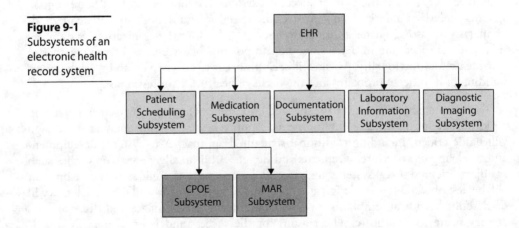

The Systems Development Life Cycle (SDLC)

A systems development project is a planned undertaking that produces an HIS. The development of any new information system involves analysis, design activities, and implementation activities. *Systems analysis* refers to the process of understanding and specifying in detail what the HIS should do. The results of a systems analysis form the foundation or basis for a specific system design. *System design* refers to the process of specifying in detail how the components of the HIS should work together to achieve desired functionality. A *systems analyst* is an IT professional who uses analysis and design techniques to solve healthcare problems using HIT. *Systems implementation* uses the results of the analysis and design processes to build, test, and deploy the system in a healthcare setting.

A central concept in HIS development around which activities, methods, and approaches are considered is the systems development life cycle (SDLC). The SDLC is a term used to describe the process and stages in the development of new HISs. The SDLC provides guidance to HIS developers by providing structure, methods, and a checklist of activities needed to successfully develop an HIS. As shown in Figure 9-2, the typical phases in the SDLC are the following:[1]

1. Planning phase
2. Analysis phase
3. Design phase
4. Implementation phase
5. Support phase

The Planning Phase

The first phase—the Planning phase—involves coming up with the initial idea for an HIS development project. This includes identifying a healthcare problem that needs to be addressed and defining what aspects of the problem can be improved using healthcare information technology. During this phase, a feasibility study may be undertaken where the objectives and scope of the project are presented, the current problems with the existing situation are considered, and a recommended HIS solution is proposed. This phase may involve input from a manager and systems analysts working together to come up with a proposal for an organization to develop an HIS. At this point, if the project

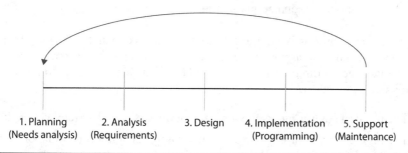

1. Planning   2. Analysis   3. Design   4. Implementation   5. Support
(Needs analysis) (Requirements)   (Programming)   (Maintenance)

Figure 9-2   The systems development life cycle

appears to be worth pursing (i.e., the projected benefits outweigh the costs), the project will then move into the Analysis phase.

The Analysis Phase

In the Analysis phase, a detailed assessment of the current situation is undertaken to determine where and how an HIS can be applied to solve healthcare problems. This may involve systems analysts going into a particular hospital setting (such as an emergency department or clinic) and collecting information about information gaps and problems that might be improved through the use of HIT. During this phase, the systems analysts involved in the project begin to gather information about the requirements for the new HIS that will be developed. This includes determining *technical requirements* for the HIS. Some examples of technical requirements include the following:[1]

- The HIS must run in a Windows 10 environment.
- The response time of the system to user queries must be less than one second.
- The data in the system must be backed up at the end of each day.

The *functional requirements* of the HIS describe the specific functions the HIS should support, with some examples of functional requirements for an HIS including the following:[1]

- The system will allow physicians to enter medication orders.
- The system will allow nurses to view medication orders.
- The system will provide automated alerts when entering a medication that the patient is allergic to.

Nonfunctional requirements make up the third major category of requirements for HIS; they include requirements for the system that are neither technical nor functional but are essential, such as the requirement that the system have a high level of usability and that the system functions can be learned easily by users with minimal prior computer experience.[3]

 TIP Systems analysis refers to describing what a system should be able to do and involves specifying system requirements (i.e., technical, functional, and nonfunctional requirements).

Requirements gathering is a major activity that occurs during the Analysis phase. This may involve a team of analysts whose aim is to understand the current work situation and determine the requirements for the new HIS. This includes describing each of the following (see Figure 9-3):

- The physical environments in which the newly developed system will be deployed
- The different types of interfaces to other computer systems (e.g., laboratory data or other data may need to be obtained directly from other systems)

- User and human factors considerations that will need to be addressed
- The actual functionality of the system
- The level of quality assurance (i.e., how error free must the system be)
- The security considerations
- The human, computing, and other resources needed to operate the system
- The data inputs and outputs
- The technical and user documentation to use, update, and safely run the system

Systems analysts use a range of methods to obtain the requirements of an HIS, including the following:

- Distributing questionnaires to stakeholders and end users (e.g., to physicians, nurses, and allied professionals who will be users of the system being developed) to assess issues with current systems and requirements for new ones
- Reviewing organizational documentation, existing reports, forms, and procedure descriptions
- Conducting interviews with end users (e.g., physicians, nurses, allied health professionals)
- Observing current work practices (e.g., watching health professionals in an emergency setting to determine requirements for a new emergency room information system)

From the software engineering literature, as well as from the growing literature describing HIS implementations worldwide, there are two key points that need to be considered. One key consideration is that weak analysis of system requirements (i.e., performing an incomplete requirements analysis before proceeding with system design) will lead to "shortchanged user requirements," which have been highly associated with failed projects, because incomplete requirements form an insufficient base for design of effective systems.[4] The complexity of the environments where an HIS is deployed, the many

Figure 9-3
Summary of types of requirements in an HIS

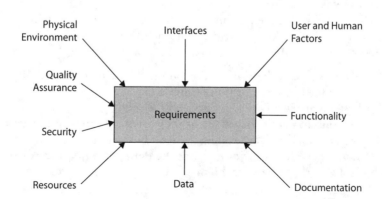

and varied uses, and the variety of users of systems (ranging from clinics to hospitals to users of systems including physicians, nurses, and allied health professionals) all make gathering "sufficient" information about requirements difficult and challenging. The literature is full of examples of system development that has led to HISs that have not met user needs, that have not worked, or that had to be "turned off." The other key consideration for an HIS is that research in software engineering has indicated that perhaps the single greatest factor in the failure of complex systems is a lack of end-user input and involvement.[4] To avoid system failure and to ensure effective system design, consultation with end users should begin in the systems Analysis phase and continue throughout the whole SDLC through completion of the system's development and testing. This will be described in the following sections.

Use Case 9-1: Conducting Interviews to Determine Problems with a Hospital System

In this case study, we will examine the interview protocol that was created for gathering requirements about a new HIS that was to be implemented in order to replace an existing system, which had been reported to have a number of problems. In this example, a set of questions was created that were to be asked of physicians in the clinic where the new system would be implemented. The questions focused on understanding what the problems with the existing system were. The following is the set of questions that was developed for this purpose:

- How often do you use the current system?
- For what purposes?
- Have you had any problems using the system?
- Can you give me some examples of problems you have encountered?
- Are there new features you would like to see in an improved system?

These questions were used to drive interviews with 20 physicians who were the end users of the current system. The interviews were recorded and transcribed for analysis in order to identify all problems with the current system that needed fixing. The following is the transcript from one of the first physicians interviewed (with responses in bold):

Systems analyst: How often do you use the current system?
Doctor: **About two or three times a day.**
Systems analyst: For what purposes?
Doctor: **To check the values of the patient for abnormal levels.**
Systems analyst: Have you had any problems using the system?
Doctor: **Well, I am finding that the data presented is not correctly updated and also that I have problems accessing the system from home.**

Systems analyst: Can you give me an example of the data not being current?

Doctor: Yes, some of the records do not contain reports that were generated at other hospitals, and the data from this hospital sometimes is mixed up with data from other patients.

Systems analyst: Really, can you show me an example?

Doctor: Yes I'll show you this one I just printed out.

Systems analyst: Anything else?

Doctor: Yes, X-ray reports do not show on the system for at least several days.

Systems analyst: Are there new features you would like to see in an improved system?

Doctor: I would like to see guidelines about how to interpret abnormal lab values presented to me on the screen when an abnormal value appears.

Based on an analysis of all 20 interviews, it was clear a number of problems or themes kept reappearing from the interviews, such as the problem of information not being updated correctly and data being incorrectly displayed, as well as long delays in getting patient data. Based on these findings (and results from other forms of requirements gathering, including giving out questionnaires to both physicians and nurses), the requirements were specified for a new system that would replace the old one and that would address these issues. Specifically, the new system would be required to provide more timely updates of patient information, always present correct patient data, have a reduced period of time for providing physicians with reports, and have online guidelines for users to help them in interpreting abnormal lab values.

In general, the activities involved in conducting requirements analysis include the creation of a report, or a requirements specification, with a number of major sections, including the following:[5]

- **Analysis method**   A list of end users consulted and a description of the methods used to obtain requirements (e.g., observation, interviews, or questionnaires).

- **Statement of user requirements**   The objectives of the system, as well as all the technical, functional, and nonfunctional requirements that are listed. The potential impact of the system on end users and the need for training are discussed.

- **Statement of system constraints**   The constraints of the system when it will be implemented in the real setting of use.

- **Documentation**   Summaries of interviews and questionnaire results, as well as a set of diagrams describing the system requirements.

The requirements specification includes a number of key diagrams in the Documentation section. These diagrams form the basis or foundation upon which the sound design of the system will be based. The diagrams included in the report will depend on what type of approach is being used to collect and specify system requirements, as will be described.

There are many approaches and tools that are used to aid in collecting and specifying system requirements. One such approach is known as the *traditional*, or structured, approach to systems analysis and design. This approach includes a number of different diagramming techniques and tools. One such diagram that has traditionally been used in structured systems analysis is known as the *data flow diagram* (DFD); see Figure 9-4 for a simple HIS example of a DFD, along with a key indicating the meaning of the symbols used in the diagram. In the diagram, computer processes are depicted as rounded rectangles, while data stores or entities that are used by the processes are depicted using open-ended rectangles. The arrows show the flow of data from external agents into and out of processes, and the types of data are labeled on the arrows. In this example, Drug Order data flow into the Process Drug Request process from the Doctor, and data labeled Confirmation flow back to the Doctor after the drug request is processed. This type of diagram can be used to show how information flows and is processed in a healthcare organization to describe the current, or "as is," situation. It can also be used to describe how information will flow in the proposed HIS that will replace the current situation.[1]

Other types of diagrams and tools associated with traditional structured analysis include entity relationship diagrams (ERDs) that describe the relationship among the

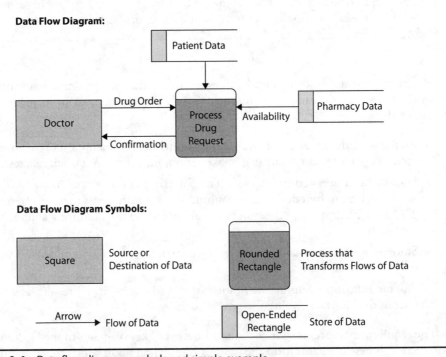

Figure 9-4   Data flow diagram symbols and simple example

"things" of interest for designing a system, such as patient data, pharmacy data, and so on, which are depicted as boxes in the ERD and labeled as shown in Figure 9-5. In this figure, there are three entities: Patient, Doctor, and Patient Record. Within each box representing an entity are its attributes. For example, within the entity Patient, the attributes are Name, Address, and Patient Number. Each Patient is associated with (can have) only one Patient Record (in this hospital system), and likewise each Patient Record can be associated with only one Patient. The two small vertical lines on the horizontal line between Patient and Patient Record indicate this relationship. Likewise, there is the line connecting Patient and Doctor, showing there is a relationship between these two entities, with crow's-feet markings (the small circles with three small lines coming from them) to indicate that Patients can have zero or more (could be many) Doctors and alternatively that Doctors can have or be associated with zero or more Patients. These diagrams are very important in that they form a blueprint for creating and designing the databases that underlie HISs, with entities in such diagrams being implemented as relational database tables.[1]

TIP   Entity relationship diagrams and data flow diagrams are examples of diagrams associated with structured systems analysis.

In contrast to traditional structured systems analysis and design, more recent approaches have appeared, including object-oriented (OO) systems analysis and design, which defines a newer set of associated diagramming techniques and tools to support work in the Analysis phase.[6] OO systems analysis and design involves using a set of diagrams that are defined in the Unified Modeling Language (UML). UML diagrams have become a standard way of representing user requirements for many HISs and are

Figure 9-5
Example of an
entity relation-
ship diagram

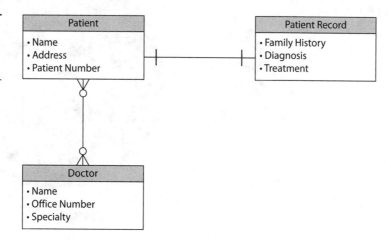

commonly used to represent key aspects of current and proposed HISs in terms of system requirements. One such UML diagram that is commonly used to describe HIS requirements is known as the *use case diagram*.[6]

Figure 9-6 illustrates a use case diagram for a computerized physician order entry system. In the diagram, a figure represents an *actor* (i.e., a type of user of the system to be developed), in this case a physician. The main outer circle represents the automation boundary, which separates the computer system to be developed from manual parts of the system and end users outside of the automation boundary. In Figure 9-6, the three smaller circles inside the larger circle represent three use cases, which are the individual activities that the system can carry out. The arrows from the physician to the three use cases indicate that the actor is involved in each of the use cases (i.e., the physician user initiates each of the use cases). In the diagram there are three use cases shown: Order New Medication, Review Medication, and Stop Medication. Note that this type of diagram indicates who the users of the system will be (i.e., the actors) and also indicates what they can use the system to do. Since this diagram is constructed in the Analysis phase, it describes what the system will do, not how it will be done. (The description of how the system will carry out the functions illustrated in the use case diagram will be described during the Design phase, which follows the Analysis phase.) This type of diagram is increasingly used in order to give a clear view of system requirements. Each use in the diagram can be expanded to include a detailed text description of how the actors and the use case interact (i.e., scenarios describing in detail the interactions between the user and the system in carrying out a use case like Order New Medication).

Figure 9-6
Use case diagram
for CPOE system

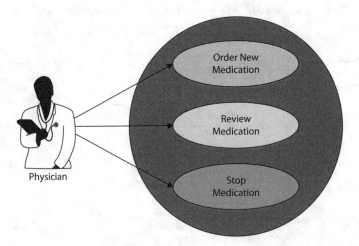

Use Case 9-2: Representing Requirements for an HIS in UML

Based on requirements gathered during the Analysis phase, a patient record and scheduling system are being designed for use in a doctor's office by receptionists, nurses, and doctors. The receptionists will use the system to enter new patient information when first-time patients visit the doctor and to schedule all appointments. The nurses will use the system to keep track of the results of each visit and to enter information about patient care. The nurses will also be able to print patient reports or the history of a patient's visits. The doctors will primarily use the system to view the patient's history and enter patient diagnostic and treatment information, as well as print patient information. Figure 9-7 shows the use case diagram for describing the requirements for the system based on this description. The three actors (i.e., receptionist, nurse, and doctor) are represented as figures, while the use cases (i.e., the activities the system will need to carry out based on the earlier description) are represented as the smaller circles within the larger circle representing the entire system.

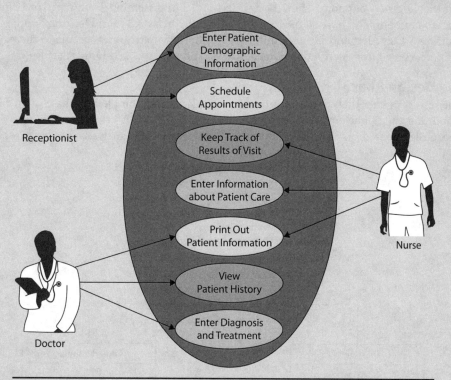

Figure 9-7   Use case diagram for patient record system

Another diagram initially developed during the Analysis phase when using the OO approach to systems analysis and design is called the *class diagram*.[6] The class diagram is used to represent the "objects" in the work environment that need to be modeled and included in the HIS being developed. Objects have some surface-level similarities to the entities in the ERD described earlier, from a traditional structured systems analysis and design standpoint. However, the class diagram is different from the ERD in a number of important ways. For example, in developing a clinical decision support (CDS) module of an HIS, as depicted in Figure 9-8, several types, or classes, of objects need to be understood and modeled. In the figure there are three classes of objects depicted in rectangles: Clinical Decision Support, Drug Alert, and Drug Reminder. Each class of objects has its own attributes. For example, the attributes of Clinical Decision Support are Invocation Style, Message Text, and Message Format, thus indicating that all types of clinical decision support have a particular way of being invoked, have some text to be displayed to users, and have some particular format for messages to users. The classes Drug Alert and Drug Reminder are subclasses of Clinical Decision Support, which is shown by the arrow with a triangle leading up to Clinical Decision Support. This means they *inherit* all of the attributes of Clinical Decision Support. Thus, Drug Alert and Drug Reminder are types of Clinical Decision Support and have all the features of their superclass Clinical Decision Support. In addition, Drug Alert and Drug Reminder have their own attributes specific to them. For example, every Drug Alert has an Urgency Level and an associated Drug Alert Rule.

The Design Phase

The results of the Analysis phase provide a foundation for the Design phase of an HIS. Obtaining the "right" information from the Analysis phase is critical to the success of HIS design. Based on the requirements gathered during the analysis, the design of the

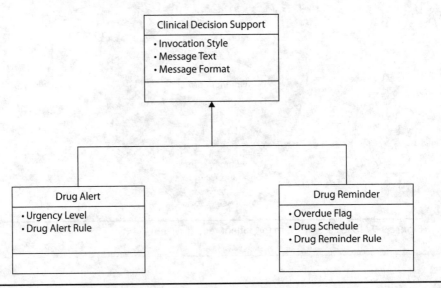

Figure 9-8 Class diagram for clinical decision support components

system is specified during the Design phase. The design can be considered the blueprint that specifies how the system will work. This is in contrast to the Analysis phase, which focuses on what the system will be able to do; in the Design phase, you move on to the consideration of *how* the system will do it. System design also involves the intensive use of diagramming and modeling techniques, as will be described. A wide range of design approaches and methodologies can be used to drive the design of complex systems such as an HIS. These range from traditional structured approaches to object-oriented approaches.[1] There are a number of considerations to keep in mind when moving from the Analysis phase to the Design phase, including the following:

- Has there been sufficient requirements gathering on which the design can be based?
- Will there continue to be sufficient end-user feedback during the design of the system?
- Is the appropriate design methodology being used for designing the system?

The design of an HIS includes the specification of the following:

- Designing the application architecture (i.e., describing how each system activity and function specified from the Analysis phase is carried out)
- Designing and integrating the network needed (i.e., specifying how the various parts of the system will communicate)
- Designing the user interface (i.e., specifying how users will interact with the system)
- Designing system interfaces (i.e., specifying how the system will work with other systems)
- Designing the underlying database (i.e., specifying how the system will store data)

As will be discussed, it is often recommended that an HIS design be carried out using an iterative approach that includes developing prototypes (partially working, limited versions of the system design) that can be quickly shown to end users to gain input and feedback into design (well before the design is finalized).[7] The result of the Design phase is essentially the "blueprint" for the HIS; this includes a range of models and diagrams that specify the needed components of the system and provide detail on how they will work and interact.

One of the most commonly used diagrams used for traditional structured HIS design is known as a *structure chart*, as depicted in Figure 9-9. The structure chart shows the modules of a system and their relationships. A module, which is represented by a box in the figure, is an identifiable component of a system that performs a desired function. This diagram shows a top-down hierarchical depiction of modules of a system. For example, the top module called Create New Medication Order has three immediate submodules below it: Record Medication Information, Process Medication Order, and Produce Confirmation. In turn, the module Record Medication Information can be broken down into the four modules below it: Enter Med Name, Enter Med Dose, Enter Med Route, and Enter Med Frequency. The lines in the chart show the calling structure from high-level modules down to ones at the bottom of the chart. For example, in Figure 9-9 you can see that from left to right, the top, or *boss*, module Create New Medication Order will first invoke or call Record Medication Information (e.g., to obtain input from the user about the medication to be recorded); then the boss module will call Process Medication Order (to actually process the medication order, check for drug interactions, send the information about it to a medication database, etc.), which is finally followed by the boss module calling the module Produce Confirmation (which displays to the end user a confirmation that the order has been made). It should be noted that some of these modules will themselves likely need to be broken down further. For example, Process Medication Order could be broken down to multiple submodules during the design process. This is known as *stepwise refinement*.

Using the object-oriented approach to systems design, an important type of diagram is called the *sequence diagram*.[6] With each use case developed during the Analysis phase, a corresponding sequence diagram is created to show how the use case actually works. For example, Figure 9-10 shows a corresponding sequence diagram for the use case Order New Medication (listed as one of the use cases from Figure 9-6). An important part of sequence diagrams is the concept of sending "messages" to objects that are needed to carry out functions required in a certain sequence over a period of time. The sequence diagram shows how the user initiates the interaction with the CPOE by first sending the message Create Order to the User Interface object, as shown in the top-left horizontal arrow from the actor to the User Interface object. The Create Order message includes in it the parameters for the following: the name of the medication to be ordered (i.e., Med), the dose, and the frequency (Freq). Next, the User Interface object sends the message Check Order to the CPOE object. That object in turn sends a Record Order message to the Patient Record object. Next, notice the arrows going in the other direction from the Patient Record object back to the CPOE object, back to the User Interface object, and finally back to the user, providing the user with a confirmation of the order. This simple example shows that the sequence diagram can elaborate on and provide design details for how a single use case works by showing how different system components interact

Figure 9-9
Structure chart
for the activ-
ity Create New
Medication Order

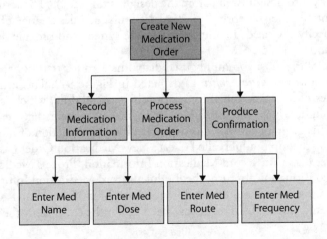

with each other by sending messages to each other in sequence over time to carry out an activity such as CPOE.

You should consider many principles of good design when developing HISs. For example, the concept of designing components of systems so that they are modular is one of the most important concepts. By good modularity we mean that the components or modules of a system have high *cohesion*, which means that each module focuses on one task and does that task well, as opposed to carrying out many functions. If a module is associated with more than one main task, it should be broken up or decomposed into submodules. Additionally, good modularity is associated with *loose coupling*, where the system modules do not interact closely with each other but are somewhat self-contained and do not inadvertently cause side effects with other modules.[1]

In addition to good modularity, a range of other good system design principles exist. For example, design patterns have emerged as sets of templates to speed up OO system development.[8] One group of design patterns states that systems should be developed in layers that can be easily interchanged or modified. For example, a typical three-layer system architecture consists of the following layers:[1] the user interface, or *view layer*; the business logic layer (containing the programming logic to run applications); and the data layer (the underlying database that the system reads and writes data to). The user interface, or view layer, is the part of the system that the user interacts with. If it is designed in a modular and self-contained way, with only a few well-defined connections and easily locatable interfaces to the layer immediately below it (the business logic layer), then

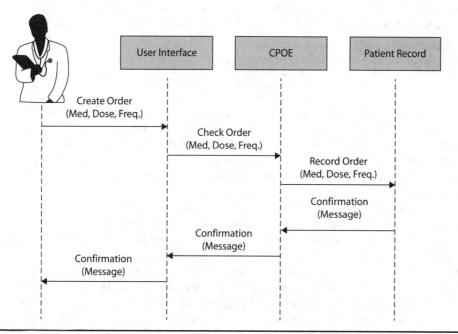

Figure 9-10 Sequence diagram for entering medications into a CPOE

as user interface technology improves, a new user interface can be added to the system easily by replacing that one layer. However, this will become difficult to do, or next to impossible to do easily, if the system's user interface calls or interacts extensively with the business logic layer below it. Likewise, if there are only a few clear and easily identifiable interfaces between the business logic layer and the underlying database layer, a new, more modern type of underlying database can be installed that will not require extensive reprogramming of the layers above it.

The Implementation Phase

Upon completion of the Design phase, the development project moves into the Implementation phase, where the design is translated into a working system by building running program code. This is the phase where the software of the HIS is constructed (or programmed), integrated with the required hardware, tested, and made ready for use in healthcare settings. The approach taken for implementation will depend on the system analysis and design methodology chosen and the type of programming languages and programming tools available. For example, if the traditional structured approach was used with the system analysis and design, then diagrams such as the structure charts would be developed to show how modules work together. In transitioning from design to implementation, the modules contained in the structure chart, as shown in Figure 9-9, are described in detail in terms of the programming code needed to carry out the function of each module. For example, the corresponding pseudocode (i.e., English-like specification of programming steps) for the top-level boss module Create New Medication Order in Figure 9-9 would serve to "call" the three modules directly below it (Record Medication Information, Process Medication Order, and Produce Confirmation). To do this, the pseudocode corresponding to this top-level module might look like the following:

```
Do until no more orders
Call module Record_Medication_Information;
Call module Process_Medication_Order;
Call module Produce_Confirmation;
```

This program-like code will be translated into the actual programming language used to implement the HIS, such as the C programming language or Java. Likewise, all the modules specified during the Design phase and represented in diagrams such as structure charts will be elaborated during the Implementation phase with programming code, as shown in Figure 9-11. This will eventually lead to a set of fully functional modules or a fully functioning HIS.

Top-down development refers to starting the development process (programming) with the module at the top of the structure chart. In contrast, *bottom-up development* refers to starting with the modules at the bottom of the structure chart, elaborating those modules with programming code first.[1] With the object-oriented methods, we approach this a slightly different way typically, by *scheduling* (i.e., elaborating with code) use cases. The first use cases to be scheduled are those that are judged by the developers to be most critical, risky, or important in the development of the HIS, such as a use case that other components of the HIS may rely on or that must work in order for all the other functions of the system to work.[8] We then proceed with developing use cases judged to be less

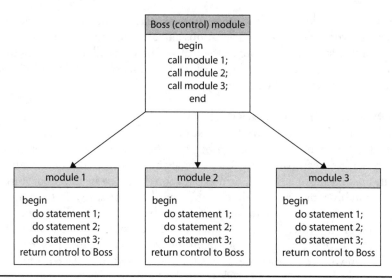

Figure 9-11 Example of a structure chart, with pseudocode programming statements

critical, once the main or most critical ones have been shown to work, at least as partially working prototypes.

These resulting program codes that correspond to different modules (or use cases) in the system's design can be tested individually through *unit testing*, where code corresponding to a module is tested on its own, or all program codes can be tested together with *integration testing*. Testing software systems and HISs in particular is an important area, and we refer you to complete books on this topic.[9] Here, we will briefly define two main approaches to testing of HIS software: black-box testing and white-box testing.

Black-box testing, also known as *testing with blinders on*, refers to testing a system by giving the system specific inputs and then testing to determine whether the right outputs result.[10] For example, you may black-box test a clinical decision support system that produces drug alerts in response to the entry of drugs that a patient might have an allergy to. You can do this by creating a list of drugs to be inputted into the system that should trigger the system to output drug alerts. The output of the system, in this case alerts, would then be compared to expected outputs to determine whether the system is working properly for all test cases (i.e., the system produces alerts when expected and does not produce alerts when not expected to). Black-box testing does not require that the testing team have knowledge of the underlying computer processes or software and is often used to test commercial vendor–based systems in hospitals when they are initially installed to check their correctness and safety.

In contrast, *white-box testing*, also known as glass-box testing, requires knowledge of underlying program code and internal aspects of a system. With this type of testing, specific parts of the software's underlying logic are "stepped through" (examined by a team of programmers and analysts) to determine whether the computer logic is working as expected.[10] It is important to note that as important as white- and black-box testing are,

HISs are typically deployed in healthcare contexts that are much more varied and complex than other types of computer applications and also require extensive user acceptance testing, usability testing, and testing in the real setting of use.[11] These methods focus on user interactions to determine whether the HIS is usable, safe, and enjoyable (or not) to use in real and complex healthcare settings.

The Support and Maintenance Phase

Once the HIS has been put into place in a healthcare setting, the ongoing process of support and maintenance of the system begins. The system may be in place for a long period of time; however, over time, there are always changes that need to be made to improve it, make it more efficient, or make it more likely to be adopted. Furthermore, HISs are inevitably replaced over time as their hardware or software becomes obsolete. Therefore, over time new systems analysis has to be conducted to determine requirements for system modification or termination. Thus, system development is seen as being cyclical, where the progress from planning to support/maintenance then eventually begins again when existing systems need to be updated or replaced. This is depicted in Figure 9-2 by the arrow going back from the Support (Maintenance) phase to the Planning (Needs Analysis) phase.

Trends and Issues in HIS Analysis and Design

Approaches to the development of complex systems such as HISs have evolved considerably over the past few decades. The traditional model for developing systems is often called the *classic waterfall life cycle*. This approach to the SDLC involves the stages described earlier (Planning, Analysis, Design, Implementation, and Support) following one another in such a way that one follows the other in strict sequential order (see Figure 9-12). Once Analysis is complete, the requirements are finalized, and the project moves to the Design phase. Once the Design phase is complete, the project moves to the Implementation phase, and once that phase is complete, the project moves to the Support phase. The approach is like a waterfall, since as the development process moves down to the next phase, it is difficult to go back to the previous phase. Therefore, the project "flows" downward. At each phase, the results, or the requirements specification produced from the Analysis phase, are typically "signed off" as complete by both the developer and the client before moving to the next phase. After the system is in place, the up arrows in the figure indicate that parts of the process may need to be modified or updated. This is typically costly and difficult to do once the system has been implemented. This type of model has been used successfully for many types of IT applications, particularly for traditional software applications such as standard business systems such as payroll applications.[1] For more complex types of applications such as complex EHRs, clinical decision support systems, patient applications, or public health informatics systems, this approach has the drawback of expecting that most if not all user requirements can be gathered once and for all during the Analysis phase. Likewise, once the design of the system is set in the Design phase, it may be difficult and costly to try to go back to the Analysis phase as the project moves on and the Analysis phase has already been signed off as completed.

In applications that are complex and that may require some piloting or experimentation, this approach may not be the best. Likewise, applications such as advanced EHRs, clinical decision support systems, and many emerging types of health applications typically require continual user evaluation and input, particularly if they are highly interactive systems.[7]

An alternative to the classic waterfall approach is known as *rapid prototyping*. This approach, which has become increasingly popular as systems become more complex, involves cycles of design, construction, and refinement of prototypes (which are incomplete but partially working versions of the system) and evaluation with end users (see Figure 9-13). In this approach, it is not assumed that initial requirements will be completely obtained at the very beginning of the development process but rather that enough requirements need to be gathered in order to start developing a working and testable prototype that is then evaluated to determine whether more requirements and design are needed (i.e., the arrow going from the Evaluation box back to the Requirements Gathering box in Figure 9-13). This cycling may continue until no more iterations are needed, such as when an evaluation indicates that final engineering of the system can be carried out or until time or money runs out. Variations of this may involve setting a fixed length of time for each iteration (an approach known as *time boxing*), in which testable and continual progress can be demonstrated in developing software components.[12]

Agile software development is an approach to developing systems that involves prototyping and that has emerged as a way to develop systems rapidly. Some key principles of Agile development are the following:[12]

- Make customer/user satisfaction the main goal through early and continuous delivery of valuable and useful software.

- Changing requirements are welcome, even in later stages of system development.

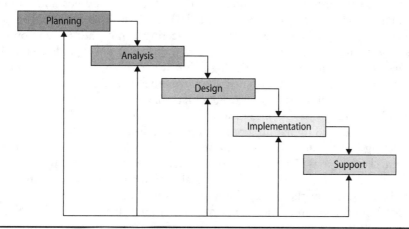

Figure 9-12   The classical "waterfall" life cycle

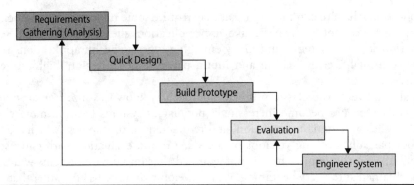

Figure 9-13 Rapid prototyping

- Prototypes and working software should be delivered at frequent intervals.
- End users and developers should work together daily throughout the project.
- Face-to-face communication is effective for conveying information during design.
- Working software is the main measure of progress.
- There should be continuous attention to technical excellence.
- Simplicity is a goal.
- Self-organizing teams should be encouraged.
- The team should reflect on progress at regular intervals.

These principles of system design and implementation should be considered in HIS development as they have been shown to be important in delivery of systems that are more likely to be adopted by end users.[13]

We refer you to other books to obtain details about the many possible variations of the previous models for carrying out the SDLC.[4] Because HIS development is complex, a thorough understanding of the options in selecting approaches to developing such systems is becoming ever more critical. Some of these variations include combining the advantages of rapid prototyping with the classic waterfall approach. For example, for applications where there is uncertainty about whether technical requirements can be met, as in some complex HIS initiatives, a first phase of rapid prototyping might be appropriate in order to assess whether the system is technically feasible and to gain information that can be used in planning out a more fixed development process. In this case, after obtaining information about technical and user requirements from building prototypes, the classic waterfall approach can be initiated in order to develop and complete the HIS. The advantages here include a better ability to estimate the time and difficulty of the different stages of the waterfall approach as well as the reduction of the risk of system development failure. Prototyping may determine that a planned HIS may not be as achievable as initially conceived before going in to an expensive and difficult-to-modify waterfall development phase. Many of these ideas are now incorporated in OO systems analysis and design, with approaches such as the aforementioned Agile programming, which promotes considerable flexibility in the ordering and sequencing involved in developing a system; the Unified Process, which employs time boxing as described earlier; and Extreme Programming, which involves carrying out fast and iterative cycles of system development. For more information about these approaches, we recommend you look at McConnell and other sources.[4]

As a final consideration, it should be noted that in HIT, many organizations, particularly hospitals or health authorities, may be involved in a combination of "building" system components and "buying" and subsequently integrating system components. This distinction is often referred to as the *buy versus build* distinction, where the management of healthcare organizations must decide which parts of an HIS will be developed and programmed from scratch and which will be purchased either as completed software systems or as software components to be integrated with existing healthcare IT. This has a number of implications, including deciding whether a healthcare organization has the capability to develop a system or should purchase a completed solution from an HIS vendor. A related decision is with regard to what extent a healthcare organization's HISs should be purchased from the same vendor or from a variety of different vendors (also known as the *best-of-breed* approach). Regardless of whether you are involved in development of HIT and HIS from scratch, such as developing HIT applications from planning through to design and implementation, or you are working in an organization considering buying a completed off-the-shelf HIT or HIS, an understanding of the principles of health information systems analysis and design is essential for successfully deploying information technology that has a good chance of supporting and improving healthcare.

Chapter Review

The development of HISs is complex, and systems that are used in healthcare settings must be carefully designed to meet the intended needs safely and efficiently. The core of development of an effective HIS is good systems analysis and design. This involves understanding the information needs of healthcare professionals, including the technical, functional, and nonfunctional requirements for a new HIS. In addition, the concept of the systems development life cycle is central to systems analysis and design, because it provides a framework from which to consider the development of systems, from the initial Planning phase all the way through to the Analysis and Design phases and then finally to the implementation and deployment of the system in a healthcare facility. In this chapter, we described a variety of diagramming and modeling tools that are routinely used to support HIS analysis and design. The traditional, structured approach includes data flow diagrams, entity relationship diagrams, and structure charts. The alternative approach, known as OO systems analysis and design, employs use case, class, and sequence diagrams. It is important for anyone engaged in systems analysis and design in HIT to be familiar with these approaches, tools, and methodologies. In addition, it is becoming increasingly important for those designing HISs to have an understanding of the trends in the analysis, design, and testing of HISs.

Questions

To test your comprehension of the chapter, answer the following questions and then check your answers against the list of correct answers at the end of the chapter.

1. Which is an example of an object-oriented diagram that depicts overall system requirements?

   A. Sequence diagram

   B. Use case diagram

   C. Data flow diagram

   D. Entity relationship diagram

2. What does the SDLC do?

   A. Provides guidance in system development

   B. Provides a checklist of activities

   C. Provides a set of stages for system development

   D. All of the above

3. What does the classic waterfall life cycle do?

   A. Assumes that most requirements can be obtained early on in the SDLC

   B. Allows for flexibility in carrying out systems analysis and design activities

   C. Allows for easily redoing phases

   D. Is well suited for the development of a complex interactive HIT application

4. Black-box testing refers to what?

   A. Testing the internal logic of a health information system

   B. Testing system components in isolation

   C. Testing system components in an integrated manner

   D. Testing systems without considering underlying program logic

5. What is rapid prototyping?

   A. It involves iterative cycles of development and testing.

   B. It is often associated with object-oriented development approaches.

   C. It is useful in designing complex or highly interactive systems.

   D. All of the above.

   E. None of the above.

PART II

6. Which of the following is *not* true about Agile design?

    A. Ensuring end user satisfaction is the highest goal.

    B. Requirements should not be changed after the system design phase is complete.

    C. Time-boxing can be used to drive iterative cycles of development.

    D. The best designs often emerge from self-organizing teams, so this should be encouraged.

Answers

1. **B.** An example of an object-oriented diagram that depicts overall system requirements is a use case diagram.

2. **D.** The systems development life cycle (SDLC) involves the following phases: Planning, Analysis, Design, Implementation, and Support. It involves activities and phenomena such as guidance in system development, a checklist of activities, and a set of stages for system development.

3. **A.** The classic waterfall life cycle assumes that most requirements can be obtained early on in the SDLC and that those requirements remain fundamentally static and stable during the entire SDLC.

4. **D.** Black-box testing refers to testing systems without considering underlying program logic.

5. **D.** Rapid prototyping involves iterative cycles of development and testing, is often associated with object-oriented development approaches, and is useful in designing complex or highly interactive systems.

6. **B.** Using the Agile approach, changes to requirements are welcome throughout the entire process of system development, even during later stages and after initial system design has been completed.

References

1. Satzinger, J. W., Jackson, R. B., & Burd, S. D. (2002). *Systems analysis and design in a changing world*. Course Technology—Thomson Learning.

2. Shortliffe, E., & Cimino, J. (2006). *Biomedical informatics: Computer applications in health care and biomedicine*. Springer.

3. Cysneiros, L., & Leite, J. (2004). Nonfunctional requirements: From elicitation to conceptual models. *IEEE Transactions on Software Engineering, 30*, 328–350.

4. McConnell, S. (1996). *Rapid development: Taming wild software schedules*. Microsoft Press.

5. Martin, M. P. (1991). *Analysis and design of business information systems.* MacMillan.

6. Satzinger, J. W., & Orvik, T. U. (2001). *The object-oriented approach: Concepts, system development, and modeling with UML.* Course Technology—Thomson Learning.

7. Kushniruk, A. W. (2002). Evaluation in the design of health information systems: Applications of approaches emerging from systems engineering. *Computers in Biology and Medicine, 32,* 141–149.

8. Larman, C. (2002). *Applying UML and patterns: An introduction to object-oriented analysis and design and the unified process.* Prentice Hall.

9. Patton, R. (2001). *Software testing.* Sams.

10. Kaner, C., Falk, J., & Nguyen, H. (1999). *Testing computer software.* John Wiley & Sons.

11. Kushniruk, A., Borycki, E., Kuo, M. H., & Kuwata, S. (2010). Integrating technology-centric and user-centric testing methods: Ensuring healthcare system usability and safety. *Studies in Health Technology and Informatics, 157,* 181–186.

12. Ambler, S. W. (2002). *Agile modeling: Effective practices for eXtreme programming and the unified process.* John Wiley & Sons.

13. Ratcliffe, L., & McNeil, M. (2012). *Agile experience design: A digital designer's guide to Agile, lean and continuous.* New Riders.

CHAPTER 10

Fundamentals of Health Workflow Process Analysis and Redesign

J. Michael Kramer, Sheila Ochylski, Jane Brokel

In this chapter, you will learn how to

- Explain essential steps in design and development of a large electronic health record system and present an implementation method for large-scale process change
- Participate in the design of processes and information flows for clinical practice using engineering methods that accommodate evidence-based safety practices, quality improvement, and reporting
- Participate in developing within a healthcare system a sustainable plan for a revised and optimized clinical workflow that integrates professional practices and meaningful use of information technology
- Plan, analyze, and develop a process map for given clinical workflows within a complex healthcare system
- Critically analyze and document clinical and healthcare business processes by identifying gaps between current and desired states, areas of redundancy, delays, inefficiencies, work volume, task times, and elapsed times in order to redesign or optimize workflows
- Design, test, and implement information technology that supports effective teamwork, fosters open communications and care coordination, and enables shared decision making to achieve quality patient care
- Design and apply information technology and standardized practices that support documentation of compliance with applicable healthcare industry, regulatory, organizational safety, and quality standards

Implementing health information systems across an organization brings an unprecedented magnitude of change to that organization. This chapter reviews two major tools necessary to manage such change: process modeling and organization-wide change management. Before we discuss utilizing these tools, we will consider an important step in the life cycle of change. Traditional "project management," discussed in Chapter 11, considers project closure as a phase of a change. At the project closure of a large-scale health information technology (HIT) implementation project, the team is often redeployed to other work, and the change is largely considered complete. However, the need to constantly apply new scientific evidence to clinical practice as well as frequent rapidly evolving healthcare accreditation, certification, and regulatory standards necessitates another approach. Sustained resources (certainly less than the large infusion of the many extra resources during the implementation project, but extra resources nonetheless) are necessary to sustain major HIT systems in an ongoing manner after the system has been implemented. Having the appropriate skills and teams to manage ongoing change is necessary to control the continuing work. Therefore, the concept of project closure per se is obsolete if organizations expect to leverage their newly implemented information systems to achieve higher levels of quality and safety.

Life Cycle of Major Information Technology Implementation and Organizational Change

To understand how health information technology can be managed, an appreciation for the larger context of change is necessary. As the United States implements electronic health records (EHRs) in every hospital and medical practice, EHRs become central to each organizations' operations.[1, 2, 3] Therefore, the responsibility and need to sustain systems in a practice or hospital does not end with the initial implementation. Each organization will choose how to support and maintain its systems differently with varying leadership models, teams, and reporting structures. See Chapter 18 for a more detailed discussion on governance.

No matter the model of support, we have observed a very clear life cycle in implementing EHRs across our combined experience in 35 hospitals and several large ambulatory practices. The phases of large-scale HIT change can be described as planning with analysis, implementation, stabilization, optimization, and transformation. This is depicted in the first row of Figure 10-1. Planning and implementation require a great deal of thorough analysis and traditional project management, which is clear to most organizations. The time it takes post-implementation to reset to new normal and stabilized operations, with productivity and other new EHR/transformation gains realized, is not always appreciated. In our experience, the movement from implementation to transformation varies across organizations. The characteristics, risks, benefits, and the HIT professional role with each phase are listed and further described in Table 10-1. Despite rigorous planning and thoughtful and careful implementation, there is still the risk of end-user workarounds and suboptimal benefits realization.

TIP   A *workaround* is a way to use the system in a fashion that was not designed or intended. Workarounds result in unplanned and unexpected outcomes.[4] A physician might not find a lab test so instead enters an electronic order to the nurse with a typed comment to order the blood test. This workaround results in a delay in the lab completing the test because of the extra steps required for the nurse to clarify the order for completing the test.

Phase	Characteristics	Best Practices and Other Considerations
Planning and Analysis	This phase usually uses traditional project management approaches, which include project conception, initiation, planning, analysis and project tracking. Analysis requires verification, validation, and reliability testing on activities to solve problems prior to implementation.	Participation and contribution require carefully identifying and tracking project activities. Information gathering for assessing resource requirements and providing updates on tasks/deliverables. Help define and prioritize requirements for interoperability and apply approved data management and information practices.
Implementation	Go-live and activation of the software, which may be phased or all at once, occurs in this phase. Communication activities are in place with users, support team, technical team, and management team to find issues and observe software use. Overall, this phase requires more detail than any other phase.	User support and training must be carefully planned by clinician or workforce educators in collaboration with HIT professionals. Documentation of issues with analytical tools/database to follow and later optimize with quality improvement methods. Monitoring usage and tracking unexpected outcomes or harms that occur.
Stabilization	This is the period in which an organization has not yet returned to normal operations. Support resources may be less numerous. Users are finding gaps between previous workflows and new workflows.	Evaluation of the implemented solution with business requirements is necessary. This is a period of greatest user frustration and highest risk for workarounds and errors of omission of care.[5] Participate in the identification of workarounds or reoccurring issues and logging a need for solutions. Use best practice methodologies to develop a maintenance plan to address changes.
Optimization	After weeks or months, an organization returns to the new normal level of patient care. Clinicians and support personnel have identified most of the workarounds or best practices in order to continue operations.	Without careful management, users will circumvent major safety and other benefits of the system to manage day to day. This will place the system benefit at risk. Participate in development of proposals that include recommended approaches and solutions and recognize major risks or benefits associated with different solutions.
Transformation	An organization begins to understand how to manage the system. They embrace change and leverage data in the system to improve their practice/operations and inform stakeholders of their performance.	Transformation elevates an organization to a higher level. Failure to recruit or train experts on the new technology will limit this opportunity. Develop proper documentation for requests for information and maintain documentation on the compatibility of software, hardware, and network components to evolve the EHR use cases in the future (e.g., information exchange) for continuity of care.

Table 10-1 Summary of the Life Cycle of Large-Scale HIT Change and HIT Role

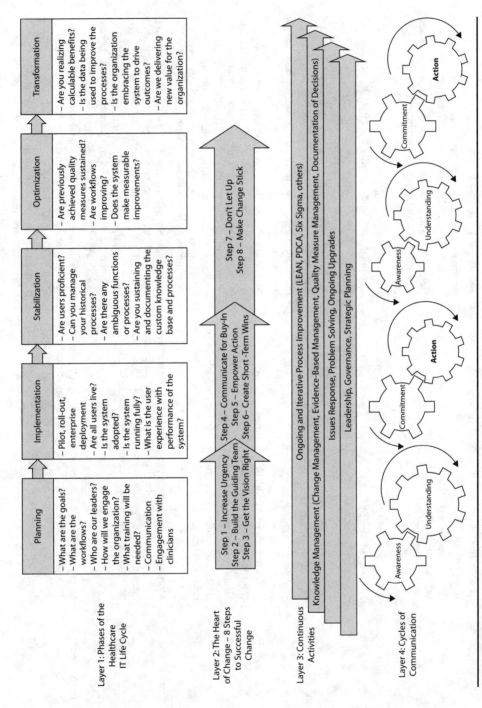

Figure 10-1 Activities across the life of a major healthcare IT implementation

In addition to the stages of implementation described in Table 10-1, Figure 10-1 introduces three additional organizational approaches to managing large-scale change that are illustrated in the second through fourth layers of the diagram: Layer 2: The Heart of Change—8 Steps to Successful Change, Layer 3: Continuous Activities, and Layer 4: Cycles of Communication. Large-scale organizational change management planning can reduce provider dissatisfaction, a prolonged stabilization phase, and a number of work-arounds. Organizational change management is discussed further later in this chapter. Layer 2 is credited to Kotter and Cohen and provides a framework to develop four core activities that will help manage large-scale organizational change.[6] Layer 3 with its four long arrows within the life cycle of change display how organizations must develop approaches to ongoing evolution and change in the system. These activities include maintaining the system knowledge base. Chapter 20 addresses the importance of maintaining and updating the system's content (e.g., order sets, rules, and workflows) to stay current with advances in medical science, health regulation, and quality measures. Finally, with each change, organizations must maintain multiple cycles and methods of communication with all stakeholders. This is represented by the cogs in Layer 4 of Figure 10-1.[6] Effective communication increases the awareness of the need to change, the understanding of the processes, the commitment to change, and the actions to achieve the desired changes and outcomes. These concepts are part of a theoretical model of change that is very helpful in creating a sequence of communications around major change.

Process Management and Process Improvement

When mapping processes for healthcare services, the opportunity exists to continuously improve patient care delivery by using safety and quality practices and reporting methods that are the best available based on scientific evidence. In this section we describe a process hierarchy for workflow analysis that HIT professionals can use to support stakeholders who are planning and implementing changes. A central theme to workflow analysis and redesign of care is keeping the patient and their information centered in the approach. This section discusses five levels of process mapping (see Table 10-2) that guide designers

Level	Description
Level 1: Enterprise to Enterprise	This workflow describes referrals, full service, and community care among multiple locations for a population of patients (e.g., care for child with genetic-oriented disability involving a broad team for full range services).
Level 2: Venue to Venue	This workflow describes care for a service line in a given setting (e.g., emergency services or obstetrics).
Level 3: Roles to Patient	This workflow describes the interactions of providers with patients and with each other (role-based, patient-centered).
Level 4: Task to Task	This workflow describes the detailed steps for a procedure of care (e.g., ordering).
Level 5: Application Function	This workflow describes the use of data or information within an EHR, decision support, or exchange application (e.g., data use within clinical rules and messages produced).

Table 10-2 Descriptions for Levels of Mapping Processes

to consider the scope and standards of practice for key healthcare professionals, the accreditation and regulatory requirements, the Centers for Medicare and Medicaid Services (CMS) EHR meaningful use incentive program requirements, quality and patient safety goals, and new legislative requirements such as the Medicare Access and CHIP Reauthorization Act (MACRA).

Process Hierarchy: Levels of Mapping Processes

A process hierarchy for workflow analysis and design can be an effective approach to meet stakeholder needs in planning and implementing initial and ongoing changes. Stakeholders in this context include administrators, clinicians, department staff, and individuals who have specific tasks and functions.

Level 1: Enterprise to Enterprise

The first level is used by senior leaders who organize care among multiple settings for a population that will need full-service healthcare through community and referral providers. This first level is described as enterprise-to-enterprise mapping with a patient-centric viewpoint. This viewpoint ensures there are services available and that region-wide health information exchange of standard documents such as continuity of care documents—which include a patient's problem list, medication profile, allergies, immunizations, and care plan—can enable sharing and movement of data between entities to accommodate the patient's needs for holistic healthcare. This first level will capture the patient's broad experience of moving in and out of provider venues and processes that support the clinical practice and patient needs, financial compensation and accounting, and public health obligations (e.g., immunizations, disease surveillance). Figure 10-2 illustrates what the patient may experience using healthcare services starting with the call for help and ending with a return home to self-manage their health.

Level 2: Venue to Venue

While patients perceive their care as being across visits and encounters with the healthcare system, many providers focus on care within one site such as a hospital or clinic. The second level in the leveled process mapping approach, venue to venue, consists of major service lines such as emergency, surgical, or oncology services. The service line director and clinical team are stakeholders who understand care delivery. This level proceeds from the first level by explaining the clinical processes the patient and family are involved in. Reuse of common processes reduces variation in the healthcare professional's workflow, such as medication management that applies to most venues and all service lines of care. This standardization of process activities supports safety and quality across the service lines of care so that the process steps for medication ordering, medication databases with allergy or drug-drug interaction alerting (some medications interact with each other in patients such that the combination can be dangerous; drug-drug interaction alerting at the time of medication ordering is a HIT safety feature), medication dispensing, medication administration, and medication evaluation with documentation of therapeutic or side effects and adverse events are consistent and harmonized across the services.

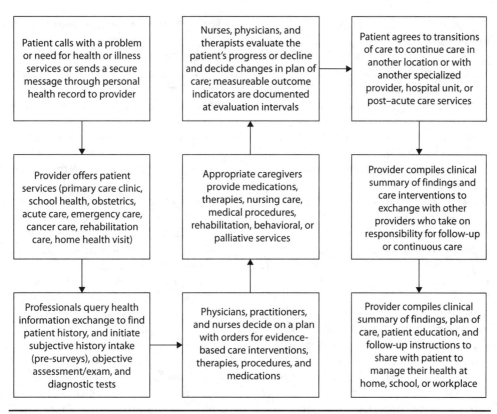

Figure 10-2   Enterprise-level processes for data, information, and knowledge use

---

TIP   For a patient undergoing surgery, typical processes include registration, pre-admission testing activities, surgical and anesthesia preparations, intraoperative procedures with pathology examination for specimens, postoperative care, shift change or handoff activities, daily care coordination, transfer and/or discharge, quality monitoring and reporting, as well as hospitalist consultation, diagnostic radiology, laboratory, and pharmaceutical services. Viewing the delivery of care as a modular activity allows reuse of defined processes within multiple venues and across multiple scenarios.

Level 3: Roles to Patient

The third level involves engineering role-based workflows within the clinical processes identified at the second level. "Roles to patient" reflects the reality that in many healthcare delivery processes, even modestly complex ones, there are many different types of healthcare professionals and healthcare workforce members that interact interdependently with patients to throughput patients through the system while striving for optimal outcomes for patients. This level will assist healthcare workforce members, professionals, and managers/leaders to emphasize interactions with the patient while specifying multiple process and documentation requirements established by federal agencies and states who license physicians, nurses, pharmacists, therapists, and technicians. The HIT professional evaluates these processes as implemented to identify problems and changes needed by interacting regularly with the clinical professionals. The HIT professional may be asked to present plans for potential process change to these clinicians to optimize clinical practice to meet new demands for services related to evidence-based research or regulatory updates.

Continuing our example of the medication management process at the third level, this process is viewed in more specific detail as a person-to-person workflow where three or more professional roles interact to use patient data, information, and evidence-based knowledge for clinical decisions. One decision may include a physician's order/prescription of a beta blocker for a specific patient's diagnoses and whether the nurse is to administer the medication when the patient's current vital sign assessments for blood pressure and heart rate are unstable (i.e., low). Does the existing technology used by the nurse allow visualization of current assessments in the medication administration record to support a decision to administer or not administer the medication at the scheduled time? Medications have therapeutic effects, side effects, and adverse effects that a nurse evaluates and documents before and after administering the medicine. Will the technology support or add extra steps for the nurse to ensure the medication can be given safely and according to evidence-based practices? As you will see depicted later in the chapter in the section "Role-Based Swim-Lane Workflow," the third level is a patient-centered workflow with the patient's role in the center of the swim-lane rows using a cross-functional flowchart.[7] This workflow defines the steps in each role where the communication of data, information, and knowledge within professional practices flows seamlessly to ensure proper handoffs across shifts or on a daily basis to safeguard care continuously for a patient.

 TIP Level 3 focuses on clinician interactions with patients within the workflow and addresses the following question: Does the clinician have access to the right information at the right time when performing functions such as medication administration, clinical treatments, or respiratory therapies?

Role-based workflows—such as those for physicians or nurses or pharmacists—identify the timely collection and documentation of patient information, providing access to the data for subsequent clinical decisions. In analyzing the workflow, HIT professionals need to account for each delay in getting information, potential gaps, areas of redundancy, manual work on the part of clinicians, work volume added to the clinician, task time to accomplish a process using the technology, and elapsed time between clinician process steps. Each of these could add to safety concerns, duplications in documentation of care or orders, or quality of care errors. Role-based workflows provide a framework for how EHRs are designed to manage information for decision makers and those coordinating care with other providers or departments. The availability of patient data and evidence-based knowledge resources (e.g., drug and disease databases, nurse procedure/intervention databases, cancer protocols) is necessary in the workflow to support clinical decisions and appropriate treatment steps. HIT professionals should focus on processes that are necessary in the clinicians' roles when providing care and monitor for unintended consequences of change with an EHR when a clinician's practice is not fully supported. An example of a gap is when a care practice to document the risk for aspiration and planned interventions is not possible within the EHR system and the care is forgotten or omitted. Solutions to avoid errors of omission include adding risks to the problem list, reminders, dashboards, templates, or other types of clinical decision support.[5] Person-to-person and patient-centered service-line workflows minimize the stress and better coordinate the complex activities of implementations.[8]

 TIP Standardizing the care process into modules and the various workflows (role-based person-to-person, task, and functional) is useful to transfer process knowledge from one setting to the next.

Communication of information can be accomplished via electronic methods, direct conversation, or paper methods. These person-to-person handoffs identify the professional's scope of practice to care for patients, which includes their use of trended and aggregated information to evaluate patient status over time. The role-based (person-to-person) workflows use action verbs in the process steps (rectangles) to describe the activities each healthcare professional performs in a given venue (e.g., admission, clinic visit, surgery) (see Figure 10-3 later in this chapter). This workflow displays questions to describe which physician or nurse decisions (diamonds) have to be made (e.g., medication management, transfer, discharge). In the analysis of process mapping, action steps, decisions, and movement of information are identified and documented. This process is enhanced when healthcare professionals and workforce members participate in actively informing the workflow diagrams as they are created and revised. One technique often employed by HIT professionals is to ask many questions of healthcare professionals and workforce members about the process being depicted. Another technique is to "demo" (demonstrate) system functionality that could potentially support the clinical process being depicted in a more effective or efficient way. The interaction between healthcare professionals and workforce members and HIT professionals by these and other techniques can strengthen the quality of the workflow diagrams created and the eventual HIT functionality that the diagrams inform. Besides these level 3 diagrams' primary use for designing/redesigning processes and workflows, the diagrams created at this level are used for training healthcare professionals and support personnel so they understand what the technology can and cannot do before any implementation. The workflow can avoid workarounds because the caregivers know how the technology is used or not used in the workflow to accomplish care activities.

As an example, the nurse will see the nursing process steps displayed within the work-flow and can relate nursing practice steps in their use of the EHR system. Randell et al. found that nurses are more likely to change their actions when they are involved and understand why the nursing process is better when using the EHR system.[9] Physicians respond similarly when they know why a given step is important.[3] This level of patient-centered cross-functional workflow provides a far better illustration of the steps for each role when working with patients.[3, 7, 9]

Level 4: Task to Task

The fourth level is task to task. At this level, the detailed use of a function is described. To illustrate, how does a physician order a radiologic test that requires pretest preparations and the holding of a medication prior to and 24 hours after the test? These workflows are modular in that they are specific to a task being completed by someone. This computer-ized ordering step can vary from other ordering processes, and therefore a task-oriented workflow provides the orientation to the additional steps necessary. These unique tasks are limited to a few professionals or support personnel to complete, while most others don't require this level of detail.

Level 5: Application Function

The last and fifth level of workflow is described as application function. These workflows generally are modular and depict the functioning of the application itself, or HIT system, with little human or user involvement. For example, the EHR's problem list may be used in several summary views, such as screen displays within the care planning function for nurses or ordering by physicians who need to link medications or interventions to condi-tions on the problem list. The application function workflow for this example would be very detailed and reference many modules and sub-modules of the application such as the care planning module and decision support module.

 TIP The flow of information in an EHR application, such as clinical decision support applications (covered in more detail in Chapter 20), is typically more automated than paper-based systems and often requires less human interaction.

Workflow for a functional application has a very limited focus, such as clinical deci-sion support or documenting allergies or supporting a specific decision. Although this workflow level lacks the perspective of care delivery, it is essential for achieving safety, avoiding errors, and meeting quality measures or regulatory requirements to share data.

 TIP The person-to-person development of workflows displays time-oriented interaction and steps taken for all the interdisciplinary team's processes occurring with patients.

Methodologies for Understanding Processes

There are several methods for understanding processes:

- Observation of current daily workflow
- Modeling workflow based on the formal scope of professional practice standards
- Simulation of the proposed workflow steps
- Quality-based deployment strategies such as Lean and Six Sigma
- Continuous workflow improvement with functional technology advances

Most organizations use business process management and modeling tools such as Microsoft Visio or others. Benefits and limitations for each method are described in the following pages. This discussion of methodologies for understanding processes is designed to help you critically analyze the workflow processes in a selected clinical setting, taking into account potential gaps, areas of redundancy, delays, inefficiencies, work volume, task time, elapsed time, and other factors.

Observation

Observation provides an opportunity to view settings and see various patient scenarios within each setting. This method is very good for understanding the task time, manual work, delays, and multiple variations that exist within care processes for a discipline. Observation is beneficial to highlight the typical time it takes to complete a task and to identify variations in practice among professionals. While there may be a good reason for variation, a common result is unnecessary cost and inefficiency. The Lean principle of Gemba is a tool to observe workflow. "Gemba" is a Japanese word that refers to the location where value is created. The principle behind "going to Gemba" (meaning the "place where the work is being done") is commonly used by Lean experts. The foundation of this principle is to observe the actual process to get the facts and data.[10]

Modeling Workflows for Scope of Professional Practice Standards

A second method for understanding processes is modeling that is informed by the scope of healthcare professional practice. Data, information, and evidence-based knowledge are used to analyze clinical decision-making requirements.

Professional practice standards are sources to identify who, what, when, how, and where information is needed. Information technology professionals may not understand or appreciate the differences, unique responsibilities, and accountabilities for each of the healthcare disciplines that are central to patient services. The processes followed by each clinical discipline or role (such as medical assistant, nurse, or physician) are equally important to the patient's care and treatment. As an example, the professional practice standards for pediatric nurses would be found in *Pediatric Nursing: Scope and Standards of Practice, Second Edition*,[11] which outlines the practice for nursing assessment, diagnosis, outcomes identification, planning care, implementation of care, coordination of care, health teaching and health promotion, consultation, and evaluation in all settings and inclusive of the role of parents and family with pediatric care.

TIP Spending time with clinicians (or, "going to the Gemba") as they provide care can help IT professionals appreciate the time and other resource constraints caregivers encounter and identify and take into account potential functionality or other gaps of the EHR .

Physicians examine, diagnose, and order medications and therapies to treat diseases and injuries or perform noninvasive or invasive procedures to improve a disease process or medical condition over time. Physicians can be specialized by the age groups they treat or in primary-care practice for all ages, while many more physicians focus on a specific body system such as cardiovascular, orthopedics, or psychiatry. (You can find more detail on care within and across venues and various medical roles and specialties roles in the appendix about healthcare professional and workforce roles. See Appendix C for how to access this content.) EHRs aggregate patient information and historical information along with drug and disease databases, laboratory, radiology, and other diagnostic references, and evidence-based guidelines to support physician decisions on diagnoses, plan for care, referrals, consultations, treatment, and follow-up. Table 10-3 describes processes and decisions for different healthcare professionals. When the EHR system lacks the ability to organize and aggregate pertinent data for a clinician or specialized practice, the professional frequently finds workaround alternatives to accomplish the same function and come up with a treatment plan individualized to the patient's condition.

Nurses—the largest group of healthcare professionals in acute-care and other healthcare facilities—are often the main users of EHR systems, providing around-the-clock coverage for patients in a number of venues. Table 10-3 highlights the major activities of the nursing process and decisions for the patient. While physicians are usually responsible for the overall management of a given disease, the nurses typically carry out the recommendations made by the physician and also address a number of patient responses including fear, agitation, confusion, nausea, acute or chronic pain, impaired

Roles	Activities and Decisions
Physician	• Reviews medical history (subjective); examines body systems (objective) • Orders diagnostic testing and focused assessments and care restrictions or limitations • Diagnoses disease or medical condition (e.g., diabetes, renal insufficiency) • Orders medications and treatment plan; consults other disciplines to evaluate and/or treat • Documents steps in procedures performed • Evaluates the resolution of the disease
Nurse	• Interviews and assesses human responses for functional health patterns • Diagnoses problems, risks, and needs for health enhancement • Determines what the patient and family desire for outcomes (i.e., their priorities) • Organizes and coordinates the plan of care • Schedules, educates, monitors, and documents performed interventions • Evaluates the effects of interventions and medications and records the progress/decline in patient's outcomes

Table 10-3 Processes and Decisions in Scope of Healthcare Professional Practices and Patient Care

Roles	Activities and Decisions
Pharmacist	• Reviews the patient's profile of medications, appropriate dosing, and known interactions • Verifies the medication as appropriate for indications • Consults with physician if a discrepancy in drug choice, dosing, or interactions is identified • Dispenses prescription medications • Educates and validates patient's understanding of dosing and side effects • Reviews lab tests and refills prescriptions
Therapist *	• Accepts order and schedules evaluation and treatments • Evaluates current patient capabilities (for example, a speech therapist conducts a detailed evaluation of the speaking ability of a recent stroke victim with new speech deficits) • Shares the therapy plan and timeline for patient activities • Evaluates the patient pre- and post-patient activities • Trends the progress or lack of progress in physical or occupational abilities • Reports the progress to the provider
Technician	• Identifies and changes schedule based on order urgency • Determines appropriateness of test procedure with radiologist, consults with ordering physician • Prepares the patient by way of at-home education or utilizes nursing when in facility • Conducts diagnostic test or therapeutic procedure • Evaluates patient cooperation and tolerance through test procedure • Reports critical findings to physician or nurse
Patient	• Decides to contact a healthcare professional or service • Expresses preferences and decides what patient outcomes are priorities • Learns how to recognize symptoms and manage the condition(s) • Learns when and who to contact for follow-up • Identifies who in the family is going to support them • Identifies what health resources or pharmacies to use

*Note: There are multiple types of therapists including physical, occupational, respiratory, and speech therapists.

Table 10-3 Processes and Decisions in Scope of Healthcare Professional Practices and Patient Care (continued)

skin integrity (which can lead to pressure ulcers), impaired mobility (a risk for accidental falls), and a lack of knowledge about their condition. In addition, they watch for patients who might become suicidal or aspirate (accidental entry of food or stomach contents in the airway). Nurses develop and are responsible for implementing a plan of care with evidence-based interventions to prevent problems, avoid risks, and promote healthy lifestyle changes; they use evidence-based information for nursing decisions about care that is usually different from information that guides physicians. Finally, given the amount of time they spend with the patient, they tend to have a more holistic view of the patient's care and observe/document the changes in patients.

Patients and their families have an important role in workflows because most information from assessments and ultimately the patient's outcome is gathered from them. Table 10-3 highlights the patient's role in learning about diagnostic results and changes in treatment activities. Any workflow that doesn't include the patient is missing the most important stakeholder in patient care. Given the time they spend with the patient and their training and skills in collecting detailed assessments, nurses frequently obtain the information to evaluate the patient to detect positive and negative outcomes of a given treatment and communicate the changes to others.

Pharmacists are educated in helping physicians find the best medication options for patients and are responsible for verifying the safety of medications that patients will take. In some healthcare settings they directly communicate with patients about medications, while in other settings they indirectly communicate through others, such as nurses. Data are important to pharmacists because the age, gender, height, weight, pregnancy status, allergy presence or absence, genetic variants (e.g., P450 CYP2C9, resulting in slow metabolism of many medications), and patient's condition(s) (e.g., problem list) are all relevant to safe medication dosing. Pharmacists and physicians rely heavily on laboratory results (e.g., creatinine and GFR for any kidney impairment; liver enzymes for liver impairment), vital signs, and other clinicians' observations of signs and symptoms. Table 10-3 provides some scope of practice considerations for pharmacists.

Another broad category critical to the care of patients consists of the assorted therapies: dietitians, social workers, respiratory, physical, occupational, speech pathology, behavioral, and recreational professionals. Clinical professionals in these groups normally focus on a specific aspect of the patient's care and, while normally autonomous, are typically involved and directed by physicians. Examples include treatments aimed at increasing a patient's mobility; optimizing their diet; and respiratory function support with ventilators. Table 10-3 provides some scope of practice considerations for therapists.

Technicians within laboratory, radiology, neurological testing, cardiovascular diagnostics, and other areas need information to prepare patients for a test or diagnostic exam and to ensure safe transport to perform the tests. A key responsibility of these healthcare workforce members is prompt reporting of the results and timely notification to nurses and physicians when the findings are critical because these findings can dramatically alter the course of care and treatment for the patient. Medications will influence how and when a test is conducted, so many technicians need to know what medications the patient is taking.

Simulation

HIT technology simulation can provide a safe testing environment that allows practitioners to test new clinical processes using simulation of the technology before implementing with patients. Many simulation applications involve artificial "patients" and "providers" that can test tasks and functions to simulate care and treatment, like flight simulators used by pilots.[12] The simulation environment provides a real-life opportunity to evaluate clinical and management information systems such as EHRs, secure messaging, and interactions with health information exchange networks in a realistic environment within the safety confines of a controlled artificial environment. Research using simulation approaches helps inform the design and development of electronic systems.

The HIT professionals can facilitate testing opportunities using EHR simulation applications collaboratively with clinicians to view and further optimize healthcare processes prior to implementation.

Lean Strategy

Lean/Six Sigma principles and methods have been used extensively in manufacturing and production lines to identify the most efficient production practices using less costly resources and fewer tasks while still achieving optimal value for customers. Since 2005, the Lean strategy has been widely adopted in U.S. healthcare. Good examples of this work have been published by Toussaint and Gerard, including significantly decreasing "door-to-balloon" time ("door" referring to emergency room door and "balloon" referring to balloon angioplasty, a common treatment for heart attacks) for heart attack patients at two hospitals from 90 minutes to 37 minutes.[13] The goal when using the Lean approach is to eliminate waste or redundancies in practices while providing the best possible patient outcomes.[14] Examples of waste in healthcare include waiting, overproduction, overprocessing, defects, needless motion, excessive inventory, inefficient transport, and underutilization of healthcare workforce member skills.

The Lean methodology is also very useful to engage clinicians in increasing their sense of ownership of important changes.[15] Often clinicians cannot see how broken their processes are until a methodology like Lean is applied. Such a methodology can break down resistance to change when facilitated properly. In general, that usually means the safest care at the lowest cost with the shortest stay and no complications (i.e., eliminating unnecessary tests and complications, hospital-acquired infections, pressure sores, injuries from falls, etc.). When Lean strategies are fully leveraged, the result is optimal outcome for the patient with less work volume and minimal to no redundancy in care. Most quality improvement professionals and clinical informaticians have advance training in one or more of these techniques and tools.

TIP When workflow is optimized, human interactions with the technology increase efficiency, decrease waste, and rely on scientific methods to decide which data are relevant rather than accepting prior methods, often based on paper or that were unique to an individual clinician.

The Lean approach poses critical questions to subject matter experts in a process undergoing improvement. These questions are helpful in identifying what matters most and avoiding the distraction of variation and waste. These who, what, where, how, and why questions highlight gaps, variations, unnecessary tasks, and redundancy in current practice and allow the clinical team to decide the safest and quickest ways to get to equivalent or better patient outcomes.

Business Process Management

Business process management (BPM) uses select engineering principles and practices to represent processes for the healthcare enterprise. BPM in healthcare settings often involves clinical informaticians and service-line leaders working with HIT professionals and business process managers or quality managers to analyze and improve current processes. Process improvements are part of everyday activities in healthcare and are useful to achieve meaningful use of HIT. HIT professionals should identify and work closely with business analysts and quality improvement staff members who are involved with improving practices for accreditation and certification. When planning to revise and optimize clinical workflow within the healthcare organization, EHR systems and HIT allow combining data analytical techniques yielding actionable insights on the organization's clinical and business data with evidence-based research from outside the organization that can result in significantly improved processes.

Healthcare organizations and clinics should designate someone who is accountable for managing a central database of process maps/workflows. Management of workflows facilitates decision making regarding when and where workflows apply, allows for the reuse of standardization workflows across service lines, and allows for the continuous optimizing of healthcare processes (workflows).

Workflow Mapping Tools

A structured approach enabled by standard visualization artifacts and understandable diagrams can aid efficient and effective problem solving and decision making. Figure 10-3 is an example of the basic tools associated with process mapping. Specific shapes correspond to different types of activities performed to visually represent workflow. The shapes are quite straightforward given the simple explanations in Figure 10-3. The diamond

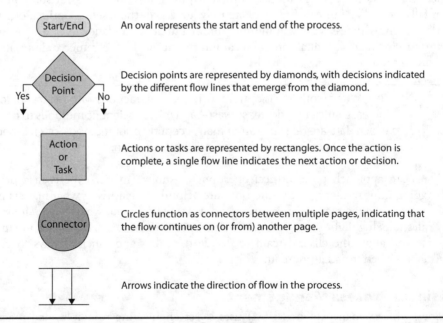

An oval represents the start and end of the process.

Decision points are represented by diamonds, with decisions indicated by the different flow lines that emerge from the diamond.

Actions or tasks are represented by rectangles. Once the action is complete, a single flow line indicates the next action or decision.

Circles function as connectors between multiple pages, indicating that the flow continues on (or from) another page.

Arrows indicate the direction of flow in the process.

Figure 10-3 Graphic representation of workflow mapping

shape, as it can be used in different ways, needs a bit more explanation to understand how it is typically used in workflow diagraming. Diamonds signify a decision-making process, usually resulting in two possible workflow directions. Most diamonds reflect a yes or no decision that has to be made; if the decision is yes, the workflow continues on the intended route, but if the answer is no, the workflow may have to go through another route to solve the problem.

Swim-lane diagrams, discussed in an upcoming section, often reduce the need for mapping roles and tasks.

Workflow Diagram Example

A workflow diagram, or map, is a graphic depiction of a course of action showing the steps in a process to accomplish a goal. Many work processes can be complex, so it is important to visually represent in detail how tasks are being completed to improve understanding and efficiency. Depending on the purpose of the map, it can be high level (abstract) or detailed. Figure 10-4 is an example of an enterprise high-level clinic visit workflow diagram to represent steps to obtain historical information on medications/allergies from the health information exchange for the patient and the patient's flow through the clinic.

Role-Based Swim-Lane Workflow

Figure 10-5 is an example of a mid-level role-based swim-lane workflow. Role-based swim lanes describe who is responsible for each stage, what documentation is needed, and the relationship to resources at each stage. Knowing employee roles and resource requirements allows management to easily determine weaknesses and alleviate bottlenecks. A bottleneck represents any aspect of the workflow that impedes overall cycle time of the process.

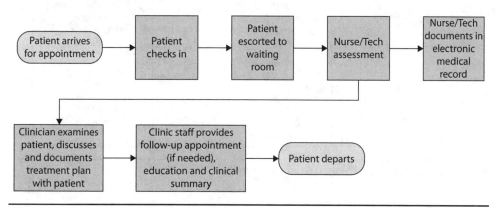

Figure 10-4   Clinic visit workflow

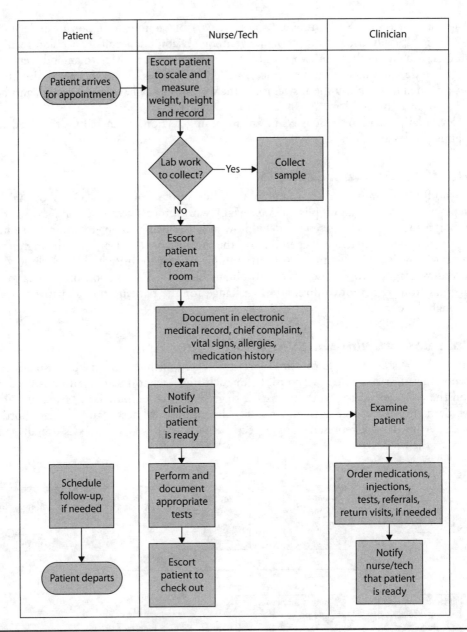

Figure 10-5 Clinic visit role-based swim-lane workflow

Value Stream Mapping

Figure 10-6 shows a value stream map. Value stream mapping is a type of process mapping or flowcharting of the value stream, which includes all of the steps (both the value-added and the non-value-added steps) in producing and delivering a service. A value stream map shows workflow from a systems perspective and can help in determining how

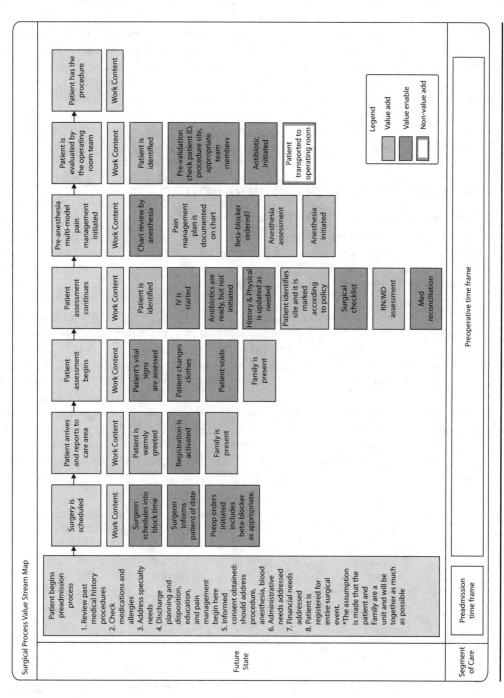

Figure 10-6 Value stream mapping

PART II

to measure and improve the system or process of interest. Without a view of the entire stream, it is possible that individual aspects of the system will be optimized according to the needs of those parts, but the resulting total system will be suboptimal. Value stream mapping in healthcare is typically done from the perspective of the patient, where the goal is to optimize the patient's journey through the system. Information, materials, and patient flows are captured in the value stream map. The key question to ask when determining whether an activity is value added is if the customer would be willing to pay for it. If the answer is no, the activity is not value added. In healthcare, an example of a non-value-added activity is waiting time. Value stream mapping is a recognized Six Sigma methodology.[10]

Success Factors for Implementing Clinical Process Change

Designing and applying information technology using standardized practices can be an extensive, time-consuming process. When possible, leverage the vendor's standardized tools and process descriptions. When these are not suitable, incomplete, or need to be extended, you must assemble a process change team with the right skill sets, as well as subject-matter experts. A moderate-sized hospital may have 200 to 300 third-level process flows. A typical ambulatory clinic may have 50 to 75 process flows. It is useful to name each of the processes and assign a priority to map these processes explicitly. One question to ask is: Is this process well defined? If not, it may require a higher priority to determine a possible future state. Complex and ambiguous processes typically create a great deal of confusion, concern, and even risk to the patient during implementation of a new or substantially changed information system or EHR. The ideal implementation has *no* ambiguous processes at go-live. A knowledge manager assigned to track and manage these processes can minimize the risk. These individuals may also be experts in identifying potential gaps and facilitating problem-solving events or in managing gaps within the vendor-supplied content or by other means without existing technology support.

 TIP Use the SIPOC (suppliers, inputs, process, outputs, customers) Six Sigma tool shown in Figure 10-7 to simplify problem solving or to plan a large process change event. A SIPOC form identifies all aspects of a process, including the beginning, the end, and all high-level steps in between. Outside of the core process, you should also identify suppliers and customers. This high-level description can be used before a more detailed process improvement activity is used.

The implementation of the actual new steps represented in a workflow diagram is the hardest aspect of process change. Organizations often do not realize the importance of understanding processes and mistakenly rely instead on technology to resolve problems. With paper-based records, many organizations had thousands of individual order sets, many unique to specific physicians and frequently outdated. With computerized

SIPOC Diagram for Physician Specialist Procedure Consult
Revised: (date) Author: (name)

Suppliers	Inputs	Process	Outputs	Customers
Specialist physician		Process Trigger: Clinician needs a specialist consult for a procedure.		Ordering physician
Ward clerk				Patient
Scheduling clerk				Primary Care physician
Transcriptionists		Step 2		Nurse
Patient				
Nursing provider		Step 3		
		Step 4		
		Step 5		
		Step 6		
		Done: Consulting physician communicates to ordering clinician the results of the procedure.		

Figure 10-7 SIPOC chart for planning workflow mapping or problem-solving event

physician order entry (CPOE), most organizations appreciate the need for standardization in workflow and reducing variation among physicians. Organization-wide recognition of process improvement is imperative, and leadership support, understanding, and communication of the reason why change is necessary are key;[3, 9] simply posting a workflow diagram on a nursing unit won't significantly impact day-to-day activities. Most workflow diagrams should include a workflow improvement strategy such as Lean, Six Sigma, or Total Quality Management as well as clear instructions on how to follow them and practice the steps.

Exercise 10-1: Create a Simple Process Model Using the SIPOC Tool

In this exercise, review Use Case 10-1, and develop a process model and overview.

1. Describe the steps in the process, including trigger and completion.
2. Identify inputs into the process.
3. Identify desired outcomes.
4. Develop a plan to engage customers and suppliers in the future state process design.
5. Advanced: After completing a process map, enhance the map by utilizing role-based swim lanes or a value stream approach.
6. Advanced: What measurement could you use to determine that the new process is being used and not a workaround?

Use Case 10-1: Physician Consult for Specialty Procedure

Mrs. Hurst is a 35-year-old woman who presented to her primary-care physician with early-onset high blood pressure. In the office she was found to have significant high blood pressure without a strong family history or other explanation. On examination, she had evidence of an abdominal bruit (an abnormal sound heard with a stethoscope over the abdomen and a sign of a narrowed renal artery). The primary-care physician treated the patient with blood pressure medications and ordered an abdominal ultrasound that identified a condition called *renal artery stenosis*. Since her blood pressure did not respond to multiple medications, the primary-care physician consults a specialist vascular surgeon who could enlarge the renal artery using balloon angioplasty.

The doctor recently started using an EHR and is unsure how to order for this patient situation and how to share the continuity of care document (CCD) with the consulting specialist through the health information exchange network. Is this an "order" like one might write for an X-ray, or is it a consult for the specialist to see the patient and then determine the appropriate course of action? Previously, the physician would communicate the intent to the nurse or office manager who would manage the details of such a workflow. Unfortunately, the physician and office manager do not know how to order the same consult or potential resulting procedure using the new EHR. After calling the supervisor superuser (an individual with additional training) and the EHR implementation team, everyone involved realizes that they had not developed a process to manage this type of problem. The implementation team needs to develop this process and communicate it to all involved quickly. While the team works on defining and implementing an electronic version of the paper process, the office returns to the previous method of handwriting the order and faxing it and the physician's visit notes to the specialist office. In addition, as the patient is at risk of losing a kidney, the office manager, following the direction of the physician who anticipates the vascular surgeon will agree with the need for renal angioplasty, calls the hospital surgical scheduling clerk, who enters the request into the surgical scheduling system.

Additional Techniques

When workflow processes are viewed in isolation, they often appear quite logical and efficient enough to accomplish the end goal. When viewed more broadly across multiple disciplines, complexities arise. Frequently missed are conflicts in the priorities of different roles in an organization (e.g., tasks that nursing is accountable for versus the pharmacy).

The suggested steps for creating a process map or workflow are as follows:

1. Assemble a stakeholder planning team. The team should consist of individuals from all clinical areas and all levels with the goal of ensuring the true process is captured.

2. Determine the level of detail desired, the methodology you will employ, and the participants needed (e.g., value stream mapping, role based, SIPOC, or simple diagramming). The level of detail will depend on the problem the team is addressing and the number of handoffs between disciplines.

3. Schedule the mapping event for the team with HIT professional support and obtain the appropriate supplies.

4. Begin the event by giving the team sufficient background on the approach you will be using. Provide initial training in the weeks before or at the start of the event.

5. Complete the mapping event. Identify the activities in your current and future state. List them and arrange them in order.

6. Create a formal chart with standard symbols for process mapping using Microsoft Visio and Excel to track questions to follow up on with the EHR technology capabilities and gaps.

7. Create an accurate picture, and check for accuracy.

8. Identify problem areas and gaps between the current and future state.

9. Prioritize projects that will address the gaps.

Identification and Prioritization of Targets for Workflow Improvement

Information technology should be designed to support effective teamwork, foster open communication, and enable shared decision making to achieve optimal, quality patient care. Once the process is mapped, gaps between the current process and best practices will become apparent. Members of the team with the most detailed understanding of the best practices can recognize gaps and highlight them for the team. A simple approach to ranking gaps using two dimensions includes "ease of implementation" and "value to the organization." Value should be defined early in the life cycle of the program. Three common primary objectives for many organizations are safety, quality, and overall patient experience, with financial and provider experience as secondary benefits.

Change Management

Change management describes a structured approach to transition individuals, teams, and organizations from a current state to a desired future state. Considered an organization imperative, change management helps employees cope with and adapt to the numerous changes every industry faces. One reason change initiatives fail is because they rely on data gathering, analysis, report writing, and presentations while not adequately factoring in human motivation, evidence-based research, political, and symbolic elements.

John Kotter, a leading thinker and author on organizational change management, describes an eight-stage model for understanding and managing change.[6] Kotter defines change management as the utilization of basic structures and tools to control any organizational change effort. Change management refers to a set of basic tools or structures intended to keep the change effort under control. Ultimately, the goal is to minimize the impact on workers and avoid distractions.

Change Management Principles

Four principles for change management are as follows:

- Elicit support from people within the system (system = environment processes, culture, relationships, and behaviors, both personal and organizational).
- Understand the current state of the organization.
- Understand where you want to be, when, why, and what the measures will be.
- Communicate, involve, enable, and facilitate involvement from people, as early, openly, and completely as possible.

Kotter's Eight Steps to Successful Change

Kotter's eight-stage approach to realizing significant change includes the following:

1. **Establish a sense of urgency**   Inspire people to move, and make objectives real and relevant. Build a compelling case for change, and assess change readiness of stakeholders.

2. **Build the guiding coalition**   Put the right people in place with the right emotional commitment and the right mix of skills. Engage sponsors in change leadership and team development to build competence and trust.

3. **Develop a vision and strategy**   Create a team to establish a simple vision and strategy and focus on emotional and creative aspects necessary to direct the change effort.

4. **Communicate the change vision for buy-in**   Involve as many people as possible, communicate the essentials simply, and respond to people's needs. Declutter communications; make technology work for you rather than against you.

5. **Empower action**   Remove obstacles, and enable constructive feedback and support from leaders. Reward and recognize progress and achievements, and encourage risk taking.

6. **Generate short-term wins**   Set aims that are easy to achieve. Recognize and reward people who made the wins possible. Finish current stages before starting new ones.

7. **Don't let up**   Foster and encourage determination and persistence, and encourage new projects, themes, and change agents.

8. **Make change stick**   Reinforce the value of successful change via recruitment and promotion, and develop new change leaders. Weave change into the culture.

Chapter Review

Ignoring or inadequately understanding workflows can lead to a decline in use of the EHR over time and the development of workaround steps. Workarounds can include both those within and outside an automated process. Analyzing workflows can help discover key factors to success: underuse and misuse of the EHR, workarounds clinicians find to collect or use patient information, and the need for aggregated information or reports to be available for decision making and sharing beyond the organization (often via health information exchange [HIE]). Working together, HIT professionals as members of an interdisciplinary team must review existing clinical workflows when technology upgrades or the clinical evidence advances to make necessary adjustments. Creating a culture focused on process and change management and understanding workflow will help guide organizations through new technology implementations and inevitable upgrades.[7, 8]

Questions

To test your comprehension of the chapter, answer the following questions and then check your answers against the list of correct answers at the end of the chapter.

1. Which of the following describes a way of using health information systems in a manner not originally designed, resulting in unplanned and unexpected outcomes?

   A. Workflows

   B. Workarounds

   C. Tracking issues

   D. Flowcharts

2. Which of the following are life-cycle phases of large-scale health information technology changes?

   A. Workflows with workarounds and testing the technology with users

   B. Planning, implementation, quality monitoring, and improvement

   C. Planning, training, testing, implementation, and closure

   D. Planning, implementation, stabilization, optimization, and transformation

3. Healthcare services are organized by many service lines of care such as surgical or obstetrical (i.e., maternal-child) services. Within each service, processes are organized such that they can be replicated across many services. Which of the following does not describe the healthcare general processes within venues of healthcare services?

   A. Registration, admission, daily care coordination, shift change, discharge

   B. Surgical preoperative visit, surgery, postoperative, same-day discharge

   C. Registration, dining, coding, billing, reporting

   D. Check-in, laboratory testing, radiology test, chemotherapy infusion visit, depart

   E. Emergency triage, registration, assessment, examination, education, discharge

4. The role-based (person-to-person) workflow describes processes by which of the following?

   A. Using swim lanes to show the roles

   B. Describing steps in the process (rectangles) with action verbs

   C. Organizing into venues for care (e.g., admission, clinic visit, surgery)

   D. Displaying physician or nurse decisions (diamonds)

   E. All of the above

5. Which workflow best describes the clinical scenario of a nurse sending a secure message using the health information exchange network to a home-care provider on research protocols which involve medication administration at very specific times for three days in the patient's home setting?

   A. Functional or application workflow

   B. Role-based workflow

   C. Enterprise-to-enterprise workflow

   D. Venue-to-venue workflow

   E. Task-to-task workflow

6. Which is a method to articulate the tasks, time, manual work, delays, and multiple variations that exist within care processes for a discipline or with a reporting process associated with many departments?

   A. Modeling workflow based on scope of professional practice standards

   B. Simulation

   C. Observation of daily activities

   D. Lean strategy, Six Sigma, and continuous improvement

   E. Business process management and modeling tools

7. The HIT professional is involved in the analysis of workflow processes. Which of the following is not a list of roles, responsibilities, and tools of the HIT professional to accomplish this analysis to avoid workarounds and to find solutions?

   A. Provide updates on tasks/deliverables; document issues within analytical tools/database to follow; monitor usage and track unexpected outcomes of harms.

   B. Define and prioritize healthcare requirements and standards for care within the workflow; provide strategies to best use technology to efficiently retrieve and document clinical processes; know the healthcare standards for safety and quality requirements for clinical practice.

    C. Evaluate implemented solution with business requirements for interoperability; develop documentation requests for information and maintain documentation on the compatibility of software, hardware, and network components to evolve the EHR use cases in the future (i.e., information exchange) for continuity of care; apply approved data management and information practices.

    D. Identify and track project activities; participate in development of proposed recommended approaches and solutions; recognize major risks or benefits associated with different solutions.

8. Kotter provides steps to help achieve successful organizational change. Clinicians are generally accustomed to making evidence-based practice change when new research advances practice on how to detect and diagnose, to test for problems or risks, or to initiate with new interventions or procedures. The change associated with electronic health records must mirror the level of constant change to ensure evidence-based practices are implemented sooner rather than later. Which one of the following least describes this level of systematic change?

    A. Quality improvement strategies: identify the focus, plan the solution, do the change, study the change through measurement, take action to implement the solution, and reinforce the value of successful change via recruitment and promotion.

    B. Establish a sense of urgency, build a team with the right people, develop a vision and plan, communicate this, reward and recognize ideas and risk taking, set aims to easily achieve, encourage new projects with change agents, and reinforce the change.

    C. Build a compelling case for change, identify a team with mix of skills to create direction, share the direction and listen for feedback, remove obstacles, generate short-term wins, encourage determination and persistence, and use change agents to weave change into the culture with successful change.

    D. Assess change readiness of stakeholders, engage sponsors, develop team competence and plan a clear direction, declutter communications, empower action, recognize wins and don't let up with new project work, and make change stick with change leaders.

Answers

1. B. A workaround is a way to use the electronic health records, other information system, or paper-based alternatives in an unintentional way. A common example is the use of nursing communication orders in place of actual departmental orders to communicate the need for a specific test. A delay occurs while the nurse contacts the physician to determine and place the correct order, with the continued risk of miscommunication. The department misreads the test and completes the test incorrectly, resulting in invalid results, and the patient needs a repeat test for diagnostic accuracy.

2. D. In summary, with large-scale HIT change, the stakeholders are involved from project conception with planning; implementation; feeling a sense of normalcy within the clinic or hospital (stabilization); optimizing practices; and embracing the change and fully using the data to determine performance to advance practice with transformation.

3. C. Processes within most venues have a well-defined start and endpoint and include a number of service lines during the episode of care. This option does not include any processes for care delivery, whereas the others depict general processes to consider where patient data and information are being collected from the patient and used to plan and deliver care.

4. E. All four answers describe how workflow is designed to display the steps and decisions within a process for those with a role in taking care of patients.

5. E. Task-to-task workflows provide additional detailed steps for less frequent activities that might occur during care delivery (e.g., a patient involved in a research study). In this scenario, the task-to-task workflow represents a process step beyond the hospital setting to ensure an intervention is coordinated between the physician, nurse, and home-care provider. When the health information exchange network is utilized to share information, the enterprise-to-enterprise workflow will work to share the patient's plan of care through a continuity of care document, but the uniqueness of a research study makes this a task-to-task workflow.

6. C. Observation of workflow will help identify some gaps, the time involved, and delays, but this method alone will not help clinicians and IT professionals in discerning all potential interactions and gaps in practice workflows.

7. B. Central to the role of clinicians (not HIT professionals) is to define and prioritize healthcare requirements and standards for practice within the workflow; provide strategies to best use technology to efficiently retrieve and document clinical processes; and know the healthcare standards, safety, and quality requirements for clinical practice. Each healthcare professional must ethically and legally provide care according to their state's or country's (if outside of the US) professional practice act and their scope and standards of practice for their specialty practices. HIT professionals would not be expected to fully understand the scope of practice for each clinical discipline or their respective specialties.

8. A. Often, systematic and cultural change requires more than quality improvement strategies because the change needs to be at an organizational level and systematic. The consequences of one change can impact the practices of others and therefore a team approach with multiple skill sets is needed to plan, measure, and implement changes.

References

1. Blumenthal, D. (2009). Launching HITECH. *New England Journal of Medicine, 362,* 382–385.

2. American Recovery and Reinvestment Act of 2009 (ARRA). (2009). Accessed on June 17, 2010, from http://frwebgate.access.gpo.gov/cgi-bin/getdoc.cgi?dbname=111_cong_bills&docid=f:h1enr.pdf.

3. Sittig, D. F., Longhurst, C. A., Russo, E., & Singh, H. (2015). Electronic health record features, functions, and privileges that clinicians need to provide safe and effective care for adults and children. In C. A. Weaver, M. J. Ball, G. R. Kim, & J. M. Kiel (Eds.), *Healthcare information management systems: Cases, strategies, and solutions, fourth edition.* Switzerland: Springer International.

4. Halbesleben, J. R., Wakefield, D. S., & Wakefield, B. J. (2008). Work-arounds in health care settings: Literature review and research agenda. *Health Care Management Review, 33,* 2–12.

5. Piscotty, R. J., Kalisch, B., & Gracey-Thomas, A. (2015). Impact of healthcare information technology on nursing practice. *Journal of Nursing Scholarship, 47*(4), 287–293.

6. Kotter, J. P., & Cohen, D. S. (2002). *The heart of change: Real life stories of how people change their organizations.* Harvard Business School Press.

7. Brokel, J. M., & Harrison, M. I. (2009). Redesigning care processes using an electronic health record: A system's experience. *Joint Commission Journal of Patient Safety and Quality, 35,* 82–92.

8. Brokel, J. M., Ochylski, S., & Kramer, J. M. (2011). Re-engineering workflows: Changing the life cycle of an electronic health record system. *Journal of Healthcare Engineering, 2,* 303–320.

9. Randell, R., Mitchell, N., Thompson, C., McCaughan, D., & Dowding, D. (2009). Supporting nurse decision making in primary care: Exploring use of and attitude to decision tools. *Health Informatics Journal, 15,* 5–16.

10. Wheeler, D. J. (2004). *The Six Sigma practitioner's guide to data analysis.* SPC Press.

11. American Nurses Association, National Association of Pediatric Nurse Practitioners, and Society of Pediatric Nurses. (2015). *Pediatric nursing: Scope and standards of practice, second edition.* Nursesbooks.org.

12. Agency for Healthcare Research and Quality (AHRQ). (2012). *Improving patient safety through simulation research.* Accessed on June 19, 2012, from www.ahrq.gov/qual/simulproj.htm.

13. Toussaint, J., & Gerard, R. (2010). *On the mend: Revolutionizing healthcare to save lives and transform the industry.* Lean Enterprise Institute.

14. Lawal, A. K., Rotter, T., Kinsman, L., Sari, N., Harrison, L., Jeffery, C., ...Flynn, R. (2014). Lean management in health care: Definition, concepts, methodology and effects reported—Systematic review protocol. *Systematic Reviews, 3,* 103.

15. Rother, M., & Shook, J. (2003). *Learning to see: Value stream mapping to add value and eliminate muda.* Lean Enterprise Institute.

Healthcare IT Project Management

Brian Gugerty, Amy Flick

In this chapter, you will learn how to
- Define the terms project, program, and project management
- Describe project critical success factors that are unique to healthcare
- Identify resources that help you learn more about project management such as the Project Management Institute and the Healthcare Information Management Systems Society
- Initiate a project, including:
  - List several project team member and project stakeholder roles and communication strategies
  - Describe how a project manager works with a project team and stakeholders to develop SMART project objectives
- Plan a project, including:
  - Construct a work breakdown structure for a healthcare IT project
  - Effectively estimate project activity durations and schedule project resources
- Execute a project, including:
  - Manage project resources and stakeholders to maintain project scope, time, quality, and budget parameters
  - Monitor and control the project in the executing phase
- Close out a project, including:
  - Describe principles and practices to effectively close out a healthcare IT project

Today's healthcare enterprises are increasingly complex, and healthcare information technology is essential to making their operations more effective and efficient. Project management is one tool that can be used to maximize the effectiveness of information technology within healthcare enterprises. In this chapter, we will define a project and project management techniques in broad, cross-industry terms, as well as begin to convey how project management works within HIT initiatives. In order to reinforce concepts in the text and demonstrate healthcare IT project management principles and practices, the chapter includes a ten-part use case centered on one project.

Projects, Project Management, and Healthcare IT

A *project* is a temporary venture undertaken to create a unique product, service, or result. A project has a defined beginning and end with specific objectives to be achieved at the completion of the project. The end of a project is reached when the project's objectives have been achieved, when it is determined that its objectives will not or cannot be met, or when the need for the project no longer exists.[1] Projects have a clearly specified objective or scope of work to be performed, a predefined budget, and usually a temporary organization whose work concludes when the project ends. While the project is temporary, the product, service, or result created is usually meant to be long lasting or permanent. Some examples of projects include building a house, designing and implementing a new business process, developing software, implementing an electronic health record, and revamping a healthcare organization's web portal. Any type of ongoing or continuous work such as manufacturing or planning the monthly schedule of nurses on a hospital unit is not a project because these tasks follow their respective organization's existing procedures and are ongoing.

A *program* is a group of projects that relate to each other and are managed together so that they can achieve benefits and goals that may not be achieved by managing them separately. A program may include additional work outside of the projects in the program that is necessary for achieving the program goals but is not part of the projects within the program. While a project may be part of a program, it can, and often does, operate independently of a program. On the other hand, a program always has projects.

Project management is the application of knowledge, skills, tools, and techniques to project activities in order to meet a project's requirements.[1] A project manager (PM) facilitates the planning, scheduling, and controlling of all activities that must be done to meet a project's objectives.

Critical Success Factors for Healthcare IT Projects

Within healthcare project management there are many interrelated elements, or success factors, that must be kept in balance in order to achieve project success. Among the most important are:

- Empowerment of a project management approach from the top of the organization
- Control over the project by the project manager
- Very high quality standards
- Effective handling of healthcare organizational and operational complexity

The foundation of successful project management is the people who manage or work on the projects themselves. Their levels of communication, leadership, negotiation, team building, decision making, and motivation combine to direct the trajectory of a project. Adding to this foundation is the culture of an organization and its values, beliefs, attitudes, behaviors, traditions, and structure. The methods employed by the organization to work both on a routine, or continuous, basis and on a project basis influence the success of a project. And, planning and information management are critical to the success of a project. The approach to a project needs to be well defined, appropriate processes need to be determined, and the work schedule needs to be developed properly. Thus, the first critical success factor for healthcare projects is empowerment of a project management approach from the top of the organization and participation in focused ways in working with project managers to organize and execute tasks on projects.

Another critical factor to a HIT project's success is control over the project by the project manager. All projects need to be controlled and directed properly in order to track the progress of the project, compare it to the original plan, take necessary corrective action, and monitor the performance of all parts of the project to ensure the project is completed in accordance with the project goals and strategies outlined in the project initiating phase.

HIT projects need to be held to very high quality standards, maybe not quite as high and exacting as the nuclear power industry, but oftentimes the quality does need to be close or equal to that level of exacting quality. Skimping on a barcode-assisted medication administration implementation may have fatal consequences, whereas skimping on the quality of certain parts of a house you are building will not. For example, opting for the lower-end shower for the guest bathroom instead of the most expensive one will hardly be noticed. Administering the wrong medication to a patient could cause a patient to become ill or even be fatal. Thus, finding a way to maintain high quality throughout the life cycle of a HIT project is a critical success factor.

Peter Drucker characterized the modern medical center as "the most complex business and social arrangement in the history of mankind."[2] There are many different organizational divisions and many, many roles in a modern healthcare enterprise. HIT projects often involve many different clinical disciplines such as doctors, nurses, respiratory therapists, and others; operational departments such as laboratory, pharmacy, radiology, and others; and both internal IT technicians and professionals and external IT consultants and vendors. Moreover, the healthcare industry has a huge number of regulations and a wide variety of highly complex payment mechanisms. Large-scale HIT projects impact most of these divisions and roles in a healthcare organization and deal with many regulations and billing challenges. For a HIT project, effectively dealing with healthcare organizational and operational complexity and the many people involved in healthcare organizations is a critical factor for success.

The Project Management Institute, PMBOK, and PMP

The Project Management Institute (PMI) is a not-for-profit membership association for the project management profession. PMI works to advance the project management profession by developing globally recognized standards, certifications, research programs, and professional development opportunities. PMI's standards for projects, programs, and

Use Case 11-1: Background of Tree Healthcare System and the EcoSys Online Labs Phase 1 Project

You are a project manager employed by Tree Healthcare System (Tree), a not-for-profit integrated healthcare delivery network. The network includes seven hospitals, the largest of which is located in downtown Forest City. Tree also has a growing provider group within the system called Tree Provider Group (TPG). TPG is composed of over 500 providers, including physicians and advanced practice providers. The Forest City Medical Center campus is considered to be the "main campus" and is where you and your project management teammates are based. The remaining six hospitals are located in communities throughout the Tree service area, which covers three counties.

The furthest hospital location from Forest City is two hours away in the rural town of Spruce. The Spruce Community Hospital location is the newest addition to Tree. Three years ago, SocialFree, a global social media services company, completed relocation of world headquarters to Spruce from Southern California. In an attempt to accelerate its ability to provide care given the explosive population growth in the community as a result of the SocialFree relocation, Spruce Community Hospital signed an integration agreement with Tree two years ago. Spruce Community Hospital is now fully integrated from a clinical, operational, and technology standpoint with Tree but has not fully addressed issues around timely access to care for area residents.

The Tree Healthcare System strategic plan calls for significant growth (50 percent) in Tree capabilities to engage directly with patients as "healthcare consumers" within three years. Per the Tree CFO, Henry Swanson, declining reimbursements coupled with increases in cost to comply with federal and state regulations make this growth goal essential to the long-term financial viability of Tree. The VP of System Patient Experience, Julie Iris, RN, MS, together with the Tree Chief Medical Information Officer (CMIO), Tony Rose, MD, have been designated as the senior leaders accountable for creating a comprehensive online experience—a portal—for all Tree patients and authorized caregivers. The primary goal is to create an online, collaborative "ecosystem" for patients and authorized caregivers to use throughout the continuum of care, whether that care is delivered in the hospital or outside hospital walls. The portal will be called EcoSys.

There are many projects that will need to be initiated and completed successfully over a period of time to create the entire EcoSys Portal. You have been assigned to manage one of the projects, Online Labs Phase 1. Your project is to create an online labs experience for patients and authorized caregivers so that they may view results from the five most common lab tests performed by Tree affiliates Acorn Labs and Walnut Creek Labs. Future phases of Online Labs will deliver additional functionality and access to lab results that is yet to be determined.

We will revisit the Tree Healthcare System EcoSys Online Labs Phase 1 Project in nine additional use cases throughout this chapter to explore each stage of managing the project.

portfolio management are the most widely recognized standards in project management across industries, including healthcare.

PMI has published *A Guide to the Project Management Body of Knowledge (PMBOK Guide)*, which is a recognized standard for the project management profession and provides guidelines for managing individual projects. We will use the *PMBOK Guide Fifth Edition* to direct this chapter's discussion of project management for healthcare IT professionals.

PMI offers a certification called Project Management Professional (PMP). The PMP is the most important and most widely recognized certification for project managers. The PMP demonstrates that the holder of the certificate has the experience, education, and competency to lead and direct projects. PMI has recently introduced a new entry-level certification for project practitioners called the Certified Associate in Project Management (CAPM). CAPM is designed for individuals with less project experience and is intended to demonstrate that those holding this certificate have an understanding of the foundational knowledge, terminology, and processes of project management. PMI believes that project managers with either of these certifications benefit from increased marketability to employers and higher salaries. As an additional resource to PMI members, PMI has created "communities of practice," which are online communities for professionals in a wide variety of industries to meet online and in other forums with other professionals in the same industry to discuss ideas and grow their community's understanding of project management. There is a healthcare community of practice that focuses on bringing an international perspective to implementing project management knowledge in the healthcare industry.[3]

Other Project Management Resources

An organization that provides training in project management is the Lewis Institute. We will use examples provided by the Lewis Institute to help you better understand project management. While the *PMBOK Guide* is a recognized standard for the project management profession, the Lewis Institute does a very good job of explaining project management concepts clearly and simply. Another reliable source of information on healthcare IT project management topics is the Healthcare Information Management Systems Society (HIMSS). HIMSS is the organization that awards the Certified Associate in Healthcare Information and Management Systems (CAHIMS), one of the two certifications this book is designed to help readers achieve. You can search on "project management" at www.himss.org and find many resources on healthcare information technology project management.

Major Project Management Constraints/Objectives

Four major variables can act as constraints, as well as objectives, in project management. These variables are

- **P** *Performance* requirements, both technical and functional
- **C** Labor and other *costs* to do the project activities
- **T** *Time* required to complete the project activities
- **S** *Scope* or magnitude of the job to be done

Figure 11-1
Project management triangle illustration of the P, C, T, S relationship

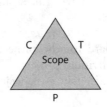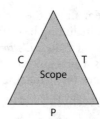

These variables directly affect the successful management and completion of a project. This is particularly true in the healthcare industry where quality is of the utmost importance. In this discussion of P, C, T, and S, you can think of performance as the equivalent to quality in HIT projects. Because a high degree of quality or performance is required in healthcare services, the costs associated with the HIT projects may be high as well. In other industries where quality or performance is less important than the cost of the product or service, a project may be able to be completed with lower costs. The project management triangles shown in Figure 11-1 illustrate the relationship between performance (quality), cost, time, and scope of a project.[4]

The performance (P) or quality lines in the two triangles in Figure 11-1 are the same length. One of the most powerful aspects of the P, C, T, S "formula" is that it reminds the project manager that if the scope of a project increases, the amount of time *and* budget required to complete the project will also almost always increase. Figure 11-1 can be described as follows: holding steady for the *performance* or quality while completing the project activities and objectives, an increase in *scope* will lead to an increase in both *time* until project completion and the *cost* of the project. So, for example, when an enthusiastic stakeholder or project team member says, "We can add computerized physician order entry to the electronic medication project and make an even bigger impact," the PM can use the P, C, T, S formula to interject the hard realities of this change into the discussion in order to keep the project on track. The PM needs to constantly monitor for "scope creep" to ensure that the costs, time, and performance remain at acceptable levels. Throughout the course of the project, the PM will need to make a variety of decisions in order to help maintain the scope of the project. The project management triangle is a very helpful tool in doing so.

 TIP If the scope of a project increases, the amount of time and budget required to complete the project will also increase. A project manager needs to make sure these increases remain at acceptable levels, or he will be faced with scope creep, which may jeopardize the project's success.

Project Team Roles and Stakeholders

The people, or organizations, who are actively interested in and involved with a project and who may affect or be affected by the results of the project are considered the project's stakeholders. A stakeholder may use their position of power to steer the project, its deliverables, and the project team members in a certain direction. The project team itself needs to identify the stakeholders and understand their expectations of the project in order to manage their influence as well as expectations so that they can ensure a successful outcome of the project.[5] Project team membership in HIT projects varies due to the large variability in types and size of HIT projects. Some of the roles of HIT project team members are project manager, clinical analyst, business analyst, network engineer, clinical application specialist, subject-matter expert, hardware/device technician, and other roles from finance, quality measurement, and compliance monitoring. Some organizations have clear delineation between project team members and project sponsors and/or project stakeholders. Some organizations have less clear delineations and one person can even have overlapping roles (i.e., project team member and project stakeholder). Use Case 11-2 presents an example where there is not a clear delineation between project team members and project sponsors and/or project stakeholders.

Use Case 11-2: EcoSys Online Labs Phase 1 Project Team Members and Key Stakeholders

The SocialFree CEO, Lorraine Hart, is eager to increase access to online healthcare information for her employees in Spruce as quickly as possible, and she is an active supporter in the community of the EcoSys Portal Program. She has explicitly approved the involvement of two SocialFree employees, Connie Hughes and Robert Kurtz, in the Online Labs Phase 1 Project to serve as "hands-on" patient testers. She has authorized up to four hours of time per week for each employee to perform a tester role on the project team for the duration of Phase 1.

As part of your PM work for the Initiating Process Group (one of five PMI process groups, introduced a bit later), you compile a roster of the key stakeholders and project team members for the Online Labs Phase 1 Project and assign project roles in discussion with the executive sponsors, the business sponsor, and the appropriate supervisors. Table 11-1 lists the multiple stakeholders and project team members and their roles in the project. The bolded and italicized roles represent project team member roles and the plain-text roles represent project sponsor or stakeholder roles.

Name	Organization Title/Role	Project Role
Tony Rose, MD	Tree Chief Medical Information Officer (CMIO)	Co-Executive Sponsor
Julie Iris, RN, MS	Tree Vice President of Patient Experience	Co-Executive Sponsor
Amie Adams, PMP	Tree Senior Project Manager	*Project Manager*
Henry Swanson	Tree Chief Financial Officer (CFO)	Stakeholder
Michael Kading, PhD	Executive Director, Walnut Creek Labs	Stakeholder and *Subject-Matter Expert*

Table 11-1 EcoSys Online Labs Phrase 1 *Project Team Members* and Key Stakeholder Roster

(continued)

Name	Organization Title/Role	Project Role
Magdalena Rosenberg, PhD	Executive Director, Acorn Labs	Stakeholder and *Subject-Matter Expert*
Dr. Luke Kelly	Tree Senior Manager of Labs	Business Sponsor
Lorraine Hart	SocialFree Chief Executive Officer (CEO)	Stakeholder
Kelly O'Grady	Tree Patient Experience Manager	*Tester*
Dan Wheeler	Tree Marketing and Brand Manager	Stakeholder
Anja Schiff	Tree IT Architect	*Cloud Services Architect*
Maya Sherman	TPG Business Analyst	Business Analyst and *Tester*
Connie Hughes	SocialFree Digital Media Coordinator	Patient User and *Tester*
Robert Kurtz	SocialFree Customer Care Representative	Patient User and *Tester*
Craig Devlin	Tree Senior Application Developer	*Website Developer*

Table 11-1   EcoSys Online Labs Phrase 1 *Project Team Members* and Key Stakeholder Roster *(continued)*

Effective Communication in Projects

Effective communication in all projects is essential to their overall success. Project managers spend most of their time communicating with the team members and stakeholders in order to ensure the project is planned and executed in accordance with the project's objectives and strategies. Project information should be available to all project team members and stakeholders as appropriate. Project documentation, minutes, status reports, and so forth should be optimally available and accessible. Many organizations have a SharePoint site, Wiki, or like repository as a "single source of truth" for the project. However the project information is shared, the project manager is responsible for making sure relevant information is available to team members and stakeholders, managing stakeholder expectations, and reporting on the performance of the project.[1]

A project manager is responsible for a wide range of forms of communications in a project, including the following:

- Internal (within the project) and external (customer, other projects, the media, the public)
- Formal (reports, memos, briefings) and informal (e-mails, ad hoc discussions)
- Vertical (up and down the organization) and horizontal (with peers)
- Official (newsletters, annual reports) and unofficial (off-the-record communications)

- Written and oral
- Verbal and nonverbal (voice inflections, body language)

The communication skills that a project manager, team member, or stakeholder possesses can directly affect the effectiveness of the communications within a project as well as the success of a project. The following communication skills are important to have and will lead to more effective communications:

- Listening actively and effectively
- Asking questions to ensure better understanding of situations
- Fact finding to find or confirm information
- Setting and managing expectations
- Persuading a person or organization to perform an action
- Negotiating to achieve mutually acceptable agreements between parties
- Resolving conflict
- Summarizing, recapping, and identifying next steps[1]

It is important to hone or develop these skills so that you can be an effective communicator and project manager.

Process Groups and the Project Life Cycle

Project management is achieved through the application of standardized processes to project activities in order to meet the project's requirements. PMI has identified 47 project management processes and has combined these into five categories, or *process groups*, by which all projects should be managed: Initiating, Planning, Executing, Monitoring and Controlling, and Closing.

These process groups, due to the more or less sequential nature of projects, have been further streamlined by the authors by combining the Executing and Monitoring/ Controlling groups and commonly put into the following project life-cycle framework:

- Starting the project (initiating phase)
- Organizing and preparing (planning phase)
- Carrying out the project work while monitoring and controlling it (executing phase)
- Closing the project (closing phase)

Projects vary in both their size and complexity. But, regardless of the size or complexity of a project, all projects follow very similar life-cycle structures.

These project management processes and the life-cycle framework by which they are often discussed apply across all industries. There is wide-ranging belief and acceptance that effectively using these project management processes will improve the chances of a project's success.

Project Initiation

While some may *not* consider the project initiation phase as important as some of the other phases of a project, such as project execution, this cannot be further from the truth. The time spent at the beginning of the project in the initiation phase is incredibly important to the success of a project. The more careful project initiation and planning that is done, the better a project's chances of success are. Projects usually don't fail at the end because of the work done on the project in the executing phase, but they often fail because not enough time and effective effort was spent in the beginning to properly initiate a project. The initiating phase often begins with a fuzzy charge from a superior to a project manager, such as "Implement an EHR system." Then, with thoughtful initial planning, a project charter and problem and mission statements are created, and finally project objectives are set and prioritized. When a PM has clear, well-defined project objectives, he or she can exit the initiating phase and is well on his or her way to successful project completion.

Project Charter and Scope

Before any work on a new project can begin, it's advisable to create, and have approved, a project charter. The *project charter* is a high-level document that outlines the objectives and requirements of the project and serves as the official authorization for the project. PMI's Initiating Process Group consists of the processes that need to be performed in order to define a new project or even to start a new phase in an existing project. The Initiating Process Group defines the scope of the project, identifies the project's stakeholders and project manager, secures the financial resources necessary to begin the project, and obtains the required authorization to begin the project or phase. The project manager and the project management team help write the project charter, which is then approved and officially authorized by the project initiator or sponsor.[1]

The project charter and scope statement begin a recurring theme throughout the life of a project that is of great importance to the success of that project: mutual understanding of a project's goals and objectives. Although this sounds simple to achieve, it isn't because of the organizational and operational complexity so prevalent in healthcare, competing demands, many different stakeholders and project team members with different foci, and other factors. Mutual understanding of a project's goals and objectives must be foremost in a PM's mind during the initiation phase and revisited during critical junctures thereafter.

Project Charter

The organization initiating a project assigns a project manager to the project. The project manager is integral to the success of the project because it is their responsibility to see that the project achieves the objectives outlined in the project charter. The PM must focus on the following:

- Achieving specified project objectives
- Controlling the assigned project resources to meet project objectives
- Managing the four project management variables (as well as risk): performance (quality), cost, time, and scope (PCTS)

The PM must constantly monitor all of these areas in order to ensure that the project is progressing in accordance with the project charter, is reaching milestones, and finally achieves the goals outlined in the project charter. As discussed, efficiently balancing the competing demands of the project's overall scope, schedule, budget, quality requirements, available resources, and risk will lead to successful project completion. It is the PM's responsibility to manage all of these factors to reach the successful completion of the project.

Project Scope Statement

Following the development and authorization of a project charter comes a more detailed description of the project and its goals through a *project scope statement*. The project scope statement is essential to the project's progress and builds upon the major factors such as required deliverables, known or assumed risks and constraints, and other variables that are identified in the project charter. Additionally, the project scope statement takes into account any other risks, constraints, or variables that may not have been known at the time the project charter was written. When the project scope statement is being developed, more information regarding the specific details of the project is available, so the scope can be defined more clearly and with greater accuracy.[1]

The *PMBOK Guide* outlines the following sources of information that the project management team uses to help develop the project scope statement:

- Project charter
- Requirements documentation (describes how individual requirements meet the business and clinical needs for the project)
- Organizational process assets (examples include policies, procedures, and templates for a project scope statement and files and lessons learned from previous projects)
- Expert judgment (examples include other units within the organization, consultants, stakeholders, industry groups, and subject-matter experts)
- Product analysis
- Alternatives identification[1]

When a project scope statement includes a sufficient level of detail and information to define the project, the project management team has a better chance of being able to successfully manage the project.

Project Problem/Vision/Mission Statements

Because proper project initiation is critical to the success of all projects, we will also walk through the principles the Lewis Institute uses to teach project initiation. Depending on the project and the project manager's and project team's preferences, the steps outlined here can substitute for the PMI scope statement process. The creation of these "statements" is best led by the PM but with the full participation of project team members

Use Case 11-3: The EcoSys Online Labs Phase 1 Project Scope Statement

Here is the EcoSys Online Labs Phase 1 Project Scope Statement:

Patients are seeking online, easy-to-use ways to view, manage, and use health information to make informed decisions about their health and the health of their dependents. Within three years, patients will consistently choose to partner with care providers who serve them in this way over providers who do not, impacting Tree Healthcare System opportunities for revenue and reimbursement from patient care.

The EcoSys Online Labs Phase 1 Project is one project within the EcoSys Portal Program. Online Labs Phase 1 will provide patients and authorized caregivers with an online, easy-to-use way to access lab results from two Tree-affiliated labs, Acorn Labs and Walnut Creek Labs. Results will be available online within 48 hours of test completion. Phase 1 of the project will deliver a functional version of the online labs experience within 12 months, displaying patient information and test results for the five most common lab tests performed by Acorn and Walnut Creek Labs, as measured by volume of tests performed in 2015. These tests are

- CBC with differential
- Hemoglobin A1c (HbA1c)
- Comprehensive metabolic panel
- Lipid panel
- Assay thyroid (TSH)

Additional lab test results or tests available from labs other than Acorn and Walnut Creek are out of scope for Phase 1 and may be considered for future project phases. The online labs experience delivered in Phase 1 must comply with the Tree System Brand Policy for Digital Marketing, Policy M-245. Future phases of online labs may deliver all remaining lab test information and results from Tree-affiliated labs.

and, when appropriate, stakeholders. The project initiating phase includes the following components:

- **Project problem statement**   A problem statement defines the problem at hand and the reason for initiating a project and helps to develop a suitable solution for the problem. It's a good starting point to then go on to construct a project's vision and mission.

- **Project vision**   The project vision provides a clear picture of what the final result will look like. The project vision communicates a shared understanding of the project's goals or endpoints to the project's team members and stakeholders. The project vision will answer the following questions: "What will the final result of this project look like?" and "How will the project deliverables affect our customers?"

- **Project mission statement**   The project mission statement describes the overarching goal or objective that the project manager and project team is hoping to achieve and reminds the team of the ultimate purpose of the project. The mission statement should satisfy the needs of the project team, customers, and stakeholders. Additionally, the mission statement can help motivate or even inspire the team to work together to reach successful completion of the project. Important questions that you should ask as you develop the mission statement are "What are we going to do?" and "Whom are we doing it for?" and sometimes "How will we do it?"

SMART Project Objectives

The project scope statement or problem/vision/mission statement exercises done by the project team ready the team to craft project objectives that will guide the project and be used to determine project success. Within a project, the project team will undertake project activities in order to reach the desired objectives or the end of the project or phase. During the project initiation phase, you should ask the following questions of the stated project objectives: "What is our desired outcome?" and "How will we know when we achieve it?" By answering these questions, you will be able to ensure that the planned project activities will lead you to the desired end state of the project. It is important to note that the objectives should not state how they are achieved. The methods that will be used to achieve the project objectives will be developed in the next phase of the project life cycle, planning.

The common acronym SMART is a helpful tool you should use when developing project objectives. Project managers use SMART objectives as a way to ensure that project phases and results are successful.

- **S**   Specific. Project objectives need to be specific and unambiguously explain what the project's objectives and plans are. Furthermore, a single objective should encompass a single concept, although it's okay to "roll up" subobjectives into one objective when setting overall project objectives.

- **M**   Measurable. An objective needs to be measurable in order to make sure the team is making progress toward successful completion of the project.

- **A**   Attainable. An objective needs to be able to be achieved with a reasonable amount of effort.

- **R**   Relevant. The objective needs to be important to the organization or make a positive impact on a particular situation.

- **T**   Time-limited. A deadline for project and/or phase completion needs to be set in order to help the team focus their efforts on completing their tasks in a timely manner. Therefore, the subject of the objective must fit into the timeframe of the project.

Developing SMART project objectives helps ensure that project managers can successfully plan, schedule, and control all of the activities that must be done to meet a project's objectives.

Use Case 11-4: SMART Project Objectives for the EcoSys Online Labs Phase 1 Project

The Online Labs Phase 1 Project objectives are defined to guide the project and align expectations on project success. As the project manager, you schedule a working session and invite the co-executive sponsors (Julie Iris, RN, MS, and Dr. Tony Rose), the business sponsor (Dr. Luke Kelly), Drs. Kading and Rosenberg, Dan Wheeler, and Kelly O'Grady to participate. As a result of the session, the following objectives are developed and approved:

- Test results in scope will be available online within 48 hours of the test completion and clinical review process at each lab.

- Users who attempt to access lab results before the 48-hour timeline will be redirected so patient-appropriate status information is provided to reduce the number of phone calls into Tree Patient Services by 25 percent from the current baseline level.

- Results will be easily sortable so that users may organize and save information for use in follow-up visits with healthcare providers.

- In the online labs experience, users will have access to patient education information regarding the test performed, potential results, and contact information for the Tree Healthcare System Patient Education Center.

- Online Labs web pages and experience will be consistent in design, appearance, and format with other pages in the EcoSys Portal and will comply with Tree System Brand Policy for Digital Marketing, Policy M-245.

- Online Labs Phase 1 will complete scope and project closure by December 31, 12 months from the start of the project, in support of EcoSys Portal Program deadlines.

 TIP Project objectives need to be specific, measurable, attainable, relevant, and time-limited (SMART) in order for the project to be well planned, scheduled, and controlled.

Planning a Healthcare IT Project

With the project charter approved, the problem/vision/mission statement written, and SMART project objectives set, a project manager and his or her team are well on their way to planning a successful healthcare IT project. The next step in successful project management that we will discuss is critical to the project and must be completed before work on the project begins. A project implementation plan must be developed before the team can begin project execution. While the project initiators or sponsors may be eager to begin the actual work of the project, it is in the best interest of the project and its stakeholders to carefully plan the work that is to be done. If you take the time up front to properly plan, you will save time and avoid costly errors in the long run. A rule of thumb is that one hour spent on planning saves three hours on execution. Equally important as developing the execution plan, the PM needs to make sure that there is a shared understanding of what is going to be done by the entire project team. Project planning will answer the following questions (who, what, when, where, why, and how):

- What must be done?
- How should it be done?
- Who will do it?
- When must it be done by?
- Where will it be done?
- Why will it be done is answered by the justification given in the project charter and/or the SMART objectives. However, for project planning purposes, why will it be done the way proposed as opposed to another way is good to ask.
- How long will it take?
- How much will it cost?
- How good does it have to be?[5]

If the project manager can ensure that he or she has developed a strong plan for the work to be done in the project as well as a shared understanding of the plan, then the PM has demonstrated one fundamental aspect of control over the project and will be able to continuously assess the project's progress and take action to correct any deviations. Without a plan, there is no control.

The Work Breakdown Structure (WBS)

One of the most important tools in project planning is the work breakdown structure (WBS). The purpose of the WBS is to organize and define the total scope of the project.

WBS Defined

Taking the project's objectives and required deliverables into account, the WBS is a diagram that outlines the actual work that needs to be accomplished by the project team. The WBS establishes the interactions between all of the various components of the project and its deliverables.[1] The process of creating the WBS breaks the project's work and deliverables down into smaller, more manageable components, which helps the project manager maintain control of the project and helps provide clear direction to the team as to what work needs to be done. A WBS creates a visual representation of the project in its entirety and is a very valuable communication tool for the project manager, project team members, and project stakeholders.[6] Said another way, a WBS is a graphic representation of a project as a whole.

WBS Principles

Before you can successfully create a WBS, you must understand the difference between a project deliverable and a project activity. A *project deliverable* is the output or product that is created by the project's activities. A *project activity* is what you need to do in order to produce the deliverable or product. A WBS is a collection of all important project activities.

TIP   A project *deliverable* is a desired end state, and a project activity is the action that leads to the desired end state.

To create a WBS for a project, the project manager will need to take the project scope statement, the project requirements from the organization initiating or sponsoring the project, and the organizational processes assets, such as policies, procedures, WBS templates, and files and lessons learned from previous projects, and break them down into smaller, more manageable components or levels until the work and deliverables are defined at the work package level. It is usually advisable to recruit the project team members and sometimes certain stakeholders into the process of creating the WBS, but ultimately, the PM is responsible for creating a comprehensive and effective WBS. Figure 11-2 depicts the levels of the WBS.

Below the Project level, all of the components are called *project activities*. Colloquially many people call project activities *tasks*. But, since Task is a level in a WBS, it's better to call all of the components of work to be done *project activities*.

How many levels should you break the work down to? That depends. WBSs in the construction industry and engineering projects commonly involve many levels, up to 20 in some cases. More than four levels (Project, Task, Subtask, and Work Package) are often unnecessarily complex for HIT projects. The rule of thumb is to break down the project only as far as you need to easily manage it. For example, if you have a great network engineer with whom you have worked on other projects, you might simply have a task that says "Manage network" with no subtasks below it. On the other hand, if you have a new network engineer on the project, you might need to have "Assess, plan new components, and test network" as subtasks, and you may even break down those subtasks further into work package activities so that together you and the new network engineer can effectively manage all the important activities related to the network infrastructure for the project.

The Work Package level is the lowest level in the WBS. Very simply, the work package groups project activities that fit together logically and that can then be assigned to one person or team to execute. Once the Work Package level has been reached, a project manager

Figure 11-2
Project
management
work breakdown
structure
illustration

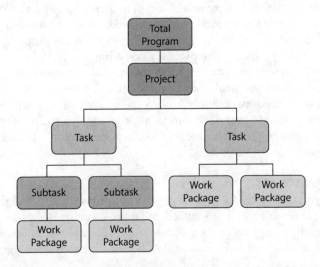

can dependably estimate the cost of the project, develop an accurate schedule for the work to be completed, and, finally, better manage and control the work.[1] For the WBS to be an effective tool for the PM, it must answer the project planning questions outlined earlier as well as ensure a shared understanding among the project team of the objectives.

TIP The project manager can reasonably estimate the cost of the project, develop an accurate schedule for the work to be completed, and effectively manage and control the project activities *after* a WBS has been created all the way down to the Work Package level.

Another important principle in constructing WBSs is that a WBS tells you nothing about sequencing. Sequencing of project tasks or activities comes in the next step, scheduling of project resources.

Use Case 11-5: The EcoSys Online Labs Phase 1 Project Work Breakdown Structure

Figure 11-3 is a partial work breakdown structure depicting Task, Subtask, and Work Package level project activities for the Online Labs Phase 1 Project for the Design and Build tasks. Note the broad similarity of the Tasks in this project to those in Figures 9-2 and 9-12 in Chapter 9. Like many projects in HIT, the EcoSys project is guided by the systems analysis framework you learned about in Chapter 9. Not depicted in Figure 11-3 are the Test, Train, Go-live, and Post-Implementation Tasks for the project. The full WBS for this project would include these Tasks as well as their Subtask and Work Package level project activities in a similar fashion to the Design and Build Tasks in Figure 11-3. The lower level project activities on this project WBS serve to guide the project team in "chunking down" the project into manageable project activities. The WBS as a whole fosters mutual understanding of the overall project for team members and stakeholders.

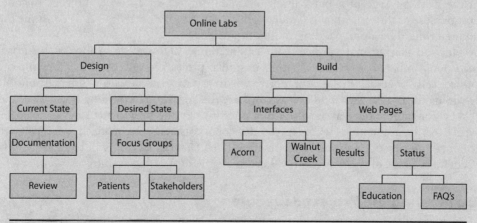

Figure 11-3　Online Labs Phase 1 Project partial WBS

Estimating Time, Cost, and Resources

Once the project manager has created the WBS all the way down to the work package level, the PM can begin estimating the time, costs, and resources necessary to successfully achieve the project's objectives. After these estimates have been created, the PM can develop a realistic schedule, budget, and plan for the project.

Key Points About Estimating

Taking the time to properly plan a project's activities increases the probability that the team will achieve the project's objectives on time and within budget. If the project has been planned well to this point, then most likely time, cost, and resource estimates will be accurate. Here are a few key points for developing accurate estimates:

- Understand what is required.
- Prioritize activities and tasks.
- Decide who needs to be involved.

In HIT projects, usually the greatest resource expenditure is on the time of project team members (project manager, clinical analysts, business analysts, network engineers, clinical application specialists, subject-matter experts, hardware/device technicians, and others from finance, quality measurement, and compliance monitoring). Thus, the main thing the project manager will be estimating is project activity duration. This will account for the vast majority of resources and cost in most HIT projects.

Essentially, what you are estimating as the PM is the probable project activity duration. The bell curve applies here. In a project with 100 activities, some of your estimates will be over, and some of your estimates will be under the actual time required to complete those tasks. If you, your project team, and the stakeholders have done your very best to estimate the duration of each of the project activities, the over/under will average out, and your overall estimate will be reasonably accurate. A word about padding: *padding*, or increasing a project activity's estimated duration time, is common. But, padding at the work package or subtask levels or overall project level inevitably leads to more cost because of the well-known "student effect"—the project activities fully consume the allotted time. Therefore, padding should be avoided.

How do you estimate project activity durations? One way is to look at historical records of similar project activities done in similar projects in the past. How long did the project activity actually take? Another way is to ask the person who will be responsible for doing the project activity. They usually have the best idea of how long it will take, and if they don't know right away, a series of questions by the project manager or dialogue with other team members will help you develop a reasonable estimate. If you have used the methods described earlier for estimating, then chances are you will have a relatively accurate estimate of the work and will complete the project successfully.

Developing the Project Schedule

With the work necessary to achieve the project's objectives defined, the WBS created, and the project activities and costs estimated, the project manager is now ready to develop the project schedule. The PM will need to take into account the project activities, estimated time to complete the activities, required resources, and project delivery date to develop the project schedule. This is an important step in the process and one that may have several revisions throughout the life of the project. The project schedule outlines the target start and finish dates for all project activities and milestones. A *milestone* is an identifiable or noteworthy event that marks significant progress on the project.[7] Time and resource estimates will need to be reviewed, and often revised, to create an approved project schedule that will serve as a baseline to track project progress.

Purpose of Scheduling

If the project manager is able to continuously maintain a realistic schedule as project work develops and changes, the PM will be able to keep the project moving forward and will be able to inform team members and stakeholders of the project's status. If the project manager sees the project deviating from the schedule, the PM can take appropriate measures to get the project back on track or make any necessary updates to the project's budget and scope. Without having an accurate project schedule and without monitoring the progress of the project's activities and revising the schedule, as needed, it will be hard for a project manager to have good control of the project and will make completing the project on time and on budget almost impossible.

Introduction to Scheduling Techniques

In project management there are many different techniques that can be used to help develop and maintain an accurate project schedule. We will discuss several of them here. One area that is outside the scope of this chapter is a detailed discussion of project management software. Microsoft Project and many other good project scheduling and management software application products are readily available. In the vast majority of HIT projects, a software application tool will be used to develop and maintain the project schedule. These tools have many helpful features that greatly simplify creating a schedule. What we will provide here are principles, practices, and advice that will ideally make your use of these essential products more powerful and effective.

Several analytical techniques underpin the algorithms of project management scheduling software that produce Gantt chart–like project schedules. By far the most common scheduling analytical technique is the critical path method. To use a project management software scheduling application that employs the critical path method in a project with interdependent activities in order to develop a chart-like depiction of the project schedule, a project manager needs to know the following:

- All project activities that are required to complete the project (from WBS)
- The time each activity will take to complete
- The relationship between all activities

The PM will then be able to calculate the *critical path*, which is the longest path (in time) from project start to project finish. The critical path indicates the minimum time necessary to complete the entire project.[8] The longest path in the diagram is the critical path, and any activity on this path is considered a critical activity and must be executed on time to keep the overall project end date on time. Oftentimes in a project there will be activities that are not on the critical path; these are referred to as *slack* or *float* activities.

Slack or float activities have the flexibility to be delayed without delaying the total project beyond its target completion date.[9] When the float of an activity or path is negative, meaning there is no flexibility, it is called *supercritical*. As a general rule, two critical paths in one project should be avoided. And, any activities that have significant risk associated with them should be considered float activities.[9]

Scheduling Resources in Projects

All projects rely on a variety of resources to actually do the work outlined in the project documents. Resources include but are not limited to people, materials, equipment, and money. Without adequate resources, a project will have difficulty reaching the target completion date or may not achieve its objectives. At this point in the project, the project manager must identify the resources required for successful project completion and then plan, or schedule, the resources so that the team can work effectively.

Resource allocation is the process of assigning to each project activity in the plan the necessary resources that have previously been identified. Some activities may require more than one resource, and depending on the nature of the activity, the amount of resources required may vary at different points throughout project execution. The project plan may need to be revised to account for resource availability.

Scheduling resources before any work begins on a project allows the project manager to see where resources may be overloaded and make adjustments to the project plan. However, one technique frequently employed by PMs is to not worry too much about overloading resources on the first pass of project activities and focus instead on the sequencing and relationships between project activities. This is because one of the most powerful features of project management software, as well as being a significant aide to the PM, is resource leveling.

Resource Leveling

Most likely, at some point in a project the demand for a resource, or resources, will outweigh the availability of the resource(s). Resource leveling helps the project manager handle this problem and keep the project on track .The process of revising a plan's schedule (start and finish dates) in order to account for resource availability is called *resource leveling* and is used to optimize the distribution of work among resources. Figure 11-4 illustrates two types of resource leveling techniques: *time-critical leveling* and *resource-critical leveling* and the differences between them.[9]

Figure 11-4
Time-critical vs. resource-critical resource leveling

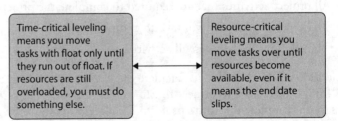

Time-critical leveling means you move tasks with float only until they run out of float. If resources are still overloaded, you must do something else.

Resource-critical leveling means you move tasks over until resources become available, even if it means the end date slips.

Resource-leveling techniques are applied to project schedules that have already been analyzed by the critical path method and can often lead to changes in the critical path as well as potentially other parts of the project.[1]

Factoring in Resource Availability

To create a schedule, the project manager will need to begin by inputting the actual time it will take to complete each project activity. Then, resource availability must be factored into the schedule to determine the duration (in calendar time) it will take to complete the project work. The PM needs to know the actual availability of their team members when developing a schedule; without this, the PM cannot create a meaningful schedule.[9] When factoring in resource availability, it is important to understand that people's productivity can be affected by the following three factors:

- **P** Personal. People must take breaks.
- **F** Fatigue. They get tired.
- **D** Delays. They are waiting for something.

It has been found that in a standard eight-hour day, you will get only about 80 percent, or 6.4 hours, of productive work from a person. This loss in productivity comes from P, F, and D.[9] Additionally, "setup time"—the time a resource takes to initiate a project activity—associated with starting each new project activity or segment of a project activity should be accounted for. If the PM can prioritize tasks and have team members working on fewer project activities at one time, setup time will be decreased, which will help the overall project schedule. One suggestion for this is to give each team member a "priority-one" activity and a backup activity. When there is a break in the work on the "priority-one" activity, team members can move to their backup activity.

Beware Multitasking

Project team members who shuttle from many different project activities, potentially across multiple projects, per day are "multitasking" and their efficiency is degraded. The pioneering work of Earl Miller, a neuroscientist at the Massachusetts Institute of Technology, has demonstrated that multitasking significantly reduces knowledge workers' efficiency and in many cases effectiveness.[10] A project manager can help project team members be much more productive by facilitating their focus on one or a few tasks in a given period of time. This may require coordination with the project team members' line manager or other project managers that have a "piece of your resource" as well.

Use Case 11-6: EcoSys Online Labs Phase 1 Project Schedule

You have finished the WBS (partially shown in Figure 11-3) and are now ready to create a project schedule:

- You consult the objectives finalized during the earlier work session (Use Case 11-4), specifically the objective concerning the project closure date. What is the objective and why is it important for scheduling?

- You work in collaboration with Maya Sherman, your business analyst, on estimates and confirming resource availabilities for the project. When discussing the testing phase, Maya states that the first round of testing will definitely require 8 hours a week per patient tester for the first 30 days. Referring to your resource availabilities for your SocialFree patient testers (Use Case 11-2), Connie Hughes and Robert Kurtz, what is the challenge? What options might you have to resolve the challenge in the schedule?

Using the principles and best practices of project management, along with the information you've learned and documented thus far, you create a first draft of the schedule, as shown in Figure 11-5.

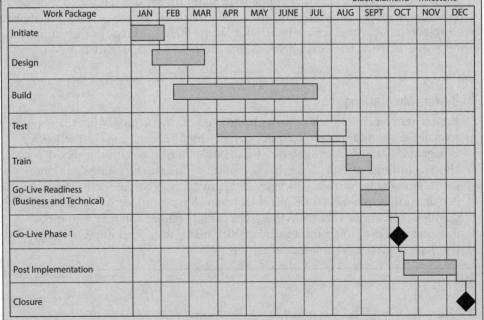

Figure 11-5   EcoSys Online Labs Phase 1 Project schedule

Executing, Monitoring, and Controlling HIT Projects

The project charter and problem/mission/vision statements have been written, the objectives have been outlined, the WBS has been created, and the time, cost, and resources have been estimated; in addition, a schedule has been developed, and resources have been allocated. So, execution of the project's deliverables is ready to begin. All of the careful, thoughtful planning that has been done up front will help ensure that execution goes smoothly, according to plan, and that the project objectives are achieved. The execution phase of a project includes completing the work outlined in the project plan in order to meet the project requirements, coordinating resources, and performing the activities in the plan.[1] Additionally, during the execution phase the project manager will need to constantly monitor the progress of the project and make any necessary changes to the plan in order to keep the project moving in the direction of achieving its objectives.

Execution Principles, Issues, and Opportunities

The execution phase of the project is the time when the work that has been planned for the project actually gets completed, a large portion of the project's budget is spent, and the plan may be updated or a new plan baseline may be established as a result of the work being done. These changes may be made because activity durations varied from the expectations in the plan, changes occurred in resource availability or productivity, or other unanticipated risks arose after execution began. If the changes are of a large enough scale, change requests will need to be initiated and subsequently approved so that the project management plan or documents can be revised and a new baseline established if necessary.[1] During the course of the execution phase, the project manager is responsible for managing the team to perform the work necessary to achieve the project's objectives. Some of the project manager's responsibilities include the following:

- Acquiring the project team, tracking their performance, and helping improve their skill sets
- Performing quality assurance audits
- Distributing important information to the team and stakeholders
- Managing stakeholder expectations[1]

 TIP During project execution, the project manager is responsible for seeing that the work that needs to be done to achieve the project objectives is completed according to the plan and, if not, for initiating project change requests.

Monitoring Progress in Projects

Throughout the course of the execution phase, the project manager is also responsible for monitoring the progress of the project. Monitoring the project includes tracking, reviewing, and controlling the progress and performance of the project as well as

Use Case 11-7: EcoSys Online Labs Phase 1 Project Issue Log

You have created an issue log for the project to track and monitor progress on issues and questions from the team. The log is stored in a shared location and high-priority items are reviewed during the weekly project team Skype calls.

Here are two issues pulled from the issue log for the EcoSys Online Labs Phase 1 Project that are discussed at weekly project team meetings. Following the discussion of the issues are questions that the PM must put on the path to resolution.

1. By mid-June, the third session to gather patient tester feedback on the online labs experience is now complete. During this round of feedback, the patient testers (Connie and Rob) had difficulty retrieving Glycated Hemoglobin (HbA1c) test results from Acorn Labs. When observing the testing, business analyst Maya Sherman noticed that clicking the link often resulted in an error message, and patients clicking the HbA1c link for Walnut Creek did not receive this error. As the PM, what are your next steps in regard to the Acorn HbA1c test results issue?

2. On the June 22 project team weekly Skype call, Dan Wheeler submits an issue to change the font used on the web pages from Arial to Helvetica Neue. He reminds the team that Helvetica Neue is the font standard approved in the Tree System Brand Policy for Digital Marketing, Policy M-245. On the same call, tester Rob Kurtz submits a new issue regarding the display of lab results. For all Walnut Creek patients, lab test results for TSH, Metabolic Panel, and CBC with differential are truncated on the page; patients cannot view their results accurately. Considering HIT project critical success factors and quality management, how would you log next steps and prioritize the resolution urgency of these two issues?

identifying and mitigating any risks that may have developed during the progress of the project; strong risk management is important to the success of the project for the following reasons:

- Improves project performance
- Ensures quality does not take a backseat to cost and schedule
- Reveals developing problems early
- Determines what needs to be done to mitigate identifiable risks
- Identifies areas where other projects should be managed differently
- Keeps clients informed of status
- Reaffirms organization's commitment to the project

Project Control and Evaluation

Project control is achieved by analyzing where one is compared to where one is supposed to be and then taking corrective action to resolve any discrepancies that exist. The project manager controls the direction of the project and helps ensure its success by regularly, and consistently, monitoring the project's performance and measuring that against the project's plan and objectives. If the PM sees the project progressing in a different way than outlined in the plan or sees any stalling, the PM needs to initiate any necessary changes to the plan.[1] Just like in all of the other phases of project management, there are systematic review techniques that the PM should use.

Kinds of Evaluation Reviews

We suggest three kinds of evaluation reviews—status, design, and process—that the project manager can use during the course of the project to systematically ensure that the project is progressing according to plan and will achieve its objectives.

- **Project status review**   The project status review should occur weekly on shorter projects and monthly on longer projects. This review looks at the current status of the project. Specifically, it reviews the P, C, T, S of the project using something called an *earned-value analysis* that we will discuss in the next section. The status of critical tasks must be updated at this time. The future status of the project is also considered in this review, including projected deviations from the schedule. Any risk factors contributing to problems in the project need to be identified and solutions need to be developed, if possible. The status of critical tasks must be updated at this time. And finally, risk management principles should be applied, if necessary.

- **Project design review**   The project design review examines a product, service, or software design to see whether it meets the project requirements. The questions that need to be asked are "Does it work?" and "Can we make it work?"

- **Project process review**   The project process review happens at major project milestones or at completion of the project; it evaluates whether the project was done well and what needs to be improved, and it develops a list of "lessons learned" from the project that can be applied to future projects.

Earned-Value Analysis

Oftentimes a project management team will use a *schedule* report to review the progress of a project. Unfortunately, this will not provide the team with a true picture of the project's status because it does not take into account the effort or work that has been put into the project, which may be greater than anticipated but slowing down the overall progress. To properly assess the status of the project and account for any deviations from the plan, the project manager should conduct an *earned-value analysis*. The earned-value system is an integrated cost-schedule tracking system that looks at the project's P, C, T, S to help the project manager, team, and stakeholders understand the true status of the project. An earned-value analysis integrates the following factors in order to accurately assess the project's performance and progress:

- **Cost variance**   Any difference between the estimated cost of an activity and the actual cost of an activity
- **Schedule variance**   Any difference between the scheduled completion of an activity and the actual completion of that activity

To determine the cost and schedule variances, the project manager will need to use the following equations:

Schedule variance = BCWP – BCWS
Cost variance = BCWP – ACWP

where:

- **Budgeted Cost of Work Scheduled (BCWS)**   The budgeted cost of work scheduled to be done in a given time period
- **Budgeted Cost of Work Performed (BCWP)**   The budgeted cost of work actually performed in a given time period (i.e., earned value)
- **Actual Cost of Work Performed (ACWP)**   The amount of money actually spent for completing the work in a given time period

Using the earned-value analysis will help provide a clear and realistic understanding of the project's progress as well as an understanding of why it may not be progressing according to the plan. With the click of a button, Microsoft Project and other project-scheduling software products produce earned-value analysis data once the schedule is updated with percent activity completion across all project activities.

TIP   An earned-value analysis looks at the project's P, C, T, S to help the project manager, team, and stakeholders understand the true status of the project, and it integrates cost and schedule variances in order to accurately assess a project's performance and progress.

Use Case 11-8: EcoSys Online Labs Phase 1 Project Status Meeting

You are about three months into the project and preparing materials for the March 15 project status meeting. Since project team members are located at many different sites (Forest City and Spruce to name just two), you have scheduled a 60-minute Skype project status call twice a month with all team members including all Online Labs sponsors.

Agenda topics for project status meetings may include the following:

- Work accomplished by the team since the last status update
- Work in process
- Work upcoming

- Issues
- Risks management and planning
- Change requests for sponsor review and decision.

Upon completing your preparations for the status meeting, most project activities, including all critical path activities, to date are on schedule:

- Drs. Kading and Rosenberg (stakeholders and subject-matter experts) met the deadline assigned for review and acceptance of the initial web page content. Craig Devlin, the project's website developer, began meeting with business analyst Maya Sherman to confirm requirements and begin coding on schedule in preparation for testing of the first prototype.

- Dan Wheeler did not meet the March 1 deadline assigned to him for review and acceptance of the initial web pages' design and format. Dan is the primary marketing and brand leader stakeholder assigned to nearly all the projects within the EcoSys Portal Program. Dan sent you an e-mail late last night and committed to completing his review by April 1.

- The resource availability issue in April for the two SocialFree patient testers has been resolved. Lorraine Hart, SocialFree CEO, has approved an additional four hours per week for both Connie and Rob in April, time needed to fulfill the work estimates needed for the first round of testing. Project change request or contingency will not be needed to address this issue.

- Earned-value analysis to date indicates that the project is spending somewhat more than the plan calls for to maintain on-schedule performance. Upon further investigation, you discover that Anja Schiff, the cloud services architect, needed to license, setup, and configure an additional web development environment two months earlier than she originally planned to support the project. Therefore, the project is simply incurring cost and resource work time earlier than planned, not additional cost and resource time. The net effect on earned-value is neutral.

- Potential risks identified for the project during the initiating phase have not manifested at this point. No new risks have been identified for management.

Changing the Plan

If after conducting project evaluation reviews and an earned-value analysis the project manager finds that there has been a significant change (+/− 5%) in P, C, T, S, then the PM may need to initiate an official change in the project's process. The PM will need to fill out an official project change form or document to request the change in the project by outlining where the change has occurred and why and how the project will be amended if the change is approved.

> ## Use Case 11-9: EcoSys Online Labs Phase 1
> ## Project Decision to Change/Add Scope or Not to Change
> At the April 30 project status meeting, the business sponsor, Dr. Kelly, says to the team that he thinks it would be a great idea if—in addition to Acorn and Walnut Creek Labs—Sunflower Labs were added into Phase 1 scope. Tree Healthcare System will be starting talks with Sunflower Labs next month about a formal affiliation agreement. You have been told by both co-executive sponsors, Julie Iris and Dr. Rose, that the Online Labs Phase 1 Project must complete in 12 months. No extension is possible because of EcoSys Portal Program deadlines.
>
> - What implications might Dr. Kelly's idea have on the project?
> - Should you create a change request? If yes, what points of analysis would you include?

Closing the Project

You have now seen how a healthcare IT project progresses from the initiation phase to the planning phase and then on to the execution phase, with its emphasis on monitoring and controlling processes. All that is left is to confirm that all aspects of the project's activities are finished so that the project can be officially complete. At the time of project closing, the following activities may take place:

- The project is accepted by the project initiator or sponsor.
- A post-project review is conducted.
- Lessons learned are documented.
- Any necessary updates are applied to the organizational process.
- Project notes are filed for use in future projects.
- Any other close-out procedures required by the project sponsor or organization are performed.

Additionally, the entire project management team should look at how the team has worked together to achieve the project's objectives. Specifically, the following team processes should be evaluated:

- Leadership
- Decision making
- Problem solving
- Communications
- Meetings

- Planning
- Giving feedback to team members and others
- Conflict management

Once a project is complete, it is important for the project team to take some time to conduct a post-mortem analysis to evaluate what went well throughout the course of the project as well as what did not go well during the project. Through this analysis, the team will develop a list of lessons learned regarding the project specifically, as well as about project management in general, and will look to carry these lessons learned over into future projects.

Use Case 11-10: EcoSys Online Labs Phase 1 Project Post Mortem

The Online Labs Phase 1 Project went live on schedule during the second week of October. All project objectives were met. Lorraine Hart, a key stakeholder from the start of the project, was very pleased with the online labs experience now available to her employees and to many others in the Spruce community. In order for progress to continue, Lorraine agreed that SocialFree will fund 50 percent of the project cost for Online Labs Phase 2, so more patients may benefit from not just five key results, but almost all lab information available online via the EcoSys Portal.

After go-live, a handful of minor issues were identified and quickly resolved during post implementation. Project closure was accomplished by December 15, about two weeks before the 12-month deadline stated in the project objectives. Post-project reviews, formal acceptance by the sponsors of the solution delivered, documentation of lessons learned, and celebration of a job well done all occurred before December 30.

During the post-project review for Online Labs Phase 1, the following conclusions were drawn:

P   Performance (quality)

- There was acceptable user satisfaction (both patients and authorized caregivers) with the Online Labs Phase 1 experience as delivered and measured by a valid and reliable survey.

- Redirection of users who attempted to access lab results before the 48-hour timeline to a new status and Frequently Asked Questions (FAQ) page resulted in a 35 percent decrease in the number of phone calls into Tree Patient Services from initial baseline level.

- The project team members and stakeholders were very satisfied with the processes and outcomes of the project.

(continued)

C Cost

- There was a 10 percent budget overrun that was considered acceptable by management. A change request was submitted, reviewed, and approved authorizing payment for an external consultant to rapidly assess the feasibility of adding Sunflower Labs into the scope of Online Labs Phase 1. The change request to retain a consultant was created in response to Dr. Kelly's request at the April 30 project status meeting. At the conclusion of the engagement, the consultant recommended against the addition of Sunflower Labs into Phase 1 scope.

T Time

- The project started and ended on time.

S Scope

- The project manager successfully managed scope through the use of project management discipline, including change management and change control processes.

The project documents, including the initiating phase reports, WBS, schedules, status reports, and post-project analysis, were archived for reference for future projects.

Chapter Review

In this chapter, we took the rather extensive subject of project management and broke it down into an easy-to-understand explanation in order to provide you with the knowledge necessary to understand how essential project management is to healthcare IT. Given the constraints of this book, we did not go into as much detail or explanation of some of the specific techniques described in the chapter, such as the WBS, critical path method, earned-value analysis, and others. We highly recommend the Project Management Institute's *A Guide to the Project Management Body of Knowledge*, the Lewis Institute, and the Healthcare Information Management Systems Society (HIMSS) as sources for additional information on the subject.

We also covered the four phases of a project (initiating, planning, executing, and closing) and broke out the major activities in each phase as they apply to healthcare information technology so that you are better equipped to work in project management in the healthcare industry. At the start of the project, or the initiating phase, you will develop a project charter and outline the project's scope and mission. Then you will need to develop SMART objectives and finally prioritize the project's objectives. After you do this, you will move into the planning phase where you will develop the WBS and estimate the time, cost, and resources needed for the project. Once you've created the WBS and have strong project activity duration estimates, you can develop the project's schedule and schedule/allocate resources for the project utilizing the critical path method and resource leveling techniques we described. Then you are ready to move to the executing phase and begin monitoring and controlling processes in earnest. In this phase, the project "work" gets done, and you will be responsible for monitoring the progress of the project and maintaining control over the project. We described several types of evaluation reviews, including an earned-value analysis that will help you monitor and control the project's trajectory. We also described how to make changes to the plan, if and when necessary. Once the work of the project is complete (and ideally the objectives have been met), you can move on to closing the project. In this phase of project management, you will conduct a post-mortem analysis of the project to see what went well and what did not, and you can develop a list of lessons learned that can be applied to other projects in the future.

You learned that a project is a temporary activity that is undertaken by a team in order to create a unique product, service, or result in a defined time period, and project management is the organization or facilitation of all of the planning, scheduling, and monitoring or controlling of all the activities or tasks that must be done to meet the project's goals or objectives. Utilizing the project management process and techniques described in this chapter will significantly increase your chances of managing projects successfully and will help you to be a more valuable asset to an organization. The project management process can be applied to projects in all industries, not just healthcare. You can take the skills you have learned here and apply them in many different situations and ideally be successful at whatever it is you have set out to accomplish.

Questions

To test your comprehension of the chapter, answer the following questions and then check your answers against the list of correct answers at the end of the chapter.

1. Project management techniques are useful tools for healthcare IT project managers to have because it helps them do what?
   A. Teach their project team how to cut corners so they can get their work done more quickly
   B. Manage computer projects better
   C. Facilitate the planning, scheduling, and controlling of projects
   D. Execute healthcare IT projects without having to create a plan

2. What is the purpose of a work breakdown structure?
   A. To create a diagram of all the people on the project team and what work they will do
   B. To break the project down so that the scope of the project is decreased and the project can be executed more quickly
   C. To create a visual representation of the project so everyone can understand the purpose of the project
   D. To break the project's work and deliverables down into smaller, more manageable components, which helps the project manager maintain control of the project and helps provide clear direction to the team as to what work needs to be done

3. What process group occurs during all phases of a project's life cycle?

    A. Monitoring and controlling

    B. Watching and listening

    C. Executing and closing

    D. Planning and finishing

4. For a project manager to accurately estimate the time, cost, and resources necessary to achieve a project's objectives, what will the project manager need to do?

    A. Understand what is required and decide who needs to be involved

    B. Prioritize project activities

    C. A and B

    D. None of the above

5. The process of moving project activities out until resources are available, even if it means the project end date slips, is called what?

    A. Time-critical leveling

    B. Scheduling adjusting

    C. Resource-critical leveling

    D. Project leveling

6. What does a project manager need to know to determine the critical path?

    A. All project activities that are required to complete the project (from the WBS)

    B. The time each activity will take to complete

    C. The relationship between all activities

    D. All of the above

Answers

1. **C.** Project management knowledge and techniques are useful tools for healthcare IT project managers to have because it helps them to facilitate the planning, scheduling, and controlling of projects.

2. **D.** The purpose of a work breakdown structure is to break the project's work and deliverables down into smaller, more manageable components, which helps the project manager maintain control of the project and helps provide clear direction to the team as to what work needs to be done.

3. **A.** The monitoring and controlling process group occurs during all phases of a project's life cycle.

4. **C.** For a project manager to accurately estimate the time, cost, and resources necessary to achieve a project's objectives, the project manager will need to understand what is required, decide who needs to be involved, and prioritize activities and tasks.

5. **C.** The process of moving tasks out until resources are available, even if it means the project end date slips, is called *resource-critical leveling*.

6. **D.** To determine the critical path, a project manager needs to know all project activities that are required to complete the project (from the WBS), the time each activity will take to complete, and the relationship between all activities.

References

1. Project Management Institute. (2013). *A guide to the project management body of knowledge (PMBOK guide), fifth edition.* Author.

2. Drucker, P. (1986). *Management tasks, responsibilities, practices.* Truman Talley.

3. Project Management Institute. (2016). *Healthcare community of practice.* Accessed on July 20, 2016, from www.projectmanagement.com/Practices/Healthcare/.

4. Lewis, J. (2010). *Project planning, scheduling, and control.* McGraw-Hill Education.

5. Project Management Docs. (2012). *What is a stakeholder? How to identify, analyze and manage project stakeholders.* Accessed on June 30, 2016, from www.projectmanagementdocs.com/articles/what-is-a-stakeholder.html.

6. Mathis, M. (n.d.). *Work breakdown structure: Purpose, process and pitfalls.* Accessed on December 1, 2016, from www.projectsmart.co.uk/work-breakdown-structure-purpose-process-pitfalls.html.

7. Mantel, S. J., Meredith, J. R., Shafer, S. M., & Sutton, M. M. (2001). *Core concepts of project management.* John Wiley & Sons.

8. Levy, F. K., Thompson, G. L., & Wiest, J. D. (1963). The ABC's of the critical path method. *Harvard Business Review, 41,* 413–423.

9. Lewis, J. (2003). *The project manager's pocket survival guide.* McGraw-Hill Education.

10. Miller, E. (2013). *Multitasking.* Accessed on August 28, 2016, from https://ekmillerlab.mit.edu/tag/multitasking/.

Assuring Usability of Healthcare IT

Andre Kushniruk, Elizabeth Borycki

In this chapter, you will learn how to

- Describe what usability is and why it is important in healthcare IT
- Employ usability engineering methods in designing and implementing healthcare IT
- Ensure health information systems operate safely
- Define human factors and human–computer interaction
- Factor in human cognition while assisting in the design of healthcare information systems
- Implement the principles of good user interface design in healthcare IT

Around the world, and currently in particular in the United States, there is a move toward widespread adoption of electronic health record (EHR) systems and related information technologies. These systems allow physicians to electronically store and retrieve patient data, document care, place orders, and access computerized decision support in the form of automated reminders and alerts about patient conditions. The ultimate goal is to electronically link individual physicians and health professionals to local, regional, and national patient data repositories. With that purpose in mind, the Health Information Technology for Economic and Clinical Health (HITECH) program was created as a component of the 2009 American Recovery and Reinvestment Act to provide financial incentives to physicians for using these systems in a clinically meaningful way, commonly called *meaningful use*.[1] One expectation is that the incentives will lead to an increased use of EHRs and other HIT-related technologies by health professionals. Adoption of EHRs by end users is highly dependent upon how easy such systems are to use and how well the technology supports and facilitates the work activities of the healthcare professionals. Additionally, it has become increasingly clear there is wide variation in how different types of user interfaces (UIs) affect a clinician's workflow, activities, and decision making. In this chapter, we will discuss a range of human factors related to designing better and more effective HIT systems from the perspective of the end user. The field of usability engineering will be introduced, and practical methods for ensuring that EHR systems are useful, usable, and safe will be described.

Besides EHRs, a wide variety of health information systems and healthcare information technology have been developed that promise to streamline and modernize healthcare. Examples of these systems include clinical decision support systems (CDSSs) along with other systems designed for use by health consumers and patients for storing and accessing their own health information, such as personal health records (PHRs). However, despite the great potential of these advances, acceptance of HIT systems by end users has been problematic.[2] Issues related to users finding some systems difficult to use and the need for increasing user input in the design of HIT systems have been identified as barriers to the widespread adoption of HIT systems by physicians, nurses, and other healthcare professionals. Problems encountered by users of HIT systems related to poor usability have been cited as contributing to the failure of a growing number of HIT projects and initiatives.[3] On the other hand, designing HIT systems that are user friendly and truly support healthcare workers and their work will lead to greater adoption of HIT systems and improved healthcare processes. This chapter will discuss some practical approaches and methods for improving the ease of use of HIT systems through the assessment of usability.

Usability of Healthcare IT

In response to the increasing complexity of user interfaces and systems, the field of usability engineering emerged in the software industry during the early 1990s. The methods that have emerged from usability engineering have been applied to improve human–computer interaction (HCI) in a wide range of fields, including HIT. Usability is a concept that can be considered as a measure of how easy it is to use an information system, how efficient and effective the system is, and how easy it is to learn to use the system.[4] In addition, usability, broadly defined, also considers the safety of healthcare IT (how safe it is to use a healthcare system) as well as the concept of user enjoyment (how enjoyable it is to use a system). Good usability is important in HIT, and some earlier systems have been rejected by end users because of poor usability. In recent years, usability has become a major issue in HIT; it has become important to avoid designing systems that are difficult to use and hard to learn and that could potentially lead to inadvertent inefficiencies and medical error.

Usability Engineering Approaches

The two main approaches in usability engineering are usability testing and usability inspection.[5] *Usability testing* involves evaluating the usability of user interfaces, prototypes, or fully operational systems by observing representative end users (e.g., physicians or nurses) as they interact with the system or user interface in the study to carry out representative tasks (e.g., use an EHR system or decision support system). For example, usability testing of an EHR system might involve observing physicians interacting with a new EHR system as they enter or retrieve patient data. Users are typically video recorded as they interact with the system (see Figure 12-1), and the computer screens are captured (which can be done with low-cost screen-recording software). During usability testing, users are often asked to "think aloud" or verbalize their thoughts while using the system to carry out tasks.[6]

Figure 12-1 Health professional being video recorded while carrying out tasks using an EHR system during a usability testing session

TIP *Usability* refers to the ease of use of a system in terms of efficiency, effectiveness, enjoyment, learnability, and safety.

The data collected from usability testing sessions, such as video recordings of users interacting with a system (including audio recordings of user verbalizations and computer screen recordings), can be played back and analyzed to identify the following:

- User problems in interacting with the system under study
- Potential inefficiencies in the user-system interaction and user interface
- Potential impact on user workflow and work activities
- Recommendations for improving the user interface and underlying system functionality[6]

Usability testing has been found to be critically important in designing, implementing, deploying, and customizing HIT systems to ensure they are efficient, effective, enjoyable to use, easy to learn, and safe to use. Furthermore, the approach can be applied across the entire systems development life cycle (SDLC) of healthcare information systems, as illustrated in Figure 12-2. The SDLC provides a timeline or life cycle for considering when and where HIT may be evaluated and improved applying usability testing.

In the early planning stages of the usability testing SDLC, testing can be applied to test early system designs and user interface ideas using mock-ups or sketches of potential

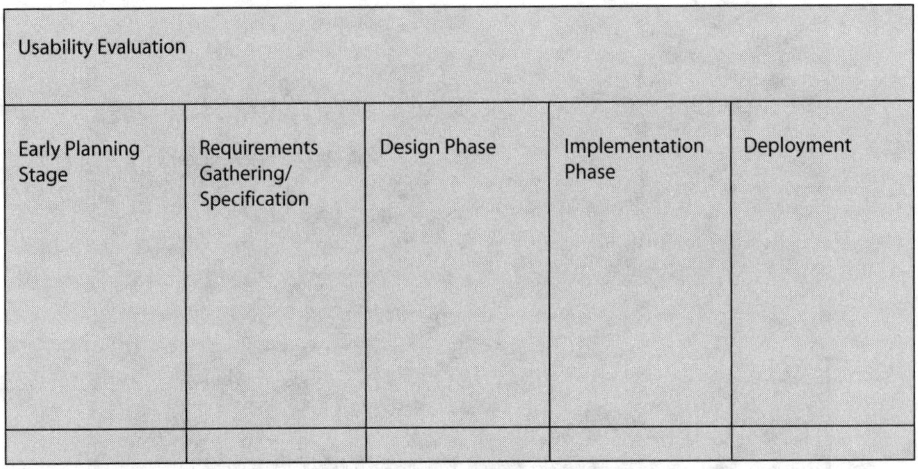

Usability Evaluation				
Early Planning Stage	Requirements Gathering/ Specification	Design Phase	Implementation Phase	Deployment

Figure 12-2 Usability evaluation in relation to the SDLC

system ideas or screen layouts that can then be shown to users for feedback. This method can also be used to help make selections among different possible candidate systems in situations where an organization, such as a hospital, is deciding among several commercial systems. In this case, potential candidate systems can be required to undergo usability testing, with information from the testing used to help decide on a system to buy. Moving to the requirements-gathering phase of the SDLC, usability testing can be used to gain information about deficiencies with systems currently in place. Also, during requirements gathering, mock-ups can be shown to potential end users to obtain feedback and refined requirements from end users. During the design phase of healthcare IT products, usability testing can be used to obtain user feedback and input in response to partially working user interfaces in iterative cycles of user testing, with the results from the usability testing sent back for use in system redesign. Once a healthcare IT system is ready for implementation, the usability testing approach can be also used to obtain information about the need for potential refinement of the system or user interface and any potential safety issues once it is to be released in a healthcare setting. Finally, once the system has been widely deployed, usability testing can be employed to determine whether the system needs to be modified, customized, or even replaced in order to continue to meet users' information and work needs.

Another main approach to conducting usability evaluations of healthcare IT is known as *usability inspection*.[7] Usability inspection methods differ from usability testing in that end users are not observed using the system under study, as in usability testing, but rather this approach involves having one or more trained usability inspectors "step through" or inspect a healthcare information system. In doing these inspections, one approach is to compare the user interface against a set of principles or heuristics for good interface design in order to identify violations of the principles or heuristics. A popular set of heuristics in this analysis was developed by Jacob Nielsen and has been widely used in the design and evaluation of healthcare IT systems.[5] The following list summarizes the heuristics:

- **Visibility of system status** The status of the system should be apparent to the user.
  Example: The users should know whether patient information that was entered by them was successfully saved in the EHR.

- **Match between the system and the real world** The terminology in the system should match that of the user.
  Example: The medical terminology used in an EHR should match the terms that physicians using the system use in their work.

- **User control and freedom** The system should support undo and redo operations.
  Example: When learning how to use an EHR, the user can explore the system's functions and features without worrying about making changes that can't be revoked.

- **Consistency and standards** The interface should be consistent throughout.
  Example: Differing modules in an EHR should use consistent formatting and labels.

- **Error prevention** The system should help users prevent errors.
  Example: An alert should pop up when a physician writes an order for a medication the patient is allergic to when using a physician order entry system.

- **Recognition rather than recall** Users should not have to remember things.
  Example: Users should be able to select a medication from a list rather than trying to remember the medication formats accepted by the system.

- **Flexibility and efficiency of use** The interface should accommodate the needs of the user.
  Example: An EHR should support nurse and physician views of relevant patient information.

- **Aesthetic and minimalist design** Simple and minimalist interfaces are often easiest to use.
  Example: The main screens on an EHR may be simple with the option of going to more advanced screens with more options.

- **Help users recognize, diagnose, and recover from errors** The system should help users recognize and fix errors.
  Example: If the user misses a field on a data entry form, then that field is highlighted in red, and a message is provided to the user that highlighted fields are missing information.

- **Help documentation** The system should provide adequate help and documentation.
  Example: If the user of an EHR needs help in using the technology, there should be online help available for them to refer to.

- **Chunking**   Information should be chunked appropriately in packets of seven plus or minus two.
  Example: A menu containing options for using an EHR should not contain more than nine items (otherwise, it should be broken up into more than one menu).

- **Style**   Prominent and important information should appear at the top of the screen.
  Example: Drug allergy information should appear at the top of the screen.

Results from conducting heuristic evaluations typically consist of a summary of the number and type of violations of usability heuristics identified in the analysis. This information is then fed back into the system and user interface customization and redesign process to improve the user interface and system.[8] For a comprehensive set of usability guidelines providing detailed guidance on development of web-based applications, refer to the excellent book, *Research-Based Web Design and Usability Guidelines* (https://www.usability.gov/sites/default/files/documents/guidelines_book.pdf).[9]

A second form of usability inspection is known as the *cognitive walk-through*.[7] In conducting a cognitive walk-through, the analyst considers the profile of potential end users: what is the level of computer expertise of the typical user, and what is their prior experience with this type of HIT? This method first involves specifying a task to be analyzed using a healthcare IT system, such as entering medications into a medication list in an EHR system. The analyst then systematically steps through the user interface to carry out the specified task. In doing so, the analyst notes and records the following:

- User goals (entering a medication)
- User steps (recording exactly what the user types or clicks)
- The system's responses to each user step
- Potential user problems in carrying out the task specified

Table 12-1 gives an example of a cognitive walk-through. The results can be used to identify the following:

- Inefficient sequences requiring too many user steps
- Inappropriate or hard-to-understand system feedback
- Potential usability problems
- Problems in achieving goals required to complete a healthcare-related task using the HIT system under study

In general, conducting usability inspections of healthcare IT is faster and may be conducted at a lower cost than doing usability testing, which involves setting up observations of real users of a healthcare IT system. However, it should be noted that usability inspection, although it is a powerful method for predicting user errors, cannot fully predict what users will actually do when faced with HIT in the hospital or clinical setting. Therefore, the two approaches (usability inspection and usability testing) are often used in conjunction, with usability inspection identifying potential errors to improve design

Goal	Order a patient's medication in an EHR.
Subgoal	Select system operation for ordering a patient medication.
Action 1	Click the medication order entry tab.
System Response	The system displays physician order entry screen.
Action 2	Click the medication text box.
System Response	The cursor appears in a text box.
Action 3	The user types in the first three letters of medication name.
System Response	A list of medications with the same three letters appears.
Potential Problem	The medication the user wants does not appear in the list, potentially causing the user to select a medication they did not want to order.
Action 4	The user selects a medication.

Table 12-1   Example of a Cognitive Walk-through for a Physician User Ordering a Medication

and subsequent usability testing with users determining whether there are serious user problems. Selecting the most appropriate usability evaluation method, given a particular system, will depend on the considerations of time and expense, with usability inspection methods requiring less investment of both. However, to ensure that systems meet user needs, observing or interviewing end users of those systems should never be replaced. Furthermore, the costs and efforts associated with conducting usability testing of HIT systems have been shown to be reasonable, and the approach can be done in a highly cost-effective way. For example, usability testing of HIT applications does not require expensive usability laboratories but rather can be conducted "on location" or "in situ" within the healthcare organizations where the system will be deployed. Furthermore, the costs associated with data collection have been shown to decrease by using low-cost video cameras and inexpensive computer screen–recording software such as HyperCam.[10, 11]

Usability and HIT Safety

In recent years, a growing body of literature on commercially available HIT and EHR systems indicates that some system features and poorly designed user interfaces may actually introduce and cause health professionals to make new types of medical errors. These errors are often not detected until the system has been released and is being used in complex clinical settings. These errors are referred to as *technology-induced errors*.[12] Furthermore, without proper testing with end users before releasing systems, it has been shown that some HIT systems may be dangerous to use, leading to potential harm to patients. Even systems that may have been tested to ensure they pass traditional software testing during their development may be found to "facilitate" or "induce" errors when used in real healthcare settings, in real work situations, and under real-world conditions that were not fully tested during commercial development.

   TIP   Healthcare information systems need to be extensively tested before going live to prevent technology-induced error.

Use Case 12-1: Simulation Testing the System

A hospital has decided to implement a medication administration system, which will allow physicians to enter medication orders for patients electronically.[13] Nurses may access the system to see what medications they should administer to their patients, including all the information about what medication to give the patient, the dosage, and so on. The system also allows the nurses to verify that the patient is the correct patient and is linked to the medication barcoding system that allows the nurse to scan the wristband of the patient to make sure the patient is the right one and also to scan the label of the medication to make sure the medication is correct. It was expected that the system would make giving medications in the hospital safer. However, through simulation testing before the system was released, it was found that under emergency situations the system could become a hazard itself. For example, the testing showed that during emergencies there was not enough time for the nurse to go through all the checking procedures that the system required. Furthermore, it was found that if one nurse was using the system for a patient and was called away, all other users were "locked" out from viewing that patient's data on the computer. Based on this pre-release testing, it was decided that in order to ensure system safety under all conditions, an emergency override function could be invoked by users if there were serious time constraints. In addition, the system was modified to allow more than one nurse or physician to access a patient record in an emergency.

Previous work has shown that HIT systems may have a number of consequences on clinical performance and cognition, which may be inadvertent and in some cases negative. For example, work by Kushniruk and colleagues has shown that certain designs of screen layouts in EHRs may lead clinical users to become "screen-driven," where they are overly guided by the order of information on the computer screen, thus relying on how information is presented on the screen to drive their interviews of patients and ultimately their clinical decision making.[6] Furthermore, suboptimal design of user interfaces can lead to errors that could potentially lead to patient harm. For example, screens that are cluttered and, as a consequence, obscure important information about drug allergies could potentially contribute to a physician giving patients medication to which they are allergic. Other examples include errors resulting from the inability of the user to navigate or move through the clinical user interface in order to find critical information, especially when needed during a patient emergency, where time is critical.

To ensure HIT safety, a variety of new methods and approaches to more fully testing healthcare information systems are beginning to appear. For example, clinical simulations are an extension of usability testing, whereby representative users are observed using a system to carry out representative tasks, much as is done in usability testing.[12] However, this type of testing is typically conducted under highly realistic conditions that closely simulate the real working environment in which a system being developed will be deployed. Once a system has been deployed, the reporting of potential technology-induced errors is also beginning to receive attention from both healthcare IT vendors and governmental organizations concerned with healthcare IT safety. Along these lines, error-reporting systems are beginning to be developed where end users can create anonymous online reports about errors that may be related to HIT that can be collected, published, and used to refine and improve the safety of commercially available HIT.[13]

Human Factors and Human–Computer Interaction in Healthcare

Human factors is the field of study focused on understanding the human elements of *systems*, where *systems* may be defined as software, medical devices, computer technology, and organizations.[1] Usability engineering can be considered a subfield of the more general human factors area. The objective of studying human factors in healthcare is to optimize overall system performance and improve healthcare processes and outcomes. Two main areas covered by human factors are cognitive ergonomics, which deals with mental processes of participants in systems, and physical ergonomics, which deals with the physical activity within a system and the physical arrangement of the system.[14] *Human–computer interaction* (HCI) is a subdiscipline of human factors that focuses on understanding how humans use computers to design systems that align with and support human information-processing activities.[4] HCI looks specifically at the user's interaction with a system, such as the keyboard or a touch screen, as well as how the interaction fits within the user's larger work context. Also important are the multitude of cognitive and social experiences that surround the use of an information system or technology. The four major components of HCI are

- The user of the technology
- The task or job the user is trying to carry out via the technology
- The particular context of use of the technology
- The technology itself

Each of these components can be further analyzed and broken down for improvement and for optimization. In healthcare there are multiple users of a given system that vary widely in their expectations, from physician to pharmacist to nurse. A given role can then be further defined by the focus of the clinician—general practice versus surgical specialty physicians. The task or job each user carries out using the technology covers a wide spectrum, from recording basic patient data to viewing and making clinical choices based on recommendations from a decision support system about a patient's treatment. The context in which technology is used might vary from the routine to complex or urgent situations and conditions that may involve more than one user or participant. Finally, healthcare technology itself may range from desktop applications for entering and retrieving patient data to mobile devices and "telehealth" applications used in remote patient monitoring. The four components of HCI listed earlier are useful in considering which aspects of user interactions within healthcare systems might need to be improved, modified, or redesigned in order to optimize the user experience. An underlying goal of HCI is to consider all four dimensions to improve HIT and healthcare systems so that users can carry out tasks safely, effectively, efficiently, and enjoyably.

User Interface Design and Human Cognition

The *user interface* is the component of a HIT system that communicates with a given clinician, healthcare worker, or healthcare consumer as they connect with that technology. The objective of user interaction with HIT systems is typically to carry out healthcare-related work tasks, where patient information can be manipulated, accessed, or created to support clinical decision making and work activities. Anyone using healthcare technology does so in the context of performing tasks related to their role that involve access to, manipulation of, or creation of data. From this perspective, HCI involves shared information processing between the machine and the end user. Given that dynamic, an understanding of human cognition and what users can and can't be expected to do using HIT systems, in a variety of contexts (i.e., emergent versus non-emergent), underlies the success or failure of the user-HIT interface. For example, an important aspect of human cognition that can be applied to improving user interactions with systems includes understanding the limitations of human ability to process large amounts of complex data. Strategies for reducing *cognitive load* (i.e., the amount of perception, attention, and thinking required to understand something) associated with task performance and improving the quality and relevance of information displayed on computers to end users are needed in order to ensure the effectiveness and efficiency of HIT systems.

Importance of Considering Cognitive Psychology

To understand how to design, develop, and implement effective healthcare IT, an understanding of key areas of cognitive psychology is relevant.[15] *Cognitive psychology* is the field that studies human reasoning and information processing (information seeking and decision making), including studies of perception, attention, memory, learning, and skill development. For example, studies of how clinicians gain experience and expertise in their area of work are relevant for designing user interfaces that better match the information processing of end users in that work area. Further, understanding the limitations of human memory has led user interface experts to develop simple heuristics "rules of thumb" that can be used to help guide the design of user interfaces and computer screens for HIT. For example, studies in cognitive psychology indicate that people can generally remember seven discrete pieces of information, plus or minus two, with seven-digit telephone numbers a good example.[4] This has led to the recommendation that the number of items in a computer menu follow that same guideline. In addition, studies of users learning how to use HIT have particular relevance to improving the adoption of complex HIT applications. A number of reports have shown that some applications are difficult to use and time-consuming to learn and master in real-world healthcare settings. Work in characterizing and finding ways of reducing the amount of time and effort to learn how to use such systems has considerable importance in deploying HIT systems, where users may be faced with the need to learn how to use multiple varied information systems and HIT in complex and stressed environments. Knowledge gleaned from the study of perception and attention is also highly relevant for HIT and has led to the following development guidelines about how to display information to users on a computer screen:

- Present information in a logical and meaningful way.
- Provide attention-getting visual cues, and highlight important or critical information.
- Help users focus their attention on important information.
- Make information needed in decision making easy to find and process.
- Avoid overloading the user with large amounts of irrelevant information.

Approaches to Cognition and HCI

The field of HCI has been influenced by two primary models of how humans interact with information technology and how they carry out tasks using computer systems. In the 1960s and 1970s, the concept of the human as the "information processor" borrowed from advances in computer science and used the metaphor of computer systems to describe human attention, information processing, and reasoning. For example, psychologists working in the area of HCI borrowed concepts such as "memory stores" and "processing units" from computer science in order to describe how humans think and process information. Five areas of focus as a result of this work are

- Describing the computer user's goals
- Describing how their goals were translated into intentions to carry out a task using computer systems
- Describing how user intentions became plans for executing an action using a computer system
- Describing how computer operations are actually performed by the user
- Describing how users interpret feedback from the computer system once the action has been completed[16]

Using the method of studying user interactions, it is then possible to understand where users are having problems in using a complex healthcare information system. Examples include the user having problems translating their intentions into computer actions by typing in the right command and having trouble interpreting error messages returned by the system as feedback to the user. While this model has been useful in analyzing HCI at a detailed level, it has been criticized for focusing only on the individual user interacting with an individual computer system in isolation, not as part of the rich and complex social context of healthcare work. As a result, more recent approaches to modeling HCI have appeared that focus on "distributed cognition" where information processing is shared among a number of people and systems in order to carry out real tasks in real social settings.[15] In an operating room, analyzing and understanding how to use a new surgical information system requires a thorough understanding of all the participants in the procedure, their roles, and their interactions with the system. Although understanding how one individual user interacts with such a system is important, it does not provide a complete picture of how the system interfaces with the activities of all the participants, including the patient. Interactions between the information-processing roles of the doctor, the patient, and the computer system used by the doctor are all important in understanding the impact of EHRs on the physician-patient relationship (see Use Case 12-2).[17]

Considering work activity as a distributed process provides a broader framework for understanding where HIT matches user needs and provides support for the goal of completing complex healthcare activities involving multiple participants. Somewhat unique to healthcare, it is important to note that many work tasks are complex, are often time-sensitive, and may involve considerable uncertainty and urgency. *Work domain analysis* is an approach used to analyze technology in these complex situations and has proven to be an effective starting point in characterizing the impact of HIT. This approach involves answering the following questions:

- Who are the classes of users in the design and testing of HIT?
- What are the tasks each class of user carries out using a technology?
- Are there situational aspects of doing the task, and did the designer consider that the task might involve time constraints or urgency?
- What are the potential problems users might encounter when using the HIT, and how can they be fixed?

All of these questions should be considered both before and after a HIT application has been implemented in a hospital or clinic.

Use Case 12-2: Observing Users Interacting with an EHR System

Observing users interacting with a system has become widely used to understand the impact of HIT on human cognition and work processes. In one such study of the introduction of a new EHR in a diabetes clinic, the vendor of the system wanted to know how the design of the system, including the way its computer screens were organized and what information it displayed to the user, would affect the interaction of the physician with the patient. This was a key consideration because the EHR was intended to be used by the physician while interviewing the patient.[17] In this study, the physician's interaction with the system was recorded while interviewing a "simulated patient" (a study collaborator who played the part of a patient). One observation of the study noted that physicians using the EHR struggled with finding the screens containing the questions they wanted to ask the patient and documenting the response. A number of physicians eventually dropped out of the study and did not adopt the system. Of those who remained, some changed their patient interviewing strategy and style and became "screen driven," asking questions based on the order of information on the screens. When interviewed about their use of the EHR, these physicians were not consciously aware that the design of the system and the layout of information had led to changes in the way they interacted with patients. The vendor used the study results to improve and streamline user training with specific examples of how to use the system while interacting with the patient.

Technological Advances in HIT and User Interfaces

A key component or dimension of HCI is the *human dimension*—or cognition, knowledge, skills, and understanding of the user interacting with a computer. The technology itself is another important consideration of HCI in healthcare. The design and build of computer-user interfaces have advanced significantly over the past several decades and continue to evolve and improve rapidly. The typical user interaction with healthcare computer systems up until the 1970s involved command-line interactions recalled from memory and entered on a keyboard to create and edit patient files and access data from laboratory and pharmacy systems. The subsequent development of graphical user interfaces (GUIs) greatly improved user interaction with those systems, and by the 1980s, those same enhancements appeared in personal and work computers. This major breakthrough in the design of user interfaces essentially extended the use of computers from only highly computer-literate end users to the larger population of work professionals and eventually the general public. The Apple Macintosh introduced the concepts of a mouse, icons, and direct manipulation of objects on the computer screen versus typing a variety of commands with only a keyboard. Operating systems such as macOS and Microsoft Windows replicated the office examples of files, folders, calendars, and spreadsheets on the computer desktop and allowed easy manipulation via keyboard and mouse. The use of this metaphor simplified user interactions with systems and allowed users to more rapidly learn how to use computer systems.[4] The World Wide Web introduced the hyperlink concept, providing links to text, images, and other media via a mouse click on the screen. In healthcare IT, these advances in organizing and displaying information on computer screens for end users have had a major impact on healthcare information system interactions and on the type of user interfaces that HIT has developed. With the introduction of the graphical user interface in other industries, EHR vendors have all evolved from the difficult-to-use command line such as Microsoft DOS to more user-friendly GUI-based systems using Microsoft Windows and macOS.[4] Improvements in the EHR user interfaces now facilitate easy access to and entry of information in a variety of source systems such as laboratory, radiology, and pharmacy. Internet or web technologies have also enhanced EHR development beyond Windows and macOS operating systems to take advantage of those capabilities.

Mobile devices such as smartphones and tablet computers, the increased use of the Web, and social media applications such as Facebook and Twitter have started a new trend in the development of collaborative/cooperative user interfaces designed to support the distributed work activities of multiple users, both health professionals and more recently patients. One example of this is the web site PatientsLikeMe (www.patientslikeme.com). Now users may be

- Located in the same place at the same time
- Geographically apart but still communicating at the same time (using video or web conferencing to discuss a patient case)
- Communicating asynchronously from different locations at different points in time (using secure e-mail to communicate with the patient or another colleague)

User interfaces are becoming increasingly important in areas such as telehealth and distance medical consultations and are providing new types of interactions that may involve multiple synchronous or asynchronous users interacting to carry out a complex task from different locations, such as conducting remote patient consultations using video conferencing. Skills and expertise in this area of HCI will become increasingly important as software/hardware for supporting collaborative healthcare activities becomes more prevalent.[18]

Input and Output Devices and the Visualization of Healthcare Data

Along with the advances in operating systems and user interfaces, improvements continue to be made in the development of more effective input and output devices for HIT. Additionally, advances in the visualization of health data are taking place, such as designing new ways for representing complex health data, supporting analysis of patient trends by health professionals, and understanding aggregated patient, health professional, and organizational data from many sources. Principles for the display of health information on computer screens include grouping information in a clinically meaningful way, avoiding overload and simplifying access to critical patient data by limiting what is presented, and standardizing information displays where possible.[4]

A variety of different approaches, styles, and technologies have been developed to support the input of health data into computer systems. Keyboards are still the most common way of entering healthcare data into a computer system, with other devices now seeing increased use. These include the computer mouse, trackballs, electronic pens, and handwriting recognition and touch screens. Voice recognition technology, as part of the EHR capturing spoken information in certain sections, is also seeing increased adoption. Each of these approaches has advantages and disadvantages, and their usefulness varies considerably depending on the context of their use in different healthcare settings. Touch screens may be useful for allowing patients to enter data in a physician's waiting room, while in infection-prone areas of a hospital they may not be recommended. Voice recognition (VR) has been useful in physicians' private offices to dictate narrative portions of a patient's history in the EHR and patient referral letters. Most VR systems work best when the user is taught how to use the program, including how to incorporate it into user workflows and "training" it to the users' speech patterns. Increasingly, with the use of networked speech files accessible from any computer and more accurate microphones, acute-care settings are now leveraging the same tools.

When considering data entry options, there are a wide variety of approaches, including using online forms that take direct data entry through the use of specific fields, using question-and-answer dialogs that prompt the user, selecting options from drop-down and other menus, directly manipulating objects on the screen using pointing devices such as a mouse, and using voice recognition, as described earlier. Across all methods, data entered in the EHR by clinicians vary widely from complete free text entered via a keyboard to very structured data where options are limited to well-defined terms and phrases the user can select from. Free-text examples include comments about how a medication might be used and the narrative in clinician notes where the patient's own words are captured. Allergies, medications, and other patient histories are more commonly captured using structured vocabularies with some options for text entry as well. Most EHRs try to find a balance of data entry methods that facilitate complete and adequate documentation but don't limit or prevent the user from performing the task in a timely fashion in the way they documented prior to using a computer. Furthermore, clinical data may be entered into fields of systems such as EHRs as free-form text (text typed in a text box in an unrestricted way) or alternatively as semistructured data (where the format of data entered is somewhat structured by the computer system) or completely structured or coded data (where the user must select only from the options displayed to them by the system, such as select from a list of medical diagnoses). For example, some EHRs will allow data on a patient's history of present illness to be entered as free text with no restrictions imposed by the computer system on what the user types. However, as electronic information in computer systems becomes more widely shared, structured or coded data using standard medical terms will be needed.[19] For example, in systems employing coded data input, a physician might enter into a text box a diagnosis of "diabetes," which will result in a menu listing agreed-upon forms of diabetes, such as "diabetes I" and "diabetes II," from which the user must select. This approach allows for the selection of coded and structured data that is sharable and understandable across systems and end users. However, some users may feel that the approach restricts their ability to express themselves and that, if not carefully selected, the choices offered by the system do not fully match their information needs or the particular medical or healthcare terminology or vocabulary they use. An anecdotal complaint from clinicians who use electronic tools to document their notes and from those who receive copies of those notes is that each one looks similar, contains more data than is needed, and doesn't tell the story compared to dictated or handwritten notes that were more common prior to electronic records. This tension between free-text entry and coded data entry still exists, and some recent work has been conducted in developing user interfaces for healthcare that automatically extract coded standardized medical terms from free text.[20]

The visualization of healthcare has also become an important area of research and development. There are many ways of visualizing health data, ranging from textual data to graphical displays including charts and histograms to three-dimensional images. Workstations capable of integrating complex images with text and graphics are becoming more common, and multimedia capabilities are becoming more standard in healthcare user interfaces. Experimental approaches to data visualization have led to user interfaces that use 3D graphics to reconstruct views of the body and to allow for remote robotically controlled surgeries and other medical procedures. One such system, known as the da Vinci system, has allowed for surgery at a micro level, where the surgeon operates using a computer display that allows for fine-tuned control of miniaturized surgical instruments that is less invasive than traditional surgeries and that has greatly improved medical outcomes.[21]

Other trends in the area of input and display of healthcare data are related to the concepts of ubiquitous and pervasive computing. *Ubiquitous computing* in healthcare refers to user interfaces that are mostly "invisible" and that the user may be largely unaware of. Examples include wearable computing, such as giving patients wired electronic shirts containing sensors that can detect cardiac problems and automatically alert healthcare professionals of impending heart-related events, often outside the normal acute-care environment. The move to pervasive healthcare includes the possibility for interaction with HIT throughout our daily lives.[22] Examples of pervasive health include use of mobile healthcare applications such as "mHealth" that allow healthcare professionals, patients, and the general public to access the latest evidence-based health information using cell phones, smartphones, tablets, and other devices. According to recent studies and reports, this trend will continue,[22] and in many countries the use of mobile devices for accessing the Internet and for text messaging has surpassed the use of desktop computing models. In the area of healthcare, many new HIT applications are being developed for supporting the promotion of health and for linking health professionals and patients through a range of innovative mobile applications. From an HCI perspective, increased use of mHealth affords new opportunities for communicating and receiving health information from a wider range of settings than previously possible.

Finally, work in the area of developing customizable and adaptive user interfaces to HIT applications is also promising. A criticism of many healthcare user interfaces and systems voiced by end users has been their perceived inflexibility, given the wide range of types of healthcare users and the even wider range of contexts in which they use HIT. Along these lines, work in developing customizable and adaptable user interfaces and the broader information systems holds considerable promise.

Approaches to Developing User Interfaces in Healthcare

Recommended approaches to the development of user interfaces for HIT include considering the design of user interfaces within the context of a "holistic" systems approach, where user input into the design and implementation is considered along the continuum from initial conception of interface metaphor to development, testing, and implementation.[4] User-centered design of HIT involves the following principles:

- Focus early on the users' needs and work situations.
- Conduct a task analysis where the details of the users' information needs and environment are identified.
- Carry out continual testing and evaluation of systems with users.
- Design iteratively, whereby there are cycles of development and testing with end users.

Along these lines, rapid prototyping of complex HIT user interfaces is recommended. The process begins with sharing early mock-ups (typically sketches or computer drawings of planned user interfaces) with potential end users, to obtain specific feedback to improve interface design, features offered, and potential alterations or revisions to the interface. As the system and user interface evolve during HIT development, continual user input and feedback through continual user testing are recommended.[4] In later stages, the testing of prototypes (partially working early versions of a system or user interface) and emerging user interfaces with end users may involve conventional methods, such as periodically holding focus groups with potential users (where groups of users are shown prototypes or early system versions and asked to react to and comment about) or individual interviews with future users about the design to obtain their feedback. Methods from the emerging area of usability engineering were described in detail earlier in this chapter.

Methods for Assessing HIT in Use

Early stages in the development of healthcare user interfaces for HIT include the creation of an initial product description and description of the context of use of the system or user interface. Here, the capabilities of the system from the end user's perspective and the requirements of the end user are defined. It is at this stage that a number of engineering method requirements can be employed. This may involve conducting walk-throughs or observations of settings in which the technology is or will be deployed. One method that has been used is known as *shadowing*, where one or more healthcare professionals are followed during a normal day to see how they perform their work, how HIT fits (or could fit) into their practice, and where problems and errors occur with current workflow and tools. A wide range of methods can be used at this stage to obtain information about users and their work, including ethnographic observational study of the work environment, time-motion studies (where the times to complete healthcare tasks with or without HIT are recorded), and interviews with health professionals about their information-processing needs. At this stage, analyses can be conducted to describe how users carry out their healthcare-related tasks and where HIT could be inserted to improve their work processes.[4] This analysis may involve observing users as they carry out real or simulated tasks of increasing complexity using HIT, including those related to managing medications: medication dispensing, patient and order verification and administration, and complex intravenous therapies.

After completing studies of end users in their work environments as described earlier, initial user interface designs and specifications are created. Similar to the previous analogies of files and folders and how those have been replicated in basic personal computing, medical analogies such as rooms can be employed to streamline and optimize workflow using other user interface options. This approach has been used in hospital bed scheduling systems, where users can click different "rooms" displayed on the computer screen and visually increase their size to focus on a particular patient bed. Decisions also need to be made about the following aspects of user interface design:

- Determining the functionality of the interface and what users will be allowed to do
- Designing the layout and sequence of computer screens that users will see
- Specifying the style of interaction with the user

- Selecting an appropriate prototyping and user interface programming tool
- Planning and scheduling continual iterative user testing

While there are a number of guiding principles that have been used for both the design and testing of healthcare information systems, several of which were described earlier in the section on usability engineering, it should be noted that a recurring theme in the design and development of applications such as EHRs has been a lack of agreed-upon national or industry user interface standards for these types of systems. A vendor may choose one type of user metaphor and lay out screen sequences and organize patient information in a way that may be quite different from another vendor, thus making it difficult for users of multiple different electronic records to remember how to use each system. Attempts at developing standards for use in the design and implementation of healthcare IT user interfaces are underway, such as the Common User Interface (CUI) project of the National Health Services (NHS) in the United Kingdom, which is in collaboration with Microsoft.[23] Its work has led to a number of nationally endorsed guidelines and recommendations for displaying health information data in an EHR in a way that is more intuitive and friendly for the user and less likely to lead to error.

Ongoing user interface review/improvement is important as technology and healthcare evolve. As described earlier, user-centered design recommends continual user input and feedback as the user interface is being developed and as soon as possible after a stable version of the user interface is available. Along these lines, an approach to the design and implementation of healthcare IT has emerged known as *participatory design*, whereby users are more closely involved in the development of healthcare user interfaces, in effect serving as "user consultants" and active participants and members of the design and implementation team, providing their expertise on what would, or would not, work from the user's perspective. Along these lines, proponents of "socio-technical design" argue that consideration of the social impact of systems, such as the effects of a new system on physician or nurse work practices and social interactions, is as important as obtaining technical requirements.[24] They further argue that lack of consideration of socio-technical issues will likely lead to lack of system acceptance and, ultimately, system failure, which has been shown to be the case in the literature regarding HIT successes and failure.

Challenges and Future Issues

In recent years, the issue of usability of HIT has come to the fore in the United States and worldwide. Along the lines described in this chapter, the American Medical Informatics Association has identified four areas of importance for which they have developed recommendations, which include: "(1) human factors in HIT research, (2) HIT policy, (3) industry recommendations, (4) recommendations for the clinician end user of EHR software."[25] From a usability and human factors perspective, there is a need to develop standardized use cases for design and testing HIT, best practices for implementation, improvement of adverse event reporting systems, and evaluation procedures for ensuring the usability and safety of HIT. Also, according to the American Medical Association (AMA), eight usability-related priorities should include (1) enhancing physicians' ability to provide high-quality patient care, (2) supporting team-based care,

(3) promoting care coordination, (4) offering configurable and modular HIT products, (5) reducing cognitive load when using systems, (6) promoting interoperability across different healthcare settings, (7) facilitating engagement among patients, mobile technologies, and EHRs, and (8) incorporating user feedback into product development design and improvements.[26]

Chapter Review

The success of HIT depends on a number of human factors and requires that the systems and technologies that we develop are both useful and usable. The usability of HIT has become a critical issue in developing HIT that will work effectively and be willingly adopted by end users. Usability is defined as a measure of how easy it is to use an information system in terms of its efficiency, effectiveness, enjoyment, learnability, and safety. A number of practical methods for evaluating HIT usability were described in this chapter. They included usability testing, which involves observing users of HIT carrying out tasks using a technology, and usability inspection (heuristic evaluation and the cognitive walk-through), which involves trained analysts "stepping through" or analyzing HIT systems and their user interfaces in order to identify potential usability problems and issues. In the chapter, the relationship between poor usability and increased chances for medical error was discussed. Along these lines, it has been increasingly recognized that some HIT systems, if poorly designed, can pose a safety hazard. Approaches for more effectively testing the safety and effectiveness of HIT systems before widespread release were described. It is important that the HIT system that is developed and deployed in healthcare settings be shown to be not only effective and efficient but also safe.

Human factors is a broad area of study that includes consideration of a wide range of human elements within healthcare systems. Human–computer interaction (HCI) is a subfield of human factors that deals with understanding how humans use computers so that better systems can be designed. There are a number of dimensions of HCI, including the technology itself, the user of the technology, the task at hand, and the context of use of the technology. It is important to consider all of these dimensions when designing and deploying HIT. Design of user interfaces in healthcare can benefit from an understanding of the capabilities and limits of human cognition. For example, knowledge about how information is best displayed to healthcare professionals borrows from fundamental work in cognitive psychology and HCI. Indeed, to design effective user interfaces, consideration of human aspects related to the processing of information, training, and potential for introduction of error must be considered. From the technological side of things, advances in user interfaces are rapidly advancing. Some of these breakthroughs have included the development of GUIs, new input and output devices, and advances in the visualization of healthcare data. Further advances include the widespread use of mobile devices and increased use of the Web and social media, allowing for access to healthcare data from many locations and supporting collaborative work practices involving multiple users. In addition, approaches to developing more effective user interfaces to HIT are also evolving, with the advent of user-centered design methods and participatory design, both of which promote increased user involvement in all stages of HIT design, implementation, and testing.

Questions

To test your comprehension of the chapter, answer the following questions and then check your answers against the list of correct answers that follows the questions.

1. Human factors can be defined as what?

   A. The study of making more effective user interfaces to computer-based systems

   B. The field that examines human elements of systems

   C. The group of methods that can be used to make systems more usable

   D. The study of technology-induced errors

2. User-centered design involves which of the following?

   A. An early focus on the user and their needs

   B. Continued testing of system design with users

   C. Iterative feedback into redesign

   D. Participation of users as members of the design team

   E. All of the above

   F. A, B, C, D

   G. A, B, C

3. Which of the following is *not* a user interface metaphor?

   A. The desktop metaphor

   B. The document metaphor

   C. The patient chart metaphor

   D. The command-line metaphor

4. What are the main methods from usability engineering?

   A. Participatory design

   B. Cognitive walk-through

   C. Heuristic inspection

   D. Usability testing

   E. B, C, D

   F. A, B, D

5. Which of the following is *not* one of Nielsen's heuristics?

   A. Allow for error prevention.

   B. Support recognition rather than recall.

   C. Use bright colors to be aesthetically pleasing.

   D. Allow for flexibility and efficiency of use.

6. Which of the following is *not* true?

   A. Usability testing can be conducted inexpensively in hospitals.

   B. Usability testing should be conducted only by human factors engineers.

   C. Lack of user input in design and testing is one of the biggest causes of system implementation failure.

   D. Nurses and physicians should be involved in systems design.

7. What can technology-induced errors arise from?

   A. Programming errors

   B. Systems design flaws

   C. Inadequate requirements gathering

   D. Poorly planned systems implementation

   E. A, B, C, D

   F. A, C

8. What are the four main components of HCI?

   A. Software, task, subtask, human factors engineer

   B. Technology, task, user, context of use

   C. Software, hardware, user, outcome

   D. User, user interface, human factors engineer, usability testing lab,

Answers

1. **B.** Human factors broadly examines human elements of systems, where systems represent physical, cognitive, and organizational artifacts that people interact with (e.g., computers).

2. **G.** User-centered design involves: (1) an early focus on users and their needs, (2) continued testing of system design with users, and (3) iterative feedback into redesign.

3. **D.** The command line is not a metaphor; it does not represent some other object in the world.

4. **E.** The main methods used in usability engineering are: (1) the cognitive walk-through, (2) heuristic inspection, and (3) usability testing.

5. **C.** Using bright colors is not one of Nielsen's heuristics.

6. **B.** Usability testing can be conducted by professionals with varied backgrounds and not just by human factors engineers. Usability engineering methods have become more widely known and have been simplified and used by different types of IT and health professionals.

7. E. Programming errors, systems design flaws, inadequate requirements gathering, and poorly planned systems implementation have all been identified as factors that cause technology-induced error in healthcare.

8. B. The four main components of HCI are the technology itself, the task, the user of the technology, and the context of use of the technology.

References

1. HealthIT.gov. (2013). *EHR incentives and certification.* Accessed on February 11, 2017, from https://www.healthit.gov/providers-professionals/ehr-incentives-certification.

2. Caryon, P. (Ed.). (2012). *Handbook of human factors and ergonomics in health care and patient safety.* CRC Press.

3. Kushniruk, A., & Borycki, E. (Eds.). (2008). *Human, social and organizational aspects of health information systems.* IGI Global.

4. Preece, J., Sharp, H., & Rogers, Y. (2007). *Interaction design: Beyond human-computer interaction, second edition.* John Wiley & Sons.

5. Nielsen, J. (1993). *Usability engineering.* Academic Press.

6. Kushniruk, A., & Patel, V. (2004). Cognitive and usability engineering methods for the evaluation of clinical information systems. *Journal of Biomedical Informatics, 37,* 56–76.

7. Nielsen, J., & Mack, R. L. (1994). *Usability inspection methods.* John Wiley & Sons.

8. Zhang, J., Johnson, T., Patel, V., Paige, D., & Kubose, T. (2003). Using usability heuristics to evaluate patient safety of medical devices. *Journal of Biomedical Informatics, 36,* 23–30.

9. Usability.gov. (2012). *Research-based web design and usability guidelines.* Accessed on June 20, 2012, from https://www.usability.gov/sites/default/files/documents/guidelines_book.pdf.

10. Kushniruk, A., & Borycki, E. (2006). Low-cost rapid usability engineering: Designing and customizing usable healthcare information systems. *Healthcare Quarterly, 9,* 98–100, 102.

11. Rubin, J., & Chisnell, D. (2008). *Handbook of usability testing: How to plan, design, and conduct effective tests.* John Wiley & Sons.

12. Borycki, E., & Kushniruk, A. W. (2005). Identifying and preventing technology-induced error using simulations: Application of usability engineering techniques. *Healthcare Quarterly, 8,* 99–105.

13. Kushniruk, A., Borycki, E., Kuwata, S., & Kannry, J. (2006). Predicting changes in workflow resulting from healthcare information systems: Ensuring the safety of healthcare. *Healthcare Quarterly, 9,* 114–118.

14. Shortliffe, E., & Cimino, J. (Eds.). (2006). *Biomedical informatics: Computer applications in health care and biomedicine.* Springer.

15. Norman, D., & Draper, S. W. (Eds.). (1986). *User centered system design.* LEA.

16. Patel, V. L., Kushniruk, A. W., Yang, S., & Yale, J. F. (2000). Impact of a computer-based patient record system on data collection, knowledge organization and reasoning. *Journal of the American Medical Informatics Association, 7,* 569–585.

17. Baecker, R. M. (1992). *Readings in groupware and computer-supported cooperative work: Assisting human-human collaboration.* Morgan Kaufman.

18. Patel, V., & Kaufman, D. (2006). Cognitive science and biomedical informatics. In E. Shortliffe and J. Cimino (Eds.), *Biomedical informatics: Computer applications in health care and biomedicine.* Springer.

19. Patel, V. L., & Kushniruk, A. W. (1998). Interface design for health care environments: The role of cognitive science. *Proceedings of the AMIA Symposium,* 29–37.

20. Da Vinci Surgery. (2012). *The da Vinci surgical system.* Accessed on June 20, 2012, from www.davincisurgery.com/davinci-surgery/davinci-surgical-system/.

21. Bardram, J. E., Mihailis, A., & Wan, D. (2007). *Pervasive computing in healthcare.* CRC Press.

22. Microsoft Health. (2012). *Microsoft health common user interface.* Accessed on June 20, 2012, from www.mscui.net.

23. Berg, M. (1999). Patient care information systems and health care work: A sociotechnical approach. *International Journal of Medical Informatics, 55,* 87–101.

24. Middleton, B., Bloomrosen, M., Dente, M. A., Hashmat, B., Koppel, R., Overhage, J. M., … Zhang, J. (2013). Enhancing patient safety and quality of care by improving the usability of electronic health record systems: Recommendations from AMIA. *Journal of the American Medical Informatics Association, 20*(e1), e2–e8.

25. American Medical Association (2014). *Improving care: Priorities to improve electronic health record usability.* Accessed on June 20, 2012, from https://www.aace.com/files/ehr-priorities.pdf.

PART III

Healthcare Information Standards and Regulation

13

Navigating Health Data Standards and Interoperability

Joyce Sensmeier*

In this chapter, you will learn how to

- Discuss the need for health data standards
- Describe the standards development process and the organizations involved in it
- Delineate the importance of interoperability
- Describe current health data standards initiatives
- Explore the value of health data standards

Standards are foundational to the development, implementation, and interoperability of electronic health records (EHRs) and other health information technology (IT) systems. The effectiveness of healthcare delivery is dependent on the ability of clinicians to access health data and information when and where it is needed. The ability to exchange health information across organizational and system boundaries, whether between multiple departments within a single institution or among consumers, providers, payers, and other stakeholders, is essential. A harmonized set of rules and definitions, both at the level of data meaning and at the technical level of data exchange, is necessary to make this possible. There must also be a socio-political structure in place that recognizes the benefits of shared information and incentivizes the adoption and implementation of such standards.[1]

This chapter examines health data standards and interoperability in terms of the following topic areas:

- Need for health data standards
- Standards development process, organizations, and categories

*Adapted from Virginia K. Saba and Kathleen A. McCormick, *Essentials of Nursing Informatics, Sixth Edition*, 101–113. © 2015 by McGraw-Hill Education.

- Knowledge representation
- Health data standards initiatives
- Business value of health data standards

Introduction to Health Data Standards

The ability to communicate in a way that ensures the message is received and the content is understood is dependent on the use of standards. Data standards are intended to reduce ambiguity in communication so that actions taken based on the data are consistent with the actual meaning of that data. In 2015, the Office of the National Coordinator for Health IT (ONC) published an interoperability vision for the future.[2] In this future state all individuals, their families, and healthcare providers should be able to send, receive, find, and use electronic health information in a manner that is appropriate, secure, timely, and reliable to support the health and wellness of individuals through informed, shared decision-making. This vision requires the ability to capture, share, and analyze data to enable improvement in the health of individuals and populations.

While current information technologies are able to move and manipulate large amounts of data, they are not as proficient in dealing with ambiguity in the structure and semantic content of that data. The term "health data standards" is generally used to describe those standards related to the structure and content of health information. At this point, it may be useful to differentiate data from information and knowledge. Data are the fundamental building blocks on which health and healthcare decisions are based. Data can be unstructured such as free-form text, or structured in the form of discrete, standardized elements such as vital signs. When data are interpreted within a given context, as well as meaningful structure within that context, they become information. When information from various contexts is aggregated following a defined set of rules, it becomes knowledge and provides the basis for informed action.[1] Data standards represent both data and their transformation into information. Data analysis generates knowledge, which is the foundation of professional practice standards.

Standards are created by several methods:[3]

- A group of interested parties comes together and agrees upon a standard.
- The government sanctions a process for standards to be developed.
- Marketplace competition and technology adoption introduces a de facto standard.
- A formal consensus process is used by a standards development organization (SDO) to publish standards.

The standards development process typically begins with a use case or business need that describes a system's behavior as it responds to an external request. Technical experts then consider what methods, protocols, terminologies, or specifications are needed to address the requirements of the use case. An open and transparent consensus or balloting process is desirable to ensure that the developed standards have representative stakeholder input, which minimizes bias and encourages marketplace adoption and implementation.

Legislated, government-developed standards are able to gain widespread acceptance by virtue of their being required either by regulation or in order to participate in large, government-funded programs, such as Medicare. The healthcare IT industry is motivated to adopt and implement these standards into proprietary information systems and related products in order to be in compliance with these regulations and achieve a strong market presence. Because government-developed standards are in the public domain, usually they are made available at little or no cost and can be incorporated into any information system; however, they are often developed to support particular government initiatives and may not be as suitable for general, private-sector use. Also, given the amount of overhead attached to the legislative and regulatory process, it is likely that maintenance of these standards may lag behind fast-paced changes in technology and the general business environment.

Standards developed by SDOs are typically consensus-based and reflect the perspectives of a wide variety of interested stakeholders. They tend to be robust and adaptable across a wide range of implementations; however, most SDOs are nonprofit organizations that rely on the commitment of dedicated volunteers to develop and maintain standards. This often limits the amount of work that can be undertaken in a certain time frame. In addition, the consensus process can be time consuming and may result in a slow development process that does not always keep pace with technologic change. Perhaps the most problematic aspect of consensus-based standards is that there is no mechanism to ensure that they are adopted by the industry, because there is usually little infrastructure in place to actively and aggressively market them. This has resulted in the development of many technically competent standards that are never implemented.

In spite of our best efforts, standards development is not always a smooth or simple process. "Conflict may occur in the development of the standards, for example, within the confines of a technical committee designing a particular standard, where participants may disagree over the nature of the standard to be developed, or where one or more participants may take part in order to block the creation of a new standard, or by virtue of competition among supporters of several incompatible extant standards."[4] The American National Standards Institute (ANSI) is the private, nonprofit organization that administers and coordinates the U.S. voluntary standards and conformity assessment system. In this role, ANSI oversees the development and use of voluntary consensus standards by accrediting the procedures used by SDOs and approving their finished documents as American National Standards.

The *United States Standards Strategy*[5] emphasizes that standards development should be open and inclusive, market driven, sector based, consumer focused, and globally relevant. The U.S. standardization system is based on the set of globally accepted principles for standards development shown in Table 12-1.

Principle	Description
Transparency	Essential information regarding standardization activities is accessible to all interested parties.
Openness	Participation is open to all affected interests.
Impartiality	No one interest dominates the process or is favored over another.
Effectiveness and relevance	Standards are relevant and effectively respond to regulatory and market needs, as well as scientific and technological developments.
Consensus	Decisions are reached through consensus among those affected.
Performance based	Standards are performance based (specifying essential characteristics rather than detailed designs) where possible.
Coherence	The process encourages coherence to avoid overlapping and conflicting standards.
Due process	Standards development accords with due process so that all views are considered and appeals are possible.
Technical assistance	Assistance is offered to developing countries in the formulation and application of standards.

Table 13-1 ANSI Principles for Standards Development

Standards Categories

Several general topic areas are used to categorize health data standards. However, as interoperability efforts advance, their boundaries increasingly overlap.[6] Health data interchange and transport standards are used to establish a common, predictable, secure communication protocol between and among systems. Vocabulary and terminology standards consist of standardized nomenclatures and code sets used to describe clinical problems and procedures, medications, and allergies. Content and structure standards and value sets are used to share clinical information such as clinical summaries, prescriptions, and structured electronic documents. Security standards include those standards used for authentication, access control, and transmission of health data.

Health Data Interchange and Transport Standards

Health data interchange and transport standards primarily address the format of messages and documents that are exchanged between computer systems. To achieve data compatibility between systems, it is necessary to have prior agreement on the syntax of the messages to be exchanged. That is, the receiving system must be able to divide the incoming message into discrete data elements that reflect what the sending system wishes to communicate. This section describes some of the major organizations involved in the development of health data interchange and transport standards.

Accredited Standards Committee X12

Accredited Standards Committee (ASC) X12 has developed a broad range of electronic data interchange (EDI) standards to facilitate electronic business transactions. In the healthcare arena, X12N standards have been adopted as national standards for such administrative transactions as claims, enrollment, and eligibility in health plans, and first report of injury under the requirements of the Health Insurance Portability and Accountability Act (HIPAA) of 1996 Privacy and Security Rules.

Institute of Electrical and Electronics Engineers

The Institute of Electrical and Electronics Engineers (IEEE) has developed a series of standards known collectively as P1073 Medical Information Bus, which support real-time, continuous, and comprehensive capture and communication of data from bedside medical devices such as those found in intensive care units, operating rooms, and emergency departments. These data include physiologic parameter measurements and device settings. IEEE standards for information technology focus on telecommunications and information exchange between systems including local area networks (LANs) and metropolitan area networks (MANs).

Current IEEE standards development activities include efforts to develop standards that support wireless technology. The IEEE 802.xx suite of wireless networking standards, supporting LANs and MANs, has advanced developments in the communications market. The most widely known standard, 802.11 (commonly referred to as Wi-Fi), allows anyone with a "smart" mobile device or computer with either a plug-in card or built-in circuitry to connect wirelessly to the Internet.

National Electrical Manufacturers Association

The National Electrical Manufacturers Association (NEMA), in collaboration with the American College of Radiology (ACR) and others, formed Digital Imaging and Communications in Medicine (DICOM) to develop a generic digital format and a transfer protocol for biomedical images and image-related information. DICOM enables the transfer of medical images in a multivendor environment and facilitates the development and expansion of picture archiving and communication systems (PACSs).

World Wide Web Consortium

The World Wide Web Consortium (W3C) is the main international standards organization for development of standards for the Web. W3C also publishes Extensible Markup Language (XML), which is a set of rules for encoding documents in machine-readable format. XML is most commonly used in exchanging data over the Internet. Although XML's design focuses on documents, it is widely used for the representation of arbitrary data structures, for example in Web Services. Web Services use XML messages that follow the Simple Object Access Protocol (SOAP) standard and have been popular with the traditional enterprise. Other data exchange protocols include the Representational State Transfer (REST) architectural style, which focuses on a specific set of interactions between data elements rather than more complex implementation details. REST enables communication via the Hypertext Transfer Protocol (HTTP), which is used in web browsers. The largest known implementation of a system conforming to the REST architectural style is the Web.

PART III

Vocabulary and Terminology Standards

A fundamental requirement for effective communication is the ability to represent concepts unambiguously for both the sender and receiver of the message. While there have been great advances in the ability of computers to process natural language, most communication between health information systems relies on the use of structured vocabularies, terminologies, code sets, and classification systems to represent healthcare concepts. Standardized terminologies enable data collection at the point of care; enable retrieval of data, information, and knowledge in support of clinical practice; and elicit outcomes. The following examples describe several of the major vocabulary and terminology standards.

Current Procedural Terminology

The Current Procedural Terminology (CPT) code set maintained by the American Medical Association (AMA) describes medical, surgical, and diagnostic services. When medical, surgical, or diagnostic services are provided, they are translated into CPT codes and reported to third-party payers for reimbursement. Every medical insurance payer recognizes CPT codes as the standard by which medical procedures in ambulatory care are described in a universal language with specific meaning. While primarily used in the United States for reimbursement purposes, CPT codes have also been adopted for other data purposes.

International Statistical Classification of Diseases and Related Health Problems: Tenth Revision (ICD-10)

The International Statistical Classification of Diseases and Related Health Problems: Tenth Revision (ICD-10) is the most recent version of the ICD classification system for mortality and morbidity used worldwide. The ICD, maintained by the World Health Organization (WHO), is designed as a healthcare classification system, providing a system of diagnostic codes for classifying diseases and health conditions, as well as procedure codes for hospital-based services and procedures. The transition to ICD-10 in the United States occurred on October 1, 2015. Moving to the new ICD-10 code sets improves efficiencies and lowers administrative costs by replacing a dysfunctional, outdated classification system.

Nursing and Other Domain-specific Terminologies

The American Nurses Association continues to advocate for the use of the ANA-recognized terminologies supporting nursing practice within EHR and other health information technology solutions.[7] Therefore, in alignment with national requirements for standardization of data and information exchange, ANA supports the following recommendations:

- "All health care settings should create a plan for implementing an ANA recognized terminology supporting nursing practice within their EHR.
- Each setting type should achieve consensus on a standard terminology that best suits their needs and select that terminology for their EHR, either individually or collectively as a group (e.g., EHR user group).

- Education should be available and guidance developed for selecting the recognized terminology that best suits the needs for a specific setting.

- When exchanging information (e.g., for problems and care plans) with another setting using Health Level Seven's (HL7) Consolidated Clinical Document Architecture (C-CDA), Systematized Nomenclature of Medicine–Clinical Terms (SNOMED CT®) and Logical Observation Identifiers Names and Codes (LOINC®) should be used. LOINC® should be used for coding nursing assessments and outcomes and SNOMED CT® for problems, interventions, and observation findings.

- Health information exchange between providers using the same terminology does not require conversion of the data to SNOMED CT® or LOINC® codes."

RxNorm

RxNorm is a standardized nomenclature for clinical drugs and drug delivery devices produced by the National Library of Medicine (NLM). The goal of RxNorm is to allow various systems using different drug nomenclatures to share data efficiently at the appropriate level of abstraction. RxNorm contains the names of the prescription formulations that exist in the United States, including devices that administer the medications in a pack containing multiple clinical drugs or clinical drugs designed to be administered in a specified sequence.

Unified Medical Language System

The Unified Medical Language System (UMLS) consists of a metathesaurus—a large, multipurpose, and multilingual thesaurus—that contains millions of biomedical and health-related concepts, their synonymous names, and their relationships managed by NLM. There are specialized vocabularies, code sets, and classification systems for almost every practice domain in healthcare. Most of these are not compatible with one another, and much work needs to be done to achieve usable mapping and linkages between them. NLM is the central coordinating entity for clinical terminology standards within the U.S. Department of Health and Human Services (HHS). NLM works closely with the Office of the National Coordinator for Health Information Technology to advance national goals toward achieving an interoperable health information technology infrastructure that improves the quality and efficiency of healthcare.[8]

Content and Structure Standards

Content and structure standards relate to the data content that is transported within information exchanges. Such standards define the structure and content organization of the electronic message/document information content. They can also define a set of content standards (messages/documents). In addition to standardizing the format of health data messages and the lexicons and value sets used in those messages, there is widespread interest in defining common sets of data for specific message types. A minimum or core data set is "a minimum set of items with uniform definitions and categories concerning a specific aspect or dimension of the healthcare system which meets the essential needs of multiple users."[9]

Clinical Data Interchange Standards Consortium

The Clinical Data Interchange Standards Consortium (CDISC) is a global, multidisciplinary consortium that has established standards to support the acquisition, exchange, submission, and archiving of clinical research data and metadata. CDISC develops and supports global, platform-independent data standards that enable information system interoperability to improve medical research and related areas of healthcare. One example is the Biomedical Research Integrated Domain Group (BRIDG) model, a domain-analysis model representing protocol-driven biomedical/clinical research. The BRIDG model emerged from an unprecedented collaborative effort among clinical trial experts from CDISC, the National Institutes of Health (NIH)/National Cancer Institute (NCI), the Food and Drug Administration (FDA), Health Level Seven International (HL7), and other volunteers. This structured information model is being used to support development of data interchange standards and technology solutions that will enable harmonization between the biomedical/clinical research and healthcare arenas.[10]

Health Level Seven International

Health Level Seven International (HL7) is a standards organization that develops standards in multiple categories including health data interchange, content, and structure. HL7 standards cover a broad spectrum of areas for information exchange including medical orders, clinical observations, test results, admission/transfer/discharge, EHR data, and charge and billing information. One of the emerging standards developed by HL7 for exchanging health information electronically is Fast Healthcare Interoperability Resources (FHIR). FHIR uses a predominantly composition approach (rather than modeling by constraint) and is organized using a combination of building blocks called resources. FHIR specifies a RESTful application programming interface (API) to access resources. Several projects are underway through standards organizations to facilitate adoption of FHIR including the Clinical Information Modeling Initiative (CIMI) and SMART on FHIR.[11]

International Health Terminology Standards Development Organisation

The International Health Terminology Standards Development Organisation (IHTSDO) is a not-for-profit association in Denmark that develops and promotes use of SNOMED CT (Systematized Nomenclature of Medicine—Clinical Terms) to support safe and effective health information exchange. It was formed in 2006 with the purpose of developing and maintaining international health terminology systems. SNOMED CT is a comprehensive clinical terminology, originally created by the College of American Pathologists (CAP) and, as of April 2007, owned, maintained, and distributed by IHTSDO. CAP continues to support SNOMED CT operations under contract to IHTSDO and provides SNOMED CT–related products and services as a licensee of the terminology. NLM is the U.S. member of IHTSDO and, as such, distributes SNOMED CT at no cost in accordance with the member rights and responsibilities outlined in IHTSDO's Articles of Association.[12]

National Council for Prescription Drug Programs

The National Council for Prescription Drug Programs (NCPDP) develops both content and health data interchange standards for information processing in the pharmacy services sector of the healthcare industry. As an example of the impact that standardization can have, since the introduction of these standards in 1992, the retail pharmacy industry has moved to 100 percent electronic claims processing in real time. NCPDP standards are also forming the basis for electronic prescription transactions. Electronic prescription transactions are defined as EDI messages flowing between healthcare providers (i.e., pharmacy software systems and prescriber software systems) that are concerned with prescription orders. NCPDP's Telecommunication Standard Version 5.1 was named the official standard for pharmacy claims within HIPAA, and NCPDP is also named in other U.S. federal legislation titled the Medicare Prescription Drug, Improvement, and Modernization Act. Other NCPDP standards include the SCRIPT Standard for Electronic Prescribing and the Manufacturers Rebate Standard.[13]

Security Standards

Information security practices are increasingly important in a world of virtual access to health data and information. These practices require guidelines and general principles for initiating, implementing, maintaining, and improving information security management within and between organizations. Chapters 25–31 provide a detailed description of the healthcare security standards and effective security management practices in use today.

Standards Coordination and Interoperability

It has become clear to many public- and private-sector standards advocates that no one entity has the resources to create an exhaustive set of health data standards that will meet all needs. New emphasis is being placed on coordinating efforts and leveraging existing standards to eliminate the redundant and siloed efforts that have in the past contributed to a complex, difficult-to-navigate, health data standards environment. SDOs and other industry groups are actively working together to develop standards that achieve technical, structural, and semantic interoperability.[14] As a result, the standards development and, more importantly, adoption process is more accelerated and streamlined, and the healthcare industry is moving closer to achieving the goal of sharable, comparable, quality data based on evidence.[15]

In addition to the various SDOs previously described, the following sections provide brief descriptions of some of the major international, national, and regional organizations involved in broad-based standards coordination and interoperability.

Health IT Standards Committee

The American Recovery and Reinvestment Act (ARRA) provided for the creation of the Health IT Standards Committee (HITSC) under the auspices of the Federal Advisory Committee Act (FACA). The committee is charged with making recommendations to the ONC on standards, implementation specifications, and certification criteria for the electronic exchange and use of health information. In developing, harmonizing, or recognizing standards and implementation specifications, the committee also provides for the testing of the same by the National Institute of Standards and Technology (NIST). Recently, the committee has formed several taskforces comprising stakeholder representatives and subject matter experts focused on precision medicine, as well as the 2017 Interoperability Standards Advisory.[16]

International Organization for Standardization

The International Organization for Standardization (ISO) develops, harmonizes, and publishes standards internationally. ISO standards are developed, in large part, from standards brought forth by member countries, and through liaison activities with other SDOs. Often, these standards are further broadened to reflect the greater diversity of the international community. In 1998, the ISO Technical Committee (TC) 215 on Health Informatics was formed to coordinate the development of international health information standards, including data standards. Consensus on these standards influences health informatics standards adopted in the United States. At times, other SDOs collaborate with ISO TC 215 to accredit international standards. For example, both HL7 and ISO TC 215 accredited the EHR System Functional Model as a set of requirements specifying the behavior of EHR systems.

Integrating the Healthcare Enterprise

Standards, while a necessary part of the interoperability solution, are not alone sufficient to fulfill the needs. Simply using a standard does not necessarily guarantee that health information exchange will occur within and across organizations and systems. Standards can be implemented in multiple ways, so implementation specifications or guides are critical to make interoperability a reality. Standard implementation guides, or profiles, are designed to provide specific configuration instructions or constraints for implementation of a particular standard or set of standards to achieve the desired interoperable result based on a domain-specific use-case scenario.

Integrating the Healthcare Enterprise (IHE) is an international organization that provides a detailed framework for implementing standards, filling the gaps between creating the standards and implementing them. Through its open, consensus process, IHE has published a large body of detailed specifications or guides, called profiles, that are being implemented globally today by healthcare providers and regional health information exchanges to enable standards-based, safe, secure, and efficient health information exchange. IHE maintains the Product Registry, which is used as a mechanism for registering and searching products that support IHE profiles. Users can then reference the appropriate IHE profiles in requests for proposals, thus simplifying the systems acquisition process and furthering the adoption of standards-based, interoperable systems.[17]

eHealth Exchange and the Sequoia Project

The eHealth Exchange (commonly referred to as "the Exchange") is a group of federal agencies and nonfederal entities organized under a common mission and purpose to improve patient care, streamline disability benefit claims, and improve public health reporting through secure, trusted, and interoperable health information exchange. By leveraging a common set of standards, legal agreement, and governance, eHealth Exchange participants are able to securely share health information with each other, without additional customization and one-off legal agreements. The eHealth Exchange connectivity spans across all 50 states and is now the largest health data sharing network in the United States.[18]

The Business Value of Health Data Standards

Clearly the importance of health data standards in enhancing the quality and efficiency of healthcare delivery is being recognized by national and international leadership. Reviewing the business value of defining and using data standards is critical for driving the implementation of these standards into applications and systems. Having health data standards for data exchange and information modeling will provide a mechanism against which deployed systems can be validated.[19] Reducing manual intervention will increase worker productivity and streamline operations. Defining information exchange requirements will enhance the ability to automate interaction with external partners, which in turn will decrease costs.

By using data standards to develop their emergency-department data-collection system, New York State demonstrated that it is good business practice.[20] Their project was completed on time without additional resources and generated a positive return on investment. The use of standards provided the basis for consensus between the hospital industry and the state, a robust pool of information that satisfied the users, and the structure necessary to create unambiguous data requirements and specifications.

Other economic stakeholders for healthcare IT include software vendors or suppliers, software implementers who install the software to support end-user requirements, and the users who must use the software to do their work. The balance of interests among these stakeholders is necessary to promote standardization to achieve economic and organizational benefits.[21] Defining clear business measures will help motivate the advancement and adoption of interoperable healthcare IT systems, thus ensuring the desired outcomes can be achieved. Considering the value proposition for incorporating data standards into products, applications, and systems should be a part of every organization's information technology strategy. The development, adoption, and use of standards-based interoperable healthcare IT will enable the achievement of better care, improved population health, and cost reduction.

Chapter Review

This chapter introduced health data standards; the organizations that develop, coordinate, and harmonize them; the process by which they are developed; examples of current standards initiatives; and a discussion of the business value of health data standards. Four broad areas were described to categorize health data standards. Health data interchange and transport standards are used to establish a common, predictable, secure communication protocol between and among systems. Vocabulary and terminology standards consist of standardized nomenclatures and code sets used to describe clinical problems and procedures, medications, and allergies. Content and structure standards and value sets are used to share clinical information such as clinical summaries, prescriptions, and structured electronic documents. Finally, security standards are used for authentication, access control, and transmission of health data. Organizations involved in the development, harmonization, coordination, and implementation of health data standards were described.

A discussion of the standards development process highlighted the international and socio-political context in which standards are developed and the potential impact they have on the availability and currency of standards. The expanding role of the federal government in influencing the development and adoption of health data standards was discussed. Finally, the chapter emphasized the business value and importance of health data standards and their adoption in improving the quality and efficiency of healthcare delivery and health outcomes.

Questions

To test your comprehension of the chapter, answer the following questions and then check your answers against the list of correct answers that follows the questions.

1. Why is the healthcare IT industry motivated to adopt and implement legislated, government-developed standards into proprietary information systems and related products?

   A. Government-developed standards are more suitable for general, private-sector use.

   B. Maintenance of government-developed standards is typically on a fast pace.

   C. Government-developed standards typically enable compliance with regulations.

   D. Bureaucratic overhead is lessened with government-developed standards.

2. Which of the following principles is *not* included in the globally accepted principles for standards development set forth in ANSI's *United States Standards Strategy*?

   A. Transparency

   B. Openness

   C. Consensus

   D. Complexity

3. What are the broad areas used to categorize health data standards?

   A. Health data interchange and transport, vocabulary and terminology, content and structure, security

   B. Health data exchange, structured, content, security

   C. Terminology, vocabulary, content, privacy

   D. Nomenclatures, code sets, protocols, and transactions

4. Which of the following organizations is involved in the development of health data interchange standards?

   A. American Medical Association (AMA)

   B. Institute of Electrical and Electronics Engineers (IEEE)

   C. American Nurses Association (ANA)

   D. National Library of Medicine (NLM)

5. Interoperability can be more rapidly advanced through coordinated, joint standards-development efforts. Which of the following is a recent example of such a joint effort between CDISC and NIH/NCI, the FDA, and HL7?

   A. EHR System Functional Model

   B. Precision Medicine Initiative

   C. Consolidated CDA

   D. BRIDG model

6. Integrating the Healthcare Enterprise (IHE) has developed a mechanism for registering and searching products that support IHE profiles. What is this mechanism called?

   A. IHE Technical Framework

   B. Consolidated CDA guide

   C. IHE Product Registry

   D. IHE Integration Statements

7. Which of the following does *not* represent a business value of health data standards?

   A. Reduced costs

   B. Decreased worker productivity

   C. Reduced manual intervention

   D. Ability to validate deployed systems

8. When New York State used data standards to develop their emergency-department data-collection system, which of the following outcomes resulted?

   A. Need for additional resources

   B. Dissatisfied users

   C. Ambiguous data requirements

   D. Positive return on investment

Answers

1. **C.** The healthcare IT industry is motivated to adopt and implement government-developed standards into proprietary information systems and related products in order to be in compliance with these regulations and achieve a strong market presence.

2. **D.** Complexity is not included in the set of globally accepted principles for standards development. The nine principles are transparency, openness, impartiality, effectiveness and relevance, consensus, performance based, coherence, due process, and technical assistance.

3. **A.** The four broad areas used to categorize health data standards are health data interchange standards (used to establish a common, predictable, secure communication protocol between and among systems); vocabulary standards (standardized nomenclatures and code sets); content standards (used to share clinical information); and security standards (used for authentication, access control, and transmission of health data).

4. **B.** The Institute of Electrical and Electronics Engineers (IEEE) has developed a series of standards that focus on telecommunications and information exchange between systems, including local and metropolitan area networks.

5. **D.** In a recent, joint standards-development effort, the Clinical Data Interchange Standards Consortium (CDISC) published the BRIDG model. This model was produced and developed through the joint efforts of the National Institutes of Health (NIH)/National Cancer Institute (NCI), the Food and Drug Administration (FDA), and Health Level Seven International (HL7).

6. **C.** IHE maintains the Product Registry as a mechanism for registering and searching products that support IHE profiles. The registry includes IHE Integration Statements, which are documents prepared and published by vendors that describe the conformance of their products with the IHE Technical Framework.

7. **B.** Having health data standards for data exchange and information modeling will provide a mechanism against which deployed systems can be validated. Reducing manual intervention will increase (not decrease) worker productivity and streamline operations. Defining information exchange requirements will enhance the ability to automate interaction with external partners, which will reduce costs.

8. **D.** By using data standards to develop their emergency-department data-collection system, New York State completed their project on time without additional resources and generated a positive return on investment. The use of standards provided the basis for consensus between the hospital industry and the state, a robust pool of information that satisfied the users, and the structure necessary to create unambiguous data requirements and specifications.

References

1. Saba, V. K., & McCormick, K. A. (Eds.). (2015). *Essentials of nursing informatics, Sixth edition.* McGraw-Hill Education.

2. Office of the National Coordinator for Health IT. (2015). *Connecting health and care for the nation: A shared nationwide interoperability roadmap.* Accessed from www.healthit.gov/sites/default/files/hie-interoperability/nationwide-interoperability-roadmap-final-version-1.0.pdf.

3. Hammond, W. E. (2005). The making and adoption of health data standards. *Health Affairs, 24*(5), 1205–1213.

4. Busch, L. (2011). *Standards: Recipes for reality.* MIT Press.

5. ANSI. (2015). *United States Standards Strategy.* American National Standards Institute. Accessed from www.us-standards-strategy.org.

6. U.S. Department of Health and Human Services (HHS). (2015). 2015 edition health information technology (health IT) certification criteria, 2015 edition base electronic health record (EHR) definition, and ONC health IT certification program modifications; final rule. 45 CFR 170. *Federal Register, 80*(60), 16804–16921. Accessed from www.federalregister.gov/documents/2015/10/16/2015-25597/2015-edition-health-information-technology-health-it-certification-criteria-2015-edition-base.

7. American Nurses Association. (2015). *Inclusion of recognized terminologies within EHRs and other health information technology solutions.* Accessed from www.nursingworld.org/MainMenuCategories/Policy-Advocacy/Positions-and-Resolutions/ANAPositionStatements/Position-Statements-Alphabetically/Inclusion-of-Recognized-Terminologies-within-EHRs.html.

8. U.S. National Library of Medicine. (2016). *Health information technology and health data standards at NLM.* Accessed from www.nlm.nih.gov/healthit/index.html.

9. HHS, Health Information Policy Council. (1983). *Background paper: Uniform minimum health data sets* (unpublished).

10. Clinical Data Interchange Standards Consortium (CDISC). www.cdisc.org/.

11. Wagholikar, K. B., Mandel, J. C., Klann, J. G., Watanasin, N., Mendis, M., Chute, C. G., Mandl, K. D., & Murphy, S. N. (2016). SMART-on-FHIR implemented over i2b2. *Journal of the American Medical Informatics Association.* Accessed from http://jamia.oxfordjournals.org/content/early/2016/06/05/jamia.ocw079.

12. International Health Terminology Standards Development Organisation (IHTSDO). www.ihtsdo.org/.

13. National Council for Prescription Drug Programs (NCPDP). www.ncpdp.org/.

PART III

14. Harris, M. R., Langford, L. H., Miller, H., Hook, M., Dykes, P. C., & Matney, S. A. (2015). Harmonizing and extending standards from a domain-specific and bottom-up approach: An example from development through use in clinical applications. *Journal of the American Medical Informatics Association, 22*(3), 545–552.

15. McCormick, K. A., Sensmeier, J., Dykes, P. C., Grace, E. N., Matney, S. A., Schwarz, K. M., & Weston, M. J. (2015). Exemplars for advancing standardized terminology in nursing to achieve sharable, comparable quality data based upon evidence. *Online Journal of Nursing Informatics (OJNI), 19*(2). Available at www.himss.org/ojni.

16. Office of the National Coordinator for Health Information Technology (ONC)/ HEALTHIT. www.healthit.gov/isa/.

17. Windle, J. R., Katz, A. S., Dow, J. P., Fry, E. T. A., Keller, A. M., Lamp, T., … Weintraub, W. S. (2016, September). 2016 ACC/ASE/ASNC/HRS/SCAI health policy statement on integrating the healthcare enterprise. *Journal of the American College of Cardiology, 68*(12), 1348–1364.

18. http://sequoiaproject.org/ehealth-exchange/about/.

19. Loshin, D. (2004). The business value of data standards. *DM Review, 14*, 20.

20. Davis, B. (2004). *Return-on-investment for using data standards: A case study of New York State's data system.* Accessed from www.phdsc.org/standards/pdfs/ROI4UDS.pdf.

21. Marshall, G. F. (2009, October). The standards value chain: Where health IT standards come from. *Journal of AHIMA, 80*(10), 54–55, 60–62.

Additional Study

The field of health data standards is a very dynamic one, with existing standards undergoing revision and new standards being developed. The best way to learn about specific standards activities is to get involved in the process. All of the organizations discussed in this chapter provide opportunities to be involved with activities that support standards development, coordination, and implementation. The following list includes the web address for each organization. Most sites describe current available activities and publications, and many have links to other related sites.

Accredited Standards Committee (ASC) X12: www.x12.org

American Medical Association (AMA): www.ama-assn.org

American National Standards Institute (ANSI): www.ansi.org

American Nurses Association (ANA): www.nursingworld.org

Clinical Data Interchange Standards Consortium (CDISC): www.cdisc.org

Digital Imaging Communication in Medicine Standards Committee (DICOM): http://dicom.nema.org/

eHealth Exchange and the Sequoia Project: www.sequoiaproject.org

Health Level Seven International (HL7): www.hl7.org

Institute of Electrical and Electronics Engineers (IEEE): www.ieee.org

Integrating the Healthcare Enterprise (IHE): www.ihe.net

IHE Product Registry: http://product-registry.ihe.net

International Health Terminology Standards Development Organisation (IHTSDO): www.ihtsdo.org

International Organization for Standardization (ISO): www.iso.org

International Statistical Classification of Diseases and Related Health Problems (ICD-10): www.cdc.gov/nchswww

National Committee on Vital and Health Statistics (NCVHS): www.ncvhs.hhs.gov

National Council for Prescription Drug Programs (NCPDP): www.ncpdp.org

National Electrical Manufacturers Association (NEMA): www.nema.org

National Institute of Standards and Technology (NIST): www.nist.gov

National Library of Medicine (NLM): www.nlm.nih.gov/healthit.html

Office of the National Coordinator for Health Information Technology (ONC): www.healthit.gov

Public Health Data Standards Consortium (PHDSC): www.phdsc.org

RxNorm: www.nlm.nih.gov/research/umls/rxnorm

Unified Medical Language System (UMLS): www.nlm.nih.gov/research/umls

World Health Organization International Classification of Diseases (WHO-ICD): www.who.int/classifications/icd/en

World Wide Web Consortium (W3C): www.w3.org

CHAPTER 14

Interoperability Within and Across Healthcare Systems

John Moehrke*

In this chapter, you will learn how to

- Explain the relationship between identity, access control, authorization, authentication, and role assignment
- Identify and explain access control to data from the perspective of patient, user, and resource, as well as in the context of information use
- Identify and explain how to apply security concepts to a healthcare information exchange (HIE)

This chapter describes how to control access to healthcare information. This includes the typical rules of any business that provides specific types of data to specific types of people while forbidding access to those who don't have a need for access. Access control is an important part of any system that holds information. Even systems that simply provide a cafeteria menu use general rules to restrict those who can change the menu.

Overall, healthcare is not that different from other industries' information systems, and for many types of access to healthcare information, the same security controls found in common IT security identity and access management (IAM) can be used. But there are aspects of healthcare, related to treatment, that require some adjustments to typical access control:

- **Patient safety**   Safety is not unique to healthcare, but in healthcare systems safety can have life-altering (even life-ending) consequences; this creates a complexity that is not as predictable as safety is in other industries.
- **Patient privacy**   Again, privacy is not a concern unique to healthcare, but in the context of healthcare and sensitive health topics, privacy is a more complex issue.

---

*Portions of this chapter are adapted with permission from John Moehrke, Healthcare Security/Privacy, http://healthcaresecprivacy.blogspot.com/. © John Moehrke.

For example, once healthcare information is released to unauthorized parties, it can't be taken back or revoked (unlike the financial world, where a breach can be recovered from by revoking the identity or transaction). In addition, although healthcare organizations would benefit from analyzing past data to make their operations better for future patients, this is not easy while also protecting the privacy rights of patients. Governments also want to mine the data to improve population health, but privacy concerns can arise.

- **Healthcare information exchange**   HIEs are groups of cooperating (and sometimes competing) organizations that must share information because of a common patient they are diagnosing or treating. HIEs are usually defined by geographic boundaries and are described later in this chapter.

User Identity

User identity is fundamental to controlling access, both for security and for privacy. The user's identity, known to the software, controls that user's access to an electronic health record (EHR).[1-8] It is this identity that is related to the certain data elements that the user is authorized to access. In addition, it is this identity that is recorded in security audit logs[9] for tracking what was done and by whom. The user identity is not specific to health professionals, though, because patients can also be users when they interact with their personal health records (PHRs). The user identity is also critical to system administration and maintenance. The user identity is leveraged by privacy controls to enable or disable access and provide appropriate accounting.

This chapter covers the specific aspects of user identity that are important to access control. This chapter does not cover everything related to user identities, such as those aspects needed by human resources and management.

Provisioning

User provisioning is the process of creating a user account, including performing the administrative steps that prove the individual represented by the user account is the correct individual. In a typical organization, provisioning is a shared responsibility among the human resources department, the managers of the department where the individual reports, and the information technology department (where the account is actually created). Larger organizations require more formal checks and balances when provisioning a user account. In addition, the process gets more complex when contractors or other short-term user accounts are needed. The provisioning step creates a user account, from which access to protected resources is provided.

In a special case of provisioning, a patient gets a user account, but there needs to be an additional step to create a binding between it and the patient identity associated with the record.

Ideally, there is only one user account per person in an organization; however, this ideal is usually never achieved. Where all systems are using the same user account per person, the user provisioning step can be simple. It is, however, common that there is some software that manages isolated user accounts, such as for laboratory, radiology, or other departmental systems. Creating all the necessary accounts is part of the user provisioning process.

Identity Proofing

Policies should be in place that document the methods used to prove that the human is who they say they are before they are allowed access to the user account, given that the user account is going to enable the individual to access sensitive healthcare information. The policies might require that a background check is done on the individual, government-issued identification is inspected, or some form of challenge and response using a previously known identifier is performed. Whatever method is used, this sets up the level of assurance that this user identity provides.

A good standard for this *identity proofing* is NIST Special Publication 800-63.[2] This document defines four levels of assurance that align well with other standards. The NIST specification is an easy-to-understand specification and is freely available, and there are many other good resources.[6, 7] The following is a summary of the levels of assurance of identity proofing (these levels are different from the levels of assurance of authentication, discussed in the section "The Multiple Factors of Authentication"):

- **Level 1**   No identity proofing is required. This is typical of free Internet services such as Facebook, Twitter, Gmail, Hotmail, and so on.

- **Level 2**   This requires the user to present government-issued identifying materials that include full name, picture, address, or nationality.

- **Level 3**   This requires that the identifying information presented be proven as authentic. This is typically done through verification with the authority that issued the credentials.

- **Level 4**   This requires in-person registration and presentation of two independent identifying materials that are verified as authentic.

A digital certificate[8, 9] is a specific type of user identity that is standards based and thus can be leveraged by many systems. Digital certificates are issued by a certificate authority. The certificate authority sets up the administrative capability for multiple organizations, individuals, or systems to "trust" the same certificate authority, and thus the certificate authority becomes known as a *trusted third party*. A specific example of a user provisioning policy that shows the aspects that should be included in user provisioning is a certificate policy (CP). This is a written policy that defines the methods used for digital certificate issuance and management. An X.509 certificate policy is defined in the IETF RFC 3647.[8] This certificate policy helps describe why the certificate authority should be "trusted." Note that digital certificates do not automatically mean a high level of assurance, because there are certificate authorities that will issue a digital certificate identity at level 1. Digital certificates are often issued to computer systems, services, or organizations.[10]

An emerging open standard is OAuth 2.0,[11] which is a significant advancement over OAuth 1.0.[12] OpenID Connect is a set of constraints on OAuth to provide a very powerful federated user identification and authentication infrastructure. The technology is more readily available on the Internet and to consumers through Facebook, Google, and so on. These standards are more conducive to use with the emerging Health Language 7 (HL7®) Fast Healthcare Interoperability Resource (FHIR®) standard (also discussed in Chapters 13 and 16). There are healthcare-focused profiles available.[13, 14, 15]

A profile in terms of "interoperability" is a set of constraints on a standard to achieve a defined outcome. Whereas interoperability standards are designed to support many outcomes, a profile is a specification that is used to assure for a given use case that two (or more) communicating parties use a narrow definition of how they are supposed to encode data and interpret that data. A profile defines vocabulary to be used (whereas the standard allows much more), specific fields to be used (whereas the standard defines them as optional), other fields that are forbidden (whereas the standard defines them as optional), and specific behaviors to be followed.

Role Assignment

Roles are the mechanism used to give user accounts access permissions. Thus, during the provisioning process, it is important to define what roles the user will need to perform their job. The initial set of roles assigned is typically simply a "starter set," that is, a minimal set of roles assigned to everyone when they first start. User accounts are assigned more roles as they take on more responsibility.

It is also important to have procedures to remove unnecessary roles as a user takes on different responsibilities. A mechanism that is used to remove unnecessary roles will keep to a minimum the number of individuals who have access to resources. Having a minimal number of individuals with access permissions to resources is a best practice but should also be weighed carefully with the need to provide care. For example, when healthcare professionals take on administrative roles, they might not need the ability to see healthcare information, but if they later need to be called upon to treat patients, then it might be best to leave access enabled.

Deprovisioning

More important than provisioning an account is to *deprovision* it when it is no longer needed. This might be when an individual retires, moves to another facility, or is dismissed. The deprovisioning should be done as soon as possible, and the date and the reason for deprovisioning should be carefully recorded.

The deprovisioning of an account in healthcare is often done through simply disabling access rather than removing the account. This is to allow the user account information to remain intact for a period of time. For example, this user account information might be needed by the medical records department to preserve the provenance of medical information, to prove signatures well into the future, or for other reasons.

User accounts that are not deprovisioned will likely stick around forever in a system, and any account that is not properly maintained presents a security vulnerability. To prevent this, an identity management system may have reports and alerts that indicate when user accounts are aging without activity. Inactivity might also be detected through the failure to change passwords on a regular basis. Regardless, there needs to be some mechanism in place to detect user accounts that are not being used so that they can be deprovisioned.

User Account Support

Not directly related to security but important to maintaining it are the user account support functions. These often include changing directory information to represent name changes or changes to a user's office location or home location.

Internal Directory vs. External Directory

A user account is often contained within a user directory, either private to the organization (internal) or public (external). Internal user directories are often richly filled with contact information including many phone numbers, e-mail addresses, physical addresses, and calendars.[16] The internal directory commonly maintains the user role assignments. In this way, an internal directory is an important asset to the operation of the organization.

External directories contain information that needs to be publicly known.[17] A specific example of this is a healthcare provider directory.[18] This kind of a directory contains information that patients and other health providers might use to discover the healthcare providers. For example, a patient might be looking for a specialist in a type of treatment they need. These external directories would contain minimal contact information, such as only the contact information of a registration or scheduling desk. An external directory would not include security roles or private contact information. An example of an external directory is one that supports the Direct Project (https://www.healthit.gov/policy-researchers-implementers/direct-project) need for certificate discovery, where the directory will contain the e-mail address and the digital certificate to use to secure the e-mail.

Authentication

Authentication in this context consists of the electronic mechanisms used to prove that someone or something is who they say they are. (This is independent of the identity-proofing step that proves that an identity is being issued correctly.) There are two types of authentication: authentication used prior to issuing an identity and authentication for the use of that identity. This section focuses on the latter type of authentication for the use of an identity in a session or transaction.

Essentially, the process of user authentication proves that a human is the one associated with a user identity (or user account). This might be the process used in a user interface to authenticate the "human" behind the keyboard. This also includes the process that is used to move that user authentication to other software that relies on it. An extreme example of this is the authentication that is used to authorize access to health information from another organization across a health information exchange (HIE).[19]

Authentication can also be used to prove that a computer system (EHR) is the system identified.[19] This can be extended to anything that can be identified, including a specific service (e.g., laboratory order manager) or whole organizations (e.g., virtual private network). Authenticating a computer system or service is often done using Transport Layer Security (TLS)[20] and digital certificate[8–10] identities.

The Multiple Factors of Authentication

Humans are hard to authenticate. When authenticating humans, security systems deal with one or more factors about that human to prove that they are indeed who they claim to be. The methods of authenticating humans have been built up over the millennium. Computers simply move these concepts to electronic technology. There are three factors[2] that we use to authenticate humans:

- Something the user knows (e.g., secret passphrase, password, personal knowledge, etc.)
- Something the user has (e.g., identity card, smartcard, security token, phone, etc.)
- Something the user is (e.g., how they look, how they behave, fingerprint, DNA, etc.)

Everyone is accustomed to using passwords to log in to computer systems. These are "secrets" that only the individual logging in knows. Even the computer should not know the actual password; rather, it knows the result of an algorithm that starts with the password (e.g., salted-cryptographic-hash). Using passwords, though, is vulnerable to "guessing," something that computers can do fast and relentlessly. This creates a need for users to create harder-to-guess passwords or change them often; however, the problem with this is that when the daily process of authenticating a user becomes hard to do, humans will get creative to thwart the system. One common example of this creativity is writing the password on a sticky note and putting it on the computer monitor for anyone to see.

Single-factor authentication, using just one of these factors, is usually not enough. Multifactor authentication, using more than one of these factors, tends to make the authentication step difficult. High-security environments or workflows might want to use at least two different factors. A good example of this is in the prescribing of narcotic drugs. Whatever method used to authenticate the user sets up another level of assurance; this is the confidence level that the user has been authenticated with for this session. Some systems, such as the Security Assertion Markup Language (SAML),[21] will indicate the method of authentication used rather than identify the level of assurance (discussed in the section "Authentication vs. Claims About Authentication (Federated Identity)" later in this chapter).

Within an organization, the level of assurance is simply a business decision or policy. This becomes far more important when the organization must trust requests coming from another organization and, therefore, the level of assurance that those identities have. If the level of assurance is not good enough, then the system should not return the resource requested. Oftentimes, much discussion and hand-wringing happens when trying to predict what level of assurance is needed to prevent unnecessary rejected requests.

Secondary Authentication

Sometimes a single authentication is not enough. For example, when requesting medical procedures, you might want to be sure that the human controlling the computer is indeed still the one authenticated. Thus, the system may need to reprompt the user for authentication credentials (e.g., password). This reprompting is part of a workflow and usually is required by legal, medical, or safety rules and policies. It is done to prevent someone else from using a system that has not yet automatically logged the original user out.

Another case where a reprompt may happen is to confirm prior to creating an electronic signature, or digital signature. This reprompting is required for signature events to make sure that the signature is indeed being done by the claimed identity.

Automatic Logoff

User identity, authentication, and access controls are all intended to enable proper access to information and functions while also forbidding inappropriate access. Automatic logoff functionality recognizes that the user may step away from the computer without logging off. This could lead to someone else walking up to the computer and seeing what is displayed and using the computer as if they were the original user. To prevent this, software tries to detect when the user might not be present and take steps to protect the system. This is referred to as *automatic logoff* and is typically implemented by noting that the user interface (keyboard and mouse) has been inactive for a defined length of time. The exact length of time usually varies depending on the kind of access and the location of the access.

The term "automatic logoff" implies that the session is terminated and the user is logged out. This isn't always done, but the spirit of the criteria is to stop access to the information on the screen and to prevent more actions under this user account, until the original user can prove that they are there again. The actual methods used can be quite complex.

Authentication vs. Claims About Authentication (Federated Identity)

So far, the concept of authentication has been about the computer system confirming that the human using the computer is the one identified by the user identity. There is another process that is also called *authentication*; this is when one computer system is using the services of a second computer system on behalf of the user. The services of the second computer system will be relying on the information that it is given and thus is called a *relying party*. Note that this concept extends well beyond just two parties. [1, 2, 3, 5, 21, 22]

For this process, a trusted third party creates a claim, which is a statement of the user identity, authentication method, roles being used, workflow purpose leading up to the request, and possibly other things. These claims are trusted because they are made by an entity that the relying party trusts and can confirm that the relying party truly did issue the claim. A claim that is not coming from an entity that the relying party trusts should be rejected. Thus, the requesting system does need to know which trusted third parties to use for specific relying parties.

The SAML[21] protocol defines a way to convey an identity and authentication claim (i.e., SAML assertion) to a relying party. Many enterprise-class authentication systems (e.g., Microsoft Active Directory) include the ability to create SAML assertions (e.g., information cards). The trusted third party is the organization, and thus there is only one trusted third party at each organization that needs to be trusted. This creates a federated identity, which is perhaps all the identity claims that your organization issues. This is similar to the OpenID and OAuth[11, 12] open standards.

Accountability

Patient care is paramount in the healthcare environment. The most effective approach to patient care involves open and cooperative access to the patient information for the diagnosis, treatment, payment, and healthcare operations. Teams of people work together to diagnose and treat a patient. Some of the team members are indirect and quite possibly remote. For example, it is common for a physician or other healthcare providers to enlist the opinion of specialists. This approach assumes and relies heavily on a well-defined and vetted user group that has been schooled in the proper ways to handle confidential information.

In a perfect world, each person who needs access to data is immediately granted access, and any inappropriate use of data is immediately blocked. The problem with this is that, given the open nature of healthcare, the boundaries between justifiable need and inappropriate are elusive. Even with proper authentication and authorization controls, there is a potential for abuse. There are two philosophies to maintaining accountability: access controls and audit controls. Both methods rely on accurate authentication of the individual user. These two different philosophies are implemented in different mixtures, but it is important to understand them.

Access Control

With this method, each user account is restricted to the patient records and product functionality that the user is authorized to access. With this type of restriction, audit trails are not that important. Accountability is maintained by the technology that keeps the individuals from doing the wrong thing.

Advantages

This method prevents any misuse of patient data. An important aspect of personal data privacy is that once data has been wrongly exposed, it is very difficult to recover.

Weakness

This method does not work well in emergency situations where qualified but not previously known individuals may need to operate the equipment. This method may interfere with diagnosis and treatment in that it restricts with whom a physician can confer. As a patient transfers from one physician to another, access control needs to be updated. This puts a large burden on the information technology (IT) staff.

Audit Control

With this method, the individuals are not restricted in any way. Audit trails[19] capture all uses of patient-identifiable data. In this method, the audit trail is very comprehensive. The accountability comes from training users on the proper use of the patient data and the knowledge that an audit trail will catch any misuse.

Advantages

This method will ensure that professional individuals are allowed the freedom to do the right thing when diagnosing and treating patients. Physicians and other healthcare providers are allowed to get second opinions for diagnostic and treatment purposes. In an emergency, new operators need only to have an account created; no complex access controls need to be created.

Weakness

The weakness of this method is that there is a huge number of audit trails that need to be managed, mined, and acted upon. This method relies on people not to abuse the personal data and to maintain ethical conduct. If there is no clear consequence to misuse, then this method will not work.

Balanced Access Control and Audit Control

A mixture of both access and audit control best achieves the balance of effectiveness versus safety versus security versus privacy. Using both access and audit controls follows the general concept of "failing into a safe state" in the healthcare treatment domain. What is safe in the banking industry is to forbid access; what is safe in the healthcare treatment domain is more of a balance. It's important to understand that it is a decision based on a good balance, not simply a declaration that access controls are hard or get in the way. This is not an easy balance, and HIT systems need to be flexible and dynamic; in other words, they need to be flexible to support expanding legitimate needs, and they need to be dynamic to adjust as issues become known.

- **Effectiveness**   Measure of success to provide healthcare
- **Safety**   Measure of physical harm to patient and caregivers
- **Security**   Measure of failure to achieve confidentiality, integrity, and availability of needed system/information
- **Privacy**   Measure of achieving patient privacy desires

This balance is not the same balance when the access of patient data is for reasons other than treatment. These other accesses are less time-critical and thus are best left in a mostly access control environment, which will require solid audit logging. The difference is that a delay in these workflows does not affect safety.

Regardless of the balance used for accountability, the security audit log must always be complete. The security audit logs are important to both security and privacy, but they are not the "accounting of disclosures" or even an "access report." These are reports that

PART III

will leverage the security audit log but will also need to be informed by disclosures that are done outside of the EHR.[23]

Roles and Permissions

This section covers the basics of access control through roles and permissions. The classic security model that is used for many large-scale organizations is role-based access control (RBAC).[24–28] What this means is that users are grouped into roles with others who have similar access control needs. A user tends to have a set of roles that they are assigned to, not just one role. These roles have permissions assigned to them that specify to the access control engine what the users assigned to this role can do. Thus, the role is simply a grouping mechanism for multiple users and multiple permissions.

What Are Permissions?

Permissions are the building block of security access control. They are an indication of the authorization of specific actions on a class of objects. The actions are a small number of specific actions often referred to as CRUDE: create, read, update, delete, and execute.

Not all objects can be executed, and typically objects that can be executed cannot be created, read, updated, or deleted. Some examples of objects that can be executed are programs, functionality within a program, and workflows. For example, in an EHR, not all users are allowed to prescribe drugs; this would require that the individual have the execute permission on the functionality to prescribe drugs.

The class of objects tends to be the usual focus of RBAC. A class of objects is a rather open definition. It is possible to define every type of attribute as a class of objects so that the user would have permissions at the most granular level. The reality is that these classes of objects are only as small as they need to be. That is, if there is no practical reason to identify two objects, then you can identify them together as an object. The class of objects does need to be reasonable to administer or efficient to operate. Another axiom is that the class of objects will have overlap but should not have overlap without good reason. These unnecessary overlaps would just cause administrative overhead without adding any value.

Use Case 14-1: Looking at Database Permissions

To see the power of permissions, look at a database: Those in billing need access to the billing data, whereas those in diagnosis and treatment should not see this information. Those in billing need to read clinical information in order to satisfy insurance requests, but they should not be allowed to create clinical information. Those in food service need access to the dietary needs, including knowledge of allergies, sensitivities, and food-related preferences.

This is a very high-level view of a simple RBAC system. Clearly, the data needs to be diced up smaller than this, and the operations such as update and delete need to be handled with care.

EXAM TIP Within an EHR, there are common user roles, also known as groups, such as Nurse, Physician, Physician Assistant, or Healthcare Unit Coordinator. HIT system administrators are able to set EHR permissions by specific functions that specific groups perform. For example, an attending physician may be permitted to read, write, and modify any clinical documentation on any patient under his care or whom he has been asked to consult on. A medical student may be permitted to read and write clinical documentation but not modify that "charting." Following an implementation of Computerized Physician Order Entry (CPOE), a Healthcare Unit Coordinator may no longer be able to write orders via the computer, but she would be privileged through the EHR to read any order on any patient on her unit.

Systems Have Roles

Note that roles are not just for human users. Systems, services, and other organizations can be assigned roles and permissions. For example, a prescription management system would recognize a specific EHR by the system authentication and, based on that system identity, find that the system is authorized to create new prescriptions or update prescriptions that it had created. This remote EHR would not be allowed to do any other permission. One graphic way to show which roles have access to which objects is a truth table.

Truth Tables

A *truth table* is simply a table that shows the roles in an organization and the class of object, with the actions allowed (such as Create, Read, Update, Delete, and Execute). Table 14-1 shows an example truth table. This example shows how different roles (rows in the table) are given different action rights (cell content) to the various classes of objects (columns in the table).

	Class of Objects					
Roles	**Billing Information**	**Demographics Information**	**General Clinical Information**	**Sensitive Clinical Information**	**Research Information**	**Dietary Information**
Registration desks	CRU	CRU				CRU
Dietary staff			R			CRU
General care provider		R	CR			CRU
Direct care provider	R	RU	CRU	CRU		CRU
Emergency care provider		R	CRU			CRU
Researcher					CRUD	
Patient or legal representative	CRU	CRU	RU	RU		CRU

Table 14-1 Example Truth Table

Multilevel Data Confidentiality

Simple RBAC is not sufficient in healthcare simply because the information has so many rules applied to it that there is no simple classification scheme that can be applied. There is a set of classes of data that requires more than the typical (normal) access control protections. These classes of data are called out in regulations such as U.S. 42 CFR Part 2,[29] which defines special handling for things such as drug-abuse and alcohol-abuse information when it is captured as part of a federally funded program. Individual states interpret these federal regulations in different ways. These are complex regulations that give us complex rules.

Some of these especially sensitive health topics are easier to handle than others. For example, it is rather easy to know whether your own organization includes federal funding of a drug-abuse program, but you still would need to differentiate that information gathered in general healthcare provision versus that which was discovered during a federally funded drug-abuse program. Where the sensitive health topics get more difficult for access control technology is when they are based on medical conditions such as HIV or sickle cell disease. These medical conditions are not always clear in every piece of health information, and humans are very good inference engines that can take multiple pieces of what seems to be normal health information and deduce that the patient is HIV positive, for example. This is where access control rules need to engage the same technology that clinical decision support systems (CDS) utilize.

Data Tagging with Sensitivity Codes

Some methods that can be used inside an EHR are to tag the data with sensitivity codes. The problem is that this tagging is being done using the current knowledge and current information in the patient chart. As you learn more about the sensitive topics, you learn what might expose the sensitive topic. As more information is gathered on the patient, you may be able to correlate that new information with historically not-sensitive information and expose sensitive topics. For these reasons, the tagging of health information, even inside a closed system like an EHR, is not a robust solution. Within a closed system, it may be the best solution. What is critical is the decision that is made upon disclosure, which must be made based on the best knowledge and information at the time.

Coding of Restricted Data

Sensitive health topics are usually identified with a confidentiality coding of "restricted." This identification does not indicate why the information is sensitive; for that, you would need to look at the policy that was used to declare that the information was restricted. The advantage of using a blunt code like "restricted" is that it doesn't expose the private condition, yet does tell the access control engine that there are special rules to be enforced.

Medical Records Regulations

Healthcare information is also ruled by regulations that are concerned not only with privacy but also with the quality and accuracy of the provision of healthcare. These regulations are not much different from any records management regulations, but their timeframes are greatly increased because they deal with a time frame of a human life span. In many cases, these regulations that mandate that records be maintained conflict with a patient's desire to have some healthcare episodes forgotten. Sometimes this can be handled through access control rules that will blind the information from the majority of potential uses. This is where the confidentiality coding of "very restricted" should be used.

Other Sources of Access Control Rules

There are other sources of rules that might need to be applied to healthcare information, such as the following:

- **Medical ethics**   Medical ethics standards show the need to have a conversation with a patient before exposing them to the results of some life-altering results. These are often implemented as temporal restrictions on the direct exposure to the patient, such as through a PHR or patient portal, until the general provider has had this discussion.

- **Court order**   Sometimes the courts will require the exposure of information to the courts or the blocking of exposure of information to anyone other than the courts. A special case is to protect a victim of domestic abuse. These cases are usually handled through nonautomated means.

Data Treated at the Highest Level of Confidentiality

Healthcare information, when communicated, needs to be protected at the highest level of confidentiality of any part of the information being communicated. This means that if a package of data is being sent to another party and most of the information is normal health information but one diagnosis is of a sensitive nature, then the whole package must be considered sensitive. If the receiving system cannot handle sensitive information, then this package cannot be sent as is. It might be possible to revise the sensitive information, but this cannot be done if it will change the authenticity of the original authored content.

As data are handled, including internal movement of data as well as data movement externally, care must be taken not to lose privacy controls. This means that healthcare information does need to contain sufficient metadata to indicate where the information came from, including specific identifiers that may be associated with access control rules. Note that although it may seem logical to have the metadata record the access control rules to be applied to the data, this is not a good solution for the long term. Policies change over time; information does not. Thus, it is important to maintain the access control rules in the policy database and have the rules point at the data the rules control. This allows for the policy to change while maintaining strict integrity on the healthcare information.

Purpose of Use

One type of context is the purpose of use, which is a specific parameter of a request for information or a request to have something done. It indicates why the request is being made and how the requester intends to use the information. A common purpose of use is for a patient's "treatment." That is, the user is asking for this information so that they can make clinical decisions related to treating the patient. If all requests were for diagnosis or treatment, then one would not need to indicate this value on each request. However, some requests for information might be for billing purposes, research purposes, population health purposes, or quality reporting. There is an emerging vocabulary around purpose of use, coming from the HL7® standards organization. Like all vocabulary, there is a meaning behind each item that both the requestor and the relying party should understand.

Patient Privacy

The biggest deviation from simple RBAC is that the information in an EHR is about a human subject and that human subject has rights and expectations about how the information is to be used. In many cases, these rights and expectations are well aligned, and there is little impact on the RBAC rules. In other cases, the deviations can be more difficult. Privacy rights are different around the globe. In some locations, they are very strict and powerful. Generally, the privacy rights fall into seven domains:

- The purpose for the data collection should be known, limited, and stated.
- The policies and practices for handling the data should be open and transparent.
- The collection of information is limited to the minimally needed information.
- The data collected should be as accurate as possible.
- The individual (patient) should have the right to see the data that has been collected and correct it if it is found to be inaccurate.
- The uses of the data should be recorded and accessible to the individual.
- The data should be controlled against any inappropriate use or access.

This list is often extended to requiring that the individual (patient) be fully informed before positively giving authorization for the use. This is the step that is often referred to as *consent* or *privacy consent* to differentiate it from "consent to diagnose and/or treat" or other cases where the patient positively authorizes something that is not privacy-related.

Privacy Consent Related to Purpose of Use and Access Control

Privacy consent, or privacy consent directive, is not a simple binary rule. Privacy consent can be a set of complex rules. Privacy consent is always a binding agreement between the individual and the controller of data about that individual. The data controller can be an individual healthcare practice but may also be a federation of multiple organizations (e.g., consent at the HIE level) or a service appointed by the patient. The binding agreement puts responsibilities upon the data controller, and thus consent rules are made up of rules that the data controller can enforce. This binding agreement needs to be captured in a way that not only meets the legal rules of evidence but also can be processed by access control enforcement, such as the policies in the IHE Basic Patient Privacy Consents (BPPC) profile.[30]

Privacy consent is distinct from privacy preferences, which are statements by the individual (patient) on how they want their data to be handled. Privacy preferences could be a very permissive set of rules or could be very restrictive, even unreasonable in the case of some individuals. Privacy preferences can be used by a data controller when formulating the binding privacy consent rules.

Where the privacy consent is aligned perfectly with organizational rules that RBAC enforces, there is no impact on the access control rules. This is the best case from a data controller perspective, because it requires no additional rules to be adhered to. In the United States, the Health Insurance Portability and Accountability Act (HIPAA) does not require a covered entity (the formal name for most data controllers in healthcare in the United States) to take on additional privacy consent rules but does give the patient the right to request their privacy preferences.

Use Case 14-2: Looking at Metadata

Some metadata explains where the data came from, some metadata explains who authored the data, and some metadata describes the type of data. The desired rule could identify a time frame that should be hidden, a type of data that should be hidden, data authored by a specific facility that should be hidden, or a specific object (report) that can be recognized by the unique identity value that should be hidden. The specific way that the privacy rules would be written would be based on the specific rule desired and the available metadata to act upon it. Note that privacy rules can leverage metadata that is not typically seen as specific to privacy.

The privacy consent is often implemented in a more generic way, as privacy rules or a privacy policy. In this case, privacy rules are special handling rules that are specific to that identified individual (patient). In this way, the privacy rules can incorporate obligation rules like "do not redisclose without getting new privacy consent from the individual."

Finally, privacy consent is often the same thing as a privacy authorization, such as when the patient authorizes a researcher to use the data for a research project. In terms of HIPAA, this is an *authorization*, but it is technically not any different from a special "Purpose of Use" in the rules of a privacy consent. That is, the patient consent authorizes some individuals or roles to have specific purpose-of-use access to their data or a subset of their data.

Privacy consent rules can be very specific rules. A common desire is to hide specific treatment episodes because of their socially stigmatizing nature. This can be included in the privacy consent rules in many ways. This is where privacy consent rules leverage metadata or the information attributes that describe the data.

Hint

When there is a need to directly bind a specific policy and a specific piece of data, the policy rules are written to identify the data to be controlled, rather than marking the data with the policy rules around how it can be used. This is an important policy pointer axiom that the policy rule should point at the data. Specifically, the data should not include policy rules. This is because policy rules tend to change over time, whereas data are a specific record at a point in time. In this way, the data stays constant over time, whereas the policy rules governing that data can change as the patient, regulation, or circumstances adjust as desired.

Summary of Basic Access Control

Access control consists of policies and access control information. The access control information falls into some general categories: patient, user, resource, and context. Policies are where all the logic resides (Figure 14-1). The access control information is simply available information that a policy may have included as part of the logic. For example, a consent policy may indicate that any data created during a specific time period in the past be kept very restricted to just the patient and the author of that data. It is the policy that is calling for the inspection of the access control information to determine what the access control rule will allow or deny. Thus, it is the policies that ultimately choose what information is needed. Policies are multiple levels deep, and thus higher-level policies will refer to the decisions made by lower-level policies; therefore, the highest-level policies are rationalizing between the decisions of the underlying policies.

Patient Information

The patient information includes different pieces of information about the patient, most importantly, the patient identifier, their admission status, and where they are located. The

Figure 14-1
Policies vs. information used by policies

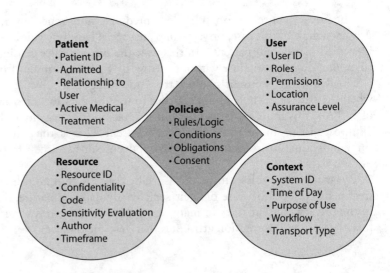

Patient
- Patient ID
- Admitted
- Relationship to User
- Active Medical Treatment

User
- User ID
- Roles
- Permissions
- Location
- Assurance Level

Policies
- Rules/Logic
- Conditions
- Obligations
- Consent

Resource
- Resource ID
- Confidentiality Code
- Sensitivity Evaluation
- Author
- Timeframe

Context
- System ID
- Time of Day
- Purpose of Use
- Workflow
- Transport Type

patient information may contain relationships to specific user identities such as "this user identification (ID) is the patient," "this user ID is the patient's general practitioner," or "this user ID is the legal guardian of the patient." The patient information does not contain the consent rules. Consent rules are policies and thus exist in the policy space. Consent policies may be managed differently, but they are logically policies, not information.

User Information

The user information clearly includes the user ID, the roles that are assigned, the permissions assigned to those roles, where the user ID exists, and what the level of assurance of the identity is.

Resource Information

The resource information is information about the healthcare information being requested, often called *metadata*. Most information has some unique identifier that may be an externally known identifier, like a laboratory order number, or an internally known item, like a database table entry. The confidentiality code is an assessment of the privacy risk, where the sensitivity evaluation would be a currently assessed value of how sensitive the information is. Policies will often reference the author of an object by individual or by their organization. Policies, especially privacy policies, sometimes will have rules about any information gathered or created during a specific period of time. There are other attributes about the resource that policies call upon that are not included here, including the complete chain of provenance.

Context Information

The context information is about this specific request here and now. It would include the system that is involved, the current time of day, the purpose of use for the request, an indicator of the workflow, and the security being used for transport. There are other attributes that policy may call upon that are considered context.

Policies: Where the Logic Resides

The important part to note is that policies are where the rules are. There may be multiple levels of rules, and there may be multiple locations where rules are managed. Policies will call upon information about the patient, user, resource, and context of the request. This makes up the space of access control information. For a more detailed discussion, see the IHE access control white paper[25] or other resources.[27, 28, 31]

Healthcare Information Exchange

Up to this point, I have discussed access control abstractly, mostly as a discussion about what happens inside an EHR. The implementation of access control within an EHR is an essential task in healthcare because it involves a patient. I will now cover how to extend access control to an HIE.[32] An HIE is simply an extension of the healthcare information across organizational boundaries, usually within a region, community, or beyond. The patient may have healthcare coverage in many geographic areas.

An important aspect of HIEs is that they are often made up of healthcare provider organizations that are otherwise competing for "customers" (patients) and "employees" (providers). This is not always the case, but it is so often the case that it affects the architecture decisions. When the different parties are not competing, they will more likely just use the same EHR system in a proprietary way. Thus, this section will focus on how to satisfy access control needs when the parties are distinct and likely competing. However, the fact that they are competing does not mean they do not get benefits from the HIE. Better care for patients is in the best interest of all parties.

Push vs. Pull in an HIE

There are two general methods of exchanging healthcare information.[32] One is where information is pushed from the organization that has the information to the organization that needs it, and the other is where the one that needs the information requests the information. The first case is often simply called *push*, and the second case is called *pull*.

Push Access Control in an HIE

In the case of a push, the access control decision is mostly made completely within the source organization. That is, the source organization has some workflow that determines that information needs to be sent somewhere. An access control decision is made based on all current policies, including some general knowledge about the recipient. Once the information is sent, it is mostly in the total control of the recipient and no longer in the control of the sender. There are exceptions to this. Utilizing callback technology such as digital rights management is an exception. These exceptions are not unique to push because pull can leverage them too; however, the exceptions must be agreed to by both the sender and the recipient.

Pull Access Control in an HIE

The rest of this chapter will mostly focus on the pull model of an HIE. The pull model offers the most complexity, and it benefits the most through the use of consistent access control models. The consistency is achieved through the use of the fundamentals that were already discussed using commonly available interoperability standards. These are considered commonly available because they are not unique to healthcare. Healthcare does, however, constrain these interoperability standards with specific vocabulary and behaviors.

Enforcement of Access Controls in an HIE

The enforcement of access control in an HIE is a group effort. All the parties involved in the HIE will get involved in some way with the access control enforcement. There are good resources[18, 25, 33, 34] that discuss access control in an HIE. There are models that indicate that the access control enforcement is the sender's responsibility, others that indicate it is the receiver's responsibility, and others that indicate that the HIE itself will enforce access control. When looked at closely, all of these are actually group efforts. Ultimately, the sender, the infrastructure, and the receiver each has a role in protecting the health information. These roles are further defined in the rule of HIE access control.

The First Rule of HIE Access Control

The first rule of HIE access control is this: If the one holding the health information is not satisfied with the access control information, then the healthcare information is simply not sent. This basic rule needs to be reiterated because many people get wrapped up in all the discussion about enabling access and forget that ultimately a deny decision is the starting point. Even if the requester has provided all the types of information that could be asked of them, the policy rules can still determine that the access control decision is "no." Ultimately, if there is no good reason to allow the information to be sent, then it clearly should not be sent. This blunt logic is not the logic that caregivers want to hear, but it is reality because sometimes their request is simply not allowed.

It is a policy decision on how this "no" is returned. The most secure way is to simply indicate no healthcare information exists, which includes denying that the patient even exists. There are others that want to enable smoother workflows through providing a hint that there is healthcare information available but the organization is not authorized to send it. The most secure method is total denial, because it doesn't expose any information, confirmed nor denied. However, there are different layers of security in an HIE. For example, if one can tell that the requesting system is a trusted system and that there are business rules in place that give assurances that the exposure is small and will be properly handled, permission might be given. Thus, a policy could determine based on the access control information what kind of a response is given.

The Second Rule of HIE Access Control

The second rule of HIE access control is this: Once the healthcare information has been transmitted, it is in the control of the recipient. This again is a rather basic rule, but it is important to the decision. If the sender is not confident that the recipient will properly handle the information, then the sender simply should not send the data (see the first rule). Thus, the sender needs to include access control rules that provide them with comfort that the recipient should be given a copy of the healthcare information. This is typically why the access control information includes the user and the context. The context speaks to the capabilities of the receiving system and how the healthcare information will be managed.

The user-based access control information speaks about the user, but it must be recognized that this is typically just the initial user who will be exposed to the information. You must recognize that for any purpose of use that includes treatment, the healthcare information disclosed will become part of the medical record at the recipient. Thus, a request for a purpose of use of "Treatment" is a request on behalf of the requesting medical record, not simply the user identified.

This rule is not as blunt as it appears; there are policies that can be communicated along with the healthcare information that would control the access at the recipient, but even in these cases, the sender must know that the recipient is going to enforce a policy before sending the healthcare information. There are standards-based methods to assure this.

Use Case 14-3: Negotiating the Policies

A policy negotiation can take place before the healthcare information is actually transferred. The policies that go along with the healthcare information are often referred to as *obligations* or *refrain policies*. The use of obligation or refrain is under the control of policies.

Everything is in the hands of the policies. These policies should incorporate federal regulations, state regulations, regional regulations, medical ethics, professional standards of practice, organizational rules, HIE rules of engagement, and the patient consent/authorizations. An HIE is really just an extension of the access control environment. The difference is that the policy space includes the whole of the HIE, including sending and receiving systems and users (recipients).

A specific example of this is a requirement of 42 CFR Part 2,[29] in which the data being communicated was gathered originally within a federally funded drug-abuse program. In this case, there is an obligation to not re-disclose the data without getting explicit privacy consent from the patient.

HIE Access Control Information

In an HIE, the access control information must come from the different parties in the HIE. This can be a challenge when communicating across organizational boundaries and with a competing organization. The interoperability standards used have been developed specifically with this in mind. The easiest way to describe this is through the example shown in Figure 14-2.

1. The user is authenticated, typically as part of their long-term session in the EHR.

2. At some point, the system queries the HIE and includes information about the user and context along with the query parameters requesting healthcare information, including the patient ID and type of data requested.

3. An access control service intercepts the transaction and inspects the system credentials that are used at the transport level, the user and context captured in the assertion, and the query parameters.

4. The access control service executes all relevant policies, including consent policies; if the policies determine that there is reason to deny access or no reason to allow access, then the access control service responds with no results found.

5. If the information is going forward, the query is forwarded to the resource that processes it normally.

6. The receiver returns the normal results.

The user identity and authentication steps are totally within the control of the organization where the user is using the EHR. It is typical of an HIE that each organization within the HIE is responsible for the user identities from that organization. In theory, there could

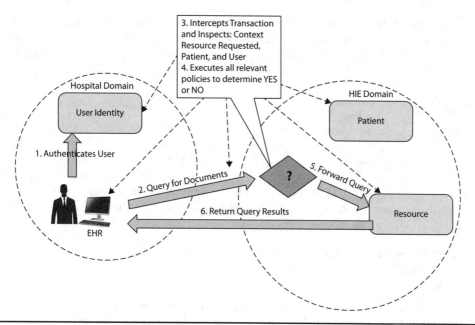

Figure 14-2 Simple HIE access control example

be a single user identity domain across the HIE, but this turns out to be too difficult to manage. Much of the concern is related to the fact that an HIE is often made up of competing organizations. Another important factor is that many of the users will have different identities within multiple organizations; these identities are different because they have different roles and responsibilities, and most importantly they are identities under the different organizations' operational environments, including medical records.

There is usually a unified patient identity domain, not just one. Unified means that there is some administrative set of rules and procedures used to create a cross-reference between the patient identifiers within each of the organizations, oftentimes with an HIE master identifier. Getting this cross-reference correct is important to access control, and specifically privacy, but is also very important for patient care and safety. There are many creative ways to do this cross-reference.

This simplified view presumes that the access control decision can be made by inspecting the query parameters and the resource access control information (metadata). Oftentimes, there needs to be more access control decisions on the return path (step 6) as well as within the EHR after the information is received. This simplified view also puts the access control decision within the HIE domain. It could be done in the hospital domain or in other types of resources. The only time that healthcare information will be returned is if the access control decision will allow it.

This simplified view shows a query and response, also known as a pull transaction. The same access control decisions can be made prior to a push transaction. The sender of the push transaction simply must predict who the user and their system capabilities are going to be. The sender clearly knows who the patient and resources are.

Each step of this use-case (1–6) would also be recorded by each system involved in an audit log. In this way, audit control can be used to confirm the system is working as expected, produce privacy reports for the patient, and support other surveillance responsibilities.

Metadata

In the context of access control, this chapter describes resource access control information, which is a specialization of more general-purpose metadata.[35] Metadata is associated with data to provide for specific data-handling purposes. These domains of data-handling purposes fall into some general categories. Each metadata element typically has more than one of these purposes, although there are some metadata elements that cover only one purpose. It is important to understand these domains and the purposes of metadata specific to an HIE.

- **Patient identity** This consists of characteristics that describe the subject of the data. This includes patient ID, patient name, and other patient identity–describing elements.

- **Provenance** This includes characteristics that describe where the data comes from. These items are highly influenced by medical records regulations. This includes human author, identification of the system that authored the data, the organization that authored the data, processor documents, successor documents, and the pathway that the data took.

- **Security and privacy** These are characteristics that are used by privacy and security rules to appropriately control the data. These values enable conformance to privacy and security regulations. These characteristics would be those referenced in privacy or security rules. These characteristics would also be used to protect against security risks to confidentiality, integrity, and availability.

- **Descriptive** This consists of characteristics used to describe the clinical value, so they are expressly healthcare-specific. These values are critical for query models and to enable workflows in all exchange models. This group must be kept to a minimum so that it does not simply duplicate the data and so it keeps risk to a minimum. Thus, the values tend to be from a small set of codes. Because this group is close to the clinical values, the group tends to have few mandatory items, allowing policy to not populate by choice. For healthcare data, this is typically very closely associated with the clinical workflows but also must recognize other uses of healthcare data.

- **Exchange** This consists of characteristics that enable the transfer of the data for both push-type transfers and pull-type transfers. These characteristics are used for the low-level automated processing of the data. These values are not the workflow routing but rather the administrative overhead necessary to make the transfer. This includes the document unique ID, location, size, types of data, and document format.

- **Object life cycle**   This consists of characteristics that describe the current life-cycle state of the data, including relationships to other data. This includes classic life-cycle states of created, published, replaced, transformed, and deprecated.

All proper metadata elements are indeed describing the data and are not a replacement for the data. Care should be taken to limit the metadata to the minimum metadata elements necessary to achieve the goal. Therefore, each metadata element must be considered relative to the risk of exposing it as metadata. A metadata element is defined to assure that when the element is needed, it is consistently assigned and processed. Not all metadata elements are required; indeed, some metadata elements would be used only during specific uses. For example, the metadata definition inside a controlled environment such as an EHR will be different from the metadata that is exposed in a transaction between systems or the metadata that describes a static persistent object.

User Identity in an HIE

User identity in an HIE is more complex than patient identity or resource information. Here is a case where managing users and their roles and permissions centrally to the HIE is simply not possible. Thus, there is a need to use federated identity. An HIE consists of multiple organizations (e.g., St. Mary Hospital and St. Luke Clinic) that are accessing each other through some HIE. Each organization needs a trust bond with the HIE. Such organizational trust is typically built through some operational certification and legal agreements. This is characterized in Figure 14-3.

For the purpose of use of "Treatment," the user identity asserted in a request for information is not as important in an HIE. This is not because user identity is not necessary but, rather, because most of the uses of an HIE are system to system or organization to organization. In this mode, the two systems (or organizations) need to trust that the

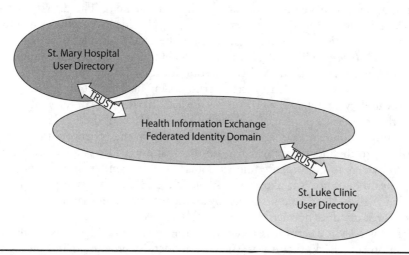

Figure 14-3   Characterization of user identity between two hospitals

other system has done the appropriate preconditions and will do the appropriate post-conditions. This is a policy: Do not let a system connect that you do not trust has the appropriate governance. In other words, you want to be sure the client machine has done the appropriate user authentication and authorization and is otherwise a secure system. The communication is highly authenticated on both the client and the server and is fully encrypted. The result returned to the client will be properly handled, the information will be exposed only to authorized individuals, and audit logs will be captured of all accesses from that point forward. If you add a user identity to this transaction, it is mostly for a little bit better audit log on the service side.

The other side of this is that even if a user identity were provided, it would be about the user who is currently connecting. The returned healthcare information will be stored in the requesting EHR, and others on the EHR will gain access. So, although the initial connection could be access-controlled, the other future accesses within the EHR must be trusted to do the right thing.

If you look at an EHR today, it has user authentication and access controls that have been built up over time to meet the requirements of being an EHR. The user authentication likely is highly flexible to support some rather complex workflows. One of the complex workflows is the ambulatory exam room, where an administrative person walks the patient to an exam room and sets up the exam room's terminal with the right patient and then "locks the screen." Next, the nurse comes in to take the chief complaints and vital signs. The nurse logs in, enters the data, and logs out. Next, the doctor comes in for the exam, again logs in to view and enter data, and logs out. Each of these people is authenticating, but the workflow on the desktop is all about the patient. These authentication methods and authorization methods are sufficient to protect the healthcare information that is maintained in that EHR. It is possible that an organization has gone to an enterprise-class authentication system like Microsoft Active Directory or more generically Kerberos or LDAP, but this is not required.

Let's look at interacting with an HIE or other organization that requires a SAML assertion, as shown in Figure 14-4 for identity management. The SAML assertion is issued by an identity provider that supports SAML. This identity provider is configured to understand specific services (relying parties) of the SAML assertions (known in SAML terms as an *audience*). The configuration will include mapping tables. Mapping tables indicate that when creating the SAML assertion for use within a specific HIE, some list of attributes needs to be added to the assertion. One likely attribute is the user's role, using a vocabulary known in the HIE versus the local EHR names of roles. Thus, a physician or other healthcare provider is known by a local EHR, but if the HIE wants the role to come from a different value set where the role within the HIE would be "caregiver," then it is up to the identity provider to do this mapping. This is a common thing for identity providers to do, because role vocabulary is not stable within any organization (not just healthcare) nor is it likely to be stable in the HIE. What is important to recognize is that the SAML assertion is issued by an identity provider that does this mapping. The user directory does not need to have the HIE roles.

When this SAML assertion is received by the service provider, it is validated. The validation process checks that it was issued by an identity provider that is on the trusted identity provider list. This allows the service provider to support many different identity

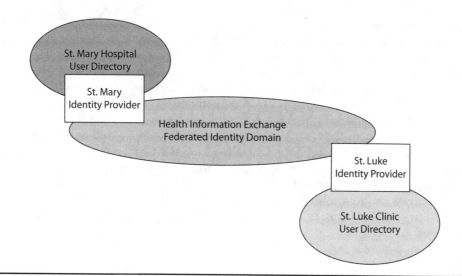

Figure 14-4 A representation of SAML

providers, likely one for each clinic and hospital connecting to the HIE. Given that all of those identity providers have normalized their roles to the HIE role vocabulary, it is clear what permissions the user should have in the context of this transaction in the HIE.

The identity provider functionality is available for most enterprise-class user-authentication systems. The WS-Trust protocol is commonly the one used to get SAML assertions issued. Federated identity decouples the task of identity management and the process of human authentication from claims of proof of authenticity within the HIE that are used for access control decisions and audit logging. The user management within any organization can be specific to that organization. Organizations are free to use proprietary means of user authentication, HTML-Forms, Kerberos, LDAP, OpenID, OAuth, or any other method. Through the conversion of these identities and authentication systems into an HIE agreed-upon federated identity, the HIE has a trusted identity system.

A few interoperability standards (such as X.509 digital certificates and SOAP) are used to support federated identity. They each have their strengths and weaknesses. The choice is often based on the technology used for the transport. Note that technologies such as SAML can bridge these environments through a trusted identity broker using WS-Trust, the interoperability standard. In this way, a user can use OpenID with their mobile device and talk to the web servers that the mobile device interfaces with. These web servers can bridge to SOAP transactions that need SAML assertions and secure e-mails that need an X.509 digital certificate.

Access Control Languages

Much standards work has been devoted to access control languages and ways to communicate policy. The most often cited is Extensible Access Control Markup Language (XACML).[35] XACML is both a policy encoding and an infrastructure for deploying access control decisions and enforcement. XACML can be used with any identity management system, although it is usually associated with SAML. There is no specific tie between SAML and XACML, although they do leverage much of the same infrastructure.

As a policy encoding language, XACML is powerful, made up of logic fundamentals that can be combined into any rules possible. The rules, however, need to invoke domain-specific vocabulary, such as for roles, permissions, object types, confidentiality codes, sensitivity evaluations, patient identities, and so on. There are also vocabularies for fractions of policies such as *purpose of use*, *obligations*, *refrain*, and *broadly applicable consent*. These vocabularies are the ones that healthcare-standards organizations are working to develop, with some of them well understood for HIE use. These vocabularies are needed regardless of whether XACML is used as the policy encoding language.

As an access control decision and enforcement system, XACML is a highly modular system; however, implementations are highly customized to fit into transactions and workflows.

Chapter Review

This chapter introduced the basics of access control and showed how to apply the controls to an EHR and a healthcare information exchange. The basics of access control rely on user identity provisioning and deprovisioning providing a specified level of assurance to each user identity. Human users will authenticate to computer systems using various types of authentication technology: combinations of something they have, something they know, and something they are. The access control decisions are based on the user identity but also information about the patient, the resources, and the context of the access to healthcare information. Policies are the rules that define what can and cannot be done and call upon the access control information to make the decisions. Patient privacy and consents are a subset of policies specific to that patient and their preferences. When extending access control across a healthcare information exchange, the various access control information comes together in a cooperative access control. The access control decision in an HIE delivers data only when the access control policies authorize the information to flow.

Questions

To test your comprehension of the chapter, answer the following questions and then check your answers against the list of correct answers that follows the questions.

1. What is the level of assurance of identity proofing that requires the presentation of a government-issued identity but does not require verification of that government-issued identity?

    A. Level 1

    B. Level 2

    C. Level 3

    D. Level 4

2. Identify the factors that a computer uses to authenticate a human user.

   A. Something you are, have, and know

   B. Something with an image of you on it

   C. Something that you know, like a secret

   D. None of the above

3. What does SAML do?

   A. Provisions user accounts

   B. Makes access control decisions

   C. Defines an identity claim

   D. Provides an audit logging system

4. What are the components of RBAC?

   A. Identity, permission, role

   B. Consent only

   C. Permission and consent

   D. Role and consent

5. What are the operations on a class of objects that make up a permission?

   A. Identity, authentication, authorization, and consent

   B. Authentication, authorization, and identity

   C. Consent, identity, and authorization

   D. Create, read, update, delete, and execute (aka CRUDE)

6. What is the policy pointer axiom?

   A. Data should not include the policy rules; the policy rules should point at the data they apply to.

   B. Data should always be pointed to in policies.

   C. Policy rules should never point to data.

   D. None of the above.

7. What is federated identity?

   A. It includes the concepts of authentication, authorization, and identity.

   B. It provides a mechanism for communicating claims of identity and authentication to a relying party in a way that can be understood and trusted.

   C. Identity can never be federated.

   D. None of the above.

8. What standard can be used to harmonize different identity and authentication systems?

   A. WS-Trust

   B. WAP

   C. Wi-Fi

   D. WEP

9. What authentication standard is best paired with FHIR®?

   A. SOAP

   B. kAuth

   C. OAuth

   D. Password

10. What is it called when one system asks another to enforce a policy fragment?

   A. Liability

   B. Obligation

   C. Commitment

   D. Permission

11. What is the critical fact about healthcare data that separates it from other data?

   A. It is large.

   B. It is detailed.

   C. It can't be changed or revoked.

   D. There is nothing special about healthcare data.

12. What type of security information is time of day?

   A. Permission

   B. Role

   C. Label

   D. Context

13. Which of the following is *not* a principle of privacy?

   A. The purpose for data collection should be known, limited, and stated.

   B. An individual (patient) should have the right to see the data that has been collected and correct it if it is found to be inaccurate.

   C. The data should be controlled against any inappropriate use or access.

   D. The data must be digitally signed.

Answers

1. **B.** Level 2 requires presenting government-issued identification that includes your full name, picture, and address or nationality; it does not require that the identity be proven as authentic.

2. **A.** Authentication factors are something you are (biometric), have (hardware token), or know (password).

3. **C.** SAML defines a way to convey an identity and authentication claim from one party to a relying party.

4. **A.** RBAC is a binding between an identity, role, and permission. Thus, it does not include consent.

5. **D.** The fundamental actions that make up a permission are create, read, update, delete, and execute (aka CRUDE).

6. **A.** Data should not include the policy rules; the policy rules should point at the data to which they apply.

7. **B.** Federated identity keeps local the identity management task by providing a mechanism for communicating claims of identity and authentication to a relying party in a way that can be understood and trusted.

8. **A.** WS-Trust is the standard used to harmonize different identity and authentication systems.

9. **C.** OAuth is considered the best security protocol for use with HL7 FHIR® along with HTTPS. Note that client certificates and SAML are also used.

10. **B.** When a sending system needs a receiving system to enforce a policy fragment, and it knows that the receiving system can enforce this policy fragment, then it would convey the policy fragment using an obligation. An obligation might be explicit or implied.

11. **C.** Healthcare data can't be changed or revoked, thus it is extra important to protect against inappropriate disclosure. Healthcare data also are often used to make life-critical or lifesaving decisions.

12. **D.** Time of day is part of the context of the transaction.

13. **D.** Digital signatures are not a principle of privacy. Digital signatures are used to provide proof of provenance, or proof of action. They might be used to sign a privacy consent.

References

1. The White House. (2011, April). *National strategy for trusted identities in cyberspace: Enhancing online choice, efficiency, security, and privacy.* Accessed from www.nist.gov/sites/default/files/documents/2016/12/08/nsticstrategy.pdf.

PART III

2. Burr, W. E., Dodson, D. F., Newton, E. M., Perlner, R. A., Polk, W. T., Gupta, & Nabbus, E. A. (2013). *Electronic authentication guideline* (NIST SP 800-63-2). Accessed from http://nvlpubs.nist.gov/nistpubs/SpecialPublications/NIST .SP.800-63-2.pdf.

3. Kantara Initiative. (2009). *Identity assurance framework: Assurance levels, draft 04.* Accessed from http://kantarainitiative.org/confluence/download/ attachments/38371432/Kantara+IAF-1200-Levels+of+Assurance.pdf.

4. Integrating the Healthcare Enterprise (IHE). (2012). *Enterprise user authentication (EUA) profile.* Accessed from www.ihe.net/uploadedFiles/Documents/ITI/IHE_ ITI_TF_Vol1.pdf.

5. IHE. (2012). *Cross-enterprise user assertion (XUA) profile.* Accessed from www.ihe .net/uploadedFiles/Documents/ITI/IHE_ITI_TF_Vol1.pdf.

6. ASTM International. (1998). *Standard guide for user authentication and authorization* (ASTM E1985-98). Accessed from www.astm.org/Standards/E1985.htm.

7. ASTM International. (1995). *Standard guide for electronic authentication of health care information* (ASTM E1762-95). Accessed from www.astm.org/Standards/ E1762.htm.

8. Chokhani, S., Ford, W., Sabett, R., Merrill, C., & Wu, S. (2003). *Internet X.509 public key infrastructure certificate policy and certification practices framework* (RFC 3647). Accessed from http://tools.ietf.org/html/rfc3647.

9. ISO. (2013). *Health informatics: Public key infrastructure—Part 1: Overview of digital certificate services* (ISO 17090-1:2013). Available at www.iso.org/iso/home/ store/catalogue_tc/catalogue_detail.htm?csnumber=63019.

10. Joint NEMA-MITA/COCIR/JIRA Security and Privacy Committee (SPC). (2007). *Management of machine authentication certificates.* Accessed from www .medicalimaging.org/wp-content/uploads/2011/02/CertificateManagement- 2007-05-Published.pdf.

11. Hardt, D. (Ed.). (2012). *The OAuth 2.0 authorization framework* (RFC 6749). Accessed from https://tools.ietf.org/html/rfc6749.

12. Hammer-Lahav, E. (Ed.). (2010) *The OAuth 1.0 protocol* (RFC 5849). Accessed from https://tools.ietf.org/html/rfc5849.

13. OpenID HEART Workgroup. (n.d.). *What Is HEART WG?* Accessed from http:// openid.net/wg/heart/.

14. IHE. (2015). *Internet user assertion profile: Profile on OAuth 2.0 for use with FHIR.®* Accessed from www.ihe.net/uploadedFiles/Documents/ITI/IHE_ITI_TF_Vol1.pdf.

15. SMART Health IT. (n.d.). *An app platform for healthcare.* Accessed from http:// smarthealthit.org/.

16. IHE. (2012). *Personnel white pages (PWP) profile.* Accessed from www.ihe.net/ uploadedFiles/Documents/ITI/IHE_ITI_TF_Vol1.pdf.

17. ISO. (2013). *Health informatics: Directory services for healthcare providers, subjects of care and other entities* (ISO 21091:2013). Available at www.iso.org/iso/home/store/catalogue_ics/catalogue_detail_ics.htm?csnumber=51432

18. IHE. (2015). *IHE IT infrastructure technical framework supplement: Healthcare provider directory (HPD)*. Accessed from www.ihe.net/uploadedFiles/Documents/ITI/IHE_ITI_Suppl_HPD.pdf.

19. IHE. (2012). *Audit trail and node authentication (ATNA) profile*. Accessed from www.ihe.net/uploadedFiles/Documents/ITI/IHE_ITI_TF_Vol1.pdf.

20. Dierks, T., & Rescorla, E. (2008). *The transport layer security (TLS) protocol: Version 1.2* (RFC 5246). Accessed from http://tools.ietf.org/html/rfc5246.

21. SAML v2.0. Accessed from https://wiki.oasis-open.org/security/FrontPage.

22. DeCouteau, D. (Ed.). (n.d.). *XSPA profile of SAML v2.0 for healthcare version 1.0.* Accessed from https://wiki.oasis-open.org/security/XSPASAML2Profile.

23. Moehrke, J. (2009). *Healthcare security/privacy blog*. Accessed from http://HealthcareSecPrivacy.blogspot.com.

24. Incits (International Committee for Information Technology Standards). (2004). *Information technology: Role-based access control*. https://standards.incits.org/apps/group_public/project/details.php?project_id=1658.

25. IHE. (2012). *Access control white paper*. See Caumanns, J., Kuhlisch, R., Pfaff, O., & Rode, O. (2009, Sept. 28). *IHE IT infrastructure technical framework white paper: Access control*. Accessed from www.ihe.net/Technical_Framework/upload/IHE_ITI_TF_WhitePaper_AccessControl_2009-09-28.pdf.

26. ISO. (2116). *ISO/CD 13606-4: Health informatics: Electronic health record communication: Part 4: Security*. Available at www.iso.org/iso/home/store/catalogue_ics/catalogue_detail_ics.htm?csnumber=62306.

27. ASTM International. (2009). *Standard guide for information access privileges to health information* (ASTM E1986-09). Accessed from www.astm.org/Standards/E1986.htm.

28. ASTM International. (2007). *Standard guide for privilege management infrastructure* (ASTM E2595-07). Accessed from www.astm.org/Standards/E2595.htm.

29. Electronic Code of Federal Regulations. (1987). *Confidentiality of alcohol and drug abuse patient records, 42 CFR Part 2*. Accessed from www.ecfr.gov/cgi-bin/text-idx?rgn=div5;node=42%3A1.0.1.1.2.

30. IHE. (2012). *Basic patient privacy consents (BPPC)*. Accessed from www.ihe.net/uploadedFiles/Documents/ITI/IHE_ITI_TF_Vol1.pdf.

31. ISO. (2014). *ISO 22600-1:2014: Health informatics: Privilege management and access control: Part 1: Policy overview and management*. Available at www.iso.org/iso/home/store/catalogue_ics/catalogue_detail_ics.htm?csnumber=62653.

PART III

32. Witting, K., & Moehrke, J. (2012, Jan. 24). *IHE IT infrastructure white paper—Health information exchange: Enabling document sharing using IHE profiles.* Accessed from www.ihe.net/Technical_Framework/upload/IHE_ITI_White-Paper_Enabling-doc-sharing-through-IHE-Profiles_Rev1-0_2012-01-24.pdf.

33. IHE IT Infrastructure Technical Committee. (2008, Dec. 2). *IHE IT white paper: Template for XDS affinity domain deployment planning.* Accessed from www.ihe.net/Technical_Framework/upload/IHE_ITI_TF_WhitePaper_AccessControl_2009-09-28.pdf.

34. Scholl, M., Stine, K., Lin, K., & Steinberg, D. (2010). *Security architecture design process for health information exchanges (HIEs).* NIST IR7497. Accessed from http://nvlpubs.nist.gov/nistpubs/Legacy/IR/nistir7497.pdf.

35. Moehrke, J. (2012, May 4). *Healthcare metadata.* Available at https://healthcaresecprivacy.blogspot.com/2012/05/healthcare-metadata.html.

CHAPTER 15

Assuring the Health Insurance Portability and Accountability Act Compliance

Chris Apgar

In this chapter, you will learn how to

- Describe, at an introductory level, the legal requirements that health IT (HIT) professionals need to be aware of
- Define the terms business associate (BA), covered entity (CE), privacy, security, and protected health information (PHI)
- Identify legal documentation requirements—what needs to be included in application development to meet legal requirements
- Understand the use of BA contracts, creation of limited data sets, and requirements related to the reduction of legal risk as HIT professionals work with healthcare organizations and vendor partners
- Describe the implications for health IT on the necessary requirements to assure privacy and security for electronic healthcare information

Introduction to the Healthcare Legal Environment

The healthcare regulatory environment is ever-changing and requires frequent monitoring to stay ahead of regulatory deadlines. The most significant change in healthcare law as it relates to privacy, security, and the exchange of administrative health data (e.g., claims, remittance advices, eligibility determinations, etc.) was the Health Insurance Portability and Accountability Act (HIPAA) of 1996 Administrative Simplification provisions.[1] Since then, privacy- and security-related requirements have expanded due to the passage of other federal and state laws.

This chapter focuses primarily on the legal requirements related to HIPAA[2] including the HIPAA Privacy Rule (45 CFR Part 160 and Part 164, Subpart E), the HIPAA Security

Rule (Part 164, Subpart C), the HIPAA Breach Notification Rule (45 CFR Part 164, Subpart D), the HIPAA Enforcement Rule (45 CFR Part 160), the Health Information Technology for Economic and Clinical Health (HITECH) Act (PL 111-5, Division A, Title XIII, Subpart D), and the Omnibus Rule of 2013 that amended HIPAA to reflect regulatory changes included in the HITECH Act as well as what can be termed as housekeeping.[3] It is important to keep in mind that the HIPAA Administrative Simplification provisions address more than privacy and security. They also establish rules related to the transmission of healthcare administrative data and define national identifiers for employers, healthcare providers, and health plans (see 45 CFR Part 162).

HIT professionals must thoroughly understand the transaction, code-set, and national-identifier rules and related transaction and code sets specifications when developing claims adjudication systems, online administrative transactions, and other applications related to nonclinical data exchange. Most HIPAA legal requirements, such as business associate contracts, fall under the umbrella of privacy and security—hence the focus on privacy and security in this chapter.

Congress and state legislative assemblies continue to pass statutes that may impact the legal side of the healthcare regulatory equation. Also, federal and state agencies periodically revise administrative rules and issue guidance to the healthcare industry. These changes often impact the legal requirements healthcare organizations are subject to.

HIPAA, HITECH Act, and Omnibus Rule Overview[2]

The purpose of this chapter is to summarize the requirements of the HIPAA Privacy, Security, and Breach Notification Rules, the HITECH Act, and the Omnibus Rule requirements, and what rules take precedence when state laws differ from HIPAA and HITECH. You can refer to the listed requirements when reviewing existing privacy and security programs and regulatory compliance.

Covered entities are required to adhere to the complete HIPAA Privacy, Security, and Breach Notification Rules as modified by the HITECH Act. A *covered entity (CE)* can be a health plan (public or private), a healthcare provider who exchanges (directly or indirectly) HIPAA-covered transactions, or a healthcare clearinghouse. CEs can be both CEs and business associates. CEs are subject to the statutory provisions and the rule provisions in general, but many CEs are not subject to all provisions of the rules. As an example, there are specific requirements included that only health plans must follow, others that only healthcare providers must follow, and another set of provisions to which only healthcare clearinghouses are required to adhere.

Business associates are required to adhere to the use and disclosure provisions of the HIPAA Privacy Rule and the complete HIPAA Security Rule and Breach Notification Rule (HITECH Act requirement). A *business associate (BA)* is a third party that uses, discloses, maintains, or transmits protected health information on behalf of a CE or on behalf of another BA (e.g., BA subcontractor). Examples of BAs include billing agencies, electronic health record (EHR) vendors, third-party administrators, health information organizations (HIOs), and accountable-care organizations (ACOs).

The Omnibus Rule of 2013 greatly expanded the number of business associates who are required to adhere to the use and disclosure provisions of the HIPAA Privacy Rule, the HIPAA Security Rule and the HIPAA Breach Notification Rule. The rule expanded the definition of business associates to include business associate subcontractors. A business associate subcontractor is a business associate that uses, discloses, maintains, or transmits protected health information on behalf of a business associate who may or may not directly contract with a covered entity.

Business associate subcontractors may themselves contract with downstream business associate subcontractors. As an example, if an electronic health record vendor contracts with a cloud vendor to provide data backup support and the data backed up is the protected health information stored in the electronic health record, the cloud data backup vendor would be a business associate subcontractor. If the cloud vendor subcontracted with a hosting vendor to provide additional backup support in an area geographically different than the cloud vendor's servers, the hosting vendor would be a business associate subcontractor of the cloud vendor. Business associate subcontractors are required to adhere to the use and disclosure provisions of the HIPAA Privacy Rule, the HIPAA Security Rule, and the HIPAA Breach Notification Rule by statute and rule, which are the same compliance requirements that business associates are required to comply with.

Protect health information (PHI) is individually identifiable health information that can be used to identify an individual and that individual's past, present, or future medical condition (acute and mental health). PHI is made up of specific identifiers listed in the HIPAA Administrative Simplification provisions. PHI includes demographic data in addition to healthcare-related data.

 NOTE This chapter is not intended to represent legal advice. If questions arise regarding the summary information presented, CEs and BAs are encouraged to refer back to the HIPAA Privacy, Security, Breach Notification, and Enforcement Rules as amended by the HITECH Act and the Omnibus Rule, other applicable state and federal privacy and security laws, and/or to contact legal counsel.

Legal Documents Review

HIPAA, the HITECH Act, and the Omnibus Rule include requirements related to the construction of several legal documents. One of the most significant legal documents referenced is the BA contract. A BA contract is a legally binding contract which spells out the privacy and security standards that BAs and their third-party vendors are required to implement and adhere to.

The HIPAA Privacy Rule also includes requirements related to the construction of authorization forms and the Notice of Privacy Practices. CEs may generate other legal documents to implement requirements outlined in the HIPAA Privacy, Security, and Breach Notification Rules, such as consent forms and requests for a copy of an individual's designated record set (DRS; medical record or claims record).

HIPAA Administrative Simplification Provisions

The Administrative Simplification Provisions of HIPAA were a part of the original legislation that was passed and signed into law in 1996. The statute was codified in federal regulations 45 CFR Parts 160, 162, and 164. 45 CFR Part 160 can be described as the general rules, definitions, and requirements governing all published HIPAA rules and includes the HIPAA Enforcement Rule. 45 CFR Part 160 includes general definitions, describes when state law preempts HIPAA, describes when the U.S. Department of Health and Human Services has authority to audit covered entities and business associates, and other general provisions that form the "rules of the road" that apply to Part 160 and the remaining Administrative Simplification provisions. 45 CFR Part 162 includes the Transactions and Code Sets Rule and the National Identifiers Rules. (This regulation is not addressed in this chapter.) 45 CFR Part 164 includes the Privacy Rule, the Security Rule, and the Breach Notification Rule.

State Law Preemption: 45 CFR 160.203

The provisions of the HIPAA Privacy Rule are preempted when state law is more stringent than the provisions of the Privacy Rule. "More stringent" is defined as providing greater protection of an individual's PHI or providing an individual greater access to their PHI.

If state law is contrary to HIPAA and is not more stringent, HIPAA preempts state law. *Contrary* is defined as a condition that would make it impossible for a CE to comply with HIPAA and state law. Certain state laws that allow collection of PHI for specific purposes, such as for public health or health oversight, are not preempted by HIPAA. If the Secretary of HHS determines that a state law is contrary to HIPAA, before the law can be effective it must be approved as an exception to HIPAA. Certain state laws, such as the monitoring and collection of PHI related to controlled substances, must be approved by the Secretary of HHS prior to the collection of PHI by states. Even when exemption has been granted, the Secretary may later revoke such exemption.

It's important to keep in mind that other federal statutes may impact which steps covered entities and business associates need to attend to when it comes to regulatory compliance. As an example, 42 CFR Part 2[4] includes more stringent requirements for protection patient information related to alcohol and chemical dependency treatment. In 2016 the U.S. Department of Health and Human Services and the Federal Trade Commission issued guidance regarding the intersection of HIPAA compliance requirements and compliance with the Federal Trade Commission's rules.

HIPAA Privacy Rule: 45 CFR Part 164, Subpart E

45 CFR Part 164, Subpart E, "Privacy of Individually Identifiable Health Information," is better known as the HIPAA Privacy Rule. Subpart E defines the privacy requirements CEs must adhere to. Especially important are the sections that outline the requirements related to the use and disclosure of PHI, individual privacy rights, and administrative requirements related to privacy. BAs and BA subcontractors are required to adhere to the use and disclosure provisions of Subpart E pursuant to the HITECH Act.

There is some duplication or joint privacy and security compliance requirements that are articulated in the HIPAA Privacy Rule and the HIPAA Security Rule. This includes training requirements, BA contracting requirements, development of policies and procedures, and so forth. The HIPAA Security Rule citations included in this section can be directly matched to requirements found in the HIPAA Security Rule.

Use and Disclosure of PHI: 45 CFR 164.502(a)

CEs and BAs are permitted to disclose PHI to an individual; for treatment, payment, and healthcare operations; when authorized by the patient/member or authorized representative; and to friends and family (as long as the patient/member is allowed the opportunity to object to such release). In addition, certain portions of an individual's PHI can be disclosed in the CE's facility directory. A facility directory is usually maintained in hospitals and other inpatient care settings. It may include the individual or patient's name, the individual's location in the CE's facility, and the individual's condition described in general terms that does not communicate specific medical information about the individual and the individual's religious affiliation. The CE may disclose this information to clergy and if asked for the information by a visitor. The CE can only disclose religious affiliation to members of the clergy. The individual may request his or her name not be included in the facilities directory.

Minimum Necessary: 45 CFR 164.502(b)

CEs and BAs are required to disclose only the minimum amount of PHI necessary to satisfy the reason for which the PHI is disclosed. The minimum necessary standard does not apply for treatment, when required by law, when disclosed to the Office of Civil Rights (OCR), for disclosures related to an individual or the individual's personal representative authorizations, and when disclosed pursuant to provisions of the HIPAA Privacy Rule to comply with the Privacy Rule.

BA Contracts: 45 CFR 164.504(e), 45 CFR 164.308(b), 45 CFR 164.314(a)

CEs and BAs are mutually responsible for entering into formal contracts or other written agreements that clearly define a BA's relationship with a CE and what PHI will be used and disclosed between a CE and BA. BA contracts (private) or other written arrangement (government) must require the BA to comply with the HIPAA Privacy Rule. CEs are required to reasonably ensure that BAs adhere to the provisions of the HIPAA Privacy Rule. In addition to the requirements included in the contract or other written arrangement as defined pursuant to 45 CFR 164.314(a), 45 CFR 164.308(b), and 45 CFR 164.504(e), the contract must specify that the BA support the CE when honoring patients' privacy rights.

Consent: 45 CFR 164.506

A CE is not required to obtain an individual's consent prior to sharing PHI for treatment, payment, or healthcare operations. Consent in this context applies only to release of PHI for treatment, payment, and healthcare operations.

Authorization Requirements: 45 CFR 164.508

Unless specifically allowed pursuant to the HIPAA Privacy Rule, disclosures of PHI are not allowed without specific authorization of the individual. This includes psychotherapy notes. A valid authorization needs to be specific and limited by time or event.

The Omnibus Rule further defines "time" and "event," giving "infinity" and "death" as examples. Authorization is required for the use of PHI for research purposes unless an institutional review board (IRB) or privacy board approves the use of PHI for research without authorization. A CE may not condition treatment on providing authorization unless the treatment is related to research (45 CFR 164.512(i)).

Further rules govern the manner in which CEs can use PHI for marketing purposes. The use of PHI for research must clearly define the purpose of such release. Marketing as defined pursuant to HIPAA requires patient authorization with limited exceptions and sale of PHI is prohibited with limited exceptions without individual authorization. Under HIPAA, an individual can object to the publication of their PHI in a facility directory.

Release Without Consent or Authorization: 45 CFR 164.512

A CE is permitted to release PHI without consent or authorization:

- To a public health authority
- To a public authority for child abuse or neglect reasons
- If the person is subject to the Food and Drug Administration (FDA) rules for tracking recalls of prescription medication, reporting adverse events resulting from certain forms of treatment, etc.
- If an individual presents for treatment of a communicable disease
- Reporting a medical incident related to a worksite injury
- In the event of domestic violence and when a personal representative is suspected of abusing or neglecting a patient
- In judicial and administrative proceedings
- When disclosing PHI to law enforcement authorities

CEs are authorized to release PHI for healthcare oversight activities to the following entities:

- The healthcare system
- Government benefit programs
- Entities subject to government oversight activities
- Entities subject to civil laws where such release is necessary to determine compliance with civil laws

Avert a Serious Threat to Safety: 45 CFR 164.512(j)

A CE may release PHI if, in the professional judgment of the CE, such release will prevent a serious threat to public safety or to the safety of another.

Disclosure for Specialized Government Functions: 45 CFR 164.512(k)

A CE may release PHI for the following purposes:

- Military activity
- Medical suitability determinations (State Department)
- National security or intelligence activity
- Correctional institutions or law enforcement custodial situations
- Protective services for the President and others
- CEs that are governmental programs providing public benefits

Limited Data Set: 45 CFR 164.514(e)

CEs may use or disclose a limited data set if the CE enters into a data-use agreement with the limited-data-set recipient. A limited data set includes PHI but excludes the following identifiers of the individual or the individual's relatives, employers, or household members:

- Name
- Postal address information, other than town or city, state, and ZIP code
- Telephone numbers
- Medical-record numbers
- Health plan beneficiary numbers
- Account numbers
- Certificate/license numbers
- Vehicle identifiers and serial numbers including license-plate numbers
- Web addresses
- Internet protocol (IP) address numbers
- Device identifiers and serial numbers
- Full-face photographic images and any comparable images
- Biometric identifiers, including finger and voice prints

CEs may use or disclose a limited data set only for the purposes of research, public health, or healthcare operations.

The HITECH Act requires CEs to disclose a limited data set instead of adhering to the minimum necessary standard if feasible until OCR formally defines "minimum necessary." At this time, OCR has not defined "minimum necessary."

HIPAA defines ways in which a CE may use certain PHI for fundraising purposes and underwriting.

PART III

Notice of Privacy Practices: 45 CFR 164.520

A healthcare provider must present a notice of privacy practices to a patient during first encounter and make every effort to obtain written verification from the patient that the notice of privacy practices was presented to the patient. Health plans are required to mail notices of privacy practices to participating members. Health plans are not required to obtain written verification from members that they received a copy of the notice. CEs are required to notify individuals when significant changes are made to the notice. If the CE maintains a web site, the notice must be prominently posted on the web site and posted publicly in a public location at healthcare provider clinics, hospitals, etc.

Patient Privacy Rights

CEs, and BAs on behalf of CEs, are required to honor certain patient privacy rights that are included in the HIPAA Privacy Rule. Those privacy rights include entitlement to

- Request restrictions on who can access a patient's record or what may not be disclosed to a third party (45 CFR 164.522(a))
- Request confidential communications (45 CFR 164.522(b))
- Obtain a copy or view designated record set (DRS; medical record) in paper or electronic form (45 CFR 164.524)
- Obtain an accounting of disclosures for purposes other than treatment, payment, or health care operations, when specifically authorized by the patient (45 CFR 164.528)
- File a complaint with the CE or the Office for Civil Rights (OCR) (45 CFR 164.530(d))

Privacy Official and Security Official: 45 CFR 164.530(a), 45 CFR 164.308(a)(2)

A CE must appoint a privacy official who is responsible for overseeing the CE's privacy program and a security official who is responsible for overseeing the CE's or BA's security program.

Workforce Training: 45 CFR 164.530(b), 45 CFR 164.308(a)(5)

A CE must provide privacy and security training to the workforce. BAs are required to provide security training to the workforce. The workforce includes employees, temporary employees, volunteers, and contracted employees.

Standard Safeguards: 45 CFR 164.530(c)

A CE must implement policies, procedures, and practices that reasonably ensure administrative, technical, and physical security of all PHI regardless of the form in which the PHI is stored.

Sanctions: 45 CFR 164.530(e), 45 CFR 164.308(a)(1)

A CE must provide for workforce sanctions in the event of a violation of the Privacy Rule, the Security Rule, or a CE's privacy and security policies, procedures, or practices. BAs are required to provide for workforce sanctions for failure to comply with the Security Rule.

Privacy and Security Policies and Procedures: 45 CFR 164.530(i), 45 CFR 164.316

CEs and BAs are required to develop and implement privacy and security policies and procedures that fully implement the requirements of the Privacy Rule, the Security Rule, and the Breach Notification Rule. CEs and BAs are required to periodically review and update policies and procedures to accommodate changes in business practices and law. CEs are also required to update and distribute their notice of privacy practices if changes in policy and procedure materially impact the provisions of the notice.

HIPAA Security Rule: 45 CFR Part 164, Subpart C

Under 45 CFR Part 164, Subpart C, "Security Standards for the Protection of Electronic Protected Health Information," CEs and BAs are required to comply with all standards. If an implementation specification is required, CEs and BAs must comply with the implementation specification. The following codes are used for the implementation specifications described in the sections that follow:

- **Required (R)**   The implementation specification must be implemented/ adhered to.
- **Addressable (A)**   Based on the risk analysis (see 45 CFR 164.308(a)(1)(ii) (A); CEs and BAs are required to conduct a risk analysis periodically), the CE or BA must implement/adhere to the implementation specification, implement/ adhere to an equivalent security safeguard, or document why the implementation specification will not be implemented/adhered to (the reason cannot be solely based on the cost of implementation/adoption).

Administrative Safeguards: 45 CFR 164.308

The administrative safeguards section of the HIPAA Security Rule addresses what can be best described as the people side of security. It is the longest section in the rule and one of the more important sections to pay attention to. Information security is more often tied to workforce compliance than the technology that has been deployed to secure CE and BA infrastructure. The best antimalware or the best firewall may be implemented, but if administrative security is lax, it may lead to breaches of PHI related to ignorance or carelessness on the part of the workforce.

Security Management Process: 45 CFR 164.308(a)(1)

This is the first administrative safeguards standard. The standard requires the implementation of policies and procedures to prevent, detect, contain, and correct security violations.

- **Risk analysis (R)** Need to complete a risk analysis periodically to assess security risks to the organization.
- **Risk management (R)** Need to establish a risk-management program that adequately implements the risk analysis findings; evaluates security incidents as they occur; and takes appropriate mitigating action.
- **Information system activity review (R)** Software applications, network servers, etc., need to be configured to create audit trails that track activities involving electronic PHI.

Assigned Security Responsibility: 45 CFR 164.308(2)

All CEs and BAs are required to appoint a security official. The security official is responsible for overseeing CEs' and BAs' information security program including the development of policies, staff training, and ensuring sanctions for violations occur consistently and in a timely manner.

Workforce Security: 45 CFR 164.308(a)(3)

This standard requires the implementation of policies and procedures to reasonably ensure that all CE and BA workforce members have appropriate access to electronic PHI (ePHI), and to prevent PHI access to workforce members who should not have access.

- **Authorization and/or supervision (A)** Processes/policies need to be implemented that provide for appropriate workforce supervision when accessing ePHI.
- **Workforce clearance procedure (A)** Need to implement policies that reasonably ensure workforce access to ePHI is appropriate.
- **Termination procedures (A)** Policies/procedures need to be implemented that reasonably ensure workforce access to ePHI is terminated when the workforce member is terminated.

Information Access Management: 45 CFR 164.308(a)(4)

The next standard requires the implementation of policies and procedures related to authorization of access to electronic PHI.

- **Access authorization (A)** Policies/procedures need to be implemented that govern authorization to access ePHI.
- **Access establishment and modification (A)** Policies/procedures need to be implemented that outline how access to ePHI is granted and modified to meet minimum necessary requirements.

Security Awareness and Training: 45 CFR 164.308(a)(5)

The following requirements were included in this subsection of the Security Rule.

- **Security reminders (A)**   Periodic security reminders need to be distributed to all workforce members.

- **Protection from malicious software (A)**   Antimalware software needs to be acquired, regularly updated, and used to ensure malware does not infect the network, applications, hardware, and portable media.

- **Log-in monitoring (A)**   An audit trail needs to be created that records when a workforce member logs on to the network or a software application.

- **Password management (A)**   Policies/procedures need to be implemented that assist in proper password management (i.e., creation, periodic changes, etc.).

Security Incident Procedures: 45 CFR 164.308(a)(6)

CEs and BAs are required to implement policies and procedures and develop an incident response plan to address security incidents. Examples of security incidents that do not involve the breach of PHI include transmission of unencrypted PHI, and a denial-of-service attack that shuts down a CE's network.

Contingency Plan: 45 CFR 164.308(a)(7)

This standard requires implementation of policies and procedures that define how a CE or BA will respond to an emergency or other disaster that could damage systems that store and utilize electronic PHI.

- **Data backup plan (R)**   Need to implement data backup and recovery processes that provide for the backing up of ePHI and proper recovery processes so the data can be recovered if data is corrupted or lost.

- **Disaster recovery plan (R)**   Disaster recovery plans need to be developed that clearly outline how critical data are to be recovered in the event of a disaster.

- **Emergency mode operation plan (business continuity plan) (R)**   Plans need to be implemented that allow access to critical ePHI in the event of a disaster and while operating in an emergency mode.

- **Testing and revision procedure (A)**   Need to implement policies/procedures that define periodic testing activity for the disaster recovery plan and the emergency mode operations plan.

- **Applications and data criticality analysis (A)**   Data need to be analyzed to determine whether it is critical and addressed as such in the disaster recovery plan and the emergency mode operation plan.

Evaluation: 45 CFR 164.308(a)(8)

This standard requires periodic technical and nontechnical evaluations to be conducted to reasonably ensure CEs and BAs comply with the provisions of the HIPAA Security Rule.

PART III

Physical Safeguards: 45 CFR 164.310

The physical safeguards section of the HIPAA Security Rule focuses on the implementation of physical safeguards to protect PHI, servers, individuals, and so forth. This section is more than just making sure there are locks on the doors. It also requires the implementation of safeguards to protect workstations, media that is used to store PHI, secure destruction of hardware and media, and protection against disasters such as the installation of a fire suppression system.

Facility Access Controls: 164.310(a)

This standard requires implementation and maintenance of facilities where PHI may be used and disclosed.

- **Contingency operations (A)**   Policies and procedures need to be implemented that accommodate emergency operation in the event of a disaster. This is directly tied to the contingency planning requirements articulated at 45 CFR 164.308(a)(7).
- **Facility security plan (A)**   A facility security plan needs to be developed, implemented, and maintained.
- **Access control and validation procedures (A)**   Policies and procedures need to be implemented that govern access management to the facility (i.e., key management, key card management, etc.).
- **Maintenance records (A)**   Policies and procedures need to be implemented that accommodate maintenance of records when access control devices are installed, maintained, replaced, or decommissioned.

Workstation Use: 164.310(b)

This standard requires CEs and BAs to adopt policies, procedures, and practices that govern workstation or class of workstation use, physical location, and function.

Workstation Security: 164.310(c)

This standard requires CEs and BAs to adopt policies, procedures, and practices that reasonably ensure the physical security of workstations used to access ePHI. This includes all mobile devices used to access or store ePHI.

Device and Media Controls: 164.310(d)

This standard requires CEs and BAs to adopt policies, procedures, and practices to physically secure hardware and media.

- **Disposal (R)**   Proper practices need to be implemented that accommodate secure disposal of electronic media and hardware used to store ePHI when no longer needed or usable.
- **Media reuse (R)**   Proper practices need to be implemented that provide for complete destruction or erasure of ePHI stored on electronic media or hardware when the media or hardware will no longer be used to store ePHI but will be used for other purposes.

- **Accountability (A)**   Practices need to be implemented to record movement of electronic media or hardware and the individuals authorized to approve movement.

- **Data backup and storage (A)**   Practices need to be implemented to create an exact copy of ePHI stored on hardware that is to be moved before the actual move.

Technical Safeguards: 45 CFR 164.312

Technical safeguards address what many think of as core to information security. While important, as noted earlier, administrative safeguards, if not adhered to, represent a more significant security deficiency. That said, this section focuses on what information technology systems need to include as at least basic functionality. As an example, systems need to support assigning users a unique ID and an associated way to authenticate a user such as the use of a password to access an electronic health record.

Access Control: 164.312(a)

This standard requires the implementation of technical controls to permit only access to PHI that meets the minimum necessary standard of the HIPAA Privacy Rule.

- **Unique user identification (R)**   Workforce members must be assigned unique logon IDs.

- **Emergency access procedure (R)**   Practices must be implemented to reasonably ensure access to ePHI in the event of an emergency.

- **Automatic logoff (A)**   CEs and BAs need to implement technical processes that automatically terminate workforce members' access after a period of inactivity.

- **Encryption and decryption (A)**   Proper technical processes need to be implemented to encrypt and decrypt ePHI transmitted over an open network and when at rest.

Audit Controls 164.312(b)

This standard requires CEs and BAs to implement technical processes that accurately record activity related to the creation, modification, and deletion of ePHI. When technically feasible, access to ePHI should also be recorded.

Integrity: 164.312(c)

This standard requires CEs and BAs to implement processes to reasonably ensure ePHI is not improperly altered or destroyed.

- **Mechanism to authenticate ePHI (A)**   Processes need to be implemented that validate that data have not been improperly altered or destroyed.

Person or Entity Authentication: 164.312(d)

This standard requires CEs and BAs to implement controls that accommodate the proper authentication of an individual or entity before allowing access to ePHI.

PART III

Transmission Security: 164.312(e)

This standard requires CEs and BAs to implement policies, procedures, and practices that secure ePHI that is transmitted over an open network (the Internet).

- **Integrity controls (A)**   CE and BAs need to implement integrity controls that check for improper modification or destruction of data in transit across an open network.

- **Encryption (A)**   ePHI transmitted over an open network must be properly encrypted.

Policies and Procedures and Documentation Requirements: 45 CFR 164.316

CEs and BAs are required to adopt policies that document how CEs and BAs comply with the HIPAA Security Rule. Policies, training material, risk analysis reports, and other HIPAA Security Rule compliance–related documentation must be retained for a minimum of six years.

Lack of required documentation or documentation that is inaccurate or not current represents one of the most significant regulatory risks to healthcare entities. For example, policies need to be current, accurate, and enforceable. Proper and timely execution of required legal documents is critical to avoid regulatory, legal, and other risks. The document requirements may change over time, so it is important to regularly review and update or amend these documents as needed.

Breach Notification Rule: 45 CFR Part 164, Subpart D

The HIPAA Breach Notification Rule was added as a compliance requirement with the passage of the HITECH Act in 2009. The rule was published as an interim final rule on September 23, 2009, and was finalized as part of the Omnibus Rule of 2013. The rule requires CEs to notify individuals and the Office for Civil Rights in the event of a breach of unsecure PHI and requires BAs to report any breach of unsecure PHI to its CE customers or, if the BA is a BA subcontractor, to notify its BA customer.

Breach Definition: 45 CFR 164.402

Breach means the acquisition, access, use, or disclosure of PHI which compromises the security or privacy of the PHI. *Breach* excludes:

- Unintentional use or disclosure of PHI by a workforce member or person acting under the authority of a CE or a BA, if use or disclosure was made in good faith and does not result in further use or disclosure.

- Inadvertent disclosure by a person who is authorized to access PHI at a CE or BA to another person authorized to access PHI at the same CE or BA, and the information received as a result of such disclosure is not further used or disclosed.

- A disclosure of PHI where a CE or BA has a good faith belief that an unauthorized person to whom the disclosure was made would not reasonably have been able to retain such information.

Unauthorized use or disclosure of PHI is presumed to be a breach unless the CE or BA demonstrates that there is a low probability that the PHI has been compromised. The finalization of the Breach Notification Rule (included in the Omnibus Rule) changed how CEs are required to evaluate whether or not notification is required. Prior to the rule finalization, CEs were required to notify individuals and OCR only if the CEs determined that the breach may cause significant harm to those individuals. The final rule now requires CEs to assume notification is required until proving to themselves otherwise by conducting a four-factor risk assessment. The required risk assessment must include at least the following factors:

- The nature and extent of the PHI involved, including the types of identifiers and the likelihood of re-identification
- The unauthorized person who used the PHI or to whom the disclosure was made
- Whether the PHI was actually acquired or viewed
- The extent to which the risk to the PHI has been mitigated

Unsecured PHI means PHI that is not rendered unusable, unreadable, or indecipherable to unauthorized persons through the use of a technology or methodology specified by OCR. CEs and BAs may conduct the four-factor risk assessment described in 45 CFR 164.402. Even if the BA conducts the four-factor risk assessment, the BA is required to notify CEs of any breach of unsecure PHI (45 CFR 164.410).

General Breach Description Notification Requirements: 45 CFR 164.404(a–c)

CEs have an obligation to notify individuals and OCR of the breach.

- A breach is considered to be discovered as of the first day the breach is discovered or should reasonably have been discovered.
- Notifications must be made "without unreasonable delay" but no later than 60 calendar days after the breach discovery by the CE. The same notification requirements applies to BAs and BA subcontractors as it relates to notifying its CE or BA customer.
- The CE or BA has the burden of demonstrating that notifications were made in a "timely" manner. This includes retaining appropriate documentation related to breach notification.
- CEs are regulatorily required to notify individuals, the Office for Civil Rights, and potentially the media in the event of a breach of unsecure PHI where the risk of compromise is determined to not be low. CEs may delegate this responsibility to BAs but, from a regulatory perspective, if the BA doesn't properly notify, the CE is ultimately responsible for rule compliance.

PART III

Methods of Notification: 45 CFR 164.404(d)

Notice must be provided to the individual using the following form:

- It is the responsibility of the CE to notify affected individuals even if the breach was reported to the CE by the BA.

- Written notification must be sent by first-class mail to the individual (or the next of kin of the individual if the individual is deceased) at the last known address or, if e-mail is the specified notification preference of the individual, by e-mail.

- If there is insufficient or out-of-date contact information (including phone number, e-mail address, or available contact information) that prevents direct individual notification of ten individuals or more, a substitute notice is required. The substitute notice includes conspicuous posting of the breach for 90 days on the home page of the web site of the CE or notice in major print or broadcast media, including major media in geographic areas where the individuals affected by the breach likely reside.

- Media and/or web notices need to include a toll-free phone number that is active for no less than 90 days so that the individual can call to learn whether the individual's unsecured PHI was or potentially was a part of the breach.

- If the notice is made through the media, the notice must be made to well-known media outlets in the state or jurisdiction. Also, if the breach involved more than 500 residents of a given state or jurisdiction, media announcement is required (45 CFR 164.406).

Notification Delay for Law Enforcement Purposes: 45 CFR 164.412

If a law enforcement official determines that required notification would impede a criminal investigation or cause damage to national security, notification shall be delayed for the period defined by law enforcement.

Specific CE Requirements: 45 CFR 164.404

In the event of a breach, a CE that stores, uses, or discloses unsecured PHI is required to notify each individual whose unsecured PHI has been, or is reasonably believed to have been, breached or inappropriately accessed by an individual or entity (includes internal and external breaches/inappropriate disclosure) within 60 days.

CEs are required to notify OCR within 60 days of when the breach was discovered or should have been discovered if it involves 500 or more individuals (45 CFR 164.408). If the breach involved fewer than 500 individuals, the CE is required to maintain a breach log. The breaches recorded in the breach log must be reported to OCR within 60 days following the end of the calendar year. OCR maintains a list on its web site that lists all CEs who have reported a breach involving 500 individuals or more.

Specific BA Requirements: 45 CFR 164.410

In the event of a breach, a BA that stores, uses, or discloses unsecured PHI is required to notify the CE of the breach. The notice needs to include the identification of each individual whose unsecured PHI has been, or is reasonably believed to have been, breached or inappropriately accessed (includes internal and external breaches/inappropriate disclosure) and sufficient detailed information to accommodate the CE's individual notification requirements. Lack of required documentation or documentation that is inaccurate or not current represents one of the most significant regulatory risks to healthcare entities. For example, policies need to be current, accurate, and enforceable. Proper and timely execution of required legal documents is critical to avoid regulatory, legal, and other risks. The document requirements may change over time, so it is important to regularly review and update or amend these documents as needed. For example, the HITECH Act significantly changed how business associates are treated—they are now directly required to adhere to certain HIPAA rules. Prior to HITECH, business associates were required to adhere to HIPAA but not directly—only through contract with covered entities.

HIPAA Enforcement Rule: 45 CFR Part 160

The HIPAA Enforcement Rule was augmented when the Enforcement Interim Final Rule became effective. The final rule was included in the Omnibus Rule of 2013. The purpose of the rule is to define "willful neglect" and to move to the HITECH Act–related increases in civil penalties that CEs and BAs may be required to pay in the event of a HIPAA rule violation.

Willful neglect is defined as cases in which the entity knew of a violation of the HIPAA rules or should have known. This means willful neglect may be found and lead to much higher civil penalties or monetary settlements when noncompliance is related to ignorance or incomplete knowledge of the compliance requirements.

The HITECH Act included language that significantly changed the level of civil penalties that could be levied against CEs and now BAs. The categories of civil penalties were expanded and associated penalties increased. OCR may also reach a monetary settlement with CEs and BAs rather than levying what could be higher civil penalties. Since 2011, OCR has imposed civil penalties and reached monetary settlements with a number of CEs and, in 2016, a BA. OCR can levy penalties up to $50,000 per violation up to $1.5 million for the same violations that occur within a calendar year.

As an example, if OCR investigates a CE or BA and finds violations, such as the lack of a completed risk analysis or a breach of unsecure PHI that resulted from deficient security safeguards (for example, from the lack of encryption of a mobile device), a separate violation occurs each day the covered entity or business associate is in violation of the provision. So, if the CE or BA has not completed a risk analysis, that counts as one type of violation and if, in addition, the CE or BA failed to encrypt the mobile device and a breach resulted, that counts as another type of violation. In this example if the CE or BA failed to conduct a risk analysis for 365 days, that's 365 violations of the same type, so OCR can levy civil penalties of up to $1.5 million for that type of violation. In addition, if the mobile device should have been encrypted and was not for a period of 60 days, that would represent 60 violations of the same type. This means that OCR could levy civil penalties of more than $1.5 million (365 days x $50,000) because a risk analysis wasn't conducted, and an additional $300,000 (60 days x $50,000) because a mobile device wasn't encrypted, resulting in a breach of unsecure PHI.

The HITECH Act mandates OCR conduct regular compliance audits of CEs and BAs. The OCR audit program was launched November 2011 (Phase 1) and only CEs were audited as part of the Phase 1 audits. The Phase 2 audits were launched in March 2016. Phase 2 audits will include desk and comprehensive audits of CEs and BAs. The audit program does not replace other enforcement and other compliance-related investigations that may be conducted by other federal agencies and reported to OCR if another federal agency believes a CE or BA is not compliant with HIPAA.

Additional Guidance

OCR has been publishing guidance to the healthcare industry since 2003, with expanding guidance on HIPAA and compliance requirements beginning in 2015. Guidance of note includes

- Mental health disclosures (www.hhs.gov/hipaa/for-professionals/special-topics /mental-health)
- De-identification of data for research purposes (www.hhs.gov/hipaa/for-professionals/privacy/special-topics/de-identification/index.html)
- Patient right to access health information (www.hhs.gov/hipaa/for-professionals /privacy/guidance/access)
- Compliance training resources (www.hhs.gov/hipaa/for-professionals/training /index.html)

Other resources are available from the OCR web site (www.hhs.gov/hipaa/index .html) and the Office of the National Coordinator for Health Information Technology (ONC; www.healthit.gov).

Chapter Review

The HITECH Act coupled with the Omnibus Rule expanded the reach of HIPAA by adding subcontractors of BAs to the list of entities that are required to comply with HIPAA. This represented a significant change in the number of vendors who now need to pay attention to HIPAA.

HIPAA, HITECH, and state law require CEs and BAs to implement sound privacy and security practices and a sound breach notification process. This includes addressing:

- Use & Disclosure of PHI
- Minimum Necessary

- Individual privacy rights
- Policy development
- Staff training
- And so forth

The HIPAA rules are foundational when it comes to privacy, security, and regulatory compliance. Not adhering to HIPAA can lead to violations, sanctions, and civil penalties imposed by HHS. CEs and BAs need to implement privacy and security programs that are consistent with HIPAA requirements and to periodically monitor compliance. CEs and BAs also need to be in a position to demonstrate compliance through retained documentation and demonstrated action. The OCR HIPAA Audits that kicked off in 2016 included the publication of audit protocols that address in detail what CEs and BAs are required to document and prove. For example, are staff complying with privacy and security policies? Are authorizations to disclose PHI accurate? Do CEs provide individuals copies of their designated record set in a timely manner? This also amounts to more than just retaining documentation—for example, the adoption of privacy and security policies and procedures. CEs and BAs need to be in a positon to demonstrate that, in this example, the workforce is adhering to adopted policies and have been provided training regarding what is expected when it comes to the workforce and privacy and security responsibilities. CEs and BAs need to periodically evaluate compliance with HIPAA because of the regulatory mandate and because not complying can have an adverse impact on the business of healthcare and its customers.

Questions

To test your comprehension of the chapter, answer the following questions and then check your answers against the list of correct answers that follow the questions.

1. From a regulatory perspective, what are the differences between what a BA is required to adhere to when it comes to the HIPAA rules and what a CE must adhere to?

   A. There are no differences.

   B. The BA is required to adhere to the HIPAA Privacy, Security, and Breach Notification Rules, but the CE is not required to adhere to any of them.

   C. The BA is required to adhere to the use and disclosure provisions of the HIPAA Privacy Rule and the full Security and Breach Notification Rules, and the CE is required to adhere to the Privacy, Security, and Breach Notification Rules and the other HIPAA Administrative Simplification provisions.

   D. The BA is required to adhere to the full Security and Breach Notification Rules, and the CE is required to adhere to the Privacy, Security, and Breach Notification Rules and the other HIPAA Administrative Simplification provisions.

2. What enforcement action can OCR take if a CE violates provisions of HIPAA's Administrative Simplification provisions?

   A. OCR has no enforcement authority.

   B. OCR may levy up to $50,000 for any level of violation with a maximum of $1.5 million per calendar year for the same type of violation.

   C. OCR may levy up to $25,000 for any level of violation with a maximum of $500,000 per calendar year for the same type of violation.

   D. The penalty depends on the severity of the disclosure.

3. What are the privacy rights afforded patients pursuant to the HIPAA Privacy Rule (45 CFR Part 164, Subpart E)?

   A. The maximum rights of quality, efficiency, and effectiveness.

   B. Patients must be informed of disclosed PHI other than for treatment, payment, and healthcare operations.

   C. The patient has the right to request a copy of their legal medical record.

   D. The patient has the right to register a complaint with the U.S. Department of Health and Human Services, Office of the Inspector General.

4. A state law that is more stringent than the HIPAA Privacy Rule preempts HIPAA. What does stringent mean?

   A. Stringent is defined as providing greater protection of an individual's PHI or providing an individual greater access to their PHI.

   B. Stringent is defined as a state law that is in conflict with HIPAA.

   C. Stringent is defined as covering more serious disclosures.

   D. Stringent means allowing more enforcement.

5. What are the document creation and retention requirements for CEs?

   A. CEs are required to retain medical records for a minimum of six years.

   B. CEs are required to create and retain for a minimum of six years all disclosures, complaints, mitigations, compliance reviews, and EHR audit reports.

   C. All document retention requirements are for one year only.

   D. CEs are required to retain all elements of PHI information indefinitely.

6. Are vendors required to adhere to HIPAA?

   A. Yes, if the vendor contracts with a CE.

   B. Only if the vendor is a software vendor or a cloud services vendor that uses, discloses, maintains, or transmits PHI on behalf of a CE.

   C. Only if the vendor has not passed a HIPAA certification course recognized by OCR.

   D. Only if the vendor uses, discloses, maintains, or transmits PHI on behalf of a CE or another BA.

7. The Omnibus Rule expanded the number of entities who are required to adhere to HIPAA. Which new category of entity was added to entities that are required to adhere to HIPAA?

   A. SaaS vendors

   B. Vendors who contract with CEs and have access to PHI

   C. Vendors who contract with a CE or a BA and who can view PHI

   D. Vendors who contract with a CE or a BA and who use, disclose, maintain, or transmit PHI on behalf of the CE or BA

8. What does "unsecure PHI" mean?

   A. PHI that is not rendered unusable, unreadable, or indecipherable to unauthorized persons through the use of a technology or methodology specified by OCR

   B. PHI that is electronic and not encrypted

   C. PHI that is left in an area where patients and visitors can view the PHI

   D. PHI that is not totally and completely destroyed

9. When may a CE disclose a limited data set?

   A. If the CE is contracting with an outside vendor to conduct marketing on behalf of the CE

   B. Only for the purposes of research, public health, or healthcare operations

   C. When requesting payment from a health plan

   D. If the CE is contracting with an outside vendor to conduct fundraising on behalf of the CE

10. The HIPAA Security Rule requires PHI to be encrypted in which circumstance?

    A. If the PHI will be transmitted over an open network.

    B. If the PHI is stored on a USB drive.

    C. If the risk of the exposure of PHI that is stored or transmitted is significant, such as when stored on mobile devices or emailed to an entity or individual outside of the CE or BA's network environment.

    D. All PHI must be encrypted at all times.

Answers

1. **C.** The business associate is required to adhere to the use and disclosure provisions of the HIPAA Privacy Rule and the complete Security and Breach Notification Rules, and the covered entity is required to adhere to the Privacy, Security, and Breach Notification Rules and the other HIPAA Administrative Simplification provisions.

2. B. OCR may levy up to $50,000 for any level of violation with a maximum of $1.5 million per calendar year for the same type of violation.

3. B. Patients must be informed of disclosed PHI other than for treatment, payment, and healthcare operations.

4. A. Stringent is defined as providing greater protection of an individual's PHI or providing an individual greater access to their PHI.

5. B. Covered entities are required to create and retain for six years all disclosures, complaints, mitigations, compliance reviews, and EHR audit reports.

6. D. Any vendor who uses, discloses, maintains, or transmits PHI on behalf of a CE or another BA is required to adhere to HIPAA.

7. D. The Omnibus Rule expanded the type of entities that are required to adhere to HIPAA. The new category of entities are BA subcontractors who use, disclose, maintain, or transmit PHI on behalf of a CE or a BA.

8. A. Unsecure PHI is PHI that is not rendered unusable, unreadable, or indecipherable to unauthorized persons through the use of a technology or methodology specified by OCR.

9. B. CEs may use or disclose a limited data set only for the purposes of research, public health, or healthcare operations.

10. C. The HIPAA Security Rule requires the encryption of PHI when PHI is transmitted over an open network, if the risk of exposure of stored PHI is significant. This would include the need to encrypt the PHI when stored on mobile devices or portable media and, wherever feasible, when the PHI is stored in an application, such as when PHI is stored in an electronic health record.

References

1. Public Law 104-191, 104th Congress. *Health Insurance Portability and Accountability Act of 1996.* Section 1, Title II, Subpart F (HIPAA Administrative Simplification provisions).

2. Public Law 104-191, 104th Congress. *Health Insurance Portability and Accountability Act of 1996.* 45 CFR Parts 160 and 164 (HIPAA privacy, security, breach notification, and enforcement rules).

3. Public Law 111-5, 111th Congress. *American Recovery and Reinvestment Act of 2009.* Division A, Title XIII, Subpart D (ARRA/HITECH privacy, security, and enforcement provisions).

4. Ibid. 42 CFR Part 2 (alcohol and chemical dependency privacy rule).

NOTE The legal documents referenced in this chapter are available from Apgar & Associates, LLC. More information is available at http://apgarandassoc.com.

CHAPTER 16

Health Information Technology and Health Policy

Allison Viola

In this chapter, you will learn how to

- Describe key issues in health information technology and health policy in the United States
- Explain the Precision Medicine Initiative and the impact on health information technology
- Identify the policies and challenges remaining to attain interoperability
- Discuss how financial incentives have changed the use of health information technology
- Describe the new privacy and consent management landscape
- Explain the changes in the ONC Health IT certification program
- Describe the Quality Data Model to enhance quality reporting

The Linkage Between Health Policy and Health IT: Why It's Important

With increasing pressure to reduce healthcare costs and to improve patient health and the care experience, the U.S. healthcare system has used, and continues to use, technological advances to help achieve those goals. But with the opportunities technology can offer, there is also the need to develop a supporting framework of nationwide policies. Jumpstarting these efforts was the passage of the American Recovery and Reinvestment Act (ARRA) of 2009 that established the Centers for Medicare and Medicaid Services (CMS) Electronic Health Record (EHR) Incentive Program and codified the Office of the National Coordinator for Health Information Technology (ONC) to implement standards and certification requirements to support the meaningful use of EHRs. Regulations ensued that helped build the policy foundation from which thousands of eligible hospitals and eligible providers have adopted, implemented, and meaningfully used

EHRs. Pushing the healthcare industry forward with the passage of federal, state, and local policies has accelerated the movement toward digitized records. With this foundation, there is increasing demand for data capture—structured and unstructured—to promote new programs and capabilities such as President Barack Obama's Precision Medicine Initiative (PMI), which was launched in 2015, and computable privacy to electronically satisfy patient consent rights without the need for human intervention. New payment models have emerged with these technological abilities through the introduction of the Medicare Access and Children's Health Insurance Program (CHIP) Reauthorization Act of 2015 (MACRA) that transitions the healthcare payment system from a fee-for-service model to one that rewards value-based service and improved outcomes.

All of these initiatives and more cannot be successful without health information transmitted from one provider to another that supports patient care and research. Interoperable health IT and health information policies have been implemented to enable the movement of data through privacy protections, as well as standards, governance, and certification requirements. Without these guardrails, the U.S. healthcare system cannot truly be a system.

Precision Medicine Initiative

The terms "personalized medicine" and "precision medicine" have been used interchangeably. For consistency, the more recent term "precision medicine" is used in this chapter. Over the last few years, precision medicine has captured the healthcare industry's attention as it struggles to reduce medical costs, improve patient care, and achieve better health for populations. Due to the rising costs of pharmaceuticals, the rising prevalence of chronic diseases such as diabetes, cardiovascular disease, and obesity, and the increasing attention given to patient safety issues, precision medicine has risen to the top of our national debate on healthcare and finding solutions to these challenges. As stated in a White House press release from 2015, "As a result of our traditional 'one-size-fits-all-approach [to healthcare],' treatments can be very successful for some patients but not for others. This is changing with the emergence of precision medicine, an innovative approach to disease prevention and treatment that takes into account individual differences in people's genes, environments, and lifestyles. Precision medicine gives clinicians tools to better understand the complex mechanisms underlying a patient's health, disease, or condition, and to better predict which treatments will be most effective."[1]

On January 20, 2015, during his State of the Union address, President Obama announced the PMI and called for $215 million in fiscal year 2016 to support this effort. More specifically, he sought $130 million in funding for the National Institutes of Health (NIH) to build a national, large-scale research group (cohort) composed of one million or more Americans who volunteer to participate in precision medicine research through the contribution of their data. The data collected will be quite diverse—including medical, genetic, metabolic and microorganism, environmental and lifestyle, patient-generated, and device-collected data.[2] To conduct research and enable clinicians to tailor their treatments for individuals, this data must be readily available and portable to support the purposes described previously. This cohort, now called the All of Us Project, will enable researchers to analyze a wider range of diseases and allow for statistical determinations to associate between genetic and/or environmental exposures. The rich data from this cohort will enable researchers to

- Develop ways to measure risk for a range of diseases based on environmental exposures, genetic factors, and interactions between the two

- Identify the causes of individual differences in response to commonly used drugs (commonly referred to as pharmacogenomics)

- Discover biological markers that signal increased or decreased risk of developing common diseases

- Use mobile health (mHealth) technologies to correlate activity, physiological measures, and environmental exposures with health outcomes

- Develop new disease classifications and relationships

- Empower study participants with data and information to improve their own health

- Create a platform to enable trials of targeted therapies

The PMI consists of two main components: a near-term focus on cancers and a long-term focus on generating knowledge that is applicable to a wider range of health and diseases. To support these goals, the following federal agencies are working in concert to help push this initiative forward and implement the necessary components as described in the following list:

- The National Institutes of Health (NIH) is responsible for building the cohort program and collecting data from the one million or more U.S. volunteer participants. Specifically, the National Cancer Institute is working to expand cancer precision medicine clinical trials, examine drug resistance in cancer patients, develop new preclinical models, and establish a national cancer knowledge system.

- The Food and Drug Administration (FDA) is developing new regulatory approaches to evaluate next-generation genomic sequencing technologies. The agency launched precisionFDA in late 2015, a crowd-sourced, cloud-based platform where next-generation sequencing (NGS) software methods can be tested, developed, and validated.

- The Office for Civil Rights (OCR) is developing regulatory guidance and other tools to help individuals and Health Insurance Portability and Accountability Act (HIPAA) covered entities understand their rights to donate information for research.

- The Department of Veterans Affairs (VA) and Department of Defense (DoD) are collaborating to enroll veterans and active-duty men and women through the Million Veteran Program.[2]

PART III

The interoperability of health IT plays a critical role in developing a framework for the future, one in which data stored in disparate EHRs and other health IT solutions can be accessed, shared, and used in far greater ways than are being accomplished today. Once this is achieved, the ability to leverage the data as a resource—particularly for such data-intensive initiatives as PMI—is endless.

Interoperability

An emerging complex and technological healthcare system, such as what we're experiencing now, requires the ability for patients, providers, hospitals, and other stakeholders within the health ecosystem to exchange health information and be able to use that information for informed decision-making about care delivery. Successful interoperability allows for healthcare IT systems to work together within and across organizational boundaries in order to advance effective delivery of healthcare to individuals and communities. Three levels of interoperability exist to achieve this goal:

- *Foundational interoperability* allows for data exchange from one healthcare IT system to another and does not require interpretation of the data.

- *Structural interoperability* defines the format of data exchanged where there is uniform movement of healthcare data from one system to another. The clinical or operational purpose remains the same as it moves throughout the system and has the ability to be interpreted at the data field level.

- *Semantic interoperability* at the highest level allows for two or more systems or elements to exchange information and use the information that has been exchanged. This level of interoperability leverages the structuring of the data exchange and the classification of the data so that the receiver has the ability to interpret the data.[3]

As a result of the CMS EHR Incentive Program implementation that encouraged the adoption, implementation, and use of healthcare IT, Congress enacted the Medicare Access and CHIP Reauthorization Act of 2015. Through this law, Congress declared it a national objective to achieve widespread exchange of health information through interoperable certified EHR technology nationwide by December 31, 2018.[4] MACRA defines interoperability as "the ability of two or more health information systems or components to exchange clinical and other information and to use the information that has been exchanged using common standards as to provide access to longitudinal information for health care providers in order to facilitate coordinated care and improved patient outcomes."[4] As a result of this legislation, CMS has issued proposed regulations to implement the requirements outlined in the law provisions.

New Payment Models

Since 1997, when the Medicare Sustainable Growth Rate (SGR) was designed and subsequently implemented to rein in Medicare Part B spending, Congress has continually passed legislation to prevent the inevitable payment cuts to providers. Despite these efforts, a permanent solution to this risk had not been developed until the passage of MACRA, which repeals the SGR. Not only does this legislation provide assurance, it also makes significant changes in the way Medicare issues payment to providers, by transitioning away from the "fee-for-service or quantity" model to one that supports value and the care rendered to patients. Payments will now be "value based," thus supporting the quality of care.[5]

In preparation for this transition toward "value" over "volume," earlier in 2015 Health and Human Services (HHS) Secretary Sylvia Burwell outlined new payment goals that center on alternative payment models (APMs). APMs emphasize improved patient outcomes and thus require provider accountability for the quality and cost of care patients receive. The following list provides some examples of improving outcomes and how APMs work hand in hand to support the U.S. healthcare system:

- **Bundled payment model**   Providers are reimbursed together for the entire cost of an "episode of care." An example is a hip replacement where the lab tests and other services are all paid for in the same lump sum—whether those tests or services are conducted once, twice, or five times. This circumstance creates an incentive to deliver better care that makes patients healthier, reduces duplicate or redundant unnecessary services, and lowers readmission rates.

- **Accountable-care organizations (ACOs)**   Within an ACO, providers partner together on a patient's care and are rewarded when they are able to deliver better care at lower cost. In a patient-centered medical home (PCMH) model, instead of doctors working individually, care coordinators oversee all the care a patient receives. The results of this collaborative effort mean patients are more likely to receive the right tests and medications rather than getting duplicative tests and procedures. The PCMH model typically offers patients access to a doctor or other clinician 7 days a week, 24 hours a day, including through extended office hours on evenings and weekends.

In her announcement, Secretary Burwell outlined the department's goals and timeline in shifting away from volume and toward value:

- The first goal is for 30 percent of all Medicare provider payments to be in APMs that are tied to how good providers care for their patients, instead of how much care they provide—and to do it by 2016. The goal would then be to get to 50 percent by 2018.

- The second goal is for virtually all Medicare fee-for-service payments to be tied to quality and value; at least 85 percent in 2016 and 90 percent in 2018.

On May 9, 2016, CMS issued a proposed rule that repeals the SGR methodology for updates to the physician fee schedule (PFS) and substantially changes the way Medicare-enrolled practitioners are reimbursed (hospitals are currently not included in this program). This new proposal, Merit-based Incentive Payment System (MIPS), aims to streamline three existing programs, the Physician Quality Reporting System (PQRS), the Physician Value-based Payment Modifier (VM), and the Medicare EHR Incentive Program for Eligible Professionals (EPs). To avoid program and reporting duplication and burden for providers, this program will establish a new framework for rewarding quality reporting, resource use, and use of certified EHR technology (CEHRT) accomplished via a unified approach called the Quality Payment Program that will transition over a period of time from 2015 through 2021 and beyond and allow participants to choose from two pathways—MIPS and the Advanced APMs. (The EHR Incentive Program will evolve into the Advancing Care Information (ACI) component of the MIPS program.)[6]

The MIPS program reimbursement is based upon a Composite Performance Score (CPS) that is divided among the following four weighted categories and, based upon the score achieved, will determine the payment that clinicians receive. Under the proposed rule, the first performance period for MIPS will begin on January 1, 2017, and run throughout the calendar year, with the first MIPS payment period beginning in 2019.

- **Quality**   Eligible clinicians will report a selection of six quality measures with an emphasis on outcome measurement.
- **Resource Use**   CMS will assess all available resource use measures, which will be based upon claims data and thus will require no reporting from clinicians.
- **Clinical Practice Improvement Activity**   As a new category not currently part of the existing reporting programs, this includes care coordination, shared decision making, safety checklists, and expanding practice access.
- **Advancing Care Information (ACI)**   MACRA restructures the concept of "meaningful use of certified EHR technology" into the ACI category and requires the selection of current quality reporting measures adopted by the Stage 3 Meaningful Use program, from six objectives: protecting patient health information, e-prescribing, patient electronic access, coordinated care through patient engagement, health information exchange, and public health reporting. The EHR Incentive Program ("Meaningful Use") is not being withdrawn; rather, it is being integrated into the MIPS program to improve efficiencies and value.

Computable Privacy

As individuals' information continues to become more digitized—with the enactment of the CMS EHR Incentive Program—so does the increased risk of a breach. HIPAA was passed in 1996 to address the use and disclosure of individuals' health information—called protected health information (PHI). This was the first time a set of national standards was established to protect certain health information.[7] Since that time, technology has advanced to the point where it enables the automation of privacy compliance requirements. This concept is referred to as *computable privacy*, which is the "technical representation and communication of permission to share and use identifiable health information, including when law and applicable organizational policies enable information to be shared without need to first seek an individual's permission. Once integrated effectively, using technology for privacy compliance saves time and resources, and can build trust and confidence in the system overall."[8]

To support this effort, three essential layers of computable privacy must be implemented. HIPAA serves as the initial foundation allowing for disclosure of health information for the necessary treatment, payment, and operations (TPO). It also establishes the nationwide framework for these uses regardless of state requirements and laws. The second layer, basic choice, refers to the choice an individual makes about the use and disclosure of their health information, including the electronic exchange of health information regardless of the default rules such as HIPAA. The third, more detailed layer is a patient's granular choice. At this level, an individual has choices regarding the distinction between legally sensitive clinical conditions, such as mental health or HIV/AIDS status, and allows for those choices to adjust over time to support decisions regarding the disclosure of this information to specific recipients within the healthcare system.[8]

Despite the technological advances in capturing and storing health information within an EHR and other healthcare IT solutions, compliance challenges continue to exist due to a variety of factors, one of which is varying state privacy laws and the ability to exchange information across state lines. Currently there are conflicting privacy and confidentiality laws, regulations, and policies that serve as an obstacle in implementation of electronic consent management, or computable privacy. These laws, regulations, and policies address consent rights and categories of information that are considered sensitive and may apply at different levels. These variations may create a complex environment based upon where the patient and provider are located, as the requirements may be in conflict. As a result of these challenges, software vendors and system developers must create more flexible systems that can support conflicting and changing privacy and confidentiality laws and requirements.

Other notable challenges exist that hinder the ability to deploy a comprehensive and common computable privacy program: the lack of structured data in patient consent forms and the lack of interoperability between healthcare IT systems. The current method most commonly used for collecting patient consent is through paper forms. Although these forms may be converted into a PDF image file, users are unable to capture discrete data elements and allow for machine-readable capabilities. Scanned consent forms do not contain structured electronic data, which is data that can be tagged or occupies searchable fields (e.g., name or address fields).[9] To process consent decisions electronically, the data must be captured, tagged, and stored to allow for automated processing. As an example of this, should a patient choose to not disclose information regarding a diagnosis or other sensitive information, these data elements must be identified by the healthcare IT systems as such and be prevented from being shared with specified individuals.

The current consent management landscape can be separated into three distinct components and maturity levels:[9]

- **Phase I, Current State**   Consent is captured on paper forms and is then scanned and stored into a healthcare IT system. There is no structured data in this process, so the information must be reviewed and analyzed by staff to determine the level of desired consent.

- **Phase II, Current Growth** This phase is experiencing both paper collected consent and then entered into the system manually as well as consent captured electronically from the beginning. Although this demonstrates an automated approach, there is little flexibility in preferences.

- **Phase III, Future State** Consent is collected electronically and structured data are collected through a standard process. This phase allows for healthcare IT to automatically interpret and process consent preferences as well as comply with all applicable laws and regulations. Granular decisions may be applied to certain data elements, such as mental health or HIV status, which are prevented from being shared with other providers. Although Phase III is not widely implemented, pilot programs have been testing this approach and have successfully demonstrated this capability through electronic means.

EHR Incentive and Certification Programs

The American Recovery and Reinvestment Act of 2009 (ARRA) was enacted on February 17, 2009, and subsequently implemented by CMS in 2011.[10] This program was created to incentivize eligible professionals (EPs), eligible hospitals, critical access hospitals (CAHs), and Medicare Advantage organizations to adopt and meaningfully use interoperable healthcare IT and qualified EHRs. The program was divided among three stages for providers, hospitals, and healthcare IT vendors and other stakeholders to prepare and meet the requirements as defined in the regulation.

Since 2011, there have been several regulatory modifications to the program and the industry is now preparing for and/or implementing stages 2 and 3. As of this writing, the OCR reports:[11]

- As of 2015, 95 percent of all eligible and critical access hospitals have demonstrated meaningful use of CEHRT through participation in CMS EHR Incentive Programs. Ninety-eight percent of all hospitals have demonstrated meaningful use and/or adopted, implemented, or upgraded (AIU) an EHR.

- As of the end of 2015, 56 percent of all U.S. office-based physicians (MD/DO) have demonstrated meaningful use of CEHRT in the CMS EHR Incentive Programs.

Some additional changes to the certification program include the publication of the 2015 Edition Health Information Technology (Health IT) Certification Criteria, 2015 Edition Base Electronic Health Record (EHR) Definition, and ONC Health IT Certification Program Modifications final rule. In this rule, ONC made changes to the certification program that strengthen the testing, certification, and surveillance of healthcare IT. ONC also clarified and expanded the responsibilities of ONC-Authorized Certification Bodies (ONC-ACBs) regarding surveillance of certified EHR technology and other certified healthcare IT under the program, requiring ONC-ACBs to conduct more frequent and more rigorous surveillance in the field. ONC-ACBs are entities that have received authorization from ONC to participate in the ONC Health IT Certification Program and make certification determinations for healthcare IT modules based upon test results that have been supplied by Accredited Testing Laboratories.[7, 9, 12, 13, 14]

To further expand and define its role with certification, ONC published a proposed rule, "ONC Health IT Certification Program: Enhanced Oversight and Accountability" on March 2, 2016, which proposes to expand ONC's role to strengthen its oversight authority to directly review and evaluate the performance of certified healthcare IT in certain circumstances, such as in response to issues that could pose a public health or safety problem, compromise the security or privacy of patients' health information, or other exigencies.[15]

Quality Measures

As both the digitization of health information and the adoption, implementation, and use of EHRs increase, so does the emphasis and importance placed on the value of care delivery. This is evidenced by the passage of MACRA in 2015 followed up by the MIPS/APM Incentive Payment proposed rule in 2016. Traditionally, quality measures have been reported through claims (administrative) data that are submitted to CMS for payment purposes and have not typically been clinical data. With the increased ability of EHRs to capture, store, and report clinical and administrative data, reporting quality measures has become less complex by allowing for a more consistent and standard way of reporting data to meet quality measurement requirements.

To improve and support the transition of quality measurement reporting from a claims-based process to one that is driven by clinical data collected in EHRs, the need to establish a model framework was evident. Therefore, based upon a request from ONC, the Agency for Healthcare Research and Quality (AHRQ) funded the development of a Quality Data Model (QDM). The QDM is a model of information that allows for the description of clinical concepts in a standardized format so that stakeholders who monitor clinical performance and outcomes can clearly and concisely communicate information and reduce ambiguity within performance measurement.[16]

The QDM also describes information in a way that enables healthcare IT vendors to interpret the data in a consistent manner and locate the required information within the healthcare IT system so that users of electronic health information have a mutual understanding. Currently, the QDM is used in over 90 measures within the EHR Incentive Program and other quality reporting programs that require electronic measure (eMeasures) reporting.

Recently, a new generation of standards framework has emerged that can easily be assembled, implemented, and used within a wider variety of contexts—mobile phone applications, cloud communications, EHR-based data sharing, and more.[17] Fast Healthcare Interoperability Resources (FHIR-pronounced "FIRE") was developed by Health Level 7 International (HL7), a not-for-profit, standards-developing organization dedicated to providing a comprehensive framework and related standards for the exchange, integration, sharing, and retrieval of electronic health information that supports clinical practice and the management, delivery, and evaluation of health services.[18] FHIR is currently a Draft Standard for Trial Use, but trial use has already begun because of the many advantages it offers. With the development of FHIR and the opportunities it provides for flexibility within healthcare IT, particularly the quality measurement realm, this new framework has been in place to align it with the QDM. Stakeholders had already begun to work with the QDM to reduce its complexity by merging the QDM with Virtual Medical Record for Clinical Decision Support (vMR-CDS) to give rise to the Quality Information and Clinical Knowledge (QUICK) model. This model was then further refined to align structurally and semantically as close as possible with FHIR to allow for common quality and interoperability but will also support future quality initiatives.[19]

Chapter Review

The U.S. healthcare industry is undergoing a profound transformation, particularly within healthcare IT, that will challenge policy makers, industry professionals, and other stakeholders to rethink the way clinical and business solutions are provided. The PMI is just the beginning in seeking cures for patient diseases, interoperability of technology and information, research, pharmacogenomics, privacy and security challenges, mobile health, and others. The success of this program requires cross-collaboration and engagement with a variety of federal agencies and other stakeholders to push this initiative forward and allow for the unprecedented collection and use of genomic data to improve health and healthcare. Despite this initiative, interoperability of technology and health information continues to present challenges, and much work is still needed in this area to support the PMI, new payment models, and other initiatives that require the collection, aggregation, and use of data. By implementing such programs and requirements as the ones announced by Secretary Burwell, CMS will be obliged to comply and thus push the industry forward on the interoperability journey.

Computable privacy has emerged as a solution to address increased privacy and security concerns and supporting legislation as our health information becomes more digitized. However, as our electronic data increases, so does the potential for breaches and other unauthorized access to that data. Therefore, the ability to drill down to the data element level and protect it permits more flexibility and peace of mind, particularly with sensitive data. Not only has data protection changed, but also providers are experiencing an improved process in quality data reporting with the integration and streamlining of quality reporting programs proposed by CMS. After years of prompting by stakeholders to align and harmonize quality reporting programs to reduce their burden, CMS, through the MIPS program, has enhanced reporting.

Questions

1. The Precision Medicine Initiative cohort that is composed of one million or more Americans will provide researchers with the ability to do which of the following?

    A. Develop new disease classifications and relationships

    B. Identify the causes of individual differences in response to commonly used drugs

    C. Empower study participants with data and information to improve their own health

    D. All of the above

2. What are the three levels of interoperability?

  A. Structural, pseudonym, and biological

  B. Foundational, structural, and semantic

  C. Semantic, workflow, and classification

  D. Technological, structural, and foundational

3. What did the Medicare Access and CHIP Reauthorization Act (MACRA) of 2015 repeal?

  A. The Sustainable Growth Rate (SGR) Model

  B. The EHR Incentive Model

  C. The Physician Quality Reporting System

  D. None of the above

4. Which three programs does the Merit-based Incentive Payment System aim to streamline to substantially change the way practitioners are reimbursed?

  A. Physician Quality Reporting System (PQRS), Physician Vendor-based Payment Modifier (VM), and Medicare EHR Incentive Program for Eligible Practitioners (EPs)

  B. Physician Quality Reporting System (PQRS), Physician Value-based Payment Modifier (VM), and Medicare EHR Incentive Program for Eligible Professionals (EPs)

  C. Physician Querying Release System (PQRS), Physician Value-based Payment Mediator (VM), and Medicaid EHR Incentive Program for Eligible Professionals (EPs)

5. Which of the following lists two examples of alternative payment models?

  A. Bundled payment model and synchronized payment model

  B. Bundled payment model and integrated payment model

  C. Integrated payment model and accountable-care organizations

  D. Bundled payment model and accountable-care organizations

6. The current consent management landscape is separated into which of the following three components and maturity levels?

  A. Phase I, Current State: Consent is captured on paper forms.
     Phase II, Current Growth: This phase is experiencing both paper collected manually as well as consent captured electronically from the beginning.
     Phase III, Future State: Consent is collected electronically and structured data are collected through a nonstandard process.

  B. Phase I, Current State: Consent is captured on paper forms.
     Phase II, Current Growth: This phase is experiencing both paper collected consent and then entered into the system manually.
     Phase III, Future State: Consent is collected electronically and structured data are collected through a standard process.

    C. Phase I, Current State: Consent is captured on paper forms and is then scanned and stored into a healthcare IT system.
Phase II, Current Growth: This phase is experiencing both paper collected consent and then entered into the system manually as well as consent captured electronically from the beginning.
Phase III, Future State: Consent is collected electronically and structured data are collected through a standard process.

    D. Phase I, Current State: Consent is captured on paper forms and not scanned and stored into a healthcare IT system.
Phase II, Current Growth: This phase is experiencing both paper collected consent and then entered into the system manually.
Phase III, Future State: Consent is collected electronically and structured data are collected through a nonstandard process.

7. FHIR stands for:

    A. Fast Healthcare Interoperability Reasons

    B. Fast Healthcare Interactive Resources

    C. Frequent Health Integrated Resources

    D. Fast Healthcare Interoperability Resources

8. The Quality Information and Clinical Knowledge (QUICK) model is composed of:

    A. Merging the Quality Data Model (QDM) with Virtual Medical Record for Clinical Decision Support (vMR)

    B. Merging the Query Decision Model (QDM) with Virtual Medical Record for Clinical Decision Support (vMR)

    C. Merging the Quality Data Model (QDM) with Virtual Medical Record for Clinical Quality Decisions (vMR)

Answers

1. **D.** The PMI cohort of one million or more Americans will provide researchers with the ability to develop new disease classifications and relationships, identify the causes of individual differences in response to commonly used drugs, and empower study participants with data and information to improve their own health.

2. **B.** The three levels of interoperability are foundational, structural, and semantic.

3. **A.** The Medicare Access and CHIP Reauthorization Act of 2015 (MACRA) repealed the Sustainable Growth Rate (SGR) model.

4. B. The Merit-based Incentive Payment System (MIPS) aims to streamline Physician Quality Reporting System (PQRS), Physician Value-based Payment Modifier (VM), and the Medicare EHR Incentive Program for Eligible Professionals (EPs) to substantially change the way practitioners are reimbursed.

5. D. Examples of alternative payment models are the bundled payment model and accountable-care organizations.

6. C. The current consent management landscape is separated into the following levels of maturity: Phase I Current State: Consent is captured on paper forms and is then scanned and stored into a healthcare IT system. Phase II Current Growth: This phase is experiencing both paper collected consent and then entered into the system manually as well as consent captured electronically from the beginning. Phase III Future State: Consent is collected electronically and structured data are collected through a standard process.

7. D. FHIR stands for Fast Healthcare Interoperability Resources.

8. A. The Quality Information and Clinical Knowledge (QUICK) model is composed of merging the Quality Data Model (QDM) with Virtual Medical Record for Clinical Decision Support (vMR).

References

1. The White House Office of the Press Secretary. (2015). *Fact sheet: President Obama's Precision Medicine Initiative.* Accessed from www.whitehouse.gov /the-press-office/2015/01/30/fact-sheet-president-obama-s-precision-medicine-initiative.

2. The White House. (n.d.). What is the Precision Medicine Initiative? In *The Precision Medicine Initiative.* Accessed from www.whitehouse.gov/precision-medicine.

3. HIMSS. (n.d.). *What is interoperability?* Accessed from www.himss.org/library /interoperability-standards/what-is-interoperability.

4. Public Law 114-10, 114th Congress. *Medicare Access and CHIP Reauthorization Act of 2015.* Accessed from www.congress.gov/114/plaws/publ10/PLAW-114publ10.pdf.

5. Cragun, E. (2015, April 20). *The most important details in the SGR repeal law.* The Advisory Board Company. Accessed on October 4, 2016, from www.advisory.com /research/health-care-advisory-board/blogs/at-the-helm/2015/04/sgr-repeal.

6. Merit-Based Incentive Payment System (MIPS) and Alternative Payment Model (APM) Incentive Under the Physician Fee Schedule, and Criteria for Physician-Focused Payment Models Proposed Rule. (2016, May 9). Accessed from https://www.federalregister.gov/documents/2016/05/09/2016-10032/medicare-program-merit-based-incentive-payment-system-mips-and-alternative-payment-model-apm.

7. U.S. Department of Health and Human Services. (n.d.) *Summary of the HIPAA Privacy Rule*. Accessed on October 4, 2016, from www.hhs.gov/hipaa/for-professionals/privacy/laws-regulations/.

8. Precision Medicine Task Force. (2016, Feb. 26). *Task force meeting* [PowerPoint slides]. Accessed on October 4, 2016, from www.healthit.gov/FACAS/sites/faca/files/PMTF_Meeting_Slides_2016-02-26.pptx.

9. MITRE Corporation. (2014, Oct. 29). *Electronic consent management: Landscape assessment, challenges, and technology.* (Prepared for the ONC Office of the Chief Privacy Officer.) Accessed on October 4, 2016, from www.healthit.gov/sites/default/files/privacy-security/ecm_finalreport_forrelease62415.pdf.

10. Centers for Medicare and Medicaid Services. (n.d.). *Electronic health records (EHR) incentive programs.* Accessed on October 4, 2016, from www.cms.gov/Regulations-and-Guidance/Legislation/EHRIncentivePrograms/index.html?redirect=/ehrincentiveprograms/.

11. Office of the National Coordinator for Health Information Technology (ONC). (2016). Quick stats. *Health IT Dashboard.* Accessed on October 4, 2016, from http://dashboard.healthit.gov/quickstats/quickstats.php.

12. Merit-Based Incentive Payment System (MIPS) and Alternative Payment Model (APM) Incentive Under the Physician Fee Schedule, and Criteria for Physician-Focused Payment Models; Proposed Rule, 81 Fed. Reg. 28161 (May 9, 2016) (to be codified at 42 CFR pts. 414 & 495). Accessed on October 4, 2016, from www.federalregister.gov/documents/2016/05/09/2016-10032/medicare-program-merit-based-incentive-payment-system-mips-and-alternative-payment-model-apm.

13. ONC. (n.d.). *ONC Health IT certification program.* Accessed on October 4, 2016, from www.healthit.gov/policy-researchers-implementers/about-onc-health-it-certification-program.

14. ONC. (n.d.). *Health IT dashboard.* Accessed on October 4, 2016, from http://dashboard.healthit.gov/index.php.

15. National Quality Forum. (n.d.). *QDM and vMR harmonization.* Accessed on October 4, 2016, from https://www.healthit.gov/archive/archive_files/.../qdm_vmr_harmonization.pptx.

16. National Quality Forum. (n.d.). *Quality Data Model (QDM): Technical questions and answers.* Accessed on October 4, 2016, from www.qualityforum.org/Projects/n-r/Quality_Data_Model/Quality_Data_Model_(QDM)__Technical_Questions_and_Answers.aspx.

17. Health Level Seven International. (2015). *Introducing HL7 FHIR.* Accessed on October 4, 2016, from www.hl7.org/fhir/summary.html.

18. HL7 International. (n.d.). *About HL7 International.* Accessed from www.hl7.org/.

19. Slabodkin, G. (2016, May 19). *CMS says meaningful use will live on in MACRA.* Health Data Management. Accessed on October 4, 2016, from www.healthdatamanagement.com/news/cms-says-meaningful-use-will-live-on-in-macra.

CHAPTER 17

The Electronic Health Record as Evidence

Kimberly A. Baldwin-Stried Reich

In this chapter, you will learn how to

- Discuss the sources and structure of law within the United States and federal agencies that provide oversight of the nation's healthcare system, including the laws, rules, and regulations governing healthcare delivery
- Examine the importance of privacy and security of health information in regulatory investigations and the admissibility of electronic health records into a court of law
- Delineate the differences between federal, state, and local courts
- Describe the process of the discovery of the electronic health record and ensuring its admissibility as evidence into a court of law
- Explore the role that technology plays as the underpinning of the nation's healthcare information infrastructure
- Explain the impact the 2016 HIPAA access rules are having on the release of information and definition of the legal health record
- Review the 2015 amendments to the Federal Rules of Civil Procedure and the 2016 amendments to the Federal Rules of Evidence and understand their impact on the process of electronic discovery of the EHR and its production in a court of law

This chapter explores the primary role the electronic health record (EHR) plays in support of direct and indirect patient care activities and the secondary role it serves as evidence in legal, administrative, investigative, and regulatory proceedings. This chapter examines the legislative process and the federal agencies that oversee the nation's healthcare system and promulgate the laws that serve as the underpinning of the nation's health information infrastructure. It also examines the evidentiary impact of the 2015 amendments to the Federal Rules of Civil Procedure (FRCP), the 2016 Health Insurance Portability and Accountability Act (HIPAA) rules, and the 2016 amendments to the Federal

Rules of Evidence (FRE). Finally, this chapter anticipates the impact that the passage of the Cures Act in 2016 will have on the future of healthcare delivery and the nation's health information infrastructure.

Sources and Structure of U.S. Law

U.S. laws establish the standards of behavior, the means by which standards are enforced, and the mechanism to guide conduct. There are four primary sources of law within the U.S. legal system:

- Federal and state constitutions
- Federal and state statutes
- Decisions and rules of administrative agencies
- Decisions of the court

In this chapter we discuss the sources and structure of U.S. law to understand how each branch of the U.S. government operates. We examine how the branches of government work together to provide oversight of the nation's healthcare system, as well as to establish the laws, rules, and regulations that govern the nation's healthcare delivery system, including the admissibility of the EHR as evidence into a court of law. Through this appraisal of the legal system and overview of the structure and function of the federal government, we gain a better understanding of how the Constitution underpins all branches of government and serves as the ultimate source of law.

Three Branches of U.S. Government Responsible for Carrying Out Government Powers and Functions

The healthcare industry is one of the most (if not *the* most) highly regulated industries in the United States today. As such, it is important to understand the structure of the federal government, how laws are created, and the role the government plays in oversight and enforcement of the laws, rules, and regulations that impact the nation's healthcare delivery system. A law is defined as "any system of regulations to govern the conduct of the people of a community, society, or nation, in response to the need for regularity, consistency, and justice based upon collective human experience."[1] A regulation is defined as "a rule of order having the force of law, prescribed by a superior or competent authority, relating to the actions of those under the authority's control."[2]

The three branches of the government—legislative, executive, and judicial—are responsible for carrying out the governmental powers and functions and creation of laws, rules, and regulations. Each of the three branches of government has a different primary function. The following is a summary of the primary functions of each of the three branches of the U.S. government:

- **Legislative branch**   The legislative branch is the law-making branch of government, made up of the Senate, the House of Representatives, and agencies that support Congress. The primary function of the legislative branch is to enact laws.

- **Executive branch**   The president is the head of the executive branch of the government, which includes many departments and agencies. The primary function of the executive branch is to enforce and administer the law.

- **Judicial branch**   The judicial branch is made up of the Supreme Court, lower courts, special courts, and court support organizations. The primary function of the judicial branch is to adjudicate and resolve disputes in accordance with the law.

The three branches of government operate under a concept known as the separation of powers. Under this concept, no branch of the government shall have more power or control than the other two branches in the exercise of its functions and activities.

Executive Branch: President, Vice President, and Cabinet

Under Article II of the Constitution, the power of the executive branch is vested in the President of the United States, who also serves as head of state, leader of the federal government, and Commander in Chief of the armed forces. The president and the vice president comprise the executive branch. The president appoints the heads of the federal agencies, ambassadors, and other high-ranking officials, including members of the cabinet who also serve as members of the president's administration. The president and the president's administration are responsible for the execution and enforcement of the laws, rules, and regulations written by Congress. Fifteen executive departments, each led by an appointed member of the president's cabinet, are responsible for the day-to-day administration of the federal government. They are joined in this responsibility by other executive agencies such as the Department of Health and Human Services (HHS) and the Department of Justice (DOJ), the heads of which are not part of the president's cabinet but operate under the full control and authority of the president.[3]

The president also appoints the heads of more than 50 independent federal commissions, such as the Federal Trade Commission (FTC), and is empowered to enact special boards, commissions, or committees, such as President Bill Clinton did in 1997 when he created the President's Advisory Commission on Consumer Protection and Quality in the Health Care Industry.[4] The president also makes appointments to the Supreme Court, appointments of federal judges, appointments of ambassadors, and appointments to other federal offices. The Executive Office of the President (EOP) is composed of the immediate staff to the president, along with entities such as the Office of Management and Budget and the Office of the United States Trade Representative.

The president is vested with the power to sign legislation into law or veto bills enacted by the Congress, although Congress is vested with the power to override a presidential veto with a two-thirds vote in both the Senate and the House of Representatives. The president has broad authority to manage national affairs and establish the priorities of the government. The president also conducts diplomacy with other nations and has the power to negotiate and sign treaties. In addition the president has the power to issue rules, regulations, and instructions called executive orders,[5] which have the force and effect of law by carrying out a provision of the Constitution, a federal statute, or a treaty. Executive orders are published in the *Federal Register* to notify the public of presidential actions.

The president has unlimited power to extend pardons and clemencies for federal crimes, except in cases of impeachment. Article II, Section 2 of the Constitution states that the president "shall have Power, by and with the Advice and Consent of the Senate, to make Treaties, provided two-thirds of the Senators present concur." This means that two-thirds of the Senate must approve a treaty in order for it to be ratified.

Article II, Section 3 of the Constitution further stipulates that, with these powers, the president shall "from time to time give to the Congress Information of the State of the Union, and recommend to their Consideration, such Measures as he judge necessary and expedient."[6]

The president has the power and duty to make recommendations to Congress that the president deems "necessary and expedient." However, the judgment as to what a president determines as "necessary and expedient" has been argued in the courts. In the landmark opinion *Youngstown Sheet & Tube Co. v. Sawyer*[7] (1952), the Supreme Court ruled that President Truman lacked either constitutional or statutory authority to seize the nation's strike-bound steel mills. Instead, the court ruled that Congress would have had constitutional authority to do so.

This landmark decision is important to understand because it teaches us both about the Constitution, the role of Congress, the separation of powers doctrine, and the limits of presidential powers in issuing executive orders. Although the framers of the Constitution did not expressly enjoin the system of checks and balances of power our nation enjoys today, *Youngstown* demonstrates "that significant separation of powers depends on the existence of some effective counterweight to the executive ruler, which in turn presupposes a disposition to restrain the ruler that does not come from the ruler himself."[8]

Legislative Branch: The Senate and the House of Representatives

Under Article I of the Constitution, the legislative branch is made up of the Senate and the House of Representatives, which together form the United States Congress. The Constitution vests the Congress with the power to enact legislation, confirm or reject presidential nominations, establish congressional investigations, and declare war.

The Senate is composed of 100 senators, two from each of the 50 states. The vice president serves as the president of the Senate and may cast the decisive vote in the event of a tie in the Senate. The Senate has the power to ratify treaties to confirm presidential appointments that require the consent of the Senate.

The House of Representatives is composed of a total of 435 elected officials, divided among the 50 states proportional to their population. In addition, there are six nonvoting members in the House of Representatives that represent the District of Columbia, the Commonwealth of Puerto Rico, and four other U.S. territories. The Speaker of the House of Representatives is elected by the House of Representatives and is third in line in succession to the presidency. The House has several exclusive powers, including the power to initiate revenue bills, to impeach federal officials, and to elect the president of the United States in the event of a tie in the electoral college.

In order to pass legislation, the House of Representative and the Senate must pass the same bill by majority vote in order to send it to the president for his signature. The president has the power to veto legislation sent by the Congress, but the Congress may override a presidential veto by passing the bill again in each chamber with at least two-thirds of both bodies voting in favor of the bill.

The Legislative Process

Before a bill is signed into law, the first step it must undergo is its introduction to Congress. Anyone can write a bill, but only members of Congress can introduce legislation. The president traditionally introduces some bills, before Congress, such as the federal budget. However, after a bill is introduced to Congress, it may (and generally does) undergo drastic changes before it is signed into law.

Once a bill is introduced to Congress, it is referred to the appropriate committee for review. There are 17 Senate committees, with 70 subcommittees, and 23 House committees, with 104 subcommittees. The numbers, scope, and responsibility of the committees change with each new Congress. Each committee is responsible for the oversight of a specific policy area, and subcommittees take on more specialized policy areas or responsibilities. For example, the Senate Committee on Health, Education, Labor, and Pensions is composed of three subcommittees: Subcommittee on Children and Families, Subcommittee on Employment and Workplace Safety, and Subcommittee on Primary Health and Retirement Safety.

The election of Donald J. Trump as the 45th President of the United States on November 8, 2016, is expected to bring about "significant legal and regulatory changes."[9] There is no greater insight into some of the significant changes that the nation is about to undertake in reforming and reshaping the nation's healthcare delivery system than is evidenced by President Trump's appointment to lead the Department of Health and Human Services (HHS).

On February 10, 2017, Rep. Tom Price, a retired orthopedic surgeon from Atlanta, was confirmed as Secretary of HHS. In this new role, Secretary Price will oversee the Medicare and Medicaid Programs and the National Institutes of Health, making the Department of HHS a $1 trillion agency, the largest of any budget in the president's cabinet. Secretary Price is also expected to implement the repeal and the replacement of the Affordable Care Act. During his confirmation hearing, Rep. Price said this about health care coverage and his vision for the future:

> What I commit to the American people is to keep patients at the center of health care. And what that means to me is making certain every single American has access to affordable health coverage.[10]

The details as to what the repeal and replacement of the Affordable Care Act will look like are unknown at this time, but it is the current administration's stated commitment to reform the healthcare delivery system and to assure all Americans have access to affordable health care coverage.

PART III

On February 27, 2017, President Trump hosted a listening session with the CEOs of some of the nation's largest health insurance companies. During this session President Trump appealed to the CEOs of the nation's largest health insurance plans to work with Secretary Price to "stabilize the insurance markets and ensure a smooth transition to the new plan."[11]

President Trump's appointment to lead the Centers for Medicare and Medicaid (CMS), Seema Verma, was expected to be confirmed in early March, 2017. The CMS administrator "has the power to drive our nation's healthcare transformation—from volume to value…and innovations in healthcare delivery and services in Medicare can set the course for the entire healthcare industry."[12]

On February 28, 2017, in his first address to a joint session of Congress, President Trump reconfirmed to the nation his commitment to reshaping the nation's healthcare delivery system by promising to replace the Affordable Care Act "with reforms that expand choice, increase access, lower costs, and at the same time, provide better healthcare."[13]

In the coming months, the scope and direction of the healthcare delivery system and the laws, rules, and regulations impacting it will become clear once the president's cabinet appointments are confirmed and the membership of Congressional committees is solidified.

Administrative Agencies

The rules and decisions set forth by administrative agencies are other sources of law. Administrative agencies are established under Article 1, Section 1 of the Constitution, which states that "[A]ll legislative Powers herein granted shall be vested in a Congress of the United States."[14] The legislature has delegated to numerous administrative agencies the power through Article 1, Section 8, Clause 18, "…to make all Laws which shall be necessary and proper for carrying into Execution the foregoing Powers, and all other Powers vested by this Constitution in the Government of the United States, or in any Department or Officer thereof."[15] A summary of the powers and authorities of the administrative agencies are outlined in the sections that follow.

The Department of Health and Human Services[16] The Department of Health and Human Services (HHS) represents almost a quarter of all federal outlays. It administers more grant dollars than all other federal agencies combined. HHS's Medicare program is the nation's largest health insurer, handling more than 1 billion claims per year. Medicare and Medicaid together provide healthcare insurance for one in four Americans, and today with the addition of the Health Insurance Marketplace and the Children's Health Insurance Program (CHIP), at least one in three Americans receives some sort of coverage under HHS.

HHS works closely with state and local governments, and many HHS-funded services are provided at the local level by state or county agencies or through private-sector grantees. The department's programs are administered by eleven operating divisions, including eight agencies in the U.S. Public Health Service and three human services agencies. The department includes more than 300 programs, covering a wide spectrum of activities. In addition to the services they deliver, the HHS programs provide for equitable treatment of beneficiaries nationwide and enable the collection of national health and other data.

The Centers for Medicare and Medicaid Services[17]　The bill that led to the establishment of Medicare and Medicaid was signed into law on July 30, 1965, by President Lyndon B. Johnson. Formerly known as the Health Care Financing Administration (HCFA), the Centers for Medicare and Medicaid Services (CMS) has been providing health insurance coverage for Americans since 1966. CMS operates as part of HHS and administers the Medicare, Medicaid, CHIP, and Health Insurance Marketplace.

CMS is headquartered in Baltimore, Maryland, and maintains ten Regional Offices (ROs) throughout the country based on the agency's key lines of business: Medicare Plans Operations, Financial Management and Fee for Service Operations, Medicaid and CHIP, Quality Improvement, and Survey and Certification Operations. The ROs are the state and local presence and provide oversight, outreach, and education to beneficiaries, healthcare providers, state governments, CMS contractors, community groups, and others.

As the steward of the nation's healthcare funds, CMS is committed to strengthening and modernizing America's healthcare system. CMS does this by developing mechanisms to assure program integrity (reducing fraud, waste, and abuse), establishing value-based incentives to reward providers' clinical performance, and tying provider payments to expected clinical outcomes.

The Office for Civil Rights[18]　The HHS Office for Civil Rights (OCR) is the federal agency designated to provide administrative oversight and enforcement of the HIPAA Privacy and Security rules. The OCR has been responsible for oversight of the HIPAA Privacy Rule since April 14, 2003, and the HIPAA Security Rule since July 27, 2009. The OCR ensures that people have equal access and opportunities to participate in certain healthcare and human services programs without unlawful discrimination.

The goals of the OCR are accomplished by

- Teaching health and social service workers about civil rights, health information privacy, and patient safety confidentiality laws
- Educating communities about civil rights and health information privacy rights
- Investigating civil rights, health information privacy, and patient safety confidentiality complaints to identify discrimination or violation of the law and take action to correct problems

The Office of the National Coordinator[19]　The Office of the National Coordinator for Health IT (ONC) was created in 2004 under Executive Order and was legislatively mandated in the Health Information Technology for Economic and Clinical Health (HITECH) Act of 2009. The ONC is located within the Office of the Secretary of HHS and is the federal agency responsible for coordinating nationwide efforts to implement and use healthcare information technology (healthcare IT) and to facilitate the exchange of health information. The ONC serves as a resource to the entire healthcare system and was created to support the federal government's efforts to advance the adoption of healthcare IT.

PART III

On July 19, 2016, the ONC, OCR, and Federal Trade Commission (FTC) jointly published a report to Congress entitled *Examining Oversight of the Privacy and Security of Health Data Collected by Entities Not Regulated by HIPAA.*[20] This groundbreaking report was developed to specifically address the oversight gaps that exist today between HIPAA covered entities that collect and process health data from individuals and those that are not regulated by HIPAA but also collect and process health data from individuals.

The health data that are collected, used, and shared by entities not currently covered by HIPAA can be valuable for clinical decision making or relevant in a court of law. As such, this report is an important first step in advancing the standards and processes surrounding the searching, preservation, collection, processing, and production of such information as evidence, whether for clinical decision-making purposes or for submission to a court of law.

At the present time, while the ONC is at the forefront of national initiatives to advance the adoption of healthcare IT, it does not have administrative oversight responsibility for the design, usability, safety, or clinical functionality of healthcare IT or information exchange systems or any of the consumer devices in use today. The ONC is solely focused on advancing the implementation of healthcare IT and exchange of health information.

The passage of the 21st Century Cures Act on December 13, 2016, also established new requirements under HIPPA which specify that a researcher's remote access of protected health information (PHI) held within a covered entity's EHR does not constitute the removal of the PHI from the covered entity, provided that HIPAA-compliant privacy and security safeguards are in place within the covered entity and the researcher, and the researcher does not copy or otherwise retain any PHI.[21]

This provision was enacted in an effort to reflect the shift from paper-based medical records to maintenance of digital records. While the Cures Act directly addresses questions posed by covered entities about remote access, further legislative or regulatory activity appears to be necessary to clarify what constitutes the "premises" of the covered entity, as many covered entities do not maintain their EHR systems via local storage (digital or otherwise) but instead rely on third-party business associates.[22] In addition, the Cures Act does not provide direction as to harmonization of HIPAA and the Federal Policy for the Protection of Human Subjects (aka Common Rule) with respect to how such preparatory research activities should be structured. The Common Rule definition of research contained in 45 CFR 46.102(d) also includes "research development." Given that definition, more rules regarding the privacy and security of PHI regarding research activities conducted by the National Institutes of Health (NIH) and/or other federal agencies may be developed in the future.[22]

The Federal Trade Commission[23] The Federal Trade Commission (FTC) conducts a variety of activities to promote competition in healthcare, including outreach and education to businesses and consumers on healthcare privacy and security practices.

The FTC enforces federal consumer protection laws that prevent fraud, deception, and unfair business practices and provides guidance to market participants—including physicians and other health professionals, hospitals and other institutional providers, pharmaceutical companies and other sellers of healthcare products, and insurers—to help them comply with the nation's privacy and antitrust laws.

As part of the American Recovery and Reinvestment Act (ARRA) of 2009, the FTC issued a final rule requiring certain web-based businesses to notify consumers when the security of their health information is breached. In 2010, the FTC began enforcing the HIPAA Breach Notification rule, which applies to the following entities:[24]

- Vendors of personal health records (PHRs)
- PHR-related entities
- Third-party service providers for vendors of PHRs or PHR-related entities

In addition, the FTC has a Mobile Health Apps Interactive Tool to help developers learn the privacy and security rules and regulations they need to follow when creating their health apps for mobile devices.[25]

The Food and Drug Administration[26]   The Food and Drug Administration (FDA) has the following responsibilities:

- Protecting the public's health by assuring that foods are safe, wholesome, sanitary, and properly labeled, and that human and veterinary drugs, vaccines, other biological products, and medical devices intended for human use are safe and effective
- Protecting the public from electronic product radiation
- Assuring that cosmetics and dietary supplements are safe and properly labeled
- Regulating tobacco products
- Advancing the public's health by helping to speed product innovations
- Helping the public get the accurate, science-based information they need to use medicines, devices, and foods to improve their health

The FDA's responsibilities extend to all 50 states, the District of Columbia, Puerto Rico, Guam, the Virgin Islands, American Samoa, and other U.S. territories and possessions.

The Internal Revenue Service[27]   The Internal Revenue Service (IRS) is organized to carry out the responsibilities of the secretary of the Department of the Treasury under section 7801 of the Internal Revenue Code. The secretary has full authority to administer and enforce the internal revenue laws and has the power to create an agency to enforce these laws. The IRS was created based on this legislative grant. Section 7803 of the Internal Revenue Code provides for the appointment of a commissioner of internal revenue to administer and supervise the execution and application of the internal revenue laws.

On June 28, 2012, the U.S. Supreme Court ruled on several key issues affecting the Affordable Care Act (ACA)[28] in *National Federation of Independent Business, et al. v. Sebelius, et al.*[29] The Court ruled that the "individual mandate" to require individuals to purchase health insurance was constitutional. However, the Court also ruled as unconstitutional the provision that would permit the secretary of HHS to withdraw all of the

Medicaid funding provided to a state if that state chooses not to expand Medicaid to certain thresholds set forth in the ACA.

Until recently, the IRS served as the administrative agency responsible for providing the administrative oversight and review in the collection of all taxes and penalties to be assessed on individuals who do not have health insurance in accordance with the Supreme Court decision handed down on June 28, 2012. However, on January 20, 2017, when Donald J. Trump was sworn into office, he signed an executive order aimed toward the ultimate replacement of the ACA, which reads in part:

> Sec. 2….[T]he heads of all other executive departments and agencies (agencies) with authorities and responsibilities under the Act shall exercise all authority and discretion available to them to waive, defer, grant exemptions from, or delay the implementation of any provision or requirement of the Act that would impose a fiscal burden on any State or a cost, fee, tax, penalty, or regulatory burden on individuals, families, healthcare providers, health insurers, patients, recipients of healthcare services, purchasers of health insurance, or makers of medical devices, products, or medications.[30]

In accordance with this executive order, the IRS will no longer be responsible for the collection of taxes or penalties on individuals who do not purchase health insurance. And furthermore, this executive order also lays forth the foundation for another restructure and redesign of the nation's healthcare system.

The Office of Inspector General[31]   Established in 1976, the Office of Inspector General (OIG) is part of HHS and is the largest inspector general's office in the federal government. The OIG provides oversight of the Medicare and Medicaid programs, as well as the Centers for Disease Control and Prevention (CDC), NIH, and the FDA.

The vast majority of the OIG's resources are dedicated to fighting fraud, waste, and abuse in Medicare, Medicaid, and more than 100 other HHS programs. The OIG carries out its mission through audits, investigations, and evaluations that result in cost-savings or policy recommendations for decision-makers and the public. The OIG also educates the public and the healthcare industry about fraudulent schemes, including what to look for and how to report them, and develops and distributes resources to assist the healthcare industry in their efforts to fight fraud, waste, and abuse.

The Federal Bureau of Investigation[32]   Established in 1908, the Federal Bureau of Investigation (FBI) reports to both the U.S. Attorney General, who serves as the head of the Department of Justice (DOJ), and the Director of National Intelligence (DNI). The FBI maintains dual responsibilities for law enforcement and intelligence. The mission of the FBI is to protect the American citizens and uphold the U.S. Constitution.

The FBI employs over 35,000 people, working in 56 field offices located in major cities throughout the United States, 350 resident agencies located in cities and towns across the country, and more than 60 international offices located in U.S. embassies worldwide.

Combating and rooting out healthcare fraud is a high priority for the FBI because healthcare fraud impacts both the nation's economy and the lives of American citizens.

The FBI serves as the principal investigative agency involved in the fight against health-care fraud and maintains jurisdiction over both federal and private healthcare insurance programs. Healthcare fraud investigations are an integral area of focus for the FBI, and personnel in each of the 56 field offices are specifically assigned to investigate matters involving healthcare fraud.

To promote the exchange of facts and information between the public and private sectors in an effort to reduce the prevalence of healthcare fraud, the FBI works collaboratively with other federal agencies such as the OIG, FDA, and Drug Enforcement Administration (DEA); with state and local agencies; with private insurance groups, and with public-private entities such as the Healthcare Fraud Prevention Partnership (HFPP)[33] and the National Health Care Anti-Fraud Association.[34]

The Department of Justice[35]   The Judiciary Act of 1789 created the Office of the Attorney General. The Act specified that the Attorney General, originally a part-time position, must be "learned in the law," with a duty "to prosecute and conduct all suits in the Supreme Court in which the United States shall be concerned, and to give his advice and opinion upon questions of law when required by the President of the United States, or when requested by any of the heads of the departments, touching on any matters that may concern their departments."[35]

The DOJ officially came into existence on July 1, 1870, when Congress empowered it to handle all criminal prosecutions and civil suits in which the United States had an interest. In 1870, Congress also created the Office of the Solicitor General, who was charged with the responsibility of representing the United States in matters argued before the Supreme Court and to support and assist the Attorney General.

The 1870 Act was foundational to the establishment of DOJ, but over the years, with the addition of the Offices of Deputy Attorney General and Associate Attorney General and the formation of various components, offices, boards, and divisions, the DOJ has grown into the world's largest law office and the chief enforcer of all federal laws. The DOJ plays a crucial role in the enforcement of the laws, rules, and regulations governing the healthcare delivery system. The detection and elimination of healthcare fraud and abuse is one of the top priorities of the DOJ, along with advocacy to promote competition in the healthcare industry. The Antitrust Division of the DOJ enforces the antitrust laws in healthcare to protect competition and to prevent anticompetitive conduct.

HIPAA established a national Health Care Fraud and Abuse Control Program, under the joint direction of the Attorney General and the Secretary of HHS, acting through the HHS Inspector General (HHS/OIG), designed to coordinate federal, state, and local law enforcement activities with respect to healthcare fraud and abuse. In May 2009, the Attorney General and Secretary of HSS announced the creation of the Health Care Fraud Prevention and Enforcement Action Team (HEAT), an initiative designed to enhance collaboration between the DOJ and investigative agencies, such as the FBI. With the creation of the new HEAT effort, the DOJ pledged a cabinet-level commitment to prevent and prosecute healthcare fraud.[36] HEAT is composed of top-level law enforcement agents, prosecutors, attorneys, auditors, evaluators, and other staff from DOJ, HHS, and their operating divisions, and is dedicated to joint efforts across government to both prevent fraud and enforce current antifraud laws around the country.

Since its inception, HEAT has charged more than 2,300 defendants with defrauding Medicare of more than $7 billion and convicted approximately 1,800 defendants of healthcare felony fraud offenses.[36] The medical record is a key source of evidence used by federal investigators to root out and convict suspects of healthcare fraud. For example, a federal jury in the Southern District of Texas convicted a Houston-based home-health agency owner for her role in a $13 million Medicare fraud and money laundering scheme.[37] The home-health agency provider falsified medical records to make it appear as though the Medicare beneficiaries qualified for and received home-health services.

Judicial Branch: Structure and Function of the U.S. Court System

The U.S. court system is divided administratively into two separate systems: the federal district courts and the state courts. Each court system operates independently of the executive and legislative branches of government. The federal court system is set forth in Article III, Section 1 of the Constitution, which states that "[T]he judicial Power of the United States shall be vested in one supreme Court, and in such inferior Courts as the Congress may from time to time ordain and establish. The Judges, both of the supreme and inferior Courts, shall hold their Offices during good Behavior, and shall, at stated Times, receive for their Services, a Compensation, which shall not be diminished during their Continuance in Office."[38] While both the federal and state court systems are responsible for hearing certain types of cases, neither system is completely independent of the other, and the systems do interact on occasion.

Federal Court System[39]

The federal court system is composed of 94 district courts, 13 circuit courts, and one Supreme Court with at least one bench in each of the 50 states, as well as benches in Puerto Rico and the District of Columbia. A total of 1 to 20 judges preside in each district. District judges are appointed by the president and serve for life. Cases handled by federal district court include: cases involving violation of federal law and/or allegations of Constitutional violations; cases directly involving a state or federal government; maritime disputes; and/or cases involving foreign governments, citizens of foreign countries, or in which citizens of two or more different states are involved.

The courts of appeals are directly above the federal district court. The court of appeals system is composed of 13 judicial circuit courts throughout the United States, plus one court of appeals in the District of Columbia. There are a total of 6 to 27 judges in the courts of appeals. In addition to hearing appeals for their respective federal district courts, the courts of appeals also have jurisdiction to hear cases involving a challenge to an order of a federal regulatory agency.

The Supreme Court is located in Washington, D.C., and is also known as "The Highest Court in the Land." It is the only court that is explicitly mandated by the Constitution. The Supreme Court is composed of one chief justice and eight associate justices. When there is a vacancy on the Supreme Court, the president makes a nomination for membership and the Senate confirms or rejects the nomination. Like federal judges, once confirmed, a Supreme Court justice serves for life. When the Senate is in recess, the President may make a temporary appointment, called a recess appointment, to any federal position, including the Supreme Court, without Senate approval in accordance with Article II, Section 2, Clause 3 of the Constitution. A recess appointment shall last for one year or until such time that a nomination is confirmed by the Senate. The Supreme Court hears cases from state appellate courts on federal or constitutional matters. The Supreme Court has the authority to decline to review most cases and maintains final jurisdiction over all cases it hears.

State Court System[40]

The state court system is large and diverse. Currently, there are more than 1,000 various types of state courts and judges. State courts, which are also referred to as local courts, include magistrate court, municipal court, justice of the peace court, police court, traffic court, and county court. These courts are called the inferior courts. The more serious cases are heard in a superior court, also sometimes known as state district court, circuit court, or by a number of other names. The majority of healthcare medical malpractice cases are heard in the state superior court system.

State superior, district, or circuit courts are generally organized by counties, hear appeals from the inferior courts, and have original jurisdiction over major civil suits and serious crimes. Most of the nation's jury trials occur in state superior court. The highest state court is usually called the appellate court, the state court of appeals, or state Supreme Court and generally hears appeals from the state superior courts and, in some instances, has original jurisdiction over particularly important cases. A number of the larger states, such as New York, may also have intermediate appellate courts between the superior courts and the state's highest court. Additionally, a state may also have a wide variety of special tribunals, usually on the inferior court level, including divorce court, mental health court, housing court, juvenile court, family court, small-claims court, and probate court.

The Judiciary

The fourth source of U.S. law arises from judicial decisions, also known as case law (discussed in further detail in the next section). Today, many of the legal rules and principles applied by U.S. courts are rooted in the traditional unwritten law of England, based on custom and usage known as "common law." Today, "almost all common law has been enacted into statutes with modern variations by all the states except Louisiana, which is still influenced by the Napoleonic Code. In some states the principles of Common Law are so basic they are applied without reference to the statute."[41] In the process of deciding an individual case, the courts interpret regulations and statutes in accordance with the relevant federal or state constitution. The court will create and establish the "common law" when it decides cases that are not controlled by regulations, statutes, or a constitution.

The courts are responsible for making determinations as to whether specific regulations or statutes are in violation of the Constitution. The case of *Marbury v. Madison* established that all legislation and regulations must be consistent with the Constitution and that the courts hold inherent powers to declare legislation invalid when it is unconstitutional.[42] Some state courts have established specific sets of rules for interpretation of conflicting regulations and statutes.

PART III

Administrative agencies also have discretion as to how regulations or statutes are applied—and disagreements over the application of a specific regulation or statute can and do arise frequently. While the decision of an administrative agency can be appealed to the courts, the courts generally defer decisions to the relevant administrative agency and will limit their review of the matter unless the following conditions were not met:

- A delegation of the matter to the administrative agency was constitutional.
- The administrative agency acted within its authority and followed proper procedures.
- The agency acted on a substantial basis and acted without discrimination or arbitrariness.

Case Law   Case law is defined as "reported decisions of appeals courts and other courts which make new interpretations of the law and, therefore, can be cited as precedents. These interpretations are distinguished from 'statutory law,' which are the statutes and codes (laws) enacted by legislative bodies; 'regulatory law,' which are regulations required by agencies based on statutes; and in some states, the 'common law,' which is the generally accepted law carried down from England. The rulings in trials and hearings which are not appealed and not reported are not case law and, therefore, not precedent or new interpretations."[43] The term "common law" is often used interchangeably with case law.

CAUTION   Avoid using the terms "common law" and "case law" interchangeably, because "common law" refers to the traditional unwritten law of England, while "case law" refers to the laws that were established by judicial decision.

The Medical Record

An individual's health information, irrespective of its form, format (paper, EHR, EMR PHR, mHealth, telemedicine, health social media, or e-prescription), or location, contains vital clinical information to support the diagnosis and justify the care and treatment rendered to the patient. Certain information—including the patient's history, physical examination results, radiology and laboratory reports, diagnoses and treatment plans, as well as orders and notes from doctors, nurses, and other healthcare professionals—is routinely recorded into an individual's medical record when the individual is treated as an inpatient or an outpatient in a care facility.

EHR stands for "electronic health record" and is a computerized record system that originates and is controlled by physicians, hospitals, or clinics. EMR stands for "electronic medical record" and is a digital version of the patient's paper chart in the clinician's office. The EHR is viewed within the industry as the patient's "legal medical record." An EMR contains the medical and treatment history of the patient in one practice.[44] Oftentimes, the terms EHR and EMR are used interchangeably, but the EHR is intended to refer to a much more robust health record system versus the medical record of a physician office.

The PHR stands for "personal health record" and is a computerized record system that is maintained by the patient or a patient's caregiver or family member. The PHR is a tool that is used to collect, track, and share past and current information about a patient's health. At this time, in the absence of legal standards for preservation data from PHI, the "PHR is separate from, and do[es] not replace, the legal record of any health care provider."[45] In today's digital era, the fact that the PHR is not defined as a "legal record" presents a perplexing dilemma for patient care. For providers and organizations in malpractice claims, this information that may reside in a patient's PHR or other third-party devices can be valuable and clinically relevant, yet it may or may not be shared with the provider.

mHealth stands for mobile-health. This term refers to the delivery of medicine and public health using mobile devices, including smartphones, tablet computers, and laptops.

Telemedicine is a term used to refer to the evaluation, diagnosis, and treatment of patients at a distance using telecommunications technology.

Health social media is a term that generally refers to Internet-based tools that allow individuals and communities to gather and communicate; to share information, ideas, personal messages, images, and other content; and, in some cases, to collaborate with other users in real time.

The quality and integrity of the information contained in a medical record are essential for clinical, legal, and fiscal purposes, for correct and prompt diagnosis and treatment of the patient's condition, and for continuity of care. Therefore, all providers and entities alike should have some protocol in place to verify the authenticity and integrity of the information that is recorded into an individual's medical record, especially information obtained from external sources, such as PHRs, mHealth, and health social media.

According to Matthew Murray, MD, Chairman of the Texas Medical Association's Ad Hoc Committee on Health Information Technology, "Whether we're copying and pasting information from an old note to a new note or using templates that automatically bring in clinical information…it is our responsibility to make sure that the information that got pulled is accurate."[46]

In addition to assuring that the information that is pulled into the EHR is accurate, when providers or entities are presented with recordings or results from mHealth devices, PHRs, or health social media from their patients, the copies of these recordings, or notations, should be placed into the patient's medical record. The provider receiving such information should document that the results from the mHealth device or PHR were reviewed and discussed with the patient along with the actions, or recommendations, if any, that were made. Although there are benefits to incorporating data from PHRs, mHealth devices, and health social media into the medical record, it must be noted that, at this point in time, there are also risks associated with these data.[47] There is no way for providers or entities to assure the quality or integrity of data from these sources, yet providers and entities alike are now charged with a duty to review and discuss this health information with their patients when it is presented to them. Furthermore, it is distressing that because there are no standards related to the preservation of PHI data from PHRs, health social media, and other third-party devices, providers may be left unaware of the existence of valuable clinical data on these devices that may help defend them in the face of a malpractice claim.

PART III

Although the primary use of the medical record is to serve as a tool for the planning and communication of the patient's treatment and care, it also serves as a secondary source of information for other uses. It provides support and documentation for insurance claims, legal matters, utilization review, case management, care coordination, professional quality and peer-review activities of prescribed treatments and medications, and the education and training of health professionals. Medical records also contain useful statistical and research information for public health and resource-management planning purposes. They contain data for clinical studies, evaluation and management of the costs associated with treatment, and the assessment of population health.

Medical records also often serve as a vital piece of evidence in a court of law.[48] Today, with the widespread adoption of electronic health records, attorneys and providers now find themselves struggling to verify the accuracy and make sense of all the information contained in today's EHR systems, so much so that some states, such as Texas, have adopted position statements on the maintenance of accurate medical records.

In April 2015, Wynne M. Snoots, MD, released a position statement on behalf of the Texas Medical Board (TMB). It reads in part as follows:[49]

> While the Electronic Medical Record (EMR) was intended to improve patient care, to date EMRs have primarily functioned to administer, structure, and memorialize the individual encounters, which is only a portion of the care process. Since the adoption of EMRs nationwide, this deviation from the initial intended primary function of the EMR to the actual function of the EMR has impacted the patient care process and caused some fragmentation of that process. Specifically, EMRs generate a much larger mass of often repetitive data which obscures key clinical medical information that is relevant to patient care and continuity of care, thus camouflaging the patient centric and longitudinal data that is crucial for improving the overall health of populations and for evaluating and treating patient-level medical problems.

> To fulfill the overall objective of improving patient care while using EMRs, the necessary data elements must be properly identified, recorded, verified, and tagged in order to facilitate: 1) identification of relevant information; 2) accessibility to the information; and 3) transfer of information to patients and practitioners.

> Therefore, it is incumbent on healthcare practitioners to be proactive and insure that their EMRs improve patient care by verifying that EMR data/information:

> - Reflects accurate and complete information relevant to patient care.
> - Memorialize each patient's care over time.
> - Facilitate communication and coordination among all members of a patient's healthcare team.
> - Guide those providing future care.
> - Is transferred and exchanged with patients.
> - Satisfies all regulatory duties.
> - Assists in tracking for patient recall in the event of new health threats or new treatment options.

EMR technology, implementation and utilization are rapidly evolving and have presented numerous challenges along the way. In recent years, TMB has observed progressive difficulty obtaining medical decision making information from current records, which interferes with the accomplishment of our mission. It is not the role of the TMB to endorse EMR software or regulate technology. However, it is clearly within the TMB's scope and oversight duties to set forth standards and expectations for creating and maintaining a useful, meaningful and readable medical record. Accordingly, the Texas Medical Board is confident that current information technology can meet this challenge, if the right focus is applied by practitioners; thereby fulfilling the priorities for clinicians, patients, administrators and all others who use the medical record for their own purposes—while keeping patient care paramount.

Perhaps one of the best examples of one of concerns expressed by the TMB about EHRs is that, unlike paper-based medical records, the EHR is proving to be a difficult witness in a court of law.[50] Providers and attorneys alike are finding the outputs and screenshots from the EHR look nothing like the actual computer screen or data entry fields the provider saw, clicked, or keyed at the time he or she saw a patient or made a clinical decision. This dilemma is causing many problems for providers and attorneys alike because it is difficult for attorneys to take a deposition of a provider using the outputs from an EHR. In the paper era, the record was the paper record and the record reflected what the provider wrote and thought at the time the provider recorded or dictated his or her note. In the digital era, the providers and attorneys are finding that because EHR screenshots and the outputs look nothing like the tool the provider used to record his or her entries on a patient, it is very difficult for a provider to verify the authenticity of the information contained in the medical record. As a result, attorneys and a new team of expert witnesses now are tasked with spending hours reading, tracing, and reviewing the meta-data audit trails.[51] Those jobs didn't exist in the paper-based medical record era. Rather than being efficient tools, EHRs are now actually adding time and cost to the discovery process because there is no easy way to conduct testimony from providers or to search, cull, process, and produce relevant data from EHR systems today.[51]

To add further confusion about the medical record as evidence in a court of law, the introduction of new technologies, such as PHRs, mHealth devices,[52] health social media, telemedicine, e-prescribing, interoperability, and the electronic exchange of health information all add a new dimension to the legal process of discovery, especially e-discovery. These new technologies may contain important and/or clinically relevant information about a patient, but the information may be inaccessible to the provider as it may reside in locations outside the patient's EHR, or in a system or device outside the provider's or organization's control.

In some cases, a provider may have referenced or relied upon this information to make a treatment decision for a patient, and will have copies of the patient's medical records obtained from other sources incorporated into the EHR system for reference. All relevant or potentially relevant information is discoverable. However, this information, along with other potentially relevant information, such as the patient's genetic or genomic information, which presently resides outside of the EHR[53] but is not considered to be part of the "legal medical record" or part of the individual's HIPAA-designated record set, is released upon request for disclosure purposes.

Yet, under 45 CFR 164.524 an individual is entitled to their genetic or genomic information if they request it, along with "any item, collection, or grouping of information that includes PHI and is maintained, collected, used, or disseminated by or for a covered entity."[54]

Under 45 CFR 164.524, organizations may be left unaware of the existence of an impending lawsuit in today's digital era. A savvy attorney or plaintiff interested in going on a fishing expedition can request "complete copies" of "any and all of their PHI, in any form, or location wherever it may exist" (including all electronic PHI) and the organization under this rule would be required to provide the individual potential to their information.

It is generally easier for plaintiffs to identify and obtain anything potentially relevant they may need to initiate a malpractice claim than it is for a defendant to obtain all of the relevant clinical information that they may need to defend themselves. This is because at this time, there are no standards for the preservation of PHI from PHRs and other third-party medical devices, nor are PHRs, social health media, or other third-party medical devices defined as "legal medical records." And sometimes, crucial clinically relevant information that may help a provider or an organization defend themselves against a malpractice claims may exist in a PHR, mHealth device, social media platform, or other medical device.

This presents a perplexing dilemma for the healthcare defense attorney because when it comes to the legal process of discovery, especially e-discovery, the process can be time consuming, expensive, and technically overwhelming. Yet, the need to obtain all relevant information is crucial to the defense of a lawsuit. The process will be even more challenging if the provider, organization, or legal counsel has not established a litigation response team that can respond to e-discovery requests, testify about the organization's EHR systems, and address other information and record keeping systems within the organization. Paper-based record outputs no longer tell the complete story—rather, a team of technical experts is now needed to obtain the complete set of digital and paper records to reconstruct the events of a case. This is further complicated by the fact that there are no standards for easily searching, culling, processing and producing relevant clinical information from today's EHR systems, not only for litigation, but for any clinical encounter. EHR systems, to be of any value in improving population health while reducing care delivery and litigation costs, will have to evolve to become more efficient and useful tools that are easily searchable and able to produce just the right clinical information at the right time. At the conclusion of the patient's encounter, the clinical data in the EHR should accurately tell the patient's story while justifying the diagnoses, treatment, length of stay, documentation, coding, and billing without providers, attorneys, and technical experts having to spend hours reconciling paper outputs, screen shots, HIPAA audit logs, metadata and data sets, and staffing logs in order to figure out what happened to a patient and why.

Until such time that standards are developed for the preservation of PHI from PHRs, health social media, and other third-party medical devices, or unless providers and organization are able to obtain copies of relevant clinical data from a patient's PHR, health social media, or other medical devices through discovery, they will often be at a disadvantage because they are left unaware of the existence of crucial clinical data that they may need to defend themselves in a malpractice case.

Because there are no legal standards or systematic approaches for the submission of the EHR as evidence into a court of law, there continue to be privacy and security gaps, along with varying approaches in how health information is collected, stored, and used by entities not covered under HIPAA. The federal e-discovery rules that were enacted in 2006 and amended in 2010 and 2015 (and have been modeled in some state court systems) are the closest thing the industry has today as a standard approach for the discovery of information of EHR systems.

As we will examine later in this chapter, the federal e-discovery and evidence rules have begun to converge and overlap with the HIPAA 2016 OCR access rules. Covered entities, vendors, and legal professionals alike are now being mandated to take a close look at their organizations' release-of-information processes and how their medical records are accessed and used as evidence in a court of law and for regulatory investigations.

As these processes conduct reviews of their systems, it is hoped that through the changes they are now undertaking, they will ultimately lead to the development of new standards, systems, and processes related to the definition of an organization's HIPAA designated record set for disclosure purposes, and that the policies and procedures the organization will undergo when responding to various requests for patient information from patients and attorneys will be improved. It is also hoped that EHRs will evolve to become not only more interoperable but also searchable and able to produce the right summary of data at the right time based on the user's query.

The USA PATRIOT Act, signed into law in October, 2001, by President George W. Bush, also significantly expanded the search and surveillance powers of the federal government and provides federal officials with greater access to medical records. This law impacts HIPAA privacy and security rules, and how a medical record can be used as evidence in a legal procedure.

Furthermore, the passage of the 2016 Cures Act has laid the foundation for a new era in the nation's health information infrastructure through healthcare IT standards development to advance interoperability, assignment of penalties for blocking the sharing of electronic health records, development of registries through the exchange of EHR data and review, and development of HIPAA privacy and security rules governing human subjects protection (Common Rule) and the confidentiality of EHRs of individuals with behavioral health and substance use disorders.

The efforts CMS is establishing to innovate and strengthen Medicare coupled with demands by consumers, providers, and payers that they be given access to their health information that exists in a wide variety of forms, formats, and locations (even outside the EHR) are causing many entities and providers to rethink the processes by which they manage health information, giving rise to a new era known as health information governance.[55]

This paradigm shift from the centralized management and processing of the release of health information requests to a more decentralized process in which the individual's medical record can be more quickly and easily searched for the relevant information in a variety of forms, formats, and locations is necessary in order to meet the OCR's goal of providing individuals with timely and robust access to their health data so they can be empowered and engaged in the care coordination and decision-making process.

Furthermore, as national security, surveillance, and the rooting out of terrorism become increasingly important to the federal government, the government is placing new demands upon healthcare organizations. These demands are to develop new health information and records management policies that include the ability to quickly and easily search the records of individuals suspected of involvement in federal crimes or terrorist activities, and establish policies that notify individuals of their privacy and security rights under both HIPAA and the USA PATRIOT Act.

Under HIPAA, medical records can be used as evidence for law enforcement purposes. Law enforcement officials can obtain an individual's medical record without a warrant under the following circumstances:[56]

- To identify or locate a suspect, fugitive, witness, or missing person
- Instances where a crime has been committed on the premises of the covered entity
- In a medical emergency in connection with a crime

Under Section 215 of the USA PATRIOT Act,[57] the FBI Director and/or his/her designee has the power to obtain a court order under the Foreign Intelligence Surveillance Act (FISA), "requiring the production of any tangible things (including books, records, papers, documents, and other items) for an investigation to protect against international terrorism or clandestine intelligence activities, provided that such investigation of a United States person is not conducted solely upon the basis of activities protected by the first amendment to the Constitution." Like the provision under HIPAA that allows a law enforcement official to obtain copies of an individual's medical records without a warrant, the FBI has the power to obtain medical records of individuals suspected of engaging in terrorism or clandestine intelligence activities.

EHR Standards for Records Management and Evidentiary Support

Electronic health records are a complex and evolving ecosystem. As such, the Health Level Seven (HL7) standards development organization (SDO) has developed an EHR system standard known as the Records Management and Evidentiary Support Functional Profile (RM-ES FP). This profile serves as a framework for the functions and conformance criteria for EHR systems to follow in the design and implementation of an EHR system. On a regular and ongoing basis, an HL7 volunteer workgroup meets to review and discuss EHR conformance criteria for the RM-ES profile. The HL7 RM-ES workgroup charter is as follows:[58]

> The charge of the RM-ES project team is to provide expertise to the EHR work group, other standards groups and the healthcare industry on records management, compliance, and data/record integrity for EHR systems and related to EHR governance to support the use of medical records for clinical care and decision-making, business, legal and disclosure purposes.

The RM-ES Functional Profile is based on the premise that an "EHR-S must be able to create, receive, maintain, use, and manage the disposition of records for evidentiary purposes related to business activities and transactions for an organization. ... This profile establishes a framework of system functions and conformance criteria as a mechanism to support an organization in maintaining a legally-sound health record."[59] Given this purpose, it is recommended that vendors and organizations alike regularly review this profile to receive guidance and updates for these purposes. The progress of the workgroup can be followed on the HL7 wiki.[60]

The Role and Use of the Medical Record in Litigation and/or Regulatory Investigations

As previously discussed, one of the important secondary uses of the medical record is to provide support and documentation for legal matters regardless of its form, format (paper, electronic as an EHR, EMR, PHR, mHealth device, etc.), or location, or who the custodian of the record is. The patient's medical record also serves as an important form of evidence that is often used in the litigation process or as evidence in regulatory investigations. Yet the process by which medical records are discovered and admitted into evidence continues to change, evolve, and grow as rapidly as our nation's health information infrastructure. Vast and significant differences exist between the role and use of paper versus EHRs as evidence in a court of law and whether or not the official custodian of the medical record is the provider who treated the patient or the individual who maintained the information on their PHR or mHealth device. The remainder of this chapter will focus on the legal process of discovery and the role of the medical record as evidence in a court of law.

Paper-based Medical Records vs. Electronic Health Records in Discovery

There are vast and important differences between paper-based medical records and electronic health records and the process by which the information is collected, preserved, processed, and produced for litigation and/or regulatory investigations. Table 17-1 provides a synopsis of these important differences. It is important to review and understand these differences because they describe how and why the legal process and standards surrounding the discovery of electronically stored information (ESI) from EHRs in litigation and regulatory investigations is in a state of constant growth and evolution.

Although the federal mandate to implement EHRs was to improve healthcare quality and patient safety while reducing cost by an estimated $78 billion, the reality is that there are unintended consequences that also go along with the implementation of EHRs.[61] These unintended consequences include but are not limited to design flaws and data entry and documentation errors, all of which can result in harm, or even death, to a patient.[62] In Illinois, for example, a Chicago law firm won a record-breaking $8.25 million wrongful death settlement on behalf of a Chicago couple who suffered the loss of their infant son at only 40 days after a pharmacy technician typed the wrong information into a field in the hospital's EHR system and the infant died from an excessive sodium overdose.[63]

Difference	Description
Volume and reproducibility issues	• EHRs exist in substantially greater volumes. • Electronic information can be replicated automatically. • Paper does not need a device such as a computer to be read. • EHRs must conform to HIPAA standards for transmission of PHI.
Dynamic content and nature of electronic data	• EHRs are easier to change than paper. • The content of electronic information can change without human intervention. • The transmission and transfer of EHR data are not fixed in final form.
Metadata	• EHRs contain metadata; paper does not. • System, application, and/or user metadata are not readily apparent. • Metadata adds new set of retention and preservation obligations.
Lifespan/persistence of electronic data	• EHRs are much harder to dispose of; paper can be shredded and easily discarded. • Electronic data are not easily deleted.
EHR and information exchange environment	• EHRs and electronically exchanged data may be incomprehensible when separated from their environment. • Migrating from a legacy system to an EHR system involves a significantly different process that does not require imaging of documents.
Search, cull, and retrieval of electronic data	• Electronic data may reside in numerous locations and on numerous digital devices. • Paper documents are usually consolidated and maintained in single file folder. • EHRs and the exchange environment may obscure the origin, completeness, or accuracy of the information.

Table 17-1 Synopsis of Differences Between Paper-Based Medical Records and EHRs

To this day, this case serves as a call for action for some sort of regulatory oversight of the safety of EHR systems.

Litigation and regulatory investigations are a fact of life. With the advent of EHRs, EMRs, PHRs, and mHealth devices, the discovery process has become more complex and time consuming than ever before. It is very different from paper-based discovery. With EHRs and digital devices, a whole new team of professionals with very specific skills and background is needed to conduct forensic examinations of the digital data so testimony can be taken before the court as to what happened in a case and why. According to healthcare defense attorney and e-discovery expert Chad Brouillard, "healthcare institutions will be footing the bill for increasing demands by litigants who want access to the data, metadata, and the original displays of data as originally viewed by the clinicians. Those demands come with significant technical, administrative, and legal expenses, which are born solely by the parties in healthcare."[51]

Discovery and Admissibility of the EHR

Whether a record that is requested for litigation is actually discoverable or will be admitted as evidence during the course of a trial may significantly affect the outcome of a lawsuit. Therefore, it is important to distinguish between the discoverability versus the admissibility of a record as evidence into a court of law. Following is a summary of the differences between discovery and admissibility:

- **Discovery**   Discovery is defined as "the entire efforts of a party to a lawsuit and his/her/its attorneys to obtain information before trial through demands for production of documents, depositions of parties and potential witnesses, written interrogatories (questions and answers written under oath), written requests for admissions of fact, examination of the scene and the petitions and motions employed to enforce discovery rights. The theory of broad rights of discovery is that all parties will go to trial with as much knowledge as possible and that neither party should be able to keep secrets from the other (except for constitutional protection against self-incrimination)."[64] Often much of the fight between the two sides in a suit takes place during the discovery period.

- **Admissibility**   Admissibility denotes "evidence which the trial judge finds is useful in helping the trier of fact (a jury if there is a jury, otherwise the judge), and which cannot be objected to on the basis that it is irrelevant, immaterial, or violates the rules against hearsay and other objections. Sometimes the evidence an attorney tries to introduce has little relevant value (usually called probative value) in determining some fact, but prejudice from the jury's shock at gory details may outweigh that probative value. In criminal cases the courts tend to be more restrictive on letting the jury hear such details for fear they will result in 'undue prejudice.' Thus, the jury may only hear a sanitized version of the facts in prosecutions involving violence."[65]

The Federal Rules of Evidence (FRE)[66]

The Federal Rules of Evidence (FRE) are civil code adopted under the Rules Enabling Act that governs civil and criminal proceedings in federal court. The FRE are designed to secure judicial fairness, eliminate unjustifiable expense and delay, and promote the growth and development of the law of evidence. They provide for the exclusion of hearsay and exceptions to that rule. They also provide rules related to the authentication of evidence. For example, FRE Article X (Contents of Writings, Recordings and Photographs), Rule 101(1) sets forth the rules for the admission of digital writings, recordings, and photographs into a court of law. Under FRE Article X, writings and recordings are defined to include magnetic, mechanical, or electronic recordings. This means digital photographs that are stored on a computer are considered to be an original, and any exact copy of the digital photograph is admissible as evidence. (You should check your state's rules of evidence for admissibility of digital recordings and photographs. Most states have enacted their own rules related to the admissibility of digital evidence into a court of law.)

The FRE have the force of statute, and the courts interpret them as they would any other statute. The Supreme Court promulgates the FRE, and they are amended from time to time by Congress, as they were in 2008, when FRE 502 was enacted to provide limitations on the waiver of attorney-client privilege and work product protection.

In September 2016, proposed amendments to FRE 803(16), *Exceptions to the Rule Against Hearsay – Regardless of Whether the Declarant Is Available as a Witness – Statements in Ancient Documents*, and FRE 902, *Evidence That Is Self-Authenticating*, were approved by the Judicial Conference Committee and submitted to the Supreme Court.[67, 68] Barring any unforeseen changes, the amendments are expected to go into effect on December 1, 2017.

Medical Records as Hearsay

Hearsay is defined as "second-hand evidence in which the witness is not telling what he/she knows personally, but what others have said to him/her."[69] Under traditional rules of evidence, medical records are considered to be hearsay by a court of law. Hearsay is generally not admissible as evidence into a court of law, because the person who made the original statement is not available to be cross-examined. EHR systems and the electronic exchange of health information sometimes add more challenges to the hearsay rule because of the distinction between electronically stored information that was generated by the computer versus information that was entered by a user into a computer system. That said, "The courts have acknowledged the distinction between computer-generated and computer-stored information. 'If the system made the statement it is "computer-generated." If a person inputs a statement into the system that then preserves a record of it, it is "computer stored" evidence.'"[70]

Exceptions to the Hearsay Rule

Medical records are considered to be hearsay in the eyes of the court. However, they generally are admitted as evidence on other grounds. The most common way in which medical records are admitted as evidence into a court of law is through FRE 803. This rule is titled "Exceptions to the Rule Against Hearsay" and is also sometimes called the "business records exception." It applies regardless of whether the declarant is available as a witness. Under FRE 803, there are 24 key exceptions to the rule against hearsay, regardless of whether the declarant is available as a witness:[71] Summarized below are the most common exceptions to the hearsay rule that are used to admit medical records as evidence into a court of law.

- **Present sense impression** A statement describing or explaining an event or condition, made while or immediately after the declarant perceived it.

- **Excited utterance** A statement relating to a startling event or condition, made while the declarant was under the stress of the excitement that it caused.

- **Then-existing mental, emotional, or physical condition** A statement of the declarant's then-existing state of mind (such as motive, intent, or plan) or emotional, sensory, or physical condition (such as mental feeling, pain, or bodily health), but not including a statement of memory or belief to prove the fact remembered or believed unless it relates to the validity or terms of the declarant's will.

- **Statement made for medical diagnosis or treatment** A statement that is made for—and is reasonably pertinent to—medical diagnosis or treatment and describes medical history, past or present symptoms or sensations, their inception, or their general cause.

- **Recorded recollection** A record that is on a matter the witness once knew about but now cannot recall well enough to testify fully and accurately, was made or adopted by the witness when the matter was fresh in the witness's memory, and accurately reflects the witness's knowledge. If admitted, the record may be read into evidence but may be received as an exhibit only if offered by an adverse party.

- **Records of a regularly conducted activity** A record of an act, event, condition, opinion, or diagnosis that is admissible when it meets all of the following conditions:

  - The record was made at or near the time by—or from information transmitted by—someone with knowledge.

  - The record was kept in the course of a regularly conducted activity of a business, organization, occupation, or calling, whether or not for profit.

  - Making the record was a regular practice of that activity.

  - All these conditions are shown by the testimony of the custodian or another qualified witness, or by a certification that complies with Rule 902 or with a statute permitting certification.

  - The opponent does not show that the source of information or the method or circumstances of preparation indicate a lack of trustworthiness.

- **Absence of a record of a regularly conducted activity** Evidence that a matter is not included in a record if the evidence is admitted to prove that the matter did not occur or exist when the record was regularly kept for a matter of that kind; and the opponent does not show that the possible source of the information indicates a lack of trustworthiness. The FRE and some states contain provisions that also make medical records admissible under the hearsay exception for public or official records, along with various other types of records such as marriage, birth, and death certificates and records from religious organizations.

You should check to determine if hearsay exception rules exist within your state. If so, understand what those exceptions are with regard to medical records and what the process is to authenticate and admit a medical record as evidence within your state. Medical records are also admissible in most states under workers' compensation laws.

Physician-Patient Privilege

In certain circumstances, patients or healthcare providers may wish to safeguard protected health information from discovery by asserting a physician-patient relationship, thus shielding the protected health information from discovery. Nearly all states maintain statutes that protect the communications of a physician-patient relationship from disclosure in judicial or quasi-judicial proceedings under certain circumstances.

PART III

The purpose of the physician-patient privilege doctrine is to encourage the patient to discuss and disclose all information for care and treatment.[72]

Incident Report Privilege

An incident report is a useful tool for making decisions regarding liability issues that may stem from the event for which the report was generated. As a general rule, incident reports are protected from discovery. However, in 2014, supreme court decisions in three states—Kentucky, Utah, and North Carolina—addressed the discoverability of incident reports and focused on three distinct aspects of the issues.

In *Tibbs v. Bunnell*[73] the Kentucky Supreme Court held that data collected, maintained, and utilized as part of the Commonwealth of Kentucky's Patient Safety Evaluation System (PSES) was not privileged under the Patient Safety Quality Improvement Act (PSQIA) and may be discovered.

In *Allred v. Saunders*[74] the Utah Supreme Court adjudicated an important discovery dispute between a hospital and a physician. The plaintiffs sought discovery of the physician's credentialing file from the hospital as well as the incident report from the patient's lithotripsy procedure. The hospital and the physicians petitioned for a protective order pursuant to Utah Rule of Civil Procedure 26(b)(1) that provides the following:

> Privileged matters that are not discoverable or admissible in any proceeding of any kind or character include all information in any form provided during and created specifically as part of a request for an investigation, the investigation, findings, or conclusions of peer review, care review, or quality assurance processes of any organization of health care providers…for the purpose of evaluating care provided to reduce morbidity and mortality or to improve the quality of medical care, or for the purpose of peer review of the ethics, competence, or professional conduct of any health care provider.

The Court held that this petition ought to have been granted, conditional on a proper factual foundation, since Utah R. Civ. P. 26(b)(1) created a broad evidentiary privilege. The Court then remanded the case back to the district court for an individualized assessment of the applicability of the privilege.

In *Hammond v. Saini*[75] the plaintiff was injured in a fire that occurred in an operating room that was part of a county health system. The defendants argued the establishment of a Root Cause Analysis (RCA) team constituted a medical review committee, and the documents created by the RCA team were shielded from discovery. The North Carolina Supreme Court found that an affidavit from the county health system's risk manager was insufficient in meeting the required medical criteria as defined under N.C.G.S. § 131E–76(5)(c). Furthermore, the North Carolina Supreme Court ruled that the RCA Policy was also insufficient in demonstrating the applicability of N.C.G.S. §§ 131E–76(5) and 131E–95(b), in part, because the Court found that it did not appear that the RCA Policy had been adopted by the governing board or medical staff of the county health system. As a result, the Court held that the documents created by the RCA Team did not constitute a medical committee and thus their documents were not shielded from discovery.

Even if incident reports are not protected from discovery by state statute, the incident reports may be determined to be inadmissible as evidence under the hearsay rule. Incident reports serve not only to document the details, circumstances, and witnesses to an unusual event but also to alert defense counsel or insurers about potential liability issues that may arise at a future date. As is the case with records of peer-review activities, the first step in determining whether the records of the organization's incident reports are discoverable or admissible is to examine state statutory and case law for an understanding of how the statutes were applied by the court.

Similar to records of peer-review activities, incident reports hold significant evidentiary value to individuals and attorneys who are suing the organization for damages that may have occurred to them as a result of the untoward event. Therefore, the scope and application of any privilege that may protect incident reports from discovery is highly dependent on state law; the allegations contained in the lawsuit; and the nature, scope, and duties of the individual(s) responsible for reviewing the incident report, investigating the circumstances, and developing the report surrounding the event. Based on the decisions in the Kentucky, Utah, and North Carolina state supreme courts, entities are being challenged now to review their organizational policy and procedures. Organizations must establish information governance programs that include quality improvement, risk management, and litigation response planning activities as foundational components of their programs. Legal counsel and risk management staff must be knowledgeable about local, state, and federal rules of evidence and civil procedure surrounding the submission of evidence into a court of law.

The Scope and Procedures of E-Discovery Process

The scope and procedure for the process of discovery of information that may be relevant to litigation is contained in Rule 26(b) of the FRCP (Duty to Disclose; General Provisions Governing Discovery; Discovery Scope and Limits), which states:

> Unless otherwise limited by court order, the scope of discovery is as follows: Parties may obtain discovery regarding any non-privileged matter that is relevant to any party's claim or defense and proportional to the needs of the case, considering the importance of the issues at stake in the action, the amount in controversy, the parties' relative access to relevant information, the parties' resources, the importance of the discovery in resolving the issues, and whether the burden or expense of the proposed discovery outweighs its likely benefit. Information within this scope of discovery need not be admissible in evidence to be discoverable.[76]

Like the FRE, the FRCP are amended periodically by Congress. They underwent significant changes in 2006, 2010, and 2015 to address issues related to the discovery of electronically stored information in federal district courts. As the following excerpts indicate, these e-discovery amendments have been adopted by many states:

- As Thomas Allman notes in "E-Discovery in Federal and State Courts: The Impact of Rulemaking – Past and Future," "Thirty-two states have adopted e-discovery amendments as part of their civil rules inspired in whole or in part by the provisions of the 2006 Amendments."[77]

- As Chad Brouillard, an attorney practicing in Boston, observes in "Not a Bang, a Whimper: The Silent E-Discovery Revolution," "...e-discovery has impacted our state practice in a subtle, not dramatic fashion."[78]

The subtle changes at the state and local court levels combined with the proliferation of electronically stored information now being utilized in the state and local court systems are further driving the need not only for legal counsel, the judiciary, and healthcare professionals to understand the design, structure, and function of today's EHR systems, but also for the establishment of standardized systems and approaches in the culling, searching, preservation, collection, processing, and analysis of information in order to produce relevant information from EHRs, PHRs, eHealth devices, and other healthcare systems, such as eHealth Exchange data, e-prescribing, and telemedicine encounter data.

Impact of the 2015 Amendments to the E-Discovery Process

Despite the 2006, 2010, and 2015 amendments to the FRCP, legal counsel and judges are continuing to engage in discovery disputes and struggle with issues pertaining to the identification, preservation, collection, and production of electronically stored information (ESI) in the digital era. Furthermore, these challenges are becoming particularly perplexing when it comes to the healthcare e-discovery process. As Chad Brouillard writes in "EHR Audit Trails Might Reveal More Than You Think: Hall v. Flannery, a Sign of the Times:"

> [T]hose who work in healthcare are themselves confused about what an EHR actually is...in truth, the EHR digital data *is* the electronic medical chart. It does not exist to create anything in printed form; it is meant to remain electronic. It can create a printed paper or electronic image display (such as PDF or TIFF) of a subset of its data, but that representation will always be imperfect, incomplete, limited, and subject to change as time goes on. A printout of the record is an afterthought to the EHR vendor; they want us to forget paper.[51]

On December 1, 2015, the third set of amendments involving the discovery of ESI were made to the FRCP, which govern civil litigation in the federal courts.[79] These amendments highlight the important role electronic discovery continues to play in both litigation and regulatory investigations. The 2015 amendments reflect a diligent effort on the part of the drafters to reduce the costs and burdens that are associated with discovery and a continued concentrated effort to streamline the process and advance cooperation between the parties and to involve the court in the process.

It remains to be seen what, if any, impact the amendments will have in reducing overall discovery costs and burdens until such time that the courts apply and interpret them. Many experts predict increased costs in the initial stages of litigation, as some of the new rules shift certain actions to earlier in the proceedings.

To date, the courts that have dealt with these new amendments have found that, by and large, they have not radically altered the nature of the discovery process.

The key 2015 FRCP amendments are summarized in Table 17-2.[79]

Rule	Synopsis of Revisions/Change(s)
1	The rule now makes clear that the FRCP should be construed, administered, and employed by both the court and the parties to secure a just, speedy, and inexpensive determination of every action.
4(m)	The time to serve a defendant was reduced from 120 days to 90 days.
16(b)(1)	The court must issue a scheduling order after receiving parties' Rule 26(f) report or consulting with the parties via direct simultaneous communication. Those communications may be in person, by telephone, or by a more sophisticated electronic means.
16(b)(2)	The court must issue a scheduling order within prescribed time limits unless it finds good cause for delay. The prescribed time limits are the earlier of 90 days after defendant was served or 60 days after any defendant has appeared.
16(b)3(B)(iii)	The scheduling order may provide for disclosure, discovery, or preservation of ESI.
16(b)3(B)(iv)	The scheduling order may include agreements reached under Federal Rule of Evidence 502.
16(b)3(B)(v)	The scheduling order may direct that before moving for an order relating to discovery, movants must request a conference with the court.
26(b)(1)	The parties may discover information about any nonprivileged matter where the information is both relevant to any party's claim or defense, and proportional to the needs of the case. Factors to be considered to determine proportionality are The importance of the issues at stake in the action The amount in controversy The parties' relative access to relevant information The parties' resources The importance of the discovery in resolving the issues Whether the burden or expense of the proposed discovery outweighs its likely benefit
26(b)(2)(C)(iii)	The court must limit the frequency or extent of discovery if the court determines that the proposed discovery is outside the scope permitted by Rule 26(b)(1).
26(c)(1)(B)	The court is explicitly authorized to issue protective orders that allocate expenses for disclosure or discovery. This change is not meant to suggest that cost-shifting should become a common practice.
26(d)(2)(A)	A party may deliver Rule 34 requests to another party more than 21 days after that party has been served, even though the parties have not yet had a Rule 26(f) conference.
26(d)(2)(B)	Early Rule 34 requests are considered to have been served as of the date of the first Rule 26(f) conference, without regard to the date of actual delivery.
26(d)(3)	Parties may stipulate to, or the court may order, case-specific sequences of discovery.
26(f)(3)(C)	The parties must state their views and proposals on any issues about disclosure, discovery, or preservation of ESI in their discovery plan.

Table 17-2 FRCP 2015 Amendments (*continued*)

Rule	Synopsis of Revisions/Change(s)
26(f)(3)(D)	The parties must state their views and proposals on issues about claims of privilege or protection, including whether to ask the court to include their agreement in a Federal Rule of Evidence 502 order, in their discovery plan.
30(a)(2)	When determining whether to grant leave to take a deposition, the court needs to consider proportionality as set forth in Rule 26(b)(1).
30(d)(1)	When determining whether to allow additional time for a deposition, the court needs to consider proportionality as set forth in Rule 26(b)(1).
31(a)(2)	When determining whether to grant leave to take a deposition of written questions, the court needs to consider proportionality as set forth in Rule 26(b)(1).
33(a)(1)	When determining whether to grant leave to serve more than 25 written interrogatories, the court needs to consider proportionality as set forth in Rule 26(b)(1).
34(b)(2)(A)	Party responding to Rule 26(d)(2) early document requests must deliver responses within 30 days of Rule 26(f) conference.
34(b)(2)(B)	Parties objecting to document requests must specify the grounds for objecting.
34(b)(2)(C)	Parties objecting to document requests must state, with each objection, whether they are withholding any responsive materials on the basis of that objection.
37(a)(3)(B)(iv)	Requesting party may bring motion to compel if responding party fails to • Produce documents • Respond that inspection will be permitted • Permit inspection
37(e)	Rule 37(e) was replaced entirely and is a completely new rule. It now "authorizes and specifies measures a court may employ if information that should have been preserved is lost, and specifies the findings necessary to justify these measures," according to Committee Note. Rule 37(e) applies only to ESI. The court takes action only if: • ESI has been lost, • The lost ESI should have been preserved in the anticipation or conduct of litigation, • The party failed to take reasonable steps to preserve the ESI, and • The ESI cannot be restored or replaced through additional discovery.
37(e)(1)	If the court finds that another party has been prejudiced by the loss of the information, the court may order measures no greater than necessary to cure the prejudice.
37(e)(2)	If and only if the court finds that the other party acted with intent to deprive another party of the information's use in the litigation, the court may take one of three actions, as described in Rules 37(e)(2) A, B, and C.
37(e)(2)(A)	Presume the lost information was unfavorable to the party.
37(e)(2)(B)	Instruct the jury that it may or must presume the lost information was unfavorable to the party.
37(e)(2)(C)	Dismiss the action or enter a default judgment.

Table 17-2   FRCP 2015 Amendments (*continued*)

Figure 17-1 shows the Electronic Discovery Reference Model (EDRM), a leading standards organization for the e-discovery and information governance marketplace acquired by Duke Law in August 2016.[80] The EDRM provides a conceptual view of the ESI discovery process and demonstrates how and why the management of health information involves the adoption of good information governance policies and procedures regarding privacy, security, and the storage, retention, and destruction of information. In addition, covered entities should establish data maps and information management plans to help legal counsel and regulatory agencies understand the uses of data and how data flow in and out of the organization.

The 2006, 2010, and 2015 FRCP amendments, coupled with widespread adoption of EHRs, continue to mandate the need for new HIT standards and approaches to support the discovery of health information from EHRs, PHRs, mHealth devices, e-prescription management, telemedicine, and eHealth information exchange systems. Chad Brouillard addresses this need in "EHR Audit Trails Might Reveal More Than You Think: Hall v. Flannery, a Sign of the Times":[51]

> What do we mean now when we say a "medical chart" in an EHR? Is it a printed, hard copy approximation of what we could hold in our hands in the paper chart paradigm? Or is it the underlying data, metadata, and functionality of a true electronic health record that only resides in the EHR servers and is usable only with unique, proprietary software, but useless outside that environment?

As Brouillard concludes, the answers to these questions will have a direct and profound impact on litigation, especially as it relates to the discovery of health information from EHRs and other related devices and the disruptive impact that EHRs are having on litigation costs.

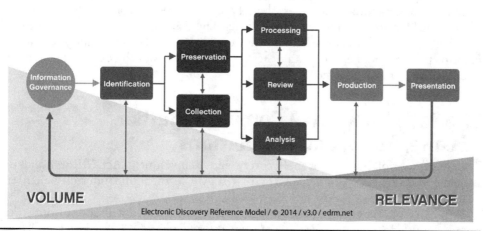

Electronic Discovery Reference Model

Electronic Discovery Reference Model / © 2014 / v3.0 / edrm.net

Figure 17-1   Electronic Discovery Reference Model

PART III

The passage of the 21st Century Cures Act will also further advance the development of standards for EHR usability and interoperability for both the clinical and legal processes. The new healthcare IT standards that will be developed through the implementation of electronic exchange will help to drive down discovery costs, and improve innovation techniques to be used to aid in the searching, culling, preservation, and production of PHI data.[21]

Duty to Preserve Relevant Evidence and Establishing Legal Holds

A classic series of precedent-setting caselaw decisions regarding e-discovery arose out of the case *Zubulake v. USB Warburg* between 2003 and 2005. The decisions, issued by Judge Shira Scheindlin in the U.S. District Court for the Southern District of New York State, are known as *Zubulake I–V* and are significant because they were utilized in the development of the 2006 and 2015 amendments to the Federal Rules of Civil Procedure. *Zubulake IV* remains known as the "gold standard" caselaw decision regarding the duty to preserve evidence. In this landmark decision, the court determined "The obligation to preserve evidence arises when the party has notice that the evidence is relevant to litigation or when a party should have known that the evidence may be relevant to future litigation."[81]

To comply with the *Zubulake IV* standard, a component of any litigation response plan should include the identification of specific events or occurrences known as "litigation triggers," in which the organization or provider immediately identifies, preserves, and establishes a legal hold on all information (paper and electronic) that may be relevant to a legal action or regulatory investigation. Furthermore, an organization with a well-established information governance program should be able to easily assess and value the risk of a potential case the moment it knows or reasonably should have known of a potential risk to the organization.

Once an organization or provider has established a legal hold (which should always be in writing and issued at the direction of legal counsel, risk management, or corporate compliance as appropriate), a process should also be in place to confirm that all custodians and the IT department have received the legal hold and understand it. Once the legal hold has been issued, the organization must establish a process to routinely review and monitor the legal hold and expand or retract it as the facts of the case or investigation into a potential threat become known.

The Path Forward: A Coming Together of Laws, Rules, and Regulations

The enactment of the American Recovery and Reinvestment Act (ARRA) and the Patient Protection and Affordable Care Act (ACA) laid the foundations of the current healthcare system.

In June 2014, the ONC released a high-level report, created with input from stakeholders, entitled *Connecting Health and Care of the Nation: A 10-Year Vision to Achieve an Interoperable Health IT Infrastructure*. This document describes the ONC's broad vision and framework to develop the nation's healthcare IT infrastructure of tomorrow and to work to establish a clear pathway toward interoperability.[82] This report was created to invite healthcare IT stakeholders—clinicians, consumers, hospitals, public health, technology developers, payers, researchers, policymakers, and many others—to join the ONC in developing a defined, shared roadmap that would allow the nation to collectively achieve healthcare IT interoperability as a core foundational element of a learning health system.

The healthcare IT infrastructure that has been outlined by the ONC will have a direct impact on local, state, and federal civil procedural rules as the discovery of ESI will be more commonplace than paper discovery and new skills, systems, and processes will be required to access, preserve, and produce relevant health information.

The ONC remains at the forefront of healthcare IT advancement efforts. Meanwhile, the establishment of the eHealth Exchange (introduced in Chapter 13) and the development of standards for interoperability are working to realize the vision set forth in the President's Council of Advisors on Science and Technology (PCAST) report.[83] These forces of federal and non-federal agencies are coming together with a common mission and purpose to improve patient care, streamline disability benefit claims, and improve public health reporting through secure, trusted, and interoperable health information exchange.

The HITECH Act

As part of the ARRA of 2009, the HITECH Act expanded HIPAA Privacy Rule requirements. Section 13402 of the HITECH Act also established a new federal security breach reporting requirement for HIPAA covered entities (CEs) and their business associates (BAs). Section 13402 requires a CE that "accesses, maintains, retains, modifies, records, stores, destroys, or otherwise holds, uses, or discloses unsecured protected health information" to "notify each individual whose unsecured protected health information has been, or is reasonably believed by the covered entity to have been, accessed, acquired, or disclosed as a result of such breach."[84]

The Health Insurance Portability and Accountability Act

The enactment of HIPAA established a complex and comprehensive federal scheme for the privacy and security of PHI. While federal law takes precedence in conflicts between federal and state law, HIPAA contains provisions that determine when HIPAA will pre-empt state law in matters relating to privacy and security. Generally, the more stringent rule—federal or state—is the law that will apply in matters related to the protection of health information. HIPAA regulations establish an array of individual rights with respect to the maintenance and access to their health information. For more information on HIPAA, see Chapter 15. For brevity, the information about HIPAA in Chapter 15 will not be repeated here. Instead, salient aspects of HIPAA as they apply to legal record concepts are discussed in this section.

Individuals, agencies, and organizations that meet the definition of a covered entity under HIPAA are responsible for the protection of the privacy and security of health information and must provide individuals with certain rights with respect to their health information, irrespective of in whatever form, format, or location it may exist.

If a CE utilizes a BA to help it carry out its healthcare activities and functions, that CE must also establish a written BA contract or another contractual arrangement with the BA that establishes specifically what the BA has been engaged to do and requires the BA to comply with the HIPAA requirements to protect the privacy and security of PHI. In addition to these contractual obligations, BAs are also directly liable under HIPAA for their actions and may be subject to civil and, in some cases, criminal penalties for making uses and disclosures of PHI that are not authorized by its contract or required by law.

The HIPAA Privacy Rule has always provided individuals with a right to access and copy their health information. Historically, the Health Information Management (HIM) Department or Medical Records Department often served as the central clearinghouse within the organization for the receipt, review, and processing of the requests for health information. Today, however, the widespread adoption of EHRs coupled with changing regulations and care delivery models and settings are demanding that individuals and their agents be given access to their health information not only in a wide variety of forms and formats, ranging from paper to electronic means, but also more quickly, easily, in real time, and on demand.

The OCR maintains that individuals have a basic right to their health information and also believe individuals should be engaged in the healthcare decision-making process. One of the best ways providers and organizations can achieve both is to empower individuals by giving them robust access to their health data.

On January 7, 2016, the OCR took a groundbreaking first step in reducing what some describe as long-standing obstacles and barriers that have hindered individuals and requesting parties in obtaining copies of medical records and other health information from providers, hospitals, and health insurance plans.[85] The OCR released for the first time a series of frequently asked questions (FAQs) to educate individuals and entities alike about an individual's right to access their health information under HIPAA and to help them take advantage of this right.

These FAQs have had the practical effect of becoming a first step in transforming the healthcare release of information (ROI) and e-discovery processes as the rules continue to overlap and converge closer to one another—topics we reviewed in the sections regarding the amendments to the FRCP and their impact on the e-discovery and ROI processes. The following sections compare and contrast the ROI and e-discovery processes.

The Convergence of E-Discovery and Release of Information Processes

The discovery of electronically stored information is growing and evolving almost as rapidly as our healthcare information infrastructure.[86] This has been due in large part to the enactment of the 2006, 2010, and 2015 FRCP amendments, as well as the steady adoption of e-discovery rules in state courts. To date, over two-thirds of the state courts have established some form of e-discovery rules.

"Electronic medical records can overwhelm—and often change—the course of a medical liability lawsuit," says defense attorney Catherine J. Flynn.[87] The EDRM previously presented in Figure 17-1 depicts the process by which information is searched, preserved, culled, analyzed, and produced for litigation. As the diagram depicts, a vast amount of information is initially collected and preserved, yet only a very small amount of data is actually produced and presented at trial.

The adoption of EHRs, electronic exchange of health information (interoperability), PHRs, mHealth devices, and health social media, all of which share health information with providers, will make this process even more challenging in the years ahead and will require trained legal and clinical professionals to review the information contained in an EHR and testify before a court of law.

In addition, as previously mentioned, one of the more notable phenomena arising in healthcare today is the overlap and interrelationship between the ROI and e-discovery processes. An examination of FRCP Rules 34 and 45 overlaid against the 2016 OCR HIPAA access requirements demonstrates how and why the e-discovery and ROI processes are now converging and overlapping with one another. These once separate functions have now become closely and inextricably linked and related to one another, and are crucial components of any information governance program. There are six crucial components to any information governance program, each of which builds and depends on the others, as depicted in Figure 17-2 and briefly described here:

- **Tapestry of state, federal, and other regulatory requirements** The foundational state and federal e-discovery rules, along with other state and licensing requirements that healthcare organizations and providers must comply with. They include, but are not limited to, Medicare, Medicaid, and state requirements; regulatory standards required by the Joint Commission, National Committee for Quality Assurance (NCQA), and URAC; and health plan database reporting requirements set forth by the Healthcare Effectiveness Data and Information Set (HEDIS).

Figure 17-2
Information governance program building blocks

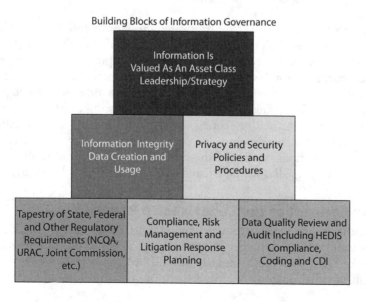

Building Blocks of Information Governance

- **Compliance, risk management, and litigation response planning**   The organization's ability to measure and assess its risk and to review and respond to risk management occurrences, including but not limited to security breaches, patient safety incidents, unexpected patient deaths, regulatory compliance and litigation matters, and organizational policies for the review and establishment of legal holds.

- **Data quality review and audit**   The establishment of internal and external controls on the review of the quality and integrity of documented clinical and financial data, including the existence of a clinical documentation improvement program.

- **Information integrity during data creation and usage**   The establishment of standards and time checks to ensure that the information created from the organization's EHR and other HIT systems is accurate and time synchronized properly.

- **Privacy and security policies and procedures**   The establishment of written policies and procedures that describe who has access to the organization's EHR and other HIT systems, how passwords are used and maintained, and what privacy and security training is required of all individuals within the organization.

- **Information is valued as an asset class**   This is the highest tier. It requires leadership and the ability to use information strategically. Organizations with mature information governance programs will have a formal means to place a numeric value on their information to assess risk, establish defensible legal holds, and reduce threats. At this level of operation, the entity can more easily identify a threat (HIPAA or cybersecurity breach or litigation threat) early on in the matter, assign a value to the case, and investigate the matter and readjust the value of the case as the facts become known.

As shown in Table 17-3, historically, the Health Information Management (HIM) Department was designated as the official custodian of the patient's medical record. As such, most HIM departments are experienced in processing and responding to state and local court subpoenas, as the vast majority of malpractice litigation occurs at those levels. However, in the new and changing health information governance paradigm, organizational procedures related to the access and processing of PHI, processing of subpoenas, and release of information requests are going to change and evolve dramatically as more PHI that providers rely upon for decision making (such as genetic and genomic data) resides in locations outside of the EHR, including but not limited to e-mail, mHealth devices, social media, voicemail, and other digital files and formats.

The Concept of the Legal Health Record

Healthcare providers, attorneys, and the courts all rely upon, utilize, and exchange "relevant" information, whether their case is a clinical one or a legal one. The combination of FRCP Rule 26(b) and the new HIPAA access rules is compelling healthcare and legal providers alike to rethink the nature, composition, and content of the patient's

Release of Information	E-Discovery
The process of making determinations as to whether or not an external requestor is authorized to access an individual's health information	The process of compiling, storing and securing digital information (including an individual's PHI), such as e-mail, documents, databases, voicemail, social media, etc., in response to a request for production in a lawsuit or regulatory investigation
Traditional Health Information Management (HIM) Function	New and Evolving HIM Function
The Director of Medical Records/HIM Department was generally named as the official custodian (or "keeper") of the individual's medical record	The Individual(s) with administrative control over the physical and remote storage and protection of records throughout their retention period.
One Official Custodian	Multiple Custodians
The types of requests varied, ranging from individual requests, to internal requests, but also requests for litigation and regulatory investigations	The types of requests are not varied. E-Discovery focuses on requests for litigation, regulatory investigations and/or administrative tribunals.
ROI: A critical component of the healthcare organization's Information Governance Program	E-Discovery: A critical component of the healthcare organization's Information Governance Program

Reprinted with permission from The Sedona Conference®[88]

Table 17-3 Contrast and Comparisons of Release of Information vs. E-Discovery Processes[88]

medical record. The rethinking of the composition of the medical record facilitates setting aside elements of the record included by other designations, such as HIPAA's designated record set, which is usually of no interest in discovery, to thinking about other aspects of the medical record that were traditionally not elements of a discovery request. Data items such as HIPAA audit trails, clinical decision support functions, or data from biomedical devices may be in scope in a given litigation setting.[89] These and other considerations are mandating the need for the establishment of new standards, systems, and processes for the culling, searching, processing, and production of health information for both discovery and release of information purposes, along with the establishment of information governance programs which now value data as an asset class and are demanding processes in place to measure and assess risk.[89]

The concept of "relevancy" is an important decision-making factor in both the clinical and legal process. The legal industry has long understood this concept, and for that reason, the concept of relevancy is incorporated into the e-discovery rules. The further challenge the healthcare industry, attorneys, and the courts have before them now is how to rethink and redefine: (1) the form, format, content, and location of the "legal health record" within changing, expanding, and system-to-system variability in the nature and scope of "relevancy," and (2) aging concepts for defining sufficiency for release of information for disclosure purposes, as in the "legal health record" concept.

To date, there have been many attempts to define or redefine the "legal health record" to bridge from paper to digital environments. The following are representatives of the many definitions and principles surrounding the composition of the "legal health record":

- **Definition of the legal health record**   "A legal health record (LHR) is the documentation of patient health information that is created by a health care organization. The LHR is used within the organization as a business record and made available upon request from patients or legal services."[90]

- **Defining the legal health record: A guiding principle**   "Defining the legal record – A healthcare organization collects a variety of information on individuals (clinical, financial, administrative). Organizations must identify, and declare, in policy the content of the formal health record that will be the official representation of a stay, encounter, or episode of care and disclosed upon request."[70]

These definitions and principle are now inadequate and passé when measured against the backdrop of the intent of federal, state, and local e-discovery rules that mandate the requester be given access to any/all "relevant" information in today's mix of paper and digital records. No longer is it appropriate for a provider or healthcare organization to declare what is the "official representation" of a stay, encounter, or episode of care that will be disclosed upon request. Rather, the new HIPAA access requirements now support the concept of allowing an individual access to any/all "relevant" PHI and specifically define a "record" as follows:

> Any item, collection, or grouping of information that includes PHI and is maintained, collected, used, or disseminated by or for a covered entity.[91]

Under the new HIPAA access rules, individuals have a right to a broad array of health information about themselves maintained by or for CEs, including medical records, billing and payment records, insurance information, clinical laboratory test results, medical images such as X-rays, wellness and disease management program files, and clinical case notes, among other information used to make decisions about individuals. In responding to a request for access, a CE is not, however, required to create new information, such as explanatory materials or analyses, that does not already exist in the designated record set.[91]

This paradigm shift now requires the healthcare industry to rethink the defining characteristics and supporting principles of the HIPAA designated record set, along with a means to assure the quality and veracity of the data for each of multiple designated end uses. Significant rethought is expected in the context of e-discovery rules and OCR access requirements as it is becoming clearer how to establish the associated new information governance and ROI processes that embrace the concept of "relevance" in the context of leveraging the improved capabilities for EHRs to produce outputs designed to meet various end-use requirements and specifications.

Furthermore, as national security and intelligence interests continue to rise, investigators will require access to records, including medical records, for the conduct of lawful intelligence, counterintelligence, and other national security activities authorized by the National Security Act.

The 21st Century Cures Act also lays forth new requirements for the electronic exchange and interoperability of EHR systems (Title IV—Delivery) and calls upon the OCR to establish additional guidance that would further clarify the permitted uses and disclosures of PHI of patients undergoing or seeking behavioral health or substance use disorder treatment (Title XI—Compassionate Communication on HIPAA). This guidance includes requiring HHS to develop model education and training programs to educate stakeholders on the permitted uses and disclosures of such information.[21]

Because of these changing paradigms, it is becoming clear that the concept of the "legal health record" is becoming obsolete because it erroneously conveys the misconception that the provider or entity can establish through policy what is and what is not "legal" for discovery and disclosure purposes. The problematic nature of this concept becomes clear, especially when measured against OCR guidance regarding what covered entities should define as an individual's designated record set for disclosure purposes under HIPAA.[92]

No better example of the struggle to define the HIPAA designated record set and concept of relevance can be found than in the evolving field of genomics. As Kannry and Williams state in *Integration of Genomics into the Electronic Health Record: Mapping Terra Incognita*, "To date, no commercial EHR system has been described that systematically integrates genetic or genomic data, let alone uses this information to translate disease risk into treatment recommendations."[93] As Kannry and Williams find, today, genomic data is not integrated into a patient's EHR. Therefore, when it comes to a traditional ROI disclosure request for a patient's medical record, this important, and what could be argued clinically relevant, piece of clinical data cannot be produced as part of the patient's EHR because these data reside outside of it.

As such, the principle that "organizations must identify, and declare, in policy the content of the formal health record that will be the official representation of a stay, encounter, or episode of care and disclosed upon request[70] is troubling when measured against the new HIPAA access rules that state that individuals be provided access to "any item, collection, or grouping of information that includes PHI and is maintained, collected, used, or disseminated by or for a covered entity."[91]

Healthcare IT and HIM professionals have vital roles in helping legal and compliance professionals preserve, search, cull, and produce information that may be relevant to litigation or regulatory investigations. They may also potentially serve as expert witnesses in litigation and regulatory investigations in helping attorneys and the courts assess and interpret the quality and integrity of the ICD, CPT, SNOMED CT, and LOINC coded information contained in the patient's medical record. (For more information on these code sets, see Chapter 13.) As the OCR continues to educate consumers on their right to access their health data, it is predicted that new systems and processes will be established to provide individuals with more robust, direct, real-time access to their health information to be used for a variety of purposes, ranging from the management of their health to litigation, all of which point to a need for accessible and trustworthy data. Furthermore, preservation and access rules governing the clinical data contained on PHRs, health social media, and other devices may be of tremendous value to a provider in the face of impending litigation. However, they are often left unaware of the existence of this information because of the lack of standards, rules, and regulations governing the use, preservation, disclosure. and protection of this information.

A New Era in the Nation's Health Information Infrastructure

On July 1, 1944, President Franklin D. Roosevelt signed the Public Health Service Act[94] into law. This groundbreaking piece of legislation led the way toward the development of the healthcare delivery system that the nation enjoys today. Many of the federal regulations that govern the nation's healthcare delivery system stem from the Public Health Service Act. At the time of the signing of the Public Health Service Act, President Roosevelt said:

> [T]he Public Health Service Act is an important step toward the goal of better national health. A constituent of the Federal Security Agency since 1939, the U.S. Public Health Service is one of the oldest Federal agencies—and one in which the people have great confidence because of its excellent record in protecting the health of the Nation.
>
> The Act signed today gives authority to make grants-in-aid for research to public or private institutions for investigations in any field related to the public health. It authorizes increased appropriations for grants to the States for general public health work. It strengthens the Commissioned Corps of the Public Health Service for the enormous tasks of the war and the peace to come. Authority is granted to commission the nurses of the Public Health Service, just as the nurses of the Army and the Navy are commissioned.
>
> It provides for the establishment of a national tuberculosis program in the Public Health Service. Since adequate public health facilities must be organized on a nationwide scale, it is proper that the Federal Government should exercise responsibility of leadership and assistance to the States.
>
> In establishing a national program of war and postwar prevention, we will be making as sound an investment as any Government can make; the dividends are payable in human life and health.[95]

Over seventy years later, the nation is on the precipice of a new era in the nation's health information infrastructure. Yet a look back upon President Roosevelt's statement reveals that many of those guiding principles that motivated the enactment of the Public Health Service Act, such as the goal of improving national health, remain true today.

Cures Act

On December 13, 2016, President Barack Obama signed into law the 21st Century Cures Act, previously discussed. This legislation received wide bipartisan support. The Senate passed the bill by a vote of 94–5, and the House passed an almost identical version of the Senate bill at 392–26.[21] The Cures Act covers many topics, mostly surrounding new drug discovery and medical devices. The Act also contains provisions to improve behavioral health and substance abuse treatment and to improve patient access to new therapies, and includes new rules and provisions related to HIPAA, PHI, and the interoperability of healthcare IT.

The Act is a milestone piece of legislation in the evolution of the nation's health information infrastructure and the future of healthcare. There are several provisions in the Act that will further the growth, development, and advancement of healthcare IT, and facilitate providers to utilize EHR data and other relevant information to reduce variations in care, improve outcomes, and better coordinate the care delivery process.

NIST[96]

Founded in 1901, the National Institute of Standards and Technology (NIST) is one of the nation's oldest physical science laboratories and is part of the U.S. Department of Commerce. Congress established NIST to remove challenges the U.S. once faced from industrial competitors such as Germany, the United Kingdom, and other nations.

Through the establishment of NIST, the U.S. became a leading innovator and maintains a broad and far reaching role in the design, build, and support of the nation's technological infrastructure. Whether it is the smart electric power grid, atomic clocks, advanced nanomaterials, computer chips, build of the cybersecurity framework, or the development and testing of core healthcare IT standards for EHRs,[97] the nation relies in some way on the technology, measurement, and standards provided by NIST.

As a new era in the design and build of the nation's health information infrastructure begins, reliance on NIST standards for EHRs, cybersecurity, and science and medicine all become integral components of the infrastructure and healthcare delivery of tomorrow.

As Figure 17-3 depicts, existing federal health insurance programs such as Medicare, Medicaid, and CHIP and laws such as HIPAA form the foundation of today's healthcare

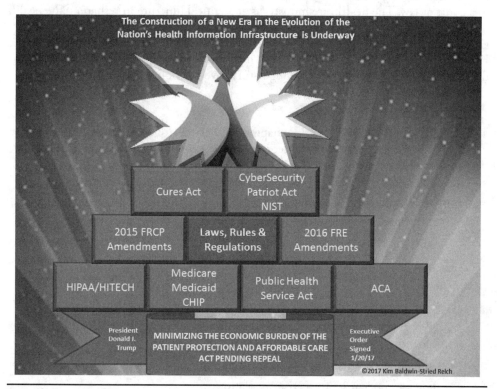

Figure 17-3 A new era in the evolution of the nation's health information infrastructure is underway.

delivery system. Laws, rules, and regulations serve as their cornerstone, and are supported by the 2015 and 2016 amendments to the FRCP and FRE. The passage of the Cures Act[21] coupled with development of NIST healthcare IT standards[98] increased focus on cybersecurity, and, most importantly, President Trump's executive order "Minimizing the Economic Burden of the Patient Protection and Affordable Care Act Pending Repeal"[30] will set forth a new vision and direction for the healthcare delivery system and information infrastructure of tomorrow.

Chapter Review

The ARRA, ACA, HIPAA, and the HITECH Act laid the foundation for the design and build of the nation's health information infrastructure. In 2014, the ONC high-level report *Connecting Health and Care for the Nation: A 10-Year Vision to Achieve an Interoperable Health IT Infrastructure* provided further direction and vision for the nation's health information infrastructure.[82] The recent passage of the Cures Act[21] and the signing of the executive order "Minimizing the Economic Burden of the Patient Protection and Affordable Care Act Pending Repeal"[30] have begun a new era in the evolution of the nation's healthcare delivery system and information infrastructure of tomorrow.

Local, state, and federal rules governing the discovery of ESI play an important role in the discovery of health information contained in EHRs and other devices as evidence in a court or law. The healthcare industry is at a critical juncture in reshaping the health information infrastructure of tomorrow. It is important, then, that all healthcare professionals understand the structure and sources of law in the United States and how the EHR serves not only as an important tool for providers in care delivery, but also as evidence in a court of law or to aid in a regulatory investigation.

Questions

To test your comprehension of the chapter, answer the following questions and then check your answers against the list of correct answers that follows the questions.

1. Which of the following is *not* one of the four goals of the HITECH Act?

   A. Savings

   B. Investment in HIT infrastructure

   C. Government oversight

   D. Establishment of the Health Insurance Marketplace

2. The OCR published a new series of FAQs in 2016 to educate individuals about which of the following?

   A. Procedures for enrollment in the Health Insurance Marketplace

   B. How to file a discrimination complaint

   C. Individuals' rights to access their health information

   D. Fines and penalties for HIPAA violations

3. What is the name of the agency that oversees the privacy and security of health data collected by entities not regulated by HIPAA?

  A. FTC

  B. CMS

  C. FDA

  D. No federal agency has been designated to oversee the privacy and security of health data collected by entities not regulated by HIPAA.

4. What is the name of the federal agency that is responsible for oversight of certified healthcare IT?

  A. AHRQ

  B. ONC

  C. No federal agency is responsible for assuring that certified healthcare IT systems are safe and secure.

  D. FDA

5. Which is the principal investigative agency in the fight against healthcare fraud?

  A. FBI

  B. HHS

  C. OIG

  D. HFPP

  E. OIG

  F. All of the above

6. The political doctrine of constitutional law in which the three branches of government are kept separate to prevent an abuse of power is known as which of the following?

  A. Common law

  B. Executive powers

  C. Separation of powers

  D. Judicial powers

  E. All of the above

  F. None of the above

7. The passage of the 21st Century Cures Act lays forth which of the following?

  A. Interoperability and healthcare IT standards

  B. A new era in the evolution of the nation's healthcare delivery system and information infrastructure

  C. HIPAA provisions for access to PHI in research

  D. All of the above

  E. None of the above

8. Which two of the following choices accurately describe differences between paper-based medical records and EHRs?

   A. Paper records are easier to change than EHRs.

   B. EHRs are easier to change than paper records.

   C. Paper records exist in substantially greater volumes than EHRs.

   D. EHRs exist in substantially greater volumes than paper.

9. A medical record is generally admitted as evidence into a court of law under the _____.

   A. HIPAA rule

   B. Hearsay rule

   C. Federal Rule of Civil Procedure 37(e)

   D. Federal Rule of Evidence 803

   E. All of the above

   F. None of the above

Answers

1. **D.** The establishment of the Health Insurance Marketplace is not one of the four goals of the HITECH Act. The four main goals of the HITECH Act are government oversight, investment in HIT infrastructure, savings, and the establishment and enforcement of stricter federal privacy and security laws.

2. **C.** The OCR published the new set of FAQs to educate individuals about their rights to access their health information. The Privacy Rule generally requires HIPAA covered entities (health plans and most healthcare providers) to provide individuals, upon request, with access to the protected health information (PHI) about them in one or more designated record sets maintained by or for the covered entity.

3. **D.** At the present time, oversight gaps exist between HIPAA covered entities that collect health date from individuals and entities that are not regulated by HIPAA but also collect health data. There is no federal agency with oversight for the latter group.

4. **C.** There is no federal agency responsible for regulating or overseeing healthcare IT system design or safety standards.

5. **A.** The FBI serves as the principal investigative agency involved in the fight against healthcare fraud and maintains jurisdiction over both federal and private healthcare insurance programs.

6. **C.** The three branches of government operate under a concept known as the separation of powers. Under this concept, as established by the framers of the Constitution, no branch of the government shall have more power or control than the other two branches in the exercise of its functions and activities.

7. D. The Cures Act is a milestone piece of legislation in the evolution of the nation's health information infrastructure and the future of healthcare.

8. B, D. As outlined in Table 17-1, EHRs are easier to change than paper-based medical records and EHRs exist in substantially greater volumes than paper-based medical records.

9. D. Although medical records are considered to be hearsay in the eyes of the court, they generally are admitted as evidence on other grounds. The most common way in which medical records are admitted as evidence into a court of law is through FRE 803, which is titled Exceptions to the Rule Against Hearsay.

References

1. Definition of "law." *Law.com.* Accessed on February 4, 2017, from http://dictionary.law.com/Default.aspx?selected=1111.

2. Definition of "regulation." *FreeDictionary.com.* Accessed on February 4, 2017, from http://legal-dictionary.thefreedictionary.com/regulation.

3. The White House. (2017). The Executive Branch: The President, the Vice President, Executive Office of the President, the Cabinet. *Whitehouse.gov.* Accessed on January 30, 2017, from https://www.whitehouse.gov/1600/executive-branch.

4. The President's Advisory Commission on Consumer Protection and Quality in the Health Care Industry. (1998). *Quality first: Better health care for all Americans—final report.* Accessed on January 30, 2017, from https://archive.ahrq.gov/hcqual/.

5. Federal Register, National Archives and Records Administration. (2017). *Reader aids: Insight into FR publications–Executive orders.* (2017) Accessed on February 28, 2017, from https://www.federalregister.gov/executive-orders.

6. U.S. Constitution, art. II, § 3, Constitutional Powers of the President. Accessed on January 30, 2017, from http://law2.umkc.edu/faculty/projects/ftrials/conlaw/prespowers.html.

7. Youngstown Sheet & Tube Co. v. Sawyer, 343 U.S. 579 (1952). Accessed on January 30, 2017, from www.casebriefs.com/blog/law/constitutional-law/constitutional-law-keyed-to-stone/the-distribution-of-national-powers/youngstown-sheet-tube-co-v-sawyer-2/.

8. Dry, M. (1967). The separation of powers and representative government. *Political Science Reviewer 3*, 43. Accessed on February 28, 2017, from https://isistatic.org/journal-archive/pr/03_01/dry.pdf.

9. Wolters Kluwer Editorial Staff. (2016, Dec. 19). *Trump's win expected to bring significant legal and regulatory changes.* Accessed on January 31, 2017, from https://lrus.wolterskluwer.com/.

10. NPR. (2017, Jan. 18). *Transcript Senate Health Committee questions Rep. Tom Price in HHS confirmation hearing.* Accessed on March 1, 2017, from www.npr .org/2017/01/18/510472472/senate-health-committee-questions-rep-tom-price-in-hhs-confirmation-hearing.

11. The White House, Office of the Press Secretary. (2017, Feb. 27). *Remarks by President Trump in listening session with health insurance company CEOs.* February 27, 2017 Accessed on March 1, 2017, from https://www.whitehouse.gov/the-press-office/2017/02/27/remarks-president-trump-listening-session-health-insurance-company-ceos.

12. Kang, J. (2017, Feb. 28). Three priorities for Seema Verma as she nears CMS confirmation. *HealthcareDive.* Accessed on February 28, 2017, from www .healthcaredive.com/news/three-priorities-for-seema-verma-as-she-nears-cms-confirmation/437083/

13. NPR. (2017, Feb. 28). *Trump's address to joint session of Congress.* Accessed on March 1, 2017, from www.npr.org/2017/02/28/516717981/watch-live-trump-addresses-joint-session-of-congress.

14. U.S. Constitution, art. 1, § 1. Accessed on July 10, 2016, from https://www.law .cornell.edu/anncon/html/art1frag1_user.html#art1_hd4.

15. U.S. Constitution, art. 1, § 8, clause 18. Accessed on July 10, 2016, from http://press-pubs.uchicago.edu/founders/tocs/a1_8_18.html.

16. U.S. Department of Health and Human Services (HHS). (2016). *HHS.gov.* Accessed on July 25, 2016, from https://www.hhs.gov/.

17. Centers for Medicare and Medicaid Services. (2016). *CMS.gov.* Accessed on July 25, 2016, from https://www.cms.gov/.

18. HHS, Office for Civil Rights. (2016). *HHS.gov.* Accessed on July 25, 2016, from https://www.hhs.gov/ocr/.

19. Office of the National Coordinator for Health Information Technology. (2016). *HealthIT.gov.* Accessed on July 25, 2016, from https://www.healthit.gov/.

20. Office of the National Coordinator, Office for Civil Rights, Federal Trade Commission. (2016, July 19). *Examining oversight of the privacy and security of health data collected by entities not regulated by HIPAA.* Accessed on July 25, 2016, from https://www.healthit.gov/sites/default/files/non-covered_entities_report_june_17_2016.pdf.

21. 21st Century Cures Act, H. R. 34, 114th Cong. (2016, Dec. 13). Accessed on January 30, 2017, from https://www.congress.gov/bill/114th-congress/house-bill/34/text.

22. Federal Policy for the Protection of Human Subjects, 82 Fed. Reg. 7149 (2017, Jan. 19). Accessed on February 5, 2017, from https://www.gpo.gov/fdsys/pkg/FR-2017-01-19/pdf/2017-01058.pdf.

23. Federal Trade Commission (FTC). (n.d.). *Competition in the health care marketplace.* Accessed on July 25, 2016, from https://www.ftc.gov/tips-advice/competition-guidance/industry-guidance/health-care.

24. FTC. (n.d.). *Health breach notification rule.* Accessed on July 25, 2016, from https://www.ftc.gov/system/files/documents/plain-language/bus56-complying-ftcs-health-breach-notification-rule.pdf.

25. FTC. (n.d.). *Mobile health applications interactive tool.* Accessed on July 25, 2016, from https://www.ftc.gov/tips-advice/business-center/guidance/mobile-health-apps-interactive-tool.

26. U.S. Food and Drug Administration (FDA). (2016). *FDA.gov.* Accessed on July 25, 2016, from https://www.fda.gov/.

27. Internal Revenue Service (IRS). (2016). *IRS.gov.* Accessed on July 25, 2016, from https://www.irs.gov/.

28. Patient Protection and Affordable Care Act, H. R. 3590, 111th Cong. (2010), Pub. L. No. 111-148. Accessed on July 10, 2016, from https://www.congress.gov/bill/111th-congress/house-bill/3590.

29. National Federation of Independent Business et al. v. Sebelius et al., 132 S. Ct. 2566 (2012, June 28). Accessed July 12, 2016, from www.casebriefs.com/blog/law/health-law/health-law-keyed-to-furrow/health-care-cost-and-access-the-policy-context/national-federal-of-independent-business-et-al-v-sebelius/.

30. President of the United States. (2017, Jan. 20). *Executive Order: Minimizing the economic burden of the Patient Protection and Affordable Care Act pending repeal.* Accessed on February 3, 2017, from https://www.whitehouse.gov/the-press-office/2017/01/2/executive-order-minimizing-economic-burden-patient-protection-and?

31. HHS, Office of Inspector General. (2016). *OIG.HHS.gov.* Accessed on July 25, 2016, from https://oig.hhs.gov/.

32. Federal Bureau of Investigation (FBI). (2017). *FBI.gov.* Accessed on February 2, 2017, from https://www.fbi.gov/.

33. Healthcare Fraud Prevention Partnership (HFPP). Accessed on February 2, 2017, from https://hfpp.cms.gov/.

34. National Health Care Anti-Fraud Association (NHCAA). (n.d.). *Who we are.* Accessed on February 2, 2017, from https://www.nhcaa.org/about-us/who-we-are.aspx.

35. U.S. Department of Justice (DOJ). (2016). *Justice.gov.* Accessed on July 25, 2016, from https://www.justice.gov/about.

36. HHS and DOJ. (2017). *Stop Medicare fraud: Health Care Fraud Prevention and Enforcement Action Team (HEAT) task force.* Accessed on February 2, 2017, from https://www.stopmedicarefraud.gov/aboutfraud/heattaskforce/.

37. DOJ. (2016, Nov. 11). Jury convicts home health agency owner in $13 million Medicare fraud conspiracy. *Justice.gov.* Accessed on February 3, 2017, from https://www.justice.gov/opa/pr/jury-convicts-home-health-agency-owner-13-million-medicare-fraud-conspiracy.

38. USA.gov. (2016). *Branches of government.* Accessed on February 28, 2017, from https://www.usa.gov/branches-of-government.

39. DOJ, Offices of the United States Attorneys. (2017). *Justice 101: Introduction to the Federal Court System.* Accessed on February 3, 2017, from https://www.justice.gov/usao/justice-101/federal-courts.

40. U.S. Courts. (2017). *Comparing federal and state courts.* Accessed on February 4, 2017, from www.uscourts.gov/about-federal-courts/court-role-and-structure/comparing-federal-state-courts.

41. Definition of "common law." *Law.com.* Accessed on July 12, 2016, from http://dictionary.law.com/Default.aspx?selected=248.

42. Marbury v. Madison, 5 U.S. (1 Cranch) 137 (1803). Accessed on July 25, 2016, from https://supreme.justia.com/cases/federal/us/5/137/case.html.

43. Definition of "case law." *Law.com.* Accessed on July 11, 2016, from http://dictionary.law.com/Default.aspx?selected=148.

44. Seidman, J., & Garrett, P. (2011, Jan. 4). EMR vs. EHR: What is the difference? *HealthITBuzz.* Accessed on February 28, 2017, from https://www.healthit.gov/buzz-blog/electronic-health-and-medical-records/emr-vs-ehr-difference/.

45. HealthIT.gov, National Learning Consortium. (2017). *What is a Personal Health Record? FAQs: The basics.* Accessed on February 28, 2017, from https://www.healthit.gov/providers-professionals/faqs/what-personal-health-record.

46. Berlin, J. (2015). Physicians work with TMB to usher medical records rules into the electronic age. *TexasMedicine, 11*(7), 53–58. Accessed on July 27, 2016, from https://www.texmed.org/Template.aspx?id=33909.

47. Ventola, L. C. (2014). Social media and health care professionals: Benefits, risks, and best practices. *Pharmacy and Therapeutics, 39*(7), 491–499, on 520. Accessed on July 25, 2016, from https://www.ncbi.nlm.nih.gov/pmc/articles/PMC4103576/.

48. Powell, R. E. (1961). Admissibility of hospital records into evidence. *Maryland Law Review, 21*(1). Accessed on February 4, 2017, from http://digitalcommons.law.umaryland.edu/mlr/vol21/iss1/4/.

49. Texas Medical Board. (2015, April). *EMR position statement: The medical board's position statement on maintaining accurate electronic medical records.* Accessed on July 26, 2016, from www.tmb.state.tx.us/idl/1FDE72F2-F7E7-781B-986A-B5F1AD32BC3D.

50. Dimick, C. (2010, Sept. 24). EHRs prove a difficult witness in court. *Journal of AHIMA.* Accessed on July 26, 2016, from http://journal.ahima.org/2010/09/24/ehrs-difficult-witness-in-court/.

51. Brouillad, C. P. (2015). EHR audit trails might reveal more than you think: Hall v. Flannery, a sign of the times. *Inside Medical Liability* (third quarter), 18–20. Accessed on July 27, 2016, from www.mgma-gkc.com/wp-content/uploads/2015/10/IML-3Q-2015-pp-18-20.pdf.

52. Kumar, S., Nilsen, W., Abernethy, A., Atienza, A., Patrick, K., Pavel, M., … Dallas, S. (2013). Mobile health technology evaluation: The mHealth evidence workshop. *American Journal of Preventative Medicine, 45*(2), 228–236. Accessed on July 26, 2016, from https://www.ncbi.nlm.nih.gov/pmc/articles/PMC3803146/.

53. Kannry, J. L., & Williams, M. S. (2013). Integration of genomics into the electronic health record: Mapping terra incognita. *Genetics in Medicine, 15,* 757–760. Accessed on July 25, 2016, from www.nature.com/gim/journal/v15/n10/full/gim2013102a.html.

54. U.S. Department of Health and Human Services, Health Information Privacy. (2017). *Individuals' right under HIPAA to access their health information.* 45 CFR §164.524. Accessed on March 1, 2017, from https://www.hhs.gov/hipaa/for-professionals/privacy/guidance/access/

55. AHIMA (American Health Information Management Association). (2016). *Information governance basics: AHIMA's commitment to healthcare–Information governance.* Accessed on July 25, 2016, from www.ahima.org/topics/infogovernance/igbasics?tabid=overview.

56. The Health Insurance Portability and Accountability Act: Uses and disclosures for which an authorization or opportunity to agree or object is not required, 45 C.F.R. 164.512(f) (2002). Accessed on February 4, 2017, from https://www.law.cornell.edu/cfr/text/45/164.512.

57. Intelligence Authorization Act for Fiscal Year 2002, Pub. L. No. 107–108, 50 U.S.C. § 501(a)(1) (2002). Accessed on February 4, 2017, from https://www.congress.gov/bill/107th-congress/house-bill/2883/text?overview=closed.

58. HL7 International. (2016). *EHR Records Management and Evidentiary Support (RM-ES) project overview.* Accessed on July 11, 2016, from http://wiki.hl7.org/index.php?title=EHR_RM-ES#Project_Overview.

59. HL7 International. (2016). *EHR RM-ES functional profile.* Accessed on July 11, 2016, from http://wiki.hl7.org/index.php?title=Product_EHR_RMES_FP.

60. HL7 EHR RM-ES Workgroup wiki. Accessed on January 9, 2017, from http://wiki.hl7.org/index.php?title=EHR_RM-ES.

61. Conn, J. (2014, Nov. 14). Vital Signs: Researcher projects $78 billion cost savings on EHRs. *Modern Healthcare.* Accessed on July 26, 2016, from www.modernhealthcare.com/article/20141124/blog/311249995.

62. Harrison, M. I., Koppel, R., & Bar-Lev, S. (2007). Unintended consequences of information technologies in health care: An interactive sociotechnical analysis. *Journal of the American Medical Informatics Association, 14,* 542. Accessed on July 25, 2016, from https://academic.oup.com/jamia/article/14/5/542/719675/Unintended-Consequences-of-Information.

PART III

63. Burkett v. Advocate Lutheran General, "Hospital agrees to pay 8.25 million in baby's death from overdose." *CBS Local News*, April 5, 2012. Accessed on September 28, 2016, from http://chicago.cbslocal.com/2012/04/05/babys-death-yields-record-settlement-of-more-than-8m/.

64. Definition of "discovery." *Law.com*. Accessed on February 21, 2017, from http://dictionary.law.com/Default.aspx?selected=530.

65. Definition of "admissible evidence." *Law.com*. Accessed on February 21, 2017, from http://dictionary.law.com/Default.aspx?selected=2339.

66. Federal Rules of Evidence. Accessed March 7, 2017 from https://www.law.cornell.edu/rules/fre

67. U.S. Courts. (n.d.). *Amendments approved by the Standing Committee.* Accessed on January 30, 2017, from www.uscourts.gov/rules-policies/pending-rules-and-forms-amendments.

68. U.S. Courts. (2016, Sept. 28). *Judicial Conference of the United States.* Accessed on January 30, 2017, from www.uscourts.gov/file/20238/download.

69. Definition of "hearsay." *Law.com*. Accessed on January 30, 2017, from http://dictionary.law.com/Default.aspx?selected=858.

70. Baldwin-Stried Reich, K., Ball, K., Dougherty, M., & Hedges, R. (2012). *E-discovery and electronic records,* p. 162. AHIMA Press.

71. Federal Rule of Evidence 803: Exceptions to the rule against hearsay. (n.d.). Accessed on January 30, 2017, from https://www.law.cornell.edu/rules/fre/rule_803.

72. Wakefield, W. E. (1981). *Physician-patient privilege extending to patient's medical or hospital records.* Annot., 10 A.L.R.4th 552.

73. Tibbs v. Bunnell, 448 S.W.3d 796 (Ky. Aug. 21, 2014), as corrected (Sept. 10, 2014), petition for certiorari filed 83 U.S.L.W. 3772 (Mar. 18, 2015). Accessed on July 25, 2016, from www.chpso.org/sites/main/files/file-attachments/tibbs_petition_3_18_15.pdf.

74. Allred v. Saunders, 342 P.3d 204 (Utah Oct. 21, 2014). Accessed on July 26, 2016, from www.utcourts.gov/opinions/supopin/Allred20141021.pdf.

75. Hammond v. Saini, 766 S.E.2d 590 (N.C. Dec. 19, 2014). Accessed on July 26, 2016, from https://scholar.google.com/scholar_case?case=17380717623516984806&hl=en&as_sdt=6&as_vis=1&oi=scholarr.

76. Federal Rules of Civil Procedure, Rule 26: Duty to disclose; general provisions governing discovery. (n.d.). Accessed on February 5, 2017, from https://www.law.cornell.edu/rules/frcp/rule_26.

77. Allman, T. Y. (2014, Jan. 1). *E-discovery in federal and state courts: The impact of rulemaking – Past and future.* Accessed on February 11, 2017, from www.americanbar.org/content/dam/aba/events/criminal_justice/midyear14_Document_Management_EDiscovery_Rules.authcheckdam.doc (note: automatic file download).

78. Brouillard, C. (2009). Not a bang, a whimper: The silent e-discovery revolution in state court practice. *Massachusetts Bar Association—Section review.* Accessed on August 1, 2016, from www.massbar.org/publications/section-review/2009/v11-n1/not-a-bang,-a-whimper.

79. U.S. Courts. (2015). *Federal Rules of Civil Procedure.* Accessed on February 28, 2017, from www.uscourts.gov/sites/default/files/rules-of-civil-procedure.pdf.

80. Duke Law News. (2016, Aug. 24). *Duke Law acquires e-discovery standards organization, EDRM.* Accessed on February 4, 2017, from https://law.duke.edu/news/duke-law-acquires-e-discovery-standards-organization-edrm/.

81. Zubulake v. UBS Warburg, LLC, 220 F.R.D. 212 (S.D.N.Y. 2003) (*Zubulake IV*), pp. 3–4. Accessed on February 28, 2017, from http://smu-ediscovery.gardere.com/Zubulake%20IV.pdf.

82. The Office of the National Coordinator for Health Information Technology. (2014, June 5). *Connecting health and care for the nation: A 10-year vision to achieve an interoperable health IT infrastructure.* Accessed on February 28, 2017, from https://www.healthit.gov/sites/default/files/ONC10yearInteroperabilityConceptPaper.pdf.

83. President's Council of Advisors on Science and Technology (PCAST). (2010, December). *Realizing the full potential of health information technology to improve healthcare for Americans: The path forward.* Accessed on August 8, 2012, from www.whitehouse.gov/sites/default/files/microsites/ostp/pcast-health-it-report.pdf.

84. American Recovery and Reinvestment Act of 2009, 111th Cong. (2009), Pub. L. No. 111-5, 42 U.S.C. 17932 § 13402 (notification in the case of a breach). Accessed on August 8, 2012, from https://www.hhs.gov/ocr/privacy/hipaa/understanding/coveredentities/hitechact.pdf.

85. HHS. (n.d.). *OCR release of public information re HIPAA.* Accessed on July 28, 2016, from https://www.hhs.gov/hipaa/for-professionals/privacy/guidance/access/#newlyreleasedfaqs.

86. Kohn, P. (2014, June 1). E-data explosion in business law: Growth in electronic information drives new costs and approaches to litigation. *ColumbusCEO.* Accessed on February 4, 2017, from www.columbusceo.com/content/stories/2014/06/08/e-data-explosion.html.

87. American Medical News. (2012, Mar. 5). Legal risks of going paperless. *Amednews.com.* Accessed on February 5, 2017, from www.amednews.com/article/20120305/profession/303059945/4/.

88. Artigliere, R., et al. (2017, forthcoming). Diagnosing and treating legal ailments of the electronic health record: Towards an efficient and trustworthy process for discovery and release of information. *Sedona Conference Journal, 17.* Accessed on February 3, 2017, from https://s3.amazonaws.com/IGG/EHR.pdf.

PART III

89. Bock, L. J., Demster, B., Dinh, A. K., Gorton, E. R., & Lantis, J. R., Jr. (2008). Management practices for the release of information. *Journal of AHIMA, 79*(11), 77–80. Accessed on July 27, 2016, from http://bok.ahima.org/doc?oid=85544# .V3mZnrgrLP4.

90. TechTarget Network. (n.d.). *Search HealthIT: Definition of legal health record.* Accessed on July 27, 2016, from http://searchhealthit.techtarget.com/definition/ legal-health-record.

91. HHS. (2016). *Individuals' right under HIPAA to access their health information, 45 CFR § 164.524.* Accessed on July 4, 2016, from https://www.hhs.gov/hipaa/ for-professionals/privacy/guidance/access/.

92. Haugen, M. B., Tegen, A., & Warner, D. (2011). Fundamentals of the legal health record and designated record set. *Journal of AHIMA, 82*(2), 44–49.

93. Kannry, J. M., & Williams, M. S. (2013). Integration of genomic into the electronic health record: Mapping terra incognita. *Genetics in Medicine, 15,* 757–760. Accessed on July 25, 2016, from www.nature.com/gim/journal/v15/ n10/full/gim2013102a.html.

94. 42 U.S. Code Chapter 6A, Public Health Service, Pub. L. No. 114-38. Accessed on March 1, 2017, from https://www.law.cornell.edu/uscode/text/42/chapter-6A.

95. Roosevelt, Franklin D. (1944, July 1). *Statement of the President on the signing of the Public Health Service Act,* July 1, 1944 American Presidency Project. Accessed on March 1, 2017, from www.presidency.ucsb.edu/ws/?pid=16528.

96. National Institute of Standards and Technology (NIST), U.S. Department of Commerce, (2017). *About NIST.* Accessed on March 1, 2017, from https:// www.nist.gov/about-nist.

97. NIST, U.S. Department of Commerce (2017). *Healthcare: Standards and testing.* Accessed on March 1, 2017, from https://www.nist.gov/itl/ssd/systems- interoperability-group/healthcare-standards-testing.

98. NIST, U.S. Department of Commerce (2017). *Healthcare IT.* Accessed on February 28, 2017, from https://www.nist.gov/topics/healthcare-it.

PART IV

Implementing, Managing, and Maintaining Healthcare IT

Effective Organizational Communication for Large-Scale Healthcare Information Technology Initiatives

Liz Johnson

In this chapter, you will learn how to

- Describe the importance of communications in the healthcare IT initiatives
- Define the essential role of the customers
- Identify the components of the communications plan
- Understand the roles of federal agencies and federal regulations
- Discuss the role of social medial and mobile devices

In America's twenty-first-century healthcare system, landmark federal reform legislation enacted since 2009 has served to progressively modernize care-delivery organizations with enhanced healthcare information technologies (healthcare IT) that began with the widespread adoption of electronic health records (EHRs). Most notable of these laws are the American Recovery and Reinvestment Act (ARRA) and its Health Information Technology and Economic and Clinical Health (HITECH) Act provision, which established the Centers for Medicare and Medicaid Services (CMS) EHR Incentive Programs (known as Meaningful Use and often abbreviated to MU) to encourage the meaningful use of EHRs.[1] These programs, one for Medicare providers and one for Medicaid providers, earmarked billions of dollars in incentive payments for eligible physicians and healthcare providers who successfully meet increasingly stringent requirements for EHR adoption and use. The incentive payments began in May 2011, and in early 2016, CMS reported that over $35 billion had been paid to more than 513,000 healthcare providers.[2]

However, the journey to successful integration of healthcare IT by providers industry-wide has been fraught with challenges. Tremendous complexities exist throughout healthcare organizations working on healthcare IT reform initiatives, and these complexities create a critical need for effective communication campaigns that run throughout the life cycle of acquiring, implementing, adopting, and continuously optimizing the use of EHRs in both inpatient and ambulatory settings. Efforts such as these, with effective communication programs in place as a core strategy, continue to support the six aims for improvement in care-delivery quality set forth by the Institute of Medicine in 2001: make it safe, equitable, effective, patient-centered, timely, and efficient.[3]

Without such communication strategies, success is far less likely. Stories of EHR implementation failures began to hit the mainstream media in the late 1990s. In 2002, for example, a major West Coast academic medical center invested heavily in the implementation of computerized provider order entry (CPOE) and encountered significant physician resistance. In large part, the clinician unwillingness to use CPOE occurred because physicians had been insufficiently informed about and inadequately trained in the use of the clinical decision support (CDS) tool being implemented.[4] Stories like these continue today. According to Charles et al., "The success of the adoption and implementation of a CPOE system in urban hospitals depends on teamwork among medical staff, clinical support services, and the hospital administration."[5] Although there are any number of obstacles to a successful EHR/CPOE implementation, three are the most challenging and typically overlooked or minimally addressed: lack of communication, lack of training, and lack of use of a standard terminology. To ensure and maintain a successful implementation after go-live, there will be a repeating cycle of user optimization and technical improvements throughout the life of the system, requiring embedded programs that support communication, training, and standard terminology development.[6]

Numerous provider organizations have encountered similar challenges with healthcare IT implementations over the past decade.[7, 8] Such costly, high-risk experiences—especially in an increasingly patient-centric healthcare industry—have underscored the importance of effective, cross-enterprise, patient-focused communications plans and strategies that include physicians and clinicians, administrators, IT professionals, and the C-suite—all of whom play critical roles as new technologies are introduced. As a result, effective communication programs are now a high priority for hospitals and physician practices as they continue to adopt and optimize the use of EHR, CPOE, and similar broadly impactful HIT systems throughout the industry.

The purpose of this chapter is to provide an overview of communication strategies that have proven effective in driving the implementation of EHRs to support the needs of patients, physicians, and the caregiver workforce. The chapter covers the importance of communications in healthcare IT initiatives, the customers and players, components of the communications plan, and industry considerations (roles of federal agencies, federal regulations, and the burgeoning role of mobile applications, social media, and health information exchange).

Importance of Communications in Health IT Initiatives

Rouse noted that healthcare organizations exist as complex adaptive systems with nonlinear relationships, independent and intelligent agents, and system fragmentation.[9] While variation among them is diminishing through increasing standardization of practices and systems geared toward patient care continuity, many provider cultures still struggle with decentralization and reliance on disparate legacy systems.[10] As with other industries, consolidation among acute and ambulatory providers has also helped drive standardization. As organizations across the nation continue on the journey of implementing, adopting, and optimizing the use of EHRs in the inpatient and ambulatory settings, effective enterprise-wide communications plans, which include both strategic and tactical elements, are essential. This section provides insight on the importance of communications in healthcare IT programs: in governance, the structure of a governance model, and rules for governance efforts. Specific governance models and success factors are also addressed in Chapter 20.

Leadership and Governance

The introduction of EHRs in healthcare organizations has driven transformational change in clinical and administrative workflows,[11] organizational structure (i.e., that which exists among physicians, nurses, and administrators),[12] and relationships among the frontline workers, physicians, administrators, and patients. Understanding the risks posed by the disruptive facets of organizational and process change is critical to ensuring the effectiveness of all healthcare IT programs, including the continued implementation, adoption, and optimization of EHRs. Vital to mitigating risks of failure is strong physician leadership and management support.[13] An essential element of risk mitigation in care-delivery reform through healthcare IT is the planning and implementing of organizational communication initiatives that help to achieve the aims of an enterprise-wide governance team.

To succeed, responsibilities for such communication initiatives should be shared between health system leaders, champions, and those charged with oversight of the implementation of healthcare IT systems, all of whom have a role to play in governance structures whose processes are grounded in a strong communications strategy. Morrissey summarized the importance of such an approach for transforming healthcare organizations: "This IT governance function, guided from the top but carried out by sometimes hundreds of clinical and operations representatives, will be evermore crucial to managing the escalation of IT in healthcare delivery…." In fact, without such an informed governance process, he states, "IT at many hospitals and health care systems is a haphazard endeavor that typically results in late, over-budget projects and, ultimately, many disparate systems that don't function well together."[14]

Accountability begins at the care delivery level and rises through the enterprise level. Messaging—through electronic, in-person, or video media—from chief executive officers and board members solidifies the importance of enterprise-level healthcare IT projects.[15]

However, both governance structures and the communications that support them require tailoring depending on the nature of every health system.

Governance models in healthcare organizations provide a structure that engages stakeholders to work through critical decisions and ensure that risks associated with changes in policy, technology, and workflow are mitigated to maintain or improve the quality of patient care. A strong example of such a working model is provided by my own health system, Tenet Healthcare Corporation, where I serve as Chief Information Officer, Acute Care Hospitals and Applied Clinical Informatics (ACI). Tenet's nationwide, multiyear EHR implementation program, directed by my office, was labeled IMPACT: Improving Patient Care through Technology. The mission of IMPACT, to implement a system-wide EHR and patient health record (PHR) system for all Tenet facilities and patients by 2015 while ensuring staff and physician adoption of the system throughout the process, was one of the largest and most successful projects of its kind in the nation.

Tenet is one of the largest integrated healthcare delivery systems in the United States, employing more than 130,000 in over 80 hospitals across the country. Figure 18-1 illustrates the structure of Tenet Healthcare's IMPACT program and the importance of communications as it was built into the implementation of the IMPACT EHR system.

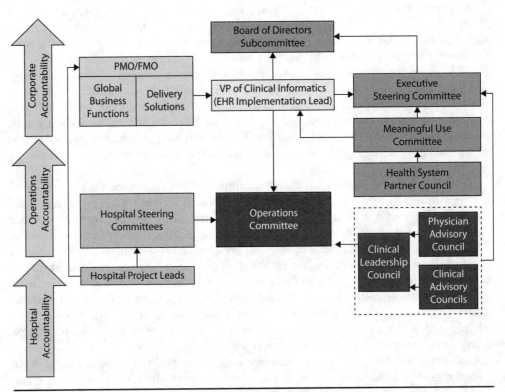

Figure 18-1 EHR implementation and oversight governance

A key to the success of Tenet's IMPACT governance was a three-tiered organizational structure that engaged the corporation, regional operations, and the hospitals themselves in a coordinated effort. Another key success factor was early commitment to key roles, including clinical informaticists, physician champions, training and communications leads, and healthcare IT leads. Binding the program together with unified, shared, and consistent messaging was a foundational strategy that supported all aspects of IMPACT's execution.[16]

Hoehn summed up the importance of communications in governance: "Today, clinical IT is finally being universally viewed as a critical component of healthcare reform, and we are only going to get one chance to do this right," she wrote. "This means having everyone in the organization, from the Board Members to the bedside clinicians, all focused on the same plan, the same tactical initiatives, and the same outcomes."[17]

Rules for Governance

Effective governance committees require a solid set of rules, since hospitals are matrixed organizations composed of multidisciplinary staff and leaders from across a healthcare organization. Morrissey provides the following set of "rules to live by" for governing IT:[14]

1. Hardwire the committees
2. Set clear levels of successive authority
3. Do real work every time
4. Form no governance before its time
5. Put someone in charge who can take a stand

The following describes each success factor:

1. **Hardwire the committees**. Ensure that the chairs of lower-level committees participate at the next level in the committee structure and hierarchy. Their role is to bring forward recommendations and issues to the higher-level committee, including issues needing resolution from a higher authority, as well as issues to be communicated from the higher committee down. "A structure with unconnected levels of governance will break down."[14]

2. **Set clear levels of successive authority**. Committee responsibilities should be well defined so members know issues they can address and issues beyond their level of authority.[17] To avoid having most decisions forwarded to the uppermost level, each committee needs a well-defined set of criteria to determine which decisions they can and can't make at that level.

3. **Do real work every time**. Focus meetings on important issues in need of clinician engagement. Setting an agenda and sharing it prior to the meeting helps facilitate consistent decision making. If there are no critical items, cancel the meeting and send out status reports electronically.

4. **Form no governance before its time**. Recognize that different organizations will not be prepared to embrace a governance structure at the same time or to the same degree as others.

5. **Put someone in charge who can take a stand**. The leader of the top committee must be someone who commands respect and possesses operational authority to enact recommendations.

Focus on Customers and Players

Those who are engaged in EHR implementation initiatives should also be involved in communications associated with these multiyear programs. Figure 18-2 illustrates the spectrum of customers and players.

In the provider setting, each of these groups will have a different type of communications engagement. The media and vehicles used may be different, but the strategic focus is the same: improving the quality of patient care through strategic adoption and ongoing user optimization of healthcare IT that is in turn enabled by smart communications. To be effective, multiple communication approaches may be required.

Patients and Communities

In its 2001 report "Crossing the Quality Chasm: A New Health System for the 21st Century," the Institute of Medicine established the need for patient-centered communications and support as part of the six aims for improving healthcare, as noted in the introduction to this chapter.[18] Since then, patient-centric healthcare and the emergence of care-delivery models such as the patient-centered medical home (PCMH) have become central to healthcare reform. Integral to the PCMH concept are seven joint

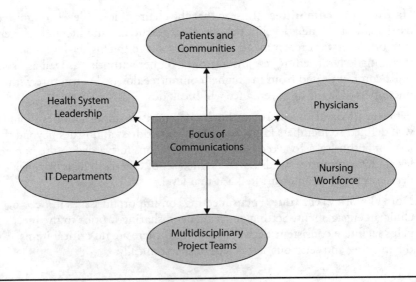

Figure 18-2 Focus of communications

principles, established in 2007, one of which calls for a "whole-person orientation." This means each personal physician is expected to provide for all of a patient's lifetime health service needs,[19] which drives the requirement for comprehensive physician-to-patient communications and shared decision making.

Such communication is also required to support healthcare reform at the community level, as demonstrated in CMS's 2011 establishment of the Three Part Aim for the Medicare Shared Savings Program (e.g., Medicare ACO) with its focus on "better care for individuals and better health for populations."[20] In its final rule for the Medicare ACO, CMS mandated the requirement for advancing patient-centered care through accountable-care organizations (ACOs), stating "an ACO shall adopt a focus on patient-centeredness that is promoted by the governing body and integrated into practice by leadership and management working with the organization's health care teams."[21]

Physicians

As discussed in the introduction of this chapter, no adoption of EHRs by health systems or practices would have succeeded without the endorsement and ownership of the physician community. Change has been and continues to be a constant in healthcare, and physicians in particular continue to experience substantial shifts to their working environment and long-established workflows. When included from the outset of any healthcare IT transformation initiative, "physician champions" are powerful and effective communicators, assisting colleagues through healthcare IT adoption. The Office of the National Coordinator for Health IT (ONC), through its regional extension centers, had started recruiting "physician champions" who were meaningful users of EHRs to help others in their area get over the hurdles of digitizing their medical records.[22] Some organizations use formal and informal processes and tools to identify more influential physicians in the organization and determine their overall attitudes toward the project. Those with strong opinions both for and against are deemed "highly influential" and need to be engaged by project leaders in different ways,

Communication that supports not only ongoing training initiatives and the management of ever-changing procedural requirements but also an understanding of the dynamics of legislated healthcare reform itself is needed through all stages of healthcare IT adoption and user optimization.[23] However, such need often continues to be unmet. For example, a survey of more than 250 hospitals and healthcare systems demonstrated that significant percentages of respondent physicians had inadequate understanding of the EHR Incentive Programs (meaningful use) requirements; others cited a lack of training and change-management issues.[24] The findings of this survey highlight the need to directly engage physicians in healthcare IT implementations, adoption, and user-optimization programs through comprehensive communication initiatives.

Nursing Workforce

For patients in both inpatient and ambulatory settings, nurses constitute the front line of patient care. But for health systems everywhere, they are also on the front line of healthcare IT reform. "Nurses are the biggest users of the EHR and are responsible for a large portion of the documentation that addresses quality measures, safety measures and the overall clinical picture of the patient," said Patricia Sengstack, former president of the American Nursing Informatics Association and CNIO at Bon Secours Health System."[25] As with their physician colleagues, therefore, the role of communication is not limited to the continued training of nurses in the use of EHR systems but rather extends to fully engaging them in the ongoing design, testing, implementation, and user optimization of EHRs to support improved care coordination, continuity of care, and quality measurement. Throughout the healthcare industry, health systems' chief information officers (CIOs) have found that the success of large health IT projects and programs depends not only on the willingness of floor nurses to accept enhanced technology, but also on the strength of the IS-nursing management connection.[26] Therefore, ongoing and consistent communication with the nursing community, key for both nurse champions and nurse users of healthcare IT, is a strategic necessity.

Engagement of nursing in the process has been a part of the IMPACT program at Tenet since its inception. IMPACT's Nursing Advisory Team (NAT) functions as a decision-making body, and NAT's decisions became the standard for the implementation of core clinical EHR applications. How these leaders communicated their decisions proved to be integral to promoting safe, quality patient care and improving outcomes for patients and families while supporting the Tenet Clinical Quality initiatives and the standards associated with the IMPACT Program itself.[16]

IT Departments and Multidisciplinary Project Teams

IT departments and project teams are responsible for meeting the challenges of new-system introductions as well as managing the continuous upgrades to existing ones. To support this work, their roles in communication efforts will involve engaging clinicians in staff positions, confirming commitments, managing change, and setting EHR deployment and revision update strategies.[27] It is also critical to recognize that Health Information Management, Laboratory, Pharmacy, and other ancillary departments are essential to the overall successful adoption of an EHR. Inclusion of these disciplines in communication efforts, governance, and other activities will significantly improve chances for success.

Use Case 18-1: *The IMPACT Insider*

Many organizations use internal newsletters as a communication tool to engage the variety of project stakeholders. First published in May 2010, *The IMPACT Insider*, Tenet's weekly, cross-enterprise e-newsletter for the IMPACT program, is used to continuously inform the health system's employees on the acute care hospital EHR implementation progress by highlighting events at the local levels, as well as providing insight into federal government drivers that may impact the EHR design and workflow standards. *The IMPACT Insider* of March 2016 contains information on the Interoperability Pledge, which was introduced by Health and Human Services Secretary Sylvia Burwell and signed by Tenet earlier in the year. This pledge was introduced to unite EHR providers and leading health systems with the goal of making it easier for patients to use the information in their EHRs.[28]

Healthcare System Leadership

As noted in the earlier section "Leadership and Governance," communication led by an executive-level steering committee, often chaired by a health system's CEO or COO, represents both the beginning and the end of successful healthcare IT implementation processes. Senior leadership not only establishes the size of the investment the organization is prepared to make but also communicates "the broad strategy for IT in advancing business goals and, ultimately, acting on the result of a consistently applied proposal and prioritization regimen."[14]

Components of a Communications Plan

Kaiser Permanente (KP) noted in its 2011 HIMSS Davies Enterprise Award application for its KP HealthConnect EHR that its "national communications plan established positioning, messages, and strategies to create awareness, build knowledge, manage expectations, motivate end users, and build proficiency."[29] As part of its communications plans, KP included vehicles such as a central intranet site, leadership messaging, weekly e-newsletters, regional communication tactics, and videos. Other health systems also employ e-mail updates, end-user training, superusers who function as subject matter experts, and champions to secure buy-in for system adoption.

A 2013 primer from the National Learning Consortium (NLC) entitled *Change Management in EHR Implementation*[30] offers other ideas for a communications plan, such as

- Vendor demonstrations, videos
- Role playing
- Simulated question/answer (Q/A) communication
- Staff visits to practices that have had successful EHR implementations

Another perspective is provided by a 2005 *JHIM* article by Detlev Smaltz, PhD, FHIMSS, and his colleagues, in which they discuss the importance of project communications plans focused on stakeholder groups and meeting their needs. Table 18-1 provides a sample of this plan for three stakeholder groups.[31]

Project Phases and the Communication Functions

Healthcare IT projects and programs often unfold over multiyear periods with the following four major phases:[32]

- Pre-adoption (selection)
- Pre-implementation (planning)
- Implementation (go-live)
- Post-implementation (outcomes, adoption, and ongoing optimization)

Therefore, it is important that communications plans be built and integrated within these phases, because the information needs of stakeholders will vary as projects evolve and mature. Furthermore, a variety of formal and informal communications media will

Stakeholder	Objective	Media	Content
Executive Management	Update on cost, benefits, service quality, and milestones	In-person meeting and briefing	Status update and impact on outcomes
Nursing	Maintain awareness of progress; engage in design effort	Nurse educators Nursing leadership Collateral Unit meetings Intranet web site	Project methodology Design participation Educational info Outcomes impact
Medical Staff	Maintain awareness of progress; engage in design sessions	Medical executive committee Clinical chairs Targeted newsletter	Project methodology Design participation Educational info Outcomes impact

Table 18-1   Sample of Healthcare IT Project Communications Plan

be needed to reach different health-system groups, a point made in a 2009 *Journal of AHIMA* article entitled "Planning Organizational Transition to ICD-10-CM/PCS."[33] The article further states that because points of urgency and risks to be mitigated are also critical to key stakeholders, they should also be considered among the key elements of an effective communication strategy.

Communication Metrics

The best metrics to measure communication program effectiveness are arguably the same used to present the stories of successful healthcare IT projects and programs themselves. As is the case with Tenet Healthcare, a large nationwide independent delivery network (IDN), strong governance programs supported by a pervasive and adaptable communications strategy helped to drive 49 successful EHR go-lives from early 2011 to 2015. This success continues as new hospitals are added to the Tenet portfolio. These results were and continue to be supported by the Tenet e-newsletter *The IMPACT Insider*; local hospital site-specific communication campaigns; future state workflow localization; change readiness assessments; at-the-elbow support for providers from superusers and subject matter experts throughout the go-live processes; physician partnering; post go-live support; and 24/7 command centers for ten days post go-live.

Key Industry Considerations

While the focus of much of the communication supporting the implementation, adoption, and user optimization of new EHR systems and related healthcare IT programs and projects is directed inside an individual health system, those who are responsible for building communication strategies must do so in the context of industry change beyond the traditional four walls of a health system. With the arrival and rapid entrenchment of the digital age over the past two decades, inclusion of mobile devices and social media platforms has expanded, enriching communications options to support successful healthcare IT integration and information interoperability. Furthermore, the actions of the federal government to ensure secure health information interoperability constantly redefine how and what the healthcare industry can expect to communicate across the continuum of care. Therefore, communications planning in support of healthcare IT initiatives must continue to reflect the forces driving such change: an expanding world of media, the roles of federal healthcare agencies, and the adoption of regulatory standards as they continue to drive the evolution of the interoperability of health information.

The Expanding World of Media

Physicians and clinicians across the industry are now regularly communicating among themselves and with their patients through the use of social media and mobile health device technology. In a recent Black Book Market Research survey of 6,000 physicians, greater than half of the responders reported they use their mobile devices to reference data at work or view patient records.[34] Such technologies have continued to improve and clinicians now rely heavily on them to document patient visits, manage clinical workflows, conduct research on technical and clinical issues, and receive alerts regarding patient conditions.

While the upside to this continued rapid increase in communication technologies is tremendous, the deployment of such devices in the marketplace has outpaced the ability for most organizations to maintain safety and security. As reported by the Brookings Institution in May 2016, 23 percent of all data breaches happen in the healthcare industry. Over the past six years, health records of more than 155 million Americans have potentially been exposed in 1,500 separate breaches—the per-record cost of which is $363, the highest of all industries.[35]

Beyond devices, digital media vehicles encompass a multitude of healthcare-specific social media web sites, which bring new opportunities to improve provider-to-provider communications with physician-centric channels. In a 2015 Forbes Advisor Network interview, Dr. Kevin Campbell, an internationally recognized cardiologist, explained that he uses social media to communicate with patients, communicate with physician colleagues, interact with scientists across the world, educate himself and others, and share ideas.[36]

As with mobile devices, the many positive effects to be gained from participation in social media must be considered alongside concerns for the privacy and security of protected health information (PHI). Supported by the Health Insurance Portability and Accountability Act (HIPAA) Privacy and Security Rules passed in 1996, healthcare organizations have become more vigilant in establishing rules and policies governing participation in social media. Such heightened awareness was noted in the April 2012 Federation of State Medical Board's *Model Guidelines for the Appropriate Use of Social Media and Social Networking in Medical Practice*.[37] Even so, as these communication platforms continue to evolve, addressing issues of privacy and security will continue to be

PART IV

a primary concern for the industry, physicians, health systems, patients, and the healthcare reform movement as a whole.

Role of Federal Healthcare Agencies

Healthcare reform during the past decade has been defined, spearheaded, and guided by federal government agencies armed with ARRA and HITECH legislation in providing funding, oversight, and industry-level guidance on the implementation and adoption of healthcare IT throughout the United States.[38] Leading the government's healthcare initiatives is the U.S. Department of Health and Human Services (HHS).[39]

For HIT purposes, two key divisions of HHS are CMS and the ONC, both introduced earlier. In addition to Medicare (the federal health insurance program for seniors) and Medicaid (the federal needs-based program), CMS oversees the Children's Health Insurance Program (CHIP), HIPAA, and the Clinical Laboratory Improvement Amendments (CLIA), among other services. Also, under HITECH, CMS was charged with advancing healthcare IT through implementing the EHR Incentive Programs, helping define meaningful use of EHR technology, drafting standards for the certification of EHR technology, and updating health information privacy and security regulations under HIPAA.[40]

The ONC and two critically important federal advisory committees operating under its auspices have had considerable influence on healthcare IT development and implementation the past seven years. The first of those committees is the Health IT Policy Committee, which makes recommendations to ONC on development and adoption of a nationwide health information infrastructure, including guidance on what standards for interoperability of patient medical information will be required.[41] The second is the Health IT Standards Committee, which focuses on recommendations from CMS, ONC, and the Health IT Policy Committee on standards, implementation specifications, and certification criteria for the electronic exchange and use of patient health information (PHI).[42]

Understanding the roles of these agencies and committees—and keeping abreast of their actions—is an important responsibility for those engaged in planning and delivering communications that support healthcare IT adoption. Individually and collectively, they continue to help drive the definition of incentive payment requirements across the three stages of EHR meaningful use. Each stage has created new healthcare IT performance requirements for a given health system. These requirements also define the kinds of information exchange and interoperability required between healthcare entities across the entire continuum of care, including those directly focused on the patient and the community. Figure 18-3 provides a snapshot of each stage's objectives:

- **Stage 1** Beginning in 2011 as the EHR Incentive Programs' starting point for all providers, stage 1 meaningful use consisted of transferring the collection of data to EHRs and being able to share information, such as electronic visit summaries for patients.

- **Stage 2** Stage 2 meaningful use includes additional standards such as online access for patients to their health information and electronic health information exchange between providers.

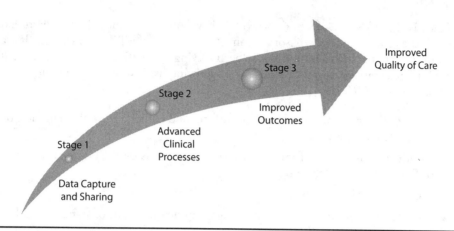

Figure 18-3 Three stages of EHR meaningful use

- **Stage 3** Stage 3 meaningful use, which is optional for participating providers to attest to in 2017 and mandatory for all but a few special classes of providers to attest to in 2018 and beyond, is defined to include demonstrating that the quality of healthcare has been improved.[43]

Consistent with the ever-changing healthcare and healthcare IT landscape, new programs and proposed rules focused on healthcare reform continue to be introduced to revamp payment approaches for healthcare services. In the past, providers were incented based on the volume of services provided, with a small percentage tied to quality metrics. The new incentives are shifting primarily to the quality of care given, with potential financial penalties for care that is deemed unnecessary. This new approach is sometimes referred to as "value versus volume." An example of this is the Medicare Access and CHIP Reauthorization Act of 2015 (MACRA) and the implementation of the Merit-based Incentive Payment System (MIPS). In testimony before the Senate Finance Committee in July of 2016, Andrew Slavitt, Acting Administrator for CMS, said the MACRA reforms aim to replace a "patchwork of programs," in which he included the Medicare EHR Incentive Programs (meaningful use), and modernize Medicare and simplify quality programs as well as payments for physicians.[44] Given the IT implications of programs such as these, their impact and complexity warrant attention and should be included as part of the overall communications plan.

Role of Regulatory Standards and the Evolution of Health Information Exchange

In today's era of healthcare reform, numerous standards in the area of health, health information, and communications technologies help to guide our industry toward interoperability between independent entities and systems. The goal is to support the safe, secure, and private exchange of PHI in ever-increasing volumes to improve the quality of care.

As advised by ONC, CMS, and the HIT Policy Committee, the HIT Standards Committee is the primary federal advisory committee working to fulfill this mandate. It is also a committee upon which I have proudly been serving since 2009 at the appointment of then HHS Secretary Kathleen Sebelius. The following list summarizes the duties of this committee under ARRA:[45]

- Harmonize or update standards for uniform and consistent implementation of standards and specifications
- Conduct pilot testing of standards and specifications by the National Institute of Standards and Technology
- Ensure consistency with existing standards
- Provide a forum for stakeholders to engage in development of standards and implementation specifications
- Establish an annual schedule to assess recommendations of HIT Policy Committee
- Conduct public hearings for public input
- Consider recommendations and comments from the National Committee on Vital and Health Statistics (NCVHS) in development of standards

The HIT Standards Committee established over the course of its deliberations a number of important workgroups as subcommittees to the parent committee. These workgroups met periodically to discuss their topics, present their findings at HIT Standards Committee meetings, and make recommendations to the HIT Standards Committee. Specific areas of focus of the subcommittees included clinical operations, clinical quality, privacy and security, implementation, vocabularies, and a variety of other subject areas that fall under what ONC and CMS called the Power Team Summer Camp.[46] Although the HIT Standards Committee and other ONC advisory groups are undergoing reorganization at the time of this writing, these important areas of focus are likely to be carried on.

Communications resulting from the work of the various subcommittees are critical for ensuring that current regulations and notices of proposed rulemaking (NPRM) are brought into the public arena. As an example, the Implementation Workgroup, which is dedicated to ensuring that what is being asked of the greater health-system and physician-practice communities is actually feasible in terms of adoption and meaningful use, employs extensive communication tools. A strong public communications strategy is core to the work of this group, which holds hearings with broad healthcare industry representation (including health systems, physicians, and EHR and other healthcare IT vendors and developers, among others) and maintains active liaison relationships with the sister HIT Policy Committee. As a result, the Implementation Workgroup will continue to bring forward "real-world" implementation experience into the Standards Committee recommendations with special emphasis on strategies to accelerate the adoption of proposed standards (or mitigate barriers, if any).[47]

All HIT Policy and Standards Committees and related workgroup meetings are held in public with the notices for each meeting posted on the ONC web site and in the Federal Register.[48] Public comments are always welcome.

Chapter Review

ARRA, HITECH, and the EHR Incentive Programs have helped the healthcare industry make a paradigm shift in care delivery through the accelerated use of healthcare IT. CMS, ONC, and its HIT Policy and Standards Committees continue to drive communications at the industry level to provide all stakeholders with a common set of rules to follow for selection, design, implementation, and adoption of EHRs. Challenges still persist, however, when effective communications plans are not developed and followed in complex healthcare IT programs and projects that can affect physicians, nurses, administrators, and patients alike.

This chapter has addressed issues regarding the importance of communications and the development of effective communication strategies in strengthening initiatives ranging from governance efforts to physician-to-patient partnerships—all as part of successful EHR implementations and ongoing user optimization. Key takeaways from this chapter include

- Coordinated, cross-enterprise communications strategies are critically important parts of healthcare IT programs and projects, including the development of governance structures supporting the implementation, adoption, and ongoing user optimization of EHR systems.

- The customers and players engaged in communications include patients and communities, physicians, nurses, project teams and IT departments, and health system leadership. Remember that a patient-centered focus, consideration of the EHR meaningful use program, and physician and nurse engagement are all critical factors in the communication initiatives for these participants.

- Vehicles in a communications plan can include an intranet, use of FAQ documents and interactive "Ask a Question" links, print media, road shows, town hall meetings, and standard meetings, all of which can be used through all phases of a project. The success of such projects is frequently the best measure of the communications plan's effectiveness.

- Some of the most powerful forces driving change include the use of social media platforms, use of mobile devices, and continued complex healthcare reforms requiring portability and interoperability of patient information.

- The committees of ONC, the HIT Policy and Standards Committees, and subcommittees such as the Implementation Workgroup are key drivers of national communications important to all stakeholders involved in working toward the meaningful use of EHRs.

- Tenet Healthcare's IMPACT EHR program, with its governance structure and effective communications efforts, serves as one example for healthcare IT program communications.

As the healthcare industry grows increasingly interconnected through healthcare IT and other technologies, effective communications plans will remain essential parts of the process. With a commitment to the development and execution of communications

PART IV

strategies around the continued implementation, adoption, and user optimization of emerging healthcare IT, higher levels of ownership and commitment by professionals will help to ensure the success of the U.S. healthcare reform movement in years to come.

Questions

To test your comprehension of the chapter, answer the following questions and then check your answers against the list of correct answers at the end of this section.

1. Effective communication programs support the goal of achieving the Institute of Medicine's six aims for improvement in quality care delivery. Which of the following is *not* one of the six aims?

    A. Effective

    B. Safe

    C. Noteworthy

    D. Equitable

2. What caused the lack of clinician adoption and resistance toward use of CPOE in 2001 at a major West Coast academic medical center?

    A. Insufficient funding

    B. Insufficient information and inadequate training on clinical decision support tools

    C. Lack of leadership

    D. Poor implementation

3. What is a key to the success of Tenet's IMPACT governance model (used as a governance example model)?

    A. Uses a three-tiered organizational structure

    B. Uses a bottom-up approach

    C. Engages multidisciplinary staff

    D. Uses technology effectively

4. What is *not* one of the "rules to live by for" governance committees article?

    A. Hardwire the committees.

    B. Set clear levels of successive authority.

    C. Form no governance before its time.

    D. Have concise committee meeting agendas.

5. Who did the ONC regional extension centers recruit to help others get over the hurdles of digitizing their medical records?

   A. Physician champions

   B. Nurse executives

   C. Industry researchers

   D. Hospital CEOs

6. Which of the following does the National Learning Consortium's *Change Management in EHR Implementation* primer suggest including in a communications plan?

   A. Vendor demonstrations, videos

   B. Role playing

   C. Simulated question/answer (Q/A) communication

   D. Staff visits to practices that have had successful EHR implementations

   E. All of the above

7. With the arrival of the digital age, innovations in _____ have enriched communications options to support successful healthcare IT integration.

   A. Speech communications

   B. Transportation services

   C. Mobile devices and social media

   D. Fiber-optic cable

8. Which subcommittee of the HIT Standards Committee was dedicated to ensuring that what is being asked of the greater health-system and physician-practice communities is actually feasible in terms of adoption and meaningful use?

   A. Operations

   B. Strategic Planning

   C. Public Relations

   D. Implementation

Answers

1. **C.** In the Institute of Medicine's 2001 seminal report, "Crossing the Quality Chasm: A Health System for the 21st Century," six aims for improving the quality of healthcare were identified as safe, equitable, effective, patient-centered, timely, and efficient.

2. **B.** A well-known West Coast academic medical center experienced significant resistance to its CPOE implementation because it provided insufficient information and inadequate training on CDS tools, and this proved to serve as a strong lesson-learned case example for the industry on the importance of effective communication on CPOE and EHR implementation projects.

3. **A.** Tenet Healthcare's governance model engages the corporation, regional operations, and their hospitals in a coordinated effort as part of the three-tiered organizational structure.

4. **D.** While having well-planned meetings is important, it was not one of the "rules to live by" for governance committees. Options A, B, and C were part of the rules to live by, along with putting someone in charge who can take a stand and doing real work every time.

5. **A.** Regional extension centers recruited physician champions to serve as role models and share best practices and lessons learned in becoming meaningful users of EHRs.

6. **E.** NLC's *Change Management in EHR Implementation* offers these ideas and more for including in a communications plan.

7. **C.** These two types of innovations have strengthened communication options, increasing the success of EHRs and other healthcare IT.

8. **D.** Out of six subcommittees of the ONC-HIT Standards Committee, the Implementation subcommittee has a strong public communications strategy and maintains an active liaison role with the HIT Policy Committee.

References

1. Blumenthal, D., & Tavenner, M. (2010). The "meaningful use" regulation for electronic health records. *New England Journal of Medicine, 363*(6), 501–504.

2. Centers for Medicare and Medicaid Services (CMS). (2016). *EHR incentive programs: Data and program reports.* Accessed on February 26, 2017, from https://www.cms.gov/Regulations-and-guidance/legislation/EHRIncentivePrograms/DataAndReports.html.

3. Institute of Medicine, Committee on Quality of Healthcare in America. (2001). Executive summary. In *Crossing the quality chasm: A new health system for the 21st century* (pp. 5–6). National Academies Press.

4. Bass, A. (2003, June 1). Health-care IT: A big rollout bust. *CIO Magazine.* Accessed on July 17, 2016, from www.cio.com/article/2442013/infrastructure/health-care-it--a-big-rollout-bust.html.

5. Charles, K., Cannon, M., Hall, R., & Coustasse, A. (2014). Can utilizing a computerized provider order entry (CPOE) system prevent hospital medical errors and adverse drug events? *Perspectives in Health Information Management.* Accessed on February 27, 2017, from http://perspectives.ahima.org/can-utilizing-a-computerized-provider-order-entry-cpoe-system-prevent-hospital-medical-errors-and-adverse-drug-events/#.

6. Vaidya, A. (n.d.). *Five healthcare leaders discuss the challenges of EMR adoption, implementation.* Accessed on May 2, 2016, from www.beckershospitalreview.com/healthcare-information-technology/5-healthcare-leaders-discuss-the-challenges-of-emr-adoption-implementation.html.

7. Shortliffe, E. H. (2005). Strategic action in health information technology: Why the obvious has taken so long. *Health Affairs, 24*(5), 1222–1233.

8. Baron, R. J., Fabens, E. L., Schiffman, M., & Wolf, E. (2005). Electronic health records: Just around the corner? Or over the cliff? *Annals of Internal Medicine, 143*(3), 222–226.

9. Rouse, W. (2008). Healthcare as a complex adaptive system: Implications for design and management. *Bridge, 38*(1).

10. Kaplan, B., & Harris-Salamone, K. D. (2009). Health IT success and failure: Recommendations from literature and an AMIA workshop. *Journal of the American Medical Informatics Association, 16*(3), 291–299.

11. Campbell, E. M., Sittig, D. F., Ash, J. S., Guappone, K. P., & Dykstra, R. H. (2006). Types of unintended consequences related to computerized provider order entry. *Journal of the American Medical Informatics Association, 13*(5), 547–556.

12. Bartos, C. E., Butler, B. S., Penrod, L. E., Fridsma, D. B., & Crowley, R. S. (2008). Negative CPOE attitudes correlate with diminished power in the workplace. *AMIA Annual Symposium Proceedings 6,* 36–40.

13. Ash, J. S., Anderson, J. G., Gorman, P. N., Zielstorff, R. D., Norcross, N., Pettit, J., & Yao, P. (2000). Managing change: Analysis of a hypothetical case. *Journal of the American Medical Informatics Association, 7*(2), 125–134.

14. Morrissey, J. (2012, February). iGovernance. *Hospitals and Health Networks Magazine.* Accessed on July 17, 2016, from www.hhnmag.com/articles/6008-igovernance.

15. College of Healthcare Information Management Executives (CHIME). (2010). Chapter 9: Communication dispels fear surrounding the EHR conversion. In *The CIO's guide to implementing EHRs in the HITECH era.* CHIME Report.

16. Johnson, E. O. (2012, Apr. 10). *IMPACT journey program briefing.* Tenet Healthcare Corporation internal corporate briefing.

17. Hoehn, B. J. (2010). Clinical information technology governance. *Journal of Healthcare Information Management, 24*(2), 13–14.

18. Institute of Medicine, Committee on Quality of Healthcare in America. (2001). Chapter 2: Improving the 21st century healthcare system, patient-centeredness. In *Crossing the quality chasm: A new health system for the 21st century* (pp. 48–50). National Academies Press.

19. Patient-Centered Primary Care Collaborative. (2007). *Joint principles of the patient-centered medical home.* Accessed on July 17, 2016, from www.pcpcc.net/content/joint-principles-patient-centered-medical-home.

20. Overview and Intent of Medicare Shared Savings Program, 76 Fed. Reg. 67,804 (Nov. 2, 2011), I(C).

21. Processes to Promote Evidence-Based Medicine, Patient Engagement, Reporting, Coordination of Care, and Demonstrating Patient-Centeredness, 76 Fed. Reg. 67,827 (Nov. 2, 2011), II(B)(5).

PART IV

22. Mosquera, M. (2011, Mar. 4). "Physician champions" help other docs with EHR adoption. *Government HealthIT.* Accessed on July 17, 2016, from www .govhealthit.com/news/physician-champions-help-other-docs-ehr-adoption.

23. Scher, D. L. (2014, Oct. 25). *Five reasons why physician champions are needed.* Accessed on May 2, 2016, from www.kevinmd.com/blog/2014/10/5-reasons-physician-champions-needed.html.

24. National Latino Alliance on Health Information Technology (LISA). (2012, Apr. 25). Providers make progress in EHR adoption, challenges remain. *iHealthBeat.* Accessed on July 17, 2016, from https://listahit.wordpress .com/2012/04/25/providers-make-progress-in-ehr-adoption-challenges-remain-by-miliard-healthcare-it-news/.

25. Herman, B. (2014, Nov. 1). Nurse CIOs are taking on bigger roles in healthcare. *Modern Healthcare.* Accessed on July 17, 2016, from www.modernhealthcare .com/article/20141101/MAGAZINE/311019980.

26. Mitchell, M. B. (2012, Feb. 21). *Role of the CNIO in nursing optimization of the electronic medical record (EMR).* HIMSS (Health Information Management Systems Society) 2012 Annual Conference Presentation.

27. CHIME. (2010). Chapter 3: Assessing the organization's current state in IT, charting a new course; Chapter 7: Considering new role players for your EHR implementation. In *The CIO's guide to implementing EHRs in the HITECH era* (pp. 13, 31). CHIME Report.

28. Tenet Healthcare Corporation. (2016, Mar. 18). Tenet, ACI play leading roles in National Patient Safety Week. *IMPACT Insider: Acute Care Hospital Implementation News.*

29. Health Information Management Systems Society (HIMSS). (2011). *Davies Enterprise Award for Kaiser Permanente: Management section* (p. 5). Accessed on February 27, 2017, from http://s3.amazonaws.com/rdcms-himss/files/ production/public/2011%20Davies%20Full%20App_final_11072011_ additional%20info.pdf.

30. HealthIT.gov. (2013, Apr. 30). *Change management in EHR implementation: Primer.* Accessed on May 2, 2016, from https://www.healthit.gov/sites/default/ files/tools/nlc_changemanagementprimer.pdf.

31. Smaltz, D. H., Callander, R., Turner, M., Kennamer, G., Wurtz, H., Bowen, A., & Waldrum, M. R. (2005). Making sausage: Effective management of enterprise-wide clinical IT projects. *Journal of Healthcare Information Management, 19*(2), 48–55.

32. Rodríguez, C., & Pozzebon, M. (2011). Understanding managerial behavior during initial steps of a clinical information system adoption. *BMC Medical Informatics and Decision Making 11,* 42.

33. D'Amato, C., D'Andrea, R., Bronnert, J., Cook, J., Foley, M., Garret, G., ... Yoder, M. J. (2009). Planning organizational transition to ICD-10-CM/PCS. *Journal of AHIMA, 80*(10), 72–77.

34. Wike, K. (2015, Aug. 20). *More than half of physicians use mobile to access patient data.* Accessed on May 5, 2016, from www.healthitoutcomes.com/doc/more-than-half-of-physicians-use-mobile-to-access-patient-data-0001.

35. Miliard, M. (2016, May 5). *Brookings calls out OCR on HIPAA audits, offers security.* Accessed on May 5, 2016, from https://www.healthcareitnews.com/news/brookings-calls-out-ocr-hipaa-audits-offers-security-tips-healthcare-organizations.

36. Belbey, J. (2015, Sept. 24). *Can doctors improve patient outcomes with social media?* Accessed on May 3, 2016, from www.forbes.com/sites/joannabelbey/2015/09/24/can-doctors-improve-patient-outcomes-with-social-media/.

37. Federation of State Medical Boards (FSMB). (April, 2012). *Model guidelines for the appropriate use of social media and social networking in medical practice.* Accessed on May 10, 2016, from www.fsmb.org/Media/Default/PDF/FSMB/Advocacy/pub-social-media-guidelines.pdf.

38. Robert Wood Johnson Foundation (RWJF). (2009). Chapter 4: Recent federal initiatives in health information technology. In *Health information technology in the United States: On the cusp of change.* Accessed on July 17, 2016, from www.rwjf.org/pr/product.jsp?id=50308.

39. Office of Disease Prevention and Health Promotion. (n.d.). HealthyPeople2020: Health communications and health information technology. *HealthyPeople.gov.* Accessed on July 17, 2016, from www.healthypeople.gov/2020/topicsobjectives2020/overview.aspx?topicid=18.

40. CMS. (n.d.). *SearchHealthIT.* Accessed on July 17, 2016, from http://searchhealthit.techtarget.com/definition/Centers-for-Medicare-Medicaid-Services-CMS.

41. Office of the National Coordinator for Health Information Technology (ONC-HIT). (n.d.). *Health IT Policy Committee.* Accessed on July 17, 2016, from https://www.healthit.gov/facas/health-it-policy-committee.

42. ONC-HIT. (n.d.). *Health IT Standards Committee.* Accessed on July 17, 2016, from https://www.healthit.gov/facas/health-it-standards-committee.

43. CMS. (n.d.). *Fact sheet: EHR incentive programs in 2015 and beyond.* Accessed on July 17, 2016, from www.cms.gov/Newsroom/MediaReleaseDatabase/Fact-sheets/2015-Fact-sheets-items/2015-10-06-2.html.

44. Bazzoli, F. (2016, July 14). Support swells for flexibility in implementing MACRA. *HealthData Management.* Accessed on July 17, 2016, from www.healthdatamanagement.com/news/support-swells-for-flexibility-in-implementing-macra?tag=00000151-16d0-def7-a1db-97f0366e0000.

PART IV

45. RWJF. (2009, May). Chapter 4: Recent federal initiatives in health information technology. In *Health information technology in the United States: On the cusp of change, 2009*; American Recovery and Reinvestment Act, H. R. 1, 111th Cong., § 3003(b), HIT Standards Committee, Duties.

46. Office of the National Coordinator for Health Information Technology (ONC). (n.d.). *HIT Standards Committee Workgroups.* Accessed on July 17, 2016, from https://www.healthit.gov/FACAS/health-it-standards-committee/HITSC-Workgroups.

47. ONC. (n.d.). *Implementation Workgroup.* Accessed on July 17, 2016, from https://www.healthit.gov/facas/health-it-standards-committee/hitsc-workgroups/implementation.

48. ONC. (n.d.). *Upcoming Health IT Standards Committee meetings.* Accessed on July 17, 2016, from https://www.healthit.gov/FACAS/meetings/25.

Non-EHR HIT: From Architecture to Operations

Alistair Erskine, Bipin Karunakaran

In this chapter, you will learn how to
- Understand overall HIT department organizational structure
- Describe HIT roles in healthcare organizations
- Understand the technology environment for non-EHR systems
- Identify clinical and nonclinical systems that are critical to every healthcare organization
- Identify commonalities in design and operation between the various non-EHR systems
- Understand interoperability between critical clinical and nonclinical systems

As discussed in detail throughout this book, one of the major clinical HIT systems is the electronic health record (EHR) system, which helps clinicians with important clinical functions such as viewing patient charts, preparing clinical notes, and ordering medications for both acute and ambulatory settings. This chapter, while acknowledging the central importance of EHR systems in today's healthcare organizations, focuses on the other major information systems and information technologies that complement EHR systems and, together with EHR systems, support healthcare operations. We describe major clinical and nonclinical "non-EHR" HIT systems and applications. This coverage is not meant to be exhaustive, as the incredible diversity of HIT systems and applications used in healthcare today is huge and would preclude such coverage here. Rather we provide a framework to allow the reader to understand the main divisions within HIT and some important examples within each of the divisions and subdivisions. To begin, we'll discuss how the HIT functions in healthcare organizations are organized, including HIT department governance and roles and how key functions are operationalized.

The Healthcare IT Organization: Challenges, Structures, and Roles

The common goals of healthcare information technology (HIT) departments in healthcare organizations are to improve quality of patient care, increase provider efficiency for care delivery, and support the administrative and revenue cycle IT needs of the organization. Attaining these goals is challenging in healthcare delivery systems that are often fragmented, where most patients receive care from disparate providers. Even large, resource-rich integrated health systems encounter challenges in coordinating multiple centers of excellence and campuses.[1] Healthcare information technologies and HIT departments benefit from being organized to enable the smooth flow of information between clinicians, technologists, nonclinicians, and technology systems. A clear understanding of organizational strategy, the current state of services, and future technical, clinical, and business directions is needed both by HIT department leaders and managers as well as key HIT department stakeholders. A common standard practice for delivery of technology services is essential for a HIT organization to be successful.

Most medium- to large-size healthcare organizations have a central HIT team supporting diverse specialty practices, medical centers, and campuses. The HIT team is often led by a physician, a nurse informaticist, or a technology administrator partnered with a physician. The head of the HIT team is a C-level executive, often with the title chief information officer (CIO), with various HIT department heads reporting to the CIO. Especially when a healthcare organization has a technologist CIO, as opposed to a licensed clinical professional CIO, a chief medical information officer (CMIO) may be part of the HIT team leadership. The CMIO is often a physician, but increasingly nurses and other clinicians are assuming these roles. Typically, major clinical systems such as radiology, lab, and pharmacy and nonclinical systems such as supply chain, finance/revenue cycle management and patient relationship management are organized as separate subdepartments under the CIO. These systems are described in depth in the next section.

Medium- to large-size healthcare organizations usually organize basic IT infrastructure functions such as networks, phone switches, computer servers, and data-center operations within the HIT department to be performed by a single centralized core infrastructure team. Similarly, user-facing phone systems, PCs, laptops, tablets, and helpdesk support are handled via a central user support team.

For HIT organizations to be successful, there is a need for close alignment and interaction with various departments/service lines of the health system. For example, the radiology department needs close alignment and interactions with the technology department working on radiology systems. This close alignment and interaction enables effective communication between the radiologists and the technologists. For example, this enables the radiology team (composed of select radiology department business and clinical staff) to quickly communicate needed business changes to the tech team, and enables the tech team to communicate to the radiology team changes in the technology landscape that may provide new clinical or business opportunities to the radiology team.

Even though HIT is a central organization under the CIO, the close alignment between the tech teams and the health system departments is essential for the best service experience. To enable effective collaboration, efficiency, and alignment, major health system departments often have one or more dedicated tech personnel enhancing and maintaining specific department systems. This arrangement of having a few dedicated technologists in major departments/service lines working closely with the IT department is becoming more common, creating a hub-and-spoke model of service. A business relationship manager (BRM) assigned to one or more health system departments plays a critical role as a conduit between the health system department(s) and the HIT department. In their role, a BRM is seen as the person representing the needs of the department(s) to the HIT department. The BRM often works with individual department heads, their representatives, or the tech teams embedded in the department to create a business case for modifications to existing software systems or the purchase or build of new software systems. The BRM works closely with the HIT governance committee to present business case proposals with the intent of gaining approvals. The BRM also communicates status of various departments or enterprise-level project status to the department heads and representatives.

Figure 19-1 shows an example of a HIT team's organization. The goal of centralizing systems under one umbrella is to enable economies of scale for technology management and uniformity in practice for providing the best patient care using technology as an enabler. Figure 19-1 represents a very general organizational structure due to the large variability of how healthcare HIT functions and departments are organized—therefore there is no one best organizational structure for HIT. We encourage you to view Figure 19-1 in relation to the "Healthcare IT Workforce Roles" section of Appendix D (see Appendix C for how to access this content), which lists several dozen of the HIT workforce roles active in healthcare organizations today, and then mix and match your own HIT subdepartment dream teams. For example, the EHR team members in a large organization may include a computer and information systems manager (reporting directly to the CIO), two project managers, two business relationship managers, four system analysts, four application

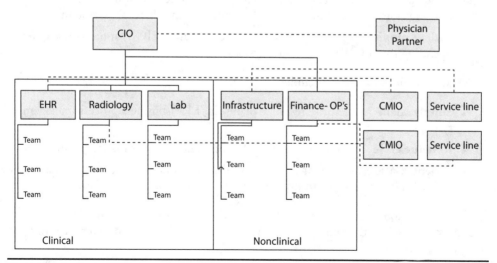

Figure 19-1 Typical HIT team organization

specialists, and two nurse informatics (who work closely with the CMIO). The infrastructure team may have one computer and information systems manager (reporting directly to the CIO), one project manager, three computer hardware engineers, two computer network architects, two computer programmers, one information security analyst, two network and computer systems administrators, one software developer, and two electrical engineering technicians. The enterprise-wide computer help desk may also be part of the infrastructure and have a dozen or more help desk support technicians.

HIT Major Non-EHR HIT Systems and Applications

All of the major systems and applications in the non-EHR space fall into two major categories: clinical systems and nonclinical systems. One or more application data interchange systems integrate clinical and nonclinical systems data. Figure 19-2 depicts these major non-EHR systems and applications. For some vendors, these "ancillary" components are part of the core EHR system. For others, interfaces are used to connect to separate "best of breed" systems. For example, subsystems such as admission/discharge/transfer (ADT) and operating room management are tightly integrated with the EHR system, while other systems, like PACS and supply chain systems, have a more detached relationship.

Major clinical ancillary departments and the clinical systems that can stand alone and be integrated with an EHR system *or* a subsystem/module of an EHR system include:

- **Radiology**   Picture archiving and communication system (PACS), radiology information system (RIS), speech recognition system
- **Pharmacy**   Pharmacy management system, pharmacy workflow system, pharmacy dispensing system
- **Clinical laboratory**   Laboratory management system, automated cellular imaging system, microbiology blood culture system, blood bank system
- **Patient monitoring**   Electronic intensive care unit (EICU) monitoring system, operating room (OR) monitoring system

Major nonclinical systems include

- **Supply chain**   Enterprise resource planning (ERP)/business process management systems
- **Revenue cycle**   Billing, accounting, finance, and contract management systems
- **Patient relationship management**   Similar to customer relationship management (CRM) software in other industries, a relatively new concept in healthcare

The application data interchange (ADI) is the application data and message interchange system for both internal system-to-system interchange and external interoperability across entities.

Figure 19-2
A model of
select HIT clinical
systems

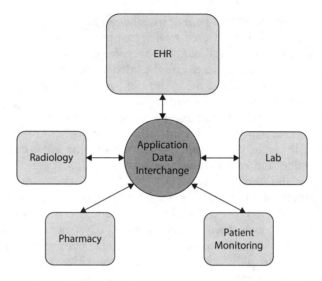

Working with Enterprise HIT Systems

Major HIT systems satisfy various needs of the clinical and nonclinical staff and assist in providing the best care for patients. Every health system has a core technology infrastructure that typically interfaces with other important systems. The core infrastructure consists of computer networks, phone systems, data centers with server farms, and various network switches directing network traffic internally as well as externally. Security systems such as firewalls prevent unauthorized network traffic from entering the internal network. Running on top of the core infrastructure are all systems and applications, both clinical and nonclinical.[2]

As patients enter the healthcare system, one of their first touch points is an online patient portal or a patient contact center. Increasingly, patients schedule appointments via the contact center or the online portal and are then seen in an ambulatory setting. Sometimes, due to the nature of the illness, patients are moved from an ambulatory setting to an acute care setting. In a few cases patients enter the system directly through the emergency department (ED). From the entry point to discharge and all throughout their care in an ambulatory or acute care facility, technology and technology systems play an important role in the care of the patient.

A patient can register online for an online account to schedule their first visit. Once an online patient account is created, subsequent visits can be scheduled online using the same account. Using the online portal, a patient can view their lab results, e-mail their provider, view and pay their bills, and so on. The online portal is one of the many systems that the HIT team builds and maintains. As the patient is scheduled for different appointments, a patient schedule management system maintained by the HIT team is used for matching patient appointments with provider availability. The schedule management system provides workflow support and reminders for patient coordinators, nurses, and providers.

As care is delivered to a patient in either an inpatient or outpatient setting, a variety of other HIT systems are used to deliver optimal patient care. A radiologist uses the PACS to store and read radiology images. A microbiologist uses the blood culture system to find an infection. To ensure the safety of donated blood, all donated blood must be tested in the lab. Blood banks are unique to the health system and one of the few functions that require FDA certification. Patient monitoring systems are used by the ICU physicians to closely monitor patient progress and their response to care. Pharmacy systems receive patient medication information as prescribed by the physician either electronically or in paper form. Pharmacy systems track medications for patients— dosage, refills, and so on. Pharmacy management software in many health systems is now part of the core EHR system.

An example of a nonclinical system is the supply chain system, which track supplies, inventory levels, and cost of supplies. Storage and movement of supplies across the health system are also tracked within a supply chain system. The supply chain system automatically orders drugs based on inventory levels, delivery timelines, and pricing. Other examples include billing systems, which are used by the revenue cycle team to create accurate billing statements for patients, and business intelligence (BI) and data systems, which are used by clinicians, operations personnel, and nonclinicians to analyze trends and future opportunities using data and analytics.

Systems that are not part of the core EHR system typically interoperate with each other via an application data interchange system. These systems facilitate exchange of data between multiple systems with guaranteed delivery mechanisms built in. For example, lab orders entered in the EHR system are sent to the lab management system via the application interchange; results from the lab management system are sent back to the EHR system also via the application interchange. This enables the labs to get information on the orders and match up the samples with the orders. The physicians see the lab results back in the EHR in a timely manner.

Vendor-Specific Systems: Acquisition, Installation, and Maintenance of HIT Systems

Healthcare information technology systems are a mix of purchased vendor software systems, usually making up the majority of systems, and internally developed custom software systems. Keeping track of the multiple enterprise-wide and more focused vendor software systems requires vendor management, which includes financial and contract management, software patching, and upgrades.

Most HIT departments have an annual budget, with a portion allocated to capital expenditures (CAPEX) and another portion allocated to operational expenses (OPEX). Dollars in the CAPEX budget are used to build or purchase new software systems, while OPEX budget dollars are used to maintain existing software system assets. Most HIT organizations have an annual budget-planning process. As part of the planning process, and based on the organization strategy and financial strength, funds are allocated to both capital and operational budgets. The budgets are managed closely by the HIT management team so that actual expenses meet the planned budget.

New software systems are purchased and implemented after a thorough vetting process, starting with a requirements analysis that includes assessing whether existing HIT within the organization meets new needs. This is followed by the researching of new solutions, which then leads to a Request for Proposal (RFP) and often involves a vendor proof of concept (PoC) implementation, as shown in Figure 19-3. A common decision point for most organizations is whether to purchase the non-core EHR components from their primary EHR vendor or to rely on stand-alone suppliers. Usually two or more vendors are vetted through the entire process before a final choice is made. The decision to select a particular vendor software system is usually based on the following four major criteria:

- System features meeting the needs of the organization
- Cost
- Vendor technical and financial strength
- Maturity of the core-EHR vendor's solution and risks/benefits of relying on an interface to third-party applications and systems

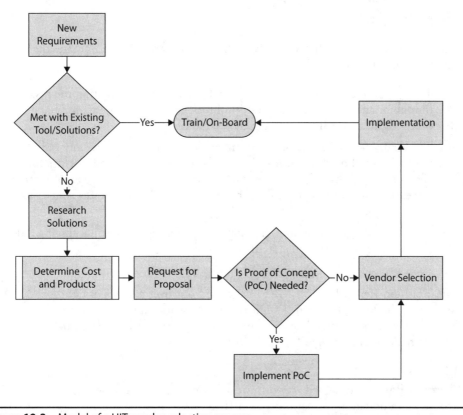

Figure 19-3 Model of a HIT vendor selection process

Radiology Systems

Radiology departments use three major technology systems: picture archiving and communication system (PACS), radiology information system (RIS), and speech recognition system.

PACS

The picture archiving and communication system is used to store and display radiologic images. The standard digital format for PACS data is Digital Imaging and Communications in Medicine (DICOM).[3] Radiology departments employ a variety of modalities, each designed for a particular focus. Some examples include

- General X-ray or digital radiography (DR)
- Computed tomography (CT)
- Ultrasound (US)
- Magnetic resonance imaging (MRI)
- Nuclear medicine (NM)
- Positron emission tomography (PET)
- Mammography (MG)

Originally, all radiographic images were printed on film. PACS eliminates the need for film. Additional benefits of PACS are

- The ability to store and retrieve images digitally, thus eliminating the need for film librarians to process a request, find the films, deliver them, and hang them onto a lightbox for interpretation by the radiologist.
- The ability to access the images from any location. This allows any radiologists in one hospital or clinic to read images from another hospital or clinic. It also allows for "nighthawk" coverage, where, for example, radiologists in Australia can easily cover the night shift for hospitals in the United States (since our night is their day).
- Allows for integration and interfacing with other digital hospital systems, such as the radiology information system (RIS) and EHR system.

PACS allows for more efficient image interpretation. Instead of looking at images in a linear fashion (reviewing 150 MRI images laid out over a series of lightboxes), PACS allows the radiologist to sit at a high-resolution workstation and zoom through the images on the Z-axis, much like watching a movie. This has distinct clinical advantages over film radiographic images.[4]

RIS

Whereas a PACS is designed to optimize the viewing of radiology images for clinical purposes, a radiology information system (RIS) is an information management system specifically designed for tracking radiology operations. A RIS manages patient identification and flow, including scheduling and tracking the patient and storing the results of their radiology test, as dictated by the radiologist.

The RIS is a database designed to track functions such as

- Scheduling and defining the exam (the provider determines the tests and evaluates the conditions of a particular patient) to be performed
- Ordering the exam
- Tracking the patient while in the radiology department
- Storing the radiologist's result of the interpretation of the images of the exam
- Billing for the exam

The RIS most often interfaces with other hospital systems, notably the EHR system and likely a speech recognition system that is used to interpret the radiologist's dictation into text. Often, the RIS interfaces with the EHR system via an interface engine that passes electronic messages among various hospital systems such as the EHR system, lab, and radiology systems. The protocol used for this interface is typically Health Level 7 (HL7) versions 2.xx, 3, or Fast Healthcare Interoperability Resources (FHIR). See Chapter 8 for more details about the HL7 standards.

Speech Recognition System

Much of a radiologist's responsibilities lie with two functions:

- Interpreting the image(s)
- Documenting their findings related to the image(s)

In most instances, when a radiology exam is ordered, the ordering physician (primary care doctor or specialist) is interested in having the images interpreted by the radiologist as quickly as possible so that the physician can provide the next step of care based on the results of the exam. A typical radiologist's workflow for documenting their findings involves reviewing and interpreting the image while simultaneously dictating into a dictation microphone or telephone dictation system. The radiologist's voice recording is stored in an analog dictation repository. Later, a transcriptionist listens to the recording and keyboards the report into the RIS. When the draft report is available, the radiologist accesses the report via the RIS, reads the transcribed report, and, if there are no errors, approves it.

With a speech recognition system, the radiologist typically views the images on a PACS workstation and simultaneously inputs his or her findings by speaking through a microphone headset. The speech recognition system converts the speech to text in real time, so that once the radiologist has completed dictation, he or she can immediately review the text, correct any errors, and electronically sign the report. The report is immediately sent to the RIS and/or the EHR system. This technology has allowed for significantly improved efficiencies in the generation of radiology reporting.

PART IV

Pharmacy Systems

Typically, a pharmacy system has the following major modules:

- **Drug information system**   A drug information system is an online, Internet-based reference tool used by pharmacists to obtain information about drugs.

- **Order-filling system**   A robot-based order-filling system is used to fill prescriptions. The system interfaces with the EHR computerized provider order entry (CPOE) module to receive medication orders directly and then, once a pharmacist has approved them as valid, fill them via a robot installed in an inpatient pharmacy. There are regularly scheduled "cart-fill" processing runs as well as ad hoc filling of "first-dose" orders in the system. The system is usually server based and has several workstations located in a central location for access and operation of the order-filling process. Generally, the order-filling system vendor maintains a 24/7 support structure including proactive monitoring of vital system functions.

- **TPN compounder system**   A total parenteral nutrition (TPN) compounder system is usually two separate applications that are used together to accomplish mixing custom TPN solutions. A compounder application is used by pharmacists to create formulas of TPN compounds for patients. This is a server-based, client/server application that references a database containing information about various elements and proper proportions for mixtures. The compounder is used to create custom mixtures for patients; its primary output is a text file for each formula that is stored on the server. A separate application (or separate module of a combined TPN compounder system) reads the formula files created by the compounder and then, via its interface with a specialized pump, combines up to 24 different elements to create an intravenous (IV) solution based on the pharmacist's formula for administration to a specific patient.

- **Prescription workflow solution**   In many inpatient settings, unit doses are required. The U.S. Food and Drug Administration (FDA) defines a unit dose as "The delivery of a single dose of a drug to the patient at the time of administration for institutional use, e.g., hospitals."[5] A prescription workflow solution includes software and hardware designed to provide a complete pharmacy workflow solution, including unit dose packaging. As such, the workflow solution fulfills the inventory management and drug distribution needs of the central pharmacy by providing barcode verification of dispensed drugs from the pharmacy to the patient's bedside. The hardware side consists of two core products: a carousel and a packager. Some customers may purchase only one or the other, as these products can work independently. A software package usually controls the devices to automate the retrieval, inventory management, and packaging.

- **Pharmacy management system**   A pharmacy management system is composed of the following functions: e-prescribing, inventory management, barcode and Universal Product Code (UPC) scanning, workflow management, integrated voice response (IVR) system, drug maintenance updates, fax, long-term care functionality, reporting packages, and a web portal for patients to refill prescriptions.

- **Pharmacy workflow system**   As a key entry point into pharmacy automation, a pharmacy workflow system delivers comprehensive workflow management, in-depth quality control, and real-time prescription tracking. To ensure filling accuracy, workstations establish quality checkpoints by employing barcode scanning, digital imagery of medications and original paper prescriptions, and high-quality software protocols at every stage of the prescription fulfillment process. To achieve continuous improvement, the information management tools provide full visibility into the pharmacy's daily activity, enabling informed decision-making and best practices, which lead to increased profitability.

- **Infusion system**   An infusion system or module of a broader pharmacy system allows for viewing real-time infusion data, drug library management, drug library uploading, and clinical reporting. This system includes large-volume IV pumps that use real-time communications with a server across a wireless local area network (WLAN) connection. While the pumps actually operate completely independent of the server, the connectivity is used to allow pump infusion libraries to be centrally maintained and selectively pushed out to the pumps as well as to allow pumps to transmit metrics back to the server to report on their operation.

- **Drug verification/inspection system**   This system includes patient safety and process improvement software solutions for difficult-to-manage processes of a hospital pharmacy. Software uses the medication barcode as a control measure for the prevention of medication restocking errors, including those stemming from look-alike or sound-alike items. The system also continually monitors all locations for medications that are near expiration to allow for timely removal prior to use. The system has different audible sound alerts at the time of medication scanning to indicate whether the medication scanned is equivalent to the one assigned. This system saves the pharmacy staff time during the restocking process and serves as an important patient safety check. The planning tool provides pharmacy leadership an easy way to plan, schedule, and monitor inspections of everywhere that medications are stored throughout the hospital. It can provide customizable e-mail alerts when inspections are overdue, provide quality assurance and compliance reports, and provide documentation for all medications removed from stock due to expiration date.

- **Automated medication dispensing cabinets**   Each automated medication dispensing cabinet consists of a computer that is touch-screen accessible as well as accessible via an integral keyboard and touchpad. The computer is used to control access to the various medications that are stored in the cabinet. The cabinets have a wide variety of physical configurations available to accommodate the storage and dispensing for various medications in various containers and forms. Each cabinet is custom designed to best suit the particular location of operation. A provider, most typically a nurse, logs into the cabinet using a personal identification. Each cabinet has screens showing the patients that are currently in that area along with medication profile information regarding the drugs that they are currently prescribed. This information is kept current via data interface feeds from various hospital systems. A specialized cabinet is typically used to store controlled substances; the backend database for this cabinet stores inventory and creates detailed tracking and reporting for each transaction.

- **Refill mobile app**   This is an application for mobile telephone devices that allows the user to refill prescriptions through the outpatient and mail-order pharmacies from their iPhone or Android mobile device. The app talks to the interactive voice response (IVR) server, which then sends the prescription information to the pharmacy software for refill.

Lab Systems

A clinical laboratory—often divided into an anatomic pathology lab and a clinical pathology lab—is where tests are done on clinical patient specimens in order to obtain information pertaining to the diagnosis, treatment, and prevention of disease.[6] An anatomic pathology lab, sometimes known as the tissue lab, includes histopathology and cytopathology among its divisions. A clinical pathology lab—sometimes known as the test tube lab—includes microbiology, chemistry, hematology, and genetics among its subdivisions.

Following are the major technology/information systems for clinical laboratories:

- **Laboratory management system**   This system includes microbiology, blood bank lab processing, and a specimen tracking module.

- **Laboratory test results system for anatomic and clinical pathology**   This provides physician clients with disease-oriented pathology reports that convert laboratory data on various tests into information and knowledge applicable at the patient's bedside. This system correlates the patient's status with the collective experience of the world's literature and ensures greater patient safety.

- **Laboratory information system (LIS)**   This system automates and drives workflow for the clinical pathology lab. This system interfaces with software applications and instruments in the lab to create a powerful integrated lab workflow system. It streamlines lab processes to decrease specimen handling time, increase productivity, and improve turnaround time. As an example, a patient's blood test result can be automatically reported to an EHR.[7]

- **Quality management system**   Because high quality of results in a lab is critical, this system tracks and reports on various quality issues in registration, accessioning, histology, and transcription. Issues like block labeling are critical as the tests have to be repeated for the patient. Block labeling occurs when a pathologist slices a "tissue block" removed from a patient by a surgeon into very thin layers and places them on a glass slide for examination under a microscope. Each slide has to be labeled carefully in reference to the tissue block and patient.

Block labeling issues are tracked very closely and remediation steps and controls monitored and adjusted to meet thresholds of quality.[8]

- **A system for Internet access to lab orders and results**   This web-based system is directly interfaced to several other lab and non-lab systems.

The laboratory's systems are also interfaced to the billing system for inpatient admissions, discharges, and transfers (ADT) and outpatient registration and all billing functions. Usually, an order-entry and results-reporting interface is available in the EHR clinical repository and web-based laboratory system via an application interface engine.

The laboratory takes advantage of all the advanced features of these systems including, but not limited to, bar-coded sample and patient identification, bidirectional instrument interfacing, distributed patient report printing, image processing, rules processing, and Internet-based access.

In addition to meeting the care needs of the patients, these systems enable the health system to market the medical lab as a referral laboratory, develop partnerships with other organizations, and support substantial enhancements in overall productivity. In addition, they allow effective and seamless integration among separate facilities and interface with existing and future corporate and clinical information systems.

Technical support is provided by a central IT team or a lab information support team.

Patient Monitoring Systems

Patient monitoring systems are almost universally present in the intensive care units (ICU) and operating rooms (OR) of inpatient settings, but they are also found in "step-down" units that transition patients from ICUs and ORs to less acute care units prior to their discharge. A new setting for patient monitoring systems is the home where clinicians use mobile health technology solutions to connect patient monitors worn by patients continually or intermittently in their homes with clinicians who evaluate the patient monitoring data remotely. Two of these applications of patient monitoring systems are further explored here.

EICU Monitoring Systems

A bedside physiologic monitor monitors patient vitals in an inpatient setting. An EICU system consists of a monitor in each room, tying back to a central server for processing of the monitored data. The unvalidated output of the monitors is transmitted through an interface engine to a care application (part of the monitoring software) for review by the care manager. The monitoring hardware and software are maintained by a combination of the clinical engineering department, the HIT department, and the vendors.

There is a second feed sourced from the EHR system containing validated monitoring data from specific vital-sign flowsheet records. The specific monitor-sourced, EICU-processed entries (e.g., temperature, heart rate, blood pressure) into the patient's record within the EHR system can—if all the parts are working together effectively—give a valid representation of the patient's status.

In addition, other datasets such as lab results and medications are interfaced to the EICU care application interface. The care application system uses algorithms from the various vitals, labs, and meds (all interfaced to the EHR system) to determine the patient's status; it alerts the staff when a defined threshold is met.

OR Monitoring Systems

This group of monitoring systems includes not only the systems dedicated to hospital ORs but also the systems present in any procedure rooms with anesthesia capability, such as endoscopy, interventional radiology, cardiac catheterization, and MRI. Data capture software is used to interface the monitored data into the EHR system. To start the process, an anesthesiologist manually connects the data capture device to the EHR system. The data flows from the OR monitoring hardware to the EHR system. Most EHR systems have an anesthesia module to store data collected from monitoring systems as part of the medical record. All patient vital data from an anesthesia machine are recorded and transferred to the EHR system. This is unvalidated data that flow unfiltered to the EHR system for temporary storage. A nurse typically reviews the whole dataset and selects the appropriate vital signs for permanent submission into the EHR system. After 72 hours, all unvalidated data are purged from the EHR system.

Supply Chain Systems

The supply chain function of a healthcare organization typically consists of centrally managed core operations and strategically placed decentralized operations. A supply chain services division of a healthcare organization provides oversight management for contract support and all capital and related service acquisitions. Clinical integration for all product and equipment decisions occurs through the application of the Clinical Use Evaluation (CUE) or similar process. This process is a system-wide, structured, interdisciplinary process to review all aspects of product utilization, product selection, new products, and product formulary development and cost effectiveness. It facilitates review of product data and outlines product evaluations for recommendations and discussion leading to the formulation of an action plan to implement and measure the impact of change in the supply chain.

The following are the main CUE objectives:

- Aid in the cost-effective delivery of high-quality patient care through clinically driven product selection and utilization management
- Educate and involve staff in the process
- Develop a product formulary

By using the CUE process, members of supply chain services staff are able to review all products and equipment used throughout the organization. This process allows avoidance of duplication, reduction of inventory, and reduced costs. To help achieve these goals, the main system used in the supply chain department is an ERP software system, described next.

ERP Software Systems

An enterprise resource planning (ERP) software system is typically used by organizations to organize and maintain a set of integrated applications and associated data for operations. ERP systems support key operational functions like manufacturing, distribution, purchasing, accounting, and inventory management. Supply chain departments use ERP software because of the integrated nature of the applications in the ERP software, enabling the department to track products, utilization, and purchasing in a central place. This eliminates the need to use multiple applications and move data from one application to another.

Finance and Operations Systems

Patients in a hospital must be registered and tracked from location to location as they progress through different care areas. The services, treatments, medicines, and equipment they use must likewise be tracked and accounted for. Similar requirements exist in ambulatory settings. "Billing systems," used for tracking patient expenses and billing them or their insurers, were some of the first HIT systems to be used in hospitals. They were started as simple systems in the 1960s and '70s but over the years became more sophisticated as healthcare organizations became more complex. As this evolution occurred, the term "revenue cycle management" was coined to identify the increasingly complex functions in healthcare financial systems. At first this took the form of simply more robust billing systems, but over time these systems became more common and multifaceted. They are now either part of or interfaced with EHR systems and serve to automate financial and operational functions in healthcare.

Basic revenue cycle management systems contain the subsystems or modules in Table 19-1. It is important to note that as this is written, revenue cycle systems are changing to adapt to an increasingly consumer-directed healthcare environment and new forms of healthcare delivery such as retail health.[9]

Module	Key Features or Functions
Billing	• Generate patient bills based on patient type and payer/payer healthplan or medical service • Validate that all necessary information has been entered based on payer/payer health plan billing requirements • Generate interim billing • Provide for UB-04 and 1500 CMS billing forms • Support electronic billing of third-party payers with automatic verification of transmittals, retransmission of corrected transmittals, and cancellation of prior transmittals • Support the operation of a Central Billing Office serving multiple facilities and office locations with the ability to consolidate functions while maintaining separate accounting buckets

Table 19-1 Revenue Cycle Management System Modules and Key Features/Functions *(continued)*

Module	Key Features or Functions
Charging	• Provide a Charge Master File enabling charge definition, multiple prices for different payers, and effective date and historical date range prices • Automatic generation of room and bed charges based on Room and Bed Master files • Ability to "explode" bundled charges into individual components for revenue and statistical reporting
Contract-Based Reimbursement	• Provide a contract file which includes payer information including addresses, contacts, expiration dates, etc.; and contract terms grouped into contract packages that apply to specific encounters, e.g., inpatient, maternity, outpatient surgery, emergency, transplants, etc. • Ability to calculate reimbursement, adjustments, identified underpayments, and payment variance reporting that compares the expected payment amount to the actual payment by contracted payer
Account management	• Provide an encounter numbering system that allows the identification of admissions, visits, and/or medical episodes independently of medical record numbering • Allow identification of receivables based on various criteria including patient or guarantor name or number, Social Security number, and date of birth
Collections	• Allow for operation of internal and external secondary business offices for collection of receivables • Ability to define and monitor special payment arrangements by individual account • Produce consolidated patient statements by guarantor showing all related patient or family accounts • Electronically accept claim denials and perform tracking and appeal processing
Payments	• Support electronic remittance for Medicare and selected insurance carriers • Support multiple point-of-service cashiering sites with separate cash draws, receipts, and balancing functions • Apply payments to an account or line item level
Reporting	• Generate enterprise reports for the health system while maintaining ability to drill down to facility and departmental information • Provide the ability to store all reports, bills, and statements in an integrated document repository • Provide accounts receivable (AR) reports by service/location, providers, Insurance Payer/Healthplan, and other parameters • Provide for generation of an AR aging report

Table 19-1 was adapted from the HIMSS Revenue Cycle Management Vendor Requirements Checklist.[10]

Table 19-1   Revenue Cycle Management System Modules and Key Features/Functions

Clinical Decision Support (CDS)

The Office of the National Coordinator of Health Information Technology (ONC) broadly defines CDS as follows:

> Clinical decision support (CDS) provides clinicians, staff, patients or other individuals with knowledge and person-specific information, intelligently filtered or presented at appropriate times, to enhance health and health care. CDS encompasses a variety of tools to enhance decision-making in the clinical workflow. These tools include computerized alerts and reminders to care providers and patients; clinical guidelines; condition-specific order sets; focused patient data reports and summaries; documentation templates; diagnostic support, and contextually relevant reference information, among other tools.[11]

Lobach et al. found evidence showing that CDS has significant impact on clinical process outcomes such as the ordering of preventive, clinical, and treatment services, as well as the enhancement of clinician's knowledge pertaining to a medical condition.[12] This study and the ONC point to CDS broadly and importantly impacting increased quality of care, enhanced health outcomes, avoidance of errors and adverse events, and improved cost outcomes.

CDS is manifest in HIT in many ways. It is integral to many modules of an EHR system; for instance, a CPOE module of an EHR system relies on CDS to issue drug interaction alerts. CDS is also integral to applications that support "hot links" to clinical practice guidelines available to a clinician as he or she is treating a patient or documenting care, whether as a stand-alone app or embedded within an EHR clinical documentation module. A well-known and highly regarded resource for those who would like to learn more about this very important field within HIT and informatics is *Improving Outcomes with Clinical Decision Support: An Implementer's Guide, Second Edition*, by Osheroff et al.[13]

Patient Relationship Management Systems

Patient relationship management is a relatively new concept that is being adopted in the healthcare industry. A patient relationship management software system maintains a list of all patients and their important personal preferences and attributes, such as preferred appointment times, the last contact via phone or e-mail the patient had with the contact center, and the length of time the patient has been associated with a particular health system. The patient relationship management system stores these and many more of their personal preferences and attributes and makes them easily accessible to contact center users. The goal of the patient relationship management software is to provide the best quality care and a personalized experience for patients. The patient relationship management system meets both these goals by providing tools and data in a single system.

Application Data Interchange Systems

Application data interchange systems are typically used to provide reliable connectivity within hospitals, information exchanges, and public health organizations. The application data interchange is one of the key systems helping in the delivery of consistent, efficient, quality patient care.[14]

An application data interchange system encompasses three main functional areas and two management console options:

- The interface engine is the main messaging service that implements communication, inter-format mapping, persistent message delivery, and message routing.[11]

- An integrated development environment (IDE) has an easy-to-learn graphical user interface to configure the functionality of the application data interchange system.

- The management console is usually a web-based application that displays system status and performance monitoring. It also allows the sorting, viewing, editing, and resending of messages and real-time monitoring of system logs and error conditions. It has two optional components:

  - A mobile app that provides the basic monitoring capability of the management console on a smartphone or tablet.

  - A web-based dashboard application that displays the notifications and system health of multiple application interface engines in a single monitoring-centric view.

Chapter Review

Healthcare information technology (HIT) systems play a critical role in improving patient care and enabling healthcare organizations to operate more effectively and efficiently. EHR and non-EHR systems enable better patient care through the use of technology. The HIT function in a healthcare organization, just like the IT function in companies or institutions, is led by a CIO in most cases. Many healthcare organizations also have a CMIO, which is a prominent position within or alongside the CIO's department that is usually held by a physician or other clinician trained in informatics. These HIT leaders oversee a wide array of application specialists, system analysts, programmers, support technicians, project managers, and many other roles if the organization is large. The structure of HIT departments within healthcare organizations varies, but it often involves divisions or sub-departments with managers overseeing the EHR system. These "ancillary" systems include lab, pharmacy, and radiology; revenue cycle or other nonclinical systems; infrastructure (such as hardware and networks); and user support such as the help desk function.

In this "age of the EHR," other systems crucial to the functioning of a healthcare enterprise are often overlooked. Clinical and operational systems in the lab, radiology, and pharmacy (either as part of the EHR system or otherwise) are critical for tracking patient workflow, recording results, providing quick access to records for both patients and providers, and storing digital information for long periods. These clinical systems also improve the quality of care by automating various functions, catching and alerting on errors in workflow. These systems integrate data into the EHR system via the central interface engine, making all information about the patient available in one place for providers to make better and faster decisions.

Nonclinical systems such as supply chain, finance, billing, and data interchange services provide the core support services that keep health systems in operation and financially viable. Supply chain systems provide ordering, tracking, and efficient movement of supplies through the health system.

Many technologies, information systems, and people work together to deliver clinical and operational support in today's modern healthcare enterprises.

Questions

To test your comprehension of this chapter, answer the following questions by selecting the best available choice and then check your answers against the list of correct answers at the end of the chapter.

1. Due to the increase in use and importance of the electronic health record (EHR) in healthcare organizations, _____.

   A. non-EHR systems are no longer needed

   B. non-EHR systems usually interface or integrate with the EHR system

   C. non-EHR systems have been entirely replaced by EHR modules

   D. non-EHR systems have not proliferated

2. Which of the following is a major clinical system, whether a stand-alone system interfaced with the EHR system or a module of the EHR system?

   A. Supply chain system

   B. Patient relationship management system

   C. Clinical laboratory system

   D. Revenue cycle system

3. A(n) _____ is usually part of the vetting process when a healthcare organization is acquiring a new software system.

   A. Request for Proposal (RFP)

   B. Proof of Perquisites (PoP)

   C. Exit Plan (EP)

   D. Federal Government Audit (FGA)

4. Which of the following best describes a business relationship manager (BRM) in a healthcare IT department?

   A. The information systems department manager who handles human relations issues

   B. A quality improvement professional

   C. The person representing the needs of the clinical and nonclinical departments to the HIT department

   D. The person representing the needs of the vendors to the HIT department

PART IV

5. A radiologist uses speech recognition software to accomplish which of the following?

   A. Automatically classify images

   B. More easily document findings related to images

   C. Interpret communication from patients and staff members who speak other languages

   D. Keep track of tasks

6. A laboratory information system can interface to a(n) _____.

   A. laboratory instrument and instantly report a result of a patient's blood chemistry test to an EHR

   B. pharmacy system and direct a nurse to administer a unit of blood

   C. radiology system, resulting in an automatic order for an X-ray

   D. EHR system by route of a cybersecurity module of the healthcare organization interface engine

7. Finance and operations systems are used for which of the following?

   A. Clinical decision support

   B. Clinical case management

   C. Priority management

   D. Billing

8. Which one of the functional areas of an application data interchange is *not* considered a main functional area?

   A. The interface engine

   B. The integrated development environment (IDE)

   C. The management console

   D. Mobile smartphone-mediated management

Answers

1. **B.** Due to the increase in use and importance of the EHR in healthcare organizations, non-EHR systems usually interface or integrate with the EHR system.

2. **C.** The clinical laboratory is a major clinical system, whether it is a stand-alone system interfaced with the EHR or a module of the EHR system.

3. **A.** The Request for Proposal (RFP) is usually part of the vetting process when a healthcare organization is acquiring a new software system.

4. **C.** The business relationship manager (BRM) is usually the person representing the needs of the clinical and nonclinical departments to the HIT department.

5. B. A radiologist uses speech recognition software to more easily document his or her findings related to the images.

6. A. A laboratory information system can interface to a laboratory instrument and instantly report a result of a patient's blood chemistry test to an EHR system.

7. D. Finance and operations systems are used for billing.

8. D. The interface engine, integrated development environment (IDE), and management console are considered the three main functional areas of an application data interchange. A mobile app that supports smartphone-mediated management may be an option. Another management console option that is not listed in the choices is a web-based dashboard.

References

1. Medicare Payment Advisory Commission. (2016, June). *Report to Congress: Medicare and the healthcare delivery system.* Accessed on August 15, 2016, from www.medpac.gov/docs/default-source/reports/june-2016-report-to-the-congress-medicare-and-the-health-care-delivery-system.pdf?sfvrsn=0?.

2. Vitalari, N. P. (n.d.). *A prospective analysis of the future of the U.S. healthcare industry.* Accessed on August 20, 2016, from http://merage.uci.edu/ResearchAndCenters/CDT/Resources/Documents/N%20Vitalari%20A%20Prospective%20Analysis%20of%20the%20Healthcare%20Industry.pdf.

3. PACS History web site. Accessed on August 1, 2016, from www.pacshistory.org/documents/index.html.

4. Forsberg, D., Rosipko, B., & Sunshine, J. L. (2016). Factors affecting radiologist's PACS usage. *Journal of Digital Imaging, 29*(6), 670–676.

5. U.S. Food and Drug Administration. (2015). Unit dose labeling for solid and liquid oral dosage forms (section 430.100). In *Compliance policy guides.* Accessed on November 28, 2016, from www.fda.gov/ICECI/ComplianceManuals/CompliancePolicyGuidanceManual/ucm074377.htm.

6. Farr, M., & Shatkin, L. (2004). *Best jobs for the 21st century* (p. 460). JIST Works.

7. Futrell, K. (2013). *The value of the laboratory in the new healthcare model.* Accessed on July 29, 2016, from www.orchardsoft.com/files/white_paper_value_lab.pdf.

8. MUSC Laboratory Information Services Team. (2014). Cerner CoPath. *Documentation: Histology section.* Accessed on November 28, 2016, from https://www.musc.edu/pathology/website/labservices/anatomic/CoPath/index.html?introduction.htm.

9. HIMSS Revenue Cycle Improvement Task Force. (2015). *Rethinking revenue cycle management.* Accessed on April 6, 2017, from www.himss.org (membership login required).

10. HIMSS. (2010). *Revenue cycle management vendor requirements checklist.* Accessed on April 6, 2017, from http://www.himss.org/revenue-cycle-management.

11. Office of the National Coordinator of Health Information Technology. (2014). *Clinical decision support (CDS).* Accessed on November 19, 2015, from https://www.healthit.gov/policy-researchers-implementers/clinical-decision-support-cds.

12. Lobach, D., Sanders, G. D., Bright, T. J., Wong, A., Dhurjati, R., Bristow, E., … Kendrick, A. (2012, April). *Enabling health care decisionmaking through clinical decision support and knowledge management.* Evidence Report / Technology Assessments, No. 203. Agency for Healthcare Research and Quality.

13. Osheroff, J. A., Teich, J. M., Levick, D., Saldana, L., Velasco, F. T., Sittig, D. F., … Jenders, R. A. (2012). *Improving outcomes with clinical decision support: An implementer's guide, second edition.* HIMSS.

14. Office of the National Coordinator of Health Information Technology. (2016). *A 10-year vision to achieve an interoperable health IT infrastructure.* Accessed on July 22, 2016, from https://www.healthit.gov/sites/default/files/ONC10yearInteroperabilityConceptPaper.pdf.

CHAPTER 20

EHR Implementation and Optimization

Diane Hibbs, Julie Hollberg

In this chapter, you will learn how to
- Understand the success factors necessary for effective governance, including executive buy-in, integration with existing governance structure, and multidisciplinary participation
- Describe the migration from paper processes or an existing electronic health record (EHR) to a new EHR system including organizational strategy, planning, decision-making techniques, training, and implementation strategies
- Document and support downtime procedures
- Propose strategies to minimize major barriers to adoption of EHRs
- Track issues and resolve problems while simultaneously providing high-level customer service
- Assist with verifying that the expected benefits are achieved (e.g., return on investment, benchmark, and user satisfaction)

With the passage of the American Recovery and Reinvestment Act (ARRA), which included the Health Information Technology for Economic and Clinical Health (HITECH) legislation, implementations of electronic health record (EHR) systems have increased dramatically over the past five years.[1] While some health systems or physician offices are implementing an entirely new EHR system to replace paper-based processes, many others with existing EHR implementations are now focusing on creating more integration across venues throughout a health system or on implementing new functionality to optimize current workflows. Alternatively, a growing number of organizations are transitioning from one EHR system to a completely different one in order to facilitate organizational and technical integration, or perhaps as the result of acquiring new practices and/or hospitals, or simply due to dissatisfaction with their current EHR system.

Combined, we have many years of experience working in complex acute and ambulatory healthcare systems. Our respective organizations, Banner Health (Dr. Hibbs) and Emory Healthcare (Dr. Hollberg), have been using EHRs for over a decade and both recently underwent optimization and replacement projects. This chapter will reference the experiences of these two health systems to illustrate the core concepts and necessary ingredients for successful EHR implementations, incorporating numerous examples and lessons learned throughout the chapter.

Banner Health implemented a new ambulatory EHR as an expansion of its current inpatient system to ensure that patients would have a unified EHR reflecting both inpatient and outpatient encounters. Emory Healthcare began its EHR implementation journey over 20 years ago and has had a unified inpatient and outpatient medical record since 1999; however, the ambulatory clinics were still using paper for all billing and for all orders except prescriptions prior to its optimization project in 2015.

Both Banner Health and Emory Healthcare, coincidentally, have been using Cerner Corporation's EHR product for many years and are currently using that product in new ways to help in their healthcare optimization efforts. Cerner's EHR product has achieved Certified Electronic Health Record Technology (CEHRT) designation and is one of the leading EHR systems as defined by U.S. market share, but there are many other EHR products that have the CEHRT designation as well as substantial market share. You are encouraged to learn about the many CEHRT products that can be found on www.healthit.gov web pages that provide more information on the ONC Health IT Certification Program. The many different EHR and HIT products from different vendors provide a rich variety of choices for today's diverse mix of healthcare organizations.

Using HIT and EHRs for Organizational Transformation

This section will introduce the strategic initiatives Banner Health and Emory Healthcare implemented using HIT and EHRs to improve and transform their organizations. Throughout the rest of the chapter, specific examples detailing the use of HITs and EHRs in these organizations will be given. Governance of and change management approaches for large HIT and EHR initiatives, again using Banner Health and Emory Healthcare as examples, will be covered as well. The principles and practices discussed here can be adjusted as needed and allied to other large HIT and EHR initiatives.

Banner Health

Banner Health is a large health system that spans seven states, primarily in the western United States, and is composed of 29 acute care facilities ranging from critical access hospitals to university medical centers. Banner Health has more than 200 ambulatory clinics and employs over 1,500 physicians, with thousands of additional independent physicians practicing in their facilities. These numbers change frequently as more clinics and facilities are either acquired or built.

The acute care facilities implemented Cerner EHR (PowerChart) in two phases:

- Implementation of computerized provider order entry (CPOE) began in 2005
- Implementation of the physician documentation solution began in 2009

Prior to 2015, the Banner Health ambulatory clinics were using at least six different documentation/ordering methods, including some clinics that were still using a paper system, and none of the clinics using an EHR system were using the same EHR system used in Banner Health acute facilities. As a result, patients lacked a unified medical record and clinicians had to refer to two or more sources of information for their patients and do a lot of manual work—signing in to multiple systems, printing, copying, faxing, and scanning—to find important clinical information and ensure that it was available in each venue for critical clinical decisions.

Banner's Strategic Initiative

Banner's project scope statement, an internal document, for this initiative connected the implementations' objectives to the mission of the organization with the following statement:

> Banner Health is committed to providing seamless, integrated care to our patients, and to accomplish this goal, it is imperative that a patient's complete medical records are readily accessible wherever in the Banner system a patient visits—any Banner Health Center or Clinic or Banner Medical Center.

Replacement of the non-Cerner ambulatory EHR systems with PowerChart Ambulatory occurred in waves, roughly based on geography but with consideration for the number of providers and the different specialties in each wave. The first wave started in June 2015 and the majority of the ambulatory providers had transitioned by the end of 2016.

Emory Healthcare

Emory Healthcare is the largest, most comprehensive health system in Georgia and attracts patients from throughout the southeastern United States. It is the healthcare arm of Emory University, and many of the Emory School of Medicine faculty practice within Emory Healthcare facilities and clinics. Included in the system are six acute care hospitals, more than 100 clinic locations, and nearly 2,000 providers (attending physicians, nurse practitioners, and physician assistants). The Emory Clinic refers to the faculty practice and completed more than 3 million outpatient visits last year. For both the inpatient and the ambulatory settings, prior to 2015, the EHR had rich functionality for nursing, radiology, lab, and pharmacy. All of those clinical areas were documenting electronically and the care teams were able to review results from each of those areas (e.g., view the medication administration record and medication list, lab result flowsheets, and radiology results flowsheets). However, the experience for CPOE was very different between the inpatient and outpatient environments.

While the six acute care hospitals had been using CPOE since 2009, the ambulatory clinics all used paper for billing and ordering (except prescriptions). Consequently, the providers performed a lot of duplicative documentation because orders for referrals, lab, radiology, and other diagnostic tests all required different pieces of paper and each required diagnosis documentation. After completing the orders, the provider also had to transcribe the diagnosis onto the paper billing form. While Emory Healthcare had developed a robust EHR over time (see Table 20-1 for a timeline), the physicians, nurse practitioners, and physician assistants were limited to a generic view of the chart based solely on their venue—inpatient, outpatient, or emergency room. Data needed to deliver care in each specific specialty were not readily available, which decreased efficiency. Summing up the set of issues Emory outpatient providers faced succinctly, a urologist said, "I don't really care about the vaccinations…I need the med list, my past office notes, any cystoscopies, CT of the abdomen and pelvis to all be face up so that I don't have to click around so much to find the data."

Timeframe	Area of EHR System Implementation
1989–2004	• Laboratory • Data repository • Pharmacy • Radiology (PACS) • Emergency room departments and enterprise-wide master patient index (EMPI) • Order entry • Multiple document interfaces that crossed departments
2005–2010	• Acute care orders sets • Decision support • Ambulatory EMR (Emory's preferred name for an outpatient EHR system that was fundamentally integrated with their inpatient EHR system) • Charge services and document imaging • Documentation • Patient portal • Surgical case tracking • Downtime solutions • Cardiac cath scheduling • Order entry • Physician documentation in various departments as well as across all acute facilities • Physician messaging • ePrescribing • Medication reconciliation advancements • Health maintenance alerts • Evidenced-based nursing care • Transplant services

Table 20-1 Emory Healthcare Electronic Health Record Development/Implementation Timeline

Timeframe	Area of EHR System Implementation
2011–2015	• Medical home • Additional patient portal capabilities • Core measure and public health reporting and other meaningful use requirements across most facilities • An HIE across the organization • Anesthesia • Flowsheet documentation • Advanced critical care viewing • ICD-10 transition • Clinical trials • Lab advancements and updated software • Infusion center • Chart searching • Physician optimization efforts and enhancements • Telemetry department • Transplant and oncology department order entry • Positive patient ID • Reference lab interfaces • Ophthalmology • Pharmacy dispensing system integration • Ambulatory order entry • Specialty specific EMR enhancements • Enterprise dragon voice recognition • Completion of anesthesia rollout • Direct standard for EMR communication • Enhancements to physician documentation

Table 20-1   Emory Healthcare Electronic Health Record Development/Implementation Timeline *(continued)*

In addition to the less than optimal provider documentation support from the EHR, the Emory Clinic was facing the looming transition from ICD-9 to ICD-10, which had the greatest impact on medical coders but also impacted providers and clinicians, and frustration among physicians was still high as a result of the additional work necessitated by the HITECH meaningful use requirements. Executive leadership was concerned that the decreased efficiency resulting from the extra time required to find a specific ICD-10 code would further frustrate physicians and that a proposed workaround using paper billing with a limited set of the most commonly used ICD-10 codes was unsustainable.

Based on feedback from the broader organization, executive leadership realized that overall provider satisfaction could be improved and workflow made more efficient by further optimizing the Emory EHR, and as a result Emory undertook a significant optimization project in 2015. This project was known as "Provider Workflow

Optimization." Each clinical division or department created their own workflow EHR view, which included the specific clinical data that they wanted readily available, as well as a quick orders page, similar to a superbill that many providers were familiar with. This quick orders page included their specialty's most commonly used orders and billing codes. The project had a very aggressive timeline, largely due to the ICD-10 transition deadline. Emory successfully completed 37 go-lives in just five months. Technically, each go-live required creating a new specialty position within the EHR and two new workflow pages. Operationally, each go-live required implementation of changes for all of the practice sites for that specialty. Emory had just over 100 geographically distinct ambulatory practice locations.

Emory's Strategic Initiative

The goals of the Provider Workflow Optimization project were to to leverage HIT to make it easier to deliver high-quality healthcare and to improve the patient and the provider experience. To operationalize those goals, project objectives such as bringing the right data to the right provider at the right time and facilitating the transition to ICD-10 were identified and helped to guide the project.

Governance of Large HIT and EHR Initiatives

Effective governance is essential to the success of any healthcare IT implementation project. Key characteristics of effective governance HIT implementation include[2]

- It is inclusive of and accountable to all relevant stakeholders.
- Governance and guiding principles are based on the organization's mission and those principles are incorporated into the work of the team.
- It strives for transparency to all constituents to assure decisions are fair and equitable for all parties involved.
- The team leaders utilize online collaboration tools (e.g., Google documents, SharePoint, Box) to facilitate optimal involvement in the discussion and dissemination of the decision-making process and the knowledge coming from the organization and governance teams.
- It is responsive and highly communicative within the organization.

Executive Leadership

Every successful company spends a considerable amount of time identifying, planning for, and then achieving its corporate initiatives each year in all areas of its business. For a hospital or healthcare system, these initiatives may be financial, regulatory, and/or clinical. Implementation of an EHR extends into all these areas, as outlined in Table 20-2.

Successful implementation and, more importantly, subsequent adoption of a new EHR requires corporate initiatives to be translated into "What's in it for me?" (WIIFM) for the clinical staff, especially physicians. Executive leadership must be willing and able to recognize and remove barriers encountered by the implementation teams.

Healthcare Organization Initiatives Category	Potential EHR Implementation/Optimization Impacts
Financial Initiatives	• Decrease rejected claims • Increase revenue generation by improving documentation of care rendered • Capture incentives for EHR implementation • Avoid penalties
Regulatory Initiatives	• Ability to mine the data entered in the EHR to ensure regulatory measures are met or exceeded • Report on clinical outcomes
Clinical Initiatives	• Reduce medical errors • Improve patient care

Table 20-2   Potential EHR Implementation/Optimization Impacts of Healthcare Organization Initiatives

Leveraging Existing Governance Structure

Healthcare organizations have a complex hierarchy of committees, councils, and boards. Adding EHR discussions to regularly scheduled meetings of these entities is preferable (when possible) because it minimizes the difficulty of organizing more meetings and avoids repetitive discussions. However, the breadth and pace of an EHR implementation will likely require creating specific separate meetings to ensure effective, broad decision making. When asked to describe their governance structure, many hospitals and ambulatory clinics can produce impressive organizational charts and documents. However, effective governance is more than a simple list of committees and representatives.

Multidisciplinary Participation

Healthcare requires an entire clinical care team—doctors, nurses, medical assistants, pharmacists, radiology and lab personnel, dieticians, physical therapists, and many others—collaborating and relying on each other to perform their work. Beyond the clinical care, healthcare operations require an even broader team including reception and scheduling staff, billing experts, coders, IT staff, compliance and privacy officers, and medical records personnel. The scope of a project determines who needs to participate on the various governance committees, and all stakeholders should be represented at the appropriate level of governance within the project.

A steering committee will likely have oversight of the project. This committee may be composed of executive leadership, IT leadership, and clinical leadership, and may have vendor stakeholders as well. This committee will meet less frequently and will review updates from the various teams that report to it.

A project team will meet very frequently. This team will be led by a project manager and will have heavy participation from both the vendor and the healthcare organization side. This team will hash out the details of the implementation. It is imperative to have a strong and effective project manager leading this team, one who isn't afraid to ask the hard questions and hold people accountable for their responsibilities.

PART IV

While it seems intuitive that the right stakeholders should participate in the right meetings, it tends to be easy to forward all the meeting invitations to more and more people, and generally the more people in a meeting, the harder it is to make a decision. Try to invite only the necessary people to participate in each meeting. By the same token, be sure the attendees include the people who can move the project forward. An important lesson learned at Banner was that meetings lasting longer than 30 minutes rarely included the required decision-maker. As a result, the next question was usually "Who needs to be invited to the next meeting to get this decision made?" Banner learned that involving too many people in meetings often resulted in wasted time because no decision was actually made.

Clinical Stakeholders

It is imperative to have clinical leadership involved from the beginning, even before the initial decision is made as to which system will be implemented. This clinical buy-in will prove invaluable in the change management process and in identifying and communicating the importance of the changes. The best clinical representatives are known for their clinical expertise, are influential, and are highly regarded by their peers. Consider specialty-specific leaders who will have relevant and meaningful input regarding content, workflows, and the order sets they and their peers will use.

Banner's Governance

Clinical care at Banner is managed as a system and is therefore very standardized. The Care Management Council, led by the system-wide chief medical officer (CMO), is composed of Clinical Consensus Groups (CCGs) for each specialty. These groups include representatives from each facility and all the pertinent disciplines—physicians, nurses, pharmacy representatives, and so on. These CCGs create evidence-based Clinical Practices that define the standard of care and drive the policies and procedures for the entire health system.

The strategic initiative guiding the ambulatory EHR implementation at Banner was developed by the senior leadership team and was led by the chief medical informatics officer (CMIO). These corporate stakeholders were joined by clinical stakeholders from the various CCGs to form the needed governance for this implementation. The importance of this governance structure is that it was clinically driven, rather than IT-focused.

Emory's Governance

The operational sponsors of the project involved senior leaders within Emory Healthcare and included the CMIO, the CMO of the Emory Clinic, and the director of revenue cycle. Each week, they met for 3–4 hours with the leaders of the four teams that were very hands-on with each of the clinical sections. See Figure 20-1. The operational sponsors presented to the executive sponsors for one hour every other week throughout the project. This level of hands-on leadership was essential to remove barriers and make decisions so that the project could stay on schedule.

Each clinical division or department was required to identify at least one physician leader for the entire optimization project. The physician leader was partnered with an administrator and clinical operations manager as well and these triads were responsible

Figure 20-1
Project
leadership
team for
Emory Provider
Workflow
Optimization
project

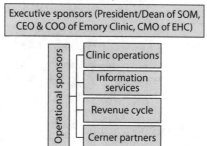

Leadership Team

Executive sponsors (President/Dean of SOM, CEO & COO of Emory Clinic, CMO of EHC)

Operational sponsors
- Clinic operations
- Information services
- Revenue cycle
- Cerner partners

for designing the new workflows and for being available during the go-live to make any workflow decisions that had not been addressed during the project planning.

Change Management

An EHR implementation can involve one physician's office or an entire multihospital health system. As described in this chapter, it can involve state-wide or multistate groups of providers. In all these cases, change management is a critical component. Chapter 10 describes a multilevel change management process that can be applied to EHR and other HIT implementations and is consistent with the implementation principles and practices in this chapter. To the process described in Chapter 10, we add the following:

- People handle introduction of innovations or technology differently.
- It is essential to identify WIIFM for the end users from the very beginning.

Everett Rogers' theory of diffusion of innovations is a common theory that change managers have applied to many areas, from farmers' views on soil conservation to mass marketing advertisements and much more.[3] It is likewise a very useful theory to help EHR and HIT implementers understand and deal with the different types of responses people have to large-scale technological change. The theory identifies classes of adopters of a message, belief, or technology: innovators, early adopters, early majority, late majority, and laggards. Figure 20-2 presents alternative names for these classes that may resonate in modern organizations more. Whatever the names associated with the types of adopters, the important concept is that in a large organization, adoption of a new technology varies significantly across individuals. This has many implications for governance, stakeholder buy-in, communication about the initiative, end-user training, and more.

Physicians are typically motivated by the opportunity to improve patient care or to save time, or both. Understanding and leveraging the WIIFM perspective for physicians helps immensely throughout the implementation of EHRs. Despite the perception of frequently objecting to or complaining about things that change their workflows,

PART IV

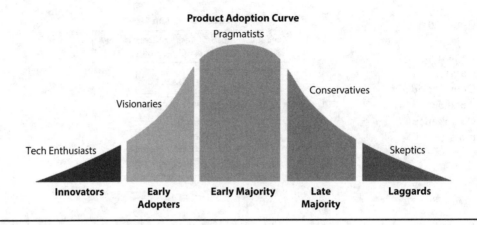

Product Adoption Curve

Pragmatists

Conservatives

Visionaries

Tech Enthusiasts

Skeptics

Innovators   **Early Adopters**   **Early Majority**   **Late Majority**   **Laggards**

Figure 20-2   Product adoption curve

clinicians ultimately care about their patients and about delivering high-quality care. Tapping into these values can help articulate the WIIFM. Examples include

- As a physician, have you ever had a patient who had previously been treated in your hospital, whose old records would have been very helpful in your decision making but could not be located by the medical records department?

- How many times have you consulted another physician for help on your patient but the dictated report from the consulting physician was not available to you for several hours or days?

- How many hours have you spent in the medical records department with a stack of charts that needed your signature?

- As a physician, have you ever received a phone call from a hospital regarding your patient while you were in your office or at home and you had to rely on someone else to look at the chart and decipher the handwritten notes and orders already on the chart?

- Have you ever mistakenly prescribed two drugs that interacted with each other because you didn't realize they interacted?

These are salient examples of things that matter to practicing physicians, and if you can help them see how patient care will improve through the use of an EHR system, they will be much more likely to not just accept the new EHR but to truly adopt it.

Managing the Project

So far this chapter has covered the high-level concepts and keys to a successful EHR selection and implementation. Ultimately, as with any successful project, the details are critical. Healthcare organizations have widely adopted and adapted the practices and principles of the discipline of project management of large HIT initiatives. The project manager leads the teams and manages all the tasks and timelines. It is imperative that the project manager create and maintain a master document that lists all the tasks, who is responsible for completion of each task, when each task is scheduled to be completed and is actually completed, and any dependencies for completing the work. See Chapter 10 for much more information on project management practice and principles that can be applied to EHR implementations and optimizations. What follows are a few of the more important details every EHR implementation project should include as part of the project plan.

A Good Product and Team

It is assumed in this chapter that the EHR solution has already been carefully vetted and chosen. As part of the selection process, the organization responsible for implementation should also be identified. A very knowledgeable team that understands the specific system being implemented and how to localize and optimize it for your organization is invaluable to your success. As you begin discussions about design, setting preferences and privileges for the users, and developing specific workflows, the downstream effects of those decisions may not be readily apparent. Including in those discussions either vendor representatives/consultants or knowledgeable third-party consultants as a partner, with their considerable experience from similar implementations at other sites, is imperative. These team members will know the vendor's core recommendations as well as other best practices you might need to consider. They will know the effects of each decision on downstream applications across roles and venues, especially if these recommendations are not heeded. A caveat when leveraging third-party implementation resources is that you should ensure they have current knowledge and recent experience with the specific EHR system, as systems are constantly changing with new functionality and changes to existing capabilities.

Some organizations think it will be less expensive if they do all the design, build, and implementation themselves in an effort to save money. However, when the cost of the time and resources required to "figure it out" on your own is factored in, it very well might be less costly to use expert external resources for this purpose.

Banner Health partnered with Cerner Corporation to implement Cerner's EHR solutions in the ambulatory clinics. This was a multiyear, strategic partnership, with many Cerner associates actually relocating and permanently working within the walls of Banner every day of the project in the Alignment Office (while remaining employees of Cerner). They became members of the Banner implementation team and their role was to ensure successful implementations, help with adoption of new technology, and foster new ideas and innovations.[4]

Emory Healthcare lacked the technical bench strength needed to customize, build out, and test all of the new desired EHR functionality, so it also partnered with Cerner. The internal Emory application experts, who were either experts on clinical workflow themselves or who had experience working with Emory subject matter experts, gathered all of the requirements and then leveraged a large Cerner team to complete the technical build.

The Orders Catalog and Order Sets

Physician and provider orders have been and continue to be a central and far-reaching function in hospitals and other types of healthcare delivery organizations. Their orders initiate a cascade of activities that, in aggregate, impact every department and area of a healthcare organization as well as some external clinical or business entities such as pharmacies and laboratories not owned by the healthcare organization. Order catalogs are organized collections of all of the "orderable" diagnostic or therapeutic treatments and/or services that a provider can choose from that they wish their patient to receive. Order sets are a collection of two or more individual orders that are often organized around a transition of care. Examples are a hospital admission order set or an ambulatory physical therapy order set. Order sets are also organized around conditions, such as community acquired pneumonia or a well child provider visit.

Prior to the existence of EHR systems, physicians wrote out each of the tasks they wanted performed on paper order sheets that looked very similar to notebook paper. In this "paper ordering paradigm" the order written by Physician A may not have been the same as the order written by Physician B for the same task. For example, a diet order from Physician A may read "Regular diet" while Physician B enters "House diet." Order entry modules of hospital information systems (HISs), a precursor to EHRs, enabled a nursing unit clerk to interpret a physician's paper order and either key it into the HIS or use pull-down menus in the HIS to select the desired order. Errors cropped up in this semi-automated approach due to non–provider order entry staff misinterpreting providers' handwriting or entering an order that best fit what the entry staff member thought the physician wanted.

To deal with this, over the past ten years, most healthcare systems have widely adopted the computerized provider order entry (CPOE). CPOE is a clinical information system, these days usually a module of an EHR, that allows clinicians to record patient-specific orders (tests, treatments, management plans, and the like) for communication to other patient care team members and to other information systems. A challenge with CPOE is standardizing all these various orders and communicating to end users how these orders will be searchable in the new EHR system. One solution is to have order aliases that all point to the same order; for example, ordering a "CBC" or ordering a "Complete Blood Count" would both show up in the lab as the same order.

For new EHR implementations from paper, an order catalog will need to be created that includes all the orders that all the physicians will ever want to write—certainly no small task. On the other hand, if your implementation is a conversion from one EHR system to another, this will be a good time to review available orders from the existing legacy EHR order catalog and remove outdated ones. In either case, this task will require significant time and resources to complete.

Creating order sets will ease CPOE as well as drive standardized practices. These standard order sets should be developed by the departments who will be using them, with added input from ancillary service lines (e.g., lab, pharmacy, radiology, etc.). A great example of this is in the use of chemotherapy order sets by oncologists. These highly specialized, evidence-based order sets are very detailed and prescriptive, with certain drugs being given on certain days and labs being drawn at defined intervals.

These order sets, and most other types of order sets, if implemented well, can reduce the chance of human error. Other good examples of order sets are those used for clinical emergencies (e.g., codes). Using order sets in these cases eliminates having to remember and then laboriously search for individual orders when time is especially critical. Additionally, as organizations shift from fee-for-service care to value-based care, electronic order sets or quick orders pages are a way to make it easier for clinicians to practice evidence-based medicine.

Documentation Templates and Note Hierarchy

Similar to standardized order sets, clinical documentation standards can be encouraged with the use of templates. Clinical stakeholders, representatives from the healthcare information management (HIM)/medical coding, and billing personnel all should participate in the development of these templates. Templates may be different for each specialty and for each venue; for example, an obstetrical office note is much different than an inpatient cardiology note. These templates can be created to include any required fields to ensure compliance with regulatory measures or health system standards. Caution should be used with required fields, however, as the trigger used to identify a required field as such (highlighting, asterisks, etc.) may inadvertently guide the provider to only fill in the required fields and skip over other important fields.

In addition, the HIM department should be included when developing a standard approach to the note hierarchy or filing structure within the electronic record. This ensures clinical documentation is easy to navigate and key information can be quickly located when needed.

Migrating Data

Any patient seen in a clinic or within an acute facility that is part of the healthcare organization implementing a new EHR system has data in some system prior to the current implementation, whether that is another EHR or even a paper chart. The usual assumption of clinicians is that all data from all dates should be migrated from the old system into the new one and be easily accessible moving forward. Unfortunately, this is not realistic and the focus will need to shift to determining which data are most needed and how that data will be translated. In many cases, it is a better decision to actually enter new data when the patient is next seen for care (i.e., as if the patient were new instead of an existing patient). This will mitigate the problem of a data mismatch where the data in one system's database is not a one-to-one match for the new system's database. Data migration, in any form, will require considerable time and resources to accomplish.

If the EHR implementation is taking place in the acute setting, it is imperative to have recent (from the current encounter) clinical information at least available for review either as a printed report or as read-only information in the legacy system. Ideally, that clinical information will be migrated to the new system just prior to conversion in order to provide seamless patient care. Conversely, in the ambulatory setting, this migrated information is nice to have but is less urgent, especially if it will remain available for review within the old system. Old information becomes most valuable when it is available in the expected locations in the new system (e.g., the patient's home medication list appears in the Home Medications section of the EHR). This may require manual data entry to accomplish the most seamless and accurate results. In the ambulatory setting, if the quality of the existing data is suspect or if challenges are expected with migrating data from one electronic system to another, it is helpful prior to the patient visit to have a team member reference the previous record and manually enter a minimal set of data including the problem list, medication list, and allergies. Consideration must be given to how long historical data that are not migrated will be available for review in a legacy system, and this will likely be determined by the cost of maintaining that system.

Extraction, then Conversion

To migrate data from an old system to a new one, the data must be extracted from the old system and then, depending on the format of that data, converted into a format that the new system can handle. As described previously, some data may actually be more accurate if reentered as new data, though that decision may be met with some opposition from providers. There is a cost both in time and money when data must be entered manually. Migrating allergy data is a good example. If the designation of an allergy extracted from the old system does not match a discrete data element in the new system or was even entered as free text, it will be migrated inaccurately or not at all, leading the provider to see the wrong information in the new system. At Banner, to ensure allergy data were migrated accurately, the Physician Informatics team manually matched thousands of allergies on a spreadsheet of data extracted from existing ambulatory systems to their corresponding data elements in the Cerner EHR system.

Some organizations know the data quality is unreliable and instruct clinicians to "clean up" core lists, such as patient problem and patient medication lists, post-conversion. The other option is to have staff or physicians edit/update existing core lists prior to conversion. Both approaches can be effective but each has its pros and cons.

An excellent checklist resource for data migration is provided on the HealthIT.gov web site.[5] Table 20-3 shows sample questions to ask and consider.

Develop Workflows

The clinical leaders should develop workflows appropriate to their specialty and clinical need. At a minimum, the following workflows should be addressed:

Ambulatory:

- New patient visit
- Established patient visit
- Sick (or problem-focused) patient
- Between-visit phone calls
- Prescription refill requests

Data Migration Element	Questions
Previous lab results	Which results and how far back?
Radiology documents and results	Which results and how far back? Will these be entered as discrete data or as scanned documents? May be specialty-specific
Patient medications	Should we migrate patient medications or enter de novo next time the patient is seen? Pros of migration: • Available immediately to next provider Cons against migration: • If discrete data fields are not an exact match, the data will be incorrect or incomplete. • If data is migrated inaccurately, no way to know that and the information may be used as is.
Allergy list	Should we migrate allergies or enter de novo next time the patient is seen? Pros of migration: • Available immediately to next provider Cons against migration: • If discrete data fields are not an exact match, the data will be incorrect or incomplete. • Some information may have been entered as free text and will therefore not match anything in the new system.
Histories (procedural, medical, social)	Should we migrate histories or enter de novo next time the patient is seen? Data fields may not match and information may be incomplete or incorrect.
Scanned patient documents: Progress notes Consults Patient letters Old (outside) records Financial documents Consents	Determine where this information should "live." Will it all be in Old Records or will the individual documents be filed as the type of document they are, e.g., pathology reports within pathology, ECGs within cardiology, etc.?

Table 20-3 Questions to Consider for Data Migration During EHR Implementations

Acute:

- Patient requiring admission from clinic
- Daily management of hospitalized patient
- Transfers within or between facilities; e.g., medical unit to critical care or to and from surgery
- Handoffs between clinical care teams
- Medication reconciliation (reviewing medication list accuracy on admission and discharge)
- Discharge from hospital, including to home or to some type of transitional care

Emergency Department (ED):

- ED visit only
- ED visit with admission to hospital

These workflows should include all roles and should clearly identify the tasks within the workflow for which each role is responsible. Representation in the development of these workflows from all disciplines (including nursing, physician, pharmacy, radiology, etc.) will ensure that the workflows have been thoroughly evaluated from the perspective of all those affected. Each workflow should be documented and approved by the clinical stakeholders, and any changes should go back to these stakeholders for governance through the accepted change process. Figure 20-3 is a graphic representation of a "Discharge from Women's Health" workflow. It is an example of the steps required of a provider and a nurse to efficiently and effectively discharge a Women's Health patient from a clinical setting. Note the separation of responsibilities by role into "swim lanes." For more information on process and workflow management, see Chapter 10.

Policies Affect Workflows

Consider the policies you either currently have in place or plan to implement, and how they will affect your new EHR. How do those policies fit into current workflows and how might they be different with new electronic workflows? For example, medication reconciliation is required by the Centers for Medicare and Medicaid Services (CMS) for meaningful use compliance.[6] Most, if not all, organizations have a policy requiring physicians to perform a medication reconciliation (i.e., review and make decisions regarding the patient's current medications—continue or stop them—at each encounter for care). However, compliance with the policy following the implementation of a new EHR requires developing a workflow that is easy and makes sense to the provider who is expected to perform it. Too often these policies are created by a group of administrators who may not ever use the EHR at all and may inadvertently create an unrealistic workflow for the busy provider. Providers will then either neglect to perform the task at all or create a cumbersome workaround that is unlikely to be successfully performed on each

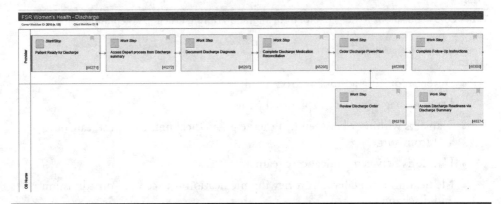

Figure 20-3 Example workflow diagram depicting a patient discharge from a clinical setting

patient, and thus the policy is not followed. Having providers involved in the development of the expected workflow will help to ensure the highest chance for success, and this workflow can then be considered when writing or rewriting the policy.

Another common example of conflict between policy and workflow occurs with CPOE. CPOE is also mandated by CMS and is a part of most organizations' policies. The easier it is for providers to enter their own orders in the EHR, the higher the CPOE rates will be. In examining why an organization is falling short of their goal for CPOE (or any other metric), it is imperative to carefully scrutinize both the current workflow and the expected workflow and determine where the opportunities exist to streamline and improve. If the expectation is 100 percent provider entry of orders through CPOE, access must be available on multiple platforms. In addition to the standard PC workstations on the hospital units or within clinics, this access must include laptops and mobile devices and should allow VPN access as well. Attention must be given to how those various platforms accommodate the workflows. It is unrealistic to require 100 percent CPOE if your providers are not physically inside the hospital and have no other way to enter the orders. Consideration for these realistic situations when writing a CPOE policy, and other similar "new system" policy, is imperative.

Verbal and telephone orders are two situations which require additional consideration and planning. In general, physicians are asked and expected to enter all orders in the EHR themselves. This policy often places nurses in a precarious situation when physicians ignore or don't follow policy. When a physician attempts to give a verbal order (assuming the physician is also capable of personally entering the order), following the policy means the nurse would potentially have to refuse to carry out the (verbal) order of the physician, thereby putting the patient at risk. While this is extreme, it illustrates the need to consider EHR workflow when writing and amending policies.

Testing

Every part of the EHR build will need to be tested to ensure that the expected responses are achieved. This will require many hours and multidisciplinary resources. For instance, when an admission order set is created, it will need to be validated by the clinical stakeholders to ensure that all the intended orders have been included. The pharmacy stakeholders will need to ensure that the medication orders actually reach the pharmacy when they've been placed, as do radiology, laboratory, dietary, and every other affected department with their departments' respective orders. Similarly, when an order is placed for periodic vital signs, a nurse should actually be notified in a reliable fashion of this recurring task. and if the process is working as expected. Similar testing will need to be performed for each part of the EHR, including documentation, printing, and so forth.

Another important part of the HIT department's work, at least as important as functionality testing, is usability testing. In other words, can the user perform the tasks as expected? Step-by-step, realistic clinical scenarios should be written and available for testers to walk through. Ideally, end users will be able to test these workflows prior to go-live to ensure things do indeed work as expected. Engaging end users in this testing will have the added benefit of allowing them to become more comfortable with the change prior to go-live.

Training

We will give you some practical guidance on EHR implementation training here that is meant to complement the more formal and comprehensive EHR and HIT training information in Chapter 21.

We recommend making baseline training mandatory and requiring that it be completed before access is granted to the EHR. While the training venues and platforms will vary—e.g., classroom, web-based training, 1:1 coaching—most clinicians, even technically savvy ones, will not be able to effectively learn how to use a new EHR while simultaneously trying to continue delivering patient care at their normal pace. Most people can relate to having bought a new high-end computer, stereo, or automobile with a number of options only to become frustrated with minimal or no training and ultimately end up discovering and using only a small percentage of the capabilities.

Mandatory EHR training is easier to achieve for employed physicians than for independent practicing physicians, especially those who practice in your facilities only sporadically. Some specialists practice at several hospitals in a given community and may only see a handful of patients at one hospital in a given month. Making training a requirement to maintain privileges is one procedural way to achieve this goal. Appealing to a physician's desire to maintain patient safety and deliver care as efficiently as possible can also be persuasive and lead to longer-term acceptance and success. Having the message and requirements communicated by clinical leadership rather than primarily by the technology leadership is crucial. As with other clinical skills, having end users trained appropriately is essential to a successful implementation. Additionally, some level of competence should be demonstrated either in one-on-one sessions or in a skills assessment following training.

Traditional training has often been focused on functionality rather than on the providers' workflows. (One example of a provider's workflow in this context is the way a provider works and the process steps the provider takes during a visit with the patient and clinic staff.) In contrast, training to a workflow will provide much more of a realistic framework for the end user to truly get a feel for the way the new system will function in practice; for example, the physician is trained on how to use the EHR from admission to discharge instead of only being taught how to enter an order or how to write a progress note. Determine the one best way to perform the workflow, even if there are many other ways, and then train to that workflow. It is important not to try to teach every possible nuance in a single training session. After learning and using the "basics" for some period of time, those users who would like additional training can learn the advanced "tricks" of the system and become even more proficient and efficient.

Reduce Schedules for Go-Live

During and after go-live, giving physicians time to learn while caring for patients requires that they reduce their schedules to some degree. There is considerable debate and no real consensus about the ideal amount of reduction and timeframe required, and determining this will depend upon the extent of the change as well as the specialty.

Banner reduced schedules by 25 percent for two weeks before go-live and by 50 percent for the two weeks following. The time prior to go-live was used to set up preferences, create "favorites" or commonly used orders and document templates, and increase familiarity with the system. The reduction of schedules for two weeks after go-live afforded the providers time to develop their workflows and learn to complete the work in real time without excessive delays in patient care. The schedule was then increased to 75 percent the third and fourth weeks and was back to 100 percent by week five.

Since Emory Health did not compensate physicians for the lost revenue had they all chosen to reduce schedules, actually taking the step of reducing schedules was left to the discretion of each clinical service line or specialty. Individual specialties approached this differently, from blocking 20 percent of appointments to restricting double bookings in specialties with high rates of no-shows. Furthermore, some Emory clinical service lines or specialties also scheduled all appointments as new patient appointments (typically longer appointments than for returning patients) for a period of time to allow more computer time per patient.

While the financial impact on the organization can be significant, and these examples of schedule reduction may seem excessive and unnecessary to some, there are many challenges that only become apparent with the go-live. Reducing schedules will give providers a chance to become proficient with the new system without sacrificing patient satisfaction. Reducing schedules can minimize the stress of transitioning to a new EHR and also learning while using the system.

Ambulatory implementations present unique challenges where physicians are the rate-limiting step in patient throughput. For many physicians, the transition from paper to an electronic record or from one electronic record to another is very disruptive. Ideally, the electronic work will be performed in real time during patient care, but that can be overwhelming when there are five patients waiting to be seen and the provider is trying to place an order but can't figure out how. It is important to communicate to providers that the way they practice medicine is not changing, only how they document that care and place orders. Some organizations take a "big bang" approach, implementing all the system's capabilities, and then expect physicians to adopt all of the new tools at once. Others find that a gradual approach is more tenable. For example, providers who traditionally dictate their notes could alternate between using traditional transcription and using the new documentation system on the first day and by the end of the week transition completely to the new documentation system. In an effort to minimize the negative impact on revenue during the implementation, giving providers some kind of "credit" for the patients they would have normally seen may be helpful in gaining buy-in and increasing their engagement.

It is important to realize that some providers will want to return to their normal routine faster than the prescribed schedule. However, an alternative for these providers would be to have them assist some of the other providers during the free times they have during reduced schedules. This approach fosters *esprit de corps* and helps the whole clinic return to a normal level of productivity faster. Also important to remember in the clinic setting is that associates in registration, billing, and scheduling and medical assistants also see dramatic changes in how they do their work, and their efficiency directly impacts the physician. Until they become fully proficient, physicians can expect their productivity to also be impacted.

Downtime Procedures

Ironically, as much as clinicians complain about having to shift their paper processes to electronic ones, over several months they become dependent upon the electronic system and rapidly forget how they used to function without it. Unfortunately, no system is fool-proof. There will be times when the system is unavailable for some or all of its functions. Downtimes may be scheduled or unscheduled and may include situations such as a temporary loss of network connectivity, malfunction of interfaces, or even scheduled time to perform system upgrades. Downtimes are inevitable and preparing for them is an essential part of any implementation. This preparation is often neglected in the midst of focusing on the go-live.

Downtime preparation post-EHR implementation requires the entire multidisciplinary team to plan for how they can deliver patient care in the absence of the EHR. The length of the downtime may also affect the processes that are developed and, to the extent the downtime can be estimated initially, which procedures should be implemented. For example, Emory hospital nurses document vital signs on paper for downtimes greater than two hours and that documentation is then scanned into the medical record after the patients' discharge. Only the medication administration record (MAR) is retrospectively updated after a prolonged downtime.

Being prepared for downtimes is more than merely keeping all of the old paper forms and processes. For example, Emory's transition from paper billing to electronic billing coincided with the transition to ICD-10. Emory had not created ICD-10-compliant paper encounter forms, so preparing for downtime post-optimization required the revenue cycle team to work with each clinical group to develop new backup processes.

After an organization has created its processes and downtime forms, a thoughtful communication plan must be developed, especially for large systems that have clinics spread geographically and/or hospitals with multiple units. Options to consider include

- Having a system-wide paging list
- Phone trees
- A process for e-mail notification
- Alerts when signing into the system (if the system is still partially functioning)

While creating the communication plan initially can be a lot of work, it is also imperative to review the list of personnel, phone numbers, and clinic locations quarterly since healthcare is an ever-changing business.

Go-Live Support

Using a new system while simultaneously trying to deliver patient care at the same pace is challenging. Earlier in this chapter, we discussed the importance of reducing the clinicians' schedules, if feasible, to enable them to begin using the new EHR without becoming frustrated and prolonging patient wait times. Another way of minimizing the pain of adoption is at-the-elbow support, which may be accomplished by using adoption coaches at go-live and by having plenty of superusers trained and available. Superusers typically work for the organization that is implementing the new system or functionality and receive additional training beyond what is required for the typical user. Adoption coaches also receive additional training, are often employed by a third-party vendor or consulting firm, and may focus on a subset of users, such as physicians.

Regardless of how fabulous or thorough training classes are, adult learners often need hands-on experience using the actual system in order to absorb the material. Many physicians only start asking more advanced questions once they are using the new EHR to provide patient care. A frequent observation is that physicians want help in the exact moment that they need it—not ten minutes before, not ten minutes after—and the implementation team's ability to accurately predict those moments is close to zero. One way to tackle that challenge is to locate trainers, adoption coaches, and superusers throughout the clinical areas so that the physician literally has someone at the elbow whenever a question arises. If that is not an option because fewer support staff are available, paging and cell phone notification can expedite their movement. Distinctive clothing is an easy way to identify staff dedicated to supporting physicians or other clinical roles. During the first week of go-live, the ideal ratio of coaches to doctors often is 1:1 or 1:2, but thereafter that ratio can be increased relatively quickly to 1:3 or 1:4. However, we recommend having ongoing coaches either stationed in the clinical setting or rounding throughout multiple clinical settings for at least four weeks after go-live.

In settings where physicians may have diverse responsibilities and are not in the same setting every day, it may be necessary to extend the local support longer. For example, at Emory, many of the faculty have less than three half days of clinic per week, so they required more weeks of at-the-elbow support in order to receive the same net amount of support on the new system. While no organization can afford to maintain trainers and supporters indefinitely, physician adoption, satisfaction, and learning are all higher when their questions can be answered promptly.

Superusers are the next line of support. They may or may not be technologically superior to their peers, but they have a very thorough knowledge base of the system and the expected workflows. Almost more important than their technological skills are their motivation, respect by their peers, and ability to share the vision of the future state. Superusers should be trained ahead of the general users, both on how to technically use the system and on the new processes and workflows. Superusers must understand the new workflows and often are helpful in designing and testing them. Training these people ahead of others will allow your team to hear questions that you may not have considered and to polish the answers. It is also important that the superusers and the training team be on the same page in terms of teaching what the entire implementation team considers the optimal workflow for that specialty. Most EHR systems offer some flexibility in how a specific process can be carried out and the order of steps within a workflow. Superusers should teach the agreed-upon optimal workflow even if they prefer a different, "outside-the-box" way of doing things.

Emory Go-Live Coaches

Emory invested heavily in coaches for go-live. Coaches were available in 1:1 or 1:2 ratios for all physicians, nurse practitioners, and physician assistants for the entire first week of go-live. Support ratios were then increased (e.g., to 1:5 or 1:8) over the next three weeks.

Because the project was so large, a coaching leader was designated to work with each of the IT project managers and the local clinical leadership triads to identify which users required additional support (i.e., continuation of 1:1 support) versus those transitioning to only needing answers to occasional questions.

Emory also learned that it was important for the IT or clinical operations manager to intentionally pair a specific coach with a specific physician. When introducing the coach to the physician, we set expectations that the coach was going to stay in close proximity to the physician for the entire clinic session. These introductions were in response to a lesson learned after the first couple of go-lives, during which some physicians told their coach that they would call him or her when needed. That physical distance resulted in the physician not asking as many questions because the coach wasn't literally at the elbow. It was also very helpful for the superusers to receive 1:1 training with a coach prior to go-live and to practice walking through each of the workflows. This exercise enabled the coaches to learn the practice's workflows and gave the physician superuser greater confidence, which in turn enhanced that individual's leadership abilities during go-live.

During and Post Go-Live Communication

During the go-live, frequent communication is imperative, especially if more than one location is going live concurrently. One strategy Banner used was to keep a conference line available for anyone to call into when an issue arose. Banner also held daily status calls that allowed everyone to hear the challenges and the successes from all the sites. These calls included corporate leadership, site leaders, end users, and IT leadership and staff. Plan for daily calls for at least a week and, depending upon the magnitude of change, longer as needed. Additionally, provide a way for end users to make suggestions for improvements and enhancements and develop a system of tracking those requests and the outcomes. As these suggestions come in, it will be necessary to prioritize them according to urgency. Finally, provide transparency as to the status of those requests to encourage everyone to continue to submit them as they encounter opportunities to improve workflow and overall system functionality.

Banner's system was to prioritize issues and suggestions based on the following:

- Issues that were affecting patient care or had significant financial consequences
- Suggestions that could provide similar results or functionality as the previous system
- Helpful suggestions that were generally good ideas but considered nice-to-have functionality

Emory conducted debrief conference calls at the end of each day during go-live. These calls were facilitated by one of the project's operational sponsors or an IT director, and a member of the leadership triad from each practice was required to participate to answer three questions for that practice:

- What went well today?
- What didn't go well today?
- What are you going to do differently tomorrow?

These debriefings enabled all of the clinicians living through the change to connect, empathize, and strategize. Because they had staggered go-lives, they had one call each day for the practices that had gone live that week and another call for any practices that were in their second week or beyond. Each practice site was required to participate for at least two weeks, and as things stabilized, the length of the calls shortened as the focus centered on the ongoing problems and potential solutions.

The issues and suggestions list was collected from people who called into the conference line, from input during the debriefing calls, and from leadership rounds during and after go-live. In total, over 1,300 issues were collected over the two months of go-lives and they ranged from simple requests for access changes to requests for significant enhancements. The issues were categorized based on urgency, clinical specialty, and type of request (e.g., minor change to fix now, future functionality, broken functionality). By the end of the project, 700 issues were resolved and the remaining 600 were analyzed to determine the focus for the next wave of optimization.

Monitoring Success

Keep in mind, a go-live is really just the first day of the next phase in your project. You may have implemented the best of the best systems, but if the people on the front lines are not using that functionality as intended or have developed a number of work-arounds, you may have wasted a substantial amount of money. Leveraging usage data from the EHR enables the team to identify users who are struggling and opportunities for improvement across the system. Many of the EHR vendors now offer analytics capabilities that are detailed enough to provide specialty and user-level reports.

Emory Provider Go-Live Metrics

During Emory's optimization project, ten metrics were monitored:

- Total Time in the EHR per patient (sum of documentation, orders, chart review, and other work in the EHR/patient)

- Documentation time (average amount of time spent using the documentation tools per patient)

- Orders time (average amount of time spent using the ordering tools per patient)

- Chart review time (average amount of time spent using the chart review tools per patient)

- Percent of Transcription (percent of notes completed using traditional transcription)

- Percent of Orders entered electronically versus via paper

- Total number of orders entered electronically

- Percent of Dynamic Documentation (percent of notes completed using Cerner's newer documentation tool)

- Percent of PowerNote (percent of notes completed with Cerner's older electronic documentation tool)

- "Pajama time," or time spent outside normal clinic hours (typically the amount of time in the EHR between 6 P.M.–6 A.M. Monday to Friday plus weekend time)

Emory exported the data into Excel spreadsheets, developed for each specialty, that tracked each of these metrics for all of the attending physicians. Both the mean and the median for the metrics were calculated across each specialty to ensure that outliers would not skew identification of who might benefit from additional coaching. When using any analytics tool, it is essential to understand the definitions of the numerators and the denominators. Emory's patient count in the denominator was based on the number of signed notes; thus, if a physician was behind in signing notes, the denominator would be smaller and significantly increase his or her average time for each metric. For this reason, several months after go-live, Emory began delaying review of the data by a month to give the providers time to complete their notes and thus increase the accuracy of the denominators.

Emory used the data to determine which physicians would be targeted for one-on-one coaching. Initially Emory targeted all physicians who were above average in their use of traditional transcription, since one of the project goals was to reduce the cost of transcription. Emory also targeted physicians who were above the mean or median for the total amount of time per patient or pajama time. During the first round of targeted coaching, 175 providers received additional assistance, the benefits of which are shown in Table 20-4.

Emory continues to monitor data monthly and uses it to proactively reach out to physicians who may be struggling or have opportunities to increase their efficiency. Prior to analytics, our support team had to wait until a physician or administrator complained, and usually by that time, the physician had been unhappy or struggling for a prolonged time. Having the analytics has significantly increased our training team's efficacy. Additionally, they use the data to assess whether the coaching had an impact after a given intervention.

Banner Provider Go-Live Metrics

Banner's go-live plan included a ten-wave implementation spanning nine months, with a target of bringing up 490 providers across 110 clinics.

The initial goal and timeline was to implement 25 providers per wave in the first two monthly waves, increase to 50 providers per wave as the process was improved, and finally increase to 75 providers per wave. Interestingly, as the initial waves were implemented

Metric	Before Coaching	After Coaching	Total Change	% Change
Time Per Patient	0:19:01	0:17:19	0:01:42	9%
Orders Time	0:01:33	0:01:24	0:00:09	10%
Chart Review Time	0:06:12	0:05:42	0:00:30	8%
Chart Review Page Time	0:02:12	0:01:37	0:00:35	27%
Transcription	11%	7%		4%

Table 20-4 Select Provider Metrics Before and After a Focused Coaching Intervention During an EHR Optimization Project

successfully, providers who were scheduled in future waves began to request to move up their go-live dates. As the implementations progressed, Banner was able to exceed its goal by more than 25 percent above projections by the tenth wave and all ambulatory providers were fully implemented by the end of 2016. See Figure 20-4.

Figure 20-4
Cumulative number of providers and clinics that "went live" during a ten-wave EHR implementation, projected vs. actual

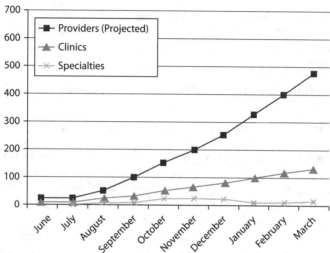

Projected Implementations

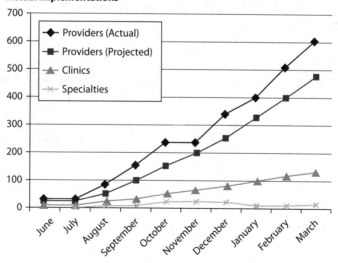

Actual Implementations

Chapter Review

Following a proven plan for implementing an EHR will increase the likelihood of your success. Understanding what challenges you might encounter will help you to prepare for those obstacles or perhaps even avoid them.

The following points summarize critical success factors for large-scale EHR implementations discussed in this chapter:

- Begin with your organization's guiding principles based on its mission and then connect those principles to project goals like standardizing care or decreasing medical error.

- Ensure that a governance structure has been developed to navigate the changes.

- Create a very detailed project plan that will guide you and keep you on track through the project.

- Identify and enlist clinical leaders from the beginning.

Recognize that the success of your implementation depends on how well you manage the change. After all, implementing a new EHR is not as much an IT project as it is a change management project and behavioral modification. Help your providers to understand that to really get the most out of an EHR system, they must realize that it is not simply a re-creation of the paper chart in a digitized form. It is a dynamic, ever-changing record, and the quality of what can be retrieved from the system is only as good as what the user puts into it. When physicians can see this true value, they will begin to use the system differently, inputting more useful information. Only then will they be able to move from merely *accepting* the new electronic changes to actually *using* the system fully to improve patient outcomes.

Questions

To test your comprehension of the chapter, answer the following questions and then check your answers against the list of correct answers that follows the questions.

1. Rogers' theory called diffusion of _____ has been used as a change management framework to guide healthcare EHR implementation projects.

   A. electronic health records

   B. electronic medical records

   C. transformation

   D. innovations

   E. technology

2. HIT large initiative governance has which of the following hallmark(s)?

   A. It includes and is accountable to all relevant stakeholders.

   B. Guiding principles based on the organization's mission.

   C. It is transparent to all constituents to assure decisions are fair and equitable.

D. Its project leaders use online collaboration tools to optimize involvement and dissemination.

E. All of the above.

3. Members of executive leadership must be willing and able to recognize and remove barriers encountered by the EHR and HIT implementation teams. Which of the following is an effective way for them to accomplish this?

A. Active involvement on an HIT or EHR steering committee

B. Receiving "back channel" communication from important physicians in the organization

C. Attending weekly project management meetings

D. Sponsoring celebrations upon completion of major project milestones

4. Which of the following is an important consideration for creating order sets?

A. They should only be created after go-live.

B. Since physicians sign the order sets, they should be the only clinical care team members involved in their development.

C. Since order sets have a significant effect on the work of many different care team members, representatives of those disciplines should participate in order set development.

D. Order sets should be evidence-based and as such should never be adjusted for local healthcare organization reasons.

5. Clinical documentation templates _____.

A. cannot vary across clinical or medical specialties

B. include required fields to foster compliance with regulations or standards

C. can accommodate any possible permutation of healthcare

D. should not be used, as the best practice for clinical documentation is free text entry

6. Which of the following workflows should be addressed during an EHR implementation?

A. Pharmacy prescription dispensing

B. Disaster preparedness

C. Handoffs between clinical care teams

D. Executive leadership participation in important project meetings

7. EHR downtimes can occur due to _____.

A. temporary loss of network connectivity

B. malfunction of interfaces

C. scheduled time to perform system upgrades

D. all of the above

8. Which of the following metrics is used to assess provider performance and/or satisfaction after EHR or HIT go-lives?

   A. Orders time (average amount of time spent using the ordering tools per patient)

   B. Issues documentation time (average amount of time spent documenting issues with the system per provider)

   C. Boot camp time (minutes spent in remediation training per provider)

   D. Global job satisfaction scores

Answers

1. **D.** Rogers' theory called diffusion of innovations has been used as a change management framework to guide healthcare EHR implementation projects.

2. **E.** HIT large initiative governance has the following hallmarks: it includes and is accountable to all relevant stakeholders, with guiding principles based on the organization's mission; it is transparent to all constituents to assure decisions are fair and equitable; and its project leaders use online collaboration tools to optimize involvement and dissemination.

3. **A.** An effective way for members of executive leadership to recognize and remove barriers encountered by the EHR and HIT implementation teams is to be actively involved on a HIT or EHR steering committee.

4. **C.** Since order sets have a significant effect on the work of many different care team members, representatives of those disciplines should participate in order set development.

5. **B.** Clinical documentation templates include required fields to foster compliance with regulations or standards.

6. **C.** Handoffs between clinical care teams should be addressed during an EHR implementation.

7. **D.** EHR downtimes can occur due to temporary loss of network connectivity, malfunction of interfaces, and scheduled time to perform system upgrades.

8. **A.** A metric used to assess provider performance and/or satisfaction after EHR or HIT go-lives is orders time (average amount of time spent using the ordering tools per patient).

References

1. Charles, D., Gabriel, M., & Searcy, T. (2015). *Adoption of electronic health record systems among U.S. non-federal acute care hospitals: 2008–2014.* ONC Data Brief, no. 23. Office of the National Coordinator for Health Information Technology.

2. McCormick, K., & Gugerty, B. (2013). *Healthcare information technology exam guide for CompTIA® Healthcare IT Technician and HIT Pro™ certifications.* McGraw Hill-Education.

3. Rogers, E. M. (2003). *Diffusion of innovations, fifth edition.* Simon and Schuster.

4. Monegain, B. (2015, Apr. 3). Banner Health, Cerner tackle big change. *HealthcareIT News.* Accessed on June 9, 2016, from www.healthcareitnews .com/news/banner-health-cerner-take-big-change.

5. Office of the National Coordinator for Health IT (ONC). (n.d.). *Chart migration and scanning checklist.* Accessed on June 30, 2016, from https://www.healthit .gov/providers-professionals/implementation-resources/chart-migration-and-scanning-checklist.

6. ONC. (n.d.). *Meaningful use definition & objectives.* Accessed on November 28, 2016, from https://www.healthit.gov/providers-professionals/meaningful-use-definition-objectives.

PART IV

CHAPTER 21

Training Essentials for Implementing Healthcare IT

Cheryl A. Fisher

In this chapter, you will learn how to
- Plan, design, develop, deliver, and evaluate technology-based instruction
- Plan and implement an instructional needs assessment
- Construct a lesson plan using appropriate instructional methods
- Incorporate adult learning principles into program design
- Create a custom presentation using principles of effective multimedia presentation and current Internet technologies
- Plan and conduct an effective student assessment and program evaluation
- Discuss new trends and future directions for teaching with technology

Implementing new technology into the healthcare setting can be a costly and resource-intensive undertaking. Training requirements for new technologies include an enormous amount of time, effort, commitment, and change management on the part of the organization. Training is required for those who will be involved in the initial implementation of the healthcare organization's new systems so that they will be familiar with the new capabilities and functionality now available. Because of this investment, it is imperative that best practices and sound educational design principles are applied to ensure success. Traditional face-to-face computer lab training presents many challenges and is time-consuming and resource-intensive. Because of a diverse workforce and varying schedules of healthcare providers, technology-supported design models can potentially address these limitations. This chapter will address training considerations when faced with the implementation of new technologies in healthcare settings and conclude with a look at future directions for training in new technologies as the field continues to evolve.

Models and Principles

The first step in developing a training program is to put together a team that understands the healthcare organization's mission, the content to be delivered, the educational design considerations, and the end user's perspective. This team must then develop a training plan that is flexible, dynamic, personalized, and reflective of post-implementation training requirements in order to reinforce the concepts and to drive the successful utilization of technology adoption. Vendor-provided training sometimes falls short because of generic content delivery that does not align with the organization or is not customized enough to meet the end-user requirements.

Several models should be considered when implementing training for new technologies in healthcare settings. These models guide the training developer through the appropriate steps and facilitate the incorporation of all considerations necessary for success. Instructional design is the analysis of learning needs followed by the systematic development of instruction to meet those needs. If such models are followed, they will facilitate the transfer of knowledge, skills, and attitude to the learner.[1] The ADDIE model, for example, is a generic instructional design model that is used by instructional designers and training developers. The model consists of five phases: analysis, design, development, implementation, and evaluation. Table 21-1 describes what occurs in each step of the model.

One commonly accepted improvement to this model is the use of rapid prototyping. This is the idea of receiving continual or formative feedback while instructional materials are being created. This model attempts to save time and money by catching problems early while they are easy to fix.[1] For example, if an institution was implementing a new technology for a new device, the course developer would incorporate evaluation and concept refinement after each step of development to provide corrective action along the way.

In the ADDIE model, each step has an outcome incorporated in the subsequent step. *Instructional design* (ID) is a general term for a family of systematic methods for planning, developing, evaluating, and managing the instructional process effectively in order to promote successful learning by students.[2] *Instructional systems design* (ISD) is a problem-solving process that has been applied to the development of training since the 1940s. Since then, more than 100 instructional design models have emerged based on the fundamentals of the ADDIE model.

Table 21-1 ADDIE Steps and Actions	ADDIE Step	Action(s) Within Step
	Analyze	Determine needs and performance gap
	Design	Write learning objectives, plan the training, and develop evaluation plan
	Develop	Build the course
	Implement	Teach or make training available
	Evaluate	Measure effectiveness or impact

Assessing Basic Skill Level

One of the most challenging aspects of training is determining baseline skill level and the learning needs of the end users. Assessment is the process of determining these needs in order to write learning objectives directed toward these needs, and one method is through a *learning or training needs assessment*. A *training needs assessment* is a study done in order to design and develop appropriate instructional and informational programs and material in order to fill in the gaps.[3] However, a learning needs assessment allows you to consider both formal and informal learning needs. That is, what do they need to be trained on, and how can you best support their informal learning needs? In other words, how are the end users supported outside of the classroom?

TIP Oftentimes the end users don't know what they need to know. Setting up general overview sessions of a new system in an auditorium prior to training and go-live can help users to start developing questions.

The next step is to determine the student's baseline knowledge and experience related to the technology to be learned. People do not learn from point zero, rather from the standpoint of their own knowledge and experience. The model seeks to motivate the student via prior experience and context to come closer to the idea of the topic. During this step, defining or describing the problem under study and sharing the objectives of the training process between trainer and participant are key.[4] Questionnaires and structured interviews are the most commonly reported methods of needs assessments. Other ways to gather information related to learning needs include observations, surveys, or group discussions. Some questions to consider when gathering information for the needs assessment include the following:

- Who is the audience, and what are their characteristics?
- What is the new behavioral outcome?
- What types of learning constraints exist?
- What are the delivery options?
- What are the online design considerations?
- What is the timeline for project completion?

Here is an example of the steps to follow when conducting a needs assessment:

1. Write objectives of what you hope to gain from the needs assessment.
2. Select an audience to sample. Consider the sample across multiple age groups, and consider those with English as a second language.
3. Collect data from participants.
4. Analyze data.

PART IV

Once this information is gathered, the trainer will have a much better understanding of the baseline knowledge of the learners and any issues that seem to be prevalent among the learners. This will allow the training developer to ensure that potential problem areas receive additional attention.

Next-generation learners are now posing additional challenges and have been the focus of educators and national initiatives in order to keep pace with evolving needs. One approach to keep up with these changing needs focuses on personalized, relevant, flexible, and engaging experiences that offer effective learning.[5] With video being one of the most popular means for delivering educational and training offerings, developers must keep in mind that cell phones, laptops, digital readers, and tablets are all popular devices for accessing content. The focus now for the digital-savvy generations is on the right tool for the task.

Design Elements

Once the learning needs are assessed, the learning objectives for the training program should be established. The general purpose for the training should be clearly defined, followed by the specific learning outcomes. The learning outcomes or objectives should be measureable and criterion-based. For example, "at the end of this module (given a set of conditions), you will be able (action verb and behavior) to (criterion with level of accuracy)." Here's a sample objective: *at the end of this module, the learner will be able to document medications with 100 percent accuracy.* When evaluating the objectives, you should look to determine completeness, practicality, feasibility, and consistency. The goal of training should be more than just knowing how and where to enter the data. The overall goal should support users to think logically and critically about how to best use the system to maximize the benefits that the system has to offer the healthcare organization and the patients. The training team and healthcare organization management have the challenge at this point of obtaining user buy-in by developing program objectives tailored to the workflow of each person's role utilizing the system. Emphasis should be placed on attitudes and benefits of the system to enhance patient outcomes. With a major focus now on measuring impact and outcomes, it should be clear within the objectives of the training what the intended outcomes hope to achieve. To achieve the full potential of what health information technology has to offer, including increased patient safety, improved healthcare quality, and reduced costs, healthcare providers must be both willing and able to use the technology effectively.[5]

Additional design considerations should include the order of the instructional program. According to Gagne's nine events for learning, the instructor should do the following, in this order:

1. Gain the learner's attention
2. Inform the learner of the objectives
3. Stimulate recall of prior learning
4. Present information
5. Provide guidance
6. Elicit performance

7. Provide feedback

8. Assess performance

9. Enhance retention and transfer

Gagne's process steps for learning were developed based on an information processing model of the mental events that occur when adults are presented with various stimuli.[6] To put this model into action, the instructor could tailor learning modules toward particular surgeon groups. These modules would use pre-op and post-op orders already familiar to the surgeons and provide them with the opportunity to translate new knowledge to their already familiar work.

A major consideration for designing and developing training pertains to the delivery method of the instruction. Whether the training will be conducted face-to-face, completely online, or using a hybrid format that includes a mix of online and face-to-face training will depend on the preference of the organization and the available resources. Training can be done by internal resources, third-party providers, or the EHR vendor, and a determination needs to be made about which groups offer the best chance for success. There are pros and cons to all approaches, and often the cost or resource impact will ultimately determine a healthcare organization's decision. The goal is to develop comprehensive training in the shortest amount of time.

Often, the end users have little time and patience for training, yet it is critical that they develop the skills and competency required to safely use the new system. Additional challenges include small training budgets, often with no minimum standard or time requirements ensuring adequate training. On average, online instruction and face-to-face instruction require similar time commitments for end users. Instructional strategies to enhance feedback and interactivity typically prolong learning time but in many cases also enhance learning outcomes.[7] Online learning has advantages such as overcoming time and distance barriers and the ability to use innovative multimedia and virtual instructional methods. It is the challenge of any instructional designer to incorporate meaningful instructional strategies that engage the learners and enhance the learning. It is also up to the organization to determine whether they have trained instructional designers on staff or whether they have the resources to outsource the required training and follow-up. Oftentimes, combinations of online and face-to-face instructional strategies are utilized to address the many facets of training required. Here are some examples:

- Web-based tutorials for general concepts and higher-level learning

- Instructor-led classroom training workshops facilitated by clinical subject-matter experts as well as training team members

- One-on-one short training sessions with end users for each phase of the project led by superusers, focused on clinical care and efficient interactions with the system applications

- On-request support for assistance or clarification just after go-live

- On-the-spot training via walking rounds using clinical experts to offer support

- Web-based or instructor-led training on advanced features and new enhancements after go-live and ongoing as appropriate

There are multiple ways of delivering training materials and content during educational sessions in addition to user guides, pocket reference guides, and quick-tip sheets. Posters can be developed and placed in staff workstations in order to reinforce visual displays and contact information for the user help desk. Regardless of the approach, the goal is ultimately to develop a user-friendly rapport with the staff in order to answer questions and help problem solve. If users find they cannot get the help they need in a timely fashion, they will develop shortcuts or "workarounds" that may be difficult to correct later and could compromise patient safety.

The Adult Learner

When designing educational training programs for adults, success can depend on the adherence to adult learning principles that need to be embedded throughout the program. Adult learners have unique learning needs and expectations that set them apart from their younger counterparts. Adult learning has received increasing attention among educators, and a significant body of literature has established clear areas of emphasis for adult educators. These areas are typically recognized in the principles of andragogy developed by Knowles, which stress the following as hallmarks of adult learners:[8]

- **Need-to-know**   Adult learners in training situations, as opposed to general learning courses, are focused on content and instruction that they feel is directly relevant to their job and/or functions they are asked to perform. Another aspect of this need is wanting to know why they should invest the time in the new content or task.

- **Immediacy of application**   Distant or theoretical applications of the knowledge are not as valued by adult learners as what they feel they need to know immediately for tasks at hand or upcoming in the near future.

- **Sharing of life experiences as a source of knowledge**   This hallmark has an internal and external application. Internally, the adult learner often references the new concepts or tasks to similar concepts or tasks in content, importance, or other factors to what they have experienced or know and thereby readily tap into successful strategies from past experience. Externally, they bring valuable experience to group learning situations.

- **Affinity for real-life learning**   Stemming from the three previous hallmarks, adult learners have a preference for real-life scenarios closely related to their job or job functions in the classroom or online, as opposed to abstract concepts that might be tied back to their job. They also tend to enjoy learning on the job.

- **Independence and self-direction**   Adult learners are ready to learn when the need arises, often self-motivated, and frequently need less guidance and feedback during the learning process than non-adult learners.

- **Ownership**   Adult learners frequently accept responsibility for the educational offering's learning objectives, sometimes somewhat modified and personalized, and take personal control of how to achieve those objectives.

When developing training with adult learners in mind, the developer must ensure that relevant training scenarios are utilized and that learning is self-paced and possibly self-directed. This can be done by creating training scenarios for different healthcare roles (e.g., physician, nurse) and by allowing for test-out options so as not to waste the time of the professional adult learner. For example, online training modules could be developed for physicians that focus specifically on order entry. Given specific concepts and opportunities for transferring knowledge, the physicians could be tested at the end of the module to demonstrate competency through applying their new knowledge. Training environments could also be made available for specific disciplines to practice their new skills. This simulated training environment should resemble the production system as closely as possible, should be accessible from every desktop, should include a realistic amount of data (with fictitious patient names), and should enable staff to practice navigation.

Game-based learning is also popular with both teens and adults and produces a range of cognitive responses that includes high levels of engagement, concentration, enjoyment, and active participation by the adult learner. Interdisciplinary teamwork, problem solving, and interacting with role-playing virtual patients produce opportunities for medical learners to apply the content being learned to relevant case scenarios.[9]

Constructing a Lesson Plan

Once the needs assessment is completed and the objectives are developed, it is time to develop a lesson plan for the targeted population. When put into simple terms, "tell, show, do, and review" is a good way to remember the steps. A sample outline for this plan could include the following:

I. Principal goal of the training
  A. Module I
    i. Learning objectives
      a. Tell: Didactic content (PowerPoint or video)
      b. Show: Demonstration of new skills to be learned (PowerPoint, video, or screen capture)
      c. Do: Learning activity to apply learned concepts (application of learned content using case scenarios)
      d. Review: Evaluation of learning (knowledge test, return demonstration)
  B. Module II (repeat previous steps)
  C. Additional resources and supporting materials

Training content should be focused on job roles and associated workflow. The key being that the training content is reflective of the actual EHR content and not a previous or outdated version of the system. Vendors usually provide the initial training materials and a limited amount of training services—often bundled with other, broader implementation services—which should be used to train the project team and the initial set of users or superusers. These superusers will then become resources to train other staff and to problem solve, support end users, and reinforce concepts at the unit or department level. The training department should then develop customized supporting materials that are consistent with workflow and the healthcare organization's policies and procedures.

In short, a successful training program must be tailored to an organization's environment. The materials developed should address the user roles and clinical workflow scenarios that will be familiar to the end user's daily practice. The training should focus on workflow and ultimately enhance safe patient care.

 TIP The change in workflow for end users cannot be underestimated. This is often one of the primary reasons why staff will resist change and develop workarounds. When changing from one electronic record to another, users try to translate what they used to do into the new workflow. To circumvent this, good relationships are critical so that staff will utilize available resources to facilitate problem solving.

Multimedia as a Method of Delivery

As multimedia and social media become more commonly used as instructional tools, researchers are finding that more than one modality (i.e., visual and auditory) is better than a single modality (visual alone) in any instructional environment for engaging students in active learning.[10] The implementation of multimedia can effectively enhance learning performance and retention. Incorporating multimedia tools at an appropriate time can enhance learning interests. The use of gaming technology to demonstrate complex concepts has been shown to have no gender difference in terms of preference. Also, the presentation of reciprocal representations can enable students to have an in-depth understanding of a course and extend the effect of learning retention.[10]

Instructional quality of online delivery is still a common concern. Quality assurance requires a comprehensive framework of several perspectives of learners' and instructors' needs including critical analysis of teaching and learning practices with the technology platform.[11] The use of high-quality instructional and course design standards by instructors in online learning has numerous benefits as well as challenges. Moving from traditional methods of teaching to online delivery methods of instruction requires a shift in the perspectives of both the instructors and the learners.[12] When constructing instructional tutorials using presentation software, you must consider basic principles for the adult learner that will ensure the message is communicated and conveyed clearly. Here are some examples:

- Combine images with verbal text (less is more when it comes to graphics).
- Present content in logically grouped sections that allow the learner to organize for recall.
- Use a text of font size 28 to 30 (and limit the font to one or two text styles).

- Don't use more than five lines per slide, and avoid using all capital letters.
- Use a title font size of 40 or larger.
- Minimize background colors and textures so as not to distract from the content, and be sure text color contrasts with slide background.
- Use consistent transitions.
- Unify slides and align text using bullets.
- Avoid using animation unless it is value added.

These principles are important to apply because they make the content easier to understand and avoid distraction from the information to be learned. When developing training tutorials, one of the most effective approaches includes the use of software that guides the learner through the navigational pathways. A videotaped lecture can be used for an instructional demonstration prior to allowing the participants to practice on their own. Instructional modules longer than 20 minutes tend to lose teaching effectiveness. Information overload is a real possibility, and the instructor must decide on the important points to be learned.[13]

Current Internet Technologies

Current Internet media and technologies that are easily accessible, modifiable, and publishable by an online community were coined Web 2.0 in late 1999, but the term began to be widely used in 2004. Features and functionality that allow for user interaction and information sharing such as blogs and social networks enhance communication, productivity, and sharing and continue to be the focus of a dynamic Internet.[14] Despite the increasing use of current Internet technologies and tools in education, there appears to be a lack of empirical evidence detailing the process educators have taken to implement them in the classroom. Identification of the vast and varied technologies available can help the course designer to choose an appropriate Internet technology to meet the teaching and learning requirement. Providing guidance to educators on key practical issues to consider when introducing new technical features into the classroom is important because it provides direction on how to overcome any unforeseen issues when undertaking this process.[15] With little guidance on how to leverage new Internet technologies in the educational context of healthcare information technology, examples and practical recommendations cited in the literature regarding implementation in organizations referenced document sharing sites, Facebook for announcements and group discussion, YouTube for uploading recorded lectures, and Twitter and others for streaming video.[16] Because current Internet technologies can be used for knowledge sharing, learning, and social interaction, these tools are now prominently used in the classroom. The tools are acknowledged in the literature to have the potential to support different educational design approaches that facilitate both self-directed and collaborative learning. The primary concerns regarding the adoption of new Internet technologies are usefulness, advantages, compatibility, technology availability, and now privacy and security. Secondary concerns are resource-facilitating conditions, healthcare organizations' technical policies, and senior management attitudes.[16]

Training Delivery and Accommodation

For any training program to be successful, the first consideration is the audience. In other words, to whom are you speaking? It is critical to know the answers to the following:

- What do you want to communicate?
- How will the messages best be conveyed?
- When will the training be seen as most relevant?
- Where will the training take place?
- Why should the individual participate in the learning?[17]

While it might seem obvious, it is critical to keep the message clear and concise and to keep all information simple.

When formulating a training plan, consider the needs assessment findings, the diversity of your audience, and any special needs of the individuals. For example, if the didactic portion of your training has been videotaped with audio recordings and you have a participant who is hearing impaired, you will need to ensure that your training has transcripts available for this individual to read. Likewise, if you have a participant who is visually impaired, does your training meet the requirements for using screen readers or assistive devices? All training delivered online must meet the requirements of the Americans with Disabilities Act. It is required by law that all participants have equal access to educational training or that special accommodations be made if required.

Training schedules need to be flexible, and given the 24/7 nature of healthcare, it may be necessary to offer late evening or weekend training classes in order to accommodate all staff. Training content should be introduced over a period of time to avoid information overload and to progress from novice to expert concepts. This can be done using a series of modules that build on previously learned content. Readily available and easy-to-use reference material can help support the formal learned content and can reinforce learning.

TIP It has been the standard that the training for implementing a new EHR should occur about six weeks prior to go-live and should be delivered in no more than three-hour blocks of time. This approach will facilitate learning and retention of information. Within the three-hour blocks of time, breaks should be given, and the "tell, show, do, review" process steps should be followed.

Evaluating Learning

Effective training should focus on the user role and should be workflow-based. A common misconception of how to train is to focus on features and functions of the system. While basic knowledge of how to navigate and what icons/buttons do is important, the training ultimately should be competency-based. It is less important for users to know every button or system function than it is for users to be able to accomplish their day-to-day tasks and to ensure patient safety. While some level of basic education is needed, physicians in particular respond best when training is clinically focused on content encountered in daily practice. Case scenarios are particularly useful when focused on complex areas of healthcare such as handoff communication for transfers of patients between clinical areas. However, considerations must also be made for cross training (for example, when nurses or medical assistants are entering orders as agents for physicians) and training within specialty areas (for example, the operating room), which will help to facilitate seamless work among the varied roles within a specialized environment through better care coordination.

Student learning and program evaluation are critical in order for the trainer to know whether they accomplished their task in delivering training. Two current working methodologies of formative and summative assessment stress involving students in generating and using assessment information as a key assessment function. Utilizing Kirkpatrick's method of evaluation,[18] questions to ask include the following:

- Were the students satisfied with their learning?
- Did it meet their needs?
- Would they recommend it to others?
- Did their behavior (or performance) change as a result?
- Did the organization achieve its desired results from the training?

A successful training evaluation must be aligned with the organization's mission and goals, it should be a systematic process, it should be data-driven, and it should be focused on continuing improvement. The best methods for assessing student learning can be obtained from participant feedback, tests, and performance. Examples include surveys, structured interviews, and formal or informal tests. The trainers, peers, or supervisors can also make behavioral observations. The purpose for assessing student learning is primarily to determine whether knowledge gains have occurred. If the users say the training was useful and relevant, it was targeted correctly to the learning needs.

It is important to note that training does not stop at the end of the formal training sessions. Successful user adoption requires ongoing follow-up and follow-through in order to ensure that users are not creating a workaround, which happens frequently when they are unable or do not understand how to perform a task in the correct way. Follow-up is also important in identifying any previous paper-based or outdated workflows that may have been missed as part of the initial review and that clinicians are still utilizing. Once these individuals are identified, superusers can focus their training time on those most in need. Walking rounds and focus groups can provide useful sources of information that require follow-up in addition to the opportunity for understanding particular areas of challenge for the users. Optimization of training has become more important in healthcare organizations as the adoption of new technology and improvements are leveraged with current tools. Chart audits and reviews are helping organizations to focus on specific users who may be requiring additional time on tasks, to target them for additional support or training as needed.

Program Evaluation

The overall program can be evaluated using satisfaction surveys, interviews, and knowledge outcomes.[19] The purpose is to incorporate the data and findings into the program for the purposes of improvement. Feedback can also provide useful information for necessary revisions to the overall program design and delivery, which will then become the orientation program content for new employees. A Likert rating is a five-point (or some other number from 3–9) scale that allows an individual to indicate how much they agree or disagree with a statement. Questions specific to the overall program could include the following and should be answered using the commonly accepted Likert rating:

Please indicate your level of satisfaction with each of the following:

- Whether the program met your expectations
- Program content
- Ability of presenter to communicate
- Presenter's knowledge
- Content and usefulness of handouts
- Location in which program was held
- Convenience of program day and time
- Overall program

Utilizing a Learning Management System

Once the training program is designed and developed, one of the most efficient ways to implement the electronic content is by using a learning management system (LMS). An LMS is a software application used for the administration, documentation, tracking, and reporting of training programs. A robust LMS should do the following:

- Centralize and automate administration
- Use self-service and self-guided services
- Assemble and deliver learning content rapidly
- Support portability and standards
- Personalize content and enable knowledge reuse
- Implement healthcare organization–wide initiatives seamlessly with the opportunity to run reports on completion status

These platforms are particularly used to make the course materials, such as lecture slides, exercise sheets and solutions, and assignments, accessible.[20] During the past fifteen years or so, LMS deployments have been utilized in most traditional educational institutions, not only to replace face-to-face instruction (e-learning) but also to combine it with computer-based instruction or hybrid learning. In addition to the delivery of learning content to students, LMSs often support interaction and cooperation with discussion, news forums, wikis, blogs, and quizzes, thus creating collaborative learning. LMSs also enable instructors to evaluate students electronically and to generate student databases where grades and progress can be charted.[20] E-learning course management systems provide educators with new tools and media to aid their teaching. For example, students can learn at their own pace at whatever time they want. These systems are not simple turnkey operations that can be implemented without some level of customization. They require an understanding of instructional design and demand a considerable amount of planning configuration, integration with user accounts, migration of course content, and testing.[13] Human resources are a major consideration from the perspective of system administration and system maintenance.

Although most LMSs are commercially developed, some have an open source license, which allows for their source code to be shared. One popular set of open source software licenses includes those identified by the Open Source Initiative (OSI), an organization dedicated to promoting open source software.

In recent years, e-learning has changed the traditional teaching and learning styles from teacher-centered to learner-centered. It emphasizes that the learner actively participates in the process of knowledge construction. The Sharable Content Object Reference Model (SCORM) has become the standard for the tracking of records in LMSs, based on previously developed standards by the Aviation Industry CBT Committee (AICC). SCORM facilitates content acquisition from multiple providers with a single, real-time interface for recordkeeping and administration purposes. By definition, SCORM refers to a set of specifications that produce small, reusable e-learning objects when applied to course content. One advantage is these objects can be reused with other training materials.[21] For example, video clips, graphics, or learning modules might fall into this category. SCORM is a set of rules specified by the Advanced Distributed Learning (ADL) initiative that specify the order in which a learner may experience the training materials, such as using bookmarks to track progress and the opportunity to take breaks from learning without having to start over. SCORM also tracks test scores and feedback to the users. The office of the U.S. Secretary of Defense originally developed these standards in 1997.[22]

New Directions

Currently, training is offered as a one-size-fits-all approach that is not always what is needed by the learner. Adaptive learning is now evolving and can provide next-generation learners with information they need on demand in a format that is best suited to each particular learner and situation. Although there is currently no widespread agreement of what is personalized or adaptive learning, the U.S. Department of Education Office of Educational Technology offers the following helpful way of understanding different kinds of adaptive learning:[23]

- **Individualization**   Learning goals are the same for all students, but students can progress through the material at different speeds.

- **Differentiation**   Learning goals are the same for all students, but the method of instruction varies according to the learning preferences.

- **Personalization**   The learning objectives and content as well as the method and pace may vary.

Adaptive learning is a method for delivery as opposed to a technology, but it is easy to see how systems or design can support flexibility to meet a spectrum of learner needs.[24]

And finally, from the educational offering developer's perspective, mobile technology can add important flexibility to learners, as was also mentioned earlier in the chapter. Mobile learning offers great opportunities for education; however, while more demand exists for mobile learning, technical issues and design challenges related to mobile learning content delivery platforms still need to be further developed.[25]

Chapter Review

The task for instructional designers to train large numbers of employees on electronic medical records is a large and complex undertaking. It is increasingly apparent that innovations in information technology can deliver instruction more effectively in a wider range of contexts.[2] Anecdotal evidence suggests that projects for developing online instruction, particularly in educational settings, are often challenged by limited staff, funding constraints, and quick turnaround times. With increasingly limited resources, corporate and governmental departments responsible for designing online instruction have been reduced. Large projects requiring complex instructional design have been replaced by smaller, less complex, and less resource-intensive initiatives.[26] Having transformed traditional learning styles and sparked the interest of business communities and schools, e-learning is now regarded as an effective way to save labor and money, while enhancing learning performance.[10] Online learning using web-based computer programs and emerging mobile technology for teaching can facilitate learning with instructional efficacy similar to that of traditional teaching approaches. Key topics in this chapter include the following:

- Instructional systems design and the ADDIE model as a guide for developing training

- Principles of adult learning theory and the importance of incorporating these principles into training programs

- Lesson plans and the various methodologies for developing educational content along with suggestions for evaluating student learning and program evaluation

- The use of a learning management system, open source software, and the incorporation of Web 2.0 technology to enhance learning

- New trends in adaptive learning designs and mobile technology

Ultimately, it is not the amount of time spent training or the method of delivery that is important but the competency of the end users and their safe practices with system use that matter.

Questions

To test your comprehension of this chapter, answer the following questions and then check your answers against the list of correct answers at the end of the chapter.

1. Utilizing an instructional systems design model can facilitate the transfer of which of the following?

   A. Knowledge

   B. Attitude

   C. Skills

   D. All of the above

2. The best way to conduct a needs assessment is to do which of the following?

   A. Conduct a survey

   B. Conduct a focus group or structured interview

   C. A and B

   D. None of the above

3. During which step of the ADDIE model is it appropriate to write the learning objectives?

   A. Analyze

   B. Design

   C. Develop

   D. Implement

4. Characteristics of adult learners include which of the following?

   A. Are responsible for their learning, are ready to learn when the need arises, and are task-oriented

   B. Are autonomous, need direction, and do not feel responsible for their learning

   C. A and B

   D. None of the above

5. When developing content using presentation software, good design principles include which of the following?

   A. An abundance of animation and a variety of background colors

   B. Consistency and uniformity of text and font sizes

   C. Excessive use of graphics and text to convey the message ("eye charts")

   D. Cartoons and humor to hold the learner's attention

6. The benefits of using a learning management system (LMS) to implement a training program include all of the following except which one?

   A. Automatic tracking of user grades and participation

   B. Incorporation of SCORM standards

   C. Administrative management

   D. Turnkey technology

7. Why is Web 2.0 (or current Internet) technology becoming popular in education and training?

   A. Younger generations are familiar with this technology.

   B. Many frameworks exist for the use and incorporation of this technology into training.

   C. Research is beginning to show the effectiveness of this technology in collaborative learning.

   D. None of the above.

8. Which of the following is a true statement about mobile learning?

   A. It is now a preferred method of learning.

   B. It should be an option for all courses developed.

   C. It is not yet fully developed.

   D. None of the above.

Answers

1. **D.** Use of an instructional systems design model to develop a training program can facilitate the transfer of knowledge, attitude, and skills to the learner.

2. **C.** The best way to conduct a needs assessment is a survey or a structured focus group.

3. **B.** The design step of the ADDIE model includes writing the objectives.

4. **A.** Characteristics of adult learners include responsibility for their learning, are ready to learn when the need arises, and are task-oriented.

5. **B.** When developing content using presentation software, good design principles include consistency and uniformity of text and font sizes.

6. **D.** The benefits of using a learning management system (LMS) to implement a training program include all of the options given except that it is not turnkey technology.

7. **C.** Web 2.0 technology is increasingly popular in education and training because initial research is showing its effectiveness in collaborative learning.

8. **C.** Mobile learning is not yet fully developed.

References

1. InstructionalDesign.org. (2016). *Home page.* www.instructionaldesign.org/.

2. Dick, W., Carey, L., & Carey, J. O. (2005). *The systematic design of instruction, sixth edition.* Pearson/Allyn and Bacon.

3. Rossett, A., & Sheldon, K. (2001). *Beyond the podium: Delivering training and performance in a digital world.* Jossey-Bass/Pfeiffer.

4. Del Val, J. L., Campos, A., & Garaizar, P. (2010). *LMS and Web 2.0 tools for e-learning: University of Deusto's experience taking advantage of both.* Paper presented at the IEEE Conference, Madrid, Spain.

5. Bredfeldt, C., Awad, E., Joseph, K., & Snyder, M. (2013). Training providers: Beyond the basics of electronic health records. *BMC Health Services Research, 2*(13), 503.

6. Gagne, R., Briggs, L., & Wagner, W. (1985). *Principles of instructional design.* Wadsworth.

7. Cook, D. A., Levinson, A. J., & Garside, S. (2010). Time and learning efficiency in Internet-based learning: A systematic review and meta-analysis. *Advances in Health Sciences Education, 15,* 755–770.

8. Knowles, M. (1975). *Self-directed learning: A guide for learners and teachers.* Association Press.

9. Walsh, K. (2014). The future of e-learning in healthcare professional education: Some possible directions. *BMJ Learning, 50*(4), 309–310. Accessed on May 18, 2016, from www.scielosp.org/pdf/aiss/v50n4/02.pdf.

10. Chen, Y. T., Chen, T. J., & Tsai, L. Y. (2011). Development and evaluation of multimedia reciprocal representation instructional materials. *International Journal of Physical Sciences, 6,* 1431–1439.

11. Lewis, K. O., Baker, R. C., & Britigan, D. H. (2011). Current practices and needs assessment of instructors in an online master's degree in education for healthcare professionals: A first step to the development of quality standards. *Journal of Interactive Online Learning, 10,* 49–63.

12. Pinheiro, M., & Simoes, D. (2012). Constructing knowledge: An experience of active and collaborative learning in ICT classrooms. *Turkish Online Journal of Educational Technology, 11*(4), 382–389.

13. Chan, C. H., & Robbins, L. I. (2006). E-learning systems: Promises and pitfalls. *Academic Psychiatry, 30,* 491–497.

14. Bower, M. (2015). *A typology of Web 2.0 learning technologies.* Educause. Accessed on May 18, 2016, from https://library.educause.edu/~/media/files/library/2015/2/csd6280-pdf.pdf.

15. Amgad, M., & AlFaar, A. S. (2014). Integrating Web 2.0 in clinical research education in a developing country. *Journal of Cancer Education, 29*(3), 536–540.

PART IV

16. Lau, A.S.M. (2011). Hospital-based nurses' perceptions of the adoption of Web 2.0 tools for knowledge sharing, learning, social interaction and the production of collective intelligence. *Journal of Medical Internet Research, 13*(4), e92.

17. MindTools.com. (2011). *Understanding communication skills.* Accessed on March 5, 2017, from www.mindtools.com/CommSkll/CommunicationIntro.htm.

18. Kirkpatrick, D. L., & Kirkpatrick, J. D. (2006). *Evaluating training programs: The four levels, third edition.* Berrett-Koehler.

19. O'Neil, C., Fisher, C., & Rietschel, M. (2014). *Developing online learning environments in nursing education.* Springer.

20. Foreman, S. (2013). The six proven steps for a successful LMS implementation. *Learning Solutions Magazine.* Accessed on May 18, 2016, from https://www .learningsolutionsmag.com/articles/1214/the-six-proven-steps-for-successful-lms-implementation-part-one.

21. Boggs, D. (2010). *SCORM/AICC standards used in web-based learning management systems.* Syberworks.

22. Advanced Distributed Learning. (2004). *SCORM 2004, fourth edition.* Accessed on May 18, 2016, from https://www.adlnet.gov/adl-research/scorm/scorm-2004-4th-edition/.

23. U.S. Department of Education, Office of Education Technology. (n.d.). *Learning: Engage and empower.* Accessed on March 5, 2017, from https://tech.ed.gov/netp/learning-engage-and-empower/.

24. Kerr, P. (2016). Adaptive learning. *ELT Journal, 70*(1), 88–93.

25. Guler, C., Kilic, E., & Cavus, H. (2014). A comparison of difficulties in instructional design processes: Mobile vs. desktop. *Computers in Human Behavior, 39*(C), 128–135.

26. Van Rooij, S. W. (2010). Project management in instructional design: ADDIE is not enough. *British Journal of Educational Technology, 41,* 852–864.

CHAPTER 22

Using Healthcare IT to Measure and Improve Healthcare Quality and Outcomes

Floyd P. Eisenberg

In this chapter, you will learn how to

- Understand the structure and components of a quality measure to help implement the components in electronic health records (EHRs)
- Determine whether there is sufficient precision in a quality measure definition to implement it in an EHR and obtain consistent results
- Consider clinical workflow to capture and manage data in an EHR for use in clinical decision support or quality measure reporting
- Identify evolving standards used for electronic quality measurement

Why Measure Quality?

"If you cannot measure it, you cannot control it. If you cannot control it, you cannot manage it. If you cannot manage it, you cannot improve it."[1] But while the concept of measurement is not new,[2] the method to apply measurement to health and healthcare has evolved over the past few decades through work by many organizations (Table 22-1).

Though a goal of measurement is to help increase the consistency with which basic healthcare is delivered, studies have shown that care provided by different organizations or providers is not the same.[3, 4, 5] Many have turned to measurement to provide the forcing function to standardize and consistently apply care processes that evidence strongly suggests will improve patients' health. Using consensus standards will improve the ability to evaluate and compare the quality of care provided. That is why many government

Organization	Measurement Focus
The Joint Commission[6]	Core measures of hospital quality[7]
The National Committee for Quality Assurance (NCQA)	Healthcare Effectiveness Data and Information Set (HEDIS) to evaluate care quality for people covered by healthcare plans[8]
American Medical Association convened Physician Consortium for Performance Improvement (PCPI™)	Quality measures for clinical practice, primary care, and specialty[9]
National Quality Forum (NQF)[10]	Measure endorsement using a formal consensus development process (CDP) to carefully evaluate and endorse consensus standards, including performance measures, best practices, frameworks, and reporting guidelines[11]

Table 22-1 Some Quality Measurement Organizations

programs use NQF-endorsed measures to evaluate their network of providers. NQF is a not-for-profit, membership-based organization that works to increase healthcare value, make patient care safer, and achieve better outcomes. Among other things, NQF is a consensus–standards setting organization for healthcare quality. As such, NQF helps healthcare quality measure developers—which are often healthcare professional societies/organizations like the American Medical Association (AMA) and the American Nurses Association (ANA)—create feasibly measurable, broad-based, and impactful measures of healthcare quality. Actually, anyone or any organization defining how to quantify healthcare performance and outcomes is a measure developer. NQF provides the rigorous consensus process to substantiate that measures it endorses are impactful, reliable, valid, feasible, and useful. In the next section, we'll jump right into some considerations that healthcare quality developers might have when they are working to develop healthcare quality measures that come from clinicians' normal daily use of electronic health records (EHRs). We'll then use that practical foundation in exploring other aspects of healthcare electronic quality measurement.

Defining Quality Measures for EHR Queries

Let's get started by going through two example measures to explain the kind of detail needed to ask a question of an EHR. The EHR is primarily a database. It will provide data only if you ask in a way it can understand. And if the question is somewhat ambiguous, so will be the answer, if an answer is possible at all. To start, refer to Table 22-2 for a list of measure components.

While we walked through some basic information about patients and how to specify the measure, it is important to note that some information needed may be stored outside the EHR in the form needed. One example is a cancer (oncology) diagnosis that includes staging criteria. The laboratory pathology database may contain structured information about the diagnosis, the number of lymph nodes, and the known location of metastases

Component	Description
Initial population	All patients who share a common set of specified characteristics. The measure can focus on all events (e.g., procedures or patient encounters) rather than individual patients. In the latter case, "population" can also refer to events. For example, the focus of the measure may be all coronary artery bypass procedures to evaluate the outcome of each. In that case, any patient with more than one procedure would be included more than once because the focus is on the procedure rather than the patient.
Denominator	May be identical to the initial population or a subset of it to further specify the purpose of the electronic quality measure (or eMeasure).
Denominator exclusions	Information about the patients or events that should be removed from the eMeasure population and denominator. These are generally used to remove patients who were excluded from the research studies, and also clinical guidelines. Exclusions are used to be sure the measure evaluates only those patients for whom the information in the numerator should apply, based on the available evidence.
Numerator	The interventions (processes) that are expected or the outcome that is expected, based on the evidence, for all members of the denominator.
Denominator exceptions	Some measures remove patients or events from the denominator only if the numerator interventions or outcomes are not met. These exceptions are used to allow providers to exercise clinical judgment and make decisions about care individually for each patient in cases that do not meet the strict requirements of the guideline on which the measure is based. Denominator exceptions allow for adjustment of the calculated score for those providers with higher-risk populations. This measure component is not universally accepted by all measure developers. It is included here so you understand its purpose.
Measure population	Used only in continuous variable measures because they do not have a denominator or numerator. This component defines the patients or events that are evaluated by the measure.
Measure observations	Used only in continuous variable measures. This component describes how the individual results are to be compared. The most common comparisons are count, average (mean), and median.

Table 22-2   Quality Measure Structure

(where the cancer has spread), each in separate fields. However, that information is often present in a narrative text report (or as an image in a PDF format) in an EHR database and, therefore, such details may be difficult to extract directly from the EHR. Another example is a cardiac left ventricular ejection fraction, a measurement of the amount of blood pumped out of the left ventricle with each contraction of the heart. A cardiac catheterization laboratory database or the radiology department's cardiac ultrasound database may store such information in discrete, structured fields. However, the report stored in the EHR may present the information in a narrative text report or as an image in PDF format, limiting the ability to extract the information directly. Measure developers need to evaluate the preferred sources of data and assure they are available in determining the feasibility of their measures.

Use Case 22-1: Defining a Quality Measure, Example 1

Request: Identify all children with normal blood pressure.

Let's assume we are working for the measure developer in this case. We need to break down the question into its component parts to be sure the EHR provides the right information to calculate the result. The first question is, "What is the time period of interest?" To clarify, we can state this:

Population: All children seen during the calendar year 2016.

Now the time period is clear, but we need to be specific about which children—all of those living in the city, all of those insured by a local health plan, or all of those seen at least twice in the office practice. We will choose the last group because it is something the EHR can find for us.

Population: All children seen in the office at least twice during the calendar year 2016.

Getting a bit deeper in the review, we find that the EHR doesn't identify people as "children" or "not children." So, we need to define what we mean by the term. We generally want to use a common definition, so we will add the following:

Population: All people who are 18 or younger as of the day prior to the calendar year 2016 and who are seen in the office at least twice during the same year.

Now we are pretty sure we know those of interest to the measure. This population is our denominator; the group we will evaluate. But now we find that providers don't record blood pressure as "normal blood pressure" or "abnormal blood pressure." Rather, they measure and record every blood pressure as two values: the *systolic* (the pressure when the heart is beating) and the *diastolic* (the pressure when the heart is resting between beats). An example of a blood pressure reading, measured in millimeters of mercury (mmHg), would be recorded as 118/74; the first, higher number is the systolic reading, and the second, lower number is the diastolic reading. So, now it is important to define what level of blood pressure is considered "normal." We were asked to create the measure because there is a set of charts available based on evidence that the National Heart, Lung, and Blood Institute (NHLBI) published to define what is "normal."[12]

 TIP Reliable sources of evidence are those produced by government agencies and specialty organizations.

Using those charts, a provider can compare any given child's height, sex, and age to find how that child compares to other children in the United States. The result is a percentile rank. Children in the ninety-fifth percentile or higher for systolic blood pressure are considered to have *hypertension* (their systolic blood pressure is higher than 95 percent of all children). Those children ranking between the ninetieth and ninety-fifth percentiles are considered to have *prehypertension*, and all those ranking less than the ninetieth percentile are considered to have *normal* blood pressure. So, now we have a definition, and we can state our measure as follows:

Population (denominator): All people who are 18 or younger as of the day prior to the calendar year 2016 and who are seen in the office at least twice during the same year.

Numerator: All people in the population (denominator) whose systolic blood pressure is less than the ninetieth percentile based on age, sex, and height according to the NHLBI blood pressure tables.

Our measure is now specific, but there are still two missing facts that will give different results to those who try to use it. First, children seen during a calendar year have several blood pressure readings. Which reading is the one we want the EHR to report: the first, the most recent, or an average of all systolic blood pressure readings? We decide that the most recent systolic blood pressure reading is best for our measure. When we measure at the end of the year, the most recent will be the last reading during that year, whenever it happened.

Population (denominator): All people who are 18 or younger as of the day prior to the calendar year 2016 and who are seen in the office at least twice during the same year.

Numerator: All people in the population (denominator) whose most recent systolic blood pressure is less than the ninetieth percentile based on age, sex, and height according to the NHLBI blood pressure tables.

Now for the second missing fact: most providers don't record the percentile rank for systolic blood pressure when recording blood pressure values. The EHRs do have fields for systolic blood pressure, height, sex, and birth date, so all are available to compare to the NHLBI charts and find a percentile rank. However, the information will not be available as a field in the EHR unless the EHR automatically calculates it or providers routinely record it manually. The measure would need to ask for all data required (the birth date, the sex, the most recent height, and the most recent systolic blood pressure) and provide the NHLBI charts with a string of code that any EHR can read to perform the calculation for reporting. Alternatively, EHR products could provide the feature as a standard component, but since that is not a consistent EHR process, we can't rely on it for our measure. That is why many measures rely on information that can be expected in existing EHR products.

Based on the information we just reviewed, we now tell our measure developer that we have two options. The first is to encourage better standard use of EHRs and work with some EHR vendors to include pediatric blood pressure percentile ranking because it adds value to clinical care. Our second option is to abandon the measure or look for other information that might support our needs. For this hypothetical case, we will take the first option and work with some vendors to develop best practices (evidence) and encourage other vendors and providers to follow their example.

PART IV

Use Case 22-2: Defining a Quality Measure, Example 2

Request: Identify all adults who have diabetes and whose condition is controlled over time.

Let's again assume we are working for the measure developer in this case. Just like in the first case, we need to break down the measure into its component parts to be sure the EHR provides the right information to calculate the result. The first question is, "What is the time period of interest?" To clarify, we can state the following:

Population: All adults with diabetes seen during the calendar year 2016.

Now the time period is clear, but we need to be specific about which patients—all of those living in the city, all of those insured by a local health plan, or all of those seen at least twice in the office practice. So, we will choose the last group because it is something the EHR can find for us.

Population: All adults with diabetes seen in the office at least twice during the calendar year 2016.

Getting a bit deeper in the review, we find that the EHR doesn't identify people as "adults" or "not adults." So, we need to define what we mean by the term. We generally want to use a common definition, so we will add the following:

Population: All people with diabetes who are at least 18 years of age on the first day of the calendar year 2016 and who are seen in the office at least twice during the same year.

Now we are pretty sure we know those of interest to the measure. We need to be clear, though, about what we mean by "diabetes." Are we comfortable that the presence of a diagnosis on the problem list is enough to find all diabetics? Or do we also want to find all patients who are receiving medications that are used to treat diabetes so we don't miss anyone? If we do that, we have to consider excluding any patients receiving such medications for reasons other than diabetes (e.g., those with a diagnosis of polycystic ovarian syndrome). We conclude for this example that the diagnosis on a patient's problem list is sufficient. This population is our denominator, the group in which we have interest.

Now we need to define what is meant by good control. Reviewing the evidence, we find that a blood test, hemoglobin A1c (HbA1c), is a good indicator of diabetes control over a period of several months. So, we have a way to measure blood glucose control. And we find several reports about what level of HbA1c should be used to decide whether that control is *good.* So, we ask a panel of experts to convene and conclude which level should be used in the measure so that the measure identifies patients who are well controlled but is not set so low that that it might lead to possible harm, or *unintended consequences.* By setting the level too low, we could find that some providers manage their patients too strictly so they perform well on the measure but that strict management causes some patients to have significant side effects and harm from blood sugars that are too low. Remember, any decisions we make in this example are presented only as examples for this hypothetical case. Panels of experts will come to different conclusions than those presented here, but the example is included to show the real concerns measure developers deal with every day.

Now, based on our review, we decide not to look for a specific value of HgA1c to determine good control. Instead, we decide to look for patients who have results that most agree are out of control (HgA1c values greater than or equal to 9) and who improve over time.

Population (denominator): All people with diabetes who are at least 18 years of age on the first day of the calendar year 2016 and who are seen in the office at least twice during the same year.

Numerator: All patients in the denominator with HgA1c values >= 9 who improve their control during the measurement year.

Now we are a bit clearer, but we still haven't noted what is meant by improvement. So, we specify that improvement should be a change in the HgA1c result of at least 1. But we also need to define over what time frame that improvement should be expected. Based on the nature of the test we are using to determine control or lack of control, we conclude that there should be at least a six-month interval between the tests. That means that only patients whose first test was performed between January and June will qualify for the measure, and we realize we need to add to our denominator. We also decide (again for this example) that a second HgA1c test should be expected for all patients not in control during the measurement year.

Population (denominator): All people with diabetes who are at least 18 years of age on the first day of the calendar year 2016 and who are seen in the office at least twice during the same year and who have HgA1c results obtained in the first six months of the year with a result of >= 9.

Numerator: All patients in the denominator with HgA1c values >= 9 who have a second HgA1c result obtained at least six months after the first that occurs during the measurement year and whose HgA1c value is less than the initial value by at least 1.

This is a bit more complex than our first example. Now we need to figure out how to tell the EHR to find the two values and to calculate the difference. Providers don't routinely document change over time in any standard way, but EHRs do capture results. So, we define a measure element *delta* (change over time) and explain to the EHR from what data the change should be derived.

Population (denominator): All people with diabetes who are at least 18 years of age on the first day of the calendar year 2016 and who are seen in the office at least twice during the same year and who have HgA1c results obtained in the first six months of the year with a result of >= 9.

Numerator: All patients in the denominator with HgA1c values >= 9 who have an HgA1c delta of >=1 derived from the first HgA1c result during the measurement year and the most recent HgA1c result that was performed at least six months after the first, and both must occur during the measurement year.

Now the EHR vendor and provider are clearer about exactly what we want to be reported.

 TIP For questions about the specific elements used in a quality measure, go directly to the developer of the measure to clarify anything that seems ambiguous.

What Makes a Quality Measure Worth Measuring?

It is important to avoid measuring for the sake of measurement—that is, to avoid the inclination to measure merely because it is in vogue. Measurement should be based on an established need to change the status quo (e.g., insufficient care, too much care, unsafe care, or less than desirable outcomes) for which evidence shows that a change is effective. Evaluating evidence of processes that work requires some basic understanding of research and how such research is used to recommend guidelines for clinical practice. A research study is a process that records information (data) for a group of people to answer questions about a healthcare problem.[13] Definitions of types of studies used to evaluate evidence for measurement are available from the Agency for Healthcare Research and Quality (AHRQ) and the National Cancer Institute (NCI).[13, 14]

Evidence-Based Clinical Practice Guidelines

Medical specialty societies, government agencies, and other organizations develop clinical practice guidelines intended to help providers and patients directly apply the findings of the research into the care patients receive.[15] Because clinical studies often carefully select patients for evaluation, the guidelines developed from them generally are careful to recommend treatments only to patients who are similar to those evaluated in the studies. Those patients who are similar to those in the clinical studies are generally *included*. That means a guideline based on a study of treatment for a specific disease in patients younger than 65 might apply only to patients 65 and younger. Patients older than 65 may be excluded. Criteria such as gender, age, type of disease being treated, previous treatments, and other medical conditions can be used as inclusion or exclusion criteria.[16] It has become increasingly common for clinical practice guidelines to carefully evaluate the strength of the evidence for each recommendation (based on the number and types of research studies) and to grade the recommendations. A carefully developed evaluation and grading method was developed and is maintained by the U.S. Preventive Services Task Force (USPSTF). The USPSTF assigns letter grades to its recommendations (A, B, C, D, and I). An "A" recommendation has the strongest support, and "D" is not supported; "I" is inconclusive.[16] The USPSTF further ranks the certainty (the level of evidence) as high, moderate, or low. Many medical specialty societies and other clinical guideline developers use the same or modified grading for their recommendations to help providers and patients decide how to apply the guidelines to their own care.

Clinical practice guidelines have been available for some time. A good source for established clinical practice guidelines is the Agency for Healthcare Research and Quality (AHRQ) National Guideline Clearinghouse.[17] But changing practice based on the research and the guidelines does not happen automatically. Translating research into practice can take up to two decades.[18] Even with good evidence and clinical practice guidelines, a large percentage of people in the United States were still not receiving routine preventive services in 2003.[19] For that reason, many have put their hopes in the electronic health record to help turn the tide and deliver the right care at the right time. EHRs provide the opportunity to influence the provider's behavior at the time they interact with it to enter or retrieve information. Actions designed to provide that influence are often called *clinical decision support* (CDS). Much has been written about CDS, and you can refer to Chapter 19 for an introduction and to other sources for further details.[20]

What Is the Connection Between Clinical Decision Support and Quality Measurement?

It is important to note the direct connection between CDS, efforts to influence behavior at the right time within the process of care, and quality measurement that evaluates whether the expected services were provided or whether the patient's status improved as expected. For example, CDS helps to make sure a diabetic patient has a hemoglobin A1c (HbA1c) blood test to make sure their diabetes is controlled over time. After all is said and done, quality measurement evaluates whether the test was performed and whether the result shows good control of the patient's diabetes. Both rely on the same information: that the HbA1c blood test was ordered and processed by the clinical laboratory and that the result is available and in normal range. But each uses that information differently. If CDS determines the test was not performed or the result is out of range, it can be programmed to encourage the provider to order the test, or if the result is high, it can be programmed to take action to improve the patient's blood sugar control. The quality measure uses the same information to see, over time, what percentage of the provider's patients with diabetes had the test done and how many had results in normal range. Rule-based CDS relies on a *trigger or triggers* that activate a rule, *input data* that the rule uses to evaluate what needs to happen, a set of *interventions* the computer system can choose from to deliver information to the provider, and *action steps* delivered to the provider to recommend how to help the patient improve (Figure 22-1).

In summary, Figure 22-2 shows the close linkage between quality measures and clinical decision support. Both are driven by the same clinical knowledge. Each requires similar data, and each plays a role in evaluating clinical performance.

Figure 22-1
Clinical decision support requires four components: the triggers, input data, interventions, and action steps.[21]

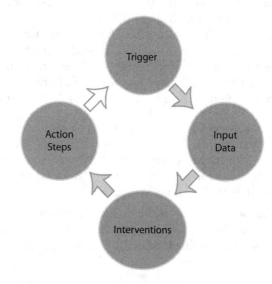

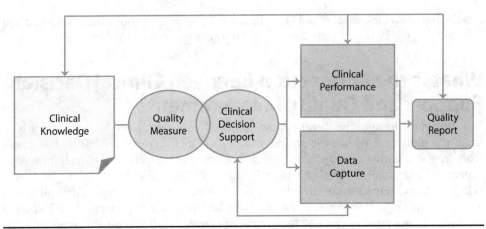

Figure 22-2 Relationship of clinical knowledge, CDS, and quality measures to encourage data capture and reuse to enhance clinical performance and report on quality processes and outcomes[21]

What Is the Measure of a Measure?

To ensure that measures meet the needs of those who use them, it is important to manage the quality, the impact, and the value of the information they produce. Regulatory and governmental organizations require the reporting of financial and clinical patient-level data for performance measurement. Some of these programs incorporate a pay-for-performance component such that healthcare organizations and clinicians are held accountable for their performance by variation in reimbursement.[22] The Affordable Care Act allows the Centers for Medicare and Medicaid Services (CMS) to develop new models of payment for care that share cost savings between CMS and the accountable-care organizations (ACOs). These payments are directly linked to the ACO's performance in quality measures that affect patient and caregiver experience of care, care coordination, patient safety, preventive health, and health provided for at-risk populations and the frail or elderly.[23] To ensure the measures used have the impact expected to support the ACO programs, a stringent process of review is needed. National Quality Forum (NQF) supports that need by using a formal consensus development process to endorse measures for quality performance and public reporting.[24] Criteria are summarized here, including importance to measure, scientific acceptability, usability, and feasibility:

- **Importance to measure and report** The extent to which the measure focus is important in order to make significant gains in healthcare quality (safety, timeliness, effectiveness, efficiency, equity, patient centeredness) and to improve health outcomes for a specific high-impact aspect of healthcare where there is variation in overall poor performance.

- **Scientific acceptability of the measure properties** The extent to which the results of the measure are consistent (reliable) and credible (valid) if it is implemented as specified. Scientific acceptability assessment includes reviewing reliability, validity, exclusion criteria, risk assessment strategy, scoring methods, the comparability of multiple data sources, and the methods to determine potential disparities in care provided. Also highly important is the extent to which those who will use the measure can understand the results and use them to make meaningful decisions (usability) and the extent to which the data required to compute the measure are readily available without undue burden and can be implemented (feasibility).

Endorsement evaluates the rigor of the measure. It is also important to select measures for use in individual programs that evaluate care provided. NQF convenes the Measure Application Partnership (MAP), a public-private partnership to providing input to the U.S. Department of Health and Human Services (HHS) about what performance measures it should select for public reporting and performance-based payment programs as required in the Affordable Care Act. The MAP is a comprehensive, multistakeholder group that includes input and comment from the public at large to share expertise on aspects of improving healthcare. Guided by the National Quality Strategy,[25] measures are recommended and provide input that addresses national healthcare priorities and goals, such as making care safer and ensuring that people and families are engaged as partners in their care.[26]

What Are the Types of Measures, and How Are They Different?

Measures can evaluate performance related to different aspects of health and healthcare. Several classification systems are available to describe measures. Donabedian defined three dimensions of quality that have become the backbone of how the industry defines measurement: structure, process, and outcomes.[27]

What Are the Expectations for the EHR to Perform Measurement?

The current process for measuring quality using EHRs is evolving. Most existing measures have not been written in a format to allow direct queries to EHRs to extract data. Much of the information needed to evaluate these existing measures is based on information from claims submitted for payment or from human abstractors who review medical records in detail to know whether the measure criteria are met. Some measures use clinical data included in claims attachments, specifically laboratory results and pharmacy-dispensing data. Using such *clinically enriched* claims information is a step forward for measurement, but it is not able to take advantage of the potentially rich information present in the EHR. So, to implement measures that describe clinical data, the process continues to use traditional manual methods to interpret the measure to evaluate available information. This effort can include medical record abstraction, natural-language processing methods to find information from unstructured (free text) fields in the EHR, or specific fields in the EHR for clinicians to enter the data using drop-down menus or check boxes.

Adding additional fields for clinician data entry is very costly. It takes significant time and effort, it increases the likelihood of incorrect entry of information, and it is not part of the patient care workflow, so it takes time away from caring for the patient. Using check boxes further limits the value of the data since the information is an interpretation of what should be captured directly as a result of the patient interaction, in other words, the provider's statement about that interaction or confirmation. For example, checking a box that the patient's systolic blood pressure is less than 140 mmHg makes the provider interpret a result already captured and attest it is correct. Capturing the result itself from the EHR as it is initially entered is preferred since it is more accurate and less prone to error. It also comes with the benefit of knowing more information about that result (metadata) such as the method used to obtain it and the date and time it was performed.

Some data can be captured only by checking a box (or performing a similar manual action) to confirm a process has occurred. A good example is medication reconciliation. *Medication reconciliation* is the process of reviewing the patient's complete medication regimen at the time of admission, transfer, and discharge and comparing it with the regimen being considered for the new setting of care to avoid duplication, to avoid inadvertently omitting critical medications, and to prevent avoidable interactions among the medications the patient is receiving.[28] However, there is no defined set of online clicks that has been determined to automatically know that a provider has reconciled a patient's medication lists. Therefore, the provider must attest that reconciliation has been performed and is complete by using some sort of check box or signature. Even attempts to reconfigure, or "retool," measures for the EHR platform used concepts intended for a manual abstraction or provider confirmation process. And the underlying standards (discussed in the next several sections) are still evolving to enable direct queries to an EHR database. So, there is still manual intervention required to use EHR data for measurement. Figure 22-3 shows a stylized process for implementing quality measures in EHRs as it exists today.

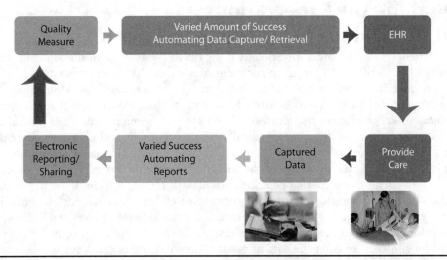

Figure 22-3   Implementing a quality measure in an EHR in 2016 still requires manual effort to interpret the measure and fit it into the provider's workflow in the EHR.

TIP   Ideally, information collected for measures that use EHRs as a data source should include only the data captured as a result of directly caring for patients and only the data that are important to the concurrent (day-to-day) care of the patient. Any request for additional data entry merely for the purpose of administrative or measurement processes will result in dissatisfaction among providers and also reduce the time available to interact with patients.

To resolve potential conflict between measure and clinical care requirements, measurement (i.e., queries to an electronic data source and/or EHR) should be defined using standard terminology and should address clinical workflow and context consistent with that used in the direct process care delivery. Clinical organizations and clinicians will be able to more clearly address quality performance through retrospective analysis and to develop clinical decision support interventions by using carefully defined query formats that are readable by both humans and computers.

There is much work in progress to evolve toward an automated process for measuring quality using electronic information from EHRs. The Centers for Medicare and Medicaid Services (CMS) has an Electronic Clinical Quality Improvement (eCQI) Resource Center that provides access to the most current activities in this area.[29] Another fundamentally important resource and organization for the important work of electronic clinical quality improvement, as well as other HIT standards efforts, is HL7, a HIT data standards organization. (Please see Chapter 8 for more information about HL7.) Much of this work originated in 2009 with the HL7 Draft Standard for Trial Use, the Health Quality Measure Format (HQMF). The current work uses an updated version of the HQMF (version 2.1) for the structure, or wrapper, that contains the measure; a data model, or grammar, called the Quality Data Model (QDM), to provide standard data definitions; and a standard grammar and structure to express the information required for the measure elements (Figure 22-4).[30] For each concept in the QDM, measure developers create value sets (lists of specific terms and codes that define clinical concepts from standard vocabularies). The QDM concept and the value set more clearly identify the information needed.

The National Library of Medicine (NLM) Value Set Authority Center (VSAC) provides measure developers with the tools to create value sets from standard vocabularies, keep them up-to-date, and share and reuse them.[31] The measure developer can then combine the QDM concepts with the value set to create phrases (also called phenotypes) they can use to construct a measure. The measure developer enters the resulting electronic clinical quality measure (eCQM) in the CMS Measure Authoring Tool (MAT), which constructs an HQMF file containing underlying XML code for use at practice sites (Figure 22-5).[32] The HL7 Clinical Quality Information Workgroup maintains the HQMF and an implementation guide for using it with the QDM (QDM-based HQMF Implementation Guide).[33] EHR software then implements the measure by extracting information from the measure-specific HQMF file, retrieving the data, and reports the results in a report file called the Quality Report Document Architecture (QRDA).

PART IV

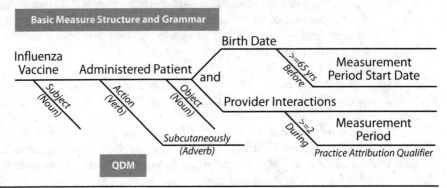

"All patients 65 years of age or older with at least two provider visits during the measurement period receiving influenza vaccine subcutaneously."

Basic Measure Structure and Grammar

Figure 22-4 Similar to diagramming a sentence, the QDM provides grammar to allow the developer of a measure to state what is needed in a consistent way.

QRDA has two versions—QRDA Category I allows reporting of a single patient's measurement data; QRDA Category III allows reporting of a summary report of all patients who meet measure criteria for a hospital or ambulatory provider. The initial intent was to create a middle tier, or Category II standard, to allow reporting detailed data for all patients who meet measure criteria but the detailed requirements were never fully defined.

 TIP The HQMF is the standard to incorporate eCQMs into the EHR.

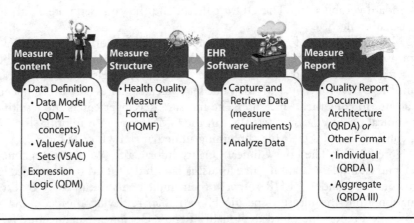

Figure 22-5 Measure development infrastructure—2016 version

What Changes Are Needed to Enable Electronic Clinical Quality Measures?

The initial implementation of eCQMs provides significant insight to decide what works and what needs to be modified. Several reports highlight challenges with implementing the first round of eCQMs.[34, 35, 36] Three main challenges are noted: measure focus, EHR readiness, and standards maturity.

Measure focus, the first challenge, has two components: legacy measure focus and overcomplexity. Measure focus previously addressed what was available: claims and paper or electronic chart data that could be abstracted manually. Unfortunately, the first round of eCQM development merely retooled or converted existing claims or abstraction-based legacy measures. This created expectations that providers would capture structured, discrete data that previously were extrapolated from other existing information and created excessive clinical workflow changes. It produced less reliable information captured so as to navigate through computer screens more quickly. Measures can also be overburdened by potentially unnecessary exclusions and complex measure logic because they are based on a different paradigm of data capture. Ideally, EHRs are not designed to replicate a paper process. They should be designed and implemented in combination with efforts to improve workflow and enhance a provider's ability to provide direct patient care. By re-engineering existing measure concepts and creating measures *de novo*, addressing information as captured during routine clinical care workflow, eCQM feasibility should increase.

The second challenge is EHR readiness. Much of the workflow included in clinical software has been designed to capture information, often replicating the paper documentation process. Addressing information capture without consideration for multiple uses often leads to information that must be reinterpreted or extracted from narrative text for subsequent analysis. While measure developers seek to take advantage of EHR data as a rich source of information, it is not necessarily safe to assume that EHRs consistently have data structured in a way that it can be easily used. In addition, more recent attention to clinical outcomes creates a need to capture structured information about changes in patient status. Previously, it was sufficient to indicate such information in narrative text assessment. As EHR and other clinical software improve mechanisms to capture data to improve clinical quality using CDS consistent with clinicians' workflow, more information will be available for performance analysis. Focus on these capabilities should increase with greater focus of CMS and insurers on paying for value rather than services provided (i.e., value-based purchasing).[37, 38, 39, 40]

The third challenge for eCQM development and implementation is standards maturity. The process used in 2016 is that it addresses measurement, but CDS activities use different standards and require a more computable expression language. The Office of the National Coordinator for Health Information Technology (ONC) established the Standards and Interoperability (S&I) Framework Clinical Quality Framework (CQF) initiative to merge, or harmonize, the measure development and CDS efforts and thus achieve a single method to improve and evaluate clinical performance.[41] Initiated in March 2014, the CQF efforts developed new standards to address clinical quality, combining the measure and CDS requirements, and shepherded them through HL7.

PART IV

These standards created a more operational data model, Quality Information and Clinical Knowledge (QUICK); a more readable expression language that is also computable, Clinical Quality Language (CQL); and a new structure to contain the logic expressions for both measurement and CDS, Clinical Reasoning. Clinical Reasoning is a component of a new HL7 initiative called Fast Healthcare Interoperability Resources (FHIR), which is developed based on information that 80 percent of EHRs can manage, reducing the complexity of previous versions of HL7 standards. These new standards (QUICK, CQL, FHIR) are in development and being used for pilot and demonstration projects at the time of this writing, but they have significant promise to provide simpler, more usable standards for sharing information for clinical care and for quality improvement.

As part of the transition to these standards, eCQMs intended for implementation in 2019 should be using the QDM data definitions with CQL logic while still using HQMF. Figure 22-6 depicts a future vision for the quality improvement infrastructure, managing the same information for measurement and CDS to enable performance improvement and determine what works and what needs adjustment.

Figure 22-6 demonstrates how measure developers in the future may use a harmonized data model that addresses needs for measurement and clinical decision support (QUICK) and values or value sets from VSAC. They will use CQL as a more human-readable method to express relationships of data elements to each other that can be interpreted by computers. They will enter the measure information in the Measure Authoring Tool (MAT), which produces a Clinical Reasoning file that provides CDS and measure content. EHR software will then coordinate clinical workflow to enable care improvement and data capture and retrieval, and analyze the data to report results using Clinical Reasoning reports (individual or aggregate).

Data Modeling: Example from the International Health Information Terminology Standards Development Organization

The International Health Information Terminology Standards Development Organization (IHTSDO) defines two methods of modeling.[42] A *model of meaning* represents the underlying meaning in a way that is common to and reusable between different use cases.

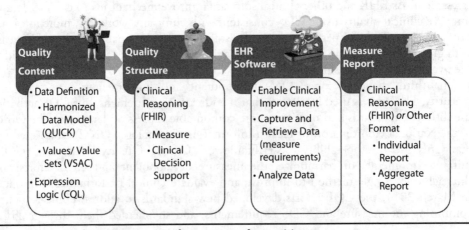

Figure 22-6 Quality improvement infrastructure—future vision

In contrast, a *model of use* structures information based on a specific intended use. If, in a hypothetical case, the intended use of a patient's blood pressure result is for a clinician to view it and make decisions, the information can be captured as text showing the systolic value over the diastolic value similar to an equation (e.g., 136/74). The data were captured and stored based on the use model that defined only a single result without the need for any specific structure. When the clinician decides it is important to follow the blood pressure over time and trend it on a graph, the EHR then needs to parse the result into its component parts and store the systolic value (136) as a number and the diastolic value (74) as a number, both of which are from the same reading.

The new use model requires trending over time, and so the data are now structured. If the original modeling were based on the intended meaning, the EHR vendor would have had to provide an enhanced display, but no change in the underlying data would have been required. Many EHRs managed data input based on use requirements determined at a point in time. Similarly, quality measurement was also based on the use model of human intervention (confirmation or chart abstraction). As both EHRs and measure developers look at achieving clinical outcomes, reuse of captured data becomes increasingly important. Restructuring the process of collecting data based on the data's meaning will enhance the potential for reusing information and reducing the need for redundant data entry and information restructuring and will enable less cumbersome clinical care, CDS, and quality measurement. In addition, the measurement infrastructure and data can itself be leveraged to encourage standardized data, coding, and tools across the healthcare continuum in a manner that has not yet been seen.

 TIP   This can occur through use of a standardized data model and standardized value sets.

How Are Value Sets Standardized?

Measures list data elements as criteria. To be sure those implementing the measures enter the right patients and the right information into the analysis, they must carefully explain what information from the clinical record is needed. For example, the term "blood pressure" seems specific, but as discussed earlier, blood pressure is actually a combination of two clinical findings: a *systolic* blood pressure (when the heart is contracting, or beating) and a *diastolic* blood pressure (when the heart is resting between beats). Each is measured at the same time. Blood pressure can also be taken at rest; during or after exercise; or in a lying, sitting, or standing position. Each of these qualifiers (metadata) about the blood pressure is important to understand how the finding should be used. So, a measure evaluating diastolic blood pressure to look for improvement needs to clearly indicate what is intended. There are several ways to state what is meant.

- Diastolic blood pressure (qualifier: resting; position: sitting)
- Resting diastolic blood pressure (position: sitting)
- Sitting, resting diastolic blood pressure

The first example uses a basic concept, diastolic blood pressure, and separately describes the attributes, or metadata, required—resting and sitting. It can be stated to *post-coordinate* an expression, breaking it down into its component parts, each of which has a concept in available code systems (e.g., Systematized Nomenclature of Medicine—Clinical Terms, SNOMED-CT).[43] The next example *pre-coordinates* the concept (i.e., suggest a single concept that incorporates all metadata into one code).

Traditionally, measures have used claims codes to specify which values are acceptable for each data element in their measures. This method has been successful when capturing data from claims, but it is more challenging when looking for information captured during a clinical interaction between a provider and a patient. Claims codes provide general information, but they do not allow clinicians to express what is needed to provide direct care. For example, the provider may want to indicate a specific interaction with the patient through e-mail exchange. The coding system used for most encounter- and procedure-related claims is Clinical Procedural Terminology (CPT),[44] which includes a code for an evaluation/management visit for an established patient at different levels of intensity. To accommodate e-mail exchange, CPT added a code, but interactions between other clinicians and patients are not clearly expressed in CPT. A clinical terminology such as SNOMED-CT allows more expression of additional interactions.

As EHRs and quality measures together require more clinical data for evaluation and trending, the use of SNOMED-CT is expected to become prevalent. It is also expected that the information in the EHR will need to be mapped to claims-related code systems for billing purposes. While EHRs may capture the information at the level of detail indicated, they do not consistently store it as a post-coordinated expression. Therefore, collaboration between measure developers and EHR vendors and implementers will be important to resolve potential conflicts.

The terms, or values, used to clearly explain each data element are called a *value set*. A value set is a set of codes derived from a particular code system, or *taxonomy*.[45] For the previous example, all of the codes for diastolic blood pressure would be included in one value set. Value sets are not static. The code systems from which the values are derived update on a regular basis, retiring some concepts and adding new ones. Therefore, value sets need to be maintained and versioned over time. A clear understanding of the code system used is also critical to be sure the values selected for a value set are complete and correct. To encourage greater consistency, the NLM Value Set Authority Center provides measure developers with access to code systems that allow them to develop and share valid, complete, and reusable value sets.[31] The NLM VSAC also curates the value sets to be sure the code system is used as intended and also assists with harmonization of concepts among measure developers to avoid duplication of value sets. The VASC recommends code systems based on recommendations of the Health Information Technology Standards Committee and Policy Committee.[46]

Moving Forward: Retooling vs. Creating Measures de Novo Based on Data in EHRs

Creating measures de novo based on data in EHRs will take a collaborative effort among measure developers, EHR vendors, data warehouse third-party providers, frontline clinicians, and also patients. The essential issue is to provide the appropriate meaning by asking for the information actually needed from the appropriate individual (e.g., ask for information about education provided by asking the patient if the expected information was learned, as compared to asking the provider to use a check box).

Chapter Review

This chapter discussed some of the challenges inherent in using EHRs to manage data intelligently so that data can be entered once as part of the workflow for usual patient care and reused to improve the care process concurrently with clinical decision support and retrospectively by measuring quality. The change from capturing and reporting information based on a model of use to a model of meaning is not easy, but it has the potential to significantly increase timeliness, efficiency, effectiveness, and safety while reducing redundancy. A consistent model to express information within and among systems is important to enable clear understanding. The Quality Data Model (QDM) provides an initial common technological framework for defining the clinical data necessary to measure performance and accelerate improvement in patients' quality of care.[30] By providing a common grammar to describe the information within quality measures, the QDM enables quality measurement from a variety of electronic sources, and it is applicable to all care settings a patient is likely to interact with in a lifetime. The structure of the QDM describes a data element as the combination of a category of information, the context in which it is used (the state), and specific attributes, or metadata, that help clarify exactly what is needed to evaluate the measure.

Here are the general steps an eCQM developer undergoes:

1. Measure developers decide on the information needed for the measure.

2. The developers use the QDM grammar to describe the category and state (or context) that is acceptable to meet their needs and any related information (attributes).

3. The developers select from existing value sets or create new value sets to indicate the information they need (e.g., the specific medications) using the NLM VSAC. The NLM VSAC provides tools and curation to develop value sets and keeps them current.

4. The developers combine the newly developed data elements with their value sets into phrases that describe more detail about the information needed (e.g., medications administered within one hour before the start of a surgical procedure).

5. The developers combine the phrases into components of the measure (e.g., denominator, numerator). The QDM provides the backbone structure to help those who read the measure to understand clearly what is meant in each measure statement or phrase. The purpose of this process is to let those implementing measures look for the data that is structured in the EHR and report the same information regardless of the EHR product used in each practice or hospital.

PART IV

This chapter described a combination of efforts to move toward a fully implementable query to measure the quality of care from an EHR. Efforts include a common data model (QDM), the NLM VSAC to standardize and curate value sets, the S&I Framework Clinical Quality Framework to harmonize standards for quality measurement and clinical decision support moving forward, and HL7 to improve existing standards and establish newer standards that can be more easily processed by EHRs and other clinical software. These activities will lead to infrastructure to enable the end-to-end processing of data for measurement. But change requires more than infrastructure. The most effective way to accelerate the movement to fully electronic measurement is through collaboration. Measure developers are increasingly working with EHR vendors and individual practices and hospitals to evaluate feasibility as they develop eCQMs and to test the measures once they are complete. Other efforts, such as the Clinical Quality Framework, enable pilots and demonstration projects using new standards to improve quality through CDS and performance measurement. Development of new, harmonized standards should improve the ability to manage quality from the standpoint of CDS as well as measurement and reporting. You can follow such efforts at the eCQI Resource Center (http://eCQI.healthit.gov).[29]

Questions

To test your comprehension of the chapter, answer the following questions and then check your answers against the list of correct answers at the end of the chapter.

1. What is a value set?

   A. A range of numbers that are normal results for laboratory tests

   B. A set of codes chosen by a measure developer to define a data element in a measure

   C. The relative strength of recommendations as supported by evidence for the interventions expected in a quality measure

   D. The combination of a measure's validity, reliability, and feasibility that describes its potential use in value-based purchasing programs

2. The chief medical officer of your organization asks you to set up a measure for his research study for all of his patients with high blood pressure whose blood pressure improves after six months, regardless of treatment given. How do you define high blood pressure?

   A. Systolic blood pressure of <120 mmHg as you found at the National Heart, Lung, and Blood Institute web site.

   B. Diastolic blood pressure of <80 mmHg as you found at the National Heart, Lung, and Blood Institute web site.

   C. Blood pressure less than the ninetieth percentile by height, age, and gender per the National Heart, Lung, and Blood Institute web site.

   D. You don't have enough information to proceed and thus ask the CMO for more clarity.

3. You are asked to measure how often doctors in your network evaluate a newborn baby's home environment for factors that might put them at risk. The factors include lead paint in the home; if the baby's mother has been screened for postpartum depression; if she has been screened and tested positive and is under treatment; and if there are pets in the home. You cannot find specific fields in your EHR for each of these items. What actions do you take?

   A. Immediately add fields to the EHR patient demographic section for Yes/No/Not Applicable responses to (1) lead paint in the home, (2) mother screened for depression, (3) if depressed mother is on treatment, and (4) pets in the home.

   B. Request input from an appropriate group of practicing clinicians to determine the workflow to capture and evaluate such information and implement a solution consistent with existing best practice to which the majority agree.

   C. Immediately add fields to the EHR patient demographic section for Yes/No/Not Applicable responses to (1) lead paint in the home and (2) pets in the home, and you look in the family history section of the EHR for evidence of depression in the mother.

   D. Search the literature to find a screening tool shown to work for another organization and implement it directly in your EHR.

4. Which of the following is the acronym for the standard used to structure the format of an eCQM?

   A. QRDA

   B. Consolidated CDA

   C. HQMF

   D. S&I Framework

5. What is a preferred method for creating an eCQM for use in a clinical setting?

   A. Scour the literature, find a clinical guideline, develop value sets and create the measure using QDM in the Measure Authoring Tool, then pilot the measure in a clinical setting.

   B. Identify the clinical outcomes most significant to the patient population seen by your organization, meet with local clinical experts to evaluate best practices to achieve those outcomes, incorporate capturing the required data as part of routine clinical workflow and assure it works, then prototype the measure for review prior to entering it into the Measure Authoring Tool for testing.

   C. Identify the clinical outcomes most significant to the patient population seen by your organization, meet with local clinical experts to select the most relevant clinical guideline, identify existing value sets in VSAC and create new ones as needed, then enter the measure into the Measure Authoring Tool for testing and modification of clinical workflow.

   D. Select a measure that already exists and consider how to adjust local clinical workflow to capture the required data, retrieve it, and measure.

PART IV

6. What are three dimensions of quality defined by Donabedian that have become the backbone of how the industry defines measurement?

   A. Performance, quality, and risks

   B. Performance, risks, and security

   C. Structure, outcomes, and risks

   D. Structure, process, and outcomes

7. Which agency of the government has the Value Set Authority Center (VSAC)?

   A. AHRQ

   B. NLM

   C. FDA

   D. CMS

8. Which standards organization developed the Health Quality Measure Format?

   A. The ONC Standards Committee

   B. ANSI

   C. NCQF

   D. HL7

Answers

1. **B.** A value set is a set of codes chosen by a measure developer to define a data element in a measure.

2. **D.** You don't have enough information to proceed and ask for more clarity. Measures require precise definition and often require inclusion and exclusion criteria. The information provided by the chief medical officer was not precise as to the definition of blood pressure and high blood pressure is age dependent.

3. **B.** Request input from an appropriate group of practicing clinicians to determine the workflow to capture and evaluate such information and implement a solution consistent with existing best practice to which the majority agree. Adding additional fields to "hardwire" a solution has the potential for causing dissatisfaction and adding additional burden to the clinician's workflow without adding substantial benefit. Using fields intended for a different purpose (e.g., family history to determine whether the child's mother is currently depressed) can lead to finding inaccurate information to support clinical decisions or measure reports. If the information is relevant to the active management of the patient's care, there is opportunity to configure the EHR and the workflow efficiently.

4. **C.** The standard to write an eMeasure is HQMF, the Healthcare Quality Measure Format, an HL7 standard.

5. B. The most preferred method for creating an eCQM is to identify the clinical outcomes most significant to the patient population seen by your organization, meet with local clinical experts to evaluate best practices to achieve those outcomes, incorporate capturing the required data as part of routine clinical workflow and assure it works, then prototype the measure for review prior to entering it into the Measure Authoring Tool for testing.

6. D. The three dimensions of quality defined by Donabedian that have become the backbone of how the industry defines measurement are structure, process, and outcomes.

7. B. The Value Set Authority Center (VSAC) is in the National Library of Medicine (NLM).

8. D. HL7 is the standards organization that developed the Health Quality Measure Format (HQMF).

References

1. Harrington, H. J. (1991). *Business process improvement: The breakthrough strategy for total quality, productivity, and competitiveness.* McGraw-Hill.

2. ASQ: Global Voice of Quality. (n.d.). *History of quality.* Accessed on September 10, 2016, from http://asq.org/learn-about-quality/history-of-quality/overview/overview.html.

3. Chassin, M. R. (2002). Achieving and sustaining improved quality: Lessons from New York State and cardiac surgery. *Health Affairs, 21*(4), 40–51. Accessed on September 10, 2016, from http://content.healthaffairs.org/content/21/4/40.long.

4. California Health Care Foundation. (2003). *Variations in healthcare quality: Racial, ethnic, and economic disparities in Medicare fee-for-service in California.* Accessed on September 10, 2016, from www.chcf.org/publications/2003/07/variations-in-health-care-quality-racial-ethnic-and-economic-disparities-in-medicare-feeforservice-in-california.

5. Dartmouth Atlas of Healthcare. (2016). *Home page.* Accessed on September 10, 2016, from www.dartmouthatlas.org/.

6. The Joint Commission. (2016). *About the Joint Commission.* Accessed on September 10, 2016, from https://www.jointcommission.org/about_us/about_the_joint_commission_main.aspx.

7. The Joint Commission. (2016). *Performance measurement.* Accessed on September 10, 2016, from https://www.jointcommission.org/performance_measurement.aspx.

8. National Committee for Quality Assurance. (n.d.). *HEDIS® and performance measurement.* Accessed on September 10, 2016, from www.ncqa.org/hedis-quality-measurement.

PART IV

9. PCPI. (n.d.). *Welcome to PCPI*. Accessed on September 10, 2016, from www .thepcpi.org/.

10. National Quality Forum. (2016). *Home page*. Accessed on September 10, 2016, from www.qualityforum.org.

11. National Quality Forum. (2012). *Consensus development process*. Accessed on September 10, 2016, from www.qualityforum.org/Measuring_Performance/ Consensus_Development_Process.aspx.

12. National Heart, Lung, and Blood Institute. (2008). *High blood pressure*. Accessed on September 10, 2016, from www.nhlbi.nih.gov/health-pro/guidelines/current/ cardiovascular-health-pediatric-guidelines/full-report-chapter-8.

13. Agency for Healthcare Research and Quality. (2012). *Glossary of terms*. Accessed on September 10, 2016, from www.ahrq.gov/patients-consumers/patient- involvement/healthy-men/glossary/index.html.

14. National Cancer Institute, National Institutes of Health. (2015). *NCI dictionary of cancer terms*. Accessed on September 10, 2016, from https://www.cancer.gov/ publications/dictionaries/cancer-terms.

15. Field, M. J., & Lohr, K. N. (Eds.). (1990). *Clinical practice guidelines: Directions for a new program*. Institute of Medicine. National Academies Press.

16. U.S. Preventive Services Task Force (USPSTF). (2012). *Grade definitions after July 2012*. Accessed on September 10, 2016, from https://www .uspreventiveservicestaskforce.org/Page/Name/grade-definitions.

17. Agency for Healthcare Research and Quality. (2016). *National Guideline Clearinghouse*. Accessed on September 10, 2016, from https://guideline.gov/.

18. Agency for Healthcare Research and Quality. (2001). *Translating research into practice (TRIP)-II*. Accessed on September 10, 2016, from https://archive.ahrq .gov/research/findings/factsheets/translating/tripfac/trip2fac.html.

19. McGlynn, E. A., Asch, S. M., Adams, J., Keesey, J., Hicks, J., DeCristofaro, A., & Kerr, E. A. (2003). The quality of healthcare delivered to adults in the United States. *New England Journal of Medicine, 348*(26), 2635–2645.

20. For a general overview of clinical decision support: Osheroff, J. A., Teich, J. M., Middleton, B., Steen, E. B., Wright, A., & Detmer, D. E. (2007). A roadmap for national action on clinical decision support. *Journal of the American Medical Informatics Association, 14*(2), 141–145; *and* Osheroff, J. A., Teich, J. M., Levick, D., Saldana, L., Velasco, F., Sittig, D., … Jenders, R. (2012). *Improving outcomes with clinical decision support: An implementer's guide, second edition*. HIMSS.

21. National Quality Forum. (2010). *Driving quality and performance measurement: A foundation for clinical decision support—A consensus report*. Accessed on September 10, 2016, from www.qualityforum.org/Publications/2010/12/ Driving_Quality_and_Performance_Measurement_-_A_Foundation_for_ Clinical_Decision_Support.aspx.

22. Agency for Healthcare Quality and Research. (2014). *Setting performance targets in pay for performance programmes: What can we learn from QOF?* Accessed on September 10, 2016, from https://archive.ahrq.gov/news/newsroom/articles-of-interest/20140418.html.

23. HealthCare.gov. (2012). *Accountable care organization (ACO).* Accessed on September 10, 2016, from https://www.cms.gov/Medicare/Medicare-Fee-for-Service-Payment/ACO/index.html.

24. National Quality Forum. (2016). *Consensus development process.* Accessed on September 10, 2016, from www.qualityforum.org/Measuring_Performance/Consensus_Development_Process.aspx.

25. Agency for Healthcare Research and Quality. (2016). *The national quality strategy.* Accessed on September 10, 2016, from https://www.ahrq.gov/workingforquality/.

26. National Quality Forum. (2012). *Measure application partnership.* Accessed on September 10, 2016, from www.qualityforum.org/setting_priorities/partnership/measure_applications_partnership.aspx.

27. Donabedian, A. (2005). Evaluating the quality of medical care. *Milbank Quarterly, 83*(4), 691–729.

28. Agency for Healthcare Research and Quality. (2012). *Patient safety primers: Medication reconciliation.* Accessed on September 10, 2016, from https://psnet.ahrq.gov/primers/primer/1.

29. Centers for Medicare and Medicaid Services, Office of the National Coordinator for Health Information Technology. (2016). *Electronic Clinical Quality Improvement (eCQI) Resource Center.* Accessed on September 9, 2016, from https://ecqi.healthit.gov/.

30. Centers for Medicare and Medicaid Services, Office of the National Coordinator for Health Information Technology. (2016). *eCQI Resource Center: QDM—Introduction to the quality data model.* Accessed on September 10, 2016, from https://ecqi.healthit.gov/qdm.

31. National Library of Medicine. (n.d.). *VSAC support center.* Accessed on September 9, 2016, from https://www.nlm.nih.gov/vsac/support/index.html.

32. Centers for Medicare and Medicaid Services. (n.d.). *Measure authoring tool.* Accessed on September 9, 2016, from https://www.emeasuretool.cms.gov/.

33. HL7. (2016). *Clinical quality information wiki.* Accessed on September 10, 2016, from http://wiki.hl7.org/index.php?title=Clinical_Quality_Information.

34. American Hospital Association. (2013). *Hospitals face challenges using electronic health records to generate clinical quality measures.* Accessed on September 10, 2016, from www.aha.org/research/policy/ecqm.shtml.

PART IV

35. The Joint Commission. (2016, July). *Survey results: Challenges faced by hospitals implementing Clinical Quality Measures (eCQMs)*. Accessed on September 10, 2016, from https://www.jointcommission.org/survey_results_challenges_faced_by_hospitals_implementing_electronic_clinical_quality_measures_ecqms/.

36. The Health Collaborative. (2015, Nov. 9). *Center for Healthcare Transparency Innovation pilot whitepaper: Increasing transparency on the relative cost and quality of healthcare*. Accessed on September 10, 2016, from www.nrhi.org/uploads/grcinci-proposal-cht-innovation-pilot-rfp-2014-07-v10-final-draft.pdf.

37. National Business Coalition on Health. (n.d.). *Value-based purchasing: A definition*. Accessed on September 10, 2016, from www.nationalalliancehealth.org/Value-based-Purchasing-A-Definition.

38. Centers for Medicare and Medicaid Services. (2015, September). *Hospital value-based purchasing*. Accessed on September 10, 2016, from https://www.cms.gov/Outreach-and-Education/Medicare-Learning-Network-MLN/MLNProducts/downloads/Hospital_VBPurchasing_Fact_Sheet_ICN907664.pdf.

39. Centers for Medicare and Medicaid Services. (n.d.). *Home-health value-based purchasing model*. Accessed on September 10, 2016, from https://innovation.cms.gov/initiatives/home-health-value-based-purchasing-model.

40. Centers for Medicare and Medicaid Services. (n.d.). *Medicare Access and CHIP Reauthorization Act (MACRA) of 2105: Delivery system reform, Medicare payment reform*. Accessed on September 10, 2016, from https://www.cms.gov/Medicare/Quality-Initiatives-Patient-Assessment-Instruments/Value-Based-Programs/MACRA-MIPS-and-APMs/MACRA-MIPS-and-APMs.html.

41. S&I Framework. (2016). *Clinical quality framework*. Accessed on September 10, 2016, from http://wiki.siframework.org/Clinical+Quality+Framework+Initiative.

42. International Health Terminology Standards Development Organization (IHTSDO). (2015, January). *SNOMED-CT IHTSDO glossary (draft version, international release)*. Accessed on September 10, 2016, from http://doc.ihtsdo.org/download/doc_IhtsdoGlossary_Current-en-US_INT_20150131.pdf.

43. National Library of Medicine. (2016). *SNOMED-CT.* Accessed on September 10, 2016, from https://www.nlm.nih.gov/healthit/snomedct/index.html; *and* International Health Terminology Standards Development Organization (IHTSDO). (2016). *SNOMED-CT.* Accessed on September 10, 2016, from www.ihtsdo.org/snomed-ct/.

44. American Medical Association. (2016). *Current Procedural Terminology (CPT)*. Accessed on September 10, 2016, from https://www.ama-assn.org/practice-management/cpt.

45. HL7. (2016). *Value set definition standard project.* Accessed on September 10, 2016, from http://wiki.hl7.org/index.php?title=Value_Set_Definition_Standard_Project.

46. Office of the National Coordinator for Health Information Technology. (2011). *Health Information Technology Policy Committee: Clinical Quality Measures Workgroup and Vocabulary Task Force transmittal letter.* Accessed on September 10, 2016, from https://www.healthit.gov/sites/default/files/standards-certification/HITSC_CQMWG_VTF_Transmit_090911.pdf; *and* Office of the National Coordinator for Health Information Technology. (2016). *Health Information Technology Standards Committee: Transitional Vocabulary Task Force transmittal letter.* Accessed on September 10, 2016, from https://www.healthit.gov/sites/faca/files/HITSC_TVTF_Transmittal_Letter_2016-01-29.pdf.

PART IV

PART V

Optimizing Healthcare IT

CHAPTER 23

Big Data and Data Analytics

John E. Mattison

In this chapter, you will learn how to

- Identify some of the best opportunities for innovation
- Define a taxonomy of exponential technologies and data sources in the multiplatform ecosystem, or Plecosystem™, that enable accelerated innovation
- Describe the likely impact of several powerful new innovations on the healthcare system
- Understand how harnessing and converging multiple exponential technologies and data sources across different platforms captures big opportunities for innovation
- Examine how current gaps in healthcare represent the best opportunities for the creative reconstruction of healthcare through innovation

Some of the best opportunities for the creative reconstruction of healthcare through innovation are described in this chapter. It is often useful to look through the lens of "where is there friction?" and "what frustrates you in your work?" from the perspective of both those who give and those who receive healthcare. A useful mantra is to "convert frustration into innovation."

In this chapter, emerging technologies in the context of their respective roles in creating sustainable solutions for big data and analytics will be discussed. It is increasingly true that combining or converging different technologies or disparate data plays a key role in crafting new solutions. It is also apparent that we are experiencing exponential growth of many technologies and data sources across many platforms and that we can benefit by a deliberate consideration of the resulting multiplatform ecosystem, or "plecosystem." The concept and taxonomy for the plecosystem continues to evolve and constitutes a useful way to create more comprehensive solutions to novel problems. As many of these exponential technologies have leveraged open application programming interfaces (APIs), more usable interfaces, and open source code bases, they have become much more accessible to people with little or no software programming experience. The implications for the future of the human experience, let alone the future of healthcare information technology (HIT), are profoundly and increasingly disruptive.

This chapter will also explore a variety of opportunities and technologies, but suffice it to say that three of the more important game-changing platforms for the next five years will be artificial intelligence (AI), robotics, and virtual reality/augmented reality (VR/AR). In 2008, the first "app store" was created and now "there's an app for everything." In 2016, virtual reality became a commoditized reality that creates an opportunity to create "a VR for everything."

It would be negligent to begin a chapter on innovation in healthcare without first highlighting the central role that virtual reality will play in the immediate future. After paying homage to that currently emerging disruptive platform of today, VR/AR, this chapter will describe a taxonomy for innovation and then define some of the opportunities and disruptive innovations. Chapter 24 will then provide further examples of specific innovations in healthcare that require a multisystem platform such as genetics/genomics, mobile applications, and telehealth.

Innovation in Healthcare IT: The Creative Reconstruction of Health and Wellness

> *Nearly anyone alive today has the prospect of having a global impact.*
> –Steven Kotler, 2016

Despite abundant literature on innovation, much confusion remains about the systematic structure and process of innovation. The most prevalent problem is that simple ideation is often mistaken for innovation. True innovation usually requires the full life cycle from ideation, human-centered design, iterative evolution of usability, operationalization, commercialization of a minimum viable product (MVP), scale with widespread adoption, and then continuous improvement through iteration and expanded scope of services with each new version.

While an occasional "breakthrough" emerges out of the concentrated focus and interdisciplinary participation in a conventional "hackathon," many factors often conspire to frustrate the successful transition from ideation to implementable innovation, including each of the following: the complexity of the human experience, the journey through health and disease, the cross-disciplinary solution sets required, and a highly regulated and litigious environment where fault tolerance is minimal. In addition, innovation often requires different approaches within small tech startups versus larger tech companies, although both generally benefit from collaboration with strategic partners or potential clients. Similarly, innovation within healthcare institutions often requires strategic partnering with multiple tech companies, arrayed across the plecosystem.

There are many pitfalls to healthcare institutional innovation programs for either products or services, and it is essential to consider strategies to minimize those risks. These pitfalls and mitigation strategies have been discussed elsewhere.[1]

One of the critical elements of impactful innovation is to first identify an important problem to solve. Clever solutions to small problems that affect few individuals may be "cute," but the same creative energy, applied to a more important problem, could generate much more benefit, and a substantial revenue stream (or cost savings or new services) to support a new round of innovation. The good news is that the "programming constraints" for many of the newest disruptive technologies have been falling rather than rising.

It is also instructive when forecasting the future to recall an innovation truism and admonition known as Amara's law (coined by Roy Amara): "We tend to overestimate the effect of a technology in the short run and underestimate the effect in the long run."

Which Technologies Are Creating Big Opportunities for Innovation?

The list of technologies contributing to innovation continues to grow. Social, mobile, analytics, and cloud constitute a powerful quadriad of tools. However, they do not inherently address the real opportunity of the human-machine interface. While the predominant high-capacity input to the human brain is visual, we cannot neglect any of the other senses which also play reinforcing roles. The "killer technology" for that interface must leverage the foundational input/output (I/O) capabilities of the human experience (not just the I/O of the brain, but the emotional, social, psychological, and spiritual receptiveness of each individual to the I/O mediated through the brain, recognizing that there is variable volatility in each of these dimensions of human interaction). The single concept that most closely captures this I/O capability is the use of multiple n-dimensional avatars. We need provider avatars that represent sources of coaching, mentoring, and motivating individuals that resonate with the receptiveness of each individual at any moment in time. It is critical to realize that the receptiveness of an individual varies throughout the course of the day and the course of their life and is shaped by the emotional tone, social milieu, recent experience, and evolving sociocultural, community, family, and household norms. Personal avatars (for both providers and individual persons and their inevitable social network of avatars) must negotiate that complex context for each individual on a dynamic basis.

Further, we need tools that help us understand what communication modality and communication style and content are most effective to motivate an individual for a specific task toward a specific objective. We need deep learning to constantly mine the digital exhaust of the interaction between provider avatars and patients to continuously refine the approach and the context-sensitivity of the interaction. We need to instrument and implement real-time adjustments to how our provider avatars extend the reach of the care-delivery system to each individual person, while advancing the situational awareness of evidence-based information (how/when/what/how often/what medium/what sequence/what frequency/what time of day/what current emotional tone/what current social context) as the various motivational tools ("motivicons™" and a "motivational formulary™") are applied as a sequence and as an ensemble. These provider or health mentor avatars will be more effective to the extent that they are coherent with emerging community and cultural behavioral cues toward better health.

Ultimately, the convergence of evolving community and social health elements with those of personal contextual health coach avatar activities will create what may be termed the "behavioral symphonies of wellness, empathy, and resilience™" which help maintain and reinforce healthy behaviors. There are many ways to achieve these goals, and there are decades of innovative discovery and implementation ahead about who responds best to the avatar mentor of their mother or daughter versus a cartoon character dog or cat versus a celebrity from sports or other celebrity arenas. There is a need for a strategy for how we match which avatar to which task in which individual and maintain an avatar milieu that conforms to the constraints of human cognitive and emotional capacity. We also need to recognize and manage to both the individual temporal and the inter-individual variability of that human cognitive and emotional capacity. It is quite likely that different people will benefit most from goal-specific avatars; for example, an avatar of a granddaughter might be the best way to motivate a grandmother to quit smoking, while an avatar of a senior Olympics sports celebrity might be the best way to help her become more active. This same principle of contextual personalization applies to how different social networks will be more or less effective for different objectives in different people; for example, a social group that helps support smoking cessation will often be different than a group that helps with exercise or weight loss. Increasingly and as a direct consequence of liberated communication and travel in the digital world, we all belong to a complex intersecting array of communities, each of which contributes significantly to the attitudes, behaviors, actions, and outcomes of each one of us, within our personal array of communities.

There are also personal avatar(s) that represents each one of us in our whole life experience, including aspects that reflect health, disease, and resilience. Amazon's Echo open source platform is but the first primitive step toward a commoditized consumer avatar. The designers of Siri will soon release the next generation of extended capabilities, and every large consumer tech company is aware that these services will be a critical conduit for marketing and ad revenue, so investment and competition will increasingly intensify. Google home is another version of this type of service/product. A recent consortium of these groups was formed to collaboratively address the ethical issues and best practices, and deserves very close oversight for full social transparency.[2]

Ultimately, much of the contextualization and dynamism of how health provider avatars interact with individual people will be brokered by "dynamic digital handshakes" between the provider avatars and the personal avatars to render the most appropriate output in support of that individual's implicit/explicit goals in ways and at times that find that individual most receptive to that motivational influence. For example, motivating someone to perform a difficult task should be withheld temporarily until after that individual recovers from an acutely traumatic emotional experience. These are not distant eventualities but are emerging today, and there are many projects in stealth mode that will begin to replicate the digital "second life" experience in real time and pervasively throughout our life experiences to the extent that we find them useful and convenient.

How Do We Optimize the Human-Machine Interface?

The previous section characterized the role of avatars as digital abstractions of individuals, providers, and social networks, and explored their potential opportunities for improving each individual's health journey. In a world where information overload is pervasive, and where individuals find solace in unconsciously constructing "digital echo chambers" where they preselect only what they want to hear and from whom they want to hear it, there is a fundamental challenge of overcoming both the ambient noise level and the implicit/explicit filters that individuals have constructed as very blunt instruments to screen out all but what they think they want/need to hear. Our overriding design goals in the human-machine interface must recognize the criticality of contextualizing the interaction to the individual in ways that do not appear as "more noise" and don't get whacked by the blunt filters constructed by that individual. The best model for how to do that and for how to "get inside people's heads" historically has been the elicitation of empathy through characters in novels and movies, and now includes more sophisticated digital gaming and VR. The avatar interactions between providers and individuals must exploit the science and art of entertainment to create compelling messaging that penetrates the conscious and unconscious filters for each individual.

While visual and audio media are most pervasive, we will increasingly witness the evolution of robotic devices that can deliver motivational emotional tone and sensory inputs beyond sight and sound. The Stanford University Virtual Human Interaction Lab has developed a science and products that allow individuals to experience "physical transfer," where they can observe themselves real-time as a "third person" in their VR visual field.[3] Early findings suggest that modifying the image of that physical transfer can also result in the person maintaining a strong identity with their virtual representation, even as that representation morphs. The potential to overcome implicit biases by recognizing one's self as being that "other" entity which evokes the implicit bias are profound.

"Augmented empathy" through physical transfer of virtual reality scenarios is an incredibly exciting opportunity for growing the capacity of individuals and communities to break down bias and more broadly accept and support their communities. One of the remaining large challenges in AI and AR is referred to as "collaborative robotics" or designing robots to safely and effectively interact with humans, who are so unpredictable. Machine learning will allow robots to better anticipate human behavior, and similarly generate "social learning" between robots, and perhaps even between multiple AI personas within individual robots. The invention of Baxter is beginning to show promise for safer human-robotic interactions. Baxter is replacing many of the manual functions in industry.[4]

How Do We Accelerate Continuous Learning and Innovation?

New technologies and new business models will continue to disrupt every business vertical. It is widely accepted that education and healthcare are the two industries most ripe for such disruptions. The productivity of a population depends critically on the health of its citizens, and our ability to create and sustain advances in health outcomes relies heavily on better educational methods and outcomes. Our current educational systems have increasingly declined on both absolute and relative benchmarking scales. It is disturbing to note that concomitant with the decline in education (and the rise of individual debt from education), many metrics of innovation show a steady decline over the past several decades, with a range of speculation as to underlying causes. Most people find that decline to be counterintuitive with the obviously great innovations resulting in Google,

Facebook, Twitter, Lyft, Airbnb, and so forth. However, those are the conspicuous exceptions to what otherwise appears to be a steady decline in the number of people directly participating in the innovation economy. One metric of that decline is the rise in social inequity in advanced economies like that of the United States. There is an emerging literature on how to address the decline in innovation through disrupting our educational systems with technology and restructuring of curricula.[5]

Two of the more critical disruptive technologies to accelerate learning in healthcare (and in general) will be virtual reality and augmented reality. The ability for individuals to practice various tasks, techniques, and approaches repeatedly and feel the result of their actions (through advanced haptics) will revolutionize training, certification, credentialing, privileging, and ultimately health outcomes. VR and AR allow for this training at far lower cost than physical alternatives. VR and AR will hopefully generate more meaningful jobs than the low-skilled jobs increasingly replaced by AI/robotics. A global rise in disintermediation of people performing simple tasks otherwise threatens economic and political stability through underemployment, unemployment, and the associated consequences of social inequity and unrest.

Much of the human experience is based on learning. Learning involves transfer of new knowledge from short-term to long-term memory. There are five chemicals in the brain known to affect the efficiency of that transfer: oxytocin, dopamine, endorphins, anandamide, and serotonin. It is now known that a virtual reality experience can stimulate each of these. The VR industry is aggressively studying how to optimize the levels of all five of them in a VR experience to optimize not only the pace of learning but the experience of pleasure during learning, since each of these naturally active neurochemicals induces a pleasurable state.

The Department of Defense (DoD) has already demonstrated that various training programs using VR can accelerate learning 2.4 times over any pre-existing method.[6] The implications for these recent discoveries is that we are on the cusp of transforming learning and education across all fields, and healthcare is perhaps more in need of better learning paradigms than any other.

A Simple Taxonomy for Innovation

There are many published taxonomies for innovation.[7,8] A simple approach includes four types of innovation, as described in the following sections.

Disruption and disintermediation of old tools, jobs, and processes with new ideas, tools, and business models This is the least common type of innovation, but when successful can generate the most dramatic progress. Augmented reality is perhaps the next successor in this disruptive series.

Incremental optimization of people, process, and technology This type of innovation is the most pervasive and critical element of "blocking and tackling" after the introduction of a new technology. The vast majority of benefits from the introduction of electronic health records (EHRs) derives from this continuous, laborious, and collaborative form of optimization of both workflow and usability.[9,10] The same can be said of many of the IT innovations in healthcare.

Identify and spread local successes   This type of innovation, which includes methods such as identifying positive deviance[11,12] and hotspotting, is the most widely neglected. Numerous superb innovations remain trapped within a local context until identified as useful, and then packaged, productized, and diffused with implementation guides and effective change management. Some form of commercialization is often required, and indeed many companies have emerged from the local imagination, innovation, and implementation by the founder(s) of that company.

Cultural transformation   Cultural transformation is the most difficult of the four types of innovation and requires leadership with maturity and wisdom for how to change attitudes, values, and behavior at scale. The clearest example of cultural transformation in healthcare is the accountable-care organization (ACO) movement. Historically, Kaiser Permanente was founded on an ethos and culture of integration and value optimization across the continuum of care, which has been continuously improved and extended over many decades and generations of leadership.[13] In contrast, the migration from a fee-for-service culture to one of maximizing value, rather than widgets of reimbursed work, is a critical requirement for success in the current value-based ACO movement. There has been a failure to appreciate the primacy of powerful and wise leadership to drive this cultural transformation. It is difficult enough to integrate previously isolated services and venues of care or to provide digital integration of those sites. However, the cultural transformation necessary to succeed in that transition to value-based care dwarfs the organizational and technical challenges. That transformation can only be executed effectively by leaders who know how to translate the values and motivate change through localized narratives adapted to each affected community engaged in the new synthesis. The creative reconstruction of healthcare represented by ACOs has faltered largely for lack of the exceptional leadership required. Failure to meet this requirement is the "silent killer" of many ACO initiatives.

The Different Communities Engaged in Healthcare Delivery

There are three different communities that are engaged in healthcare delivery leading to innovations:

- Individual persons within their communities and cultures
- Professional caregivers, oftentimes working in teams
- Personal caregiver networks

Person-Centric Communities

First, it is important to recognize that traditional Western healthcare, while consuming massive resources, only addresses 10–20 percent of the factors that contribute to leading a long, healthy life.[14] Epidemiologic research reveals that communities with exceptionally long, healthy lives have four features in common: healthy diet, exercise, sufficient sleep, and social interaction. These finding emerge from the study of five communities with long healthspans and lifespans and are called "Blue Zones."[15] We have understood the benefits of healthy diet, exercise, and sleep for many years, and over the past decade the evidence supporting the social impact on health has dramatically increased.[16]

Traditional healthcare IT innovation has made huge strides in treating disease. The larger opportunities for creative reconstruction of health and wellness reside in our ability to apply innovative design and new technologies to help reverse the habits that collectively create disorders of lifestyle, which in turn are driving the epidemics of obesity, diabetes, and the directly associated rise in cardiovascular disease, cerebrovascular disease, cancer, and most forms of dementia, including Alzheimer's disease.

HIT experts have a key role to play in addressing the behavioral economics, early childhood experiences, and social determinants of health from a collaborative community perspective where healthcare and HIT professionals participate, catalyze, and at times lead these efforts.[17] There is indeed a role for technology to play and abundant opportunities for innovation, but we must truly embrace the broader root causes of disease or we will neglect the larger opportunity to build health and resilience into our communities and reduce the prevalence of disease. We are beginning to witness a concerted focus on ensuring healthier and safer early childhood experiences and a collaborative leadership of community resources to address the many aspects that can positively impact the social determinants of health.[18] While these are largely sociocultural, political, and even generational issues, there are critical opportunities for the use of technology to support and reinforce those positive cultural vectors.

While these simple steps are somewhat obvious, it is remarkable how many local initiatives neglect key elements that are necessary for success. More importantly, there are many opportunities for innovative technologies to support each and every step of this process during planning, execution, and building sustainability. These evidence-based steps must also be iterative as each community evolves and learns, and as the palette of available technologies and resources evolves.

Professional Care-Delivery Teams

A growing chorus of voices laments the problems of usability in electronic health records and the growing work associated with the digital in-basket, even to the point of slogans like "It's the in-basket, stupid." Unfortunately, the in-basket workload is just a symptom of a deeper disease in digital healthcare. Just as in treating symptoms of disease, treating usability of EHRs and in-baskets will only address a small portion of the underlying problem afflicting physicians, which is fundamentally an increase in transparency into care gaps generated by the rise of digital data while disorders of lifestyle continue to wreak havoc on our communities. We have created an exponential growth both in the science of health and disease and in our ability to quantify health and disease in every individual. While both sets of information are valuable, we have not yet delivered commensurate services to transform the collision of those two large, complex sets of information into simplified actionable knowledge.

Rather than simplifying care, the barrage of data has mostly shined a spotlight on previously unseen care gaps without a corresponding increase in our ability to address those gaps. This problem is amplified by a legitimate emphasis on focusing on "value-based care" where measurable care outcomes are increasingly incentivized. Every director of quality has a mission to raise the bar on the practice of medicine and thereby compounds this growing chasm between the transparency of problems versus the constraints upon efficiently resolving those problems. It should not be such a mystery that many physicians are experiencing burnout at historic levels. This is especially true when our toolkit for healthcare is focused on disease care, whereas the root causes reside much deeper in our behaviors as individuals and in our social fabric. Setting aside the sociocultural issues for a moment, we clearly need a sophisticated set of tools that simplifies and facilitates each of the following tasks:

- Simplify the reconciliation between each individual's digital health footprint with the exponentially growing science of medicine and behavior. These personal digital footprints have been referred to as either "the quantified self" or "N of 1." These terms have acquired a large footprint themselves.

- Deploy "deep learning on the fly" with global searches of "practice-based evidence" to match individuals with a cohort that most closely resembles each individual to learn which approaches to intervention are most appropriate for that individual based on the outcomes of different treatment options previously applied to a cohort of similar individuals.

- Efficiently identify the values and objectives of the individual within their individual, sociocultural, familial, and household contexts. We need better survey instruments to more effectively elicit and elucidate both implicit and explicit values and objectives that represent the soil into which we can plant and fertilize the behavioral changes that are appropriate and realistic for that individual to pursue. "Noncompliance" is a physician-centric construct that often disguises a failure to create solutions that are practical and sustainable within a broader sociocultural and value-based context. When a person with diabetes is "noncompliant" with their behavioral or medical prescriptions because they have undiagnosed or untreated depression, this is not a failure of compliance by the patient, it is a failure of the caring profession to identify, understand, and address the comorbidity of depression. Further, the depression may result from the fact that the person has a husband in jail and a teenage daughter who is pregnant. Treating her diabetes is not at the top of her priorities, and treating her depression requires social services in concert perhaps with an antidepressant.

- Effectively use visualization tools to array the alternative approaches to closing those gaps while exposing the differences between options in ways that reflect the values and objectives of each individual. Simple facets of that array can include each of the following:
  - Potential benefits
  - Potential risks
  - Behavioral and environmental changes required to support that option
  - Opportunities to leverage support networks within their social milieu
  - Level of effort required for behavioral change and ability of and support for the individual to commit

These visualizations must elucidate alternative options in ways that are readily accessible to each individual in the context of their basic literacy, health literacy, and ability and willingness to own and participate in their own health outcomes. Underlying those visualization tools must be access to the underlying knowledge sets, personal data, and the algorithms that connect those big data with little data. Individuals with different levels of literacy need to be able to drill down through the supportive data to understand their options to the extent they are capable of understanding (within their basic literacy and health literacy), within both sets of data (their personal health data and the larger knowledge base of health sciences).

- Leverage effective metrics and remote monitoring for progress against goals. There is a well-known element of "wearable monitoring fatigue" where digital nannies like Fitbit have a high attrition rate. We have observed for many years that the notion of a digital nanny is doomed and that we need to substitute a different behavioral model whereby we use digital monitoring for three objectives:
  - Initiate desired behavioral changes
  - Sustain motivation
  - Calibrate progress against goals periodically

Products such as MUSE and from companies such as HeartMath have adopted this philosophy and approach.

One method for shifting from the model of a digital nanny to one of mindfulness is to progressively increase the time period between checking the data (e.g., steps taken) to reinforce the internal motivations toward health, while using the digital technology for calibration of those efforts toward more mindfulness. Other behavioral tools including gamification, personal health avatar coaches, and so on will assume increasingly powerful roles as motivation toward positive change. These tools need to be applied in a personalized, evidence-based approach that is subject to continuous machine learning and adaptation.

The coordination of care across the continuum of care and the "warm handoffs" required between services have been elaborated extensively as the foundation of ACOs. The best example of how this can and does accelerate improvement in health outcomes has been provided by the few truly integrated delivery networks who were early adopters of integrated health record technology, such as Kaiser Permanente, Geisinger, Intermountain Healthcare, Group Health Cooperative, and others. These are largely issues of clinical operations and organizational structure and culture and will not be elaborated further in this chapter.

Personal Caregiver Networks

Some individuals will remain isolated in the context of managing their own health for personal health goals. Web communities such as PatientsLikeMe and Smart Patients are specifically designed to create self-assembled groups of people with similar issues to help support each other toward better health outcomes. There is a bit of a legal conundrum about how care professionals can actively moderate these micro-communities without incurring undue risk, but many entrepreneurs are tackling that issue in novel ways. These social support technologies can be placed into three categories:

- Unmonitored
- Monitored
- Active intervention

Increasingly, human-centered design reveals how critical it is to embed any form of support, including social, within native workflows and experiences. As a result, dominant social networks (Facebook, Snapchat, WeChat, etc.) will increasingly become the preferred platforms for these social support technologies. There are inherent conflicts incurred by the naturally monopolistic nature of these networks with the sensitive tradeoffs of access, privacy, and security.[1]

What Can the Impact of Innovations Be on the Future Technologies?

Any physician who can be replaced by a computer should be.

–Warner Slack[19]

Just how far can we go with new technology in healthcare? Several respected futurists have raised the existential and philosophical question of how the future of AI and robotics could fundamentally threaten the role and/or existence of the human species.[20] While the existential threat is debated, the threat to optimal levels of human employment is recognized worldwide as robotics continues to displace tens of millions of jobs.

While we discover how often machines can replace many routine and complex tasks, we simultaneously e-discover the essence of healing, where a focus on the compassion and empathy of caring can be mimicked and leveraged by the machine, but not replaced. We must *use modern technology to restore ancient wisdom and compassion*. This simple maxim will help define the human roles in our increasingly technologic future.[21] Even chatbots and health robots can model empathy and stimulate reciprocal feelings of trust when specific human characteristics are embedded in language, tone, and facial expressions of robots.

Key Gaps and How Technology Can Help Close Them

There are 14 gaps between where we are today and where we can go with better technologic support. If we close those gaps with innovative applications of technology, such as a plecosystem, there will be new opportunities in innovation to solve healthcare problems. The most important gap to close is the empathy gap, which I will discuss first.

PART V

The Empathy Gap Is the Most Important Gap to Close

For the secret of the care of the patient is in caring for the patient.
–Francis W. Peabody, MD, October 21, 1925

This simple assertion that empathy is a requirement for healing is both the most critical and the most challenging gap to close in all of humanity today, with healthcare representing a central opportunity. Great leaders such as Dr. Peabody have inspired generations of compassionate physicians. However, many factors conspire to inhibit or even rob the caring professions of their true potential for empathy. The rigors of qualifying for a competitive spot in medical school (or any of the healing arts) results in a pre-selection bias against the most empathic candidates who might not get the same grades and scores because their empathy leads them to be less self-indulgent in their own career paths. The intense training, often with sleep deprivation, delayed gratification, debt accumulation, constant time pressure, and an unspoken (and sometimes spoken) sense of futility in treating people who are not motivated to do their part to engage in a healthy lifestyle all contribute to a drain on empathy. Further, healers are not immune from the implicit bias that contributes to social disparities in health outcomes. The "empathy gap" is the most critical and first for discussion because it is truly at the core of "why" someone should be motivated to enter and practice the healing arts, and yet technology itself has, if anything, increased the distance between the healer and that empathic ethos.

If this empathy gap and related implicit bias are so critical to healing and healthcare, and if technology so far has not helped, how can the use of technology close this gap? One relatively simple approach is to use validated survey tools to quickly understand how each individual approaches their life in terms of values, attitudes, and receptiveness to different types of behavioral support and motivational tools. A variety of innovations are moving in this direction. Ultimately, we can create a palette of tools that quickly helps assess how best to communicate with and motivate each individual, with a motivational formulary adapted to them, and motivicons that resonate with their receptiveness and aspirations. The social aspects of each individual's learning style and their available personal social network support system (e.g., PatientsLikeMe or Smart Patients) augmentation of social support structures will play an increasingly important role.

As previously described, the VR-based "physical transfer" may utterly transform our ability to teach, motivate, and sustain empathy and overcome implicit bias. This single aspect of the rapidly maturing technology of VR is perhaps the most hopeful prospect for how technology can begin to directly shape the human experience in a concerted way toward a more empathic and compassionate future. It is not coincidental that the teams developing VR programs for increasing empathy and reducing implicit bias in healthcare have also targeted the most proximate existential threat to the human species, global warming, by using VR technology to create a "field trip" for the world to give large audiences the "experience" of how ocean acidification is unequivocally threatening our planet and our species. The recent unveiling of that technology will hopefully represent a milestone in our awareness and commitment to address climate change.

We are already experiencing many of the health effects of global warming, such as the epidemic spread of previously restricted mosquito-borne viruses including Zika virus, Dengue, and Chikungunya. These rising epidemics, while already serious health threats, pale in comparison to the health and social consequences of the human dislocations and associated access to clean drinking water caused by rising sea levels. Any technology can be used for good or evil purposes, and VR is no exception. There is already an association made of how "shoot-em-up" video games like *Grand Theft Auto* can desensitize game players to their impact on others and correlate with antisocial behaviors. So the biggest opportunity with VR is how we as a society and culture embrace its applications for the benefit of our societies and our planet. Facebook's acquisition of Oculus for $2.3 billion is in no small part motivated by CEO Mark Zuckerberg's personal commitment to use this technology for humanistic and philanthropic good.

Gap Between Evidence and Behavior for Disorders of Lifestyle

> *The future is already here—it's just not very evenly distributed.*
> —William Gibson, sci-fi author

Gibson's prescient assertion can be updated as follows to embrace the opportunity afforded by the exponential advances across many parallel and synergistic technologies:

> The future is already here—it's just not very evenly distributed across populations, converged across technologies, and democratized for the benefit of all.

Since traditional healthcare delivery only addresses about 10–20 percent of the root causes affecting the health of our communities,[14] we must first imagine how to more effectively get at the root causes of disease. How do we create higher levels of health and resilience for individuals and their communities?

The epidemiologic evidence paints a fairly clear picture of what leads to longer and healthier lives. Despite that evidence, sedentary lifestyles, fast-food diets, epidemic sleep disorders, and, for many, the loss of a sense of real social community have all conspired to raise the disease burden of our population. These factors combined have contributed not only to the historically high levels of obesity and diabetes, but also to the rise in prevalence of cardiovascular and cerebrovascular disease, cancer, and many forms of dementia, including Alzheimer's disease. The abundant epidemiologic evidence and detailed molecular and genetic evidence clearly indicate that the Blue Zone findings generalize to every individual, although there is some genetically based variation in susceptibility to each of the factors affecting healthspan and lifespan.[15]

However, the ability of the healthcare delivery system to address these issues by itself is clearly constrained. Several healthcare organizations, including Kaiser Permanente, have initiated aggressive campaigns to address these issues. The following projects are among many that Kaiser Permanente has sponsored:

- The "Thrive" campaign, which includes educational programs for all ages, such as "Every Body Walk" and "Exercise as a Vital Sign"
- The documentary series "Weight of a Nation"
- Increased availability of farmers' markets in "nutritional deserts" in the inner cities
- Support for the creation of safe areas for walks and recreation through collaboration with communities and policy makers

Political/social efforts to address childhood obesity represent another key example of how social policy and advocacy can make a difference. While much progress has been made and some fast-food restaurants have recently revamped their menu offerings to include healthier choices, there is still a long way to go. In concert with these political, social, and community efforts, innovative technology can offer many solutions to help initiate, motivate, and calibrate individuals toward their goals for healthier lifestyles. As described earlier, wearable sensors in combination with motivational tools that are personalized to the individual, using avatars and behavioral economics, offer huge opportunities to close this central gap for driving unhealthy outcomes, reducing the cost of healthcare, and restoring the confidence of the healthcare communities that they can indeed succeed in thwarting the current epidemic in diseases of lifestyle.

Collectively, all of these changes create a "behavioral symphony of wellness." In order to go forward, the careful integration of multiple technologies with social policies and collaborative community efforts is required. A simple example of the innovative opportunity is using new consumer-grade technologies that can quickly and reliably assess the "health value" of a particular food item, beyond what might be listed on a package label or restaurant menu.

Regular and sufficient sleep is critically important to overall health. Disruption of our circadian rhythm has pervasive consequences for health, and healthy patterns of sleep are critical for clearing the beta-amyloid (highly associated with Alzheimer's disease) from our brains.[22]

Sleep disorders are far more prevalent now as a direct consequence of both the epidemic of obesity-associated sleep apnea and the high levels of anxiety associated with the time pressures of modern life. While many innovative wearable technologies have advanced our ability to monitor our sleep, we still struggle to effectively address the root causes of sleep disorders. Aside from sleep apnea, many sleep disorders reflect the cumulative impact of unhealthy lifestyle choices and exposures during the day. The previous discussion concerning the other aspects of healthy living will likely contribute to a final common pathway of healthier sleep habits and patterns, which hopefully will initiate a virtuous cycle of healthier wakeful behavior leading to healthier sleep habits leading to healthier wakeful behavior, ad infinitum.

In addition to better support healthy habits in children with respect to all these factors, we need better methods for early screening and detection of many morbidities deriving from lifestyle disorders. Earlier detection of metabolic manifestations will both enable earlier intervention and provide better metrics for gauging progress against goals. The introduction of "mindfulness as a vital sign" would systematize the capture of this information. This is similar to what has already been done with "exercise as a vital sign" or "BMI as a vital sign." In addition, the science behind the mindfulness of many ancient healing arts, including transcendental medicine, is beginning to be elucidated at the genetic and molecular levels with evidence that brain architecture is favorably altered as well. Wearable technologies, including MUSE and HeartMath, are directly targeted at helping initiate and sustain a more peaceful, meditative, and mindful state. As we use big data analytics to better appreciate the benefits of these ancient wisdoms, we can more successfully infuse them not only into more widespread practice of integrative medicine but also into early childhood education to shape healthy habits earlier in the lifecycle where they can yield huge lifelong benefits. Effective educational programs including the use of VR for parents to help them experience the benefits of better parenting may well become a profoundly useful use case for VR globally in early parenting experiences and practices.

Environmental Disruption Gap (Chemical, Thermal, Microbial)

Our food, air, and water are contaminated with industrial toxins and carcinogens.[23] We know that both automobile particulate exhaust and synthetic carpets are highly associated with the rise in reactive airway disease (RAD). Our food is riddled with antibiotics that disrupt our microbiome that normally maintains a healthy immune system, which in turn maintains a healthy brain.[24] A pervasive herbicide impairs our natural enzymes that detoxify dietary antibiotics and disrupts the ancient evolutionary balance of bacterial ecosystems in our gut that are so essential to a healthy immune system.[24] The global pervasiveness of these modern intrusions into our environment by over 80,000 novel manmade chemicals has made it extremely difficult to identify cause and effect. The Toxic Substances Control Act of 1976[25] was nothing less than a capitulation to the industrial chemical giants that has frustrated research about the impact of new chemicals before, during, and after their introduction into our environment.

Careful toxicology of human serum and body tissues shows that even in remote parts of the world native residents have measurable levels of manmade toxins that have become globally pervasive in our food, air, and water. While we desperately need responsible social policy that funds research, and legislation that bans the biggest offenders for commercial use and release into our environment, there is once again a key role for technology and technologists to play in untangling this complex morass of toxins that now has universally contaminated every one of our bodies. The advent of big data analytics and deep learning should help us identify sources and causal relationships between specific pollutants, serum and tissue levels, impacts on our microbiomes, and specific health outcomes to help eradicate much of the unintended consequences of the otherwise salutary industrial revolution.

The dense sensor network developed by UCSD's California Institute for Telecommunications and Information Technology (Calit2) and the deep analytics behind it and similar initiatives elsewhere will help us identify and eliminate more of the toxins from our air and water as we better understand which ones pose the more serious threats and at what levels or thresholds.[26] There is a critical quadriad of technology that will dramatically enhance our ability to address this issue:

- Polyfunctional sensors (fixed and mobile)
- Pervasive testing of serum levels of toxic substances
- Identification of genetic variation in susceptibility, detoxification enzymes, and processes
- Big data analytics and visualization to suggest correlations, then validate causations

That quadriad of technologies when converged should help us identify each of the following:

- Which people are at risk of exposure to which chemicals?
- Which chemicals should be removed from commercial production?
- Which chemicals require decontamination of the environment?
- Which classes of chemicals should raise the bar for approval of any new species in that chemical class into commercial production?

Without the quadriad of technologies and innovative convergence of those tools focused on complex problems such as chemical exposure, we will continue to be creating environmental threats to the health of our global communities.

Learning/Education/Communication Gap

While better education is relevant to each of the three gaps described thus far, there is a pervasive need to provide more context-specific, validated, actionable information to individuals, communities, professionals, and policy makers. As previously discussed, VR and AR are extremely disruptive opportunities to accelerate learning. Avatars can increasingly broker personal and context-specific motivational material (including motivicons and motivational formularies). An example of matching motivational methods with individual motivational profiles is Framehealth.com. The matching occurs both at the reference level with avatar chatbots, as well as at the social level in social avatar networks and moderated escalations from both chatbot failures and avatar network failures.

In addition to the exponential rise of AI, VR, AR, and avatars as instruments of education, there is another exponential source of new and real-time information emerging from the Internet of things (IOT) that will challenge our ability to transform massive contextual information into actionable knowledge. Innovation in this space will be characterized by both the network topology and the "accordion model of learning," explained next.

IOT Data Filtering and Analytics Designed for Continuous Learning

Rather than assume that we should stream all data from all sensors into an enormous centralized or federated cloud database as a substrate for all analytics, we can appreciate the necessity of some intelligent sorting of signal from noise. As a simple example, if we're monitoring exercise, do we really need to know the GPS location of an individual at every pico-second? Clearly not, yet the technology could deliver that volume of data. So how do we decide what level of filtering of inbound information is appropriate for a specific use case or for future unknown use cases? We simply don't yet know which data abstraction is appropriate for every existing and future possible use case. However, an iterative process embedded in a network topology by design can accommodate Continuous Learning as a Service (CLaaS™).

Specifically, in the example of monitoring exercise, the total translational motion can be abstracted from the accelerometer and GPS data to effectively determine distance moved, altitude changes, and a composite score for energy consumed. Only those abstracted data relevant for the use case need be transmitted to the analytic cloud, whereas the analytics that abstract that information can reside within the wearable device itself, within a body sensor network aggregator, or in edge analytics. These filtered data could be staged for transmission with topologic buffers so that no resource in the network is unnecessarily overwhelmed. In the reverse direction from the analytic and decision-support sources, the intelligent feedback/advice to the user (e.g., "slow down, you're above ideal maximal heart rate") can be staged on the efferent loop back to the individual. As a simple example, there may be dietary advice intended for a person who has just received emotionally distressing news unrelated to their diet. We need machine learning to help determine "when" to deliver motivicons within a personal motivational formulary to an individual based on emotional and other context for that individual. Does this person respond better to the advice of "don't eat that unhealthy comfort food (donut)" when they are at peak emotional reactivity, or are they more likely to be receptive after their galvanic skin response (GSR) sensor, HeartMath, or Afectiva (www.affectiva.com) data indicate that they've partially/fully recovered from the stressor? Augmented reality sensors and displays will also play a role in informing individual decisions. Simply put, timing of the message may be as important as what the message communicates or what communication medium is used (e.g., text vs. video motivicon vs. humorous cartoon). There is an enormous goldmine of innovation to begin to instrument the data relevant to these questions, develop the behavioral science around the answers to these questions, "read" the emotional tone with tools like Afectiva, and use a network topology, edge analytics, temporal buffers that operate on appropriate inbound data and outbound alerts or deeper data interrogations, and the accordion model of learning (see below) to support both continuous and periodic learning.

The Accordion Model of Learning

The second component of this approach to continuous learning is "the accordion model of learning."™"

This refers to the fact that we may initially filter out "extraneous noise" in a data set before transmitting to a body sensor network aggregator, edge server, or a central server, but later we might subsequently learn that this "noise" has previously unrecognized signal in it. We need to elucidate and elaborate the triggers that warrant "opening that accordion" to reevaluate the filtered "noise." Those triggers consist of newer technologies for analytics, new contextual information that might influence the value of those data, or better knowledge about what is relevant to which person under what situation of health or disease—that is, advances in the global knowledge base relevant to this specific subset of data. The periodicity of opening and closing of this accordion for filtering data will vary by data type and velocity of change in both the sensing and the analytics spaces, especially in the context of big data, wherein mashup of previously isolated types of data is overcome and visualization tools help recognize relevant correlations and potential causative relationships heretofore unknown. The network topology, storage topology, and localization of analytics will need to be structured in such a way that

PART V

analytics can be moved as close as possible to the self-contained dataset but no closer, and data will be moved as far out as the analytics engine relevant to that datatype in context, and no farther.

Buffers for Staging Information Inbound and Outbound Between People, Devices, and Analytics Environments

The heuristic architecture previously described can function with or without temporal buffers, but there are two types of buffers that would assist overall performance and effectiveness:

- **Inbound (to central services) data buffers** Temporal staging for load-balancing resources (network/analytic/storage/CPU) with compromised headroom

- **Outbound (to devices or individuals) alert/advice or data interrogation buffers** Temporal staging to ensure that the device or individual is "ready" to most effectively respond to that alert/advice or interrogation

Failure and outlier detection in these contexts is a rich opportunity for innovation in AI and big data analytics and visualization. Failures of both process and outcome will become increasingly transparent and subject to both continuous and machine learning and will increasingly reinforce the paired questions "Who owns your avatar?" and "Who owns your black box?," which refer to the human oversight of the values and objectives used both directly and heuristically to guide the libraries of algorithms that drive avatars and decision-support black boxes (e.g., Amazon's Alexa as first-generation commodity). Clearly, the world of AI poses risks to the ability of any human or group of humans to truly retain control over which values and objectives are prioritized and how those values and objectives are delivered or motivated by various avatars and black boxes. Alternatively, these explicit and transparent values and objectives may be subjugated by other priorities in a variety of opaque methods.

The term "dyadarity™" as opposed to "singularity" is useful to capture this dilemma. In a dyadarity, the introduction of any new advance in AI could be deployed strictly under human direction to ask, and hopefully address, the following four questions within the existing AI infrastructure, avatars, and black boxes:

- Are the desired values and objectives both explicit and transparent?

- Are those values and objectives effectively governed by appropriately represented humans with a diversity of views?

- Are those values and objectives effectively implemented?

- Who decides who is included in any automation of the arbitration between conflicting values, and what are the limits of "auction design" in adjudicating those decisions?

David Brin's book *The Transparent Society* is a primer for considering social policy goals in the context of the digital age.[5] The emergence of powerful AI since the publication of that book in 1998 only highlights the necessity of a larger public exposure to the technologic risks and innovative opportunities.

AI/Robotics Robotics Gap

There are many lengthy treatments of the benefits and risks of the emerging AI/robotics infrastructure to the extreme of their representation as an existential threat to humans. Robots are predictable by design, whereas humans are much less so. Programming robots to be adaptive enough to anticipate the full range of human behavior is a significant challenge and hence a critical opportunity. Many of the remaining challenges for the self-driving car or truck relate to the interaction of such vehicles with either pedestrians or other vehicles driven by humans. Even intuitive heuristics from superior engineers fail to anticipate every permutation of unpredictable and/or dysfunctional behavior from individual humans.

Gap in Seamless and Reliable Human Data Entry

Integration of conventional input devices (keyboard, mouse, trackpad, joystick, etc.) with more natural inputs such as full haptics-based data capture, video capture combined with video analytics (e.g., for monitoring progress with neurologic disorders), and natural voice capture with natural language understanding (NLU) with real-time natural language processing (NLP) will advance in ways that simplify, augment, and streamline the data-capture process. Innovation in this arena will significantly relieve the current conundrum around usability of electronic health records.

Gap in Evidence-Based Virtual Care

While some have predicted that 80 percent of doctors will be rendered unnecessary by automation, that assertion assumes that the role of the human will remain static as machines replace various human tasks. The "human aspect" of care can be simulated, but it is unlikely that genuine empathy will ever be fully entrusted to devices. The evolution of commoditized "tricorder-like" diagnostic devices will raise the opportunity for virtual care, whether by e-mail, text, phone, video, app-based autonomous avatars, or other medium. One of the biggest innovation opportunities in virtual care is how to reconcile two intersecting data sets. The first is the evidence basis for what level of communication or care is appropriate for which clinical situation. The second is the evidence basis for what individual people prefer as a communication and/or motivational modality. We have already observed that sometimes individuals will demand care over the phone for what can only safely be evaluated and treated in person. The challenge will be to reconcile the evidence base for effectiveness with the evidence base for personal preference so that overall we can achieve the highest balance of access, clinical outcomes, and patient satisfaction. Where those goals are in conflict, we need to put patient safety as the top priority, but within that frame there is an opportunity for innovative intelligent routing of problems through various modalities from simple text messaging at one extreme to face-to-face encounters at the other extreme, and everything in between.

The Science vs. the Application of –omics (Genomics, Microbiomics, Proteomes, etc.) Gap

In no area of healthcare is the science of health so disrupted as in the areas of genomics and microbiomics. It is increasingly clear that the genome, microbiome, immunome, and neurome are intimately interrelated and interdependent. Collectively these areas are called the "omics." Simple examples include the fact that excessive exposure to antibiotics in children under age 5 is associated with disruption of the gut bacteria (dysbiosis), and by age 15 those children have maldistribution of gray matter in the brain, closely resembling the typical pattern for people suffering from depression and anxiety. There are huge opportunities for big data analytics and visualization to begin to disambiguate the complexity of these interactions. In genomics alone, the big opportunities currently reside in four main areas:

- Diagnosing and treating cancer
- Diagnosing and treating over 500 known inborn errors of metabolism
- Pharmacogenomics decision support (selecting drug and dosing based on pharmacogenomics profiles)
- Early diagnosis and appropriate treatment of infectious diseases (where antibiotic resistance can be detected with initial sequencing)

Many other benefits of genomic sequencing will emerge, but these appear to be among the most promising to have impact in the immediate future. It won't be long before personalized health maintenance and preventive medicine schedules are routinely informed by the genome of each individual.

The Cancer Genome Trust (CGT) concept pioneered by David Haussler at UC Santa Cruz as part of the Global Alliance for Genomic Health (GA4GH) is based on blockchain technology that promises to revolutionize our ability to do global research across many inputs to human health, including all of the conventional "omics" data, and extended to socialomics and exposomics.[27]

Each of these areas affords opportunities to integrate traditional medicine, lifestyle interventions, and integrative medicine. Traditional evidence-based medicine reflects the use of approaches for entire populations of patients. We are moving to much more personalized medicine when we use analytical tools to identify patients with like conditions to help guide care for an individual. When we can identify small cohorts of individuals who more closely resemble the individual patient under consideration, we can apply practice-based evidence in a more context specific method to each individual. This approach is at the core of both "personalized medicine" and "practice-based evidence," while not abandoning the traditional "evidence-based practice" of medicine embodied in clinical practice guidelines targeted less precisely on a population of individuals.

While CRISPR/Cas9 genetic editing technology is very promising for correcting many germ-cell line genetic disorders, there have been a variety of other genetic editing technologies discovered since CRISPR was first reported. Other related technologies such as "gene drive" offer profound opportunities for eliminating certain infectious diseases, but also carry huge concerns about unintended consequences. Both of the technologies will rely on extensive use of big data analytics and AI to model for potential unintended consequences and balance of benefits and risk.

Gap in Drones and Healthcare

In many medical emergencies such as heart attacks, strokes, narcotic overdoses, or traumatic injuries such as ruptured spleens, minimizing the time elapsed between the event and the medical/surgical response can be life-saving. First-responder drones will likely become ubiquitous so that within minutes of a 911 emergency call, a drone or multiple drones could arrive at the scene and deliver life-saving advice and care, such as cardioversion to restore normal heart rhythm or bystander-administered Narcan in the case of a verified narcotic overdose. There are many opportunities for innovation in how we design and operationalize the deployment of these drones and how we coordinate medical oversight with direct-care delivered by untrained bystanders and first responders.

In less acute situations, highly contagious diseases will be diagnosable through commoditized home/field diagnosis of infectious agents and antibiotic sensitivity so that appropriate antibiotics can be delivered quickly and efficiently to a patient anywhere in the world without the risk of exposing others to that infectious agent. Solar-powered drone-charging stations that support drones capable of delivering emergency drugs have already been field-tested in Haiti and are on the verge of widespread deployment in remote corners of Africa. This drone delivery network will become an integrated component of virtual care and remote monitoring.

Gap in 3D Printing

Simply put, the ability of 3D printers to print nearly any physical product from a rapidly growing array of materials has already led to printed functioning organelles and larger organs such as human esophagus for implant post-esophagectomy for cancer, in conjunction with stem cell therapy. Soon to follow will be autologous kidneys created from one's own stem cells, as well as other organs. There are almost limitless possibilities for how 3D printing will transform health and reverse local organ aging. There are already over 300 materials that can be used for printing, and China has already printed five single-family houses in two days as well as a five-story apartment building. What was previously unimaginable and cost-prohibitive because of complex design is becoming affordable because there is no material wastage in 3D printing, no matter how complex the design.

Gap in Chatbots, AI, Trust, and Health

An "AI psychiatrist" developed by the Department of Defense (DoD) has proved to be more trusted by users than human psychiatrists, because it is perceived as nonjudgmental as opposed to human psychiatrists.[28] This is a simple extension of the finding 30 years ago that patients were more candid with computer surveys of their illicit drug use for the same reason. The implications for scalability and bringing more relief to more sufferers of mental illness are profound. IBM has put Watson in the cloud, open-sourced the API, and put up millions of dollars to encourage use of Watson in the cloud. The possibilities are extraordinary for discovering new useful knowledge and applying it.

Gap in Transcranial Magnetic Stimulation and Health

Weak magnetic pulses to specific brain regions have created experiences including out-of-body experiences and mystical experiences resembling those of people with near-death experiences. The use of high-resolution imaging of the brain and deep-learning analytics and visualization tools will provide new probes into how the brain functions and have already provided examples of how we can begin to treat serious neuropsychiatric disorders through increasingly less invasive brain stimulation.

Gap in New Psychopharmacology Research and Previously Refractory Psychiatric States

Use of low doses of MDMA (ecstasy) in conjunction with talk therapy have created sustained recovery from severe post-traumatic stress disorder (PTSD) for up to four years.[29] Again, the use of high-resolution dynamic brain imaging and big data analytics and visualization will help guide research and treatment for an expanding array of mental illnesses, including common disorders of anxiety and depression.

Gap in Harnessing Exponential Technology

When considering the vast array of technologies that are expanding in scope and impact at an exponential pace, it is useful to cluster these exponentials into a simple taxonomy. Table 23-1 provides a brief and partial taxonomy.

There are five principles that characterize members of this taxonomy:

- **Exponential growth** As an example, it took only ten years from the introduction of the first smartphone to reach 1 billion phones; a similar exponential pattern exists for many platforms.
- **Synergy and convergence** Value rises exponentially with the number of nodes accessible, the number of data types accessible, and the number of platforms converged within any solution set.
- **Data liquidity** Amplified by federation of data, respecting local privacy values/policy. Blockchain may be a game-changer here (CGT of GA4GH as a model).
- **Person-centricity** (e.g., Matticalfe's law) The number of data types linked to a single person raises the value of each individual data type linked to that individual.
- **Open source acceleration of value** Open source communities accelerate innovation through "interoperability by design."

I reserved this final gap, "harnessing the plecosystem," for last because understanding the potential convergences of each of these dimensions of the multiplatform exponential world we now live in has given rise to what can be described as "The Sci-Fi Generation." If you can imagine it, you can create it in your own lifetime.

Platform	Examples
Service	Internet; cloud; smartphone; Amazon Alexa Voice Service (AVS voice APIs); BioCurious (for bio hackers); quantitative Polymerase Chain Reaction (qPCR) (DNA sequencer for $200); TensorFlow (for machine-learning hackers); Blockchain; Blockstack; Distributed Autonomous Organizations (DAOs); SparkFun (robotics); IoT; personal real-time IoT (aka PRIoT); AI/deep learning, robotics; smartwatch; avatars; social avatar networks; AR/VR; CRISPR/cas9; Genedrive; Cpf1-...; stem-cell therapy; 3D printers; drones; self-driving cars; etc.
Data	Panarome (gen-, transcript-, proteo-, lipid-, etc.), Digital Phenome, Microbiome, Immunome, Exposome, Socialome, Neurobiome, Connectome, Quantified Self, Wearable Sensors, etc.
API	SMART on FHIR, OMH, Apple, Samsung, Google, EHR vendors, etc.
Experience	Empathic design, Social-Connected, UX, Avatar social network (intra-individual and inter-individual, locally autonomous to globally networked) (Human value-based social networks)
Financial support for entrepreneurs	Incubators vs. Accelerators, Angels to institutional investors to IPOs, fit for purpose and stage of life-cycle
Economic	GigEconomy, Gift Economy, Sharing Economy, Relationship Economy (Tracy Saville)
Cognitive	IQ, EQ, AI, Augmented Cognition, NLP and AI for CBT/NLP (X2AI)
Sociocultural/ Geopolitical/ Value/ Ethical	Widespread difference in attitudes: Failure Fault Tolerance? Data Sharing/ Access Predominantly Masculine: Polarized/possessive/big-fast (e.g., U.S., Japan, UK, Nigeria) Predominantly Feminine: Caring, modest, graceful (e.g., Sweden, Denmark, Netherlands, Thailand)

Table 23-1   Eight-Platform Dimensional Taxonomy of a Plecosystem

PART V

Chapter Review

This chapter covered several concepts of innovation. It offered a frame of reference for the big opportunities to innovate in healthcare using healthcare IT as one of the integrated components within the broader framework of communities, social determinants of health, and behavioral and motivational frameworks. This chapter provided an understanding of how critical it is to restore empathy throughout every aspect of health and wellness and some of the emerging technologies that can help develop and reinforce empathy, alongside tools that help us personalize our behavioral and motivational tools to each individual as a major component of personalized medicine. It also examined the emerging roles of various new technologies to help accelerate both learning and the acquisition of healthier behaviors to combat the epidemics of diseases of lifestyle disorders. The chapter presented how the plecosystem can help inform healthcare IT work to exploit emerging cross-platform technologies and services to create synergy through convergence. Finally, the chapter described the principles that help accelerate innovation across the plecosystem.

Questions

To test your comprehension of the chapter, answer the following questions and then check your answers against the list of correct answers that follows the questions.

1. Which of the following are distinct types of innovation?

   A. Disruption and disintegration of old tools, jobs, and processes with new ideas, tools, and business models

   B. Incremental optimization of how a technology is operationalized and advanced

   C. Identify, scale, and spread local successes (hotspotting, positive deviance)

   D. Cultural transformation

   E. All of the above

2. How can the gap between science and action be closed to address the crippling disorders of lifestyle?

   A. There are no innovative tools that can close the gap between science and action to address the crippling disorders of lifestyle.

   B. Start in early life to develop healthy habits of sleeping, eating, exercise, and social health and use modern motivational tools and techniques to personalize the behavioral program for each individual and create a digitally enhanced "behavioral symphony of wellness."

   C. Develop new empathy tools for patients.

   D. None of the above.

3. How can you reverse the unhealthy impacts of environmental disruption?

   A. Polyfunctional sensors (fixed and mobile), pervasive testing of serum levels of toxic substances, identification of genetic variation in susceptibility, detoxification enzymes, and processes, and big data analytics and visualization methods to suggest correlations.

   B. Big data analytics and validation of causes alone.

   C. Wearable sensors alone.

   D. Big data analytics and visualization of genetic variation alone.

4. How do we architect an infrastructure for continuous learning?

   A. Feedback from sensors and avatars.

   B. Bring analytics as close to the source data as practical.

   C. Accordion model of learning, filter noise out close to the source, bring analytics close to the source, identify triggers, and leverage evidence-based practice.

   D. None of the above.

5. What approaches enhance data capture and usability?

   A. Enhanced sensor data only

   B. Enhanced video capture only

   C. Enhanced capture and analytics of genomic data only

   D. Enhanced voice capture with real-time NLP and NLU, enhanced video capture with real-time video analytics, and enhanced capture and analytics of haptics-based data as well as the increasing array of noninvasive sensor data

6. What evidence-based approaches will guide how we implement virtual care?

   A. Individual patient's preference for communication tools alone will be the best approach.

   B. Explicit methods for balancing between NLP and NLU voice capture.

   C. There are no ways that evidence-based approaches guide virtual care.

   D. Evidence basis of which form of care is most effective for an individual at a point in time, based on their complete health history as well as their current problem, patient's preferences for communication tools, and explicit methods for balancing between the evidence and the patient preference when they are in conflict.

7. What are some of the near-term wins for the role of genomics in healthcare?

   A. Diagnosing and treating cancer, diagnosing and treating over 500 known inborn errors of metabolism, pharmacogenomics decision support (selecting drug and dosing based on pharmacogenomics profiles), and early diagnosis and appropriate treatment of infectious diseases (where antibiotic resistance can be detected with initial sequencing).

   B. It is too early to determine the role of genomics in healthcare.

   C. The results of the Precision Medicine Initiative will determine the near-term wins for the role of genomics in healthcare.

   D. The only win will be in pharmacogenomics in selecting drug and dosing based on pharmacogenomics profiles.

8. Name five of the platform types in the plecosystem?

   A. Data, API, financial support, Internet, consumer service

   B. Data, economic, Internet, consumer, and API

   C. API, data, economic, Internet, and consumer

   D. Experience, financial support for entrepreneurs, economic platforms, cognitive platforms, and sociocultural/geopolitical/value/ethical platforms

PART V

9. What are the five principles of the plecosystem?

   A. Exponential growth of platforms, synergy through convergence across platforms, data liquidity, person-centricity of data, and acceleration through open source communities and components.

   B. There is only one principle of a plecosystem: it can accept sensor data.

   C. Person-centered data is the sole principle of a plecosystem.

   D. None of the above.

Answers

1. **E.** The four distinct types of innovations are (1) disruption and displacement of old tools, jobs, and processes with new ideas, tools, and business models, (2) incremental optimization of how a technology is operationalized and advanced, (3) identify, scale, and spread local successes (e.g., hotspotting, positive deviance); and (4) cultural transformation.

2. **B.** We close the gap between science and action to address the crippling disorders of lifestyle by starting in early life to develop healthy habits of sleeping, eating, exercise, and social health and use modern motivational tools and techniques to personalize the behavioral program for each individual and create a digitally enhanced "behavioral symphony of wellness."

3. **A.** You can reverse the unhealthy impacts of environmental disruption with polyfunctional sensors (fixed and mobile), pervasive testing of serum levels of toxic substances, identification of genetic variation in susceptibility, detoxification enzymes, and processes, and big data analytics and visualization methods to suggest correlations.

4. **C.** We architect an infrastructure for continuous learning by the accordion model of learning, filter noise out close to the source, bring analytics as close to the source data as practical, identify triggers that allow the accordion to reopen to "old noise" and discover a new "signal" within it as new knowledge and technologies emerge, and leverage a virtuous cycle of evidence-based practice and practice-based evidence.

5. **D.** The approaches to enhancing data capture and usability are through enhanced voice capture with real-time NLP and NLU, enhanced video capture with real-time video analytics, and enhanced capture and analytics of haptics-based data as well as the increasing array of noninvasive sensor data.

6. **D.** Evidence-based approaches that will guide how we implement virtual care include using an evidence basis of which form of care is most effective for an individual at a point in time, based on their complete health history as well as their current problem, the individual patient's preference for communication tools, and explicit methods for balancing between the evidence basis of effectiveness and the individual patient preference, when they are in conflict.

7. **A.** The near-term wins for the role of genomics in healthcare are diagnosing and treating cancer, diagnosing and treating over 500 known inborn errors of metabolism, pharmacogenomics decision support (selecting drug and dosing based on pharmacogenomics profiles), and early diagnosis and appropriate treatment of infectious diseases (where antibiotic resistance can be detected with initial sequencing).

8. **D.** Five of the platform types in the plecosystem are experience, financial support for entrepreneurs, economic platforms, cognitive platforms, and sociocultural/geopolitical/value/ethical platforms. Service, data, and APIs are also platform types, but not sole platform types.

9. **A.** The five principles of the plecosystem are exponential growth of platforms, synergy through convergence across platforms, data liquidity, person-centricity of data, and acceleration through open source communities and components.

References

1. Mattison, J. E. (2015). *Managing risk in institutional innovation programs.* Accessed on October 6, 2016, from http://medtechevents.blogspot.in/2015/10/managing-risk-in-institutional.html.

2. Weitzner, D. (2004). *The transparency paradox: Privacy design strategies for open information networks.* Accessed on October 6, 2016, from https://www.w3.org/2004/05/loc-priv-transparency-extab.html.

3. Stanford University Virtual Human Interaction Lab. (2016). Accessed on October 6, 2016, from https://vhil.stanford.edu/.

4. RethinkRobotics.com. (2017). *Baxter.* Accessed on February 27, 2017, from www.rethinkrobotics.com/baxter/.

5. Brin, D. (1999). *The transparent society: Will technology force us to choose between privacy and freedom?* Basic Books.

6. Kotler, S. (2014). *Legal heroin: Is virtual reality our next hard drug?* Accessed on October 6, 2016, from http://singularityhub.com/2014/02/24/legal-heroin-is-virtual-reality-our-next-hard-drug/.

7. Christensen, C. M. (2013). *The innovator's dilemma: When new technologies cause great firms to fail.* Harvard Business Review Press.

8. Keeler, L., Walters, H., Pikkel, R., & Quinn, B. (2013). *Ten types of innovation: The discipline of building breakthroughs.* John Wiley & Sons.

9. American Medical Association (AMA). (2014). *Improving care: Priorities to improve electronic health record usability.* Accessed on October 6, 2016, from www.aace.com/files/ehr-priorities.pdf.

10. Payne, T. H., Corley, S., Cullen, T. A., Gandhi, T. K., Harrington, L., Kuperman, G. J., ... Zaroukian, M. H. (2015). *Report of the AMIA EHR 2020 task force on the status and future direction of EHRs.* Accessed on October 6, 2016, from http://jamia.oxfordjournals.org/content/early/2015/05/22/jamia.ocv066.

11. Sternin, J., & Choo, R. (2000). The power of positive deviancy. *Harvard Business Review,* January–February 2000, 14–15. Accessed on February 15, 2017, from https://hbr.org/2000/01/the-power-of-positive-deviancy.

12. Zanetti, C., & Bhatt, J. (2014, June 28). Big data with a personal touch: The convergence of predictive analytics and positive deviance. *Huffington Post.* Accessed on February 27, 2017, from www.huffingtonpost.com/cole-zanetti-do/big-data-with-a-personal-_b_5206219.html.

13. O'Brien, A., & Mattison, J. E. (2015). Emerging roles in health and healthcare. In C. Weaver, M. Ball, M. Kim, & J. Kiel (Eds.), *Healthcare information management systems: Cases, strategies, and solutions* (pp. 199–217). Springer-Verlag.

14. Heiman, H., & Artiga, S. (2015). *Beyond health care: The role of social determinants in promoting health and health equity.* Accessed on October 6, 2016, from http://kff.org/disparities-policy/issue-brief/beyond-health-care-the -role-of-social-determinants-in-promising-health-and-health-equity.

15. Buettner, D. (2008). *The Blue Zones: Lessons for living longer from the people who've lived the longest.* National Geographic Society. See also *Harvard Business Review* (January–February 2012) and *Time Magazine* (July 1, 2016), both dedicated to happiness metrics and literature.

16. Christakis, N. A., & Fowler, J. H. (2009). *Connected: The surprising power of our social networks.* Little Brown.

17. Kaiser Family Foundation. (2016, Aug. 2). *U.S. government and global non-communicable disease efforts.* Accessed on October 6, 2016, from http://kff.org/global-health-policy/fact-sheet/the-u-s-government-and-global-non-communicable-diseases/.

18. Council of Economic Advisers, Executive Office of the President of the United States. (2015). *The economics of early childhood investments.* Accessed on October 6, 2016, from https://obamawhitehouse.archives.gov/sites/default/files/docs/early_childhood_report_update_final_non-embargo.pdf.

19. Oldenburg, J., & Grieskowisz, M. (2017). *Participatory healthcare: A person-centered approach to healthcare transformation.* CRC Press for HIMSS.

20. Zolfagharifard, E. (2015). Don't let AI take our jobs (or kill us): Stephen Hawking and Elon Musk sign open letter warning of a robot uprising. *DailyMail.org,* January 12. Accessed on October 6, 2016, from www.dailymail.co.uk/sciencetech/article-2907069/Don-t-let-AI-jobs-kill-Stephen-Hawking-Elon-Musk-sign-open-letter-warning-robot-uprising.html.

21. Human Resources for Health (HRH). (2012). Integrated health and post modern medicine. *Journal of the Royal Society of Medicine, 105*(12), 496–498.

22. National Institutes of Health, NIH Research Matters. (2013, Oct. 28). *How sleep clears the brain.* Accessed on February 27, 2017, from https://www.nih.gov/news-events/nih-research-matters/how-sleep-clears-brain.

23. Baselt, R. C. (2014). *Disposition of toxic drugs and chemicals in man, tenth edition.* Biomedical Publications.

24. Lundberg, G. (2016). Is Roundup slowly killing us? *Medscape News,* August 8. Accessed on October 6, 2016, from www.medscape.com/viewarticle/866710?nlid= 108743_3243&src=WNL_mdplsfeat_160809_mscpedit_imed&uac=126057HX &spon=18&impID=1175750&faf=1.

25. Toxic Substances Control Act of 1976. Accessed on October 6, 2016, from https://en.wikipedia.org/wiki/Toxic_Substances_Control_Act_of_1976.

26. California Institute for Telecommunications and Information Technology (Calit2). (n.d.). *Sensor network testbed proposed.* Accessed on October 6, 2016, from www.calit2.net/newsroom/article.php?id=28.

27. Global Alliance for Genomic Health (GA4GH). Accessed on October 6, 2016, from http://ga4gh.org.

28. Darcy, A. M., Louie, A. K., & Roberts, L. W. (2016, Feb. 9). Machine learning and the profession of medicine. *JAMA 315*(6), 551–552.

29. Mithoefer, M. C., Wagner, M. T., Mithoefer, A. T., Jerome, L., Martin, S. F., Yazar-Klosinski, B., ... Doblin, R. (2011). Durability of improvement in post-traumatic stress disorder symptoms and absence of harmful effects of drug dependency after 3,4 methylenedioxymethamphetamine-assisted psychotherapy: A prospective long-term follow-up study. *Journal of Psychopharmacology 27*(1), 28–39.

24

Innovations in Healthcare Impacting Healthcare Information Technology

Kathleen A. McCormick

In this chapter, you will learn how to

- Define three key healthcare innovations impacting healthcare IT
- Describe some genetic/genomics examples throughout the continuum of care in health
- Identify the major sources where new evidence can be found in pharmacogenomics
- Identify the IT challenges and uses of clinical decision support for monitoring genetics/genomics and pharmacogenomics
- Describe the volume of mobile devices and the impact on healthcare IT
- Define where telemedicine is being used in healthcare IT

While there were many innovations in healthcare IT described in Chapter 23, this chapter builds upon those innovations by describing three major sources:

- Genetics/genomics/pharmacogenomics
- Mobile devices
- Telemedicine

This chapter addresses basic concepts and current directions for each of these sources of innovation and describes the impact of each on healthcare IT.

Innovations in Genetics/Genomics/Pharmacogenomics

It is now many years since the Human Genome Project was launched in June 1989.[1] This chapter defines the implications of genomic science for engineers, computer scientists, and those in healthcare professions. The growth in genomic science has increased steadily in those years, and the volume of tools to analyze the data, diagnose patients, recommend treatments, and integrate into the electronic health record (EHR) and mobile devices has accelerated. The United States and other countries have entered into the era of Precision Medicine that includes $240 million total funding through 2017, targeted to new initiatives and more healthcare IT innovations, $300 million for the Moonshot project for cancer, and $45 million for Brain Research. The U.S. emphasis for Precision Medicine is on cancer therapeutics and resistances.[2] The million patients who consent to being studied in the Precision Medicine cohort, now called the All of Us Project, will have data collected that includes their tissue samples, EHRs, and information about their diet, exercise, lifestyles, and other health information that may be relevant to diagnosis and treatment of disease.

Three of the most important definitions for the reader to understand in the context of this chapter are

- **Genetics**   The study of individual genes and their impact on relatively rare single gene disorders (e.g., Down syndrome)
- **Genomics**   The study of all of the genes in the human genomes together, including their interactions with each other, the environment, and other psychosocial and cultural factors (e.g., cancer)
- **Pharmacogenomics**   The study of the influences of genetic variation on medication and adverse events (e.g., how metabolism of commonly used medications, such as warfarin, differs depending on a person's individual genetic makeup)

The reason these three definitions are so important is that throughout the continuum of healthcare from birth to death, the data that should be collected for an individual for purposes of improving healthcare outcomes, quality, and safety can be influenced by research in genetics, genomics, and pharmacogenomics. This research can identify the impact of variations in genes, genomes, and medication metabolism, respectively. Greater precision in data collection can also have substantial economic benefits. Healthcare outcomes previously were dependent upon clinical practice guidelines and quality measures, as described in Chapter 22. Now healthcare providers recognize that some healthcare outcomes are directly dependent on a person's individual genetic makeup, with variations in genes determining susceptibility to or increased risk of certain diseases.

These variations are known for prenatal conditions, for newborns, childhood, and adult disorders. Genetic screening tools can more precisely characterize health disorders and can improve medication choices, including drugs that may target underlying diseases caused by genomics. The genetics/genomics profiles may also help clinicians to manage common symptoms such as fatigue, pain, sleep disorders, abnormal clotting, the healing process, and skin breakdown.

Genetics/Genomics Throughout the Healthcare Continuum

Since 2013, teams of clinicians from the National Institutes of Health (NIH), National Human Genome Research Institute (NHGRI) have recognized the influences of genetics and genomics across the healthcare continuum.[3] In the *preconception period* (before a child is conceived), testing can be done to determine if the parents are carriers for genetic variants associated with such diseases as cystic fibrosis and sickle cell disease. Carriers of these diseases may require genetic counseling in the preconception period. In the preconception period, genetic testing of single cells from multiple in vitro fertilization (IVF) embryos is helpful to ensure a healthy genome when the parents are known to be at risk of a genetic disorder. *Prenatal care* occurs when the mother is pregnant. During this time in the pregnancy, samples of the baby's genetics can be tested from the mother's plasma through amniocentesis (to detect, for example, Zika virus, which can lead to genetic deformities). This test also can focus on single gene disorders, chromosomal abnormalities, congenital malformations, and other hereditary genomic conditions. Also in the prenatal period, liquid biopsy can now isolate fetal stem cells in nearly 100 percent of circulating blood in a pregnant woman and allow for full genotyping of the fetus as early as eight weeks in the pregnancy. *Newborn screening* is done with a blood sample from a child's heel at birth. Most parents are familiar with the screening test from dried blood that can determine if further genetic tests should be done for conditions such as immunodeficiency from HIV or congenital heart disease.

Disease susceptibility can be determined from genetic tests. For example, if a person has inherited the BRCA2 and BRCA3 genes, they may be more susceptible to acquiring breast and ovarian cancer. *Disease screening/diagnosis* can be done with fecal (stool) material. DNA testing is done to determine if a person has colon cancer. The family history assists in the accuracy of the genetic testing matched to treatment. The family history helps to narrow the list of candidate genes for testing based on how the condition or disease has presented within the family members in the past.

Prognosis and therapeutic decisions can test for therapies that are matching tumor type with treatment choices. An example is found in matching the mutations found in non-small cell lung cancer with a treatment choice of tyrosine kinase inhibitors. Tumors have genetic profiles that can then be matched to the correct treatment. Also, some patients who carry specific genetic enzymes are not able to metabolize certain medications or have an increased risk of adverse effects from certain medications.

Monitoring disease burden, symptoms, and recurrence occurs when a patient has a genetic enzyme that determines whether they can convert codeine into an active metabolite morphine, which would help control pain.

PART V

New Major Sources of Evidence with a Focus on Pharmacogenomics

In February 26, 2015, the Institute of Medicine (now called the National Academy of Medicine) stated, "in many instances, there is sufficient evidence to justify the use of genetic testing to inform choice or dosage of medications."[4]

The influences of pharmacogenomics on medication and observations of adverse events can be organized into five specific categories:

- Medication efficacy
- Pharmacodynamics (the study of the mechanism of action, concentration, and effect of drugs)
- Pharmacokinetics (the study of drug absorption, distribution, metabolism, and excretion)
- Target
- Toxicity resulting in inducers or inhibitors

It is estimated that the effects of genetics and genomics are adversely affecting 20–50 percent of patients receiving medications.[5]

The individual's genetic inheritance affects their body's response to drugs. Never before has it been deemed essential that the patient's ethnicity be included in the EHR. Engineers, computer scientists, and clinicians need to identify current genetic and genomic information resources, such as the Pharmacogenomics Knowledgebase (PharmGKB) web site and the Clinical Pharmacogenomics Implementation Consortium (CPIC) guidelines, which should be included in EHRs. They also need to work on policies regarding access to genomic information stored within the EHR. Lastly, they need to understand the unique issues of privacy and security related to the use and potential misuse of genomic information. Therefore, the new monitoring in healthcare is to match the individual's genome profile to deliver the best drug for the person at the best dosage that is the most effective and least likely to cause side effects. That is the new concept of personalized treatment in Precision Medicine and the documentation that drugs were administered and side effects and adverse drug reactions were monitored and outcomes evaluated.[6]

Another project funded by the National Institutes of Health is a knowledge base that collects, curates, and disseminates knowledge about the impact of human genetics variation on drugs response. The PharmGKB is a pharmacogenomics knowledge resource that encompasses clinical information including dosing guidelines and drug labels, potentially clinically actionable gene-drug associations, and genotype-phenotype relationships.[7] The data are extracted and curated from pharmacogenomics literature, and like other guidelines, include knowledge extraction, annotation, aggregation, and integration. Where available, some of the drugs in the PharmGKB have clinical interpretations and clinical implementation plans. Specific workgroup consortia are studying the pharmacogenomics of four specific drugs: warfarin, tamoxifen, SSRI class (including drugs like citalopram, escitalopram, paroxetine, sertraline), and clopidogrel.

The guidelines resulting from the extraction of evidence are produced in a database called the Clinical Pharmacogenomics Implementation Consortium (CPIC).[8] Workgroups are also implementing the CPIC guidelines into EHRs using clinical decision support (CDS). It is necessary to bring clinical decision support to the point of care information about pharmacogenomics. It is also necessary to bring clinical decision support about pharmacogenomics to patients during the entire continuum of care.

As an example of a warning that might be placed in a patient's EHR, consider a leukemia patient whose genotype result predicts that the patient will be at risk for myelosuppression (bone marrow suppression) when taking a particular drug. The patient's EHR should include a warning such as "The patient is at risk for myelosuppression with normal doses of 6-mercaptopurine. If disease treatment normally starts at the 'full dose,' consider starting at 30–70 percent of target dose (e.g., 1–1.5 mg/kg/d), and titrate based on tolerance. Allow 2–4 weeks to reach steady state after each dose adjustment."

Effective March 15, 2017, there are 36 CPIC guidelines with sufficient evidence to implement in clinical practice.[8] There are 83 more drugs in the pipeline for CPIC, and the FDA has identified pharmacogenomics biomarkers on drug labels in 155 drugs. The PharmGKB is evaluating 560 drug interactions for sufficient evidence to produce CPIC guidelines.

The IT Volume Challenge of Monitoring Genetics/Genomics/Pharmacogenomics in Healthcare

A genetic analysis of a single patient can produce about 1 terabyte of data in a single encounter.[9] Genetics/genomics may be analyzed before or at the time of diagnosis and multiple times during treatment, as well as being integrated with lab blood data, doctors' and nurses' clinical observations, tissue biopsy and other data, and imaging data (such as X-ray, MRI, CAT scans). The volume of new data is so large that healthcare information technologists will need to develop roadmaps for incorporation into their current practice and EHRs. If one studied the genetics of an individual over the continuum of care from birth to death, the amount of data, the multiple repositories in which the data are stored, the multiple formats the data are described in, and the multiple standards applied to the data would be daunting. The mining of these data over time and through different environmental locations in which the person has resided is becoming a formidable task and a new science in big data mining, storage, and retrieval.

The NIH is developing roadmaps to determine if the genetic and genomic findings are clinically relevant. The project, called ClinGen (Clinical Genome Resource), is intended to be a resource that defines the clinical relevance of genomic variants. The goal is to aid in the diagnosis and treatments for use in the Precision Medicine Initiative. ClinGen also aims to improve patient care by accelerating the understanding of genomic variation in healthcare through data sharing, knowledge curation, and technology development. Three questions are raised in considering whether a clinical variation has been found in ClinGen: Is the gene associated with the disease? Is the gene variation causative of the disease? Is this information something that can be used in describing a treatment? Working groups are establishing data models and standards for integrating these finding into EHRs.[10]

PART V

One project is being conducted to develop workflow and algorithm pathways for the inclusion of genetic, genomic, and pharmacogenomics information into user-friendly CDS formats linked to the EHR. This work is taking place at St. Jude's Children's Research Hospital. The work specifically supports a model workflow with the CDS algorithm to incorporate pharmacogenomics tests into their EHR.[11] Additionally, other national initiatives have been funded by the NIH to facilitate strategies to integrate genomics into practice, including Implementing Genomics in Practice (IGNITE) and the Electronic Medical Records and Genomics (eMERGE) Network.[12]

At the National Academy of Medicine (NAM), another relevant implementation project is Displaying and Integrating Genetic Information Through the EHR, or DIGITizE. This work is a part of the NAM Roundtable on Genomics and Precision Health. Several vendors working on this project include Cerner, Epic, and Allscripts. Roundtable members are launching pilot studies focused on pharmacogenomics with some vendors. The DIGITizE working groups are also developing an implementation guide, the Logical Observation Identifiers Names and Codes (LOINC) database, and an Allele Registry with ClinGen.[13]

Researchers and clinicians have identified the need for a toolbox or toolkit to help in the dissemination of information and implementation of the genetic scientific information on diagnosis and treatment into clinical practice. A toolkit that has been developed was made available as of March 15, 2016, through Genome.gov.[14] The toolkit provides links to resources that helps the developers identify which tests to include, how to interpret results, and how to manage genetic conditions. It specifically provides links to find specific genes, conditions, or medications and link them to ClinGen. The Guidelines for Pharmacogenomics are included in these resources. Some of the disease-specific information includes resources addressing cancer and rare disorders. Links to family history tools and for baby's first genetic tests are included. Several sources for basic and advanced education are also provided for healthcare providers and consumers.

Another team that is advancing the development of an ecosystem for sharing genomic and clinical data is the Global Alliance for Genomics and Health. It has several projects. The Beacon project is developing an open technical specification for sharing data from large-scale population sequencing projects, the clinical data, and the curated data on variations. The BRCA Challenge aims to exchange data on breast, ovarian, and other cancers that are variants in the breast cancer genes (BRAC1 and BRAC2). Another component of the global effort is the Matchmaker Exchange, a collaborative effort with the Rare Diseases Research Consortium. The advantage of an exchange is that even if the suspicious gene variant occurs in only a few people, querying the database can potentially identify cases with similar gene disruptions in common and establish the diagnosis of a rare disease. The data set can be queried for the presence or absence of a specific allele without requiring compatible data sets or compromising patient identity.[15]

Necessary Components in Electronic Health Records

Relevant to healthcare information technology is the need to ensure that the family history section in the EHR elicits a minimum of three generations and that the physical assessment section is updated regularly and includes genetic and environmental information and risk factors.[16] This assessment will uncover who the biological parents are, if they had conditions that are known to be linked to genetics, and risks associated with surgery (e.g., complications from anesthesia) and other procedures (e.g., blood clotting or unusual bleeding disorders). The Surgeon General has a free genetic screening tool on the HHS web site.[17] The family history is also a window into conditions for which an asymptomatic patient/consumer may have a genetic predisposition. For complex diseases such as cardiac disease, hypertension, or diabetes, the consumer needs to be guided about routine screening, testing, and targeted actions they can take to prevent the condition, or gain early treatment when diagnosed, and seek continuing education about new diagnostic and treatment options. Since 2010, the Centers for Medicare and Medicaid Services (CMS) requires the provider to incorporate the family history into the physical exam for the patient encounter to be reimbursed.

There are standardized symbols and nomenclature to be used in the family history. The Pedigree Association Task Force first developed them in 1995. Since 2008, recommended symbols and nomenclature have been defined.[18] When standardized tools, nomenclature, and symbols are used, integration across professional practices is possible, and interpretation is consistent between sites.

Necessary Components of the Healthcare Delivery Team

Incorporating genomics, and especially pharmacogenomics, into the delivery of healthcare necessitates adding new members to the traditional team of doctors, nurses, and pharmacists, including a geneticist, and perhaps one or more computer scientists, engineers, programmers, and security experts. This team might also include a genetic counselor if one is available in the facility. If a healthcare facility cannot support such a team, it might need consultation mechanisms with larger practices and academic settings. Genetic, genomic, pharmacogenomics, and bioinformatics competencies have been developed for training in all of these special areas.

Challenges in the IT Transfer of Genomics and Pharmacogenomics into Clinical Practice

There are challenges that remain in the integration of the genomics information into EHR implementation. The most notable are data sharing and information storage and retrieval policies related to data into the EHR from genomic resources. There are further challenges to move data from EHRs into the new mobile technologies (including wearable biosensors), telemedicine, and digital medical devices. Some small companies are beginning to develop tools that translate the CPIC guidelines into alert sheets for healthcare practitioners. Others also link the CPIC guidelines to drug databases that identify drug-drug interaction and drug overdose information. Still others are integrating the CPIC guidelines into clinical decision support tools to integrate into the EHR.

Innovations in Mobile Devices in Healthcare

Mobile devices are slated for a $57 billion growth internationally by 2020.[19] The markets include mobile devices, sensors, and smart homes. Monthly global data traffic is expected to be 49 exabytes by 2021 according to a Cisco White Paper.[20]

PART V

Wireless Communication Technologies and Standards

The foundation of mHealth is the capability of mobile devices to connect with networks in multiple ways. Rapid growth has occurred with three hardware elements enabling mobile health (mHealth). The hardware advances are larger physical device size, wireless network access, and longer battery life. Large, redundant storage capacity has become available through cloud computing services. In addition, the development of the smartphone has allowed powerful handheld computing with the ability to access the Internet.

The technology is supported by Wi-Fi, Bluetooth, and radio frequency identification (RFID). The regulation of wireless technology in the United States evolves under the direction of the Federal Communications Commission (FCC). Fourth-generation (4G) wireless supports all Internet Protocol (IP) communication and uses additional technology to transfer data at high bit rates. The International Telecommunications Union Radiocommunication Sector (ITU-R) sets the standards for International Mobile Telecommunications Advanced (IMT-Advanced) technology.[21, 22]

The ITM-Advanced standard for 4G services is a data rate of 100 megabits per second (Mbps) for communications while traveling in a car or train and 1 gigabit per second (Gbps) for communications while standing still.[23]

Wi-Fi is intended for local networks called wireless local area networks (WLANs). Bluetooth is intended for a wireless personal network (WPAN). Wi-Fi and Bluetooth are complementary.[24]

Wireless Application Environment (WAE) specifies an application framework, and Wireless Application Protocol (WAP) is an open standard allowing telephone communication access from mobile devices.[25]

Mobile devices can exchange data through Wi-Fi or connect to the Internet (in the United States) through 2.4 GHz ultra high frequency (UHF) waves and 5 GHz super high frequency (SHF) waves. Advanced hardware makes this connection through a wireless network access point, or hotspot. These standards are from the Institute of Electrical and Electronics Engineering (IEEE) standard 802.11.[25]

Protection for these wireless connections is through various encryption technologies such as Wi-Fi Protected Access (WPA) and Wi-Fi Protected Access 2 (WPA2) security protocols.[25] To assure devices can communicate with one another, Extensible Authentication Protocol (EAP) is used. Wi-Fi security concerns are covered by the National Institute of Standards and Technology (NIST) Special Publication 800-153, "Guidelines for Securing Wireless Local Area Networks (WLANs)."[26] Security of Bluetooth wireless technologies is also covered by a NIST Special Publication (800-121, Revision 1).[27]

RFID is a technology that uses radio frequency electromagnetic fields to transfer data. It is usually used to track inventory. The International Organization for Standardization (ISO) and the International Electrotechnical Commission (IEC) set standards for RFID. Security concerns are addressed using cryptography standards addressed in NIST Special Publication 800-98, "Guidelines for Securing Radio Frequency Identification (RFID) Systems."[28]

Mobile Devices Connected to the Internet

When mobile devices are connected to the Internet, the network model and communications protocols use the Transmission Control Protocol (TCP) and the Internet Protocol (IP), or TCP/IP. The Internet Engineering Task Force (IETF) maintains the standards for mobile devices connected to the Internet. Other commonly known protocols for the Internet user interface include the Simple Mail Transfer Protocol (SMTP), File Transfer Protocol (FTP), and Hypertext Transfer Protocol (HTTP). HTTP Secure (HTTPS) is a protocol for secure communication over computer networks and is used on the Internet.

When mobile devices are connected to the Internet to connect to the EHR, the application programming interfaces (APIs) require different HIT standards. The current standards are in need of change since the current standards are not inclusive of information flow into and out of the EHR. This level of standard will eventually lead to consumer mobile devices connected to EHRs for data retrieval.

Mobile Device Security Protocols

To provide encryption security protocols, Pretty Good Privacy (PCP) and GNU Privacy Guard (GPG) are used. Cryptography network protocols are Secure Sockets Layer (SSL) and Transport Layer Security (TLS). New protocols will be on the horizon to protect the mobile devices from cybersecurity threats that protect sender to receiver.[29] An alternative to TLS to monitor is the Direct Project.[30]

How Mobile Networks Are Being Used in Healthcare

As the mHIMSS Roadmap describes, "patients and providers are leveraging mobile devices to seek care, participate in, and deliver care. Mobile devices represent the opportunity to interact and provide this care beyond the office walls."[31] In a 2015 update to the mHIMSS Roadmap, the task force added the following topics: new care models (including consumer engagement), policy, privacy and security, return-on-investment and payment, standards and interoperability, and technology (infrastructure, standards, and interoperability).[32]

mHealth is identified by the National Institutes of Health as one of the key innovations to be studied in the *All of Us* Research Program (https://www.nih.gov/allofus-research-program). The program will support projects that use mHealth technologies to correlate activity, physiological measures, and environmental exposures with health outcomes.[33]

Across NIH, other studies are being conducted on mHealth. Mobile devices are being studied to facilitate anytime, anywhere access to healthcare data that extends beyond traditional clinical settings. NIH is conducting studies to develop new consumer engagement techniques and strategies for more effective and timely engagement between clinicians, patients, and consumers. Finally, mobile devices are considered a necessary ingredient going forward to determine the genetic/genomic variance in populations that are compliant with treatment, add alternative treatments such as diet and exercise to their treatments, and prevent the occurrence of persons with genetic predispositions from actually developing diseases. Mobile health is being touted as the path forward for consolidated and value-based care.

The Most Popular Mobile Health Apps

An IMS Institute for Healthcare Informatics report notes that significant variation exists in the functionality of mHealth apps available to consumers, with most having narrow functionality intended to inform, instruct, record, display, guide, remind/alert, or communicate. The report also points out that "depending on the intent of an app, multi-functionality is not always required to meet the purpose of an app and therefore should not be considered the single factor in assessing or rating mHealth apps."[34]

The most popular mobile device mHealth apps by category in 2015 were fitness apps (36%), lifestyle and stress management apps (17%), and diet and nutrition apps (12%).[34] There were over 130 fitness apps for public use. The most popular were MapMyFitness, Fitbit, and Runtastic. For disease and treatment management, the most widely used mHealth mobile apps by category in 2015 were for disease-specific information (9%), women's health and pregnancy (7%), and medication reminders and drug information (6%). In 2015, the top disease specific mHealth mobile device apps were mental health apps (29%), diabetes apps (15%), heart and circulatory apps (10%), musculoskeletal apps (7%), and nervous system apps (6%).[34]

The public utilized the apps to inform, instruct, record, display, guide, remind/alert, and communicate. The rapid advances in the devices have led to the rapid adoption and consumer-driven health wearables (watches, shoes with biofeedback, and stress relievers).

Between 2013 and 2015, there was a significant increase in the number of mHealth apps with the capability to connect to social media (up 8% from 26% to 34%). An app called QuitNow that provides real-time stats on consumption of cigarettes. Another example is C25K Couch to 5K that provides a training companion, and posts workouts and progress through Facebook.[34]

Mobile apps are available that integrate with social media for specific populations such as those with communication difficulties. The apps help people with autism, Down syndrome, amyotrophic lateral sclerosis (aka Lou Gehrig's disease), apraxia (difficulty speaking), stroke, or other conditions communicate through augmentation and alternative communication, and link to social media for support and educational community groups.

A major problem in mobile application is the sustainability rate, which was measured in 30-day usage of the app. The majority of persons with mental health issues sustain their usage only 40 percent, whereas the highest sustainability rate has been with fitness (76%), diabetes (67%), smoking cessation (63%), and caloric counting (62%). Overall app sustainability in 2015 is 59 percent.[34]

Healthcare Professionals' Use of Mobile Devices

The use of smartphones and tablets has become ubiquitous in most healthcare environments. The concept of bring your own device (BYOD) is now prominent in many healthcare settings. Healthcare professionals are bringing their Androids, iPhones, iPads, and tablets into their work environments. They are connecting to the vendor systems and integrating into the EHR. The IT departments have to secure those devices and their communications with the enterprise.

Major Barriers to Advancing Mobile Devices

The major barriers to widespread adoption of devices are the following: lack of evidence that the content changes patient outcomes; limited integration with EHR, personal health record (PHR), and patient portals; access gaps in coverage and communication;

data privacy and security; and lack of reimbursement. As mentioned previously, these are being addressed by the HIMSS task force on mHealth.[32]

Steps to Institutionalizing Genomic and Mobile Technologies

The most significant driver for both genomics and mobile technologies is the consumer. This section identifies the gaps that are common to both the genomics and mobile device areas.

The establishment of regulatory guidelines is ongoing but not complete. Security and privacy guidelines are not inclusive of genomic and mobile technologies. There is a gap in curating and evaluating the content on applications, and there is a lack of the following:

- Inclusive reimbursement models
- Strategic healthcare system buy-in to clinicians prescribing apps
- Integration of genomics and mobile devices into the clinical workflow, EHRs, PHRs, models for CDS to support the test result and interpretations, continuum of care, and optimized connectivity
- Predictors of success in consumers who should be screened for genetic tests, and those who should be prescribed mobile apps

The stakeholders moving forward are developers, regulators, institutions, payers, health systems, providers, and patients/consumers. Partnerships need to be facilitated to remove the barriers for these innovations. While there are databases of diseases and treatment and databases of pharmacogenomics, there currently are no genetic/genomics databases for symptom management (e.g., pain and fatigue).

Innovative Institutions Pushing Advances in Genomics and Mobile Devices

There are two national academic research programs (Stanford and MIT) and four companies that highlight the integration of genomics and mobile device use specifically focused on the aging population. A description of these innovative programs is as follows:

- Human Longevity, Inc. (HLI) is linking human genomics, informatics, next-generation DNA sequencing technologies, and stem cell advances to solve diseases of aging.
- The Google-owned company Calico is focused on comparative genomics to harness advanced technologies and understand the biology that controls lifespan.
- Palo Alto Investors is investing in prizes related to senescence (aging) research. They are asking questions such as why women live longer than men.
- The ABEO Smart Shoe from the Stanford Center for Longevity is sold through The Walking Company.
- The MIT AgeLab is a multidisciplinary research program that works with business, government, and NGOs to improve the quality of life of older persons.

Nine Technologies for Future Innovation Using Devices

According to the American Association of Retired Persons (AARP), the following nine technologies are still needed for innovation:[35]

- Hearing and vision, preventive aging care, cognitive and brain health, and life support tools
- Health sensors for vital sign monitoring, and diagnostic devices
- Care navigation of care records, care planning tools, and care coordination solutions
- Emergency detection and response—the integration of home security systems with sensors to detect falls, location tracking (in patients with Alzheimer's disease), and activity of daily living monitors (eating, walking, toileting)
- Physical fitness devices with enabling solutions for those persons with mobility impairments. This is also known as aging with vitality.
- Diet and nutrition tracking tools for cognitively impaired, immobile, and handicapped persons, with solutions for cooking
- Social engagement for mobility assistance, online communities, and peer-to-peer support
- Behavioral and emotional companionship solutions with support groups, self-help solutions, stress/emotional management, and grieving after loss
- Medication reminders, tracking tools, and compliance services

Social Media Being Used in Healthcare

The types of social media used in healthcare are a separate description that will not be fully addressed in this book. When healthcare providers and government agencies and officials want to get a message out to the press, they use Twitter. When they create groups for patients with similar conditions and want to educate, monitor, and evaluate groups of patients and consumers, they use Facebook. Oftentimes, a healthcare professional is a member of the Facebook group. Professionals and enterprises used LinkedIn to create communities of correspondence. All of these modes are available on smartphones, so the correspondence can be within healthcare and external to healthcare. Video platforms include YouTube for educational transmissions. Shared services utilize Skype and FaceTime to communicate with health professionals and patients/consumers.

Innovations in Telehealth

The American Telemedicine Association (ATA) defines telemedicine as "the use of medical information exchanged from one site to another via electronic communications to improve patients' health status."[36] ATA treats the terms "telemedicine" and "telehealth" as synonyms and uses them interchangeably to refer in general to the use of remote healthcare technology to deliver clinical services.[37] It clarifies the distinction sometimes made between the terms as follows: "Closely associated with telemedicine is the term 'telehealth,' which is often used to encompass a broader definition of remote healthcare that does not always involve clinical services."[36]

Telehealth is used in healthcare for live video conferencing, for consultation and remote patient monitoring and e-visits via a secure web portal. With mobile devices in patients' homes, telehealth can now be an extension of mobile health for home care monitoring in patients with chronic health conditions.

One of the advances in healthcare that makes healthcare practitioners more accessible to consumers and patients is the presence of nurse practitioners in retail clinics and pharmacies. Often equipped with telehealth, the nurse practitioner and pharmacist can triage the patient and call upon specialists and experts in academic healthcare and acute healthcare environments while the patient is in the retail clinic. When consultants are in demand for psychiatric and dermatologic needs of patients, for example, telehealth has provided a means for patients in remote and urban areas to have the advantage of a specialist consultant.

Major Services of Telehealth

Examples of major services of telehealth are defined by the ATA as follows:[38]

- **Primary care and specialist referral services** may involve a primary care or allied health professional providing a consultation with a patient or a specialist assisting the primary care physician in rendering a diagnosis. This may involve the use of live interactive video or the use of store and forward transmission of diagnostic images, vital signs, and/or video clips along with patient data for later review.

- **Remote patient monitoring**, including home telehealth, uses devices to remotely collect and send data to a home health agency or a remote diagnostic testing facility (RDTF) for interpretation. Such applications might include a specific vital sign, such as blood glucose or heart ECG or a variety of indicators for homebound patients. Such services can be used to supplement the use of visiting nurses.

- **Consumer medical and health information** includes the use of the Internet and wireless devices for consumers to obtain specialized health information and online discussion groups to provide peer-to-peer support.

- **Medical education** provides continuing medical education credits for health professionals and special medical education seminars for targeted groups in remote locations.

Delivery Mechanisms Used for Telehealth

ATA defines four delivery mechanisms that support telehealth:[39]

- **Networked programs** link tertiary care hospitals and clinics with outlying clinics and community health centers in rural or suburban areas. The links may use dedicated high-speed lines or the Internet for telecommunication links between sites. ATA estimates the number of existing telemedicine networks in the United States at roughly 200 providing connectivity to over 3,000 sites.

- **Point-to-point connections** using private high-speed networks are used by hospitals and clinics that deliver services directly or outsource specialty services to independent medical service providers. Such outsourced services include radiology, stroke assessment, mental health, and intensive care services.

- **Monitoring center links** are used for cardiac, pulmonary, or fetal monitoring, home care and related services that provide care to patients in the home. Often normal landline or wireless connections are used to communicate directly between the patient and the center although some systems use the Internet.

- **Web-based e-health patient service sites** provide direct consumer outreach and services over the Internet. Under telemedicine, these include those sites that provide direct patient care.

Chapter Review

This chapter has described healthcare innovations in three areas: genetics/genomics/pharmacogenomics, mobile devices, and telehealth. While there are other innovations and issues, barriers to implementation, and regulations affecting these and other areas, this chapter highlighted the healthcare IT needs in these three areas. The healthcare technology innovations in these areas have been embraced by consumers so rapidly that the healthcare industry and regulators are under pressure to address the hurdles of interstate licensure and reimbursement associated with these innovations. Further advances will be made in these three areas in the next five to ten years, and you can stay up to date by accessing the sources cited in this chapter. The next five to ten years will also demonstrate rapid advances in these three innovations, so primary sources have been provided for students.

Questions

To test your comprehension of the chapter, answer the following questions and then check your answers against the list of correct answers that follows the questions.

1. The importance of genomics in healthcare is to:
   A. Understand the genetics in healthcare
   B. Facilitate risk identification and diagnosis and establish prognosis and symptom management
   C. Plan for the future of healthcare
   D. Understand the actions of each gene

2. Why does genetic and genomic information require big data storage and analytics?
   A. Quality cost data has to be included in documenting genetics/genomic information.
   B. State and national healthcare data are needed.
   C. It is costly to pay for the genetics/genomics data.
   D. The diagnosis and analysis data involved in genomics requires the integration of several large databases, oftentimes requiring cloud computing.

3. What part of the continuum of care is affected by genetics and genomics?

   A. None of the continuum of care components is affected.

   B. The continuum of care from preconception to death.

   C. The continuum of care from a diagnosis to death.

   D. The continuum of care from diagnosis to treatment.

4. Where can the guidelines be found for pharmacogenomics evidence?

   A. There is no evidence in pharmacogenomics.

   B. There is evidence in the FDA guidelines for genomics.

   C. There is evidence in the AHRQ guidelines for disease treatment.

   D. The CPIC guidelines contain the pharmacogenomics evidence.

5. What best describes wireless communications?

   A. Networks that provide faster performance

   B. Networks that support only the Internet

   C. Mobile computing devices that connect with networks in multiple ways

   D. New technology transfers high bit rates

6. What best represents the future of mHealth inside healthcare facilities?

   A. Path toward consolidated and value-based care

   B. Access to TCP Internet usage

   C. Complete HL7 coverage

   D. Unified Internet communications

7. What are the most common mHealth platforms?

   A. Smartphones, electronic tablets, and remote technologies

   B. Cellular networks, wireless networks, and mobile devices

   C. Electronic tablets, mobile devices, and cellular networks

   D. Remote technologies, smartphones, and wireless devices

8. What is the correct definition of telehealth?

   A. Telehealth is the use of medical information exchanged from one site to another via electronic communications to improve patients' health status.

   B. Telehealth is the emerging field in medical informatics, referring to the organization and delivery of health services and information using the Web and related technologies.

   C. Telehealth is the field of informatics using a handheld device.

   D. Telehealth cannot be defined since it is an evolving method.

PART V

Answers

1. **B.** The importance of genomics in healthcare is to facilitate risk identification and diagnosis and to establish prognosis and symptom management.

2. **D.** The diagnosis and analysis involved in genomics requires the integration of several large databases. An actionable treatment course cannot be selected until the genes and pathways involved in the abnormality have been researched in multiple public and private databases. Both the clinical actions and the biologic actions need to determine the relevance to the treatment. These involve heuristic tools, curated and annotated databases, genomic tumor databases, and other knowledge bases that include outcome databases, genomic registries, integrative analysis tools, and machine learning systems. And in many cases, there are several possible treatment alternatives to a particular abnormality.

3. **B.** The entire continuum of care from preconception to death is affected by genetics and genomics.

4. **D.** The Clinical Pharmacogenomics Implementation Consortium (CPIC) guidelines contain the pharmacogenomics evidence.

5. **C.** Mobile computer devices that connect with networks in multiple ways best describes wireless communications. Technologies used to wirelessly communicate with mobile devices include mobile telecommunication such as Wi-Fi.

6. **A.** The future of mHealth inside healthcare facilities is best represented as a path toward consolidated and value-based care. Some of these innovations include paging and first-responder communication systems.

7. **B.** Cellular networks, wireless networks, and mobile devices are the most common mHealth platforms.

8. **A.** Telehealth is the use of medical information exchanged from one site to another via electronic communications to improve patients' health status.

References

1. Green, E. D., Watson, J. D., & Collins, F. S. (2015). Twenty-five years of big biology. *Nature, 526*(7571), 29–31.

2. Collins, F. S., & Varmus, H. (2015). A new initiative on Precision Medicine. *New England Journal of Medicine, 372*(9), 793–795.

3. Calzone, K. A., Jenkins, J., Nicol, N., Skirton, H., Feero, W. G., & Green, E. D. (2013). Relevance of genomics to healthcare and nursing practice. *Journal of Nursing Scholarship, 45*(1), 1–2.

4. Relling, M., & Veenstra, D. (2015, Feb. 26). *Implementation of pharmacogenomics: Evidence needs.* National Academy of Sciences. Accessed on February 28, 2017, from https://nam.edu/perspectives-2015-implementation-of-pharmacogenomics-evidence-needs/.

5. Lea, D. H., Cheek, D., Brazeau, D., & Brazeau, G. (2015). *Mastering pharmacogenomics: A nurse's handbook for success.* Sigma Theta Tau.

6. Relling, M. V., & Evans, W. E. (2015). Pharmacogenetics in the clinic. *Nature, 526,* 343–350. Also see Surgeon General Family History tool. Accessed on September 22, 2016, from www.hhs.gov/programs/prevention-and-wellness/family-health-history/index.html.

7. PharmGKB. Accessed on September 22, 2016, from https://www.pharmGKB.org.

8. CPIC guidelines. Accessed on March 15, 2017, from https://www.pharmgkb.org/vie/dosing-guidelines.do?source-CPIC or https://cpicpgx.org/guidelines,

9. Savage, N. (2014). Bioinformatics: Big data versus the big C. *Nature, 509,* S66–S67.

10. ClinGen (Clinical Genome Resource). Accessed on September 28, 2015, from https://clinicalgenome.org/.

11. Hoffman, J. M., Haidar, C. E., Wilkinson, M. R., Crews, K. R., Baker, D. K., Kornegay, N. M., … Relling, M. V. (2014). PG4KDS: A model for the clinical implementation of pre-emptive pharmacogenetics. *American Journal of Medical Genetics: Part C, Seminars in Medical Genetics, 166C*(1), 45–55.

12. Electronic Medical Records and Genomics (eMERGE) Network. Accessed on September 28, 2016, from https://www.genome.gov/27540473/.

13. National Academics of Sciences, Engineering, and Medicine—Health and Medicine Division. (2016). *DIGITizE: Displaying and integrating genetic information through the EHR.* Accessed on September 28, 2016, from http://iom.nationalacademies.org/Activities/Research/GenomicBasedResearch/Innovation-Collaboratives/EHR.aspx.

14. Wildin, B., & Jenkins, J. (2016). *Toolkit resources for primary care providers—Genetics in your clinic: What you can and should do now.* Accessed on September 28, 2016, from https://www.genome.gov/pages/health/healthcareprovidersinfo/vm-toolkit_20160315.pdf.

15. Global Alliance for Genomics and Health (GA4GH). (2016). A federated ecosystem for sharing genomic, clinical data. *Science, 352,* 1278–1280.

16. Feero, W. G., Bigley, M. B., & Brinner, K. M. (2008). New standards and enhanced utility for information in the electronic health record: An update from the American Health Information Community's Multi-Stakeholder Workgroup. *Journal of the American Medical Informatics Association, 15*(6), 723–728.

17. U.S. Department of Health and Human Services. (2008). *My family health portrait: A tool from the Surgeon General.* Accessed on September 28, 2016, from https://familyhistory.hhs.gov/. See also *The Surgeon General's family health history initiative.* Accessed on September 28, 2016, from www.hhs.gov/programs/prevention-and-wellness/family-health-history/index.html.

PART V

18. Bennett, R. L., French, K. S., Resta, R. G., & Doyle, L. D. (2008). Standardized human pedigree nomenclature: Update and assessment of the recommendations of the National Society of Genetic Counselors. *Journal of Genetic Counseling, 17*(5), 424–433.

19. International Data Corporation. (2016). *Worldwide mobile applications forecast, 2016–2020.* Doc. US41100816. https://www.idc.com/getdoc.jsp?containerId=US41100816

20. Cisco. (2016). *Cisco Visual Networking Index (VNI): Global mobile data traffic forecast, 2015–2020.* Accessed on September 22, 2016, from www.cisco.com/c/en/us/solutions/collateral/service-provider/visual-networking-index-vni/mobile-white-paper-c11-520862.html.

21. Federal Communications Commission. (2012). *mHealth Task Force: Findings and recommendations.* Accessed on September 29, 2016, from http://transition.fcc.gov/cgb/mhealth/mHealthRecommendations.pdf.

22. International Telecommunications Union Radio (ITU-R). Accessed on September 29, 2016, from www.itu.int/en/ITU-R/information/Pages/default.aspx.

23. International Mobile Telecommunications Advanced Technology (IMT-Advanced). Accessed on September 29, 2016, from www.itu.int/net/ITU-R/information/promotion/e-flash/2/article4.html.

24. Institute of Electrical and Electronics Engineers (IEEE). Accessed on September 29, 2016, from www.ieee802.org/15/pub/TG2.html.

25. IEEE 802 LAN/MAN Standards Committee. Accessed on September 29, 2016, from www.ieee802.org.

26. National Institute of Standards and Technology (NIST). (2012). *Guidelines for securing wireless local area networks.* NIST Special Publication 800-153. Accessed on September 29, 2016, from http://nvlpubs.nist.gov/nistpubs/Legacy/SP/nistspecialpublication800-153.pdf.

27. NIST. (2012). *Guide to Bluetooth security.* NIST Special Publication 800-121, revision 1. Accessed on September 29, 2016, from http://nvlpubs.nist.gov/nistpubs/Legacy/SP/nistspecialpublication800-121r1.pdf.

28. NIST. (2007). *Guidelines for securing radio frequency identification (RFID) systems.* NIST Special Publication 800-98. Accessed on April 9, 2014, from http://nvlpubs.nist.gov/nistpubs/Legacy/SP/nistspecialpublication800-98.pdf.

29. Institute of Electrical and Electronics Engineers (IEEE). (2013). *Revisiting past challenges and evaluating certificate trust model enhancements.* Accessed on September 29, 2016, from www.ieee-security.org/TC/SP2013/papers/4977a511.pdf.

30. Direct Project (2015). Accessed on September 28, 2016, from http://wiki .directproject.org/file/view/Applicability+Statement+for+Secure+Health+ Transport+v1.2.pdf.

31. Healthcare Information and Management Systems Society (HIMSS). (2015). *mHIMSS roadmap.* Accessed on February 28, 2017, from www.himss .org/himss-mhealth-roadmap-overview?ItemNumber=30480&navItemNumber =30479 .

32. HIMSS. (2015). *Mobile health roadmap update.* Accessed on February 28, 2017, from www.himss.org/library/mhealth

33. National Institutes of Health (NIH). (2016). *NIH precision medicine program scope.* Accessed on September 28, 2016, from https://www.nih.gov/precision-medicine-initiative-cohort-program/scale-scope.

34. IMS Health (now Quintiles IMS). (2016). *Patient adoption of mHealth: Availability and profile of consumer mHealth.* Accessed on February 28, 2017, from www.imshealth.com/en/thought-leadership/ims-institute/reports/patient-adoption-of-mhealth.

35. American Association of Retired Persons (AARP). (2014). *Health innovation frontiers II: The $30 billion social impact market in the shadows.* Accessed on February 28, 2017, from www.aarp.org/content/dam/aarp/home-and-family/ personal-technology/2014-10/2014-Health-Innovation-Frontiers-Untapped-Market-Opportunities-for-50+-Exec-Summary-AARP.pdf

36. American Telemedicine Association (ATA). (n.d.). *Telemedicine glossary.* Accessed on February 28, 2017, from http://thesource.americantelemed.org/resources/ telemedicine-glossary.

37. ATA. (n.d.). *About telemedicine.* Accessed on February 28, 2017, from www .americantelemed.org/main/about/about-telemedicine/telemedicine-faqs -.

38. ATA. (n.d.). *Services provided by telemedicine.* Accessed on February 28, 2017, from https://www.americantelemed.org/main/about/about-telemedicine/services-provided-by-telehealth

39. ATA. (n.d.). *Delivery mechanisms.* Accessed on February 28, 2017, from http:// www.americantelemed.org/main/about/about-telemedicine/delivery-mechanisms.

PART V

PART VI

Making It All Secure: Healthcare IT Privacy, Security, and Confidentiality

CHAPTER 25

Framework for Privacy, Security, and Confidentiality

Dixie B. Baker*

In this chapter, you will learn how to
- Explain the relationship between dependability and healthcare quality and safety
- Identify and explain five guidelines for building dependable systems
- Present an informal assessment of the healthcare industry with respect to these guidelines

The healthcare industry is in the midst of a dramatic transformation that is motivated by costly administrative inefficiencies, a payment system that rewards doctor visits rather than healthy outcomes, and a hit-or-miss approach to diagnosis and treatments. This transformation is driven by a number of factors, most prominently the skyrocketing cost of healthcare in the United States; the exposure of patient-safety problems related to care; advances in genomics and "big data" analytics; and an aging, socially networked population that expects the healthcare industry to effectively leverage information technology to manage costs, improve health outcomes, advance medical science, and engage consumers as active participants in their own health.

The U.S. Health Information Technology for Economic and Clinical Health (HITECH) Act that in 2009 was enacted as part of the American Recovery and Reinvestment Act (ARRA) provided major structural changes; funding for research, technical support, and training; and financial incentives designed to significantly expedite and accelerate this transformation.[1] The HITECH Act codified the Office of National Coordinator (ONC) for HIT and assigned it responsibility for developing a nationwide infrastructure that would facilitate the use and exchange of electronic health information,

*Adapted from Virginia K. Saba and Kathleen A. McCormick, *Essentials of Nursing Informatics, Sixth Edition* Chapter 10, 145–160. © 2015 by McGraw-Hill Education.

639

including policy, standards, implementation specifications, and certification criteria. In enacting the HITECH Act, Congress recognized that the meaningful use and exchange of electronic health records (EHRs) were key to improving the quality, safety, and efficiency of the U.S. healthcare system.

At the same time, the HITECH Act recognized that as more health information was recorded and exchanged electronically to coordinate care, monitor quality, measure outcomes, and report public health threats, the risk to personal privacy and patient safety would be heightened. This recognition is reflected in the fact that four of the eight areas the HITECH Act identified as priorities for the ONC specifically address risks to individual privacy and information security:[1]

- Technologies that protect the privacy of health information and promote security in a qualified electronic health record, including for the segmentation and protection from disclosure of specific and sensitive individually identifiable health information, with the goal of minimizing the reluctance of patients to seek care (or disclose information about a condition) because of privacy concerns, in accordance with applicable law, and for the use and disclosure of limited data sets of such information

- A nationwide HIT infrastructure that allows for the electronic use and accurate exchange of health information

- Technologies that as a part of a qualified electronic health record allow for an accounting of disclosures made by a covered entity (as defined by the Health Insurance Portability and Accountability Act of 1996) for purposes of treatment, payment, and healthcare operations

- Technologies that allow individually identifiable health information to be rendered unusable, unreadable, or indecipherable to unauthorized individuals when such information is transmitted in the nationwide health information network or physically transported outside the secured, physical perimeter of a healthcare provider, health plan, or healthcare clearinghouse

The HITECH Act resulted in the most significant amendments to the Health Insurance Portability and Accountability Act (HIPAA) Security and Privacy Rules since the rules became law.[2] In addition, the HITECH Act's EHR certification and "meaningful use" incentive program produced the most dramatic increase in the adoption and use of certified EHR technology the United States had ever witnessed.[3]

Capitalizing on this universal adoption of EHR technology, the Patient Protection and Affordable Care Act (ACA) enacted in 2010 changed the basis of payment from services rendered (e.g., visit, procedure) to the effectiveness of the outcomes attributable to those services, as captured in EHR data.[4] Because care may span multiple organizations, the ACA encouraged providers to participate in networks called accountable-care organizations (ACOs) through which outcome measures are reported. The ACA significantly increased the number of individuals covered by health insurance, while at the same time increasing privacy risks for individuals and security risks for healthcare organizations.

By associating coverage with individuals' Social Security numbers (SSNs), employers and providers were required to collect, store, and report SSNs, one of the most valuable individual identifiers. Thus, the healthcare organizations exchanging SSNs, along with sensitive health information, became very attractive targets for intruders. As the financial payout for medical records in the black market increased, the number of cyberattacks against healthcare systems and medical devices also increased[5] and the number of breaches of unprotected health information soared.[6] Although the certified EHR technology that providers adopted was tested against a set of standards and criteria, the certification process for security mechanisms included only conformance testing and did not include any assurance evaluation that would measure the degree to which these systems could defend against, withstand, or recover from concerted cyberattack. Thus the U.S. health system lacked the security and resilience architecture and functional components necessary to withstand a critical health infrastructure attack.[7]

As noted by former National Coordinator David Blumenthal, "Information is the lifeblood of modern medicine. Health information technology is destined to be its circulatory system. Without that system, neither individual physicians nor healthcare institutions can perform at their best or deliver the highest-quality care."[8] To carry Dr. Blumenthal's analogy one step further, at the heart of modern medicine lies "trust." Caregivers must trust that the technology and information they need will be available when they are needed at the point of care. They must trust that the information in an individual's EHR is accurate and complete and that it has not been accidentally or intentionally corrupted, modified, or destroyed. Consumers must trust that their caregivers will keep their most private personal and health information confidential and will disclose and use it only to the extent necessary and in ways that are legal, ethical, and authorized consistent with the consumer's personal expectations and preferences. Above all else, both providers and consumers must trust that the technology and services they use will "do no harm."

The medical field is firmly grounded in a tradition of ethics, patient advocacy, care quality, and human safety. Health professionals are well indoctrinated on clinical practice that respects personal privacy and that protects confidential information and life-critical information services. The American Medical Association (AMA) *Code of Medical Ethics* commits physicians to "respect the rights of patients, colleagues, and other health professionals, and shall safeguard patient confidences and privacy within the constraints of the law,[9] and the American Nurses Association's (ANA's) *Code of Ethics for Nurses with Interpretive Statements* includes a commitment to "promote, advocate for, and strive to protect the rights, health, and safety, and rights of the patient."[10] Fulfilling these ethical obligations is the individual responsibility of each healthcare professional, who must trust that the information technology she relies upon will help and not harm patients and will protect the patient's private information—despite the fact that digitizing information and transmitting it beyond the boundaries of the healthcare organization introduces risk to information confidentiality and integrity.

Recording, storing, using, and exchanging information electronically does indeed introduce new risks. As anyone who has used e-mail, texting, or social media knows, very little effort is required to instantaneously make private information accessible to millions of people throughout the world. We also know that disruptive and destructive software and nefarious human intruders skulk around the Internet of Things and insert themselves into our laptops, tablets, and smartphones, eager to capture our passwords, identities, credit card numbers, and health information. The question is whether these risks are outweighed by the many benefits enabled through HIT, such as the capability to receive laboratory results within seconds after a test is performed; to continuously monitor a patient's condition remotely, without requiring him to leave his home; or to align treatments with outcomes-based protocols and decision-support rules personalized according to the patient's condition, family history, and genome.

The ANA *Code of Ethics* acknowledges the challenges posed by "rapidly evolving communication technology and the porous nature of social media" and stresses that "nurses must maintain vigilance regarding postings, images, recordings, or commentary that intentionally or unintentionally breaches their obligation to maintain and protect patients' rights to privacy and confidentiality."[10] Along with these challenges come opportunities to engage patients in protecting their own health and the health of their families. Consumer health technology is growing at exponential rates. A 2016 study found that approximately 24 percent of consumers were using mobile apps to track health and wellness, 16 percent were using wearable sensors, and 29 percent used electronic personal health records—a trend expected to continue.[11] For healthcare professionals, this trend offers a huge opportunity to engage patients as a key player in the care team, helping to measure health indicators and monitor compliance with preventive and interventional strategies.

As HIT assumes a central role in the provision of care and in healthcare decision-making, healthcare providers increasingly must trust HIT to provide timely access to accurate and complete health information and to offer personalized clinical decision support based on that information, while assuring that individual privacy is continuously protected. Legal and ethical obligations, as well as consumer expectations, drive requirements for assurance that data and applications will be available when they are needed, that private and confidential information will be protected, that data will not be modified or destroyed other than as authorized, that systems will be responsive and usable, and that systems designed to perform health-critical functions will do so safely. These are the attributes of trustworthy HIT. The Markle Foundation's Connecting for Health collaboration identified privacy and security as technology principles fundamental to trust: "All health information exchange, including in support of the delivery of care and the conduct of research and public health reporting, must be conducted in an environment of trust, based upon conformance with appropriate requirements for patient privacy, security, confidentiality, integrity, audit, and informed consent."[12]

Many people think of "security" and "privacy" as synonymous. Indeed, these concepts are related—security mechanisms can help protect personal privacy by assuring that confidential personal information is accessible only by authorized individuals and entities. However, privacy is more than security, and security is more than privacy. A key component of privacy is autonomy—the right to decide for oneself whether and how one's health information is collected, used, and shared. Healthcare privacy principles were first articulated in 1973 in a U.S. Department of Health, Education, and Welfare report (entitled "Records, Computers, and the Rights of Citizens") as "fair information practice principles."[13] The Markle Foundation's Connecting for Health collaboration updated these principles to incorporate the new risks created by a networked environment in which health information routinely is electronically captured, used, and exchanged.[12] Other national and international privacy and security principles have also been developed that focus on individually identifiable information in an electronic environment (including but not limited to health). Based on these works, the ONC developed a Nationwide Privacy and Security Framework for Electronic Exchange of Individually Identifiable Health Information that identified eight principles intended to guide the actions of all people and entities that participate in networked, electronic exchange of individually identifiable health information.[14] These principles, described in Table 25-1, essentially articulate the "rights" of individuals to openness, transparency, fairness, and choice in the collection and use of their health information.

Principle	Description
Individual access	Individuals should be provided simple and timely means to access and obtain their individually identifiable health information in a readable form and format.
Correction	Individuals should be provided a timely means to dispute the accuracy or integrity of their individually identifiable health information and to have erroneous information corrected or the dispute documented.
Openness and transparency	Policies, procedures, and technologies that directly affect individuals and their individually identifiable health information should be open and transparent.
Individual choice	Individuals should be provided a reasonable opportunity and capability to make informed decisions about the collection, use, and disclosure of their individually identifiable health information.
Collection, use, and disclosure limitation	Individually identifiable health information should be collected, used, and/or disclosed only to the extent necessary to accomplish a specified purpose and never to discriminate inappropriately.
Data quality and integrity	People and entities should take reasonable steps to ensure that individually identifiable health information is complete, accurate, and up-to-date to the extent necessary for intended purposes and that it has not been altered or destroyed in an unauthorized manner.
Safeguards	Individually identifiable health information should be protected with reasonable administrative, technical, and physical safeguards to ensure its confidentiality, integrity, and availability and to prevent unauthorized or inappropriate access, use, or disclosure.
Accountability	These principles should be implemented—and adherence assured—through appropriate monitoring and other means, and methods should be in place to report and mitigate non-adherence and breaches.

Table 25-1 Eight Principles for Private and Secure Electronic Exchange of Individually Identifiable Health Information[14]

PART VI

Whereas privacy has to do with an individual's right to be left alone, security deals with protection, some of which supports that right. Security mechanisms and assurance methods are used to protect the confidentiality and authenticity of information, the integrity of data, and the availability of information and services; as well as to provide an accurate record of activities and accesses to information. Security mechanisms help assure the enforcement of access rules expressing individuals' privacy preferences and sharing consents. While these mechanisms and methods are critical to protecting personal privacy, they are also essential in protecting patient safety and care quality—and in engendering trust in electronic systems and information. For example, if laboratory results are corrupted during transmission or historical data in an EHR is overwritten, the healthcare professional is likely to lose confidence that the HIT can be trusted to help them provide quality care. If a sensor system designed to track wandering Alzheimer's patients shuts down without alarming those depending upon it, patients' lives are put at risk!

Trustworthiness is an attribute of each technology component and of integrated collections of technology components, including software components that may exist in "clouds," in smartphones, or in automobiles. Trustworthiness is very difficult to retrofit, as it must be designed and integrated into the technology or system and conscientiously preserved as the technology evolves. Discovering that an operational EHR system cannot be trusted generally indicates that extensive—and expensive—changes to the system are needed. In this chapter, we introduce a framework for achieving and maintaining trustworthiness in HIT.

When Things Go Wrong

Although we would like to be able to assume that computers, networks, and software are as trustworthy as our toasters and refrigerators, unfortunately that is not the case, and when computers, networks, and software fail in such a way that critical services and data are not available when they are needed, or confidential information is disclosed, or health data are corrupted, personal privacy and safety are imperiled.

In 2013, the Sutter Health System, in Northern California, experienced an outage affecting all 24 hospitals across the network. The outage was attributed to an "issue with the software that manages user access to the EHR"[15]—demonstrating that even technology designed to protect patients can cause security and safety risks. The "issue" resulted in a failure of both primary and back-up systems, and for one full day, nurses, physicians, and hospital staff had no access to patient information—including vital medication data, orders, and medical histories. Information available from back-up media was outdated by two to three days. Several days before the incident, the system had been purposely brought down for eight hours for a planned system upgrade—an unacceptable period of planned downtime for a "trustworthy" safety-critical system.[15]

Some might surmise that the risk of such outages might be mitigated by migrating systems to the cloud, where storage and infrastructure resources are made available upon demand, and services are provided in accordance with negotiated service-level agreements (SLAs). However, today's cloud environments are equally susceptible to outages. Even the largest global cloud computing infrastructures can be brought down by seemingly minor

Use Case 25-1: Stolen IDs Can Put Patient Safety at Risk

Identity theft is a felonious and seriously disruptive invasion of personal privacy that also can cause physical harm. In 2006, a 27-year-old mother of four children in Salt Lake City received a phone call from a Utah social worker notifying her that her newborn had tested positive for methamphetamines and that the state planned to remove all of her children from her home. The young mother had not been pregnant in more than two years, but her stolen driver's license had ended up in the hands of a meth user who gave birth while registered at the hospital using the stolen identity. After a few tense days of urgent phone calls with child services, the victim was allowed to keep her children. She hired an attorney to sort out the damages to her legal and medical records. Months later, when she needed treatment for a kidney infection, she carefully avoided the hospital where her stolen identity had been used. But her caution did no good—her electronic record, with the identity thief's medical information intermingled, had circulated to hospitals throughout the community. The hospital worked with the victim to correct her charts to avoid making life-critical decisions based on erroneous information. The data corruption damage could have been far worse had the thief's baby not tested positive for methamphetamines, bringing the theft to the victim's attention.[17]

factors—in some cases factors intended to provide security. One such example is a major crash of Microsoft's Azure Cloud that occurred in February 2013, when a Secure Sockets Layer (SSL) certificate used to authenticate the identity of a server was allowed to expire. The outage brought down cloud storage for 12 hours and affected secure web traffic worldwide. Over 50 different Microsoft services reported performance problems during the outage.[16]

One's personal genome is the most uniquely identifying of health information, and it contains information not only about the individual, but about her parents and siblings as well. One determined and industrious 15-year-old used his own personal genome to find his biological father, who was his mother's anonymous sperm donor.[18] Even whole genome sequences that claim to be "anonymized" can disclose an individual's identity, as demonstrated by a research team at Whitehead Institute for Biomedical Research.[19] As genomic data are integrated into EHRs and routinely used in clinical care, the potential for damage from unauthorized disclosure and identity theft significantly increases.

In July 2009, after noting several instances of computer viruses affecting the United Kingdom's National Health Service (NHS) hospitals, a British news broadcasting station conducted a survey of the NHS trusts throughout England to determine how many of their systems had been infected by computer viruses. Seventy-five percent replied, reporting that over 8,000 viruses had penetrated their security systems, with 12 incidents affecting clinical departments, putting patient care at risk and exposing personal information. One Scottish trust was attacked by the Conficker virus, which shut down computers for two days. Some attacks were used to steal personal information, and at a cancer center, 51 appointments and radiotherapy sessions had to be rescheduled.[20] The survey seemed to have little effect in reducing the threat—less than a year later, NHS systems were victimized by the Qakbot data-stealing worm, which infected over a thousand computers and stole massive amounts of information.[21]

For decades, healthcare organizations and individuals have known that they need to fortify their desktop computers and laptops to counter the threat of computer malware. However, as medical device manufacturers have integrated personal computer technology into medical devices, they have neglected to protect against malware threats. The U.S. Department of Veterans Affairs (VA) reported that between 2009 and 2013, malware infected at least 327 medical devices in VA hospitals, including X-ray machines, lab equipment, equipment used to open blocked arteries, and cameras used in nuclear medicine studies. In one reported outbreak, the Conflicker virus was detected in 104 devices in a single VA hospital. A VA security technologist surmised that the malware most likely was brought into the hospital on infected thumb drives used by vendor support technicians to install software updates.[22] Infections from malware commonly seen in the wild are most likely to cause a degradation of system performance or to expose patients' private data. However, malware written to target a specific medical device could result in even more dire consequences. Recognizing the safety risk posed by malware, the Food and Drug Administration (FDA) in 2013 published a warning addressed to medical device manufacturers, hospitals, medical device users, healthcare IT and procurements staff, and biomedical engineers regarding cybersecurity risks affecting medical devices and hospital networks.[23]

Since 2009, entities covered under HIPAA have been required to notify individuals whose unsecured protected health information (PHI) may have been exposed due to a security breach, and to report to the Department of Health and Human Services (HHS) breaches affecting 500 or more individuals. HHS maintains a public web site, frequently referred to as the "wall of shame," listing the breaches reported.[24] Between October 21, 2009, and March 2, 2017, a total of 1,850 breaches, affecting over 172 million individuals, were reported! One breach, affecting nearly 79 million individuals, accounted for almost half of the individuals affected. From the first reported breach until March 26, 2010, no hacking incidents were reported. Since that time, 283 hacking incidents have been reported, including three that together affected nearly 100 million individuals.[2]

 TIP Breaches affecting 500 or more individuals must be immediately reported to the secretary of the Department of Health and Human Services, who must post a list of such breaches to a public web site.

The bottom line is that systems, networks, and software applications, as well as the contexts within which they are used, are highly complex, and the only safe assumption is that "things will go wrong." Trustworthiness is an essential attribute for the systems, software, services, processes, and people used to manage individuals' health information and to help provide safe, high-quality healthcare.

HIT Trust Framework

Trustworthiness can never be achieved by implementing a few policies and procedures, licensing some security technology, and checking all the boxes in a HIPAA checklist. Protecting sensitive and safety-critical health information and assuring that the systems, services, and information that healthcare professionals rely upon to deliver quality care are available when they are needed, require a complete HIT trust framework that starts with an objective assessment of risk, and that is conscientiously applied throughout the development and implementation of policies, operational procedures, and security safeguards built on a solid system architecture. This trust framework is depicted in Figure 25-1 and comprises seven layers of protection, each of which is dependent upon the layers below it (indicated by the arrows in the figure), and all of which must work together to provide a trustworthy HIT environment for healthcare delivery. This trust framework does not dictate a physical architecture; it may be implemented within a single site or across multiple sites, and may comprise enterprise, mobile, home health, and cloud components.

Layer 1: Risk Management

Risk management is the foundation of the HIT trust framework. Objective risk assessment informs decision making and positions an organization to address those physical, operational, and technical deficiencies that pose the highest risk to the organization's information assets. Objective risk assessment also puts in place protections that will enable the organization to manage the residual risk and liability.

 TIP Patient safety, individual privacy, and information security all relate to risk, which is simply the probability that some "bad thing" will happen to adversely affect a valued asset. Risk is always considered with respect to a given context comprising relevant threats, vulnerabilities, and valued assets. Threats can be natural occurrences (e.g., earthquake, hurricane), accidents, or malicious people and software programs. Vulnerabilities are present in facilities, hardware, software, communication systems, business processes, workforces, and electronic data. Valued assets can be anything from reputation to business infrastructure to information to human lives.

A security risk is the probability that a threat will exploit a vulnerability to expose confidential information, corrupt or destroy data, or interrupt or deny essential information services. If that risk could result in the unauthorized disclosure of an individual's private health information or the compromise of an individual's identity, it also represents a privacy risk. If the risk could result in the corruption of clinical data or an interruption in the availability of a safety-critical system, potentially causing human harm or the loss of life, it is a safety risk as well.

Information security is widely viewed as the protection of information confidentiality, data integrity, and service availability. Indeed, these are the three types of technical safeguards directly addressed by the HIPAA Security Rule.[2] Generally, safety is most closely associated with protective measures for data integrity and the availability of life-critical

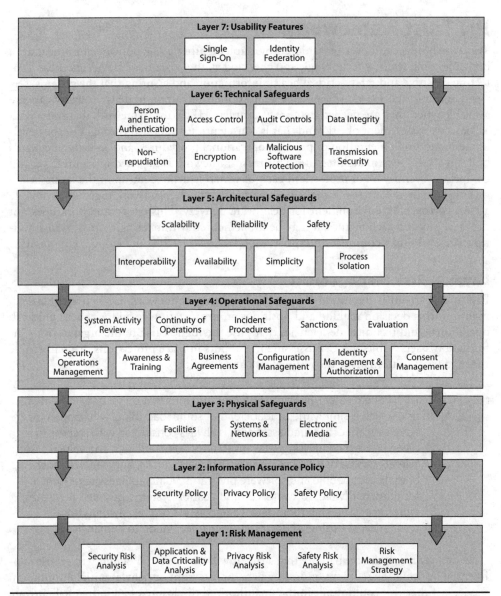

Figure 25-1 A framework for achieving and maintaining trustworthiness in healthcare IT comprises multiple layers of trust, beginning with objective risk assessment that serves as the foundation for information assurance policy and operational, architectural, and technological safeguards.

information and services, while privacy is more often linked to confidentiality. However, the unauthorized exposure of private health information, or corruption of one's personal EHR as a result of an identity theft, can also put an individual's health, safety, lifestyle, and livelihood at risk.

Risk management is an ongoing, individualized discipline wherein each individual or each organization examines its own threats, vulnerabilities, and valued assets and decides for itself how to deal with identified risks—whether to reduce or eliminate them, counter them with protective measures, or tolerate them and prepare for the consequences. Risks to personal privacy, patient safety, care quality, financial stability, and public trust all must be considered in developing an overall strategy for managing risks both internal and external to an organization. Effective risk management helps security managers determine how to allocate their budgets to get the strongest protection possible against those threats that could cause the most harm to the organization.

In bygone times, risk assessment focused on resources within a well-defined physical and electronic boundary that comprised the "enterprise." In today's environment, where resources may include cloud components, bring-your-own devices (BYOD), smartphones, personal health-monitoring devices, as well as large, complex enterprise systems, risk assessment is far more challenging and will require careful analysis of potential data flows and close examination of SLAs for enterprise and cloud services, data-sharing agreements with trading partners, and personnel agreements.

 TIP Resource virtualizations—from Internet transmissions to cloud computing—present particular challenges because the computing and networking resources used may be outside the physical and operational control of the subscriber and are likely to be shared with other subscribers.

Layer 2: Information Assurance Policy

The risk management strategy will identify what security, privacy, and safety risks need to be addressed through an information assurance policy that governs operations, information technology, and individual behavior. The information assurance policy comprises rules that guide organizational decision-making, and that define behavioral expectations and sanctions for unacceptable actions. The policy defines rules for protecting individuals' private information, protecting the security of that information, and providing choice and transparency with respect to how individuals' health information is safely used and shared. It includes rules that protect human beings, including patients, employees, family members, and visitors, from physical harm that could result from data corruption or service interruption. Overall, the information assurance policy defines the rules enforced to protect the organization's valued information assets from identified risks to personal privacy, information confidentiality, data integrity, and service availability.

Some policy rules are mandated by applicable state and federal laws and regulations. For example, the HIPAA Security Rule requires compliance with a set of administrative, physical, and technical standards, and the HIPAA Privacy Rule (2013) sets forth privacy policies to be implemented.[2] However, although the HIPAA regulations establish uniform minimum privacy and security standards, state health privacy laws are quite diverse. Because the HIPAA regulations apply only to "covered entities" and their "business associates" and not to everyone who may hold health information, and because the HIPAA regulations pre-empt only those state laws that are less stringent, the privacy protections of individuals and security protections of health information vary depending on who is holding the information and the state in which they are located.[25]

The policy that codifies the nurse's obligation to protect patients' privacy and safety is embodied in the ANA *Code of Ethics for Nurses:*[10]

- The nurse holds in confidence personal information and uses judgment in sharing this information.
- The nurse takes appropriate action to safeguard individuals, families, and communities when their health is endangered by a co-worker or any other person.

The HIT information assurance policy provides the foundation for the development and implementation of physical, operational, architectural, and security technology safeguards. Healthcare professionals can provide valuable insights, recommendations, and advocacy in the formulation of information assurance policy within the organizations where they practice, as well as within their professional organizations and with state and federal governments.

Layer 3: Physical Safeguards

Physically safeguarding health information and the information technology used to collect, store, retrieve, analyze, and share health data is essential to assuring that information needed at the point and time of care is available, trustworthy, and usable in providing quality healthcare. Although the electronic signals that represent health information are not themselves "physical," the facilities within which data is generated, stored, displayed, and used; the media on which data is recorded and shared; the information system hardware used to process, access, and display the data; and the communications equipment used to transmit and route the data are physical. So are the people who generate, access, and use the information the data represent. Physical safeguards are essential to protecting these assets in accordance with the information assurance policy.

TIP The HIPAA Security Rule prescribes four standards for physically safeguarding electronic health information protected under HIPAA: facility-access controls, workstation use, workstation security, and device and media controls. Physically safeguarding the lives and well-being of patients is central to the roles and responsibilities of healthcare professionals. Protecting patients requires the physical protection of the media on which their health data are recorded, as well as the devices, systems, networks, and facilities involved in data collection, use, storage, and disposal.

Healthcare organizations are increasingly choosing to purchase services from third parties, rather than hosting and maintaining these services within their own facilities. Third-party services include EHR software-as-a-service (SaaS) applications, outsourced hosting services, and cloud storage, platform, and infrastructure offerings. The HIPAA Security Rule requires that the providers of these services sign a business associate agreement in which they agree to meet all of the HIPAA security standards. However, if a breach occurs, the covered entity retains primary responsibility for reporting and responding to the breach. So it is essential that healthcare entities perform due diligence to assure that their business associates understand and are capable of providing the required levels of physical protection and data isolation.

Layer 4: Operational Safeguards

Operational safeguards are processes, procedures, and practices that govern the creation, handling, usage, and sharing of health information in accordance with the information assurance policy. The HIT trust framework shown in Figure 25-1 includes the following operational safeguards.

System Activity Review

One of the most effective means of detecting potential misuse and abuse of privileges is by regularly reviewing records of information system activity, such as audit logs, facility access reports, security incident tracking reports, and accountings of disclosures. The HIPAA Privacy Rule requires that covered entities provide to patients, upon request, an accounting of all disclosures (i.e., outside the entity holding the information) of their PHI except for those disclosures for purposes of treatment, payment, and healthcare operations (TPO). The HITECH Act dropped the TPO exception, and a proposed rule was published in May 2011.[26] However, in October 2014, the Office of Civil Rights announced a delay in the release of a final rule. As of this writing, no final regulation has been released.

Technology that automates system-activity review is increasingly being used by healthcare organizations to detect potential intrusions and internal misuse, particularly since healthcare has become a key target for intruders.

Continuity of Operations

Unexpected events, both natural and human-produced, do happen, and when they do, it is important that critical health services can continue to be provided. As healthcare organizations become increasingly dependent on electronic health information and information systems, the need to plan for unexpected events and for operational procedures that enable the organization to continue to function through emergencies becomes more urgent. The HIPAA Security Rule requires that organizations establish and implement policies and procedures for responding to an emergency. Contingency planning is part of an organization's risk-management strategy, and the first step is performed as part of a risk assessment—identifying those software applications and data that are essential for enabling operations to continue under emergency conditions and for returning to full operations. These business-critical systems are those to which architectural safeguards such as fail-safe design, redundancy and failover, and availability engineering should be applied.

The rapidly escalating risk to healthcare organizations is motivating them to strengthen their continuity-of-operations posture. The 2015 Cybersecurity Survey conducted by the Health Information Management and Systems Society (HIMSS) reported that 87 percent of respondents "indicated that information security had increased as a business priority" over the previous year, resulting in "improvements to network security

PART VI

capabilities, endpoint protection, data loss prevention, disaster recovery, and information technology (IT) continuity."[27]

Incident Procedures

Awareness and training should include a clear explanation of what an individual should do if they suspect a security incident, such as a malicious code infiltration, denial-of-service attack, or a breach of confidential information. Organizations need to plan their response to an incident report, including procedures for investigating and resolving the incident, notifying individuals whose health information may have been exposed as a result of the incident, and penalizing parties responsible for the incident. Individuals whose information may have been exposed as a result of a breach must be notified, and breaches affecting 500 or more individuals must be reported to DHS.

Not all security incidents are major or require enterprise-wide response. Some incidents may be as simple as a user accidentally including PHI in a request from the help desk. Incident procedures should not require a user or helpdesk operator to make a judgment call on the seriousness of a disclosure; procedures should be clear about what an individual should do when they notice a potential disclosure.

Sanctions

The HIPAA law, as amended by the HITECH Act, prescribes severe civil and criminal penalties for sanctioning entities that fail to comply with the privacy and security provisions.[28,1] Organizations must implement appropriate sanctions to penalize workforce members who fail to comply with privacy and security policies and procedures. An explanation of workforce sanctions should be included in annual HIPAA security and privacy training.

Evaluation

Periodic, objective evaluation of the operational and technical safeguards in place helps measure the effectiveness, or "outcomes," of the security management program. A formal evaluation should be conducted at least annually and should involve independent participants who are not responsible for the program. Security evaluation should include resources and services maintained within the enterprise, as well as resources and services provided by business associates—including SaaS and cloud-services providers. Independent evaluators can be from either within or outside an organization, as long as they can be objective. In addition to the annual programmed evaluation, security technology safeguards should be evaluated whenever changes in circumstances or events occur that affect the risk profile of the organization.

Security Operations Management

HIPAA regulations require that each healthcare organization designate a "security official" and a "privacy official" to be responsible for developing and implementing security and privacy policies and procedures. The management of services relating to the protection of health information and patient privacy touches every function within a healthcare organization. For large enterprises, responsibility for security- and safety-critical operations may require implementation of shared, two-person administration.

Awareness and Training

One of the most valuable actions a healthcare organization can take to maintain public trust is to inculcate a culture of safety, privacy, and security. If every person employed by, or associated with, a healthcare organization feels individually responsible for protecting the confidentiality, integrity, and availability of health information and the privacy and safety of patients, the risk for that organization will be vastly reduced! Recognition of the value of workforce training is reflected in the fact that the HIPAA Security and Privacy Rules require training in security and privacy, respectively, for all members of the workforce. Formal privacy and security training should be required to be completed at least annually, augmented by simple reminders.

Business Agreements

Business agreements help manage risk and bound liability, clarify responsibilities and expectations, and define processes for addressing disputes among parties. The HIPAA Privacy and Security Rules require that each person or organization that provides to a covered entity services involving individually identifiable health information must sign a "business associate" contract obligating the service provider to comply with HIPAA requirements, subject to the same enforcement and sanctions as covered entities. The HIPAA Privacy Rule also requires "data use agreements" defining how "limited data sets" will be used. Organizations wishing to exchange health information as part of the National eHealth Collaborative must sign a Data Use and Reciprocal Support Agreement (DURSA) in which they agree to exchange and use message content only in accordance with the agreed-upon provisions.[29] Agreements are only as trustworthy as the entities that sign them. Organizations should exercise due diligence in deciding with whom they will enter into business agreements.

The HIPAA administrative definitions draw a distinction between "business associates" and members of the "workforce" whose work performance is under the direct control of a covered entity or business associate. Although not required by HIPAA, having workforce members attest to their understanding of their responsibilities to protect privacy and security is a good business practice as part of a comprehensive risk-management program.

Configuration Management

Configuration management refers to processes and procedures for maintaining an accurate and consistent accounting of the physical and functional attributes of a system throughout its life cycle. From an information assurance perspective, configuration management is the process of controlling and documenting modifications to the hardware, firmware, software, and documentation involved in the protection of information assets.

Identity Management and Authorization

Arguably, the operational processes most critical to the effectiveness of technical safeguards are the process used to positively establish the identity of the individuals and entities to whom rights and privileges are being assigned, and the process used to assign credentials and authorizations to (and withdraw them from) those identities. Many of the technical safeguards (e.g., authentication, access control, audit, digital signature, secure e-mail) rely upon and assume the accuracy of the identity that is established when an account is created.

Identity management begins with verification of the identity of each individual before creating a system account for them. This process, called "identity proofing," may require the person to present one or more government-issued documents containing the individual's photograph, such as a driver's license or passport. Once identity has been positively established, a system account is created, giving the individual the access rights and privileges essential to performing their assigned duties, and a "credential" is issued to serve as a means of "authenticating" identity when the individual attempts to access resources. (See the "Layer 6: Technical Safeguards," section, later in the chapter.) The life cycle of identity management includes the prompt termination of identities and authorizations when the individual leaves the organization, is suspected of misuse of privileges, or otherwise no longer needs the resources and privileges assigned to them. In addition, the identity-management life cycle includes the ongoing maintenance of the governance processes.

Consent Management

Just as medical ethics and state laws require providers to obtain a patient's "informed consent" before delivering medical care, or administering diagnostic tests or treatment, a provider must obtain the individual's consent (also called "permission" or "authorization") prior to taking any actions that involve their personal information. Similarly, the Federal Policy for the Protection of Human Subjects (aka the Common Rule), designed to protect human research subjects, requires informed consent before using an individual's identifiable private information or identifiable biospecimens in research.[30] Obtaining an individual's permission is fundamental to respecting their right to privacy, and a profusion of state and federal laws set forth requirements for protecting and enforcing this right.

The HIPAA Privacy Rule specifies conditions under which an individual's personal health information may be used and exchanged, including uses and exchanges that require the individual's express "authorization." Certain types of information, such as psychotherapy notes and substance abuse records, have special restrictions and authorization requirements. Managing an individual's consents and authorizations and assuring consistent adherence to the individual's privacy preferences are complex processes, but essential to protecting personal privacy.

Historically, consent management has been primarily a manual process, and signed consent documents have been collected and managed within a single institution. However, as health information was digitized and electronically shared among multiple institutions and with the patient, paper-based consent management no longer is practical. At the same time, digitization and electronic exchange heightens the risk of disclosure and misuse. New standards and models for electronically capturing individual consents and for exchanging individual permissions are beginning to emerge. Although the original HIPAA Security Rule published in 1998 included a requirement for a digital signature standard, by the time the final rule was issued, this requirement had been omitted, placing the onus on the covered entity to ensure that digital signature methods they use are sufficiently secure and do not lead to compromise of PHI. The preamble to the Privacy Rule final rule, issued in 2002, stated "currently, no standards exist under HIPAA for electronic signatures. Thus, in the absence of specific standards, covered entities should ensure [that] any electronic signature used will result in a legally binding contract under applicable State or other law."[31] Standards for "segmenting" data for special protection also are beginning to emerge.[32]

Layer 5: Architectural Safeguards

A system's architecture comprises its individual hardware and software components, the relationships among them, their relationship with the environment, and the principles that govern the system's design and evolution over time. As shown in Figure 25-1, specific architectural design principles and the hardware and software components that support those principles work together to establish the technical foundation for security technology safeguards. In simpler times, the hardware and software components that comprised an enterprise's architecture were under the physical and logical control of the enterprise itself, but in an era when an enterprise may depend upon external services (e.g., a health exchange service, external back-up service) and virtualized services (e.g., SaaS, cloud storage), this may not be the case. Still, the design principles discussed in the following sections apply whether an enterprise's architecture is centralized or distributed, physical or virtual.

Scalability

As more health information is recorded, stored, used, and exchanged electronically, systems and networks must be able to deal with that growth. A catastrophic failure at CareGroup in 2003 resulted from the network's inability to scale to the capacity required.[33] The most recent stage in the evolution of the Internet specifically addresses the scalability issue by virtualizing computing resources into services, including SaaS, platforms as a service (PaaS), and infrastructure as a service (IaaS)—collectively referred to as "cloud" services. Indeed, the Internet itself was created on the same principle as cloud computing—the creation of a virtual, ubiquitous, continuously expanding network through the sharing of resources (servers) owned by different entities. Whenever one sends information over the Internet, the information is broken into small packets that are then sent ("hop") from server to server from source to destination, with all of the servers in between being "public"—in the sense that they probably belong to someone other than the sender or the receiver. Cloud computing, a model for provisioning "on demand" computing services accessible over the Internet, pushes virtualization to a new level by sharing applications, storage, and computing power to offer flexible scalability beyond what would be economically possible otherwise.

Reliability

Reliability is the ability of a system or component to perform its specified functions consistently and over a specified period of time—an essential attribute of trustworthiness.

Safety

Safety-critical components, software, and systems should be designed so that if they fail, the failure will not cause people to be physically harmed. Note that fail-safe design may indicate that under certain circumstances, a component should be shut down or forced to cease to perform its usual functions in order to avoid harming someone. So the inter-relationships among redundancy and failover, reliability, and fail-safe design are complex, yet critical to patient safety. The "break-the-glass" feature that enables an unauthorized user to gain access to patient information in an emergency situation is an example of fail-safe design. If, in an emergency, an EHR system "fails" to provide a healthcare provider access to the clinical information they need to deliver care, the "break-the-glass" feature will enable the system to "fail safely." Fail-safe methods are particularly important in research, where new treatment protocols and devices are being tested for safety.

Interoperability

Interoperability is the ability of systems and system components to work together. To exchange health information effectively, healthcare systems must interoperate at every level on the Open Systems Interconnect (OSI) reference model, and beyond that, at the syntactic and semantic levels as well.[34] The Internet and its protocols, which have been adopted for use within enterprises as well, transmit data (packets of electronic bits) over a network in such a way that upon arrival at their destination, the data appear the same as when they were sent. If the data are encrypted, the receiving system must be able to decrypt the data, and if the data are wrapped in an electronic envelope (e.g., e-mail message, HL7 message), the system must open the envelope and extract the content. Finally, the system must translate the electronic data into health information that the system's applications and users will understand. Open standards, including encryption and messaging standards, and standard vocabulary for coding and exchanging security attributes and patient permissions—e.g., Security Assertion Markup Language (SAML), OAuth 2.0—are fundamental to implementing interoperable healthcare systems.

At a finer level of abstraction than the "application layer" are the syntactic packages and semantic coding that together help assure that applications that process health information will interpret the information consistently across systems within an organization, and between systems at different organizations. Historically, Health Level Seven (HL7) messaging has been used for this purpose. More recently, HL7 introduced a new model for packaging and exchanging health information. Called Fast Healthcare Interoperability Resources (FHIR), the new model is designed to capitalize on the simplicity of RESTful Internet exchange by defining "resources" that are exchanged in accordance with predefined FHIR "profiles."[35] Access authorization to FHIR resources is performed primarily using the OAuth 2.0 authorization framework.[36]

Further, within these packages, health information is coded using an extensive set of controlled vocabularies that are used for different purposes, such as SNOMET-CT for clinical systems, ICD-10 for classifying diseases for reimbursement purposes, and RxNorm for drug prescribing. The complexity of health information exchange only serves to heighten the need for data integrity and system security.

Availability

Required services and information must be available and usable when they are needed. Availability is measured as the proportion of time a system is in a functioning condition. A reciprocal dependency exists between security technology safeguards and high-availability design—security safeguards depend on the availability of systems, networks, and information, which in turn enable those safeguards to protect enterprise assets against threats to availability, such as denial-of-service attacks. Resource virtualization and "cloud" computing are important technologies for helping assure availability.

Simplicity

Safe, secure architectures are designed to minimize complexity. The simplest design and integration strategy will be the easiest to understand, maintain, and recover in the case of a failure or disaster. Achieving simplicity may be an elusive goal for implementers of healthcare systems, but it is an important principle to helping minimize security vulnerabilities.

Process Isolation

Isolation refers to the extent to which processes running on the same system at different trust levels, virtual machines (VMs) running on the same hardware, or applications running on the same computer or tablet are kept separate so that if one process, VM, or application misbehaves or is compromised, other processes, VMs, or applications can continue to operate safely and securely. Isolation is particularly important to preserve the integrity of the operating system itself. Within an operating system, functions critical to the security and reliability of the system execute within a protected hardware state, while untrusted applications execute within a separate state. However, this hardware architectural isolation is undermined if the system is configured so that untrusted applications are allowed to run with privilege, which puts the operating system itself at risk. For example, if a user logs into an account with administrative privileges and then runs an infected application (or opens an infected e-mail attachment), the entire operating system becomes infected.

Within a cloud environment, the hypervisor is assigned responsibility for assuring that VMs are kept separate so that processes running on one subscriber's VM cannot interfere with those running on another VM. In general, the same security safeguards used to protect an enterprise system are equally effective in a cloud environment—but only if the hypervisor is able to maintain isolation among virtual environments. Another example of isolation is seen in the Apple iOS environment. Apps running on an iPad or iPhone are isolated such that not only are they unable to view or modify each other's data, but one app does not even know whether another app is installed on the device. (Apple calls this architectural feature "sandboxing.")

Layer 6: Technology Safeguards

Technology safeguards are software and hardware services specifically designed to perform security-related functions. All of the security services depicted in Figure 25-1 are technical safeguards required by the HIPAA Security Rule. Table 25-2 identifies a number of standards that are useful in implementing these safeguards.

Safeguard	Standard	Description
Person and entity authentication	ITU-T X.509: Information technology—Open Systems Interconnection—The Directory: Public-key and attribute-certificate frameworks	Standard for public-key infrastructure (PKI), single sign-on, and privilege-management infrastructure (PMI); includes standard formats for public-key certificates, certificate revocation lists, attribute certificates, and a certification path-validation algorithm
	OASIS Security Assertion Markup Language (SAML)	XML-based protocol for exchanging authentication and authorization data ("assertions") between an identity provider and a service provider; used to enable single sign-on
	OpenID Foundation OpenID Connect	Standard for a simple identity layer that lies on top of the OAuth 2.0 protocol
Access control	IETF OAuth 2.0 Authorization Framework; RFC 6749	Standard for enabling a third-party application (or mobile app) to obtain limited access to a web service, either on behalf of a resource owner by orchestrating an approval interaction between the resource owner and the web service, or by allowing the third-party application to obtain access on its own behalf
	INCITS 359-2012: Information technology—role-based access control (RBAC)	Specifies RBAC elements (users, roles, permissions, operations, objects) and features required by an RBAC system
	HL7 Version 3 Confidentiality Code System	HL7 V3 value set for coding confidentiality attributes
	HL7 Version 3 Role-based Access Control (RBAC) Healthcare Permission Catalog	Permission vocabulary to support RBAC, consistent with OASIS XACML and ANSI INCITS RBAC standards
	OASIS eXtensible Access Control Markup Language (XACML)	XML-based language for expressing information technology security policy
Audit controls	ASTM E2147-01(2013): Standard Specification for Audit and Disclosure Logs for Use in Health Information Systems	Specifies how to design audit logs to record accesses within a computer system and disclosure logs to document disclosures to external users

Category	Standard	Description
Data integrity	FIPS PUB 180-4 Secure Hash Standard (SHS)	Specifies five hash algorithms that can be used to generate message digests used to detect whether messages have been changed since the digests were generated
Nonrepudiation	ASTM E1762-95(2013): Standard Guide for Electronic Authentication of Health Care Information	Standard on the design, implementation, and use of electronic signatures to authenticate healthcare data
	ETSI TS 101 903: XML Advanced Electronic Signatures (XAdES)	Defines XML formats for advanced electronic signatures, based on the use of public-key cryptography supported by public-key certificates
Encryption (confidentiality)	FIPS PUB 197, Advanced Encryption Standard	Specifies a symmetric cryptographic algorithm that can be used to protect electronic data
Transmission security	IETF Transport Layer Security (TLS) protocol: RFC 2246, RFC 3546	Standard for establishing secured channel at layer 4 (transport) of the OSI model; includes authentication of sender and receiver and encryption and integrity protection of the communication channel
	IETF IP Security Protocol (IPsec): RFCs listed at https://datatracker.ietf.org/wg/ipsec/	Standard for establishing virtual private network (VPN) at layer 3 (network) of the OSI model; includes authentication of sender and receiver and encryption and integrity protection of the communication channel
	IETF Secure/Multipurpose Internet Mail Extensions (S/MIME): RFC 2633	Internet mail protocol for providing authentication, message integrity and nonrepudiation of origin (digital signatures), and confidentiality protection (encryption)
	OASIS Web Services Security (WS-Security)	Extension to the Simple Object Access Protocol (SOAP) transport protocol used to access web services; includes encryption and digital signing of messages and exchange of security tokens, including SAML assertions

ANSI: American National Standards Institute; ASTM: ASTM International (originally American Society for Testing and Materials); ETSI: European Telecommunications Standards Institute; FIPS: National Institute of Standards and Technology (NIST) Federal Information Processing Standard; HL7: Health Level Seven; IETF: Internet Engineering Task Force; INCITS: InterNational Committee for Information Technology Standards; ITU-T: International Telecommunication Union—Telecommunication Standardization Sector; OASIS: Organization for the Advancement of Structured Information Standards

Table 25-2   Many Open Standards Address Security Technology Safeguards

Person and Entity Authentication

The identity of each entity, whether it be a person or a software entity, must be clearly established before that entity is allowed to access protected systems, applications, and data. Identity management and authorization processes are used to validate identities and to assign them system rights and privileges. (See the "Identity Management and Authorization" section earlier in the chapter.) Then, whenever the person or application requires access, it asserts an identity (userID) and authenticates that identity by providing some "proof" in the form of something it has (e.g., smartcard), something it knows (e.g., password, private encryption key), or something it is (e.g., fingerprint). The system then checks to verify that the userID represents someone who has been authorized to access the system, and then verifies that the "proof" submitted provides the evidence required. While only people can authenticate themselves using biometrics, both people and software applications can authenticate themselves using public-private key exchanges.

Individuals who work for federal agencies, such as the Department of Veterans Affairs (VA), are issued Personal Identity Verification (PIV) cards containing a digital certificate that uniquely identifies the individual and the rights assigned to them. The National Strategy for Trusted Identities in Cyberspace (NSTIC) program is working toward an "identity ecosystem" in which each individual possesses trusted credentials for proving their identity.[37]

Access Control

Access-control services help assure that people, computer systems, and software applications are able to use all of (and only) the resources (e.g., computers, networks, applications, services, data files, information) they are authorized to use and only within the constraints of the authorization. Access controls protect against unauthorized use, disclosure, modification, and destruction of resources and unauthorized execution of system functions. Access-control rules are based on federal and state laws and regulations, the enterprise's information assurance policy, as well as consumer-elected preferences. These rules may be based on the user's identity, the user's role, the context of the request (e.g., location, time of day), and/or a combination of the sensitivity attributes of the data and the user's authorizations.

OAuth 2.0 is starting to be used to authorize patients to access their own health information using a web or mobile app, and to enable a provider from one organization to access their patient's information held by a different organization.

Audit Controls

Security auditing is the process of collecting and recording information about security-relevant events. Audit logs are generated by multiple software components within a system, including operating systems, servers, firewalls, applications, and database management systems. Many healthcare organizations rely heavily on audit log review to detect potential intrusions and misuse. Automated intrusion and misuse detection tools are increasingly being used to normalize and analyze data from network monitoring logs, system audit logs, application audit logs, and database audit logs to detect potential intrusions originating from outside the enterprise, and potential misuse by authorized users within an organization.

Data Integrity

Data integrity services provide assurance that electronic data have not been modified or destroyed except as authorized. Cryptographic hash functions are commonly used for this purpose. A cryptographic hash function is a mathematical algorithm that uses a block of data as input to generate a "hash value" such that any change to the data will change the hash value that represents it, thus detecting an integrity breach.

Nonrepudiation

Sometimes the need arises to assure not only that data have not been modified inappropriately but also that the data are in fact from an authentic source. This proof of the authenticity of data is often referred to as *nonrepudiation* and can be met through the use of digital signatures. Digital signatures use public-key (asymmetric) encryption (discussed next) to encrypt a block of data using the signer's private key. To authenticate that the data block was signed by the entity claimed, one only needs to try decrypting the data using the signer's public key; if the data block decrypts successfully, its authenticity is assured.

Encryption

Encryption is simply the process of obfuscating information by running the data representing it through an algorithm (sometimes called a *cipher*) to make the information unreadable until it has been decrypted by someone possessing the proper encryption key. Symmetric encryption uses the same key to both encrypt and decrypt data, while asymmetric encryption (also known as *public-key encryption*) uses two keys that are mathematically related—one key is used for encryption and the other for decryption. One key is called a private key and is held secret; the other is called a public key and is openly published. Which key is used for encryption and which for decryption depends on the assurance objective. For example, secure e-mail encrypts the message contents using the recipient's public key so that only a recipient holding the private key can decrypt and view it, and then digitally signs the message using the sender's own private key so that if the recipient can use the sender's public key to decrypt the signature, the recipient can be assured that the sender actually sent it. Encryption technology can be used to encrypt both data at rest (to protect sensitive data in storage) and data in motion (to protect electronic transmissions over networks).

Malicious Software Protection

Malicious software, also called *malware*, is any software program designed to infiltrate a system without the user's permission, with the intent to damage or disrupt operations or use unauthorized resources. Malicious software includes programs commonly called viruses, worms, Trojan horses, and spyware. Protecting against malicious software requires not only technical solutions to prevent, detect, and remove these intruders but also policies and procedures for reporting suspected attacks.

Transmission Security

Sensitive and safety-critical electronic data that are transmitted over open, vulnerable networks such as the Internet must be protected against unauthorized disclosure and modification. The Internet Protocol was designed with no protection against the disclosure or modification of any transmissions and no assurance of the identity of any transmitters or receivers (or eavesdroppers). Internet traffic is clearly visible from every server through which it passes on its journey from source to destination. Protecting network transmissions between two entities (people, organizations, or software programs) requires that the communicating entities authenticate themselves to each other, confirm the integrity of the data exchanged (for example, by using a cryptographic hash function), and assure that data exchanged between them are encrypted.

Both the Transport Layer Security (TLS) protocol and Internet Protocol Security (IPsec) suite support these functions, but at different layers in the OSI model. TLS establishes protected channels at the OSI transport layer (layer 4), allowing software applications to exchange information securely.[38, 39, 40] For example, TLS might be used to establish a secure link between a user's browser and a merchant's check-out application on the Web. It is important to note that a TLS secure channel is between two servers or between a server and a browser. If data need to flow through an intermediary, such as a load balancer, the TLS link is broken. Thus TLS does not provide true end-to-end protection, such as that provided by encrypted e-mail.

IPsec addresses this problem by establishing protected channels at the OSI network layer (layer 3), allowing Internet gateways to exchange information securely. For example, IPsec might be used to establish a VPN that allows all hospitals within an integrated delivery system to openly yet securely exchange information. Because IPsec is implemented at the network layer, it is less vulnerable to malicious software applications than TLS and also less visible to users (for example, IPsec does not display an open/closed lock icon in a browser).

Layer 7: Usability Features

The top layer of the trust framework includes services that make life easier for users. Single sign-on often is referred to as a security "service," but in fact it is a usability service that makes authentication services more palatable. Both single sign-on and identity federation enable a user to authenticate oneself once and then to access multiple applications, multiple databases, and even multiple enterprises for which they are authorized, without having to re-authenticate oneself. Single sign-on enables a user to navigate among authorized applications and resources within a single organization. Identity federation enables a user to navigate between services managed by different organizations. Both single sign-on and identity federation require the exchange of *security assertions*. Once the user has logged into a system, that system can pass the user's identity, along with other attributes, such as role, method of authentication, and time of login, to another entity using a security assertion. The receiving entity then enforces its own access-control rules, based on the identity passed to it.

Increasingly, identity is being federated across multiple organizations using an OAuth 2.0 profile called OpenID Connect.[41] For example, an individual might use her Google+ identity to log into a different application in a web browser or on her smartphone. Healthcare organizations are using OpenID Connect to enable an individual with an authenticated (and identity-proofed) credential from one organization to use that credential to log into a different organization. The OAuth 2.0 authorization protocol enables the identity to be validated and authorized.

Neither single sign-on nor identity federation actually adds security protections (other than to reduce the need for users to post their passwords to their computer monitors). In fact, if the original identity-proofing process or authentication method is weak, the risk associated with that weakness will be propagated to any other entities to which the identity is passed. Therefore, whenever single sign-on or federated identity is implemented, a key consideration is the level of assurance provided by the methods used to identity-proof and authenticate the individual.

Chapter Review

Healthcare is in the midst of a dramatic and exciting transformation that will enable individual health information to be captured, used, and exchanged electronically using interoperable HIT. The potential impacts on individuals' health and on the health of entire populations are dramatic. Outcomes-based decision support will help improve the safety and quality of healthcare. The availability of huge quantities of de-identified health information, combined with genomic sequencing data, will help scientists discover the underlying genetic profiles for diseases, leading to earlier and more accurate detection and diagnoses and more targeted and effective treatments, ultimately reaching the vision of "precision medicine."

This chapter explained the critical role that trustworthiness plays in HIT adoption and in providing safe, private, high-quality care. It introduced and described a trust framework comprising seven layers of protection essential for establishing and maintaining trust in a healthcare enterprise. Many of the safeguards included in the trust framework have been codified in HIPAA standards and implementation specifications. Building trustworthiness in HIT always begins with objective risk assessment, a continuous process that serves as the basis for developing and implementing a sound information assurance policy and physical, operational, architectural, and technological safeguards to mitigate and manage risks to patient safety, individual privacy, care quality, financial stability, and public trust.

Questions

To test your comprehension of the chapter, answer the following questions and then check your answers against the list of correct answers that follows the questions.

1. What components are included in an information assurance policy?

    A. Rules for protecting confidential information

    B. Rules for assigning roles and making access-control decisions

    C. Individual sanctions for violating rules for acceptable behavior

    D. All of the above

2. The HIPAA Security Rule prescribes four standards for physically safeguarding electronic health information protected under HIPAA. Which four are they?

   A. Redundancy, failover, reliability, and availability

   B. Isolation, simplicity, redundancy, and fail-safe design

   C. Interoperability, facility-access control, cloud control, and device control

   D. Facility-access controls, workstation use, workstation security, and device and media controls

3. Which of the following is *not* an operational safeguard?

   A. Reliability

   B. Configuration management

   C. Sanctions

   D. Continuity of operations

4. The new push for virtualizing applications, storage, and computing power offers what dimension to your architectural safeguards?

   A. Scalability

   B. Data integrity

   C. Network audit and monitoring

   D. None of the above

5. What are two types of usability features?

   A. Data encryption and authenticity

   B. Access control and audit logs

   C. Malicious network protection and isolation

   D. Single sign-on and identity federation

6. Which of these statements best describes the relationship between security and privacy?

   A. The terms are synonymous.

   B. Security deals with cybercriminals, whereas privacy does not.

   C. Security helps protect individual privacy.

   D. Privacy is a security mechanism.

7. The purpose of risk management is to help an organization accomplish which of the following?

   A. Identify its vulnerabilities, and assess the damage that might result if a threat were able to exploit those vulnerabilities

   B. Decide what security policies, mechanisms, and operational procedures it needs

   C. Figure out where to allocate a limited security budget in order to protect the organization's most valuable assets

   D. All of the above

8. Which operational process is most critical to the effectiveness of a broad range of security technical safeguards?

   A. System activity review

   B. Identity management

   C. Incident procedures

   D. Secure e-mail

Answers

1. **D.** The components in an information assurance policy include rules for protecting confidential information, rules for assigning roles and making access-control decisions, and individual sanctions for violating rules for acceptable behavior.

2. **D.** The HIPAA Security Rule prescribes four standards for physically safeguarding electronic health information protected under HIPAA: facility-access controls, workstation use, workstation security, and device and media controls.

3. **A.** Reliability is an architectural safeguard, not an operational safeguard.

4. **A.** Virtualizing applications, storage, and computing power provides the capability to scale as the need and demand for these resources increases.

5. **D.** Two types of usability features are single sign-on and identity federation.

6. **C.** Security helps protect individual privacy.

7. **D.** The purpose of risk management is to help an organization: identify its vulnerabilities and assess the damage that might result if a threat were able to exploit those vulnerabilities; decide what security policies, mechanisms, and operational procedures it needs; and figure out where to allocate a limited security budget in order to get the most "bang for the buck."

8. **B.** The operational process most critical to the effectiveness of a broad range of security technical safeguards is identity management.

References

1. American Recovery and Reinvestment Act (ARRA) of 2009, Pub. L. No. 111-5, 123 Stat. 115, 516 (Feb. 19, 2009). Accessed on March 7, 2017, from https://www.congress.gov/bill/111th-congress/house-bill/1/text.

2. Health Insurance Portability and Accountability Act (HIPAA) Privacy, Security, and Enforcement Rules, 45 C.F.R. pts. 160, 162, and 164, most recently amended January 25, 2013. Accessed on July 19, 2016, from www.ecfr.gov/.

3. HealthIT.gov. (2016). *Adoption dashboard.* Accessed on July 7, 2016, from https://dashboard.healthit.gov/quickstats/quickstats.php.

4. Patient Protection and Affordable Care Act (ACA), Pub. L. No. 111-148, 42 U.S.C. § 18001 et seq. (2010). Accessed on July 7, 2016, from https://www.gpo.gov/fdsys/pkg/PLAW-111publ148/pdf/PLAW-111publ148.pdf.

5. Federal Bureau of Investigation (FBI). (2014, Apr. 8). *Health care systems and medical devices at risk for increased cyber-intrusions for financial gain.* Accessed on July 7, 2016, from www.aha.org/content/14/140408--fbipin-healthsyscyberintrud.pdf.

6. HealthIT.gov. (2016). *Safety and security dashboard.* Accessed on July 7, 2016, from http://dashboard.healthit.gov/quickstats/pages/breaches-protected-health-information.php.

7. The White House. (2013, Feb. 12). *Presidential Policy Directive 21: Critical infrastructure security and resilience.* Accessed on July 7, 2016, from https://www.whitehouse.gov/the-press-office/2013/02/12/presidential-policy-directive-critical-infrastructure-security-and-resil.

8. Blumenthal, D. (2010, Feb. 4). Launching HITECH. *New England Journal of Medicine, 362,* 382–385. Accessed on July 19, 2016, from www.nejm.org/doi/full/10.1056/NEJMp0912825.

9. American Medical Association (AMA). (2001). AMA *code of medical ethics: Principles of medical ethics.* Accessed on March 7, 2017, from https://www.ama-assn.org/sites/default/files/media-browser/principles-of-medical-ethics.pdf.

10. American Nurses Association (ANA). (2015). *Code of ethics for nurses with interpretive statements.* Silver Spring, MD: Nursesbooks.org. Accessed on July 7, 2016, from http://nursingworld.org/DocumentVault/Ethics-1/Code-of-Ethics-for-Nurses.html.

11. Das, R. (2016). Top 10 healthcare predictions for 2016. *Forbes.* Accessed on July 7, 2016, from www.forbes.com/sites/reenitadas/2015/12/10/top-10-healthcare-predictions-for-2016/#49bef6392f63.

12. Markle Foundation Connecting for Health (Markle). (2006). *The common framework: Overview and principles.* Accessed on March 7, 2017, from https://www.markle.org/sites/default/files/CF-Professionals-Full.pdf.

13. Department of Health, Education, and Welfare (DHEW). (1973, July). *Records, computers, and the rights of citizens: Report of the Secretary's Advisory Committee on Automated Personal Data Systems.* Accessed on July 19, 2016, from https://epic.org/privacy/hew1973report/.

14. Office of the National Coordinator for Health Information Technology, U.S. Department of Health and Human Services (ONC). (2008, Dec. 15). *Nationwide privacy and security framework for electronic exchange of individually identifiable health information.* Accessed on March 7, 2017, from https://www.healthit.gov/sites/default/files/nationwide-ps-framework-5.pdf.

15. McCann, E. (2013). Setback for Sutter: $1B EHR goes black. *HealthcareITNews,* November 10. Accessed on July 12, 2016, from www.healthcareitnews.com/news/setback-sutter-1b-ehr-goes-black.

16. Microsoft Corporation (Microsoft). (2013). Details of the February 22nd 2013 Windows Azure storage disruption. *Windows Azure blog.* Accessed on March 7, 2017, from https://azure.microsoft.com/en-us/blog/details-of-the-february-22nd-2013-windows-azure-storage-disruption/.

17. Rys, R. (2008). The imposter in the ER: Medical identity theft can leave you with hazardous errors in health records. *NBCNews.com*, March 13. Accessed on July 19, 2016, from www.msnbc.msn.com/id/23392229/ns/health-health_care.

18. Stein, R. (2005). Found on the web, with DNA: A boy's father. *Washington Post*, November 13. Accessed on July 19, 2016, from www.washingtonpost.com/wp-dyn/content/article/2005/11/12/AR2005111200958.html.

19. Gymrek, M., McGuire, A. L., Golan, D. E., Halperin, E., & Erlich, Y. (2013). Identifying personal genomes by surname inference. *Science, 339*, 321–324. Accessed on July 19, 2016, from http://data2discovery.org/dev/wp-content/uploads/2013/05/Gymrek-et-al.-2013-Genome-Hacking-Science-2013-Gymrek-321-4.pdf.

20. Cohen, B. (2009). NHS hit by a different sort of virus. *Channel 4 News*, July 9. Accessed on July 19, 2016, from www.channel4.com/news/articles/science_technology/nhs+hit+by+a+different+sort+of+virus/3256957.

21. Goodin, D. (2010). NHS computers hit by voracious, data-stealing worm. *Register*, April 23. Accessed on July 19, 2016, from www.theregister.co.uk/2010/04/23/nhs_worm_infection/.

22. Weaver, C. (2013). Patients put at risk by computer viruses. *Wall Street Journal*. Accessed on March 7, 2017 from https://www.wsj.com/articles/SB10001424127887324188604578543162744943762.

23. Food and Drug Administration (FDA). (2013, June 13). *Cybersecurity for medical devices and hospital networks: FDA safety communication.* Accessed on July 12, 2016, from www.fda.gov/MedicalDevices/Safety/AlertsandNotices/ucm356423.htm.

24. Department of Health and Human Services (HHS). (2016). *Health information privacy: Breaches affecting 500 or more individuals.* Accessed on July 12, 2016, from https://ocrportal.hhs.gov/ocr/breach/breach_report.jsf.

25. Pritts, J., Choy, A., Emmart, L., & Hustead, J. (2002, June 1). *The state of health privacy: A survey of state health privacy statutes, second edition.* Accessed on July 19, 2016, from http://ihcrp.georgetown.edu/privacy/pdfs/statereport2.pdf.

26. Department of Health and Human Services (HHS). (2011). *HIPAA privacy rule accounting of disclosures under the Health Information Technology for Economic and Clinical Health Act: Proposed Rule.* 76 Fed. Reg. 31425 (May 31, 2011) (to be codified at 45 C.F.R. pt. 164). Accessed on July 12, 2016, from https://www.federalregister.gov/articles/2011/05/31/2011-13297/hipaa-privacy-rule-accounting-of-disclosures-under-the-health-information-technology-for-economic.

27. Health Information and Management Systems Society (HIMSS). (2015, June 30). *2015 cybersecurity survey.* Accessed on July 12, 2016, from www.himss.org/2015-cybersecurity-survey.

PART

28. Health Insurance Portability and Accountability Act of 1996, Pub. L. No. 104-191, § 264, 110 Stat. 1936 (August 21, 1996). Accessed on July 19, 2016, from http://aspe.hhs.gov/admnsimp/pl104191.htm.

29. Department of Health and Human Services (HHS). (2014, Sep. 30). *Restatement I of the data use and reciprocal support agreement (DURSA)*. Accessed on March 7, 2017, from http://sequoiaproject.org/wp-content/uploads/2015/03/Restatement-I-of-the-DURSA-9.30.14-FINAL.pdf?x54807.

30. Department of Health and Human Services (HHS). (2017). *Federal Policy for the Protection of Human Subjects*. 45 C.F.R. Part 46 (January 19, 2017). Accessed March 7, 2017, from https://www.gpo.gov/fdsys/pkg/FR-2017-01-19/pdf/2017-01058.pdf.

31. Department of Health and Human Services (HHS). (2002). *Standards for privacy of individually identifiable health information: Final Rule*. 67 Fed. Reg. 53181 (August 14, 2002) (to be codified at 45 C.F.R. pts. 160, 164). Accessed on July 12, 2016, from https://www.federalregister.gov/articles/2002/08/14/02-20554/standards-for-privacy-of-individually-identifiable-health-information.

32. Health Level Seven (HL7). (2014, May 13). *HL7 Version 3 Implementation Guide: Data segmentation for privacy (DS4P), Release 1*. ANSI Approved Standards. ANSI/HL7 V3 IG DS4P, R1-2014.

33. Berinato, S. (2003). All systems down. *CIO from IDG* (pp. 46–53). Accessed on July 12, 2016, from www.cio.com.au/article/65115/all_systems_down/.

34. TechTarget. (2014, August). *OSI reference model (Open Systems Interconnect)*. Accessed on July 12, 2016, from http://searchnetworking.techtarget.com/definition/OSI.

35. Health Level Seven. FHIR DSTU2. Accessed on March 7, 2017, from https://www.hl7.org/fhir/.

36. Internet Engineering Task Force (IETF). (2012, October). *The OAuth 2.0 authorization framework, RFC 6749*. Accessed on July 12, 2016, from https://tools.ietf.org/html/rfc6749.

37. National Institute of Standards and Technology (NIST). (2011, April). *National strategy for trusted identities in cyberspace*. Accessed on March 7, 2017, from https://www.nist.gov/sites/default/files/documents/2016/12/08/nsticstrategy.pdf.

38. Internet Engineering Task Force (IETF). (2008, August). *The transport layer security (TLS) protocol, version 1.2, RFC 5246*. Accessed on July 19, 2016, from http://tools.ietf.org/html/rfc5246.

39. Internet Engineering Task Force (IETF). (1998, November). *Security architecture for the internet protocol, RFC 2401*. Accessed on July 19, 2016, from www.ietf.org/rfc/rfc2401.txt.

40. International Organization for Standardization (ISO). (1996). *Information technology—open systems interconnection—basic reference model: The basic model.* ISO/IEC 7498-1. Second edition, November 15, 1994; corrected and reprinted, June 15, 1996. Accessed on March 7, 2017, from www.ecma-international.org/activities/Communications/TG11/s020269e.pdf.

41. OpenID. (2014). *Welcome to OpenID Connect.* Accessed on July 12, 2016, from http://openid.net/connect/.

CHAPTER 26

Risk Assessment and Management

Gila Pyke

In this chapter, you will learn how to
- Participate in the process of reducing the risk of any healthcare IT product or implementation
- Identify the difference between security, privacy, and other healthcare risks
- Recognize different threats and associated mitigation strategies

Risk management is the art of enabling innovation and opportunities while preparing to manage potential negative outcomes. Risk management is not about eliminating risk (that is impossible) but instead identifying it, reducing it as much as possible, informing affected parties, and preparing to respond quickly and effectively should the risk materialize.

Healthcare technology is tasked with improving patient health outcomes and reducing certain types of healthcare risk. However, as with the introduction of any new system, the introduction of technology into the healthcare space introduces the potential for new risks that must be managed. A good example of this risk-benefit balance is the introduction of healthcare information systems that provide access to health information from laboratory tests, emergency response reports, hospital discharge summaries, and patient medical histories all in one place. The benefit that this can provide to patients is obvious, but the risk that unauthorized personnel may gain access to this information is also increased as more points of access to this information are introduced. When filing cabinets contain the health files, there is only one point from which the information can be accessed. But when you have a broadly shared healthcare information system, there are many points of access.

Fortunately, once healthcare IT risks are identified and assessed, they can also be managed and additional preventative and responsive safeguards can be implemented. In the case of risks involving unauthorized access, authentication and access controls can significantly reduce such risks and enable the technology to be used more safely.

Definitions

The National Institute of Standards and Technology (NIST) is the agency of the government that produces *Guide for Conducting Risk Assessments: Information Security (NIST SP 800-30)*.[1] The guide includes many terms relevant to risk assessment for information security that are included in this chapter. In order to better enable you to discuss risk management in healthcare, the following are definitions of some key terms:

- **Asset** An asset is something that needs to be protected from harm or loss. In healthcare IT security terms, an asset can refer to health information itself or devices containing health information. In healthcare privacy, safety, and other risk areas, assets consist of sensitive health information, patient safety, emotional or physical well-being, etc.

- **Vulnerability** A vulnerability is a weakness that leaves the asset unnecessarily exposed to harm inherent in the design or implementation of software. In healthcare IT terms, a vulnerability can be an unnecessary or insecure connection from a system hosting live healthcare data to the Internet, a lack of virus protection, or an unnecessary open port on a firewall.

- **Threat** A threat is a possible danger that might exploit a vulnerability and cause harm to an asset. A threat can originate from natural causes (power failures, floods, earthquakes, etc., resulting in health information being unavailable), intentional misuse or attack (e.g., spying on a Very Important Patient (VIP) patient's files), or error (e.g., losing or misplacing valuable health information required for a patient's treatment).

- **Safeguard** A safeguard is a measure taken to protect assets against threats. A safeguard, or security control, effectively reduces or eliminates a vulnerability. For example, virus scanners (safeguard) help protect our data (assets) from exposure to viruses (vulnerability) by unauthorized individuals who want to access or destroy our data (threats or threat agents).

- **Risk**[2,3] A risk is the likelihood that a threat will exploit a vulnerability and harm an asset, resulting in an impact on the organization or the patient.[4] For example, if you are trying to protect an assault victim's health record (asset) from being accessed by an individual with the intent to cause harm (threat), and that patient's health record is accessible from a computer located in a public area that is often left logged in and does not require a password or any kind of credential to use (vulnerability), then there is a risk that an unauthorized individual may access that patient's poorly protected health record and use it to cause harm to the patient.

In risk management, our goal is to reduce either the likelihood of the risk or its potential harm or impact. The likelihood of the risk just cited can be reduced by making it harder for the threat to access the records (by implementing safeguards such as moving the computer into an area restricted to staff only and providing staff with training that emphasizes the need to log out when they are not using the system). The impact of the risk cited can be reduced by removing the patient's real name and using a pseudonym known only to authorized members of the care team to mask the patient's identity. We will explore other ways to respond to risks later in this chapter.

Exercise 26-1: Identifying, Assessing, and Mitigating Risk

Identify the asset, vulnerability, threat, risk, and impact in the following healthcare scenario. Assign a likelihood value that this scenario may occur, and identify some potential safeguards that may help lower the likelihood or reduce the severity of the impact.

Scenario   The surgical theatre in your local hospital relies on an allergy database to guide decisions on which anesthetic, medications, and other materials can be safely used on a patient during surgery. This database is also connected to the Internet for research purposes. A researcher unwittingly downloaded a virus, making the allergy database suddenly unavailable and resulting in a patient with allergies to opiates being administered morphine and suffering complications.

Risk Assessment

- **Asset**   Allergy database
- **Vulnerability**   Insufficiently protected Internet connection
- **Threat**   Virus
- **Risk**   Virus will be introduced to the system due to the insufficiently protected Internet connection and render the allergy database unavailable
- **Likelihood**   Medium or high
- **Impact**   Harm to patient health

Potential Mitigations

- Segregate database from research system, increase security of Internet connection (lowers likelihood)
- Install antivirus (lowers likelihood)
- Maintain paper backup of allergy data (reduces impact)

Risk Management in Healthcare IT

In healthcare IT, risk management is about assessing and reducing the risks along the spectrum of IT development—including healthcare device manufacturers, software developers, healthcare IT service providers, healthcare IT implementers, government organizations involved in healthcare, other third parties, healthcare providers, and—most importantly—patients.

Risk management in healthcare takes more lessons from the nuclear and aerospace industries than from the more traditional manufacturing or financial domains, in the sense that the ultimate impact of a risk in healthcare IT is the emotional or physical well-being of a patient. When risks can cost lives, the management of these risks becomes a priority component of healthcare IT development.

PART VI

The Risk-Management Process[2]

The risk-management process is a cyclical, or spiral, process that begins with identification and assessment and returns there in order to ensure continual progress toward reducing the risks inherent in any development, implementation, or use of healthcare information technology.

At a high level, these are the steps of the risk-management process:

1. **Identification of risks**   As we move through this chapter we will discuss various methods for identifying risks that may impact the security of an application, the privacy of a patient or provider, or ultimately the safety of a patient. The first step is always to identify all possible applicable risks, regardless of how likely they are. Risks will be prioritized during the assessment step.

2. **Assessment of risks**   The risk-assessment step is the prioritization or triage step. This step takes into account the relative likelihood of a risk occurring, as well as the potential impacts of that risk, and assigns it a risk rating. A higher risk rating indicates a more serious risk that needs to be addressed first during the planning of mitigations. This prioritization is also a valuable tool for communicating with risk owners and stakeholders.

3. **Mitigation planning**   Once priority risks are identified, the next step is planning ways to mitigate them (i.e., reduce their likelihood or probability of occurrence), or reduce the potential impact if the risk does occur.

4. **Risk and mitigation tracking**   In order to ensure that mitigation plans are being implemented effectively, it is important to follow up with mitigation owners at predetermined intervals to provide support and ensure that mitigation plans will succeed.

5. **Documentation**   Once the first round of risk assessment is complete, it should be documented in a report to be used to communicate to key internal and external stakeholders so that everyone is aware of how risks are being managed.

Using one or more of the methods described next for identifying risks is recommended for the initial cycle of risk identification, such as coupling a checklist with additional follow-up interviews of key stakeholders, or leveraging a standardized questionnaire with a follow-up brainstorming session with subject-matter experts. Once the initial list of risks has been identified, the risks need to be documented in a risk register. A *risk register* is a table used to document risks throughout the risk-management lifecycle, in support of each phase. Table 26-1 is an example of a risk register.[2, 5] During the first identification phase of the risk-management lifecycle, only the leftmost columns of the risk register need to be completed.

 NOTE   Table 26-1 is available for download; see Appendix C.

	Risk Identification			Risk Assessment				Mitigation Planning				Risk and Mitigation Tracking	
	Risk summary	Asset	Vulnerability/ threat scenario	Likelihood	Impact (note the category)	Risk rating	Modifiers (safeguards/detectability)	Mitigation	Owner	Due date	Status	Adjusted likelihood	Adjusted probability
1.													
2.													
3.													

Table 26-1 The Risk Register

For ongoing iterations of the risk-management lifecycle, risk identification should be based on the existing risk register. Questions such as "Have new risks been identified?" should be asked of key subject-matter experts and stakeholders, but conducting interviews or workshops will take less time. Often the checklists and questionnaires that are used are called "delta" or Δ assessments.

Risk Identification

The goal of the risk-identification step is to identify any and all possible risk scenarios that may adversely affect the project or solution. In order to identify risks, a project or system must be broken down into assets and scenarios so that vulnerabilities and threats can be identified.[1] Depending on the type of risk—security, privacy, data criticality, or safety—there are a few different approaches to help identify a comprehensive list of potential risks:

- Creating checklists
- Using technology tools
- Using questionnaires
- Conducting interviews
- Holding workshops or brainstorming sessions

A checklist example is provided next since full coverage of all the approaches is beyond the scope of this chapter.

PART VI

Checklist Example

When building a network to host healthcare applications, a list of required security controls (such as firewalls, encryption, authentication, and audit functionality) can be used to prompt risk identification. Creating a comprehensive map of the network and then verifying the checklist against each applicable path or node can create a list of gaps or vulnerabilities. Those vulnerabilities can then be combined with a checklist of the system's assets and the potential threats to those assets to identify the security risks related to that system.

There are standardized security or safety checklists available, such as the Common Criteria Evaluation and Validation Scheme (CCEVS) produced by the National Information Assurance Partnership (NIAP).[6] Organizations that routinely build or implement healthcare technology should leverage past risk assessments to build their own tailored risk-identification templates based on these and other standardized checklists.

Risk Assessment

Once a comprehensive list of risks has been identified, the next phase is to assess these risks and determine which risks must be prioritized for mitigation, which risks should be mitigated once the priority risks have been satisfactorily addressed, and which risks are sufficiently low that they can be accepted or removed from discussion. It is the responsibility of the healthcare provider to conduct the risk assessment by either utilizing staff on the healthcare IT security team or hiring consultants.

The triage of risks enables organizations to focus their resources on implementing safeguards where they are needed most. The risk-assessment process also enables subject-matter experts to communicate about priority risks with senior stakeholders using a common language of agreed-upon concepts.

Risk assessment is composed of three sequential activities:

1. Assignment of risk likelihood and impact values
2. Prioritization of risks based on assigned values
3. Reduction of risk values based on modifiers such as existing safeguards or risk detection

Assignment of Risk Likelihood and Impact Values

In order to determine the relative priority of risks, each risk is discussed in terms of two dimensions: likelihood and impact.

Risk Likelihood   A risk's likelihood is the probability that this risk will materialize in the foreseeable future. Likelihood can be measured based on quantitative statistics of past occurrence if these are available (e.g., the number of distributed denial-of-service—DDOS—attacks on a network per month, where a high number infers a high likelihood of DDOS attacks occurring in the future). If statistics are not available, then a qualitative value should be assigned.

In order to ensure that all participants in the risk-management exercise are speaking the same language, an agreed-upon likelihood table should be used to assign values. Since different projects, systems, and organizations have different risks and risk tolerances, a likelihood table should be customized to that organization. Table 26-2 is an example of a likelihood table.[2, 5]

There are five levels of likelihood in this table. High, medium, and low are intended to be used regularly, whereas very high and very low are intended to demonstrate severe outlying events. Events such as "this happens all the time, it even happened today" would be listed as very high, and "this will probably never happen, but we wanted to document the risk anyway" would be listed as very low. An example of a very low risk could be the risk of flooding negatively impacting the availability of critical healthcare information. While the impact of such a risk is high and therefore should be considered, if the healthcare information is located in an area prone to drought that has never experienced flooding and is stored several stories above ground, then the relative likelihood of that risk would be considered very low.

 TIP When the probability of occurrence is unknown due to insufficient data, a value of medium is assigned until further information is available.

Risk Impact The other dimension for discussing risks is the severity of the potential impact if that risk were to occur. As with likelihood, the scale for assessing level of impact should be customized to the organization assessing the risk and should be based on stakeholder and subject-matter-expert consensus. Where quantitative cost analysis is possible, impact should be measured in terms of cost because cost is the most measurable and widely understood impact type. Where quantitative data is not available, a qualitative value should be assigned. Often, several categories of qualitative impact are needed to be able to compare different types of risks. Table 26-3 is an example of the types of impact categories.[2, 5]

PART VI

	Probability	Likelihood Description
Very high	>80%, or daily	This event may be happening on a regular basis or will likely occur soon.
High	51% to 80%, or monthly	This event is likely to occur in the near future.
Medium	21% to 50%—less than once per month but more than once per year	This event may occur in the near future.
Low	6% to 20%, or 1–2 times per year	This event is possible but highly unlikely to occur in the near future.
Very low	0% to 5%, or less than once per 5-year period	This event is not expected to occur in the near future.

Table 26-2 Example of a Likelihood Table

	Cost (Quantitative)	Reputation	Safety	Product Functionality
Very high	Capital cost > $100M	Potential for shareholder action	Potential for multiple fatalities/ serious injuries	May not be able to deliver on most critical requirements
High	Capital cost of $10M–$100M	Serious adverse attention from media and medical establishment and/or loss of clients	Potential for fatality/serious injury/severe psychiatric disability	Major shortfalls in one or more critical requirements
Medium	Capital cost of $1M–$10M	Minor adverse attention from media and medical establishment and/or existing clients	Potential for minor physical injury/ emotional or mental distress	Minor shortfalls in one or more key requirements
Low	Capital cost of $100,000–$1M	Loss of reputation among public/ potential clients	Potential to reduce quality of healthcare/cause anxiety	A few shortfalls in desired functionality
Very low	Capital cost < $100,000	Internal loss of reputation	Impact does not affect delivery of healthcare	System should still fully meet mandatory requirements

Table 26-3　Example of an Impact Table

In order to use a table like 26-3, where multiple categories or types of impacts are possible, the relative impact of the highest risk is the one that counts. For example, if the risk materializing may result in minor adverse attention from the media from the reputation category (which has an impact value of medium) but might also result in potential for serious injury in the safety category (which has an impact value of high), assign the risk a value of high.

 TIP　As with likelihood, if the potential impact of a risk cannot be estimated, a value of medium is assigned until further information is available.

Example of Assigning Risk Likelihood and Impact　If the same risk of unauthorized access due to insufficient role-based access control is identified but there is no information yet available as to what information may be accessible, how this unauthorized access may affect a patient's emotional or physical well-being, or whether it may affect the organization in terms of reputation or eventual financial cost, the impact category would be set to medium until more information is available about what data may be accessed without authorization and by whom. If, after further analysis, it is identified that the only information that can be accessed without login credentials is limited patient demographic information (i.e., name, age, and postal code) but no full address or health information, then the impact can be reduced to very low—without home-address or health information, there is likely very little cost or reputation impact for the provider or safety impact to the patient. It is important to note the impact category in the risk register or supporting documentation in order to support risk-assessment discussion with stakeholders.

If the risk of unauthorized access due to insufficient role-based access control is identified but there is no information as to the motivation or likely frequency for such unauthorized access, then the likelihood is assigned a medium value. Later, when this risk is discussed with stakeholders and other safeguards are identified that might prevent the occurrence of the risk (such as restricted issuance of login credentials to the system, reducing the availability of access to unauthorized staff), then the likelihood may be lowered. (Conversely, the likelihood value may also be raised should data supporting the likelihood of occurrence be brought forward.)

Prioritization of Risks Based on Assigned Values[1, 2, 5]

Once each risk has been assigned a likelihood and impact value, each risk is mapped into a visual risk matrix to establish the risk's overall rating and relative priority. Figure 26-1 is an example of a risk map. In this example, the various risks are listed at the top of the map for ease of reading. They are then mapped using the likelihood and impact tables and placed in the appropriate box on the grid. The grid is divided into risk levels, with darkly shaded boxes indicating major priorities that must be addressed as soon as possible and where the majority of time and resources should be allocated. The lighter the shading in the box, the lower the priority.

 NOTE   Figure 26-1 is available for download; see Appendix C.

The risk-tolerance line indicates the risk tolerance agreed upon by the organization performing the risk assessment.[1, 2] Risks that fall below the line can be accepted. Recovery plans may still be put in place, but further efforts to reduce the likelihood or impact of the risk are not prioritized. ISO/IEC 80001 ("Application of risk management for IT-networks incorporating medical devices") describes this phenomenon in a different way.[7] It states that the organization shall decide which of the following is most appropriate:

- The estimated risk is so low that risk reduction need not be pursued. In this case the rationale for this decision must be documented.

- The estimated risk is not acceptable. In this case risk-control measures, or in the language of this chapter, mitigations, shall be implemented.

Reduction of Risk Values Based on Existing Safeguards

Existing safeguards that reduce the potential likelihood or impact of a risk should be listed in the risk register, and the risk rating should be modified accordingly. In other words, if a healthcare information system has been designed with safeguards already in place, then the impacts or likelihoods of some risks inherent in the use of the system will be lower than upon initial assessment.

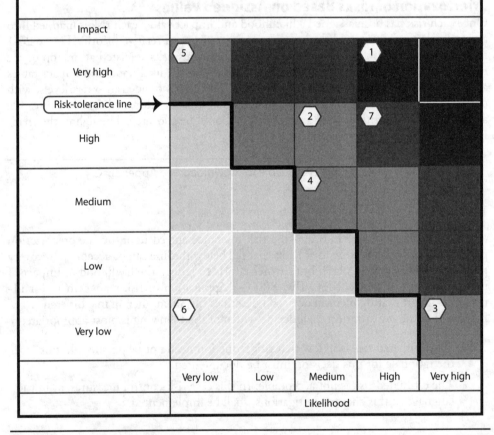

Risk 1. Lack of availability of allergy database information due to DDOS attack

Risk 2. Potential for non-identification of prescription conflicts

Risk 3. Unauthorized access to limited demographic data

Risk 4. Unauthorized access to sensitive mental or sexual health information

Risk 5. Lack of availability of laboratory results information due to flooding of server room (located in Death Valley, California)

Risk 6. Unavailability of inventory systems due to flooding of server room (located in Death Valley, California)

Risk 7. Inability to provide accounting of disclosures of patient health information upon request due to software malfunction in unpatched systems

Figure 26-1 Example of a risk map

Once initial risk ratings are mapped, the next step is to identify which risks have safeguards already in place that may lower the initial risk rating. For example, for risk 1 in Figure 26-1, the likelihood of a DDOS attack on a discoverable system is high, and the impact of unavailable allergy information is very high—it can negatively impact the lives of many patients. Therefore, the initial risk rating of risk 1 is in the dark-shaded (maximum-priority) category.

Upon discussion with the security team, the following safeguards are identified as already in place:

- A well-configured firewall and intrusion-prevention system (IPS)
- An intrusion-detection system (IDS) that raises alarms if a DDOS attempt is detected

Once the safeguards have been documented in supporting documentation along with their effect on the risk rating, the readjusted likelihood and impact should be updated in the risk register along with the mitigating factors.

Risk-Mitigation Planning[1,2]

There are four ways to respond to risk:

- **Accept** Weigh the cost of the risk versus the cost of mitigating it. Sometimes it is more prudent and effective to create a disaster-recovery plan or review audit logs regularly to identify an incident as quickly as possible than it is to try to mitigate the inevitable (or hard to avoid).

- **Transfer** Leverage insurance clauses, service-level agreements, and other contractual documentation to transfer the cost of recovery from a risk away from the organization. A prime example of this is liability insurance.

- **Mitigate** Buy antivirus software, provide awareness and training, optimize business processes, hire more people (so that staff can do their job properly without being overworked, which will reduce safety, privacy and security risks), write a profile, demand the use of encryption, or propose a controlled and well-documented activity that will reduce (not eliminate) the risk level to the point where it is either completely tolerable or at least tolerable enough that the focus of efforts can move to the mitigation of other priority risks. Formal signing of mitigation letters, or risk waivers in the case of risk acceptance, by risk owners can be an effective way of ensuring that senior stakeholders recognize risk mitigation commitments.

- **Avoid** Sometimes there is too much risk associated with something and no effective way to mitigate the risk, so we choose to do something else and avoid the risk altogether. This is often the least desirable or feasible action to take because it may result in losing the benefit of the avoided action as well (e.g., avoiding a risk by cancelling a project means that the benefits of the project are lost). In some cases of extreme risk, this may be the best approach: to scrap the plans and start over with a new design.

TIP For each risk in the risk register, identify which of these strategies will be employed, the details (such as developing a recovery or log-review plan, purchasing which kind of insurance, or implementing what kind of mitigation), who will own these risk management activities, and the deadline for when they must be implemented. This is necessary to enable risk tracking and reporting steps.

Risk-Mitigation Tracking

Once mitigation strategies have been agreed upon, assigned, and documented, the progress of mitigation plans must be tracked on a regular basis in order to identify issues or obstacles and provide support to risk owners to ensure that their risks will be mitigated. The frequency of tracking should be based on the risk rating—mitigation plans for extremely high risks should be followed up biweekly or monthly, whereas the progress of mitigating lower risks can be verified on a quarterly or even less frequent basis.

Documentation and Communication

There are two audiences for risk-management documentation:

- Internal stakeholders
- External stakeholders

Communicating About Risk with Internal Stakeholders[1]

Internal stakeholders (senior management, project owners, and internal clients) must be kept informed about risks on a periodic basis as part of established reporting mechanisms, such as quarterly risk reports to the board and weekly or monthly project meetings.

The risk register should be updated prior to each reporting cycle, including any new risks that have been identified along with their mitigations, changes to mitigation plans, updates on mitigation status, and residual risk ratings for mitigation plans that have been completed. This enables stakeholders from all levels of the organization to be kept appraised of their responsibilities as risk owners and also to provide support, such as additional resources for the mitigation of risks elsewhere within the organization.

Communicating About Risk with External Stakeholders

Communicating about risk with external stakeholders is part of the closeout phase of any project and part of ongoing maintenance of any healthcare IT system. Before a healthcare IT product can be sold to a healthcare provider, before an implementer can install the hardware and software at the healthcare provider's site, and before the healthcare provider can begin using the product, risks must be managed along the entire spectrum—from software vendor to implementer to healthcare provider to patient.

In order for this to be possible, software and hardware vendors that are aware of residual risks in their products must clearly document and report these risks to the implementers who will install these products. Implementers who conduct risk assessments on the software or hardware implementation must document and communicate the residual risks to the healthcare providers, and the healthcare providers must in turn include these risks in their own risk identification, assessment, mitigation, tracking, and documentation activities. Risks that may ultimately affect patients must be managed along the continuum of the development of healthcare IT, from the initial conception of a software or hardware product to the daily use of that product for providing healthcare.

Domains of Risk Analysis

There are many domains of risk that may affect a healthcare IT system. The diagram in Figure 26-2 categorizes the threats associated with mitigation strategies into the following five domains: safety, security, privacy, application criticality, and data criticality.

The risk-management cycle in each case follows the same steps. In many organizations a common risk register is used to document all categories or domains of risk, and common impact and likelihood tables are used to assess and prioritize them. The primary difference between these domains lies in the specific types of risks that are identified and minor deviations in the techniques used to identify them. In some cases, subject-matter experts who have a deeper knowledge of one domain (e.g., safety) versus another (privacy) are hired to conduct risk assessments.

Security Risk Analysis

Security risk analysis focuses on the triangle of security: confidentiality, integrity, and availability (CIA). All risks to healthcare IT assets are considered in terms of the confidentiality of the information contained in the assets, the integrity of the information contained in the assets, or the availability of the assets. Following are some examples of common security risks and their safeguards.

Figure 26-2
Domains of risk

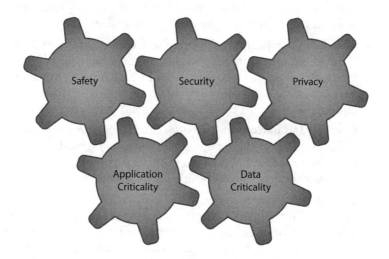

Threat: DOS or DDOS Attack

A denial-of-service (DOS) or distributed denial-of-service (DDOS) attack is an attempt to make a healthcare information system (asset) and the information hosted on it unavailable through flooding or overloading of the system.

Risk The hospital's decision-support software may become unavailable as a result of a DOS/DDOS attack. This is an availability risk.

Mitigations

- Implementation and configuration of firewalls, switches, and routers
- Implementation of specific preventative hardware and software
- Antivirus software
- Code reviews
- Antispyware
- Security scanning (early detection)

Threat: Malware

Malware obtains its name from malicious software. This is a category of software that is purposely designed to cause damage to an information system such as a healthcare information system. Following are examples of malware:

- **Viruses** A virus is malicious software that can copy itself and infect a computer without the user knowing. In order for a virus to spread, the infected file must be sent to another computer or system and executed there. Viruses can corrupt computer files and make healthcare information unavailable when it is most needed.

- **Worms** A worm is malicious software that makes copies of itself using a network rather than being embedded in a file like a virus. Worms can also result in healthcare information becoming unavailable.

- **Trojans** A Trojan is named after the Trojan horse from Greek mythology and is malicious software that appears to do something desirable (such as download music files or play a video) but contains code hidden inside it that can open a backdoor and allow a malicious user to have unauthorized access to healthcare information. This is a risk to confidentiality rather than availability.

- **Rootkits and backdoors** Rootkits and backdoors are malicious software that can be installed without a user's knowledge and provide access to a computer and the information on it to an unauthorized person. Rootkits and backdoors are a threat to confidentiality of healthcare information.

- **Spyware** Spyware is malware that collects information about a computer user, such as login and password information, without their knowledge and sends it to a third party who can use it to get unauthorized access to healthcare information. Like Trojans, rootkits, and backdoors, spyware poses a risk to the confidentiality of healthcare information.

Risk   The patient files stored at the doctor's office may be accessed (confidentiality risk) or modified (integrity) by unauthorized attackers, or the physician may lose access (availability) to critical health information that he or she needs to provide patient care.

Mitigations

- Educating users not to click on certain types of links or install certain types of software

- Restricting user accounts from being able to install software without the help of a technically savvy person

- Antivirus software

- Antispyware, or spyware removal, software

- Code reviews

- Regular security scans to detect rootkits and other malware as early as possible

Threat: Social Engineering

Social engineering is the act of manipulating people to provide confidential information or information that will permit an unauthorized person access to confidential information. In healthcare IT, social engineering could include posing as staff at a healthcare institution in order to gain access to a server room, impersonating an authorized user over the telephone, or various electronic means of posing as someone with a legitimate need for confidential information. A common example of social engineering is called phishing. With this technique the poser uses e-mail and a web page that appear to be legitimate to ask you to "verify your login information." In fact, you are being redirected to a false page and the sender is using the information you provide to gain unauthorized access to healthcare information.

Risk   Social engineering can pose a risk to the confidentiality, availability, and integrity of healthcare information.

Mitigations

- Educating users to recognize social engineering or phishing attempts.

- Effective disposal of electronic and paper media to reduce "dumpster diving." Dumpster diving is a common technique used by attackers to gain information that they can use to make their social engineering attempt appear more legitimate.

Threat: Spam

E-mail spam, sometimes known as junk e-mail, involves thousands of e-mails sent to as many recipients as possible with the intention of selling, advertising, or phishing for information from unsuspecting users. Spam can also involve sending bulk messages over instant messaging, mobile texting, and other forms of electronic communication media.

Risk   Spam can be used to transmit viruses, phishing scams, and other threats and can also result in reduced or no availability of networks and, as a result, healthcare information. In other words, spam can pose a risk to the confidentiality, integrity, and availability of healthcare information.

Mitigations

- Educating users not to sign on to untrusted sites with their e-mail addresses, how to recognize spam messages, and not to respond to them
- E-mail filtering
- Greylisting or blacklisting services

For more information on security-specific risk analysis, see NIST SP 800-30, Revision 1.

Application and Data Criticality Analysis

The purpose of application and data criticality analysis is to fulfill the HIPAA security regulation requiring healthcare organizations to have a disaster-recovery plan in place, as well as an emergency-operation plan if applications hosting critical healthcare information suddenly become unavailable. An application and data criticality analysis should identify

- Which software applications are critical to the provision of healthcare
- What data is critical to the provision of healthcare

Privacy Risk Analysis

In healthcare IT, privacy risk analysis encompasses more than the confidentiality of personal health information. It also includes

- Compliance with legislative and regulatory requirements, such as those laid out in HIPAA, and the financial or business impacts that noncompliance can have on a health organization.
- Adherence to privacy principles, such as those laid out in the OECD Privacy Principles:[8]
  - **Collection limitation**   Limiting how much healthcare information is collected and where it can be collected from. Consent must be given for the collection.
  - **Data quality**   Information collected and used should be relevant to the purposes for which it was collected and kept up to date.
  - **Purpose specification**   Communicating to patients why their information is being collected, when it will be used, and under what conditions it would be disclosed.
  - **Use limitation**   Limiting how and when data is disclosed and for what purposes the disclosure is being made.

- **Security safeguards** Security safeguards should be used to protect healthcare information.

- **Openness** Organizations should be open about their practices of using and protecting personal health information.

TIP Informing patients about what information is collected about them supports the principle of openness.

- **Individual participation** Patients should be informed about what information is collected about them, as well as with whom it will be shared, and have the ability to correct it if they can demonstrate that it is inaccurate.

- **Accountability** Healthcare providers should be held accountable for the protection of personal health information in their custody.

- **Big data and de-identification** Big data and statistical analysis is becoming more and more prevalent in the healthcare IT industry as organizations work to predict and prevent adverse outcomes based on the enormous amount of information generated by the electronic provision of healthcare services. In cases of family planning, mental health, or even broader acute care data, large collections of healthcare data may put individual patients at risk. In addition to privacy risk analysis and mitigation prior to, during, and at the end of the implementation of any big data project, de-identification is often considered to be a key mitigation for reducing the risk of identification of an individual from the data used for analysis.[9]

NOTE Privacy risk assessment should be conducted at the start, middle, and end of a project in order to support risk-based planning (Privacy by Design[10]), risk-based development, and risk-based implementation.

Safety Risk Assessment

While the risks identified by security, application and data criticality, and privacy risk analysis often relate to patient safety, independent safety risk assessments are necessary to ensure that all risks to a patient's safety have been considered. Safety risk assessment in healthcare IT is intended to identify any areas where technology-induced errors may introduce risks to patient safety and then follow the risk-management process to reduce them as much as possible.

NOTE Errors are introduced by poorly calibrated diagnostic imaging equipment.

Medical device and hardware manufacturers use an analysis method called "failure modes and effects analysis" (FMEA) to identify potential failures in their products.[3]

PART VI

Appendixes C and D of the ISO/NP 14971[11] standard for the application of risk management to medical devices contain questions to ask when assessing device safety and conducting harm analysis. These questions can be applied to safety risk assessment in software, implementation, and healthcare-setting risk analysis as well. For example:

- What is the intended use of the device/software (in the provision of healthcare)?
- Will this device come into contact with the patient (tissues or body fluids, processing of biological materials, etc.)? What are the sterilization requirements?
- What are the accuracy requirements of the measurements?

As with all other types of risk assessment, once the risks have been identified they must be prioritized, mitigations must be assigned and tracked, and risks must be communicated with all potentially affected parties.

Chapter Review

The introduction of technology into the healthcare space reduces some risks to patients but also introduces new technology-related risks that must be managed. This chapter described the five iterative steps involved in managing risk:

1. Identifying risks
2. Assessing and prioritizing risks
3. Planning mitigations and assigning ownership for mitigation activities
4. Tracking mitigation progress and residual risk posture
5. Documenting and communicating with internal and external stakeholders

This chapter also examined the differences between security, privacy, application and data criticality, and safety risk assessment and explored the techniques used to manage risk in these specific domains.

Questions

To test your comprehension of the chapter, answer the following questions and then check your answers against the list of correct answers that follows the questions.

1. You have been put in charge of performing a risk assessment for a new software product. What should you do first?
   A. Identify information assets
   B. Identify the potential safety hazards
   C. Identify vulnerabilities
   D. Identify potential impact

2. Which of the following mitigations does not reduce the likelihood of a risk?

   A. Antivirus

   B. Tape backups

   C. Awareness and training

   D. Access controls

3. Which of the following mitigations do not reduce the impact of a risk?

   A. Tape backups

   B. Disaster-recovery plans

   C. Firewalls

   D. Encryption

   E. C and D

   F. A, B, and C

4. How would you mitigate the risk of clinical decision support data being sent through a wi-fi network that may be accessed by unauthorized individuals?

   A. Encryption

   B. Awareness and training

   C. Change the network configuration

   D. A and C

   E. B and C

5. When should you perform a privacy risk assessment?

   A. At the start of a project

   B. At the start, middle, and end of a project

   C. At the end of a project

   D. In the middle of a project

6. How should you mitigate the risk of phishing?

   A. Education and awareness

   B. E-mail filtering

   C. A and B

   D. None of the above

7. Why is avoiding a risk the least desirable type of mitigation?

   A. Because it doesn't work to reduce the impact of the risk

   B. Because it doesn't work to reduce the likelihood of the risk

   C. Because all the positive opportunities associated with the avoided action are also lost

   D. Because risks are impossible to avoid

8. What is the best way to address risks introduced by big data?

   A. Risk analysis

   B. Risk mitigation

   C. De-identification

   D. All of the above

Answers

1. **A.** Always start with identifying what you are trying to protect, i.e., the assets.

2. **B.** Tape backups reduce the impact but not the likelihood of a risk by making sure that the information can be restored quickly.

3. **E.** Firewalls and encryption prevent risks but do not lower their impact if they do occur.

4. **D.** Encrypting the data will make it harder to access, as will changing the network so that the data is not sent over the public Wi-Fi.

5. **B.** You should conduct a risk privacy assessment at the start, middle, and end of a project.

6. **C.** You mitigate the risk of phishing with education and awareness and e-mail filtering.

7. **C.** Avoiding a risk often involves cancelling a feature, or even a whole project, resulting in the loss of the opportunities presented by the feature or project.

8. **D.** De-identification is a key mitigation in addition to risk analysis and mitigation for any big data initiatives.

References

1. National Institute of Standards and Technology (NIST). (2012, September). *Guide for conducting risk assessments: Information security.* SP 800-30, revision 1. Accessed on August 8, 2016, from http://nvlpubs.nist.gov/nistpubs/Legacy/SP/nistspecialpublication800-30r1.pdf.

2. HL7. (2012). *Cookbook for security considerations.* Accessed on August 8, 2016, from http://wiki.hl7.org/index.php?title=Cookbook_for_Security_Considerations.

3. Carnegie Mellon Software Engineering Institute. (1999, December). *Software risk evaluation (SRE) method description (version 2).* Accessed on August 8, 2016, from www.sei.cmu.edi/reports/99tr029.pdf.

4. IEC. (2006). *Analysis techniques for system reliability: Procedure for failure mode and effects analysis (FMEA).* IEC 60812. Accessed on August 8, 2016, from https://webstore.iec.ch/preview/info_iec60812%7Bed2.0%7Den_d.pdf (search document ID=60812).

5. IHE International. (2008, Oct. 10). *IHE cookbook: Preparing the IHE profile security section (risk management in healthcare IT) whitepaper.* Accessed on August 8, 2016, from https://www.ihe.net/Technical_Framework/upload/IHE_ITI_Whitepaper_Security_Cookbook_2008-11-10.pdf.

6. National Information Assurance Partnership (NIAP). (2011, Aug. 1). *Common criteria evaluation and validation scheme for IT security (CCEVS), version 1.2.* Accessed on August 8, 2016, from https://dev.niap-ccevs.org/Ref/What_is_NIAP .CCEVS.cfm.

7. ISO. (2012, July). *Application of risk management for IT-networks incorporating medical devices.* IEC 80001. Accessed on August 8, 2016, from www.iso.org/iso/iso_catalogue/catalogue_tc/catalogue_detail.htm?csnumber=57934.

8. Organisation for Economic Co-operation and Development (OECD). (2013, July 11). *Guidelines governing the protection of privacy and transborder flows of personal data.* Accessed on March 8, 2017, from http://www.oecd.org/internet/ieconomy/privacy-guidelines.htm.

9. IHE International. (2014, June 6). *IHE IT infrastructure handbook for de-identification.* Accessed on March 8, 2017 from https://www.ihe.net/uploadedFiles/Documents/ITI/IHE_ITI_WP_Analysis-of-DeID-Algorithms-for-FP-Data_Elements.pdf.

10. Cavoukian, A. (n.d.). *Privacy by Design: The 7 foundational principles—Implementation and mapping of fair information practices.* Accessed on June 13, 2016, from https://iab.org/wp-content/IAB-uploads/2011/03/fred_carter.pdf.

11. ISO. (2007, March). *Medical devices: Application of risk management to medical devices.* ISO 14971:2007. Accessed on August 8, 2016, from www.iso.org/iso/home/store/catalogue_ics/catalogue_detail_ics.htm?csnumber=72704.

Physical Safeguards, Facility Security, Secure Systems and Networks, and Securing Electronic Media

Dennis M. Seymour

In this chapter, you will learn how to
- Understand the necessary physical safeguards for your system, including location, access, and access-control devices
- Understand how privacy requirements impact physical safeguard requirements, including how to assess or audit compliance with privacy requirements
- Identify and explain guidelines for building systems including office hardware, environmental controls, personal controls, and storage devices
- Understand encryption and how an organization determines if it should implement it
- Understand common encryption-related terminology
- Understand guidelines for security and preservation of electronic media for storage devices and secure disposal of electronic media
- Assess your organization's risks related to physical security and conduct an assessment of your organization's practices for securing electronic media

Physical Safeguard Requirements

In ancient times (you remember—prior to the turn of the millennium), most of our sensitive medical records were created and stored on paper, often stored in dark and dingy corners of the basement of the medical center in rooms only specific staff members could access. When a patient had an appointment or came into the emergency room, a staff member had to request the paper record be retrieved for the clinical staff to review. The doors had locks, maybe the medical center was advanced enough to have key pads with access codes, and the room had sprinklers and fire extinguishers—but then every other room in the medical center also had many of those safety and security devices.

In today's medical centers, many of those old paper records may still be there, but they have most likely been scanned into the medical centers' electronic records systems and are rarely referenced. They might even be archived away in some offsite storage location or repository, or in some cases even the National Archives. The security of the location where the electronic data are stored has new considerations, in part based on compliance requirements and in part due to the differences between storing paper and electronic media. The amount of time these records are stored is largely dependent on the organization who once used them.

Often, when a healthcare organization transitions from paper to electronic records, it does so in phases and the transition is not planned in depth. Even before the health record was electronic, it is likely individual offices within the organization were already using technology such as desktop computers, facsimiles, and printers for office functions such as e-mail, scheduling, transmitting data, and billing. Initially these functions were likely running on the local desktop and not stored centrally, and in most cases there was no real network to speak of for storage. At some point the organization may have moved to using servers and networking to store the data from these office operations, without considering the specific security requirements for these data. Prior to the passage of the Health Insurance Portability and Accountability Act (HIPAA) of 1996, many organizations did not consider the requirements for the security or privacy of these data. Even after HIPAA, many small office environments did not have privacy or security professionals involved in their process for adding hardware, software, applications, and so forth to their office environment.

Locating Storage Devices, Network Hardware, Printers, and Other Devices

When we consider where we will locate or place the devices used for our healthcare practices, we must consider certain aspects of access to the data and implement an in-depth approach to the security and privacy of the data. The systems will also need to control user access. Consider not only the storage of the data but also the display, transmission, and input/output of the data contained in the system and applications. Beginning with the desktop or other device being used to access the data, we need to consider who will have access to the keyboard and display, as well as how to control who can look at the data on the computer. For example, we may have administrative staff who work in the office but should not have access to all patient data. We may have volunteers who we permit to assist patients and visitors but, again, should not have access to the network for patient data.

We must have the ability to transmit these data from the desktop to a network storage device such as a server. The organization must consider whether this will be a wired or wireless network connection. In either instance, we must determine whether an individual could attempt to gain access by either plugging in their own computer or accessing the wireless network with an unauthorized device. If we have a wired connection, we must consider where the cabling is run, whether overhead in a drop ceiling or within the finished walls. Either way, the wire will likely run to a data closet, which in smaller offices and facilities is often the same closet that stores administrative, cleaning, or other supplies. Some organizations even have switches and routers located on a shelf in the restroom or other publicly accessible areas of the office. Access to this data can be compromised when proper security fundamentals are not applied.

Securely Handling Protected Health Information (PHI)

Your organization's processes for handling PHI should be based on implementation of best practices, and it should depend on your local assessment of the threats, vulnerabilities, and risk exposure of your location, regulatory requirements such as HIPAA, and other factors. Following are descriptions of the many pieces of the physical system you need to consider in this assessment. Remember also that while the focus of this section is on security, you should consider that privacy is an element of any assessment of risk. A good rule of thumb is that privacy requirements determine what you will secure, and secure safeguards are implemented based on privacy requirements. We determine risk based on these collective requirements.

Monitor Placement

First, you should consider whether visitors or patients can view the screens used to display patient information for scheduling, billing/insurance, or electronic health record (EHR) data. Upon entering the physician's reception area, you often find the receptionist is behind a wall with a sliding window, with the monitor placed in such a way as to prevent your view. But once you enter the office area, you may walk by half a dozen or more computers on your way to an exam room, and each computer monitor may be clearly displaying radiology, lab, or other data with little regard to privacy of the patient data. The organization should consider the placement of each display screen as part of its overall risk assessment strategy.

Privacy Screens

For computer display screens, including laptops, tablets, and other devices that do not permit placement to prevent "shoulder surfing," risk mitigation might include the use of privacy screens. These screens allow the user to view the screen from a direct angle, but as you change your angle of view toward the side, the image becomes less and less visible. Information on the screen is not visible beyond a 45–50-degree angle.

Printer, Fax Machine, and Scanner Placement

Printers, fax machines, and scanners should be placed in secure areas away from public access, to prevent printed documents, received faxes, or scanned records that are not immediately retrieved by the user/recipient from being removed by unauthorized personnel. Remember that the safeguards you can implement to control electronic data on your local computer or server are not effective once the data is printed. Ideally, the organization should explore the option of secure printing, requiring the user to log in to the printer prior to the printing of the material. This may often be accomplished also by use of badge scanning, if the facility has implemented an employee badging system.

Screensavers

Most users are familiar with screensavers; however, few actually implement them securely. The best implementation requires the user to press CONTROL-ALT-DELETE and re-enter a password when they want to return to using their computer. This and the use of a time lockout (see the next section) together add to a defense-in-depth strategy. Newer operating systems, including Windows and Apple macOS, and associated keyboards often have shortcuts. For example, Windows has WINDOWS KEY-L to lock the computer. With macOS, there are two shortcuts: SHIFT-COMMAND-Q to log out of your macOS user account (you'll be asked to confirm), and OPTION-SHIFT-COMMAND-Q to log out without being asked to confirm.

Time Lockout

Most operating systems (Windows, Apple iOS, Android, etc.) include the functionality to implement a time lockout of access to the device. Best practices usually guide this requirement to be between 5 and 15 minutes. This time period begins when the last keystroke or mouse movement occurs, so simply viewing the screen for an extended period may trigger the time lockout that starts the screensaver program. Organizations must consider the operating environment for users when implementing time-based lockout. An organization's policies and procedures should include exceptions to primary requirements so that blanket requirements, such as a 5-minute-maximum timeout, do not interrupt healthcare operations. As an example, procedure rooms with access that is restricted to staff members (and the patient) might have longer timeout periods if clinicians perform procedures that take 10–20 minutes or longer and need to have access to the information on the screen without actually interacting with the keyboard or mouse.

Access to Servers, Offices, and Data Closets

The amount of data stored on a device or transmitted through a device needs to be considered when assessing risk; a device that stores or transmits a large amount of data needs to be placed higher on the risk scale than a device that doesn't store or transmit much data. For example, your laptop may have access to most of the data on the network but not store much information locally. On the other hand, a server stores thousands of times more data, and our data closets, which house routers and switches, are part of a connection which transmits most of the data used by local network devices. Individual access to these devices should be limited to the minimum necessary. For example, if a clinic clerk needs access only to her computer to do her job, that is the level of physical access she should be granted. She should not be given access to the data closets. An IT employee who supports desktop operations needs to have access to the computer used by the clerk, but likely also needs some access to network devices in the data closets. This person might not need access to the data center or even servers on the network. So, physical access to devices should be limited similarly to logical access, and the organization must ensure its policies and procedures support limited access.

The Physical and Environmental (PE) Controls section of National Institute of Standards and Technology (NIST) Special Publication (SP) 800-53 is a valuable reference for the level of security you need to consider.[1] Exercise 27-1 toward the end of the chapter provides an expanded look at this topic, detailing how you might conduct an assessment of your organization's risk relative to physical access to data. There are many security safe-guards we are not able to cover within this chapter, or even this book, so reference to SP 800-53 is a great study guide prior to taking any exam.

Data Center

The data center is the primary location where servers and other network communications gear is maintained. The security of this location may range from limited access to extreme (such as National Security Agency, Department of Defense, or secret or top-secret systems). While the level of security required is based on risk, there should always be a process in place to determine which security practices will be implemented, and the specific require-ments that have not been implemented based on cost or other considerations need to be documented. Increasingly, larger healthcare organizations are moving to managed ser-vice provider data centers or cloud services that are not at their medical centers and often are contracted to managed service providers or contracted facilities, with the organization maintaining their own equipment, often remotely. Exercise 27-1 toward the end of the chapter guides you through a risk assessment of your organization's data-center security.

Data Closets

The data closet is often located on each floor of a large facility and should be maintained with the same level of security as the data center. Access to the closet grants access to the network environment, meaning that anyone who has access can simply plug or unplug any cable or device as they desire. These closets might house network routers, switches, wireless routers, and, in some cases, even firewalls or servers. At many locations, data closets are often shared with engineering, electrical, or even janitorial employees. This can be a dangerous practice. Consider the situation where the employee working in this closet or storage room opens the door to obtain tools or cleaning materials. They might not consider the security of the area and block the door open with a cart or toolbox to ease access while they work. This grants access to anyone in the area.

Intermediate Distribution Frame / Main Distribution Frame

An intermediate distribution frame (IDF) is a free-standing or wall-mounted rack for managing and interconnecting the telecommunications cabling between end-user devices and a main distribution frame (MDF). For example, an IDF might be located on each floor (in the data closet) of a multifloor building to route the cabling from that floor down the walls to an MDF on the first floor or basement. The MDF would contain cabling that would interconnect to the phone company or to other buildings.

Backups

System backups should be completed on a regular basis and include system-level and data-level backups. These backups may be performed at different time increments; for example, the system backups that include the operating system and all settings might be conducted on a routine basis, but could even be annually for organizations whose hardware, operating systems, and applications change less frequently. Other organiza-tions whose hardware and so forth change more often might complete these system-wide backups more frequently. Data backups, which include the actual healthcare record data rather than systems, OS, and applications, might be done weekly, daily, or, as in the case of some healthcare locations, even hourly. One surprising fact is that many organizations do not apply the same principles for physical and environmental security to the location where backups are stored. Quite often the data center has moderate to high security, while backup tapes are stored in a file cabinet in the IT section.

Backup tapes should be stored with the same level of security, or perhaps even stronger security, as the data in the data center, with access to those tapes restricted to the personnel who have authorization to access the data center. Many data-loss events over the past ten years have involved backup copies of the data, not a compromise of the data center or unauthorized access to the system itself. For the purposes of disaster recovery, continuity of operations, and business resumption, copies of backups should also be maintained offsite. It is important to remember that the security of those backups when in transit or stored offsite should have the same security considerations as you implement onsite.

Access-Control Devices

Access-control devices include devices that provide access to physical facilities and devices that provide access to systems. Some devices can actually provide access to both facilities and systems, as is the case with the Personal Identity Verification (PIV) card and the Common Access Card (CAC) described in this section. Organizations who have implemented security through access-control devices must ensure they emphasize the importance of the security of these devices as part of the overall security-awareness training program.

Key Fobs

A key fob is a type of security token or small hardware device with built-in authentication mechanisms. Just as the keys held on an ordinary real-world key chain or fob control access to the owner's home or car, the mechanisms in the key fob control access to network services and information. The key fob provides *two-factor authentication*: the user has a personal identification number (PIN), which authenticates them as the device's owner; after the user correctly enters their PIN, the device displays a number that allows them to log on to the network. Because a key fob is a physical object, it is easy for the owner to know if it has been stolen. In comparison, a password can be stolen (or guessed) and used for an extended period before—if ever—the theft is detected.

Some companies now provide a service where the user's cell phone or other device can provide the same service. When the user enters their access PIN, a message is sent by the system to their cell phone with the specific number or code to enter. This code may be used only for a limited period of time and for a single login. The next time the user attempts to log in, a new code is generated and sent to their phone.

Badges

Users who are familiar with Department of Defense (DoD) systems may have seen the Common Access Card (CAC).[2] Other users of federal agency systems may use a card called the personal identification and verification (PIV) card.[3] Many non-federal organizations have begun implementing very similar cards. The primary purpose of these cards is to provide secure access to both facilities and systems for which the user has authorization based on their role—referred to as *role-based access* (RBA). Figure 27-1 describes the various

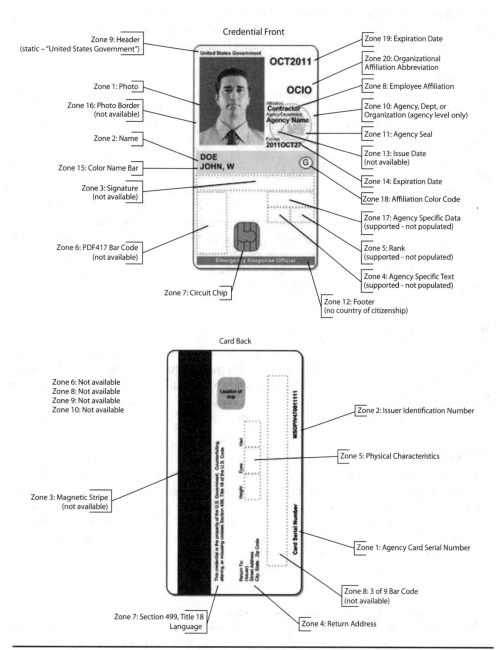

Figure 27-1 PIV card layout. Images courtesy of U.S. General Services Administration (GSA) USAccess Program, http://fedidcard.gov/credfeatures.aspx.[4]

elements of the PIV card, including displays of both the front and back of the card. This PIV card (as well as the CAC) must be implemented in a specified manner in accordance with guidelines established by the Federal Chief Information Officers (CIO) Council.

Biometrics

Over the past few years the use of biometrics has increased in many areas, especially when it comes to access to facilities and IT systems. Back in the '60s, TV shows such as *The Man from U.N.C.L.E.*, *Mission Impossible*, and *Star Trek* made biometrics seem "sci-fi," but today they are very commonplace. Whether using your finger, voice, facial recognition, or retina, biometrics use is becoming a daily occurrence. It uses the "something you have" security principle and adds to the defense-in-depth strategy. An example of a device used to gain access to a physical location is a biometric fingerprint reader placed at the entry to the data center. This reader requires the user to place their index (or other registered) finger on the biometric reader. The screen then requests that the user add a second identification code, which might be four or more characters. The combination of something you have with a PIN (described as "something you know") provides two-factor authentication. Many devices, including tablets, laptops, and desktop keyboards, now have biometric readers included in them.

Building Secure Systems

Risk identification should be part of the process of working out the details of how data will be stored, and appropriate security measures to mitigate those risks should be implemented. This includes physical and environmental controls that are often in place but frequently not fully or correctly implemented. Understanding the requirements for these areas is a vital aspect of supporting the IT infrastructure.

Office Hardware

The organization should consider security when selecting hardware, including desktops, laptops, and external storage devices. The ability to properly secure the devices, including cable locks for securing devices to the desk, should be considered. Selecting external storage devices that cannot be "locked down," including USBs and other drives, should include the ability to encrypt the device to prevent disclosure in the event of loss. Encryption is a topic later in this chapter.

Locks

Locks on safes, filing cabinets, and other storage areas must be commensurate with the risk and sensitivity of the data being stored within the area or cabinet. Consider this: at home, would you store your diamond jewelry in the same drawer as your forks and knives in the kitchen? The more sensitive the information, such as backup tapes from your IT systems, the more secure the enclosure and therefore the locks must be that secure those areas.

Door Locks

Doors should be kept locked when employees are not present, and most office areas should have both a handle lock and a deadbolt lock. Keys that access doors to areas where sensitive data are stored should be controlled, and only those employees who should have access to the area should have access to the keys to that area. Consider reworking your key-control system if you have a single key storage or, even worse, you store keys in the secretary's desk drawer. Always consider who has access to the area; if the desk is left unattended and unlocked, anyone could gain access to the keys. Also consider how often, if ever, your organization actually takes an inventory of who has keys to sensitive areas. Finally, your organization should have security officers who check secure areas on a regular basis, actually checking to ensure doors are locked and the locks function properly.

Environmental Controls

As you would expect from the name, these controls involve the environment in which the systems, storage, and communications reside. Again, the level of implementation of these controls must be based on the risk versus costs. While some controls must be implemented, not all must be implemented to the same level. We will address environmental controls in the following sections, including HVAC, lighting, surveillance, fire suppression, emergency power, UPS, and others.

Heating, Ventilation, and Air Conditioning (HVAC)

The HVAC of the data center (or other area where IT equipment is stored) is vital to the health of the equipment. Place your hand beside the area of your computer or laptop where the fan is located, or simply sit with your laptop on your lap for 10 minutes. The heat generated by the central processing unit (CPU) can be over 100 degrees. Now consider that your data center may have hundreds, and in larger medical centers or universities thousands, of servers, each generating this heat. As the external temperature increases, so too does the internal temperature of the data center, so the HVAC of the data center is extremely important. Monitoring this information is also vital, including not only the temperature but also the humidity. If the humidity is too high, even a temperature in the high 70s can lead to condensation, which can cause problems with electronic circuits.

Security Lighting

The data center and data closets should have lighting even when power is lost, whether by generator power or by battery (for short-term power loss). This is both for security and safety (so that individuals attempting to circumvent security during the power loss can be seen) and to allow IT staff to see and operate in emergency situations. Exit lights should be included in the emergency lighting plan, and in most jurisdictions emergency exit lights must be illuminated at all times.

PART VI

Surveillance

Tools to observe the data center may include video cameras, alarm systems, motion detectors, and other devices. Just as with other elements of physical security, the level of surveillance should be based on the risk assessment. In today's environment, most data centers are designed to be "dark." The data center equipment is administered remotely, although it could be from rooms adjacent to the data center. Most IT-related tasks that would routinely require physical access are automated. Individuals enter the data center only in rare situations, so there is no need to keep the facility lit. This also means that cameras and other recording devices should be implemented in such a way that they record only when motion is detected or the door records entry by use of an access device. Additionally, the storage of surveillance data should be in a controlled, secure environment, not necessarily within the data center itself. This could be in the organization's security office or in the office of a security firm hired to remotely monitor your organization's facilities.

Fire Suppression

In an effort to prevent damage due to fires, the facility should have multiple forms of fire suppression, including handheld fire extinguishers (appropriate for the size and nature of the facility and the equipment), overhead fire suppression (which might include dry-pipe, wet-pipe, or dry-chemical systems), and access to fire department standpipes for larger fire suppression. Organizations should implement dry-pipe fire suppression in data center environments. Dry-pipe systems consist of the same pipes as wet-pipe systems but do not contain water in the pipes until such time as an emergency. This prevents damage from a leak, puncture, or accidental discharge. Dry-chemical systems are optimal for data centers; however, the cost is often prohibitive for many, primarily smaller, organizations. Staff members who routinely have access to the data center and areas adjacent to it should be trained in the use of fire suppression as well as the process for turning off the system. Your organization should work with local fire department personnel to conduct routine visits to your facilities so the staff is aware of the locations of fire suppression equipment, such as standpipes, elevators, fire alarm systems, and so forth. While your facility may never experience a serious event, the ability of your local fire department to support you in an emergency is vital. Staff need to know how to the turn the system off in case of accidental discharge, to decrease the negative effects of water on electrical components.

Generator

Backup electrical power should be available, and as with other aspects of security should be based on the risk to the facility, the possibility of power disruptions, and other environmental factors. As an example, we might think a facility in an area with a history of high winds, tornados, or hurricanes would be more likely to suffer power loss than a facility in California, but a location in California might be subject to earthquakes, which could also cause the loss of power. The generator power must be implemented so that backup power is provided immediately and automatically, without requiring manual intervention.

Uninterrupted Power Supply (UPS)

The UPS provides short-term backup power to systems in the event of power loss or brownout. In an office environment the UPS might be small and provide emergency power to a computer or other equipment so as to permit access to data in the event of power loss. In a data-closet or data-center environment, UPSs might be rack-mounted and provide power to a number of devices, again for a short period of time. In general, a UPS can provide power to devices for a period of five minutes to a few hours, depending on the type of UPS and the amperage of the devices supported. The UPS is intended to bridge the time between loss of power and the implementation of alternate power, such as the generator, for the continuity of business operations over short periods of time.

Other Controls

The following controls are neither physical nor environmental; however, they do tie in very closely to the implementation of those controls.

Personnel

All personnel having access to the data center should be screened. Risk and trust are important elements of the security and privacy of your organization's data. In addition, training your staff on their responsibility to secure the organization's data is vital, but their training should also include other areas discussed in this chapter—such as the process to use when allowing visitors into the data center or closets, the use of security devices and fire-suppression equipment, and other areas that might be part of their responsibilities.

Awareness and Training

We have mentioned awareness and training throughout this chapter, but primarily the organization should focus on ensuring that all employees are aware of risks and threats specific to their role, and have the training necessary to support organizational operations related to continued business operations for their role. Examples include ensuring they know how to power down equipment and use fire suppression devices, and ensuring they have knowledge of data destruction requirements for the types of data they access such as printed PHI data, electronic PHI (ePHI) stored on storage devices, and so forth. The organization should consider the following reasons for ensuring employees are trained and aware of information security practices:

1. Compliance requirements change or their interpretation changes.

2. The organization is responsible for the actions of its employees.

3. Consumers are becoming more aware of the requirements that healthcare organizations must comply with.

Sensitivity Labels and Clearance

Data-storage devices should include appropriate labeling based on the type of data and data sensitivity. These labels should include instructions on who to contact should the devices be found in an unexpected place, for example, if lost or delayed while being transported to an offsite storage location or while being transported by a third-party vendor. It is not necessary to state that the device contains personally identifiable information (PII) or PHI; simply label it as sensitive, with instructions for contacting you, including phone number, e-mail address, or mailing address of the facility.

Securing and Preserving Electronic Media Storage Devices

Each of the storage devices discussed in the following sections needs to be considered when planning for the security and preservation of electronic media. An overall policy that includes procedures for the use of storage media is vital to every organization, and instruction on the policy should be part of employee awareness and training programs. Explaining the risks associated to the users of these devices can assist the organization in ensuring employees follow established guidance.

Flash Drives

Often referred to as flash memory, flash drives are small storage devices or cards that store data on flash memory. Flash memory is a nonvolatile computer storage chip that can be electrically erased and reprogrammed. It was developed from EEPROM (electrically erasable programmable read-only memory) and must be erased in fairly large blocks before it can be rewritten with new data. An important note is that, just as with any storage media, these drives introduce a number of risks to the organization, including the possible undetected theft of data or the introduction of viruses or Trojans. Facilities should have policies and procedures in place for the use of these devices. Because of their small physical size but large storage capacity, the risk of loss of large amounts of data via these devices is high. Many organizations go so far as to ban the use of flash drives on their networks. On the other hand, their small size means they are also easy to destroy by shredding or burning, both good processes for eliminating the threat of loss. If your organization finds the need to use these devices—and they certainly have a place in many practice areas, such as with digital cameras to record wounds (e.g., rashes or decubitus ulcers), procedures, etc.—it should develop strong policies and procedures for their use and disposal.

Personal Computers (PCs)

Personal computers, often referred to as desktop computers, frequently store at least some data locally, on the hard drive or memory. However, EHRs and other healthcare data are stored centrally on database servers, not on PCs, and PCs can be used only to access the data via the organization's network. Typically, procedures such as cutting and pasting, creating screen dumps, or otherwise storing data are not approved and are disabled. The problem is that data in EHRs and other healthcare data sometimes are generated on other devices and stored locally before being uploaded to the database server. For example, as introduced in the prior section, a digital camera may be used to document wounds or procedures, and the images typically are transferred via the flash drive to a PC before being moved to a network storage area or entered into an EHR. While the risk of loss of a PC is lower than that of a more mobile device, a PC should still be secured to a desk via a locking cable.

Laptops

A laptop is essentially a mobile version of the PC, making the risk of data loss significantly higher than with other devices. Generally, the laptop is intended to permit authorized user access to data while not physically at the facility or at a single work location within the facility. Ideally, as with other mobile devices, the hard drive of the laptop should be protected by encryption (discussed later in the chapter) so that if the device is lost or stolen, the data stored on it are much more difficult to obtain. Requiring two-factor authentication or encryption reduces risk of loss of the data. Laptops should be securable to the work location by a cable or a locking docking station. Of course, risk is further reduced if the device is both secured with a cable and the hard drive is encrypted.

Secure Digital (SD) Card

An SD card is a nonvolatile memory card format used in portable devices. In general, the SD card requires a specific slot to access the PC or laptop; it does not use the USB slot. There are various versions of these cards, including the SD, HDSD, miniSD, and microSD. As addressed in the earlier section regarding flash memory, it is important to note that, just as with any storage media, these drives introduce risks to the organization, including the possible undetected theft of data or the introduction of viruses or Trojans. On the positive side, because of their small size, they are easily destroyed by shredding or burning, both good processes for eliminating the threat of loss. As with flash storage, if your organization finds the need to use devices with SD cards, it should develop strong policies and procedures for their use and disposal.

External Drives

An external drive is usually larger and less mobile (although still easily transportable) than the flash or USB drive and resides outside the physical PC or laptop. External drives usually require their own power source, unlike USB or flash drives, which get their power through their connection to the computer. These drives should be covered in the organization's security policy and procedures, and employees who are authorized to use these devices should attest to the fact they understand and will adhere to policy.

Servers

A server is a computer attached to a network for the primary purpose of providing a location for shared disk access—that is, shared storage of computer files (such as documents, sound files, photographs, movies, images, databases, etc.) that can be accessed by the workstations that are attached to the same computer network. These devices should be secured by both device level access controls as well as enhanced physical security controls.

PART VI

Network-Attached Storage (NAS)

Network-attached storage (NAS) is file-level computer data storage that is connected to a computer network and provides data access to heterogeneous clients. NAS operates as a file server and is specialized for this task by its hardware, its software, or the configuration of those elements. NAS is often made as a computer appliance—a specialized computer built from the ground up for storing and serving files—rather than simply a general-purpose computer being used for the role. Again, these devices should be secured by both device level access controls as well as enhanced physical security controls.

Storage Area Network (SAN)

A storage area network (SAN) is a dedicated high-speed network that provides access to consolidated, block-level data storage, generally in the form of storage devices, such as disk arrays, tape libraries, and optical jukeboxes, accessible to servers. The SAN moves storage resources from the user network and reorganizes them into an independent, high-performance network. This allows each server to access shared storage as if it were a drive directly attached to the server. When a host wants access to a storage device on the SAN, it sends out a block-based access request for the storage device. Again, these devices should be secured by both device level access controls as well as enhanced physical security controls.

Encryption

Encryption is the process of encoding messages or information in such a way that only authorized parties can read it. Encryption does not of itself prevent interception, but denies the message content to the interceptor. In an encryption scheme, the intended communication information or message, referred to as plaintext, is encrypted using an encryption algorithm, generating ciphertext that can only be read if decrypted. An encryption scheme usually uses a pseudo-random encryption key generated by an algorithm.[5]

The discussion of encryption, including whether an organization should or must use encryption, can cause confusion for many in healthcare. Because HIPAA identifies encryption as an addressable implementation specification rather than a required implementation specification, some organizations mistakenly assume encryption is optional. In fact, *addressable* means that the encryption implementation specification must be implemented if, after a risk assessment, the entity has determined that the specification is a reasonable and appropriate safeguard in its risk management of the confidentiality, integrity, and availability of e-PHI. If the organization decides that the addressable implementation specification is not reasonable and appropriate, it must document that determination and implement an equivalent alternative measure, presuming that the alternative is reasonable and appropriate.[6] Implementation of encryption can be accomplished by the use of either symmetric key encryption, asymmetric encryption, or public key infrastructure (PKI).

Symmetric Encryption

In symmetric-key schemes, the encryption and decryption keys are the same. Communicating parties must share the same key before they can achieve secure communication.

Asymmetric or Public Key Infrastructure (PKI)

In public-key encryption schemes, the encryption key is published for anyone to use and encrypt messages. However, only the receiving party has access to the decryption key that enables messages to be read.

TLS/SSL

Transport Layer Security (TLS) and its predecessor, Secure Sockets Layer (SSL), both of which are frequently referred to as SSL, are cryptographic protocols that provide communications security over a computer network. Several versions of the protocols are in widespread use in applications such as web browsing, e-mail, Internet faxing, instant messaging, and Voice over IP (VoIP). SSL is no longer considered secure, and as of October 2014 should no longer be used as a security protocol. It is a good business practice to use the term TLS, not SSL when implemented.

DES

The Data Encryption Standard (DES) was once a predominant symmetric-key algorithm for the encryption of electronic data. It was highly influential in the advancement of modern cryptography in the academic world. In 1976, after consultation with the National Security Agency (NSA), the National Bureau of Standards (NBS), the predecessor to NIST, eventually selected a slightly modified version (strengthened against differential cryptanalysis, but weakened against brute-force attacks), which was published as an official Federal Information Processing Standard (FIPS) for the United States in 1977. DES is now considered to be insecure for many applications. This is mainly due to the 56-bit key size being too small; in January 1999, distributed.net and the Electronic Frontier Foundation (EFF) collaborated to publicly break a DES key in 22 hours and 15 minutes. DES has been withdrawn as a standard by NIST.

AES

The Advanced Encryption Standard (AES) is a specification for the encryption of electronic data established by NIST in 2001. AES is a subset of the Rijndael cipher developed by two Belgian cryptographers, Joan Daemen and Vincent Rijmen, who submitted a proposal to NIST during the AES selection process. For AES, NIST selected three members of the Rijndael family, each with a block size of 128 bits, but three different key lengths: 128, 192, and 256 bits. AES has been adopted by the U.S. government and is now used worldwide. The algorithm described by AES is a symmetric-key algorithm, meaning the same key is used for both encrypting and decrypting the data.

3DES

In cryptography, Triple DES (3DES) is the common name for the Triple Data Encryption Algorithm (TDEA or Triple DEA) symmetric-key block cipher, which applies the Data Encryption Standard (DES) cipher algorithm three times to each data block. The original DES cipher's key size of 56 bits was generally sufficient when that algorithm was designed, but the availability of increasing computational power made brute-force attacks feasible. Triple DES provides a relatively simple method of increasing the key size of DES to protect against such attacks, without the need to design a completely new block cipher algorithm.

PGP

Pretty Good Privacy (PGP) is a data encryption and decryption computer program that provides cryptographic privacy and authentication for data communication. PGP is often used for signing, encrypting, and decrypting texts, e-mails, files, directories, and whole disk partitions and is also used to increase the security of e-mail communications.

Secure Disposal of Electronic Media

Now that we have considered securing the data, the next step is to consider what we need to do when it is time to dispose of the data or the storage devices on which we store the data. The following sections discuss how to ensure that the devices are disposed of in a manner appropriate to the type of data and the type of device.

Secure Shredding, Degaussing, and Sanitizing

Various processes and methods are available to securely destroy data and media held on storage media including shredding, degaussing, and sanitizing. The most important factor in deciding which process or method is appropriate is again based on the organization's risk and mitigation policies. The overall goal is to prevent unauthorized access to sensitive information, including ePHI, PHI, and PII.

Secure Shredding

Data shredding is a data-destruction utility designed to securely erase a hard disk or digital storage device, completely removing the data and making the data unrecoverable. The software utilizes an overwrite method of destroying data rather than other means of data destruction (such as degaussing or physical destruction). The downside of data shredding is that it usually makes the storage device unusable. Data shredding (electronic) should not be confused with the shredding of paper documents; often some confusion occurs when only the term "shredding" is used.

Degaussing

Degaussing is the process of decreasing or eliminating an unwanted magnetic field on a magnetic medium, such as a hard disk. In layman's terms, degaussing converts the current 0s and 1s to randomized 0s and 1s to prevent reverse engineering of the data. Due to a phenomenon known as magnetic hysteresis, it is generally not possible to reduce a magnetic field completely to zero, so degaussing typically induces a very small "known" field referred to as bias. Some organizations require that degaussing occur in multiple passes—for instance, DoD practices require at least seven degaussing passes. The advantage of degaussing is that the media is not destroyed and remains reusable for new data.

Sanitizing

Sanitizing involves the use of anonymization and other techniques to purge data sets (often statistical) of PII in order to protect user privacy. Sanitizing can be used in cases where you want to remove the data and reuse the devices within the given environment.

Determining the Level and Type of Destruction

The overall goal in determining which level of destruction of data to use for the organization and the specific devices must always be to prevent unintentional disclosure or dissemination of PHI or other sensitive data. Best practices should be followed when determining the best process to follow. The type and level of destruction should be based on the type of data, the type of media, and, most importantly, the policy and procedures established by the organization. Allowing individuals to choose the process they follow without guidance could result in data loss, even minor, which could lead to financial loss or embarrassment to the organization.

Exercise 27-1: Assessing Your Organization's Facility Security Risks

If you work for a healthcare organization, follow the three sets of steps in this exercise to consider the areas covered in the chapter. Before conducting this exercise, obtain management approval to perform the assessment. Clearly, you would not want your efforts to be complicated by negative management reaction to a surveillance observation or a visitor who reports you, thinking you might be considering how to circumvent security.

Office Areas

1. Walk into an office or clinical area. Once inside the door where patients and visitors enter, look around and see if you can identify where PCs, laptops, printers, and other devices are visible. The purpose is to observe whether any sensitive information is viewable in plain sight, including computer screens with data visible, printed material left in printer or fax machine trays, and so forth. A good practice is to conduct this exercise in more than one office or clinical area, both to compare implementation of policies and procedures and to look for internal best practices. Identify the areas in which stronger processes are in place, and look for processes that perhaps exceed the actual organization policy.

2. Now act as though you are the patient being taken from the waiting room to the exam room. What can you observe en route and in the exam room? Next move from the exam room to checkout (billing, scheduling, etc.) and consider during this walk-through the same list of devices.

3. Look for signs or other evidence of where your data closets, data center (which may not be local to your office), or other communications areas are located. Look for open closets, in use by maintenance or housekeeping perhaps, and observe if network devices or equipment is visible.

Next, conduct the same type of review of the areas where the data are stored or transmitted.

Data Closets   If you are authorized access to the data closets, or if an authorized individual will provide you escorted access, proceed as follows:

1. Attempt to identify the IDF in the closet.
2. Identify the fire suppression and HVAC provided within the closet, as well as any surveillance devices.
3. Identify access-control devices, including access cards, key fobs, or biometric devices if used.
4. Identify any risks you can observe, such as access issues, lock functionality, improper temperature or humidity levels, poor lighting, and so on.

Data Center   Again, if you are authorized to access the data center, or if you can get an authorized individual to provide you escorted access, conduct a review of the following areas:

1. Prior to entering the data center, observe the signage such as warning signs, authorized-personnel-only signs, and so forth. Also, prior to entering determine the types of physical controls implemented, including key fobs, access cards, biometrics, two-factor authentication, and so on.
2. Upon entering the data center, determine the procedure for controlling employee access and visitor access to the data center, including whether the organization requires visitors to record their entry in a log book. Verify what information a visitor must place into a log when they enter. Later you can review the policies and procedures for entry to determine if the log actually requires the same data as policy dictates. As an example, I have seen policies that state the user must enter "form of ID" but there is no column to enter such information on the log. Act as an auditor here; if policy dictates a security measure, the organization must ensure they enforce it.
3. Look for fire suppression (fire extinguishers, sprinklers, etc.), security lighting, surveillance, UPSs and generators for emergency power, and HVAC.
4. Note the temperature and humidity in the data center, if displayed.
5. Note whether trash, boxes, or other items are stored in the data center. Most organizations do not permit these items in the data center to reduce fire hazards. A best practice is to destroy or shred trash, such as empty PC boxes, from the data center once they are emptied.
6. When departing, do you have to also note in the visitor log your departure time? Did your escort stay with you the entire time, and did they ensure you entered your departure time in the log?

Exercise 27-2: Assessing Your Organization's Practices for Disposing of Electronic Media

Find an individual in the organization who has knowledge of how your organization disposes of electronic media, and set up a time to discuss the practices that are in place. In the interview, determine whether the facility uses secure shredding, degaussing, or sanitization when disposing of electronic media. If the organization uses a combination of these methods, determine whether there is a documented procedure for the type of process to follow in different situations. For example, if a drive is defective and covered under warranty, what process does your organization follow when returning the drive to the manufacturer? Are there any special requirements for disposing of electronic media in your organization, such as medical devices, mobile devices, and so forth?

Chapter Review

This chapter addressed the physical safeguards required for your IT systems, including the location of storage devices, network hardware, printers, scanners, and copiers. Best practices regarding physical equipment were identified for the handling of PHI, including PC placement, privacy screens, printer placement, screensavers, and time lockout. Access points to servers, offices, and data closets are all critical considerations. The chapter discussed how determining the level of safeguards required by your facility's data center, data closets, IDF/MDF, and backups will depend on the risks to which your facility is exposed, weighed against the costs of providing those safeguards.

Access-control devices were defined and discussed, including key fobs, badges, and biometrics. The chapter presented guidelines for building secure systems, including office hardware, environmental controls, other controls, and storage devices. We discussed guidelines for securing and preserving electronic media and briefly explored encryption and types of encryption. The final topic included best practices for secure disposal of electronic media—including secure shredding, degaussing, and sanitizing—and determining the type and level of destruction of media. The end of the chapter provided two exercises on how to conduct informal assessments of your organization's risks related to physical security and assessing your organization's practices for secure disposal of electronic media.

Questions

To test your comprehension of the chapter, answers the following questions and then check your answers against the list of correct answers that follows the questions.

1. Which of the following is a dedicated network that provides access to consolidated, block-level data storage?

   A. Servers

   B. NAS

   C. SAN

   D. SD card

2. In a healthcare office environment, which of the following applications must be considered as possibly having sensitive data included within its storage media?

   A. E-mail

   B. Scheduling

   C. Billing

   D. All of the above

3. When determining the appropriate location of PCs in your organization, which of the following should you consider?

   A. Security of the location

   B. Ability to view the screen

   C. Whether privacy screens are available

   D. All of the above

4. Which of the following is a network device usually located on each floor (sometimes more than one per floor) in a larger building?

   A. MDF

   B. DMZ

   C. IDF

   D. Both A and C

5. Which of the following principles is used by two-factor authentication to grant physical access to systems?

   A. Something you have

   B. Something you know

   C. Both A and B

   D. Neither A or B

6. Motion detectors are considered to belong to which of the following classes of environmental controls?

   A. Fire suppression

   B. Surveillance

   C. Security lighting

   D. UPS

7. Why is employer-provided education and training for employees necessary?

   A. Compliance requirements change or their interpretation changes.

   B. Healthcare organizations are responsible for the actions of their employees.

   C. Consumers are becoming more aware of the requirements that healthcare organizations must comply with.

   D. All of the above.

8. What is the predecessor of Transport Layer Security (TLS)?

   A. Triple DES (3DES)

   B. Pretty Good Privacy (PGP)

   C. Secure Sockets Layer (SSL)

   D. Data Encryption Standard (DES)

Answers

1. C. A storage area network (SAN) generally provides access to consolidated, block-level data storage, generally in the form of storage devices, such as disk arrays, tape libraries, and optical jukeboxes, accessible to servers so that the devices appear to the operating system to be locally attached devices.

2. D. Even though a healthcare office may have policies in place that prohibit the use of e-mail for communications with the patient about specific sensitive healthcare diagnoses and so forth, the fact is that users and patients could be including this in their communications. As a result, you should assume that e-mail data must be stored with the same security controls as other sensitive data systems. Clearly, patient scheduling and billing applications contain personally identifiable data as well as protected health information.

3. D. All PCs, specifically those used to access sensitive information, should be placed in locations where only the intended viewers of the data can see it. They should also be located in a place that would make it impossible for an unauthorized person to simply pick up the device and walk out without being observed. If a device must be placed in a more public space, consider using privacy screens to allow only a limited field of view of the data being displayed.

4. C. The intermediate distribution frame (IDF) is usually placed in the data closet, while the main distribution frame (MDF) is more centralized and located in the data center or other communications area of the facility.

5. B. The principle of "something you know" covers passwords and personal identification numbers (PINs), as opposed to "something you have," which covers an access-control device such as a key fob or badge or a part of your person such as a fingerprint or retina.

6. B. Surveillance includes cameras, motion detectors, alarms systems, and other devices.

7. D. As compliance requirements age, they are often changed, or the interpretation of specific requirements might change. Additionally, these changes often enact fines and penalties, and although often the individual might be held accountable for noncompliance, in most cases the healthcare organizations are also responsible for the actions of their employees. Lastly, and this is often a good thing, consumers are becoming more aware of the requirements that healthcare organizations must comply with and therefore are more likely to make an effort to ensure accountability.

8. C. Secure Sockets Layer is the predecessor to TLS, though both are frequently referred to as SSL. They are cryptographic protocols that provide communications security over a computer network.

References

1. National Institutes of Standards and Technology (NIST). (2012). *Security and privacy controls for federal information systems and organizations.* SP 800-53, initial public draft. Accessed on March 7, 2017, from http://nvlpubs.nist.gov/nistpubs/ SpecialPublications/NIST.SP.800-53r4.pdf.

2. U.S. Department of Defense. (n.d.). *Common access card requirements.* Accessed on July 21, 2016, from www.cac.mil/.

3. Federal Chief Information Officer Council. (2009). *Personal identity verification interoperability for non-federal issuers.* Accessed on March 7, 2017, from https:// www.idmanagement.gov/IDM/servlet/fileField?entityId=ka0t0000000TNSVAA4 &field=File__Body__s.

4. U.S. General Services Administration, USAccess Program. (n.d.). *PIV credential features.* Accessed on July 21, 2016, from http://fedidcard.gov/credfeatures.aspx.

5. https://en.wikipedia.org/wiki/Encryption

6. https://www.hhs.gov/hipaa/for-professionals/faq/2020/what-is-the-difference-between-addressable-and-required-implementation-specifications/index.html

CHAPTER 28

Healthcare Information Security: Operational Safeguards

Sean Murphy

In this chapter, you will learn how to
- Define operational safeguards
- Apply operational safeguards within a healthcare setting
- Explain the value of an information security management process that includes information security training and awareness
- Assess risk in healthcare organizations using a framework of standards-based criteria
- Identify operational safeguard fundamentals within emerging healthcare initiatives

Operational Safeguards: A Component of Information Security

Operational safeguards are correct processes, procedures, standards, and practices that govern the creation, handling, usage, and sharing of health information. They are an important piece of the "due care" and "due diligence" any healthcare organization must perform.[1, 2] A distinction must be made between these and administrative, physical, and technical safeguards. While the administrative, physical, and technical safeguards are important by themselves, they must be integrated to completely protect health information and systems. To implement a process that provides layers of protection, like defense in depth, where a robust and integrated set of measures and actions are in place that focus in a variety of security areas, operational safeguards must be added to any overall security program to achieve compliance.[3]

Due care and due diligence relate to processes and actions a company takes that are considered responsible, careful, cautious, and practical. Due care and due diligence are defined as follows:

- **Due care**   Steps taken to show that a company has taken responsibility for the activities that occur within the corporation and has taken the necessary steps to help protect the company, its resources, and employees.

- **Due diligence**   The process of systematically evaluating information to identify vulnerabilities, threats, and issues relating to an organization's overall risk.

Conceptually, due diligence and due care are a pathway for the flexibility a healthcare organization needs to conduct information-sharing securely, yet within the constraints of information protection.

Operational safeguards apply to information security practices that are required in all industries—banking, manufacturing, retail, and so forth. But this chapter will focus on the operational safeguards required for healthcare, where there are similarities but also unique challenges for providing information security.

Operational Safeguards in Healthcare Organizations

No organization can totally eliminate the risk of improper disclosure of health information. In fact, within a healthcare organization, the Heath Insurance Portability and Accountability Act (HIPAA) of 1996 permits certain incidental uses and disclosures that happen as a by-product of another permissible or required use or disclosure, as long as the covered entity has applied *reasonable* safeguards.[4] An incidental use or disclosure does not invalidate an organization's operational safeguards.[5] Operational safeguards apply to healthcare organizations because of HIPAA and all of its amendments. The power of the federal government to enforce HIPAA compliance through fines and penalties stems from one of these amendments, the Health Information Technology for Economic and Clinical Health (HITECH) Act of 2009. The administrative simplification provisions of HIPAA called for the establishment of standards and requirements for transmitting certain health information to improve the efficiency and effectiveness of the healthcare system while protecting patient privacy.[6] HITECH as an amendment to HIPAA followed the HIPAA Privacy Rule (2002) and the HIPAA Security Rule (2003). It was enacted as part of the American Recovery and Reinvestment Act (ARRA) of 2009 to promote the adoption and meaningful use of healthcare information technology and addresses the privacy and security concerns associated with the electronic transmission of health information, in part through several provisions that strengthen the civil and criminal enforcement of the HIPAA rules.[7] HIPAA governs organizations that provide certain services using protected health information (PHI). Table 28-1 provides a foundational summary and definitions for some of the most important concepts and terms relevant to understanding healthcare information security.

Rule/Concept	Summary
HIPAA Privacy Rule	Implements the requirements of HIPAA. Addresses the use and disclosure of individuals' health information—*protected health information* (PHI)—by organizations subject to the Privacy Rule—*covered entities*—as well as standards covering individuals' rights to understand and control how their health information is used.
HIPAA Security Rule	Establishes national standards to protect individuals' electronic personal health information that is created, received, used, or maintained by a covered entity. The Security Rule requires appropriate administrative, physical, and technical safeguards to ensure the confidentiality, integrity, and security of electronic PHI (ePHI).
HITECH Act	Provides designated funding to modernize the healthcare system by promoting and expanding the adoption of healthcare information technology (HIT). HITECH supports the rapid adoption of HIT by hospitals and clinicians through Medicare and Medicaid incentive payments to physicians and hospitals for meaningful use of electronic health records (EHRs). It also authorizes grant programs and contracts that support HIT adoption by providing technical assistance to healthcare providers, especially in rural and underserved communities; training a HIT workforce; as well as developing standards for certification of EHR privacy and security.
HIPAA Omnibus Final Rule	Passed in 2013, an amendment to HIPAA that clarifies earlier provisions to the law and implements several new requirements. It provides a clear definition of a business associate and strengthens how these agents are subject to HIPAA—whether they sign a business associate agreement or not. Another key change is in the requirements for determining when a data breach has occurred. The previous standard was to determine "risk of harm" to the affected person. The new standard is "risk of disclosure," which is designed to be more objective.
Covered entity	Under the HIPAA Privacy Rule, *covered entity* refers to three specific groups—health plans, healthcare clearinghouses, and healthcare providers—that transmit health information electronically.
Business associate	A *business associate* is a person or organization (other than a member of a covered entity's workforce) that performs certain functions or activities on behalf of, or provides certain services to, a covered entity involving the use or disclosure of individually identifiable health information.
Protected health information (PHI)	PHI includes all individually identifiable health information held or transmitted by a covered entity or its business associate in any form or media, whether electronic, paper, or oral, including the following: • Information concerning the individual's past, present, or future physical or mental health or condition • Information regarding the provision of healthcare to the individual • Information regarding the past, present, or future payment for the provision of healthcare to the individual • Information that identifies the individual or for which there is a reasonable basis to believe it can be used to identify the individual (e.g., name, address, birth date, Social Security number)

Table 28-1 Understanding HIPAA: Basic Definitions

PART VI

What is important to the understanding of operational safeguards in healthcare is that all covered entities and business associates must put provisions in place to use PHI appropriately and not disclose any PHI inappropriately. When a covered entity or business associate does disclose PHI inappropriately, they may have committed a PHI breach. The U.S. Department of Health and Human Services (HHS) oversees the U.S. laws applicable to these breaches. Over the last several years, HHS has handed out numerous monetary fines (and a few jail terms) for organizations and individuals who have committed PHI breaches. Here are just a few highly publicized examples from the news headlines:

- Triple-S Management Corp., an insurance holding company based in San Juan, Puerto Rico, was slapped with $6.8 million in penalties in 2014 for improperly handling the medical records of some 70,000 individuals.[8]

- As many as 80 million customers of the nation's second-largest health insurance company, Anthem, Inc., have had their account information stolen. "Anthem was the target of a very sophisticated external cyber attack," Anthem president and CEO Joseph Swedish said in a statement. The hackers gained access to Anthem's computer system and got information including names, birthdays, medical IDs, Social Security numbers, street addresses, e-mail addresses, and employment information, including income data.[9]

- A medical group in Texas is facing a potential healthcare data breach that may have exposed patient and employee information after a hacking incident. Approximately 50,000 individuals were affected by the healthcare data security event at the Medical Colleagues of Texas, LLP. Medical Colleagues of Texas, LLP stated that it discovered an outside entity had accessed its computer network, which stored EHR and personnel data.[10]

As HITECH has opened the door for all 50 U.S. states and territories to also sue for damages due to a PHI breach, the potential for an organizationally disastrous impact of just one breach is highly likely.

 TIP Per 45 CFR 164.408, if a disclosure is determined to be a breach, it must be reported to HHS immediately if it affects 500 or more individual records. At lower levels, covered entities are required to keep a log and report breaches annually.

The operational safeguards are critical to maintaining a high level of trust between the individual and the organization that uses their information. When a patient heads to their family physician for a routine check-up or visits the hospital for a more intensive procedure, they deserve to know that the information they share is kept confidential. Patients in any medical setting want to rest assured that their personal information is not going to be available to anyone other than the physicians and medical staff involved in their care. Even if patients generally trust their care providers, studies have shown they do not extend that same level of trust when the information is digitized or transferred to electronic information. In one study, 35 percent of respondents indicated they are worried that their health information will end up widely available on the Internet. Half of the respondents believe that EHRs will have a negative impact on the privacy of their health data. Only 27 percent of respondents felt computerized health records would have a somewhat positive or significantly positive effect on their privacy. Another 24 percent said that computerized health records would have no impact on privacy at all. Interestingly, 24 percent of respondents said they don't even trust themselves with access to their own records.[11]

Beyond the impact a PHI breach can have on an organization, the impact of a healthcare provider not having access to information they need to provide diagnosis, treatment, and make any other health-related decisions can be critical. Of the traditional information security concerns—confidentiality, integrity, and availability—availability of information is uniquely and exceedingly important within healthcare. The root cause of medical and diagnostic errors is often patient information that is not available when the provider needs it—at the time of patient care. Even in nonemergency situations physicians are forced to provide care, usually by asking the patient (who may or may not provide accurate information). In worse cases, a doctor may need to rely on what the family member(s) can recollect—if anything at all. Redundant tests, inefficient care, delay in treatment, and patient safety risk are all outcomes of providers lacking information—irrespective of the confidentiality or integrity concerns that are also important. Having secure information available is vital to avoiding medical errors. This represents a major challenge for healthcare organizations and is illustrated in the seminal and still relevant Institute of Medicine's (IOM) report, *To Err Is Human* (2000). The IOM also highlights the role unavailable information has in patient safety and causing medical errors.

Another aspect of information availability is system or network downtime. While these are traditionally covered by technical controls, downtime can also be prevented and mitigated using numerous operational (nontechnical) safeguards. Measures like contingency planning, manual processes, and disaster recovery are ways an organization can build in extra security for information availability. And downtime is very expensive. For instance, downtime can cost a practice with five physicians nearly $25,000 per instance when the system is down for ten hours or more. If systems are down just 4 percent of the time, the data predicts the cost could top $234,000 annually. We also must factor in the cost of recovery from an unplanned event. A survey of healthcare providers showed, on average, that maintaining a 99 percent uptime still resulted in an average of 87 hours per solution rework annually for information systems (such as clinical patient record systems).[12] Clearly, periods of information unavailability are not only dangerous, as we have already examined, they are also costly—putting patients' lives at risk and healthcare organizations' reputations in jeopardy.

Now that we have seen how operational safeguards are integral to information security (particularly availability) specific to a healthcare setting, the next step is to examine common components of a robust, integrated operational safeguard program in healthcare. All of the components discussed in the following sections are required by HIPAA and HITECH.

PART VI

Security Management Process

One of the first operational safeguards is an obvious security management process. This is required by HIPAA for all healthcare organizations.[13] A main provision of the security management process is that the organization must designate a "security official" and a "privacy official" to be responsible for developing and implementing security and privacy policies and procedures. This is critical, because protecting healthcare information permeates the entire organization—privacy and security of patient information is integral to every medical activity.

Information Management Council

Along with corresponding policies and procedures that provide governance for proper handling and protection of sensitive data (including PHI), implementing an information management council is an important operational safeguard. Depending on the overall governance structure of the organization, this group can be a council, a committee, or even a team. What matters is that the group is a formally chartered or organized collection of decision-makers in the organization. It should have an executive sponsor and be made up of people from strategic areas in the organization—not only from security, information technology, legal, and privacy, but also from clinical and business areas.[14]

Together this team considers and provides strategic direction for various aspects of protecting information. For instance, how an organization may migrate data to the cloud or implement a bring your own device (BYOD) policy would be issues the council addresses. The council does not replace the leadership and role of established positions like information security or privacy officers. In fact, the council leverages the reach and influence these positions can have in an organization by creating enterprise-wide awareness and shared priority.

Identity Management and Authorization

This is an operational safeguard that applies across all industries that care about information security. Being able to establish and validate the identity of each individual or entity with access to the system; assigning roles and providing appropriate authorizations to each identity; controlling the accesses related to those authorizations, including authenticating the asserted identity; terminating the authorizations as necessary; and maintaining the governance processes that support this life cycle are best practices no matter what the business.[15] In healthcare, there are so many issues that are prevented or mitigated by implementing proper identity management and authorization processes. Obtaining unauthorized (free) care or illegally filled prescriptions via identity theft are prevalent issues—assuring that patients are who they say they are can mitigate those risks. Likewise, taking actions to enforce use of strong passwords and prohibit sharing of user credentials can prevent someone from using a doctor's credential to access the computerized order-entry system and sign orders unlawfully.

In fact, the use of multifactor authentication is increasingly imperative to assure identity and access management due to the growing threat of credential theft. A hacker who has a valid username and password becomes indistinguishable from the authorized user. The protection methods of information security become effectively useless.

TIP Multifactor authentication is based on having two or more elements that make up the access, authentication, and authorization credentials for a user. It is considered a best security practice, reduces the impact of credential theft, and is based on the concept of identity established and verified according to[16]
—Who the user is, which is a given: Username (e.g.)
—What the user knows: Password (e.g.). These identifiers make up single-factor authentication.
—What the user has: A biometric marker (fingerprint) or public-key infrastructure (PKI) card. These identifiers make up multifactor or two-factor authentication.

Awareness and Training Programs

The HIPAA Security and Privacy Rules require all members of the workforce to be trained in security and privacy principles. The required training should take place at least once per year. But that does not preclude real-time awareness tips and education. Keeping the importance of HIPAA, safeguarding PHI, and complying with information security requirements as priorities in an organization (with dozens of competing priorities and scarce resources) is no easy task. However, a healthcare organization where safety, privacy, and security are part of the culture as opposed to a compliance requirement has a competitive advantage. And in those healthcare organizations where all employees feel individually responsible for protecting the confidentiality, integrity, and availability of health information and the privacy and safety of patients, organizational risk will be reduced and patient safety will be improved.

Risk Assessment

Risk assessment is the heart of any information security program in a healthcare organization. From a compliance perspective, HIPAA requires that an organization "conduct an accurate and thorough assessment of the potential risks and vulnerabilities to the confidentiality, integrity, and availability of electronic protected health information held by the covered entity."[17]

Even if there were no legal or regulatory mandate, any good security management process would begin and end with a risk assessment. Within a risk assessment are objective standards that are based on industry standards and accepted practices, compliant with law, and adhere to ethical principles. Within HIPAA, a healthcare organization can defend itself against fines and penalties (and loss of public trust) by demonstrating what is called the "reasonable and prudent person" rule. As mentioned before, organizations must demonstrate due diligence and due care to convince the courts that their actions were not negligent. There are numerous examples of risk assessments. In general, they are systematic, ongoing, and conducted in identifiable phases. (This chapter does not elaborate on risk assessments; Chapter 26 examines risk assessment in greater detail.) HIPAA requires covered entities to protect against *reasonably anticipated threats or hazards* to the security/integrity of the e-PHI they create, receive, maintain, or transmit. They must also prevent *reasonably anticipated* impermissible uses or disclosures. A covered entity must reduce risk to *reasonable and appropriate* levels. The risk analysis process determines what is "reasonable."

 TIP See the HIMSS Risk Assessment Toolkit at www.himss.org/library/ healthcare-privacy-security/risk-assessment for a variety of frameworks and other resources for conducting a risk assessment. Additionally, go to the National Institute of Standards and Technology (NIST) Security Compliance Automation Protocol (SCAP) web site for access to the HIPAA Security Rule Automated Toolkit at https://scap.nist.gov/hipaa.

Software and System Development

Software and system development are important with respect to operational safeguards in that too often information security is "bolted on" at the end of development and during implementation. Operational safeguards, like risk assessments, need to be integrated into the identified phases of development—in other words, information security needs to be "built in." Managing the software and system development life cycle is akin to managing the configuration process, but it is more focused on systems or software as they are being engineered before implementation. Generally speaking, the life cycles have four development phases, listed next. However, to properly build in information security, some operational safeguards must be attended to.[18] The relative operational safeguards are listed in italics corresponding to the appropriate development phase.

- **What** Specification of WHAT the product is to do.
  - **Initiation** An initial threat and risk assessment will provide input for IT security requirements.
- **How** Specification of HOW the product does it.
- **Build** Development or BUILD of the code or components that implements HOW.
  - **Design and development** An appropriate balance of technical, managerial, operational, physical, and personnel security safeguards will help to meet the requirements determined by the threat and risk assessment.
- **Use** Operational deployment or USE of software or system that performs WHAT.
  - **Implementation** Design documentation, acceptance tests, and certification and accreditation processes are created.
  - **Operation** System security is monitored and maintained while threat and risk assessments aid in the evaluation of modifications that could affect security.

When developing software with operational safeguards built in, it is crucial to begin the process with the end in mind. A plan for disposal must also be built in to the system and software development life cycles. In accordance with archival and security standards and guidelines, the organization must plan to archive or dispose of sensitive IT assets and information once they are no longer useful.[19]

Configuration Management

Having control of how systems are developed and implemented is a crucial component of operational safeguards in healthcare organizations. Not many industries have systems as diverse as a healthcare organization. Traditionally, many systems and applications within healthcare are highly customized, commercial-off-the-shelf (COTS). For this reason, an operational safeguard for resources not fully developed by the healthcare organization is required. Configuration management controls provide the organization with a safe way to manage changes made to systems once they are in operation. Examples of bodies or systems that control configuration management are configuration control boards or system-change-request processes.[20]

Some of the types of systems that can be found within one healthcare organization fall into the following categories:

- Office automation IT (business and administrative functions)
- Financial systems connected to state and federal agencies as well as healthcare insurers
- EHR systems and clinical applications
- Medical devices regulated by the Food and Drug Administration (FDA) and manufactured/maintained by commercial vendors (e.g., PACS, telemetry, catherization labs).

Configuration management is an operational safeguard that creates processes for controlling how changes are made to a system and keeping records of those changes. It is good information security practice to control and document changes to the hardware, firmware, software, and documentation involved in protecting information assets. This configuration management process should be governed by the security management program an organization has in place. An additional measure that is an increasingly important safeguard is to use automated detection and alerting tools that identify when unexpected changes are made and notify security teams.

Consent Management

Revisiting the importance of having operational safeguards in place to ensure public (patient) trust in the organization, having a consent management process allows a patient to know how their information will be used. It also makes it possible for patients to control the use of their information. Numerous federal and state laws cover this safeguard, and HIPAA requires a consent management process. An organization must obtain a patient's consent for collecting, retaining, or exchanging his or her personal health information. And when that information concerns behavioral health or substance abuse, additional restrictions and authorizations are needed. The consent process is extremely important as it relates to promises and obligations covered entities make to the patient.

Today, these processes are primarily manual, but technologies emerging in advance of healthcare information exchanges (HIEs) and Integrating the Healthcare Enterprise (IHE) are building technical methods for obtaining and maintaining consent.

TIP   IHE refers to a group started by radiologists and information technology professionals to address and improve how computers in heathcare share information. The group started their work in 1998 based on interoperability standards for healthcare-specific transmission formats like DICOM and HL7. Today, they provide numerous resources for healthcare organizations such as technical frameworks and a product registry.

System Activity Review

A comprehensive program of operational safeguards will include system activity review. This consists of trained and qualified personnel routinely reviewing records of information system activity. These reviews can come in the form of audit logs, facility access reports, and security incident tracking reports. Being vigilant in this area can be an effective means of detecting potential misuse and abuse of privileges. The need for this activity is growing with HITECH Act's requirements for providing accounting of disclosures and notification to all patients affected by a data breach. The sheer volume of clinical and financial data is overwhelming. Where hospitals rely on manual auditing and reporting today, they will certainly be forced to move to automatic and technical solutions for running the reports. In fact, the technology exists today; it is just underused in the healthcare industry.[21]

TIP   HITECH provides that an individual has a right to receive information about disclosures made through a covered entity's electronic health record for purposes of carrying out treatment, payment, and healthcare operations.[22]

Continuity of Operations

Healthcare organizations are required to establish and implement policies and procedures for continuity of operations when unanticipated events, both natural and manmade, happen. Natural disasters, malware that causes systems to crash, and any other number of events that impede healthcare for measurable periods of time will happen. Healthcare organizations have always prepared to provide care in the face of mass-casualty emergencies or when power and water are unavailable. However, the loss of information availability or critical system access requires a different process. It is not practical to expect to go to a paper or manual process until a system or a data center is available again. Healthcare is more and more dependent on electronic health information. HIPAA requires operational safeguards that protect information continuity to be in place.[23] The plan must include a prioritization of business and clinical systems with an order of restore. When the event happens is not the time to begin deciding which systems must be restored and in what order. Those decisions must be made when all conditions are normal.

Incident Procedures

Because the data breach rules are enforced with fines and penalties, it becomes a high priority of any healthcare organization's awareness and training program to provide employees with a clear explanation of how incidents are reported. Incidents can be a virus received in an e-mail, a medical record found in a public area, or some other breach of sensitive PHI. Not all disclosures or incidents are breaches that require notification, so healthcare organizations need to design and implement a proper response that includes a full investigation. In some cases, the organization will need to notify individuals whose health information may have been exposed. There has been a significant change in data breach notifications that is important to an organization and its incident response procedures. Previously, under the HITECH Act, healthcare organizations conducted a risk assessment of the data disclosure to determine if there was any impact or harm to the patient. It was the organization's responsibility to make notification if they determined there was a likelihood of negative impact on the affected individual. Under the amendment to HIPAA called the Omnibus Final Rule in 2013, the burden shifted to determining the risk of disclosure. The law removes any measure of impact and makes the threshold simply a measure of how likely it is that the data was exposed to an unauthorized entity.[24]

Sanctions

The HIPAA law outlined penalties in the event of unauthorized disclosure, but the HITECH Act enacted severe civil and criminal penalties for sanctioning entities that fail to comply with the privacy and security provisions. In addition to patient notification requirements, healthcare organizations are required to take remedial actions, document actions taken, and discipline (up to and including firing) their employees when privacy and security policies and procedures are not followed correctly.

Evaluation

Drawing from the basic "plan, do, check, act" cycle of quality management, a healthcare organization should periodically evaluate the security management program in place. This should be done at least annually and include objective measures of success. An independent review is a key component of this yearly process. That does not preclude internal review, but every effort must be made for objectivity. Another time to evaluate operational safeguards is when material changes are made within the organization that might impact the security management program. A good example of such a change would be a merger or acquisition of a new medical group practice or the opening of a new surgical service center off campus. These changes will alter the risk to which the organization can be exposed.

Business Associate Contracts

Unique to healthcare entities subject to HIPAA, business associate (BA) contracts are a source of operational safeguards. All organizations have contractual obligations and service providers that must be considered when operating a security management program. Within healthcare, HIPAA mandates these agreements be in place and include satisfactory assurance that appropriate safeguards will be applied to protect the PHI created, received, maintained, or transmitted on behalf of the covered entity.[25] BA agreements help manage risk and bound liability, clarify responsibilities and expectations, and define processes for addressing disputes among parties. The BA contract requires that each person or organization that provides certain functions, activities, or services to the healthcare organization involving PHI is obligated to comply with HIPAA requirements. The HITECH Act subjects the BA to the same enforcement and sanctions as the healthcare organization they support.

Healthcare-Specific Implications on Operational Safeguards

The need to implement operational safeguards applies to various industries—banking, manufacturing, energy, and healthcare, to name a handful. Across these industries, information security professionals have to be flexible enough to apply information security best practices while enabling maximum business capability at appropriate cost. Across these industries, the common constraints are the unique features of the business and how these features impact implementing security measures. Healthcare is no different. Health information security professionals need to be on top of the latest advances in information technology, including operational safeguards, all the while making accommodations for the requirements of the healthcare organization.

Networked Medical Devices

Medical devices present a unique challenge within a healthcare environment. An increasing number of medical devices connect to the hospital network or use network resources to operate. Expanding on the FDA definition of a medical device, a *networked medical device* is a special-purpose computing system including an instrument, apparatus, or implant intended for use in the diagnosis of disease or other conditions or in the cure, mitigation, treatment, or prevention of disease, or intended to affect the structure or any function of the body.[26]

Some examples of networked medical devices include digital imaging machines, telemetry systems, linear accelerators, and infusion pumps. Although they are typically built upon standard IT operating systems and run well-known applications, their special-purpose nature means that the normal operational safeguards that would be appropriate in office automation IT could cause patient harm when indiscriminately applied to medical devices.[27] This fact has introduced a new term into the healthcare information security lexicon. *E-iatrogenesis* is any patient harm caused at least in part by the application of healthcare information technology (and, by extension, healthcare information security efforts).[28] This term evolves from *iatrogenesis*, which is an inadvertent adverse effect or complication resulting from medical treatment or advice from a healthcare provider.

An example of e-iatrogenesis is when a prescription for a drug is not cross-referenced with the current patient medication list and the new drug causes an adverse reaction when combined with the medications the patient currently takes. Table 28-2 highlights some real-life examples of episodes of e-iatrogenesis that have occurred at various engineering stages of medical devices.[29]

Engineering Stage	Adverse Event	Contributing Factor
Requirements specification	Linear accelerator: patients died from massive overdoses of radiation.	An FDA memo regarding the corrective action plan (CAP) notes that "Unfortunately, the AECL response also seems to point out an apparent lack of documentation on software specifications and a software test plan."
Design	Pacemakers/implantable defibrillators: implant can be wirelessly tricked into inducing a fatal heart rhythm.	Security and privacy need to be part of the early design process.
Human factors	Infusion pump: patients were injured or killed by drug overdoses.	Software that did not prevent key bounce misinterpreted key presses of 20 mL as 200 mL.
Implementation	Infusion pump: patient received incorrect dosage and experienced increased intracranial pressure followed by brain death.	Buffer overflow (programming error) shut down the pump.
Testing	Ambulance dispatch: lost emergency calls. An earlier system for the London Ambulance Service failed two major tests and was scuttled.	Ambulance workers later accused the computer system of losing calls and that "the number of deaths in north London became so acute that the computer system was withdrawn." The ambulance company attributed the problems to "teething troubles" with a new computer system.
Maintenance	Health information technology (HIT) devices: computer systems rendered globally unavailable.	Due to the configuration of antivirus software, a heart catheterization device crashed during patient care. The display screen went black and doctors had to reboot their computer. The antivirus was configured to run every hour and made it impossible for the medical device to access real-time data, which precipitated the crash.[30]

Table 28-2 Examples of Adverse Events Where Medical Device Software Played a Significant Role

Multiple-Tenant Virtual Environments

With the onset of the "cloud" computing environment, healthcare organizations looking for efficiency, cost reduction, and expert IT support are quickly entering into the virtual computing environment. Today's IT infrastructure too often suffers from single-purpose server and storage resources, which result in low utilization, gross inefficiency, and an inability to respond quickly and flexibly to changing business needs. Sharing common resources and delivering IT as a service (ITaaS) from an offsite data center or purchased from a cloud services provider (e.g., Amazon Web Services [AWS] or Microsoft Azure) promises to overcome these limitations and reduce future IT spending. The trend in IT spending is to move to the cloud instead of investing in infrastructure, with 59 percent of those surveyed in the 2017 Computerworld Forecast Study responding that software as a service (SaaS) and a mix of public, private, hybrid, and community clouds are most likely to have an impact on their organization in the next three to five years.[31]

However, within the cloud data center, typical cloud providers have numerous customers. These customers have varied IT security requirements, ranging from almost none to very secure. Because healthcare is a highly regulated industry, healthcare organizations that enter into cloud computing agreements for service must ensure that their specific operational controls are in place and exercised. While subject to HIPAA, the healthcare organization as a covered entity cannot side-step requirements to safeguard PHI because other tenants within the multiple-platform virtual environment have less rigid requirements. The lack of confidence that data and applications will be securely isolated has been a major impediment to adoption of cloud-based services in healthcare. Healthcare IT professionals must be certain that applications and data are securely isolated in a multitenant environment where servers, networks, and storage are all shared resources. Additionally, the contractual agreements that must be established between the covered entity and the business associate data center must also account for HIPAA provisions for backup and recovery processes that may be more rigorous than the processes of other tenants in the environment. A very important point, with the passing of the HIPAA Omnibus Final Rule, HHS clarified the definition of a business associate and made certain that cloud providers were subject to HIPAA.

NOTE The final rule (https://www.gpo.gov/fdsys/pkg/FR-2013-01-25/pdf/2013-01073.pdf) does not specifically mention "cloud." However, using the definitions section of the final rule and the clarification found at "Guidance on HIPAA & Cloud Computing" on https://www.hhs.gov/hipaa/for-professionals/special-topics/cloud-computing/index.html as guidance, the applicability to cloud providers is demonstrated.

The tools, processes, and people skills needed by a healthcare organization will change as the healthcare organization moves data, infrastructure, and services to the cloud. However, the requirements for assuring data protection will not.

TIP For students interested in further study on the changing nature of cybersecurity in cloud environments, the Cloud Security Alliance is useful as a starting point. Their mission is "To promote the use of best practices for providing security assurance within Cloud Computing, and provide education on the uses of Cloud Computing to help secure all other forms of computing (https://cloudsecurityalliance.org)."

Mobile Device Management

Another trend in every industry is the use of mobile devices. Healthcare is no different. Many healthcare providers are enticed by the idea of allowing caregivers, administrators, and patients to use their own tablet computers, notebooks, and smartphones to access healthcare resources. However, they are concerned about the security risks—and the impact on IT operations. In fact, the pressures for mobile device use are extensive in healthcare. Statistics such as "81% of employed adults use at least one personally owned device for business use" and "Apple shipped more iPADs in 2 years than MACs in over 20 years"[32] are eye-opening. Bring your own device (BYOD) efforts are increasing as physicians and other caregivers want to use their smartphones and tablet computers for ordering prescriptions in computerized provider order entry (CPOE).

These BYOD efforts introduce unique challenges to the operational safeguards in terms of the devices' portability, their varying configurations, and the lack of control the organization has on any third-party software already loaded on the device. Equally eye-opening statistics point to the vulnerabilities inherent in these mobile devices: "$429,000 is the typical large company loss due to mobile computing mishaps in 2011" and "1/2 of companies have experienced a data breach due to insecure devices."[32]

Operational Safeguards in Emerging Healthcare Trends

Operational safeguards impact healthcare operations in all clinical and business processes—wherever confidentiality, integrity, and availability must be assured. This is true in existing processes and legacy systems. It is also true when examining emerging healthcare trends. A few select advances and initiatives demonstrate this reality and are presented here.

Healthcare in the Cloud

As mentioned before, healthcare organizations are moving to the cloud in meaningful ways. Business associate agreements will need to become more cloud-friendly.[33] As David S. Holtzman, formerly of the Health Information Privacy Division of the Office for Civil Rights (OCR), said, "If you use a cloud service, it should be your business associate.

PART VI

If they refuse to sign a business associate agreement, don't use the cloud service" (during a speech at the Health Care Compliance Association's 16th Annual Compliance Institute).

It bears restating that cloud computing offers significant benefits to the healthcare sector. Healthcare providers desire quick access to computing and large storage facilities that are either not available in traditional settings or just too expensive. The need for healthcare organizations to routinely share information securely across various settings and geographies places a burden on the healthcare provider and the patient. There can be significant delay in treatment and loss of time, which translates into increased cost to the system. The benefits of cloud computing address these realities by giving healthcare organizations a way to improve healthcare services and operational efficiency—and reduce costs over the long term. The other side of the coin is that healthcare data has specific requirements under HIPAA and HITECH that cloud providers may not be prepared to follow.[34] Whereas in the recent past many cloud vendors did not appear to fully understand the importance of addressing the special considerations within healthcare, the HIPAA Omnibus Final Rule in 2013 clarified the issue. With respect to the definition of a business associate, HHS has been clarified to include cloud service providers. Also, HHS went on to decree that even if a cloud service provider (or any entity performing a role subject to HIPAA) does not actually sign a business associate agreement, that does not excuse them from the law. They are subject to HIPAA regardless of whether they actually sign the document.

Healthcare organizations considering cloud computing need to carefully consider the risks before taking the plunge, and then take the right steps to obtain adequate due-diligence protection. According to Rebecca Herold, CEO of The Privacy Professor, a healthcare information security professional must know the key security issues for cloud computing in healthcare:

- Cloud computing safeguards necessary to satisfy HIPAA and other privacy and security requirements
- The impact of standards, for example, accounting of disclosures
- The negotiation of a HIPAA-compliant business associate agreement with the cloud vendor
- How to effectively obtain assurance that cloud vendors are in compliance with HIPAA
- Metrics to use to determine that vendors maintain compliance on an ongoing basis
- Performance issues, including availability of data and services
- Increased complexity of e-discovery if processes and/or data storage are handled using cloud computing
- Handling the transition to another cloud vendor or back to the healthcare organization without disrupting operations or conflicting claims to the data[35]

International Privacy and Security Concerns

HIPAA security standards apply to covered entities within the United States; if your data is being hosted overseas in a cloud vendor arrangement, the same privacy and security laws may not apply. However, the international laws may be even more restrictive:

> Personal data protection is a fundamental human right....
>
> —Code of EU Online Rights (2012)

The important point is for a healthcare organization to know where their data lives and how it is transferred as it is being shared and used. The physical location of data stores brings up the varying international laws governing privacy and security that come into play—they must be addressed in business associate agreements and other binding contractual terms and conditions.[36]

Health Information Exchanges

As PHI becomes more digital and automated through EHRs, the movement toward health information exchanges (HIEs) is accelerating. For the most part, HIEs enable healthcare providers across the same or multiple organizations almost real-time access to clinical information, reducing the delay in information transfer in the traditional paper-based system. Built into the HIE is the ability to ensure information integrity if operational safeguards are integrated. Because of the availability of the PHI, HIEs may also provide a way for healthcare organizations to accomplish public health reporting, measure clinical quality, conduct biomedical surveillance, and perform advanced population health research. But this is only true if the element of trust is present and the PHI is deemed reliable from all perspectives—those of the patient, the provider, and the HIE activity.

HIEs are subject to HIPAA rules. Patients have specific rights as to how their information is used and disclosed. HIEs are required to publish their practices and inform participating patients of their individual rights. The only way to build trust is to communicate these terms and conditions clearly. The Office of the National Coordinator for Health Information Technology (ONC) has produced a Nationwide Privacy and Security Framework for Electronic Exchange of Individually Identifiable Health Information. This framework outlines principles that, when taken together, constitute good data stewardship and form a foundation of public trust in the collection, access, use, and disclosure of PHI information by HIEs. Along with the ONC framework, the OCR published a series of fact sheets to assist HIEs in building privacy policies and explain how HIPAA applies. A summary of the ONC privacy and security framework can be found in Chapter 25, Table 25-1.

Workforce Information Security Competency

HIPAA requires that within a covered entity's environment, workforce members who need access to PHI to carry out their duties must be identified.[37] As healthcare information security processes mature over time, it is important to not only identify these individuals but ensure they are trained and competent. One model for this is the U.S.

Department of Defense's Instruction 8570.01-M, Information Assurance Workforce Improvement Program.[38] It will become increasingly important to have certification programs that aid in assessing workforce competency, because the HHS Office of Civil Rights healthcare auditing process looks at workforce security competency and assesses directly against the following criteria:

Summary of Principles from OCR's Audit Protocol Edited

- Inquire of management as to whether staff members have the necessary knowledge, skills, and abilities to fulfill particular roles.

- Obtain and review formal documentation and evaluate the content in relation to the specified criteria.

- Obtain and review documentation demonstrating that management verified the required experience/qualifications of the staff (per management policy).

- If the covered entity has chosen not to fully implement this specification, the entity must have documentation on where they have chosen not to fully implement this specification and their rationale for doing so.[39]

In light of this, healthcare organizations will want to identify and qualify workforce personnel who perform information security functions focusing on the development, operation, management, and enforcement of security capabilities for the organization's systems and networks. As a condition of working information security positions, workforce competency will have to be a sustained effort, not a one-time event.

Accountable-Care Organizations

An emerging healthcare organizational construct, an accountable-care organization (ACO) is a legal entity recognized and authorized under applicable state law. It is composed of certified Medicare providers or suppliers. Participants come from both previously affiliated and unaffiliated healthcare organizations and work together to manage and coordinate care for a defined population of Medicare fee-for-service beneficiaries. The ACO has a shared governance that provides appropriate proportionate control over the new organization's decision-making process as priorities may conflict with individual member organizations' missions and objectives.

The motivation for participating in an ACO extends beyond a desire for improved population health. ACOs that meet specified quality performance standards are eligible to receive payments for shared savings. These shared savings come from reducing spending growth below target amounts in Medicare.[40] HIPAA allows the use and disclosure of PHI within a healthcare organization for treatment, payment, and healthcare operations by and between the hospital and its medical staff. ACOs extend the HIPAA guidelines beyond the internal healthcare organization. For this reason, ACOs will have to revisit their own internal operational safeguards with respect to HIPAA and ensure they are addressed in the framework of the ACO. An unauthorized disclosure of PHI by one member healthcare organization in the ACO could create significant risk both for the ACO and its participating providers.[41]

Use Case 28-1: Expensive Data Breaches Can Occur When Operational Safeguards Are Not in Place

An important operational safeguard in healthcare is the business associate agreement (BAA). This special type of contract is between a covered entity and vendor organizations that are subject to HIPAA law; that designation qualifies the vendor organization as a business associate. A primary reason these agreements are so important is that their terms and conditions outline additional operational safeguards that the covered entity will expect to be in place, such as a risk assessment requirement, written incident procedures, and a system activity review, which can include audit by the covered entity. Without these BAAs, the risk that a business associate will be the source of a data breach due to incompetence or ignorance of their obligations under HIPAA goes up measurably. One such example is the case of North Memorial Health Care of Minnesota.

North Memorial had a contractual relationship with Accretive Health, Inc. that involved access and use of PHI. When Accretive Health disclosed that they had an employee lose a laptop containing PHI that was not adequately encrypted, several operational safeguards were found lacking or missing altogether. While having the safeguards in place does not guarantee a data breach cannot happen, the risk would have been minimal had North Memorial taken the following precautions:

- Properly executed a BAA with Accretive Health so that the business associate would clearly understand its obligations to North Memorial under the law.
  - The BAA also would have addressed the acceptable uses and disclosures for PHI on the part of the business associate and held them liable for unauthorized disclosure.
- Incorporated in the BAA an encryption requirement for laptops and mobile devices.
- Adequately protected the volumes of PHI stored, especially in mobile devices.

The original accounting to HHS stated that 2,800 patients were potentially affected, but that number was later revised to add an additional 6,697 patients.

Although the actions described in this scenario happened mostly in 2011, the investigation and negotiation of a resolution agreement stretched out until March 2016. HHS announced in a press release in that month that North Memorial Health Care will pay approximately $1.5 million in HIPAA settlement fines and implement a corrective action plan (including having a properly executed BAA) and proper training for employees.[42]

PART VI

Meaningful Use Privacy and Security Measures

For healthcare organizations, meaningful use (MU) was established as a provision for financial payments of federal funds for early adopters of electronic health records under the ARRA Medicare and Medicaid EHR incentive programs. The act also established penalties for healthcare organizations that fail to implement EHRs and demonstrate MU against baseline criteria by a future date. To meet MU criteria, healthcare organizations must not only implement EHRs but also attest that security practices are in place to protect the confidentiality, integrity, and availability of electronic health information. Further, MU is a demonstrated ability to facilitate electronic exchange of patient information, submit claims electronically, generate electronic records for patients' requests, or e-prescribe. Obviously, operational safeguards and HIPAA compliance are important considerations.

HIPAA privacy and security requirements were embedded in the ARRA Medicare and Medicaid EHR incentive programs. To meet the baseline requirements in the first stage of meaningful-use adoption, eligible providers needed to "attest" that they had conducted or reviewed a security risk analysis in accordance with HIPAA requirements and correctly identified security deficiencies as part of the risk-management process.[43]

Complying with privacy and security requirements to meet MU baselines in stage 1 and subsequent stages is vital to healthcare organizations that desire to receive the ARRA stimulus funds and, later, avoid penalties. For many organizations, if not all, the stimulus money subsidized a terrific cost outlay for implementing an EHR system. But failing to take privacy and security into account can be a deal-breaker. Devin McGraw, HHS OCR Deputy Director for Health Information Privacy, asserted that providers and hospitals who are fined for significant civil or a criminal HIPAA violation should be ineligible for healthcare IT incentive payments. In short, you cannot be "meaningfully using" healthcare IT if you are willfully neglecting or intentionally violating federal health privacy and security rules.[44]

As of April 2015, the meaningful use program was effectively replaced by Medicare Access and CHIP Reauthorization Act (MACRA). A portion of that act relates to this progression of meaningful use phases from 1 to 2 to 3. MACRA sets the end date for meaningful use payments by 2018. Rather than reimbursement incentives, MACRA implements a Merit-based Incentive Payment System (MIPS), which incorporates meaningful use. The relevance to operational safeguards in this change remains. For instance, failure to meet a performance measure in the MIPS advancing care information performance category, like failure to conduct a risk analysis, results in a score of zero. For more information about the scoring methodology under MIPS, a download of the MACRA Fact Sheet "Cross Cutting Measures: Privacy & Security" is available at www.himss.org/macra-fact-sheet-cross-cutting-measures-privacy-security.

Chapter Review

Healthcare organizations are in the most exciting times of change and disruptive innovation ever. The great promise of information technology (in which EHRs and information sharing play a lead role) is that it will enable providers and researchers to improve patient care dramatically and produce an equally dramatic reduction in costs over time. But underlying these improvements are the imperative components of information availability and trust. The only way to achieve information availability and trust is to have a solid information privacy and security program within a healthcare organization. At the heart of the program are operational safeguards that include a security management program, a systematic and recurring risk assessment, and workforce training and awareness.

In this chapter you have learned what operational safeguards are and how they apply within a healthcare setting. HIT professionals will need to realize their responsibilities and become competent in operating in the healthcare environment. This chapter explained the value of an information security management process that includes information security training and awareness. Such a process will include a risk assessment process using a framework of standards-based criteria. Properly done, a risk assessment provides a roadmap for prioritizing improvements and maintaining compliance. Finally, we identified a few operational safeguard fundamentals with respect to their applicability within emerging healthcare initiatives. To capitalize on these, healthcare organizations must do more than acknowledge and comply with the HIPAA and HITECH requirements for privacy and security. They must use operational safeguards, one element of comprehensive administrative, physical, and technical controls, to lead their healthcare efforts over the next few tumultuous decades.

Questions

To test your comprehension of the chapter, answer the following questions and then check your answers against the list of correct answers that follows the questions.

1. What are the correct processes, procedures, standards, and practices governing the creation, handling, usage, and sharing of health information called?

   A. Technical standards

   B. Administrative safeguards

   C. Operational safeguards

   D. Physical standards

2. What is a covered entity that inadvertently discloses protected health information on 500 or more individuals required to do?

   A. Report a breach to the U.S. Department of Health and Human Services

   B. Conduct an investigation to recover the data so they do not have to report it

   C. Contact the patients to see if they have had any credit report issues

   D. Ensure the records were backed up so there is another copy

3. Big Bull Community Hospital signs an agreement with a "cloud" vendor to host their applications and data. The vendor will provide storage and continuity-of-operations support to include disaster recovery. As a covered entity subject to HIPAA law, Big Bull must insist on all of the following, except

   A. PHI should not be stored on shared resources with other tenants' data.

   B. Adequate bandwidth for data availability is a HIPAA requirement.

   C. Disaster recovery requirements are not lessened because other tenants compete for resources or have lesser recovery requirements.

   D. Big Bull should require the cloud vendor to sign a business associate agreement.

4. Which of these is the most recent of the HIPAA amendments?

    A. HITECH Act

    B. Omnibus Final Rule

    C. Privacy Rule

    D. Security Rule

5. Of the following, which is the appropriate approach to operational safeguards for a healthcare organization to require from a cloud services provider?

    A. Sign a contract to transfer security responsibility to the cloud services provider

    B. Reduce impact of data breach by contracting with multiple cloud service providers and spread data stores out across all of them

    C. Complement the cloud services provider's security offerings with the healthcare organization's use of a CASB

    D. Ensure an exact copy of the data is maintained within the healthcare organization's computing environment to prevent data loss

6. The security officer at Methodist Hospital expressed concern with a proposal to host a utilization management application serviced by a global cloud provider company. Which of these could be her valid concern?

    A. PHI cannot be used by non-US personnel.

    B. Global companies do not have to abide by US contracts.

    C. PHI cannot be translated into foreign languages.

    D. Global companies may be out of HIPAA jurisdiction.

7. The HIPAA Omnibus Final Rule specifically defines which of these?

    A. Unauthorized disclosures

    B. Business associates

    C. Cloud providers

    D. Minimum penalties

8. Moving data, including PHI, to the cloud has all of the benefits, except:

    A. Transferring responsibility for security to a third party

    B. Gaining specialized skillsets and certified personnel

    C. Access to security tools and techniques with moderate investment

    D. Professional services like vulnerability and patch management

Answers

1. **C.** This is the definition of operational safeguards.

2. **A.** For disclosures of 500 individuals or more, the covered entity is required to notify the U.S. Department of Health and Human Services.

3. **B.** Adequate bandwidth is a concern, but it is not applicable to HIPAA requirements.

4. **B.** HIPAA as written in 1996 has had several updates over the years, called amendments. The most recent is the HIPAA Omnibus Final Rule, which went into effect in September of 2013.

5. **C.** Of the choices, using a cloud access security broker (CASB) is a great approach to maintaining the required level of information security controls on the cloud (outsourced) environment.

6. **D.** One of the several concerns with off-shoring PHI to international third parties is the fact that they are likely not subject to U.S. law, including HIPAA.

7. **B.** The HIPAA Omnibus Final Rule of 2013 has a dramatic, important feature. It clearly identifies that anyone performing services subject to HIPAA law on behalf of a covered entity is a business associate. This significantly reduced any confusion from third parties who had any action in handling PHI for the covered entity.

8. **A.** Although any third-party agreement, particularly the business associate agreement, creates a shared responsibility, cloud services can never fully transfer responsibility. The covered entity remains ultimately responsible for the security of the data.

References

1. Baker, D. (2015). Trustworthy systems for safe and private. In V. Saba & K. McCormick (Eds.), *Essentials of nursing informatics, sixth edition* (pp. 152–154). McGraw-Hill Education.

2. Conrad, E., Misenar, S., & Feldman, J. (2016). *CISSP study guide, third edition* (p. 24). Syngress.

3. Harris, S., & Maymi, F. (2016). *CISSP all-in-one exam guide, seventh edition*. McGraw-Hill Education.

4. Centers for Medicare and Medicaid Services (CMS). (2007, March). *Security standards: Organizational, policies and procedures and documentation requirements*. 45 C.F.R. 164.314 and 164.316. HIPAA Security Series. Accessed in March 2017 from https://www.hhs.gov/sites/default/files/ocr/privacy/hipaa/administrative/securityrule/pprequirements.pdf?language=.

5. U.S. Department of Health and Human Services (HHS). (2002, Dec. 3). *OCR HIPAA Privacy: Incidental uses and disclosures*. 45 C.F.R. 164.502(a)(1)(iii). Accessed in March 2017 from https://www.hhs.gov/sites/default/files/ocr/privacy/hipaa/understanding/coveredentities/incidentalu%26d.pdf.

6. Health Insurance Portability and Accountability Act of 1996. Pub. L. No. 104-191, 110 Stat. 1936 (August 21, 1996). Accessed in March 2017 from https://aspe.hhs.gov/report/health-insurance-portability-and-accountability-act-1996.

7. HHS. (2009, Feb. 17). *HITECH Act Enforcement Interim Final Rule.* Accessed in July 2016 from https://www.hhs.gov/hipaa/for-professionals/special-topics/HITECH-act-enforcement-interim-final-rule/index.html.

8. McCann, E. (2014). Group slapped with $6.8M HIPAA fine. *Healthcare IT News,* February 18. Accessed in July 2016 from www.healthcareitnews.com/news/group-slapped-68m-hipaa-fines.

9. Weise, E. (2015). Massive breach at health care company Anthem Inc. *USA Today,* February 25. Accessed in July 2016 from www.usatoday.com/story/tech/2015/02/04/health-care-anthem-hacked/22900925/.

10. Belliveau, J. (2016). Hackers access EHR data in potential healthcare data breach. *HealthITSecurity,* May 19. Accessed in July 2016 from http://healthitsecurity.com/news/hackers-access-ehr-data-in-potential-healthcare-data-breach.

11. Caraher, K., & LaVanway, A. H. (2011, Mar. 8). *CDW healthcare elevated heart rates: EHR and IT security report.* Accessed in July 2016 from www.cdwnewsroom.com/wp-content/uploads/2014/11/CDW-Healthcare-Elevated-Heart-Rates-EHR-and-IT-Security-Report-0311.pdf.

12. Anderson, M. (2011, Feb. 11). *The costs and implications of EHR system downtime on physician practices.* Whitepaper reprinted by Stratus Technologies; rights granted by AC Group. Accessed in July 2016 from www.stratus.com/assets/Costs_and_implications_of_Downtime_on_Physician_Practices.pdf.

13. Borkin, S. (2003). The HIPAA final security standards and ISO/IEC 17799 (p. 6). *SANS Institute InfoSec Reading Room.* Accessed in July 2016 from https://www.sans.org/reading_room/whitepapers/standards/hipaa-final-security-standards-isoiec-17799_1193.

14. National HIE Governance Forum (2013, December). *Identity and access management for health information exchange* (p. 3). From a report for the National eHealth Collaborative through its cooperative agreement with the Office of the National Coordinator for Health Information Technology, U.S. Department of Health and Human Services. Accessed in July 2016 from https://www.healthit.gov/sites/default/files/identitymanagementfinal.pdf.

15. Murphy, Sean P. (2015). *Healthcare information security and privacy*—Chapter 3: Healthcare information regulation (p. 80). McGraw-Hill Education.

16. Verizon. (2016). *Verizon 2016 data breach investigations report* (p. 21). Accessed in July 2016 from www.verizonenterprise.com/verizon-insights-lab/dbir/2016/.

17. HHS. (2010, July 14). *Guidance on risk analysis requirements under the HIPAA Security Rule* (p. 20). Accessed in March 2017 from https://www.hhs.gov/sites/default/files/ocr/privacy/hipaa/administrative/securityrule/rafinalguidancepdf.pdf?

18. Donaldson, S. E., & Siegel, S. G. (2001). *Successful software development* (pp. 42–43). Prentice Hall.

19. Treasury Board of Canada Secretariat. (2004). *Operational security standard: Management of information technology security (MITS).* Accessed in July 2016 from https://www.tbs-sct.gc.ca/pol/doc-eng.aspx?id=12328.

20. Software Engineering Institute, Carnegie Mellon. (2006). *A framework for software product line practice, version 5.0.* Configuration Management. Accessed in July 2016 from www.sei.cmu.edu/productlines/frame_report/config.man.htm.

21. McGraw, D., & Hinkley, G. (2010, February). ARRA accounting of disclosures requirements: Aligning goals with emerging regulations. *eHealth Initiative.* Accessed on July 12, 2016, from https://www.cdt.org/files/pdfs/ AccountingforDisclosures.pdf.

22. HHS. (2010, May 3). *HIPAA Privacy Rule accounting of disclosures under the Health Information Technology for Economic and Clinical Health Act: Request for information.* 75 Fed. Reg. 31425, 45 C.F.R. 160 and 164. Accessed in July 2016 from https://www.gpo.gov/fdsys/pkg/FR-2010-05-03/pdf/2010-10054.pdf.

23. National Institute of Standards and Technology (NIST). (2013, Apr. 30). *Recommended security controls for federal information systems and organizations* (p. F48). SP 800-53, revision 4. Accessed in July 2016 from http://nvlpubs.nist .gov/nistpubs/SpecialPublications/NIST.SP.800-53r4.pdf.

24. Bourque, D., Gold, K., Willis, S., et al. (2013). *Breach notification rule risk assessments: Applying the new breach notification standard under the HIPAA Omnibus Rule.* Health eSource: American Bar Association. Accessed in July 2016 from www.americanbar.org/publications/aba_health_esource/2013-14/july/breach_ notification.html.

25. HHS. (2013, January). *Business associate contracts.* Accessed in July 2016 from https://www.hhs.gov/hipaa/for-professionals/covered-entities/sample-business- associate-agreement-provisions/index.html.

26. FDA. (2014, September). *Is the product a medical device?* Accessed in July 2016 from https://www.fda.gov/MedicalDevices/DeviceRegulationandGuidance/ Overview/ClassifyYourDevice/ucm051512.htm.

27. Bolte, S. (2005). *Cybersecurity for medical devices: Three threads intertwined.* PowerPoint presentation to MedSun audio conference "Cybersecurity of Medical Devices," April 12.

28. Weiner, J. P., Kfuri, T., Chan, K., & Fowles, J. B. (2007). "e-Iatrogenesis": The most critical unintended consequence of CPOE and other HIT. *Journal of the American Medical Informatics Association, 14,* 387–388.

29. Hildreth, E. A. (1965). The significance of iatrogenesis. *JAMA, 193,* 386–387.

30. FDA. (2016, February). *MAUDE adverse event report: Merge healthcare merge hemo programmable diagnostic computer.* Accessed in July 2016 from https:// www.accessdata.fda.gov/scripts/cdrh/cfdocs/cfmaude/detail.cfm?mdrfoi__ id=5487204.

31. Computerworld's Forecast 2017 Survey on IT. *Computerworld.* Accessed on March 14, 2017 from http://core0.staticworld.net/assets/media-resource/122905/ forecast_1117a.pdf.

PART VI

32. Hoglund, D. (2012). *Healthcare wireless and device connectivity: The BYOD Healthcare Challenge—2012.* Accessed in July 2016 from http://davidhoglund .typepad.com/integra_systems_inc_david/2012/05/the-byod-healthcare-challenge-2012.html.

33. CIO Council. (2010, August). *Privacy recommendations for the use of cloud computing by federal departments and agencies.* Issued by Privacy Committee and Web 2.0/Cloud Computing Subcommittee. Accessed on July 12, 2016, from https://cio.gov/resources/document-library.

34. Speake, G., & Winkler, V. (2011). *Securing the cloud: Cloud computer security techniques and tactics* (p. 80). Elsevier.

35. Herold, R. (n.d.). *Cloud computing in healthcare: Key security issues.* Webinar. Accessed in July 2016 from www.bankinfosecurity.com/webinars/cloud-computing-in-healthcare-key-security-issues-w-200.

36. Winkler, V. (2011). Cloud computing: Legal and regulatory issues. *TechNet Magazine.* Elsevier. Accessed in July 2016 from http://technet.microsoft.com/en-us/magazine/hh994647.aspx.

37. CMS. (2007, March). *Security standards: Administrative safeguards* (p. 8). HIPAA Security Series. Accessed in July 2016 from https://www.hhs.gov/sites/default/files/ocr/privacy/hipaa/administrative/securityrule/adminsafeguards.pdf.

38. U.S. Department of Defense. (2015). *Information assurance workforce improvement program,* December 19, 2005, incorporating Change 4, November 10, 2015. Accessed in July 2016 from www.dtic.mil/whs/directives/corres/pdf/857001m.pdf.

39. HHS. (n.d.). *Audit protocol edited.* Accessed in March 2017 from https://www .hhs.gov/hipaa/for-professionals/compliance-enforcement/audit/protocol-edited/index.html.

40. CMS. (2012). *Shared savings program.* Accessed in July 2016 from https://www .cms.gov/sharedsavingsprogram/30_Statutes_Regulations_Guidance.asp.

41. Dowell, M. (2011, May). *Accountable Care organization data sharing.* Health Law Alert. Accessed in March 2017 from www.hinshawlaw.com/newsroom-publications-alerts-237.html.

42. Heath, S. (2016). $1.5M HIPAA settlement fine for North Memorial Health Care. *HealthITSecurity,* March 17. Accessed in July 2016 from http://healthitsecurity .com/news/1.5m-hipaa-settlement-fine-for-north-memorial-health-care.

43. Office of the National Coordinator for Health Information Technology (ONC). (2015). *Guide to privacy and security of health information v2.* Accessed in July 2016 from https://www.healthit.gov/sites/default/files/pdf/privacy/privacy-and-security-guide.pdf.

44. McGraw, D. (2010, Feb. 18). *A good day for health privacy.* Accessed in July 2016 from https://cdt.org/blog/a-good-day-for-health-privacy/.

CHAPTER 29

Architectural Safeguards

Lisa A. Gallagher

In this chapter, you will learn how to

- Describe the importance of architectural safeguards for designing, building, purchasing, and implementing safe and secure IT systems and medical devices
- Define the relationship between reliability, availability, and safety as they impact healthcare IT systems
- Identify basic design considerations for high-reliability healthcare IT systems

The introduction of certain technology platforms, such as electronic health records (EHRs), has highlighted concerns about the privacy, security, and availability of patient records. Other examples of IT systems used in healthcare enterprises include billing/financial systems, clinical decision support (CDS) systems, and databases/data analytics software. At the same time, the evolution of the consumer-based mobile device and application market has created a desire to integrate mobility solutions into the clinical and patient workflow.

Finally, there is one other critical category of IT system/component that is used in the healthcare workflow today—medical devices. Here are the most common categories of medical devices that are currently used in healthcare organizations:

- **Monitoring** Typically used to measure and track physiological aspects of patient health (for example, a heart monitor)
- **Resuscitative** Used to restore normal brain or heart function (for example, a defibrillator)
- **Surgical** Used to aid surgical procedures (for example, medical lasers)
- **Imaging** Used to obtain a medical image for diagnostic purposes (for example, an X-ray machine)

Each category listed contains one example of medical devices that are not only implemented in technology but have evolved to contain software operating systems, connect to and share data through information networks, and even to operate remotely through wireless technical or cellular networks. Increased use of mobile medical devices is expected to be a trend as the healthcare industry looks for new, cost-saving, and safe ways to expand and improve healthcare services (for example, to reach underserved or remote populations).

When designing or building an IT system, all aspects of the system's architecture—its individual hardware and software components—must be considered. An IT system design-and-build process demands that various architectural considerations related to the components' features, functions, and desired performance (in terms of measurable attributes or parameters of the system performance) are set out as requirements, based on the needs of the users and the operational environment. The goal and the desired outcome is to design, build, purchase, and implement safe and secure IT systems and components for use in healthcare.

Reliability

One important performance trait of an IT system is its reliability. *Reliability* is the "degree to which a system, product, or component performs specified functions under specified conditions for a specified period of time."[1] Table 29-1 shows several ways to specify and measure the reliability of an IT system.

 NOTE System reliability, by definition, includes all parts of the system—hardware, software, supporting infrastructure (including critical external interfaces), operators, and procedures.

For the software components of a system, a common reliability metric is the number of software faults, usually expressed as faults per thousand lines of code. This measure, along with software execution time, is key to most software reliability models and estimates.

Relationship Between Reliability and Security

Software errors, defects, and logic flaws, often stemming from poor coding practices, can be a cause of commonly exploited software vulnerabilities. For example, programming

System Usage	Reliability Measure
System is operated frequently or continuously as a resource or workflow aid, such as most vehicles, machinery, and electronic equipment	Mean time to failure (MTTF) or failure rate
Specific mission is defined for system	Probability or percentage (without dimension)
Single mission (for example, rocket launch or airbag deployment)	Probability of one-time success
For repairable systems	Mean time to repair (MTTR)

Table 29-1 System Reliability Measures

errors in the software of an IT system can introduce security vulnerabilities (weaknesses in the system that allow exploitation) in the following areas:

- Authentication of users (for example, improperly authenticating a potential user)
- Authorization of access rights and privileges (for example, allowing unauthorized access)
- Data confidentiality (for example, allowing unauthorized access)
- Data integrity (for example, allowing unauthorized modification or deletion of data)
- Data availability (for example, preventing data from being accessed when needed)

Other problems or defects that affect security are hardware defects; inadequate site access, monitoring policies, and procedures; and lack of employee performance and monitoring policies and procedures. These are examples of "system" vulnerabilities that are not directly related to the software.

Reliability Implications for Healthcare Systems

For all IT systems, design and performance considerations are critical to meeting system mission goals and foundational to technical security considerations. The goal is to design the software and other system elements to have as few defects and failures as possible. For healthcare, the consequences of IT system failures can be severe, including

- Risk to patient outcomes, health, and lives
- Data security breaches (manifesting as unauthorized data access, compromise of data integrity, and/or system or data availability issues)
- Public health implications
- Research implications
- Cost implications
- Reputational impact
- Legal/regulatory compliance implications

Reliability goals should be considered and identified for all care scenarios and processes. For hospitals, this may mean that these goals might be defined by system, department, or workflow. For a physician office, it is likely to include the workflow and integration of the IT system.

For each system or process, failure (and how it can be detected or measured) should be defined and then reliability goals associated with the desired improvement or outcome should be set according to a reliability analysis. For example, in the emergency room, one measure of failure is the percentage of patients receiving the wrong diagnosis, treatment, or medication. A reliability analysis can be conducted at the system or component level. All analyses should include the software, hardware, physical, and employee components as discussed previously.

Understanding the relationship between reliability and healthcare is critical as IT systems are increasingly integrated into the clinical workflow.

Availability

System *availability* is the property of the system being accessible and usable upon demand by an authorized entity.[2] Simply put, availability is the proportion of time a system is functioning.

The availability of a system is typically measured as a factor of its reliability—as reliability increases, so does availability. No system can guarantee 100 percent reliability; therefore, no system can assure 100 percent availability.

Availability as a Component of Data Security

There are three main components, or goals, of data security (together, these are commonly called the "CIA" of data security):

- Confidentiality
- Integrity
- Availability

Information or data security is concerned with the confidentiality, integrity, and availability of data regardless of the form it may take—electronic, print, or other forms.

With respect to electronic health data, data availability is a critical issue. For any healthcare IT system to serve its purpose, the information (for example, patient data and ancillary data, decision support data, references, alerts, etc.) must be available when it is needed. This means that the computing systems used to store and process the information, the security controls used to protect it, and the communication channels used to access it must be functioning correctly. The goal of high-availability systems is to remain available at all times, preventing service disruptions due to power outages, hardware failures, and system upgrades. Ensuring availability also involves preventing denial-of-service attacks (attacks meant to disrupt system and/or data access by users). There are several categories of security controls used to ensure/protect data availability:

- **Technical** Security controls (i.e., safeguards or countermeasures) for an information system that are primarily implemented and executed by the information system through mechanisms contained in the hardware, software, or firmware components of the system.[3]
  Examples include firewalls and data encryption.

- **Administrative (Operational)** The security controls (i.e., safeguards or countermeasures) for an information system that are primarily implemented and executed by people (as opposed to systems).[3]
  Examples include organizational policies and procedures.

- **Physical**   Physical measures, policies, and procedures to protect a covered entity's electronic information systems and related buildings and equipment from natural and environmental hazards, and unauthorized intrusion.[4] Examples include any doors, locks, and security guards.

Maintainability

Maintainability for IT systems can be defined as the capability of the software product to be modified. Modifications may include corrections, improvements, or adaptation of the software to changes in environment, requirements, and/or functional specifications.[1] Maintainability affects both reliability and availability of IT systems and components.

Scalability

Scalability is the ability of a system, network, or process to handle a growing amount of work in a capable manner or the ability of a system, network, or process to be enlarged to accommodate that growth.[5] When an organization is considering its design or purchase requirements for healthcare IT systems, it should also consider its ability to easily and quickly enhance the system by adding new functionality and/or storage capacity. A system that can easily "scale" to meet new requirements enables an organization to invest in technology based on current needs without having to replace the system when requirements change.

The term *cloud computing* is defined by the National Institute of Standards and Technology (NIST) as "a model for enabling ubiquitous, convenient, on-demand network access to a shared pool of configurable computing resources (e.g., networks, servers, storage, applications, and services) that can be rapidly provisioned and released with minimal management effort or service provider interaction."[6] Healthcare organizations are beginning to take advantage of the ability to "outsource to the cloud" (contract for IT services or system usage) in order to address the scalability issue. This allows the organizations to facilitate rapid provisioning of additional computing, application, and storage resources and avoid some capital expenditures.

Scalability can also be thought of as a measure of how well a system or application can grow to meet increasing performance demands. In thinking this way, one can see that scalability is a factor for both availability and reliability.

Safety

"Safety" in medicine is often used to mean patient safety. The Institute of Medicine (IOM), which is now called the Academy of Medicine (NAM), has defined *patient safety* as "the prevention of harm to patients."[7] An event during an episode of care that causes harm to a patient is called an *adverse event*. Patient safety overlaps in many ways with privacy, security, and technology concerns, which we will discuss later in this chapter.

PART VI

With respect to system and software design, safety means that a life-critical system behaves as needed even when some components fail. Systems that are to be used in healthcare should be designed so that if failure occurs, it will not cause a patient to be physically harmed.

Considerations for Healthcare IT Systems

Ideally, in the early design of a system, the design is analyzed to determine what faults can possibly occur. That analysis is then used to identify the safety requirements.

 TIP The most common method used to identify possible faults is the failure mode and effects analysis (FMEA).[8]

The FMEA (see IEC 60812) provides for an evaluation of potential failure modes for processes and their likely effect on outcomes and/or product performance. Once failure modes are established, risk reduction can be used to eliminate, contain, reduce, or control the potential failures. The effects of the failure mode are described and assigned a probability based on the predicted failure rate and failure mode ratio of the system or components. Failure modes with identical or similar effects can be combined and summarized in a failure-mode effects summary. When combined with criticality analysis, FMEA is known as failure mode, effects, and criticality analysis (FMECA).

In general terms, once a failure mode is identified, it can usually be mitigated by adding extra or redundant equipment to the system. Ongoing maintenance actions are also important safety-related actions. With regard to maintenance activities, considerations must be taken to reduce operational risk by ensuring acceptable levels of operational readiness and availability.

The overall patient-safety concerns of a healthcare organization can be met only by defining system safety requirements early on in the design and/or acquisition process of a healthcare IT system and performing a FMEA and/or FMECA to identify and mitigate faults.

Safety analysis is focused on safety-critical systems or components. Reliability analysis has a broader scope than safety analysis, because noncritical failures must also be considered. Higher failure rates may be considered acceptable for noncritical systems.

Considerations for Medical Devices

Medical devices are considered safety-critical devices. They are regulated as such by the U.S. Food and Drug Administration (FDA).

 TIP The FDA reviews applications from medical-device manufacturers and approves them to sell medical devices on the open market. It also reviews any substantial changes to the medical-device system, software, or other components.

The FDA also monitors reports of adverse events and other problems with medical devices and alerts health professionals and the public when needed to ensure proper use of devices and the health and safety of patients. The FDA posts lists of recent medical-device recalls and other FDA safety communications on its safety web site, https://www.fda.gov/safety.

The FDA has also recently begun to oversee the deployment and use of mobile medical devices and mobile medical applications (apps). A mobile medical device is a device that exchanges data with other devices or computers over a wireless network. Mobile apps are software programs that run on smartphones and other mobile communications devices and in most cases communicate over a cellular network. Development of mobile medical apps is opening new and innovative ways for technology to improve health and healthcare.

Consumers use mobile medical apps to manage their own health and wellness. Healthcare professionals are using these apps to improve and facilitate patient care. These apps include a wide range of functions, from allowing individuals to monitor and input their blood levels for diabetes maintenance to allowing doctors to view a patient's X-rays on their mobile communications device. The FDA encourages further development of mobile medical apps that improve healthcare and provide consumers and healthcare professionals with valuable health information very quickly.

The FDA has a public health responsibility to oversee the safety and effectiveness of a small subset of mobile medical apps that present a potential risk to patients if they do not work as intended. In order to balance patient safety with innovation, the FDA has published guidance for manufacturers and developers of mobile medical apps, including clear and predictable outlines of FDA expectations during the approval process. The guidance, released on February 9, 2015, defines a small subset of mobile medical apps that may impact the performance or functionality of currently regulated medical devices and therefore will require FDA oversight.[9]

Beginning in 2020, the FDA requires a Unique Device Identification (UDI).[10] When fully implemented, the UDI will add to security in providing a secure distribution chain of devices globally, helping to address counterfeiting and prepare for medical emergencies. Further, UDIs will provide a standard to document device use in electronic health records, clinical information systems, claim data sources, and registries.

Considerations for Design of High-Reliability Healthcare Systems

In the design of safety-critical systems, one of the first tasks is to adequately specify the reliability and maintainability requirements as defined by the stakeholders in terms of their overall availability needs. There are several design techniques that are important to employ when designing or evaluating an IT system or component.

Fail-Safe Design

A fail-safe system is designed to return to a safe condition in the event of a failure or malfunction. A fail-safe or fail-secure *medical* system or device is one that, in the event of failure, responds in a way that is predictable and will cause no harm to other devices or danger to patients or personnel.

A system is fail-safe not because failure is impossible or improbable but because the system's design prevents or remediates unsafe consequences of the system's failure—that is, if a system fails, it remains safe, or at least no less safe than when it is operating correctly.[11]

It is important to note also that a fail-safe design may indicate that, under certain circumstances, a component should be shut down (forced to violate its functional specification) in order to avoid harming someone.

A fail-secure component of a system secures that system (or at least the portion to which the component is dedicated) in the event of a failure either of that component or elsewhere in the system.

Fail-safe designs are particularly critical for medical devices that are connected to patients and would be part of the safety testing by the FDA.

Fault Tolerance

Fault tolerance (sometimes called graceful degradation) is the capability of the software product to maintain a specified level of performance in cases of software faults or of infringement of its specified interface.[1]

For an individual system, fault tolerance can be achieved by anticipating conditions outside normal operating parameters and building the system to deal with them—in general, aiming for self-stabilization so that the system converges toward a safe state. However, if the consequences of a system failure are catastrophic, or the cost of making it sufficiently reliable is very high, a better solution may be to use some form of duplication or redundancy (discussed next). Fault tolerance is particularly sought after in high-availability or life-critical systems.

Redundancy and Failover

One of the most important design techniques is redundancy. *Redundancy* refers to the ability to continue operations in the event of component failures through managed component repetition. In the case of information technology, it can be applied to infrastructure components such as hardware, power supply, software, and information itself. Component repetition for the purpose of providing redundancy is geared toward the avoidance of single points of failure.[12] Designing with redundant or duplicate components or resources requires creating alternate operational paths, such as backups or duplicate systems or components, that will be used if particular parts of the system fail.

Failover refers to the process of automatically switching to a different, redundant system upon failure or abnormal termination of the currently active system. Failover can be applied to a cluster of servers, to network or storage components, or to any other set of redundant devices that must provide high availability because downtime would be expensive or inconvenient. It may be implemented in hardware, software, or in a combination of hardware and software.[13]

Failover and switchover are essentially the same operations, except that failover is automatic and usually operates without warning, while the term *switchover* means that the process requires human intervention. Failover capability is designed into systems requiring continuous availability and a high degree of reliability. Failover in the context of information technology refers to the process of changing the status of a standby system to become the primary system in the case of a failure in the original primary system. Failover is commonly used in database systems as part of a high-availability and disaster-recovery (HADR) design. Failover provides a high level of fault tolerance and high availability that is transparent to the end user.[13]

Simplicity

The simpler the system or component design, the more easily or predictably the system can fail and/or recover. Simplicity in design can be seen as the opposite of complexity. For example, complex software means more lines of code, more interfaces, and so on. The greater the number of code lines and/or interfaces, the greater the possibility of unforeseen errors and unsafe consequences. Complex design also results in more security concerns, because coding errors, bugs, and other factors can create greater vulnerability to security threats.

In order for a system or component to meet reliability and availability requirements and avoid security vulnerabilities, a "design-for-simplicity" approach should be used. Designs should purposefully be designed for simplicity at the component, interface, and system level and the design-review process should include consideration of simplicity.

Chapter Review

This chapter described the importance of using architectural safeguards in designing, building, purchasing, and implementing safe and secure IT systems and medical devices. When designing or building an IT system, all aspects of the system's architecture—its individual hardware and software components—must be considered. The IT system design-and-build process mandates that various architectural considerations related to the components' features, functions, and desired performance are defined in the requirements. The overall goal is to design, build, purchase, and implement safe and secure IT systems and components for use in healthcare. The reader should understand the relationships between reliability, availability, scalability, and safety. In addition, the chapter discussed the basic design considerations of a reliable system, including fail-safe design, fault tolerance, redundancy and failover, and simplicity.

Questions

To test your comprehension of the chapter, answer the following questions and then check your answers against the list of correct answers that follows the questions.

1. Which of the following is an example of an administrative control?

    A. Firewall

    B. Fence

    C. Organizational policy

    D. Security guard

2. How is a system's, product's, or component's reliability defined?

    A. The degree to which a system, product, or component performs specified functions under specified conditions for a specified period of time.

    B. The measure of the product's safety, efficiency, and effectiveness

    C. Its ease of use

    D. Assurance that the product is without fault

3. Which of the following can directly affect a system's reliability?

    A. Organizational policies

    B. Employee training

    C. Poor coding practices

    D. Unauthorized access

4. What does FMEA stand for?

    A. Federal management event archives

    B. Failure management event archive

    C. Failure mode and effects analysis

    D. None of the above

5. For which reason would a government agency be concerned about mobile devices/apps used to treat or monitor patients?

    A. The mobile device may be too expensive for the patient.

    B. The reliability and effectiveness of a mobile app used with a patient could present a potential risk to patient safety.

    C. Use of mobile medical devices is not yet reimbursable by Medicare.

    D. Use of a mobile medical app is not consistent with medical guidelines.

6. What should systems be designed to do if they fail?

    A. Roll over to a different system

    B. Do no harm to the patient

    C. Contain backups

    D. Contain an audit of failures

7. How is a system's maintainability defined?

   A. It can be modified.

   B. It is fail-safe.

   C. It is redundant.

   D. It is rolled over.

8. How is scalability defined?

   A. A system that allows integration of multiple patient records

   B. A system capable of growth

   C. A system that is geographically diverse

   D. A system that provides multiple layers

Answers

1. **C.** An organizational policy is an example of an administrative control.

2. **A.** *Reliability* is the "degree to which a system, product, or component performs specified functions under specified conditions for a specified period of time."

3. **C.** Poor coding practices can create vulnerabilities that can affect system reliability.

4. **C.** FMEA is the acronym used for failure mode and effects analysis.

5. **B.** A government agency would be concerned with the reliability and effectiveness of a mobile app to ensure that it doesn't present a potential risk to patient safety.

6. **B.** If a system fails, it should be designed to do no harm to the patient.

7. **A.** Maintainability is defined as a system's ability to be modified.

8. **B.** Scalability means a system is capable of growth.

References

1. ISO. (2001). *Software engineering—Product quality: Part 1, Quality model.* ISO/ IEC 9126-1:2001. Accessed on March 9, 2017, from. https://www.iso.org/ standard/35733.html.

2. ISO. (1989). *Information processing systems—Open systems—Basic reference model: Part 2, Security architecture.* ISO 7498-2:1989. Accessed on August 4, 2016, from https://www.iso.org/standard/14256.html.

3. National Institute of Standards and Technology (NIST). (2012, September). *Guide for conducting risk assessments: Information security.* SP 800-30, revision 1. Accessed on August 4, 2016, from http://nvlpubs.nist.gov/nistpubs/Legacy/SP/ nistspecialpublication800-30r1.pdf.

4. U.S. Department of Health and Human Services (HHS). (2012). *HIPAA FAQs for professionals: What does the Security Rule mean by physical safeguards?* Accessed on August 4, 2016, from https://www.hhs.gov/hipaa/for-professionals/faq/2012/what-does-the-security-rule-mean-by-physical-safeguards/index.html.

5. Bondi, A. B. (2000). Characteristics of scalability and their impact on performance. *Proceedings of the 2nd International Workshop on Software and Performance* (pp. 195–201), Ottawa, Ontario, Canada.

6. NIST. (2011, September). *The NIST definition of cloud computing* (SP 800-145). Accessed on August 4, 2016, from http://nvlpubs.nist.gov/nistpubs/Legacy/SP/nistspecialpublication800-145.pdf.

7. Mitchell, P. H. (2008). Defining patient safety and quality care. In R. G. Hughes (Ed.), *Patient safety and quality: An evidence-based handbook for nurses.* Agency for Healthcare Research and Quality. Accessed on August 4, 2016, from https://www.ncbi.nlm.nih.gov/books/NBK2681.

8. International Electrotechnical Commision (IEC). (2006). *Analysis techniques for system reliability: Procedure for failure mode and effects analysis (FMEA), second edition.* IEC 60812. Accessed on August 4, 2016, from https://www.saiglobal.com/PDFTemp/Previews/OSH/iec/iec60000/60800/iec60812%7Bed2.0%7Den_d.pdf.

9. FDA. (2015, Feb. 9). *Guidance for Industry and Food and Drug Administration staff: Mobile medical applications.* Accessed on August 4, 2016, from https://www.fda.gov/downloads/medicaldevices/deviceregulationandguidance/guidancedocuments/ucm263366.pdf.

10. FDA. (2015, May 6). *Benefits of a Unique Device Identification (UDI) system.* Accessed on August 5, 2016, from https://www.fda.gov/MedicalDevices/DeviceRegulationandGuidance/UniqueDeviceIdentification/BenefitsofaUDIsystem/default.htm.

11. Krutz, R. L., & Fry, A. J. (2009). *The CSSLP prep guide: Mastering the certified security software lifecycle professional.* John Wiley and Sons.

12. Schmidt, K. (2006). *High availability and disaster recovery: Concepts, design, implementation.* Springer.

13. Chen, W., Otsuki, M., Descovich, P., Arumuggharaj, S., Kubo, T., & Bi, J. Y. (2009). *High availability and disaster recovery options for DB2 on Linux, Unix, and Windows.* IBM Redbooks.

30

Healthcare Cybersecurity Technology

Mac McMillan

In this chapter, you will learn how to
- Define why healthcare is a target of cybercriminals
- Identify the threat and developing threat information resources
- Describe the importance of planning and using frameworks to help plan outcomes
- Develop cybersecurity readiness and technologies that support security
- Develop tests of your cybersecurity readiness and vulnerability

Healthcare Cybersecurity Threat

Arguably, cybersecurity became the number one information technology concern for healthcare organizations in 2015. By early 2016, there was no doubt that it was a top priority, if not the top priority. Many in the IT industry and media referred to 2015 as the year of the hack, but in the healthcare IT segment, we witnessed healthcare mature into a full-fledged battleground with cybercriminals, hackers, hacktivists, and state-sponsored attackers all becoming prominent in 2015 and 2016. For everyone in healthcare, the cybersecurity threat was finally real and inescapable, progressing from theft of data to hacking to attacks that are disruptive. This, however, should not have been a surprise to anyone involved in security, as all the conditions necessary to make healthcare the target it had become began to align as early as 2006 and took a significant leap forward in 2009 with the Health Information Technology for Economic and Clinical Health (HITECH) Act[1] that established incentives for "meaningful use" of electronic health records (EHRs) and started healthcare on the path toward increased automation and the wholesale digitization of patient information.

Over the next few years after HITECH became law, healthcare rapidly adopted EHRs and reinvented how hospitals and doctors cared for their patients, managed the enterprise, collected revenue, and measured quality. The application and data became the epicenter of how all things got done in healthcare. The expansion of the healthcare network through a growing supply chain, cloud and software service providers, increased partners, and patient-centric initiatives like telehealth and population health added to the complexity of the enterprise and increased its risks. Healthcare had what cybercriminals wanted and had now made it possible for them to get at it. Understanding the technology implications of the healthcare security ecosystem today requires an appreciation of how the threat has evolved and how it is affecting our environment. Figure 30-1 depicts through several prominent examples how the threat has evolved between 2009 and 2016.

When the HIPAA Security Rule went into effect in 2005, much of the automation that is available today did not exist yet, patient records were still for the most part in paper form, there were no smartphones or tablets, medical devices were not yet networked, and things like accountable-care organizations (ACOs), health information exchanges (HIEs), cloud services, population health, and the Internet of Things (IoT) were not yet a reality. That all began to change shortly thereafter as one innovation after another in either healthcare or information technology added an additional layer of complexity to the computing environment and, with it, increased risk of cybersecurity events. In 2009, HITECH all but ensured that healthcare would never again see a simple information security environment. The threat, as Figure 30-1 shows, evolved and escalated in sophistication, form, and impact. Today, healthcare confronts the same threats that any other industry sector confronts and is the number one target

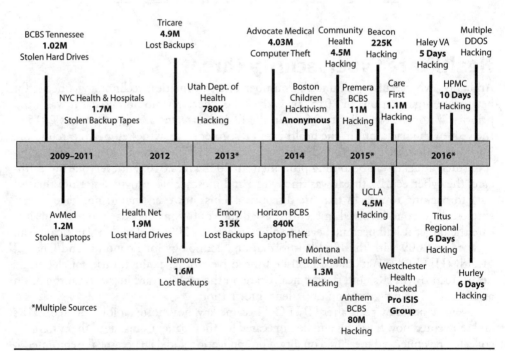

Figure 30-1 The evolution of threats between 2009 and 2016. Numbers represent records and individuals affected.

of cybercriminals because of the amount, type, and value of information it holds that they can monetize easily on the dark web (aka darknet). The cybersecurity threat today comes in many forms, and it attacks weaknesses in technology, organizational processes, and people. As an example of how threatening the cyberattackers can be, in late June of 2016, a cyber extortionist going by the name of "thedarkoverlord" offered for sale on the dark web 655,000 medical records and included an ominous threat: "Next time an adversary comes to you and offers you an opportunity to cover this up and make it go away for a small fee to prevent the leak, take the offer. There is a lot more to come." Days later the hacker posted for sale an additional 9.3 million records, seeking almost $500,000 worth of bitcoins in exchange.

In the 1990s, when the HIPAA security rules were first contemplated, the Nationwide Health Information Network (NwHIN) was just an idea, EHRs only existed in some hospitals and large practices that had a hospital information system (HIS), and HIEs (as we know them today) and ACOs, creating large networks of connected providers, payers, physicians, and vendors, did not exist. For many organizations, very few systems reached outside the four walls of the institution, and the number of users who had access to patient information was far fewer than today. In 2017, we have enterprises that involve tens of thousands of systems, thousands of applications, huge data repositories, and even more users with access than systems. Add to that the number of third-party service providers, business associates (BAs), that the average provider deals with and the numbers soar. That is the ecosystem that healthcare IT leaders find themselves confronted with today. That ecosystem is characterized by ever-evolving technologies, clinical and decision support systems, a rapid proliferation of networked and mobile devices, remote services, telemedicine to bring healthcare closer to the rural or distant patient, and home health initiatives to bring healthcare to the patient where he or she lives. The delivery of healthcare is not just in the hospital or clinic anymore, it is everywhere, and demands a ubiquitous information presence that can keep up and support it. Patient information is rapidly being digitized in larger and larger amounts and being replicated and disseminated across this ecosystem very broadly, making the information more accessible in more ways, on more devices, and to more people, and introducing more ways that the threat can compromise or exploit it.

The point is that just as healthcare IT is dynamically evolving, so are the cyber threats around it, and those involved in owning a healthcare business, delivering IT services to healthcare, or engaged in information security need to be comfortable with adapting to and managing change. Health organizations that are likely to succeed more often in meeting the threat will have three things in common:

- They will learn their adversary and understand their risk posture.
- They will develop a dynamic plan of action that focuses their cybersecurity efforts.
- They will learn to execute at a high level of precision.

The battle with cybercriminals will not be won by those who sit on the sidelines waiting for a solution to come to them.

PART VI

Think Like a Bad Guy

When assessing threats, it is always useful to identify what you have that a particular threat might want, which then enables you to recognize those threats that are of reasonable concern. It is also necessary to be objective when considering your state of security and areas of vulnerability. Often, the best way to do this is to ask someone else to evaluate your security posture for you. Another important thing to understand is the general nature of the threat, both directly and indirectly. The Ponemon Institute has conducted independent research into the cost of data breaches for many years now. Consistently, the Ponemon researchers have found that regulated industries such as healthcare pay more for breaches, that the overwhelming majority of breaches are caused by criminals, and that the longer it takes for an organization to detect and react to a breach the more it will cost them.[2] Indiscriminate threats account for a large number of network outages and lost data. Most malware attacks today are indiscriminate attacks seeking any network connected to the Internet that is not protected properly. There are also bad actors that target healthcare and patient information both from within and without the hospital. In fact, today the number of incidents perpetrated by insiders still far exceeds the number perpetrated by outsiders, and the number of incidents caused by carelessness or mishandling of systems and information far exceeds the number caused by sophisticated hacks. Therefore, it is important to understand your security weaknesses and those threats that can take advantage of those opportunities to exploit your systems and information. Many external attacks first start with an attack that targets an insider, like phishing attempts, water-cooler attacks, and so forth. These are forms of social engineering, and to understand social engineering, it is helpful to understand the con artist. Two famous con artists are Frank Abagnale, Jr. and Kevin Mitnick. You can find books by both of these individuals, and Frank's autobiography during his crime years, aptly titled *Catch Me If You Can*, was also turned into a movie.[3] Neither one of these individuals was a hacker, but what is important here is understanding the mindset of the attacker.

There is plenty of motivation for individuals who would commit theft, fraud, or a crime to target healthcare. Healthcare has a tremendous amount of valuable information. More so than any other industry, healthcare collects, retains, processes, transmits, and shares very personal and very valuable information belonging to patients. This includes personally identifiable information, health information, and financial information. At the time of writing, the average price of credit card details on the black market is $1 a number, the average price for a Social Security number is between $1 and $3, while the average price for a medical identity is $50. Healthcare entities collect and store all three of these. Prior to 2000, it was harder to steal this information because many healthcare organizations were still very paper process dominated, but that is not the case anymore. Not only is more of this information digitized, but also there are more systems, greater connectivity, and more people accessing it, all of which introduce new types of threats and attract persistent threats. When famous criminal Jesse James was asked why he robbed banks, he reputedly answered "that's where the money is." The same is true for cybercriminals. They go where they can steal the most data, and that is healthcare organizations.

The Big Four: Cybercrime, Cyber Espionage, Hacktivism, and Advanced Persistent Threats

Cybercrime, cyber espionage, hacktivisim, and advanced persistent threats (APTs) are the "four horsemen of the apocalypse" because they are coming, they keep coming, and they are relentless, persistent, and able to constantly reinvent themselves. As soon as we find a way to block them from our networks, or at least make it harder for them to get in, they find a new way. The battle with these four is also an asymmetric contest where the organizations must find and close every vulnerability in their networks and systems and the attackers need only find the one they missed, and the threat only requires periodic victories. For hackers, trial and error is not only part of the experience, it is expected, and with each failure or win, they learn something new. For organizations whose mission it is to protect against these threats, any security breach is failure. Therefore, the first thing that those who engage in cybersecurity need to know is that abnormal is normal. The second thing to know is that the threat is trying to get in continuously, 24 hours a day, 365 days a year. The third thing to know is that you will not be successful 100 percent of the time in keeping the threat out, which is why increasing cybersecurity readiness both inside and out, enhancing detection capabilities, and having solid incident response are imperative.

Cybercriminals come in many forms, from malicious insiders, to information thieves, to identity thieves, to extortionists. Extortion, most often in the form of ransomware, is especially troubling for healthcare organizations because it attacks data availability, which affects the very thing they care most about—patient care. Ransomware itself now has many different forms, from types that attack and lock up systems, to types that attack and encrypt data, to types that attack/steal the information and leave behind an encrypted copy. Extortion can take a more sinister approach when the hacker steals data and then demands a ransom to return the data, typically along with an explanation of how to fix the vulnerability and a promise not to disclose the issue. The problem with responding to extortion is that you are dealing with a criminal. You do not know if the extortionist will return all the data or keep a copy and continue the extortion, has left a back door into your environment to steal more data, or will keep the promise not to disclose the issue.

Cyber espionage is a targeted form of cybercrime. The attacker is after information for the value of the information itself—the intelligence, commercial advantage, and so forth that can be gleaned from it. The attacker could be a hacker looking for intellectual property to sell to the highest bidder, a state actor seeking strategic intelligence, or a rival corporation looking for competitive advantage. Espionage can signal massive breaches, as the attackers are after all the information they can get. These are usually more sophisticated attacks as well, and the hacker may run a ransomware or denial-of-service attack as they leave in order to throw off the investigation.

Hacktivisim is usually cause-based, or an attack based on ideology. For example, an attacker may be unhappy with some position the healthcare system has taken regarding delivery of services or some environmental impact the business is causing. Hacktivists want to make a point. They are usually not interested in stealing information or hurting anyone, but their attacks are no less serious as some have learned the hard way (e.g., Boston Children's Hospital[4] and Hurley Medical Center[5]).

PART VI

Finally, advance persistent threats, attacks against the enterprise where the attacker gains unauthorized access and is able to remain undetected for a very long time, are the last of the four horsemen. These attacks generally target the theft of information, not the disruption or destruction of the network. These attacks are typically carried out by more sophisticated attackers such as state-sponsored groups, but they could also be organized criminals looking to exploit financial systems or steal personal information and intellectual property. In many of the large breaches discovered in 2015/16, the attackers were in the target network for more than 200 days prior to discovery. Many of the largest breaches in healthcare were the result of APTs.

The four horsemen are not the only threats that healthcare needs to be aware of. Malware represents another very large concern. Just the sheer volume of malware we see now annually, as discussed previously, and the hackers' use of malware to deliver ransomware and other malicious payloads, make this last category an ongoing concern. Thankfully, there are multiple technologies that can help mitigate these threats, as we will discuss in the next section.

Cyber attacks, like other criminal activity, tend to follow the path of least resistance or the simplest means of attack. The attacker will almost always try to find the easiest means to breach the network or system. In many cases, the attacker is able to find a vulnerability or trick someone into providing information that will enable the attacker to gain access without having to resort to a complicated technical attack. Sometimes the attacker is a form of automated malware that does not discriminate with respect to who it attacks. The number of malware attacks has grown exponentially in the past 20 years such that, at the time of this writing, leading threat research centers estimate that there were 430 million unique new pieces of malware in 2015, equating to more than 100,000 new attacks daily, and more than 700,000,000 known forms of malware.[6] Even more challenging are "zero day" attacks, malware that takes advantage of a software vulnerability that the vendor is unaware of and for which there is no immediate fix. In 2015 there were 54 zero-day attacks or roughly one per week.

NOTE In previous years, reports focused on exploited zero-day vulnerabilities, and now they focus on the total number of vulnerabilities that could potentially be exploited. The new definition demonstrates potential risk more accurately, while the other spoke to actual historical risk. In 2014, the number of vulnerabilities was 4,958, in 2015 it was 4,066, and in 2016 it was 3,986.[7]

Many recent malware variants are very sophisticated, capable of morphing their appearance, disabling antivirus systems and other security controls, communicating remotely and transmitting data, and masking themselves to make it more difficult to detect and eradicate them quickly. Malware comes in many different forms and is delivered via multiple mechanisms. The volumes are so high that many traditional methods of protection such as antivirus systems that rely primarily on signature-based rules have become less effective. Today organizations must apply newer technologies that take advantage of heuristic capabilities to recognize potential malware threats. Advanced malware solutions now can detect anomalous patterns in behavior and flag threats before they traverse the perimeter.

If malware were the only threat that healthcare entities had to deal with, the task would be difficult enough, but even as big a threat as malware represents, it is not the most serious risk. In fact, loss of data, compromises, or network outages due to malware account for less than 15 percent of the total threat. The largest losses of data suffered have traditionally been through the physical loss or theft of computer devices, malicious acts or unintentional mistakes by insiders, and actions of third-party business partners. There are literally millions of discrete access events a year that must be monitored and evaluated. A single patient visit lasting a day for a simple procedure can generate more than 150 access events. A longer stay in a hospital for a more serious reason can generate thousands of access events. Taken over the course of a day, a week, a month and the entire universe of patient encounters will generate literally millions of access events. Things as seemingly simple as accounting for disclosures—who has seen a patient's record—can become a major task. Simple policies, procedures, and manual processes are not adequate to protect either today's healthcare IT environment or tomorrow's.

Staying Abreast of the Threat

Computer information security officers (CISOs) need to develop an effective system for gathering relevant threat information to inform their decisions and programs. There are many sources for threat information, such as the National Health Information Sharing and Analysis Center (NH-ISAC; https://nhisac.org/), InfraGard (https://www.infragard.org/), a partnership between the FBI and private sector, and the U.S. Computer Emergency Readiness Team (US-CERT; https://www.us-cert.gov/). In late 2015, Congress passed the Cybersecurity Information Sharing Act (CISA)[8] with the intent to establish a clearinghouse and methods of dissemination for threat information in healthcare. Some regional alliances have formed as well where member entities share threat information with one another. However, to be truly useful to a future threat, accurate information needs to be shared in a timely fashion between systems. As processing speeds increase and threats become more sophisticated, aggressive CISOs will need to turn to technology to enable real-time threat information sharing in order to support timely reaction and action. In 2025, simple personal computer speeds are predicted to be 10^{16} cycles per second (10,000 trillion cycles per second) or the equivalent processing speed of the human brain.[9] Larger, more sophisticated platforms and big data will be moving even faster. Security technology of the future will require timely threat intelligence in order to successfully protect the enterprise. The US-CERT in concert with the Department of Homeland Security (DHS) is working to automate the sharing of threat information through the use of several integrated technical specifications. Three of these specifications are

- Trusted Automated eXchange of Indicator Information (TAXII)
- Structured Threat Information eXpression (STIX)
- Cyber Observable eXpression (CybOX)

Together, these specifications provide common standards and languages to describe types of information exchanges, cyber threats, and observable cyber events.[10]

Training and education are also important for anyone engaged in cybersecurity due to its dynamic and evolving nature. What we know today will not carry us very far into the future. Seek out courses in advanced techniques of defense as well as threat information. There are many different credible sources for this type of training such as SANS, ISACA (previously known as the Information Systems Audit and Control Association), and CompTIA (Computing Technology Industry Association). All of these organizations offer multiple certifications in various security disciplines and functional areas. These organizations and others, like Black Hat, also provide forums to present and discuss threat information. Black Hat is one of the largest threat conferences hosting both hackers and security professionals who share information, know-how, and techniques regarding the latest security threats facing industries. Since 2012, healthcare has been the focus of part of its agenda. Healthcare cybersecurity professionals can glean useful information about the threats they face by attending these types of events.

Systems and cybersecurity professionals are not the only ones who will need better education and awareness. Workforce members will as well. The antiquated practices of the past that relied heavily on briefings and canned computer-based training (CBT) modules will need to be augmented by more advanced techniques using experiential approaches. Providing training to workforce members about phishing is a good example of this. Traditional methods do not work, because users do not internalize the information such that it becomes a habit (changes behavior), nor do they keep up to date on ways to recognize the latest phishing techniques. Phishing exercises repeated on a regular basis that simulate a real phishing message that the user receives in his or her e-mail stream, followed by immediate training if they open it, have proven to reduce significantly the number of repeat offenders. "With repetition, a sustained and well-executed phishing simulation program provides a significant reduction in overall exposure to risk from this *ever-changing* attack vector and improves the security posture of an organization."[11] Real-time and table-top exercises for workforce members provide the hands-on simulations that enhance the training experience and engage cognitive problem solving. Essentially, we learn better by doing.

Planning for Outcomes: Cybersecurity Frameworks and Standards

A systemic approach to cybersecurity management must begin with a clear understanding of the "big picture," which means understanding the assets to be protected, the stakeholders, and the impact to the organization given the realization of a threat. The best way to create this understanding is by using frameworks and standards to identify the controls and technology necessary to implement that vision.

The Healthcare Insurance Portability and Accountability Act (HIPAA) provides comprehensive guidance and a legally binding framework for protections applied to patient health information to assure privacy and security. However, HIPAA lacks the overall approach and the necessary guidance to marry cybersecurity to business goals, is silent on many of the current practical realities affecting cybersecurity today, and is considered far too ambiguous on many aspects of cybersecurity to be really useful for designing an effective control environment. HIPAA's one-size-fits-all design provides a basic set of recommendations that are very helpful and act as a roadmap for small organizations, but fall short when it comes to the advanced challenges of cybersecurity.[12] For those reasons, while HIPAA provides a meaningful guide for privacy and security considerations affecting patient health information, it is not considered an acceptable standard or framework to build an effective cybersecurity program. As a result, and in response to the growing cybersecurity threat, healthcare is embracing more mature security frameworks to protect their systems and data.

There are far too many frameworks and standards to discuss in this chapter, but the one most prevalent in healthcare today is the National Institute of Standards and Technology Cybersecurity Framework for Healthcare (NIST CSF). NIST as a government organization has as its primary purpose researching, developing, and publishing guidance for the protection of information technology and data. The NIST Framework for Improving Critical Infrastructure Cybersecurity is a set of industry standards and best practices to help organizations manage cybersecurity risks. The Department of Health and Human Services (HHS) in conjunction with NIST has released a useful crosswalk between the NIST CSF for healthcare and the HIPAA Security Rule. The crosswalk provides "mappings" between the many very specific requirements listed in the NIST CSF and the specifications listed in HIPAA. The NIST CSF is the result of a February 2013 Executive Order titled "Improving Critical Infrastructure Cybersecurity" and 10 months of collaborative discussions with more than 3,000 security professionals.[13]

Using frameworks for guiding program development and execution offers multiple benefits beyond simply improving our cybersecurity posture. Frameworks afford an opportunity to establish both a target state as well as a prioritization of action with respect to remediation to achieve that target state. It provides reference for discussions both internally and externally around program status, direction, budget, compliance, etc. as well as common road map for continuously mapping and reassessing the program and cybersecurity posture. More importantly it provides a plan that keeps the program focused and creates a structure that allows flexibility to make adjustments when new requirements or changes come along that need to be accommodated. Last, but not least, it promotes compliance, but in a more meaningful way, as a result of sound security. The NIST CSF was the basis for the HIPAA Security Rule and Office of Civil Rights (OCR) "Guidance on Risk Analysis Requirements under the HIPAA Security Rule" and is used across the federal government, including by both the Centers for Medicare and Medicaid Services (CMS) and the HHS Office of the Inspector General (OIG). It is also used by the national research community and by more than 60 percent of healthcare organizations, and is used as part of the Malcolm Baldrige National Quality Award criteria. Whether for meeting a regulatory requirement, meeting program mandates, seeking recognition, or just communicating security readiness to peer organizations, NIST CSF provides a common language and standard for those activities.

PART VI

Building a Secure Architecture

When building the security architecture, you should think in terms of layers (from the core to the endpoint and everywhere in between), integration, and complementary controls. An example of complementary controls would be signature-based systems and heuristic-based systems, systems that are both context aware and intelligence aware, and systems that use URL, IP address, and file reputation services. Relying solely on one technology, one capability, or one identifying technique is dangerous at best. Today's threat environment cannot be managed with simple signature-based controls. According to Symantec's 2016 Internet Security Threat Report, in 2015 there were more than 430 million new unique pieces of malware released and 54 zero-day vulnerabilities identified.[6] Greater reliance must be placed on advance detection capabilities and an integrated set of complementary controls. When developing your security architecture, you need to start with your data, then work outward and address databases, applications, infrastructure, the perimeter, and endpoints. Solving the cybersecurity challenges of tomorrow will require a combination of building and maintaining a current environment and investing in advanced security technology.

Maintaining a Current Environment

Cybercriminals continue to go after what are called Common Vulnerabilities and Explosures (CVE), meaning system vulnerabilities that are more than a year old, well known, researched and analyzed, and in most cases addressable. According to Verizon's 2016 Data Breach Investigations Report,[14] more than 85 percent of the incidents studied took advantage of a very old CVE, as much as five or six years old, while most of the remaining 15 percent took advantage of a CVE at least a year old. What this means essentially is that, as systems and cybersecurity professionals, we are our own worst enemy when it comes to making sure our enterprises are as protected as they can be because we are failing to address even the most basic of responsibilities; namely, applying hardening standards as we build out systems and deploy them, keeping those systems up to date with required service packs and patches, maintaining good discipline in managing their configurations and changes, and replacing or upgrading them when they become end of life or no longer supported. There are many reasons for this shortcoming, but the overwhelming one is usually lack of time. Considering the high tempo most modern IT shops keep just to match the rate at which new systems and applications are added and to accomplish the number of major changes or implementations required, they have little time for routine administrative or maintenance chores. The problem with this is that poor maintenance and administration leads to more downtime and greater susceptibility to exploitation. Similar to the automobile you drive, the longer you ignore maintenance, the sooner your network or systems will break down. Dissimilar to the automobile you drive, your network also has active threats attacking it constantly.

There are many examples of hardening guides that can be acquired for just about any device on the network. While there are not specific hardening guides for all systems and devices, there are hardening standards that can be acquired and used to build a guide and to turn it into a specific image to aid in build-outs. There are vulnerability scanners to aid in the identification of vulnerabilities that require patching, as well as scanners that can look for variances in policy or compliance settings on devices. These tools can also aid in the identification of systems either approaching end of life or already there. These scans can be run on schedule or ad hoc as needed. There are technologies for dynamically managing configuration to aid in the rollout of new policies, maintain configuration discipline, track changes, and enforce rules or compliance mandates. A change by an unauthorized person can be either disallowed or automatically rolled back to the original setting.

The firewall is still an important asset in protecting the perimeter and keeping the bad guys out, but today's firewalls need to be a lot smarter than they use to be. Healthcare organizations should be deploying next-generation firewalls (NGFWs) and unified threat management (UTM) platforms that provide application control and user identity awareness capabilities. UTM platforms generally integrate several protective capabilities on a single platform at the perimeter, virtual private networks (VPNs), an intrusion prevention system (IPS), security protection and management, antivirus, and other tools to provide for more thorough traffic review. Though difficult in every environment due to business needs or network and application traffic requirements, firewall rules can be enabled to block traffic from high-risk countries, related threat information, and certain lists such as bad URLs, known botnet addresses, or known hacking sites. Some advanced firewalls permit blocking of Domain Name System (DNS) queries and will stop or inspect executables. Phishing, botnet, and spam attacks can be greatly curtailed by simply blocking these queries and not allowing automatic execution of code for downloads, attachments, and so forth. Legacy firewalls are not capable of handling the cyber threat healthcare now faces. Note that there are also multiple types of firewalls. Here we discussed perimeter firewalls; we will refer to other firewall types later.

Managing Privileges

Local administrative privileges can and should be eliminated wherever possible to avoid unscheduled or unapproved changes, dangerous downloads, and other risky actions. The first step in effectively managing privileges is to inventory and eliminate those that are not necessary or improperly matched with the user. Normal user accounts should never have elevated privilege, to preclude overuse or inappropriate use. Elevated privileges should also be managed more securely. Elevated privileges include local administrator accounts, privileged user accounts, domain administrative accounts, service accounts, application accounts, and emergency accounts.

Minimally, privileges should be encrypted, especially ones with administrative rights, when traversing the network. Privileges with administrative rights should also be subject to two-factor authentication so that a simple username and password combination is not sufficient to make changes affecting the network or critical applications. A technology that vaults privileges can strengthen the protection of elevated privileges even further. Essentially, all users have a standard user ID and password, but IT personnel who are authorized can authenticate to the vault to check out a set of administrative privileges when needed. The rights are issued to the person who logged into the vault and their usage can be audited. When the IT person is finished, they simply check the admin

PART VI

privileges back in to the vault. If they forget or just fail to do so, at a predetermined time the privileges expire. This eliminates active elevated privileges on the network that can be easily compromised and then used to exploit the network.

Thwarting Cyber Exploitation

Every organization needs to know where its critical systems and data are located before it can develop a cogent strategy for protecting them. One technology that gives us the ability to do just that at a very granular level for information is data loss prevention (DLP). DLP solutions are often thought of as security solutions, but they are actually more accurately categorized as enterprise-level data management solutions that just happen to enhance protection. DLP has three main components:

- Discovery
- Network enforcement
- Endpoint protection

The first component, discovery, uses a process called fingerprinting to accurately identify and index where all of our sensitive information is located throughout the enterprise, including both structured and unstructured data. This is no trivial undertaking. Without knowing where the sensitive information is located, the DLP deployment becomes more difficult. Therefore, discovery is critical to implementing DLP effectively.[15] Fingerprinting permits very accurate identification of a document based on multiple key attributes of the document itself. Once a fingerprint has been created, the DLP system can detect the sensitive information contained in the document despite manipulation, reformatting, or modification. Most DLP systems can then identify derivative content from the original when captured in smaller passages, even when cut and pasted or retyped. This gives CISOs a very powerful tool for identifying where sensitive data are located in the enterprise and where they have greater resulting cyber risks.

The network enforcement component of the DLP solution allows for very specific rules to be enabled to allow or block certain activities based on system, user, or destination profile. This aids tremendously in reducing cyber risk by controlling where this information may be stored and transmitted, and by disallowing inappropriate actions by users. More importantly, though, this component provides a real deterrent to exfiltration of data by unauthorized individuals.

The endpoint component extends the protections and rule enforcement capabilities to platforms like desktops, laptops, and tablets, and allows the CISO to prescribe rules governing local storage, use of removable media, or functionality such as printing or thumb drives.

Isolating Cyber Threats

In 2016, multiple damaging attacks on healthcare entities were perpetrated using malware, ransomware, and zero-day viruses and caused serious disruptions to service and patient care. What aided these attacks greatly, both in the attack phase and the exploitation phase, was that many target locations were running flat networks. Flat networks, while greatly simplifying network management, offer little protection for critical assets once the perimeter has been compromised. Add to this the fact that most breaches are not detected for well over 100 days, and a flat network gives an attacker a considerable advantage. A better approach is to create a segmented enterprise that separates and allows apportionment of assets on different subnetworks to improve security. Segmentation if done properly provides many advantages in managing protected health information such as limiting or managing access, reducing risks from malware, and aiding containment and making critical or sensitive assets/databases less visible. Segmentation can be achieved by creating separate virtual LANs (VLAN). However VLANs alone will not provide the security desired. Segmentation is not effective unless enforced by either access control lists (ACLs) or firewalls.

There are many reasons why segmentation is important in healthcare. Health systems have Payment Card Industry Data Security Standard (PCI DSS) requirements for segmenting financial systems from the rest of the network. Hospitals have multiple groups accessing the network, not all created equal in access. Some hospitals seek to enhance their security posture by segmenting vendor-supported or -administered systems. Medical devices are well known for being insecure and representing a risk to the network. Many systems have legacy applications that are end of life and not capable of being secured any longer or are in the process of being replaced and not necessary in the day-to-day production environment. Segmentation firewalls permit organizations to place barriers between sensitive segments of their network or to isolate areas of greater risk. Segmentation also contributes significantly to the organization's ability to effectively triage an incident and isolate the portion of the network affected, thereby aiding containment and reducing the number of systems that might have to be restored afterward. Internal firewalls can help to achieve defense-in-depth by forcing an attacker to penetrate multiple layers of security to reach mission-critical servers or applications.[16]

Detecting Cyber Intrusions

While next-generation firewalls generally integrate an IPS capability at the perimeter, the need for this technology goes beyond the perimeter to the internal segments of the enterprise as well. Monitoring anomalous traffic and activity over the network and on critical systems is also important, to detect internal exploitation. Each healthcare organization must determine whether an intrusion detection system (IDS) or an IPS is the best approach for the environment. Some health systems are concerned that IPS, which can automatically block certain traffic, connections, and so forth, may present safety risks if critical systems, communications, or segments of the network are blocked or affected. This is a valid concern and should be considered when determining a detection strategy. If an IDS is chosen over an IPS, then greater reliance will need to be put on active monitoring and alerting. For this reason, many health systems have chosen a managed security service provider (MSSP) that is capable of real-time monitoring and alerting along with stronger algorithms for anomaly detection and false-positive reduction. In addition to network-based IDS/IPS solutions that perform traffic analysis, there are also host-based IDS/IPS solutions that monitor for deviant behavior on servers and other platforms. Hospitals should consider host-based IDS/IPS solutions for many of their high-risk assets or assets that could be easily exploited such as legacy or end-of-life assets.

PART VI

A good candidate for host-based IDS and key asset that plays a critical role in most healthcare enterprises is the Health Language 7 (HL7) Interface Engine. This asset sits between critical clinical, financial, and other applications and performs translations of data so that those systems can seamlessly communicate with one another. This system must decrypt the data from the sender before performing the translation process and forwarding the data to the receiver. Additionally, most interface engines store or archive a certain amount of the data they handle for contingency reasons. This system sits at the heart of the enterprise application environment, but is often dismissed as a part of the infrastructure because of its function. Interface engines are perfect candidates for host-based IDS/IPS due to their critical nature to operations, the sensitive data they process and retain, and the fact that only a very limited number of people need direct access to the engine.

Detecting Web-Based Threats

Many applications and services are web enabled to support the mobile workforce, collaboration with partners and vendors, and initiatives to promote patient engagement, population health, and a host of other activities. In many of these situations, connecting directly to the network is either not possible or not preferred. Web applications present a definite risk profile as assets that can be easily attacked externally. For that reason, it is highly recommended that organizations work only with reputable vendors when developing these platforms and always perform security testing of the application code to ensure its integrity. The vendors should be performing security testing throughout their development process, and it would be important to review this with them.

Testing of web application code is done from two perspectives: from the outside in, using dynamic application security testing (DAST), and from the inside out, through code review using static application security testing (SAST). Both are important and provide an understanding of the vulnerabilities of the application both from within and from outside.[17] Vulnerability scanning and penetration testing, discussed later in the chapter in "Looking for Vulnerability," is considered DAST. For most commercially acquired web applications, this type of testing is usually the norm. Testing should be conducted against both the application and the hosting platform. Web application firewalls can also be used to provide another layer of filtering and protection for assets.

Detecting the Unknown

Malicious content can enter the enterprise from a multitude of directions, pathways, and devices. Building early and accurate detection can assist incident response efforts by limiting the impact of a particular attack. There are multiple technologies that can aid in detecting and avoiding malware. Antivirus solutions, secure e-mail gateways, secure web gateways, sandboxing, advanced malware detection solutions, and mobile device management solutions are some technologies that should be incorporated into the cybersecurity strategy for protecting the network and information assets. *Antivirus solutions* have been around for a very long time, and work on a simple premise that there is a list of signatures of known bad actors. When the antivirus protection running at the perimeter or on an internal platform detects/recognizes traffic as possessing one or more of these signatures, it blocks that traffic from entering. There are many different antivirus solutions, and they do not all function the same. Ideally, more than one antivirus engine should be used on different parts of the network: at the perimeter, on the e-mail gateway, on servers and workstations, and on endpoints. *Secure e-mail gateways* provide malware and phishing detection and prevention. This technology can inspect e-mail for malicious content, attachments, web links, and executables. *Secure web gateways* work much the same way as e-mail gateways, enabling inbound inspection of web traffic as well as outbound inspection. These can work in conjunction with a cloud-based *sandboxing* capability to open and inspect questionable content before it has the chance to affect the network. *Advanced malware detection solutions* should be implemented to help detect malicious content that antivirus just cannot see. *Mobile device management solutions* are not normally thought of as advanced detection platforms, but with their ability to monitor mobile devices and ensure that they have not been tampered with or had their security features disabled, they can reduce the risk of compromised mobile devices from affecting the enterprise.

Addressing the Ubiquitous Threat of IoT

Society in general is becoming more and more connected and data aware in its quest for fast information in convenient form wherever and whenever users want it. More and more routine processes are becoming automated to enhance convenience in management of functionality. The Internet of Things encompasses many commercial devices, including smart TVs, smart locks, smart refrigeration, smart environmental controls, smart vehicles, and of course smartphones. All are networkable, usually over a wireless connection, but some are on the network itself.

The IoT extends to healthcare as well. Healthcare is being extended steadily out to wherever the patient exists, whether that is in their home, their workplace, or where they recreate. We have medical devices that are connected and communicate both across the ethernet and over the wireless network (see Chapter 31 for more information). These include various devices deployed throughout the hospital setting, devices that travel with or on the patient, and devices that monitor the patient or the patient's environment. The overwhelming majority of these devices at the time of this writing are not secure and represent a credible cyber threat to both patient safety and the enterprise. "More than 25% of cyber attacks will involve the Internet of Things (IoT) by 2020, according to technology research firm Gartner."[18] As fast as these devices are being developed they are being compromised. These devices represent a particularly attractive target for cybercriminals and hackers because they are additional gateways to the healthcare systems and networks. The numbers of connected devices after 2016 is expected to be in the tens of billions, which represents multiple devices per person. The challenge with these devices, just like medical devices, is that there is no standard architecture or security requirements that apply when companies develop them, so healthcare organizations are left with having to find ways to architect security around them.

Probably the most concerning from an IoT cyber threat perspective are distributed denial of service (DDOS) attacks. A prominent example of this is the Mirai hack that uses sophisticated malware to commandeer smart devices accessible via the Internet and

PART VI

combine them into very powerful botnets capable of launching crippling DDOS attacks. In October of 2016, thousands of critical applications, including EHR systems, were taken offline by a massive Mirai attack that used corrupted devices from all over the world to attack the DNS servers at a company called Dyn. The Mirai attacks underscore the security vulnerability of these devices and the risk they pose to network, communications, and critical services. There are ways to mitigate this risk, but they aren't easy to implement: they require manufacturers to design devices with fewer inherent flaws and consumers to rethink how they implement these devices and the security they place around them. This type of attack highlights how interconnected we all are as a society and as businesses and accentuates the need for everyone to do a better job of protecting their own environment for the sake of society in general.

Monitoring Activity

Every hospital needs to develop its auditing strategy and enable logging to support that strategy. A log is a record of the events occurring within a computer system or network. A log may be made up of many (hundreds or thousands or even millions) entries. Each entry contains information related to a specific event that has occurred within that system or network. The number and volume of computer logs have increased greatly since 2009 with the advent of EHRs and the massive automation of processes in healthcare over the last decade, creating the need for automated log management.[19] The first step is to enable logging on all systems. The second is to move those logs off the primary system to a log repository, usually a dedicated server or a storage area network (SAN). The next step is to implement a log manager. This technology will then aggregate log data and identify security, operational, and compliance events and report or alert as configured. These events can number into the thousands. Many of the mainstream log managers have industry-specific modules to facilitate the reporting and alerting process. If a hospital system has a contract with a managed security service provider, a log manager may or may not be required. If one is used, it will send its logs to the security information and event management (SIEM) system that the MSSP is using. If a log manager is not used, the MSSP usually deploys a collector that in turn communicates with the SIEM. Organizations may opt to perform manual audits of system and user activity although it is not recommended. If they do, then attention must be given to the individual who is going to review the logs/events, planning must be done for log collection and log review, and procedures must be implemented around alerts and communicating escalation, troubleshooting, identifying false positives, remediation and log retention.

Under the HITECH Act patient information was supposed to be digitized and securely held in Certified Electronic Health Record Technology (CEHRT). Organizations were told that as long as they implemented CEHRT in a meaningful way, then security would be sufficiently addressed. However, databases and those who had direct access to those databases were not adequately covered by the security requirements of that technology. Immediately, CISOs understood they had a problem. While access to the data in the EHR could be audited through the application, direct access to the database supporting the application could not. Fortunately, there is technology for this purpose: database activity monitoring (DAM). DAM audits database access, audits users with elevated privileges such as database administrators, and helps protect against cyber events. All forms of privileged user can be monitored in databases, including superusers, administrators, sysadmins, developers, help desk personnel, and third-party personnel. DAM monitors application activity matching specific database actions with specific users to identify abnormal activity. DAM can then thwart certain attacks by creating a baseline of what is normal and alerting/reporting on deviations from that baseline to security analysts.

The insider threat continues to dominate the number of incidents that occur each year, although they only account for roughly 1 percent of the records potentially compromised. However, even if small in number in terms of impact, workforce members who snoop or otherwise access patient information create real compliance challenges for health systems. Fortunately, a new set of technologies called user and entity behavior analytics (UEBA) can profile user behaviors and detect inappropriate activity. Before UEBA came Privacy Activity Monitoring, systems that essentially perform the same log or event analysis, but as it related to application access and activity related to users. Privacy monitoring is widely used in healthcare today as hospitals seek to deal with the insider threat issues, but most privacy monitors fall short of being truly effective beyond narrow compliance monitoring. They rarely catch the person or persons engaged in real crimes like identity theft or medical identity theft because they lack behavioral modeling. These early user technologies are sufficient for monitoring for compliance purposes. Organizations can define their audit program and automate checks against compliance requirements. They can also run ad hoc investigations into user activity and, depending on the number of applications, perform limited event correlation. In some cases they can even create baselines for user behaviors and then monitor against those norms to identify when a workforce member's behavior is not normal. UEBA combines monitoring of workforce members' behavior with entity events to identify when either they or third-party individuals are engaging in suspicious behaviors.

Conducting Information Correlation and Analysis

SIEM solutions have long been touted by their vendors as the holy grail of security, enticing many in security to purchase them. Unfortunately, more often than not, figuring out how to use them has proven as elusive as tracking down another well-known grail. In truth, SIEMs are at the top of the security pyramid as it relates to detection and monitoring. SIEMs are very complex solutions that require a significant amount of security expertise and experience to implement and manage. When sitting on top of a well-managed, well-architected foundation of security controls and technologies, they become very powerful correlation engines capable of connecting the dots between multiple events occurring on many systems, at different times, in different parts of the enterprise to produce a cohesive picture of a security event or policy violation. For SIEMs to be such powerful correlation engines, they must gather information from a host of network and security devices and applications, such as IDS/IPS, antivirus, malware filters, vulnerability scanners, policy compliance systems, servers, workstations, databases, application logs, and threat databases. Additionally, SIEMs require sophisticated algorithms to make sense of all the information collected and analyzed.

PART VI

The sheer volume of security events and attacks detected in the healthcare enterprise makes monitoring, correlation, and analysis all but impossible without technology and expertise. While the technology can be acquired, such as log managers, privacy application monitors, IDS/IPS, and SIEMs, very few health systems have the real expertise necessary to optimize their utility. The average hospital will produce tens of millions of events each month, with the overwhelming number of these being "noise" and only a few being actionable. The trick is being able to synthesize all of those events down to what needs attention. The expertise becomes critical when writing the rules and the algorithms necessary to carry out that synthesis. Expertise is required to know which information is critical, to understand and analyze network traffic, and to know how to optimize each technology to support the correlation process. This is an area in which MSSPs excel. They know how to tune IDS/IPS sensors for optimal performance, how to configure logging to collect the right system/user events, and how to incorporate firewall logs, vulnerability scanning results, and other feeds to facilitate correlation and analysis. They also have the advantage of extensive libraries of specific rules that they can implement and algorithms they can use to support correlation. They can provide these services better, faster, and more reliably because they monitor thousands of organizations across the globe in real time around the clock.

Looking for Vulnerabilities

To provide assurance regarding the integrity of the enterprise and its constituent systems, an organization needs to perform technical testing, a process that begins with automated vulnerability scans and culminates in a penetration test. Technical testing is an important part of any security program. This in-depth security testing allows an organization to better understand its security posture and find potential vulnerabilities before they are exploited by bad actors. Technical security testing includes two important aspects:

- **Vulnerability scanning** Vulnerability scanning should be performed frequently, often on a monthly or at least quarterly basis, to ensure new issues are identified quickly as well as to verify the remediation of previously found issues.

- **Penetration testing (pentesting)** Pentesting requires an analyst with a very specialized skill set. Because of this and the nature of pentesting, most organizations perform these tests at least annually. Pentests can be performed as frequently as quarterly.

Vulnerability Testing

Scanning for weakness in the environment is the first step. Vulnerability scanners have large databases of known vulnerabilities and their associated digital signatures. The scanning software will scan the systems within a defined scope for evidence of potential vulnerabilities based on the signatures in its database and how the systems in scope respond to specific types of requests. According to the SANS institute, "Vulnerability Scanning is the art of using one computer to look for weaknesses in the security of another computer—so that you can find and fix the weaknesses in your systems before someone else finds that there is a security weakness and decides to break in."[20]

There are numerous tools available that are used to perform automated vulnerability scanning. These tools range from very general testing tools that will test virtually any platform and can test compliance with virtually any standard, to very specific tools that test one type of appliance or system. The cost of these software packages also ranges greatly, from open source (free) to tens of thousands of dollars a year in licensing fees. The tools that have a high cost for licensing are known industry-wide and their results are relied upon universally. The open source community has provided some incredibly useful tools as well. Descriptions of some of these tools follow:

- OpenVAS (www.openvas.org) is one of the most popular of the open source tools available. OpenVAS is a fully functional, regularly updated, and reliable automated vulnerability scanning tool.

- Nessus (www.tenable.com/Nessus), offered by Tenable Network Security, is possibly the most popular general-purpose vulnerability scanning solution available. Nessus is a paid program, for commercial use, but is widely considered the gold standard in vulnerability scanning throughout the industry.

- Qualys Vulnerabilty Management (https://www.qualys.com/suite/vulnerability-management/) and Nexpose from Rapid7 (https://www.rapid7.com/products/nexpose/) are two other popular vulnerability scanning tools that are commercially available.

In general, most of the commercial vulnerability scanners available are roughly equivalent to each other, and they tend to have much the same functionality as well. The paid solutions work better for large organizations because they provide customized signatures, centralized reporting, and several other features that make any of the paid options a good choice.

Before scanning, the scope of what is to be tested must be determined as well as when the testing will be performed. This decision-making process, called *scoping*, defines the parameters of the testing process and which systems should be tested at what times. This process also specifically defines which systems should not be tested. This is an important step in healthcare, as care must be given to scanning clinical assets and systems connected to patients. Scoping conversations should always include key system owners and IT security specialists. A risk-based approach is used to make scoping decisions.

Performing the actual scan(s) comes next. All popular vulnerability scanning tools have comprehensive scheduling systems built in to make scheduling much simpler. These systems allow the analyst in charge of the program to set up scanning profiles for each type of scan that was determined during scoping. Often, it is preferred to organize assets to support reporting and/or risk concerns. Assets can be grouped by who manages them (in house/vendor) or by responsible group (server team/network team). They can be grouped by sensitivity (clinical/legacy/network), and for sensitive assets or at-risk assets, scans can be run using safer profiles to permit better observation and response if an incident occurs. After the analyst has developed or selected a preconfigured scanning profile, it is time to set up the scanning schedule. Scans can be accomplished automatically on a regularly recurring basis or performed manually on an as-needed basis. Again, careful consideration should be given to hospital operations to make sure that when scans are executed, staff is present to respond if needed.

Scanning tools have the ability to generate reports in multiple formats. Minimally, reports will list the systems scanned, the identified vulnerabilities, and severity ratings. The analyst should be prepared to generate an executive summary report for leadership and a detailed technical report for the system administrators, or owners, that will work to remediate the issues.

The most important aspect, besides the initial reporting of issues, is follow-up. This means that a system administrator or owner informs the scanning team or analyst that they have remediated the previously identified issues. At this point it is the responsibility of the vulnerability scanning analyst to scan that system again to ensure that the vulnerability is no longer present. If the scan reports that the vulnerability in question has been fixed, the vulnerability scanning analyst can sign off that the finding has been remediated.

Penetration Testing

Vulnerability scanning alone is not enough to protect an organization from attack. The next critical piece of a comprehensive technical security testing program is penetration testing. Penetration testing is a test of system or network vulnerabilities by authorized testers in which they attempt to break into the systems that are in scope. This is all done from the perspective of a malicious attacker, either from inside the network or external to the network.

Pentests typically begin with several simple network discovery scans and a vulnerability scan. The pentester will then manually verify any serious findings from the vulnerability scans. By doing this, the pentester is able to confirm the existence and exploitability of the vulnerability scanner's results. This enables the organization to better understand its security gaps and better prioritize remediation efforts based on likelihood and ease of exploiting those vulnerabilities.

The goal of pentesting is to emulate the activities of a malicious attacker. To help build in a level of consistency, several organizations have taken the time to develop in-depth pentesting frameworks. These frameworks ensure that testing and reporting follow a consistent process that is verifiable, thorough, and repeatable.

Depending on the target organization's regulatory requirements (i.e., PCI-DSS, HIPAA, Sarbanes-Oxley [SOX], etc.), there may be an annual pentest requirement. The specific framework for these tests is often prescribed. The two most common frameworks in use today are NIST Special Publication 800-115, "Technical Guide to Information Security Testing and Assessment," and the Penetration Testing Execution Standard (PTES). There are many other frameworks in existence, but the basic principles remain the same in all of them.

Both NIST 800-115 and PTES have a staged approach that follows a logical set of steps, with each step building on the previous steps. The PTES framework breaks down a typical pentest into seven phases, or stages, shown in Table 30-1.

Phase	Description
Pre-Engagement Interactions	Includes planning, scoping, etc.
Intelligence Gathering	Includes scanning, open source intelligence (OSINT) gathering, etc.
Threat Modeling	Determines potential threats in security posture
Vulnerability Analysis	Analyzes vulnerability scans and selects targets
Exploitation	Exploits discovered vulnerabilities to access target systems
Post-Exploitation	Includes privilege escalation, persistence, etc.
Reporting	Develops and delivers reports to subject of testing

Table 30-1   Seven Phases of the Penetration Testing Execution Standard (PTES) Framework

NIST 800-115 uses only four phases to present the penetration test: Planning, Discovery, Attack, and Reporting. However, all of the same actions are called for in both standards. NIST 800-115 combines the PTES Intelligence Gathering, Threat Modeling, and Vulnerability Analysis phases into the Discovery phase and combines the Exploitation and Post-Exploitation phases into the Attack phase.

There are hundreds of useful tools available to testers that vary greatly in scope, cost, and usefulness. Because of the nature of pentesting, and the hacking community it arose from, the vast majority of popular pentesting tools are open source and free to use.

Most pentesters use a particular Linux distribution called Kali Linux (https://www .kali.org), which is considered the gold standard in pentesting toolsets. This distribution is maintained and funded by Offensive Security (https://www.offensive-security.com/). Kali Linux comes with hundreds of open source tools preinstalled for almost any tester situation, and has hundreds more available for simple installation in the online repositories. There are entire books written about some of the individual tools in the Kali distribution and several books about Kali itself that cover the technical details of these tools.

The makers of Nmap, a very popular open source security tool, have developed a comprehensive list of the top 125 network security tools (www.sectools.org) that contains detailed information on each. Table 30-2 is a brief overview of five of the most commonly used network security tools available and includes links to additional information.

Tool	Description	URL
Metasploit	A framework for testing and exploiting systems	https://metasploit.com
Wireshark	Open source multiplatform network protocol analyzer	https://www.wireshark.org
Aircrack-ng	Suite of tools for 802.11 a/b/g WEP and WPA cracking	https://www.aircrack-ng.org
Netcat	Simple utility that reads and writes data across TCP and UDP connections	http://nc110.sourceforge.net
Burp Suite	Integrated platform for attacking web applications	https://portswigger.net/burp/

Table 30-2   Five of the Most Commonly Used Network Security Tools

Scoping a pentest is a little different from a vulnerability scan. In vulnerability scanning, the hostnames or IP addresses are populated in a database and scheduled to be scanned. The scanning itself is accomplished automatically. In pentesting, much of the process is completed manually, and as a result, each additional system added to the scope means additional hours the tester will need to expend. On the other hand, it is important to know that despite the time needed, the scope should be as broad as can be managed. By limiting the tester to fewer systems to test, the chances of their detecting a vulnerable system decreases.

It is also useful to remember that criminal attackers do not limit themselves with respect to scope or impacts, nor do they care about whatever policies are in place. They are breaking the law already, so they are not going to leave specific systems alone. If possible, the tester should be allowed to complete a full-scope test at least annually, meaning all systems owned and operated by the entity being tested should be in scope.

After the scope has been determined, the tester follows the steps laid out by the selected framework, starting with discovery. During discovery, the tester scans the in-scope networks and systems for live systems using a simple ping scan. Once the live systems on the network have been identified, the tester performs increasingly complex scans in order to gather as many details as possible about the targets. By the end of this phase, the tester should have a significant list of detailed information about the in-scope systems. These scans provide information such as IP addresses, hostnames, open ports, running services, operating systems, and so on.

The tester then compares what they have learned with a recent vulnerability scan report to identify the most likely targets for the exploitation phase. The exploitation phase begins with vulnerability verifications in which the tester attempts to exploit the vulnerabilities reported from the vulnerability scanner. As the tester moves through the verifications, often more potential targets and vulnerabilities are identified, which are run through the discovery phase again and moved back into the exploitation phase.

After exploitation is accomplished on the first set of systems, the tester begins post-exploitation activities. These typically include exfiltrating sensitive data, adding privileged user accounts, installing malware, and using other techniques to elevate their access and ensure they can get back in (persistence).

A pentesting report is similar to a vulnerability scan report in that it will also include discovered vulnerabilities, risk ratings, and remediation suggestions. The key difference is the analysis is performed by the tester, which provides additional insight into the security and vulnerabilities that no automated systems can match. In most cases the tester will provide the subject of the test with an executive report or presentation along with a detailed technical report for the system owners and administrators.

Red Teaming for Readiness

Another very effective set of activities that can be implemented to ensure an organization is ready for cyber incidents is a series of red-teaming activities such as cyber exercises, physical penetrations, social engineering, and phishing exercises. Each of these activities is designed to emulate an actual cyber threat experience. Red-teaming activities serve several very important purposes:

- They permit review of procedures, response times, coordination processes, team member knowledge, and so forth so that the organization can improve its performance.

- They permit learning from mistakes in a nonimpact environment so that teams can identify areas for advanced training.

- They increase familiarity and awareness among staff, which improve chances of success because staff and team members know what to expect.

Cyber exercises can be conducted as table top exercises, real-time exercises, or simulations. To be most helpful, they should be run at least twice a year. Social engineering tests and phishing exercises, which are really geared toward changing user behavior and elevating awareness of the threats, should be run more often, minimally quarterly, and should emulate actual attacker methods for both general and spear phishing types. Phishing is the number one security threat facing healthcare organizations, but only one-third of the organizations responding to a 2015 HIMSS survey considered themselves adequately trained to repel phishing attempts.[21] Anyone who responds to a phishing attempt should be directly immediately to training on what they did wrong and what they should look for in the future. This immediate feedback and refresher training is critical to achieving behavior modification. Physical penetrations can be run once or twice a year to test guards, access controls, surveillance, and so forth.

Chapter Review

This chapter covered a brief history of the changes in healthcare that have contributed to the current environment, the increase in cyber incidents, and factors that have made health information systems and patient information so attractive to the criminal element. It also explained how the healthcare information technology ecosystem has evolved to be more complex and sophisticated, adding further to the challenges in protecting health information. Since the rapid adoption of EHRs stimulated by the HITECH Act of 2009, the threat itself has also become more sophisticated and disruptive, increasingly more focused on the healthcare industry. More than 430 million new unique pieces of malware were released in 2015 and that number is expected to increase each year. The number of zero-day attacks also has risen significantly, rendering traditional signature-based security solutions all but obsolete. There has also been an escalation of targeted attacks that have disrupted services, resulting in millions of records compromised and patient safety put at risk. The types of actors who now target healthcare have also broadened from malicious insiders and cyberthieves focused mainly on fraud to state actors, cybercriminals, extortionists, and hacktivists. Healthcare organizations must increase the level of threat awareness across their workforce and implement technologies and services that provide actionable intelligence in a timely manner to aid risk avoidance and support quick response to cyber events. They should also take advantage of the abundant resources on cybersecurity threats that are made available by organizations such as NH-ISAC, US-CERT, and InfraGard (the FBI partnership).

PART VI

Organizations that use a security framework to guide their strategic plan improve their ability to build an effective cybersecurity program. The NIST CSF for healthcare was specifically developed to assist healthcare organizations in the implementation of best practices around data protection while meeting compliance objectives. Frameworks provide a common taxonomy for organizations to demonstrate their security compliance, implement continuous assessment against a standard, communicate both internally and externally on cyber readiness, and provide the structure for identifying a target end state with priorities to achieve the target end state.

Effectively combating cyber threats starts with laying a solid foundation that includes addressing the basics of network architecture, system administration, and maintenance. This includes establishing hardware and software refresh cycles to eliminate legacy or unsupported systems, and ensuring the network and systems are hardened appropriately and maintained through consistent patching, change control, and configuration management practices. It also includes ensuring adequate segmentation and restricting and protecting privileges. Elevated privileges should be eliminated, if possible, through vaulting, or at the very least encrypted in transmission and enabled by multifactor authentication.

Building a security architecture that is capable of meeting today's cyber threats requires addressing every layer of the enterprise, from the core out to the endpoints and third-party services such as Software as a Service (SaaS) via the cloud. It also requires an integrated mix of many different technologies and services that support each facet of the security framework from identification to response. In particular, organizations need to improve detection capabilities. The architecture needs to complement more traditional solutions like firewalls and antivirus with newer behavior analytic technologies like advanced malware solutions. Organizations need to improve audit and monitoring capabilities and consider seriously working with an MSSP to automate things like log management, IDS/IPS, and event correlation with SIEM.

After evaluating controls using a framework and implementing a secure architecture, organizations must be diligent in testing their security posture. Conducting risk analysis, performing security control audits, undergoing vulnerability and penetration testing, and conducting red-team efforts are all important to managing and reducing cybersecurity risks.

Questions

To test your comprehension of the chapter, answer the following questions and then check your answers against the list of correct answers that follows the questions.

1. The cyber threats facing healthcare today include which of the following?
    A. Extortion
    B. Hacktivism
    C. Espionage
    D. All the above

2. Which of the following is not typical of how external attacks are initiated?

   A. Phishing

   B. Social engineering

   C. Brute-force attack

   D. Water-cooler attack

3. The thing that makes ransomware particularly troublesome for healthcare is:

   A. It encrypts data

   B. It involves negotiating with an extortionist

   C. It undermines the health system's ability to provide care

   D. It only attacks health systems

4. While there are more physical thefts and loss of data events, hacking still represents the biggest risk because:

   A. It is the most damaging

   B. It represents the largest risk of compromised records

   C. It is conducted by cybercriminals

   D. It is bad for business

5. Using a framework like the NIST CSF provides which of the following benefits?

   A. A guideline for building and selecting controls

   B. A way of demonstrating compliance

   C. A way of communicating cyber readiness to business partners

   D. All of the above

6. Limiting access is a key component of preventing cyber events. Which of the following is not a recommended practice?

   A. Encrypting just elevated privileges

   B. Vaulting elevated privileges

   C. Applying additional authentication factors to privileges

   D. Encrypting all privileges

7. Most disruptive attacks that spread rapidly through an enterprise are aided greatly by a lack of _____.

   A. segmentation

   B. access control

   C. new hardware

   D. educated users

PART VI

8. Successfully monitoring and detection of cyber events in the future will likely involve which of the following?

   A. Use of advanced detection systems with behavioral-based approaches

   B. Advanced event correlation and analysis

   C. Partnering with a managed security service provider for expertise

   D. All the above

Answers

1. **D.** Healthcare organizations today face cyber threats in the form of extortion attempts, wholesale theft of data for espionage, as well as long-term exploitations and hacktivism when groups do not like positions that the organizations have taken on social issues.

2. **C.** Most hacking starts with social engineering, phishing, or water-cooler type attacks because they are easier and less risky.

3. **C.** Ransomware has become a very real threat to healthcare because it does affect directly healthcare's ability to deliver care by disrupting its systems, communications, and data.

4. **B.** Hacking as of 2015 now represents the greatest risk to patient information from a compromised records perspective. While physical theft and loss still account for the majority of events, hacking, by a wide margin, accounts for the greatest number of records compromised.

5. **D.** Using a framework like the NIST CSF provides many benefits, including a structure for selecting controls, a method of measuring maturity, and a way to demonstrate compliance or communicate security posture to others.

6. **A.** Encrypting all privileges, applying multifactor authentication, and vaulting elevated privileges are all recommended practices for limiting access, a key component of making the enterprise more resilient to threat. If hackers cannot get hold of privileges, their task of exploiting the enterprise is exponentially harder.

7. **A.** Lack of segmentation, typical of flat networks, is the biggest enabler of rapidly spreading viruses, ransomware, and other network attacks. Other factors contribute, of course, but lack of segmentation is the chief limiting factor in being able to stop the spread of an attack once it occurs.

8. **D.** Successful monitoring requires the integration of many systems, with advanced detection capabilities, and the use of advanced correlation and analysis tools like SIEM. This task, for most organizations, has grown too complex, and requires 365/24 coverage, which most cannot provide, making partnering with a managed security services provider (MSSP) necessary.

References

1. U.S. Department of Health and Human Services (HHS). (2009, Feb. 17). *HITECH Act: Enforcement interim final rule.* Accessed on August 15, 2016, from www.hhs.gov/hipaa/for-professionals/special-topics/HITECH-act-enforcement-interim-final-rule/index.html.

2. Ponemon Institute. (2016, June). *Cost of data breach study: Global analysis.* Sponsored by IBM. Accessed on August 15, 2016, from https://app .clickdimensions.com/blob/softchoicecom-anjf0/files/ponemon.pdf.

3. Abagnale, F. (1980). *Catch me if you can.* Grosset & Dunlap.

4. Farrell, M. B., & Wen, P. (2014). Hacker group anonymous targets Children's Hospital. *Boston Globe,* April 24. Accessed on August 15, 2016, from https:// www.bostonglobe.com/business/2014/04/24/hacker-group-anonymous-targets-children-hospital-over-justina-pelletier-case/jSd3EE5VVHbSGTJdS5YrfM/ story.html.

5. "Zack." (2016). Hurley Medical Center confirms "cyber-attack" as Anonymous hacking group threatens action over Flint water crisis. *Epoch Times,* January 22. Accessed on August 15, 2016, from www.theepochtimes.com/n3/1947837-hurley-medical-center-confirms-cyber-attack-as-anonymous-hacking-group-threatens-action-over-flint-water-crisis/.

6. Symantec. (2016, April). *Internet security threat report/healthcare, vol. 21.* Accessed on August 15, 2016, from https://www.symantec.com/content/dam/symantec/ docs/reports/istr-21-2016-en.pdf.

7. Symantec. (2017, April). *Internet security threat report/healthcare.*

8. Cybersecurity Information Sharing Act of 2015, 114th Cong., 1st Sess. (October 27, 2015). Accessed on August 15, 2016, from https://www.congress .gov/114/bills/s754/BILLS-114s754es.pdf.

9. Diamandes, P. (2015). My predictions for the next ten years. *Huffington Post,* May 6. Accessed on August 15, 2016, from www.huffingtonpost.com/peter-diamandis/the-next-10-my-prediction_b_7172978.html.

10. US-CERT. (n.d.). *Information sharing specifications for cybersecurity.* Accessed on August 9, 2016, from https://www.us-cert.gov/Information-Sharing-Specifications-Cybersecurity.

11. PhishMe. (2015). *Enterprise phishing susceptibility report.* Contributing analysis by University of Cambridge, London School of Economics and Political Science. Accessed on August 15, 2016, from https://ca.insight.com/content/dam/insight-web/Canada/PDF/partner/phishme/PhishMe-EnterprisePhishingSusceptibility.pdf.

12. Yaraghi, N. (2016, May). *Hackers, phishers, and disappearing thumb drives: Lessons learned from major health care data breaches.* Brookings Institution. Accessed on August 15, 2016, from https://www.brookings.edu/wp-content/uploads/2016/07/ Patient-Privacy504v3.pdf.

13. National Institute of Standards and Technology (NIST). (2014, Feb. 12). *Framework for improving critical infrastructure cybersecurity.* Accessed on August 15, 2016, from https://www.nist.gov/sites/default/files/documents/cyberframework/ cybersecurity-framework-021214.pdf.

14. Verizon. (2016). *Data breach investigations report.* Accessed on August 15, 2016, from www.verizonenterprise.com/resources/reports/rp_DBIR_2016_Report_en_ xg.pdf.

15. Forrester. (2016, July 7). The future of data security and privacy: Growth and competitive differentiation. In *The data security and privacy playbook for 2017.* Accessed on August 15, 2016, from https://www.forrester.com/report/The+Future+ Of+Data+Security+And+Privacy+Growth+And+Competitive+Differentiation/ -/E-RES61244.

16. SANS Institute. (2001). *Achieving defense-in-depth with internal firewalls.* Accessed on August 15, 2016, from https://www.sans.org/reading-room/ whitepapers/firewalls/achieving-defense-in-depth-internal-firewalls-797.

17. McDonald, N. (2011). Static or dynamic application security testing? Both! *Gartner Blog Network,* January 19. Accessed on August 15, 2016, from http:// blogs.gartner.com/neil_macdonald/2011/01/19/static-or-dynamic-application- security-testing-both/.

18. Ashford, W. (2016). IoT to play a part in more than a quarter of cyber attacks by 2020, says Gartner. *ComputerWeekly.com,* April 25. Accessed on August 15, 2016, from www.computerweekly.com/news/450288414/IoT-to-play-a-part-in-more- than-a-quarter-of-cyber-attacks-by-2020-says-Gartner.

19. Finn, D. (2016). The future of information security in healthcare. In D. Garets & C. M. Garets (Eds.), *The journey never ends: Technology's role in helping perfect health care outcomes.* Boca Raton, FL: CRC Press for HIMSS Media.

20. SANS Institute. (2003). *Vulnerabilities and vulnerability scanning.* Accessed on August 15, 2016, from https://www.sans.org/reading-room/whitepapers/threats/ vulnerabilities-vulnerability-scanning-1195.

21. Healthcare Information and Management Systems Society (HIMSS). (2015, June 30). *Cybersecurity survey.* Accessed on August 15, 2016, from www.himss.org/2015-cybersecurity-survey.

Cybersecurity Considerations for Medical Devices

Axel Wirth

In this chapter, you will learn how to
- Understand the fundamental security problems of the medical device ecosystem and its vulnerabilities
- Describe how these vulnerabilities translate to a variety of risks, including risks to patient safety and care delivery
- Explain how regulators and security specialists are starting to address these problems
- Describe what device manufacturers and healthcare organizations can do to minimize the risk of harm or impact to their business

Medical Device Cybersecurity and Cybersafety: An Introduction

Many IT professionals regard implementing good cybersecurity in healthcare to be more challenging than in other industries because of the complexity of healthcare workflows and supporting IT systems as well as the potential of security measures conflicting with care delivery, which often requires immediate and easy access to information. Further, healthcare is a highly regulated industry, so healthcare organizations tend to be very conservative and careful about implementing change. Although this approach is understandable, it also, unfortunately, has the potential of conflicting with the nimble approach required to maintain an up-to-date security posture and adapt to today's ever-evolving cyberthreats and attack strategies.[1]

Ever since clinicians, physicists, and engineers began to apply technology to improve diagnosis and treatment of patients,[2] medical devices have become an integral part of our healthcare delivery system, improving diagnoses and extending lives. They form a complex and sensitive ecosystem of networked devices and integrated workflows, supporting all aspects of care delivery. However, in the twenty-first century, cybersecurity of networked medical devices and the resulting risks to patient safety have become a serious concern.

This unique security challenge has developed for a number of reasons:

- Increasingly, medical devices are interconnected via standard IT networks and supported by common IT components like servers and workstations. This interconnectivity provides cost savings through staff efficiency and improves the reliability of data capture, but it also introduces cybersecurity risks that devices were previously not exposed to.

- Medical devices are strictly regulated (for example, through the Food and Drug Administration [FDA] in the United States), traditionally prioritizing a controlled engineering processes, formal testing, and well-documented market release and approval for the benefit of device safety over flexibility to address cybersecurity.

- As a result of regulation, manufacturers are often slow to release security patches or updates, and hospitals cannot deploy them or other security measures (e.g., after-market security software) without approval by the manufacturer.

- Because medical devices have a long useful product life, many systems still in operation were not designed with today's sophisticated and rapidly developing threats in mind.

- The number of devices, suppliers, and platforms is typically larger than in the traditional IT environment, making complexity part of the challenge.

- Security responsibility for devices, from purchasing to maintenance to end-of-life (EOL) disposal, is often unclear or may be separated between Clinical Engineering (CE) and IT Security departments.

All of these factors have resulted in a typically low security maturity of the individual device and a poor security posture of the integrated device networks in hospitals.

To compound the problem further, the potential damage that could result from a medical device cybersecurity incident is much higher than that of a traditional IT security incident. Although both can impact hospital operations and care delivery, a medical device event has the potential of directly harming a patient. Although not all devices are life critical or life sustaining, even the shutdown of devices in a cardiac catheterization lab (cath lab) through a computer worm,[3] for example, will delay diagnosis and be a risk to cardiac emergency patients.

As we review the challenges that exist around securing medical devices, we need to be aware of three main aspects:

- The easily exploitable vulnerability and low security posture of today's medical device ecosystem

- The resulting high risk to patient safety and care delivery

- Due to practical, economic, and regulatory limitations, the fact that the complete replacement of existing devices with modern, more secure ones will take time

The risks are real, and although there is no need to panic, we should proceed with a sense of urgency—and there are things that we can and should do now.

Medical Device Vulnerabilities and Risks: A Review

At the time of this writing, there have been no reported incidents of patient harm caused by a medical device cybersecurity incident. However, many critical device vulnerabilities have been documented by security researchers and many incidents of operational and care delivery impact have been reported by healthcare providers. Some examples include the following:

- Security researchers demonstrated that they can crack the proprietary communication of implantable medical devices and reprogram them; e.g., vulnerabilities have been found in pacemakers and implantable cardiac defibrillators[4] and insulin pumps.[5]

- In 2013, ICS-CERT (Industrial Control System Cyber Emergency Response Team within the Department of Homeland Security) issued a security alert reported to them by security researchers Billy Rios and Terry McCorkle about design vulnerabilities in 300 medical devices across approximately 40 vendors; e.g., prevalent design vulnerabilities like the use of default or even hardcoded passwords.[6] Many other ICS-CERT medical device–specific warnings have followed since.

- The ability of healthcare facilities to deliver care and clinical services is impacted due to devices being compromised by malware and computer worms (like Conficker), exploiting vulnerabilities of commercial operating systems in medical devices. Reported cases include the shutdown of a VA hospital's catheterization laboratory in New Jersey in 2010, requiring rerouting of cardiac emergency patients[3] and a malware infection of medication cabinets across multiple locations, requiring shutdown of devices and manual medication management (personally reported to the author in 2009).

- Several organizations—for example, the Mayo Clinic—have performed targeted testing on networked medical devices, all with very concerning results, showing a prevalence of vulnerabilities across a variety of devices.[7]

- Patients have been able to obtain the password of a patient-controlled analgesia (PCA) pump and increase the dosage of pain medication above the pump's safety limit, resulting in respiratory arrest of one of the patients.[8]

- Security researchers at TrapX[9, 10] and Protiviti[11] demonstrated that medical devices are actively being targeted and exploited. It is believed that they are not the primary targets but are being targeted because they are an easy entry point for a network attack and an excellent hiding point for attack-supporting malware.

There is plenty of other evidence that medical devices have significant vulnerabilities that could be maliciously exploited. To add to the concerns, in general cyberattacks have

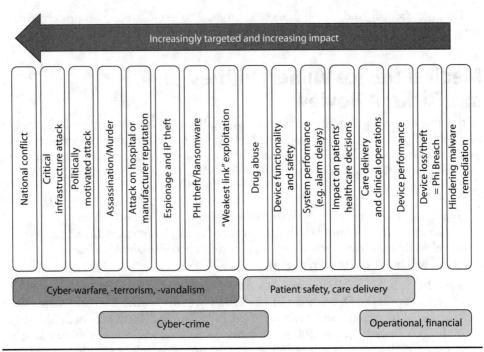

Figure 31-1 Medical device risk spectrum and implications

become increasingly targeted and sophisticated and are being performed by financially motivated criminal gangs and by well-funded and politically motivated cyberarmies and cyberterrorists. This leads to a broad spectrum of possible risks and resulting impacts ranging from harmless nuisances to catastrophic events. On the most serious end of the spectrum, devices could be targeted in nation-state conflicts and cyberwarfare attacks on our critical infrastructure. On the other, more benign end of the spectrum, attackers could hide malware in medical devices to make remediation more difficult. Figure 31-1 depicts the broad spectrum of possible scenarios and underlying implications.

We also need to differentiate between two types of attack: a targeted attack (e.g., the intent to do harm) or an opportunistic attack or coincidental malware outbreak (e.g., compromising a medical device not because of what it is but because it fits an attack profile and is an easy entry point).

Although to date there has not been a report of a targeted attack on medical devices with the intent to do harm, should this occur, the consequences could be severe and far reaching, including, for example, patients rejecting device-based treatment options based on news headlines. As discussed above, today's problems are of a coincidental or indirect nature leading to IT and care delivery interruptions. As we develop our defensive strategies, we need to do so in consideration of both scenarios.

The main risk scenarios can be summarized as follows:

- Patient harm as a direct result of a targeted attack
- Patient harm as an indirect result of compromised device performance or functionality directly resulting from a coincidental attack or malware outbreak

- Care delivery and operational impact due to device or network compromise, requiring reduction in or shutdown of certain clinical services
- Privacy breach and exposure of data due to device hack or compromise, loss or theft of device, or improperly disposed device

The following are secondary consequences of patient harm, privacy breach, or operational impact:

- Damage to reputation of healthcare provider or device manufacturer
- Revenue loss and financial impact due to service shutdown, lawsuits, and fines
- Remediation costs due to overtime, IT services, notifications, etc.
- Security compromise and exploitation of the device as an entry or hiding point for an attack on other systems, such as the EHR system (patient record theft) or business systems (financial theft)

Medical device security is, as stated initially, a highly complex problem with many moving pieces and interdependencies.

Medical Device Regulation: Impact on Cybersecurity

As mentioned before, one specific issue impacting medical devices is their regulated nature. This section will examine in more detail how regulations impact device security, but also how regulators are responding to this challenge with changing guidance.

Regulatory Background

All developed countries have some framework for regulating medical devices to assure their safety and effectiveness. Most countries take a somewhat similar approach to how pharmaceuticals are regulated. In the United States, for example, the FDA provides the regulatory framework for device manufacturers and importers through its Center for Devices and Radiological Health (CDRH), which "is responsible for regulating firms who manufacture, repackage, relabel, and/or import medical devices sold in the United States." CDRH also regulates radiation-emitting electronic products such as lasers, X-ray systems, and ultrasound equipment.[12]

The overall approach is to impose formal regulatory controls to govern engineering, manufacturing, and marketing processes, either in general (e.g., for manufacturing facilities and processes) or for each individual device (e.g., formal validation and verification testing to assure the device's "safety and effectiveness" relative to its "intended use"). This approach is intended to assure that all aspects of the device are safe: everything from handling and sterilization to mechanical, radiation, or electrical safety—including the safety of device software.

The degree of regulatory controls applied varies depending on the risk to the patient in case of device failure. For example, the risk of an electronic thermometer harming a patient is much lower than that of a proton therapy system harming a patient.

PART VI

Therefore, devices are classified into low, medium, and high risk categories (Class I, II, and III, respectively, in FDA terminology), with increasing level of regulatory controls for devices in the higher classes. For example, the FDA requires device manufacturers to file a so-called 510(k) Premarket Notification for Class I and II devices (unless the device type is considered low risk and is explicitly exempt) or to file for a more extensive Premarket Approval (PMA) for Class III devices.

Because this classification process applies to the entire device, it has had significant impact on management of a device's software, including any commercial off-the-shelf (COTS) software (e.g., the operating system) or open source software. Although the FDA has repeatedly stated that software updates or patches for the sole purpose of addressing cybersecurity do not require filing notice with or approval by the agency,[13] the manufacturer still needs to undertake formal testing and release of a device update or patch to assure that device safety is not compromised.[14] This is, in general, governed by the FDA's Quality System Regulation, also called Good Manufacturing Practices as defined under 21 CFR part 820.

Although this test-and-release approach is advisable from a general product safety perspective, unfortunately it has hindered the execution of nimble and good cybersecurity practices in the following respects:

- The formal testing performed by the manufacturer defines an approved configuration (including software version) of the device. As a consequence, the operator (i.e., the hospital) typically cannot install aftermarket security solutions (e.g., antimalware), nor apply patches (e.g., to the operating system) that are not approved by the manufacturer. In the FDA's view, "it is rare for healthcare organizations to have enough technical resources and information on the design of medical devices to independently maintain medical device software." However, organizations could issue simple patches or updates if they are willing to assume the risk.[15] It is, in the end, a tradeoff decision between the risk of the patch and the risk of the unpatched vulnerability.

- There are practical and economic limitations on how often a manufacturer can release updates and patches. Although this depends on device complexity, the quality of the manufacturer's engineering and release processes, and the overall device architecture, most manufacturers release only a few security updates per year—leaving significant security gaps between patches.

One common concern voiced by healthcare providers is that manufacturers may not release any patches at all, citing a misinterpretation of the FDA requirements, and using it as an excuse (intentionally or not) to defend poor patch release and lifecycle management practices. However, the FDA has repeatedly clarified that timely patching of device software is not only permitted, but is desired to minimize safety risks due to security vulnerabilities.

But the issue of delayed patching is not limited to the manufacturer alone. Once a patch has been released, it still needs to be deployed in the hospital environment, which typically requires careful analysis and change management beforehand so that the deployment does not interfere with care delivery and is properly synchronized between dependent devices or devices and, for example, backend servers. This adds additional time to the deployment of a security upgrade, and it is not uncommon to see a delay of months, or in extreme cases even a few years, between the release of a patch by the software manufacturer, through approval by the device vendor, to actual implementation by the hospital.

It must be understood that although timely patching is a critical security strategy, it is not the only one and should always be applied in conjunction with other security technologies and measures, as will be discussed later. For more information, medical device patching has been discussed in more detail elsewhere.[16]

Of specific concern are legacy medical devices with operating systems (or other software components) that are no longer supported by the original manufacturer, and for which security patches are no longer produced. Short of replacing the device, which may be cost-prohibitive, a hospital needs to rely on security measures outside of the device, such as network isolation.

In a sense and unintentionally, regulations have contributed to the fact that today's medical devices are insecure and cannot be as easily protected through common security measures like customer-installed security software or timely patching.

Changes in the Regulatory Landscape

The previously discussed challenges regarding medical device vulnerabilities are well understood by all stakeholders, including regulators. This understanding includes the realization that the historic focus on strict regulatory controls on one hand and the growing cyber risks on the other have created a new type of safety risk due to exploitable software flaws.

In the United States, the FDA has taken the lead in addressing this problem. For now, the FDA's approach is one of providing guidance to the industry and encouraging a collaborative approach between stakeholders. The FDA recognizes that trying to force the issue with a strong regulatory arm at this juncture would be difficult because it could lead to lack of cooperation and coordination around cyber risks, and could potentially even have an impact on device availability and, consequently, treatment options, as some manufacturers could decide to exit a certain business rather than spend the effort of upgrading or redesigning insecure legacy devices.

Similarly, on the healthcare provider side, there are practical and economic limitations on how fast existing devices can be upgraded or replaced with more secure devices.

The FDA's approach is, of course, based on today's knowledge about and view of device security risks. Should there be an actual patient safety incident, or should progress of improving device security be too slow, it is entirely possible that we will see faster action and stricter regulatory enforcement.

To date, the FDA has issued two guidance documents specific to cybersecurity and intended for the medical device industry. The first is "Content of Premarket Submissions for Management of Cybersecurity in Medical Devices" (Oct. 2, 2014),[17] which addresses the key cybersecurity functions to consider during device design and release:

- Identify and protect:
  - Limit access to trusted users (e.g., no common or hardcoded passwords)
  - Ensure trusted content (providing and securely updating software)
- Detect, respond, recover:
  - Implement features that enable users to detect, recognize, log, and act upon cybersecurity incidents
  - Recommend actions to be taken by the user upon detection of a cybersecurity incident
  - Implement features that protect critical functionality
  - Provide methods for recovery of device configuration

The 2014 guidance recommends manufacturers include the following types of information in the cybersecurity documentation that they provide as part of their premarket submission to the FDA:

- Hazard analysis, mitigation, and design considerations pertaining to intentional and unintentional cybersecurity risks associated with a device
- Traceability matrix (mapping cybersecurity controls to risks)
- Update and patch management plans
- Summary of software integrity assurance controls
- Recommended security controls appropriate for the intended use

The second guidance issued by the FDA is "Postmarket Management of Cybersecurity in Medical Devices" (Dec. 28, 2016),[18] which addresses the key aspects of device security maintenance once a device is in the market. Some of the important points include the following:

- Emphasizes that cybersecurity risk management is a shared responsibility among all the stakeholders
- Strongly recommends participation in an Information Sharing Analysis Organization (ISAO):
  - Multistakeholder model
  - Voluntary, but actionable, transparent, and trusted
  - Information shielded from release, exempt from regulatory use and civil litigation
  - Critical component of a comprehensive approach to cybersecurity
- Introduces the concept of "essential performance":
  - Assure freedom from unacceptable risk

- Provides recommendations on cybersecurity routine patches and updates:
  - Generally not required to be reported to the FDA
  - Reporting required for rare actions that pose serious adverse health consequences or unacceptable residual risk
- Provides other key manufacturer guidance on topics such as the following:
  - Threat and incident monitoring
  - Vulnerability disclosure policy
  - Receipt and processing of vulnerability reports
  - Good cyber hygiene practice

The preceding information is only a summary of the two guidance documents. For actual regulatory and legal decision making, you should refer to the latest release of the actual documents.

Obviously, both guidance documents are targeted at the medical device manufacturer, but both, and especially the postmarket guidance document, contain significant recommendations that can help healthcare providers articulate their security requirements and establish formal engagement with the device manufacturer on security topics.

Concerns around medical device cybersecurity are not limited to just the device manufacturer and healthcare provider. In fact, many aspects of this problem are of larger, socio-economic and even political concern. Therefore, the FDA's efforts are being supported by other government entities looking at the problem from their respective perspectives, including (among others):

- The White House (critical infrastructure security under the Cybersecurity National Action Plan)
- Homeland Security (national security)
- The FBI (crime prevention)
- Federal Trade Commission (consumer protection)
- Federal Communications Commission (wireless reliability)

At the time of this writing, little has been published on activities by other, non-U.S. regulators. Regulators in other countries are closely watching the development in the United States and the FDA's approach.

Implementing Medical Device Cybersecurity

Although there are multiple dimensions of complexity to the medical device security problem, there is a path forward that can be taken by the respective stakeholders as will be discussed in this section.

A Shared Responsibility

Solving the challenge of securing the medical device ecosystem is not a simple task, and will require a multiyear effort of implementing complex change and targeted improvement. This effort must be carried forward by all stakeholders together, primarily by regulators, manufacturers, healthcare providers, and security specialists, but also with the support of IT system integrators, healthcare IT developers, and IT vendors.

Further, as illustrated in Figure 31-2, the applicable solutions vary depending on which aspect of the problem is being addressed, which in turn defines the responsibilities of the manufacturer (solutions that need to be designed into the device) and the healthcare organization (solutions that help manage and minimize the security risks of the integrated system of devices).

Although all stakeholders share the underlying problem of securing the medical device ecosystem, they contribute different aspects of the solution. It will take time to upgrade the inventory of relatively insecure devices, and even then it would not be advisable to rely just on the device for defense. Modern attacks are so sophisticated that they require what in security is commonly referred to as "defense in depth," which means defending all aspects of the infrastructure.

Essentially, stakeholders need to address the four tenants of cybersecurity:

- Protect the device (and its data)
- Protect the ecosystem
- Manage the device
- Respond to and manage incidents

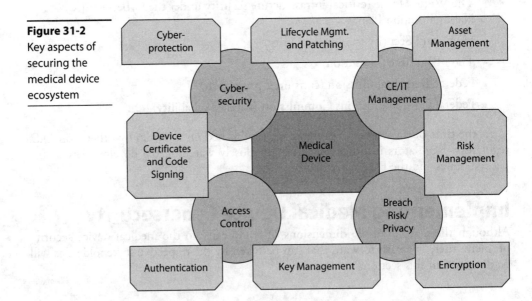

Figure 31-2 Key aspects of securing the medical device ecosystem

A variety of cybersecurity measures can be applied by medical device manufacturers and healthcare providers to achieve these tenants. Manufacturers can improve device security through the process-based measures presented in Table 31-1 and the technical measures presented in Table 31-2, and healthcare providers can improve the security posture of their device networks and operations through the process-based measures presented in Table 31-3 and the technical measures presented in Table 31-4. More detailed information on security best practices specific to medical devices has been provided elsewhere.[19]

A detailed approach and guidance for healthcare providers on how to implement risk management for networked medical devices is provided through the ISO/IEC 80001 series of standards.[21] An example on how to approach medical device network segregation is provided by the U.S. Department of Veterans Affairs' "Medical Device Isolation Architecture Guide."[22]

Risk Analysis, Assessment, and Management: Laying the Foundation

Risk analysis (analyzing threats relative to an organization's or system's vulnerabilities) and risk assessment (assigning values to risks based on impact and likelihood, providing a metric of potential consequences for the purpose of informed decision making and prioritization of countermeasures) are the foundations for a successful risk management

Measure	Description
Security education and awareness	Assure that all decision makers from engineering to field service are up to date in their security knowledge; continually educate to stay current with the developing threat landscape.
Threat awareness and monitoring	Consume threat intelligence to monitor trends in the threat landscape; analyze for relevance to the solutions and customer base.
Vulnerability reporting and disclosure	Establish capability to • Consume vulnerability reports from external sources (CERTs, security research, customers). • Maintain up-to-date communication with the customer base on newly discovered vulnerabilities; provide guidance on mitigation.
Lifecycle management and customer communication	Provide timely • Updates on vulnerabilities and threats. • Communication of mitigation and patch availability.
Document device security properties	Describe device IT and security properties as provided, for example, through the Manufacturer Disclosure Statement for Medical Device Security (MDS²) form.[20]
Regulatory compliance	Comply with FDA (or other international) regulatory requirements (Quality Systems Regulations, as discussed earlier) and specifically guidance provided on pre- and post-market cybersecurity.

Table 31-1 Manufacturer Approach: Process-Based Cybersecurity Measures

Measure	Description
Protect IT infrastructure	Protect and secure internal IT infrastructure to • Protect intellectual property. • Assure manufacturing and support infrastructure integrity.
System hardening	Follow COTS manufacturer guidance on software security best practices (e.g., Microsoft, Oracle, etc.).
Software design best practices	Establish best practices based on available guidelines (e.g., Defense Systems Information Agency [DISA], NIST, Center for Internet Security [CIS]) to minimize vulnerability exposure and attack surface.
Host intrusion detection/prevention system (HIDS/HIPS)	Protect commercial OS platforms, applications, and critical data through signature-less security technology: whitelisting, behavior control, and sandboxing.
Code signing/boot verification	Assure that only signed code can be installed and that the boot firmware is authentic.
Strong authentication	Although not always practical for clinical users, service technicians should always be required to authenticate securely (e.g., via two factor), especially for remote access, since they typically access systems at a higher level of privilege.

Table 31-2 Manufacturer Approach: Technical Cybersecurity Measures

Measure	Description
Procurement	Include device security requirements in the purchasing process (Request for Information/Proposal [RFI/RFP], contracts) and define manufacturer security obligation (e.g., patch availability, vulnerability communication, incident response support).
Asset management	Assure complete asset inventory of medical devices, including device security and IT properties; track device configuration including patch level.
Risk analysis	Provide risk score for each device type based on • Security properties/vulnerabilities. • Use case and risk to patient safety. • Other impact (operations, revenue, reputation).
Risk management and mitigation	Remediate or mitigate risks through appropriate measures (e.g., device upgrade, network segregation, and handling).
Device handling	Assure that all device handling processes are inclusive of security (e.g., new device purchase, device EOL).
Address specific device handling use cases	For example: • Control removable media use as this is a common malware infection vector. • Address high-risk use scenarios, such as leased devices and demo equipment. • Establish processes to remove electronic protected health information (ePHI) from devices at their EOL or when leaving the facility (e.g., for repair).

Table 31-3 Healthcare Provider Approach: Process-Based Cybersecurity Measures

Measure	Description
Incident response planning	Assure that the security incident response planning is inclusive of medical devices (e.g., decision making on care delivery in case of a device compromise). A good incident response plan should define responsibilities as well as a standardized process to guide through recovery and restoration, forensics, and postmortem. It should not just be internal focused but should also define external activities (e.g., press release, reporting, vendor engagement, etc.). Specifically, the postmortem should include an analysis of how the incident occurred and what updates should be made to prevent (or at least reduce the impact of) such an incident in the future.

Table 31-3 Healthcare Provider Approach: Process-Based Cybersecurity Measures (*continued*)

Measure	Description
Network segregation	Use network segregation technology (e.g., virtual local area network [VLAN], software-defined networking [SDN]) to reduce threat exposure and to contain impact should a compromise occur.
Network-based security	Use network-based security technology (e.g., security gateway) to detect external attacks or suspicious network traffic generating from the inside (e.g., by an infected device).
Security event monitoring	Monitor devices, network, and egress points (gateways, firewalls) for security events.
Device patching	Maintain latest device patch level based on manufacturer communication; assure timely deployment of patches.

Table 31-4 Healthcare Provider Approach: Technical Cybersecurity Measures

program (the continual application of policies, procedures, and practices to identify, analyze, assess, and communicate risk) and enable risk mitigation (reduction of potential adverse effects) based on business objectives.

A good risk management program should look at all possible risks, and should reduce the potential impact based on likelihood (probability of occurrence) and potential impact (harm). The practice of risk management is not unique to IT, and is used for anything from managing business risks to the risk of natural disasters to risks to human health (e.g., through an adverse event of a medical device, be it cybersecurity related or another form of device failure).

Healthcare providers typically use the risk management processes not only to address regulatory and legal requirements, but also to reduce security risks to their sensitive data housed in their IT infrastructure. Similarly, medical device manufacturers use a risk analysis approach (usually referred to as hazard analysis) to minimize the potential harm to patients. The difference between the two is that a healthcare provider performs a risk analysis based on their actual implementation and larger ecosystem, whereas a

PART VI

device manufacturer tries to mitigate risks to their individual devices for all use cases and through design, testing, documentation, and communication.

Although risk management is a well-established methodology to help organizations reduce risk, numerous problems often occur in the process. Too many risk analyses remain abstract exercises that take a checklist approach and fail to address real-life uses and risks. This results in shortcomings such as

- The risk assessment is performed against incomplete inventory.
- It is incomplete and does not cover all use cases and workflows.
- It may address regulatory compliance requirements (e.g., HIPAA), but not actual security risks.
- It is performed based on a fixed schedule (e.g., annually) rather than actual need.
- An organization performs multiple analyses addressing different areas of focus or meeting different needs, yet fails to align them, resulting in gaps, overlap, and conflict.
- It is not updated as business, technology, processes, or cyberthreats change.
- Periodic analyses are inconsistent and do not allow tracking relative to previous assessments.
- It fails to keep up with technological advances like cloud-based data storage, mobile devices, or social media.

Especially in the medical device space, these types of problems are commonplace. Many organizations perform a risk assessment for their IT environment but fail to include medical devices, even though HIPAA requires that any device containing ePHI is to be included. Alternatively, an organization may assess medical equipment safety as required by the Joint Commission but fail to include cybersecurity risks.

Often, these gaps start with the regulations. To take a simple example, a digital X-ray system may store patient data (orders, images, etc.) that would be regulated under HIPAA, but it also contains critical system data (e.g., calibration) that would be a radiation safety concern from the FDA perspective. This simple example shows how healthcare providers are challenged to meet multiple requirements and may choose to perform multiple risk analyses—or, a single but more complex process that encompasses all. The latter is obviously preferred but also more complex and challenging.

The complexity in the medical device space is significant. Commonly, hospitals have more medical devices to manage than they have regular IT components. Furthermore, the device ecosystem is more diverse and includes different types of systems from many different vendors and, consequently, of very differing levels of security maturity. A medical device risk management process must account for this complexity as well as for the challenges of managing and maintaining life-critical devices in a 24/7 operating environment.

Although healthcare providers should not install security measures without manufacturer approval, they can improve their device integration and management processes to

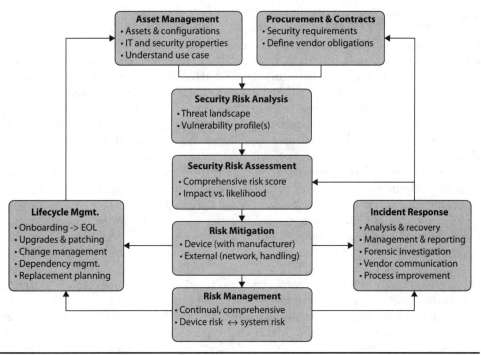

Figure 31-3 Medical device risk management framework overview

minimize their security risks. As illustrated in Figure 31-3, a medical device–specific risk management process has to be

- **Comprehensive** Starting with procurement and specification of security requirements and ending with device EOL (removal of sensitive data and network credentials).

- **Vendor-inclusive** Define security requirements and vendor obligations; include the vendor in incident response and other relevant analysis and findings.

- **Complete** Include all devices, use scenarios, and dependencies between devices and IT components.

- **Manageable** In light of the previously mentioned complexity, automation and tools are likely required to make a medical device risk management program manageable and maintainable. Although some tasks may still require manual execution (e.g., patching, as previously discussed), the processes and management of these tasks can be automated, leading to more efficient and reliable execution of the overall processes.

This approach is very much in line with the previously described four tenants of cybersecurity: protect the device (and its data), protect the ecosystem, manage the device, and respond to and manage incidents.

Chapter Review

Unlike in the traditional healthcare IT security environment where the focus is on information protection (as stipulated by the HIPAA Security Rule), in the medical device environment the focus is on safety, functionality, reliability, and operational availability. Although there are data concerns in the device space as well (e.g., a change in dosage at an infusion pump), the situation is really much more complex and sensitive, requiring a comprehensive view and understanding of the medical device security problem and related risks. A path forward has been established through regulatory guidance and by thought-leading device manufacturers and healthcare providers.

It is now up to the larger healthcare community to articulate and fine-tune an approach to collectively move forward and solve this problem as fast as possible—but without compromising the critical function that medical devices perform.

This chapter has mainly focused on discussing cybersecurity in the context of traditional, hospital-based equipment. As our care-delivery models change and as new technologies enable remote and mobile monitoring of patients' conditions, care providers can now manage chronic diseases in patients' homes, and we need to be equally concerned about cybersecurity in an even more complex ecosystem that includes personal devices, like smartphones, and public networks.

It is clear that in either case, traditional care delivery or home care equipment, we need to recognize the cybersecurity and privacy challenges and move forward with determination and a sense of urgency. Our healthcare delivery system, including the medical device ecosystem, is part of our national critical infrastructure and is exposed to the same cyber risks. However, it is woefully behind in security and implementing change.

Developing a more security-resilient approach will require overcoming systemic latency, but we have to do our best and do it soon because bad actors are creative and persistent in their approach and attacks are growing in volume and sophistication.[23] In addition, we need to be prepared in the event that a potential patient safety incident results in complex consequences.

Questions

To test your comprehension of the chapter, answer the following questions and then check your answers against the list of correct answers that follows the questions.

1. Which U.S. government agency regulates the release of medical devices and assures their safety and effectiveness?

    A. FTC

    B. FDA

    C. DHS

    D. FCC

2. What is the purpose of the FDA premarket and postmarket cybersecurity guidance documents pertaining to medical devices?

   A. They inform medical device manufacturers about expected future regulations.

   B. They define what hospitals should consider when they buy a new device as well as when they discard a device at the end of its useful life.

   C. They define what security requirements manufacturers need to meet for a device in clinical trials.

   D. They provide guidance on device manufacturers' cybersecurity responsibilities prior to market release and after market release of a medical device.

3. Why are medical devices' software patch levels difficult to keep up to date?

   A. Because of the devices' critical patient care role.

   B. Because the impact of a patch on cybersecurity is difficult to predict.

   C. Because a new patch requires a new regulatory filing.

   D. Because a new patch requires manufacturer testing and approval.

4. Are medical devices at risk of a malicious cyberattack?

   A. No, because they typically are not connected to an open network.

   B. Yes, because of their many software vulnerabilities.

   C. No, because even hackers would not stoop that low.

   D. Yes, but such an attack is highly unlikely.

5. What are the typical parts of a comprehensive security risk management program?

   A. Risk definition, assessment, and mitigation

   B. Vulnerability, threat, and impact analysis

   C. Replacement cost versus remaining life expectancy

   D. Risk analysis, assessment, and mitigation

6. What is incident response planning?

   A. Good business management practice.

   B. A process approach to prepare for an incident (e.g., a cybersecurity event) that defines responsibilities and the appropriate action to be taken.

   C. A best practice to make sure patients do not become aware if something goes wrong.

   D. A replacement strategy for medical devices as they may fail and need to be replaced.

7. What can hospitals do to protect their medical devices from cybersecurity risks?

    A. Buy only secure devices.

    B. Make sure that devices are always password protected.

    C. Nothing, because regulations prevent them from doing anything.

    D. Network segregation architecture, network-based security, security event monitoring, and device patching.

8. Is the long useful life of medical devices a security concern?

    A. Yes, because older devices were not designed with today's threats in mind.

    B. No, because devices get updated on a regular basis.

    C. Yes, because software tends to become unreliable over time.

    D. No, because they are designed for robustness and safety.

Answers

1. **B.** The U.S. Food and Drug Administration (FDA) regulates firms who manufacture, repackage, relabel, and/or import medical devices sold in the United States through its Center for Devices and Radiological Health (CDRH).

2. **D.** The FDA's premarket (October 2014) and postmarket (December 2016) guidance documents lay out the agency's interpretation of existing regulation with regard to medical device manufacturers' cybersecurity responsibilities as they release a new product to the market (premarket) and maintain its security posture once it is released and in use (postmarket).

3. **D.** Under FDA guidance, as long as a patch or update does not change a device's functionality or intended use, in most cases the device manufacturer is not required to update its regulatory filing. However, under the Quality Systems Regulation, the patch or update still needs to be approved by the manufacturer and undergo formal testing to assure system safety has not been compromised. This adds cost and overhead to each release, which makes it difficult to provide timely and frequent security patches.

4. **B.** Security researchers, healthcare providers, and government agencies have conducted medical device security testing and demonstrated vast vulnerability due to poor security design practices.

5. **D.** A complete and comprehensive risk management program should include the steps of risk analysis (threats, vulnerabilities), risk assessment (likelihood, impact), and risk mitigation (reducing risk through technical or administrative controls or financial protection such as insurance). Note that acceptance of risk is also a possible outcome, but should always be supported by a conscious decision process and an understanding of the possible impact.

6. B. A good incident response plan should define responsibilities as well as a standardized process to guide through incident recovery and restoration, forensics, and postmortem. It should not just be internal-focused but also define external activities.

7. D. Although hospitals are typically prevented from making changes to the actual devices without manufacturer approval, they can improve their devices' security posture through network segregation architecture, network-based security and event monitoring, secure handling, and configuration maintenance (including patching).

8. A. Medical devices often have a useful life of ten years or even longer. As a consequence, older devices were not designed with knowledge of today's cybersecurity threat vectors. Another concern is that older devices may include software components that are no longer supported with security patches.

References

1. Independent Security Evaluators. (2016, Feb. 23). *Securing hospitals: A research study and blueprint.* Accessed on August 23, 2016, from https://securityevaluators .com/hospitalhack/securing_hospitals.pdf.

2. Röntgen, W. C. (1895, December). Über eine neue Art von Strahlen [On a new kind of rays]. In *Sitzungsberichte der Würzburger Physik.-medic Gesellschaft* (pp. 137–147). Braunschweig: Friedrich Vieweg und Sohn. Translated by Arthur Stanton in *Nature, 53,* 274–276 (1896), available at www.nature.com/physics/ looking-back/roentgen/index.html.

3. Weaver, C. (2013, June 13). Patients put at risk by computer viruses. *Wall Street Journal.* Accessed on August 23, 2016, from www.wsj.com/articles/SB100014241 27887324188604578543162744943762.

4. Halperin, D., Heydt-Benjamin, T. S., Ransford, B., Clark, S. S., Defend, B., Morgan, W., … and Maisel, W. H. (2008, May). Pacemakers and implantable cardiac defibrillators: Software radio attacks and zero-power defenses. *Proceedings of the 29th Annual IEEE Symposium on Security and Privacy.* Accessed on March 10, 2017, from www.secure-medicine.org/public/publications/icd-study.pdf.

5. Radcliffe, J. (2011, Aug. 4). *Hacking medical devices for fun and insulin: Breaking the human SCADA system.* Black Hat 2011 Conference. Accessed on March 10, 2017, from media.blackhat.com/bh-us-11/Radcliffe/BH_US_11_Radcliffe_ Hacking_Medical_Devices_Slides.pdf.

6. ICS-CERT. (2013, June 13; revised 2013, Oct. 29). *Alert (ICS-ALERT-13-164-01) medical devices hard-coded passwords.* Accessed on March 10, 2017, from ics-cert.us-cert.gov/alerts/ICS-ALERT-13-164-01.

PART VI

7. Bruemmer, D. (2015, June 22). *Medical device security in a connected world.* NCHICA Annual Conference. Accessed on March 10, 2017, from nchica.org/wp-content/uploads/2015/06/Bruemmer-Hudson-Wirth.pdf.

8. Sarvestani, A. (2014, Aug. 15). Hospital patient hacks his own morphine pump. *MassDevice Today.* Accessed on March 10, 2017, from www.massdevice.com/hospital-patient-hacks-his-own-morphine-pump-massdevicecom-call/.

9. TrapX. (2015, June 4). *Anatomy of an attack: MEDJACK (Medical Device Hijack).* Accessed on March 10, 2017, from deceive.trapx.com/rs/929-JEW-675/images/AOA_Report_TrapX_AnatomyOfAttack-MEDJACK.pdf.

10. TrapX. (2016, June 27). *MEDJACK.2 hospitals under siege.* Accessed on March 10, 2017, from deceive.trapx.com/rs/929-JEW-675/images/AOA_Report_TrapX_MEDJACK.2.pdf.

11. Pauli, D. (2015, Sept. 29). Thousands of "directly hackable" hospital devices exposed online. *The Register.* Accessed on March 10, 2017, from www.theregister.co.uk/2015/09/29/thousands_of_directly_hackable_hospital_devices_found_exposed/.

12. U.S. Food and Drug Administration (FDA). (2015, Aug. 14). *Overview of device regulation.* Accessed on August 23, 2016, from www.fda.gov/MedicalDevices/DeviceRegulationandGuidance/Overview/.

13. FDA. (2016, Aug. 8). *Deciding when to submit a 510(k) for a change to an existing device.* Accessed on August 23, 2016, from www.fda.gov/downloads/MedicalDevices/DeviceRegulationandGuidance/GuidanceDocuments/UCM514771.pdf.

14. FDA. (2015, July 28). *Information for healthcare organizations about FDA's "Guidance for industry: Cybersecurity for networked medical devices containing off-the-shelf (OTS) software."* Accessed on August 23, 2016, from www.fda.gov/RegulatoryInformation/Guidances/ucm070634.htm.

15. Association for the Advancement of Medical Instrumentation (AAMI). (2017, Feb. 28). *Seven cybersecurity myths put to the test.* Accessed on March 10, 2017, from www.aami.org/newsviews/newsdetail.aspx?ItemNumber=4191.

16. Integrating the Healthcare Enterprise (IHE). (2015, Oct. 14). *Medical device software patching.* IHE PCD Technical Committee in cooperation with MDISS. Accessed on August 23, 2016, from http://ihe.net/uploadedFiles/Documents/PCD/IHE_PCD_WP_Patching_Rev1.1_2015-10-14.pdf.

17. FDA. (2014, Oct. 2). *Content of premarket submissions for management of cybersecurity in medical devices: Guidance for industry and Food and Drug Administration staff.* Accessed on August 23, 2016, from www.fda.gov/downloads/MedicalDevices/DeviceRegulationandGuidance/GuidanceDocuments/UCM356190.pdf.

18. FDA. (2016, Dec. 28). *Postmarket management of cybersecurity in medical devices: Guidance for industry and Food and Drug Administration staff.* Accessed on March 10, 2017, from www.fda.gov/downloads/medicaldevices/deviceregulationandguidance/guidancedocuments/ucm482022.pdf.

19. IHE. (2015, Oct. 14). *Medical equipment management (MEM): Medical device cybersecurity—Best practice guide.* IHE PCD Technical Committee. Accessed on August 23, 2016, from http://ihe.net/uploadedFiles/Documents/PCD/IHE_PCD_WP_Cyber-Security_Rev1.1_2015-10-14.pdf.

20. HIMSS, ACCE, NEMA. (2013, Oct. 7). *Manufacturer disclosure statement for medical device security (MDS²).* Accessed on August 23, 2016, from www.himss.org/resourcelibrary/MDS2.

21. AAMI. (2011, March). *Getting started with IEC 80001: Essential information for healthcare providers managing medical IT networks.* Accessed on August 23, 2016, from www.aami.org/productspublications/ProductDetail.aspx?ItemNumber=918.

22. U.S. Department of Veterans Affairs. (2009, August). *Medical device isolation architecture guide, version 2.0.* Accessed on August 23, 2016, from www.himss.org/ResourceLibrary/ResourceDetail.aspx?ItemNumber=7236.

23. Symantec. (2016, April). *2016 Internet security threat report.* Accessed on August 23, 2016, from www.symantec.com/threatreport.

PART VII

Appendixes

AHIMA CHTS Exams Domain Maps

The following tables map each official CHTS exam domain to the corresponding chapters in which the information pertinent to the domain is covered.

CHTS-CP: Clinician/Practitioner Consultant Examination

Chapter Number	Chapter Title
Domain I	*Fundamentals of Health Workflow Process Analysis and Redesign*
10	Fundamentals of Health Workflow Process Analysis and Redesign
13	Navigating Health Data Standards and Interoperability
19	Non-EHR HIT: From Architecture to Operations
Domain II	*Quality Improvement*
20	EHR Implementation and Optimization
22	Using Healthcare IT to Measure and Improve Healthcare Quality and Outcomes
Domain III	*Working with HIT Systems*
11	Healthcare IT Project Management
19	Non-EHR HIT: From Architecture to Operations
20	EHR Implementation and Optimization
Domain IV	*Health Information Management Systems*
4	Healthcare Information Technology in Public Health, Emergency Preparedness, and Surveillance
16	Health Information Technology and Health Policy
29	Architectural Safeguards

CHTS-IM: Implementation Manager Examination

Chapter Number	Chapter Title
4	Healthcare Information Technology in Public Health, Emergency Preparedness, and Surveillance
15	Assuring Compliance with the Health Insurance Portability and Accountability Act
16	Health Information Technology and Health Policy
17	The Electronic Health Record as Evidence

CHTS-IS: Implementation Support Specialist Examination

Chapter Number	Chapter Title
Domain I	*Networking and Health Information Exchange*
8	Networks and Networking in Healthcare
14	Interoperability Within and Across Healthcare Systems
16	Health Information Technology and Health Policy
19	Non-EHR HIT: From Architecture to Operations
28	Healthcare Information Security: Operational Safeguards
Domain II	*Configuring EHRs*
7	Databases, Data Warehousing, Data Mining, and Cloud Computing for Healthcare
10	Fundamentals of Health Workflow Process Analysis and Redesign
12	Assuring Usability of HIT
19	Non-EHR HIT: From Architecture to Operations
20	EHR Implementation and Optimization
Domain III	*Vendor-Specific Systems*
12	Assuring Usability of HIT
13	Navigating Health Data Standards and Interoperability
19	Non-EHR HIT: From Architecture to Operations
20	EHR Implementation and Optimization
Domain IV	*Working with Health IT Systems*
11	Healthcare IT Project Management
19	Non-EHR HIT: From Architecture to Operations
20	EHR Implementation and Optimization
Domain V	*Installation and Maintenance of Health IT Systems*
9	Systems Analysis and Design in Healthcare

PART V

Chapter Number	Chapter Title
11	Healthcare IT Project Management
19	Non-EHR HIT: From Architecture to Operations
20	EHR Implementation and Optimization
Domain VI	**Information and Computer Science**
5	Computer Hardware and Architecture for Healthcare IT
6	Programming and Programming Languages for Healthcare IT
7	Databases, Data Warehousing, Data Mining, and Cloud Computing for Healthcare
8	Networks and Networking in Healthcare
9	Systems Analysis and Design in Healthcare
25	Framework for Privacy, Security, and Confidentiality
26	Risk Assessment and Management
27	Physical Safeguards, Facility Security, Secure Systems and Networks, and Securing Electronic Media
30	Healthcare Cybersecurity Technology
Domain VII	**Terminology in Health Care and Public Health Settings**
4	Healthcare Information Technology in Public Health, Emergency Preparedness, and Surveillance
13	Navigating Health Data Standards and Interoperability
14	Interoperability Within and Across Healthcare Systems

CHTS-PW: Practice Workflow & Information Management Redesign Specialist Examination

Chapter Number	Chapter Title
Domain I	**Fundamentals of Health Workflow Process Analysis and Redesign**
10	Fundamentals of Health Workflow Process Analysis and Redesign
13	Navigating Health Data Standards and Interoperability
19	Non-EHR HIT: From Architecture to Operations
Domain II	**Usability and Human Factors**
5	Computer Hardware and Architecture for Healthcare IT
12	Assuring Usability of HIT
23	Big Data and Data Analytics
24	Innovations in Healthcare Impacting Healthcare Information Technology

Chapter Number	Chapter Title
Domain III	*Health Management Information Systems*
4	Healthcare Information Technology in Public Health, Emergency Preparedness, and Surveillance
16	Health Information Technology and Health Policy
29	Architectural Safeguards
Domain IV	*Quality Improvement*
20	EHR Implementation and Optimization
22	Using Healthcare IT to Measure and Improve Healthcare Quality and Outcomes
Domain V	*Introduction to Information and Computer Science*
5	Computer Hardware and Architecture for Healthcare IT
6	Programming and Programming Languages for Healthcare IT
7	Databases, Data Warehousing, Data Mining, and Cloud Computing for Healthcare
8	Networks and Networking in Healthcare
9	Systems Analysis and Design in Healthcare
25	Framework for Privacy, Security, and Confidentiality
26	Risk Assessment and Management
27	Physical Safeguards, Facility Security, Secure Systems and Networks, and Securing Electronic Media
30	Healthcare Cybersecurity Technology
Domain VI	*Terminology in Health Care and Public Health Settings*
4	Healthcare Information Technology in Public Health, Emergency Preparedness, and Surveillance
13	Navigating Health Data Standards and Interoperability
14	Interoperability Within and Across Healthcare Systems
Domain VII	*The Culture of Health Care*
1	Healthcare Information Technology: Definitions, Stakeholders, and Major Themes
2	U.S. Healthcare Systems Overview
4	Healthcare Information Technology in Public Health, Emergency Preparedness, and Surveillance
15	Assuring Compliance with the Health Insurance Portability and Accountability Act
22	Using Healthcare IT to Measure and Improve Healthcare Quality and Outcomes

PART VII

CHTS-TR: Trainer Examination

Chapter Number	Chapter Title
Domain I	*Usability and Human Factors*
5	Computer Hardware and Architecture for Healthcare IT
12	Assuring Usability of HIT
23	Big Data and Data Analytics
24	Innovations in Healthcare Impacting Healthcare Information Technology
Domain II	*Training and Instructional Design*
19	Non-EHR HIT: From Architecture to Operations
20	EHR Implementation and Optimization
21	Training Essentials for Implementing Healthcare IT
28	Healthcare Information Security: Operational Safeguards
30	Healthcare Cybersecurity Technology
31	Cybersecurity Considerations for Medical Devices
Domain III	*Health Care and Public Health in the U.S.*
2	U.S. Healthcare Systems Overview
3	An Overview of How Healthcare Is Paid for in the United States
4	Healthcare Information Technology in Public Health, Emergency Preparedness, and Surveillance
Domain IV	*The Culture of Health Care*
1	Healthcare Information Technology: Definitions, Stakeholders, and Major Themes
2	U.S. Healthcare Systems Overview
4	Healthcare Information Technology in Public Health, Emergency Preparedness, and Surveillance
15	Assuring Compliance with the Health Insurance Portability and Accountability Act
22	Using Healthcare IT to Measure and Improve Healthcare Quality and Outcomes
Domain V	*Information and Computer Science*
5	Computer Hardware and Architecture for Healthcare IT
6	Programming and Programming Languages for Healthcare IT
7	Databases, Data Warehousing, Data Mining, and Cloud Computing for Healthcare
8	Networks and Networking in Healthcare
9	Systems Analysis and Design in Healthcare
25	Framework for Privacy, Security, and Confidentiality

Chapter Number	Chapter Title
26	Risk Assessment and Management
27	Physical Safeguards, Facility Security, Secure Systems and Networks, and Securing Electronic Media
30	Healthcare Cybersecurity Technology
Domain VI	*Health Information Management Systems*
4	Healthcare Information Technology in Public Health, Emergency Preparedness, and Surveillance
16	Health Information Technology and Health Policy
29	Architectural Safeguards
Domain VII	*Professionalism/Customer Service in the Health Environment*
18	Effective Organizational Communication for Large-Scale Healthcare Information Technology Initiatives

CHTS-TS: Technical/Software Support Staff Examination

Chapter Number	Chapter Title
Domain I	*Networking and Health Information Exchange*
8	Networks and Networking in Healthcare
14	Interoperability Within and Across Healthcare Systems
16	Health Information Technology and Health Policy
19	Non-EHR HIT: From Architecture to Operations
28	Healthcare Information Security: Operational Safeguards
Domain II	*Special Topics Course on Vendor-Specific Systems*
12	Assuring Usability of HIT
13	Navigating Health Data Standards and Interoperability
19	Non-EHR HIT: From Architecture to Operations
20	EHR Implementation and Optimization
Domain III	*Introduction to Information and Computer Science*
5	Computer Hardware and Architecture for Healthcare IT
6	Programming and Programming Languages for Healthcare IT
7	Databases, Data Warehousing, Data Mining, and Cloud Computing for Healthcare
8	Networks and Networking in Healthcare
9	Systems Analysis and Design in Healthcare

PART VII

HIMSS CAHIMS Exam Domain Map

The following table maps each official HIMSS CAHIMS exam domain to the corresponding chapters in which the information pertinent to the domain is covered.

Chapter Number	Chapter Title
Domain 1	*General*
A.	*Organizational Environment*
1	Healthcare Information Technology: Definitions, Stakeholders, and Major Themes
2	U.S. Healthcare Systems Overview
3	An Overview of How Healthcare Is Paid for in the United States
4	Healthcare Information Technology in Public Health, Emergency Preparedness, and Surveillance
15	Assuring Compliance with the Health Insurance Portability and Accountability Act
16	Health Information Technology and Health Policy
17	The Electronic Health Record as Evidence
18	Effective Organizational Communication for Large-Scale Healthcare Information Technology Initiatives
B.	*Technology Environment*
3	An Overview of How Healthcare Is Paid for in the United States
4	Healthcare Information Technology in Public Health, Emergency Preparedness, and Surveillance
8	Networks and Networking in Healthcare
13	Navigating Health Data Standards and Interoperability
14	Interoperability Within and Across Healthcare Systems
19	Non-EHR HIT: From Architecture to Operations
23	Big Data and Data Analytics
24	Innovations in Healthcare Impacting Healthcare Information Technology

About the CD-ROM

The CD-ROM included with this book comes complete with Total Tester customizable practice exam software with more than 450 practice exam questions, a glossary and "Healthcare Professional and Workforce Roles" appendix in PDF format, a PDF risk register (Table 26-1) and example risk map (Figure 26-1) from Chapter 26, and a secured PDF copy of the entire book.

System Requirements

The software requires Windows Vista or higher and 30MB of hard disk space for full installation, in addition to a current or prior major release of Chrome, Firefox, Internet Explorer, or Safari. To run, the screen resolution must be set to 1024 × 768 or higher. The secured book PDF requires Adobe Acrobat, Adobe Reader, or Adobe Digital Editions to view.

Installing and Running Total Tester Premium Practice Exam Software

From the main screen you may install the Total Tester by clicking the Total Tester Practice Exams button. This will begin the installation process and place an icon on your desktop and in your Start menu. To run Total Tester, navigate to Start | (All) Programs | Total Seminars, or double-click the icon on your desktop.

To uninstall the Total Tester software, go to Start | Control Panel | Programs And Features, and then select the Total Tester program. Select Remove, and Windows will completely uninstall the software.

Total Tester Premium Practice Exam Software

Total Tester provides you with a simulation of the CAHIMS exam and the CHTS exams. Exams can be taken in Practice Mode, Exam Mode, or Custom Mode. Practice Mode provides an assistance window with references to the book, explanations of the answers, and the option to check your answer as you take the test. Exam Mode provides a simulation of the actual exam. The number of questions, the types of questions, and the time allowed are intended to be an accurate representation of the exam environment. Custom Mode allows you to create custom exams from selected domains or chapters, and you can further customize the number of questions and time allowed.

To take a test, launch the program and select CAHIMS or the CHTS test you want to take from the Installed Question Packs list. You can then select Practice Mode, Exam Mode, or Custom Mode. All exams provide an overall grade and a grade broken down by domain.

Secured Book PDF

The entire contents of the book are provided in secured PDF format on the CD-ROM. This file is viewable on your computer and many portable devices.

- **To view the PDF on a computer**, Adobe Acrobat, Adobe Reader, or Adobe Digital Editions is required. A link to Adobe's web site, where you can download and install Adobe Reader, has been included on the CD-ROM.

 NOTE For more information on Adobe Reader and to check for the most recent version of the software, visit Adobe's web site at www.adobe.com and search for the free Adobe Reader or look for Adobe Reader on the product page. Adobe Digital Editions can also be downloaded from the Adobe web site.

- **To view the book PDF on a portable device**, copy the PDF file to your computer from the CD-ROM and then copy the file to your portable device using a USB or other connection. Adobe offers a mobile version of Adobe Reader, the Adobe Reader mobile app, which currently supports iOS and Android. For customers using Adobe Digital Editions and an iPad, you may have to download and install a separate reader program on your device. The Adobe web site has a list of recommended applications, and McGraw-Hill Education recommends the Bluefire Reader.

Glossary and Appendix PDFs

A glossary and appendix ("Healthcare Professional and Workforce Roles") is available on the CD-ROM in PDF format. Simply click the links in the CD-ROM menu to launch the files.

Risk Register and Example Risk Map from Chapter 26

Enlarged versions of Table 26-1 (the risk register) and Figure 26-1 (example risk map) are included on the CD-ROM in PDF format for viewing in greater detail. Table 26-1 is printable so that you can use the risk register.

Technical Support

For questions regarding the Total Tester software or operation of the CD-ROM, visit **www.totalsem.com** or e-mail **support@totalsem.com**.

For questions regarding the secured book PDF, visit **http://mhp.softwareassist.com** or e-mail **techsolutions@mhedu.com**.

For questions regarding book content, e-mail **hep_customer-service@mheducation .com**. For customers outside the United States, e-mail **international_cs@mheducation.com**.

INDEX

Symbols

<% and %>, ASP commands, 125
{ } (curly brackets), in C language, 113–114

Numbers

2.4 GHz band
    mobile devices, 624
    WLAN topology, 190
2.5 GHz band, 802.11 standards, 189
3D printing, gap in, 607
3DES (Triple DES), 708
4G (fourth-generation) wireless, 624
5 GHz (ISM) band, 802.11 standards, 189–190
21st Century Cures Act, 2016, 418
45 CFR Part 160, HIPAA Enforcement Rule, 389–390
45 CFR Part 164
    Subpart C, HIPAA Security Rule, 381–386
    Subpart D, HIPAA Breach Notification Rule, 386–389
    Subpart E, HIPAA Privacy Rule, 376–381
802.1Q protocol, VLANs, 195
802.11 (Wi-Fi) standard, IEEE, 189–190, 327

A

A (Addressable) code, HIPAA, 381
AAMC (Association of American Medical Colleges), physicians, 34
AARP (American Association of Retired Persons), 628
ABCs (Active Bacterial Core surveillance), CDC, 39
ABEO Smart Shoe, 627
ABMS (American Board of Medical Specialties), physicians, 34
ACA (Affordable Care Act)
    efforts of President Trump to repeal, 10, 415–416, 420
    as foundation of current health system, 442
    individual privacy/security risks of, 640–641
    IRS responsibilities for taxes/penalties in, 419–420
    payment based on effectiveness of outcomes, 60, 640
    Prevention and Public Health Fund, 73
    provisions of, 36
    testing bundled strategies, 62
academic health centers, healthcare delivery via, 24
acceptance of risk, 682
access control
    802.11 standards, 189
    accountability, 348–350
    authentication, 345–348
    balanced with audit control, 349–350
    HIPAA Security Rule for facilities, 384
    HIPAA Security Rule for technical controls, 385
    languages, 365–366

medical records regulations, 352–353
    multilevel data confidentiality, 352
    other sources of rules for, 353
    overview of, 341–342
    personnel, 703
    physical database, 148
    physical safeguard standards, 650
    physical safeguards for devices, 698–700
    privacy consent/purpose of use and, 354–356
    review Q & A, 366–372
    roles and permissions, 350–351
    security technology safeguards, 658, 660
    summary of basic, 356–357
    user identity, 342–345
access control, in HIEs
    access control information, 360–362
    enforcement of, 358–359
    first rule of, 359
    metadata, 362–363
    push vs. pull, 358
    second rule of, 359
    user identity, 363–365
access control lists (ACLs), in threat isolation, 765
access points (APs), WLAN topology, 188–190
accordion model, of continuous learning, 603–604
accountability
    access control across healthcare systems, 348–350
    HIPAA Security Rule for device/media, 385
accounts, user. *see* user identity
accreditation, healthcare professional, 33–34
Accredited Standards Committee (ASC) X12, health data interchange, 326–327
ACGME (Accreditation Council for Graduate Medical Education), physicians, 34
ACI (Advancing Care Information), 81, 400
ACLs (access control lists), in threat isolation, 765
ACOs (accountable-care organizations)
    alternative payment model, 399
    continuum of care, 596
    as cultural transformation in healthcare, 593
    healthcare reform of, 471
    linking payment to quality measures, 566
    measuring outcomes based on, 640
    operational safeguards for, 732
    Pioneer ACO program, 64–65
action, create change via, 256
Active Bacterial Core surveillance (ABCs), CDC, 39
Active Server Pages (ASP), 124–126
acute care
    chronic care vs., 32
    EHR workflow development, 523
    types of settings for, 27–28

blood culture system, in delivery of patient care, 492

blood pressure, standardizing value sets, 573

Blue Zones, 594

blueprint, as result of Design phase, 221

Bluetooth

    intended for WPANs, 624

    NIST handling security of, 624

    wireless security and, 191

Blu-ray optical disks, 96

BMI as vital sign, 600

<body> tag, HTML, 120–121

bottom-up development, in SDLC, 224

BPM (business process management), 247–248

bps (bits per second), throughput measured by, 176

BRAIN initiative, Cures Act research into, 10

brain research, funding, 618

BRCA Challenge project, 622

Breach Notification Rule, HIPAA, 386–389

breaches, PHI data

    as expensive, 733

    HIPAA Breach Notification Rule, 386–387

    impact of, 718–719

    incident procedures as operational safeguard, 725

"bring your own device" (BYOD), in healthcare setting, 99, 729

BRM (business relationship manager), 489

Broadband Integrated Services Digital Network (BISDN), 170

broadcast mode, hub working in, 193–194

broadcasts, LAN, 182

Budgeted Cost of Work Scheduled (BCWS), earned-value analysis, 288

budgets, HIT planning process, 492

buffers, for staging information inbound/outbound, 604–605

Build, operational safeguards for software/system development, 722–723

bundled payment system, 399

Bureau of Labor Statistics, report on technicians/professionals preparation, 10–11

burn centers, acute care delivered via, 28

Burwell, Sylvia, 399

bus

    connecting components on motherboard, 94

    defined, 93

business

    in database application development, 137–138

    value of health data standards in, 333

business agreements, as operational safeguard, 653

business associate. *see* BA (business associate)

business associate agreement (BAA), 733

business continuity plan, HIPAA Security Rule contingency plan, 383

business process management (BPM), 247–248

business relationship manager (BRM), 489

business rules

    database application development, 137–138

    design ERD based on, 138–139

buy versus build, systems development, 228

BYOD ("bring your own device"), in healthcare setting, 99, 729

bytecodes, Java, 118

C

C language, 114–115

C++ language, 115–118

cabinet, United States

    executive branch powers/functions, 413–414

    Health Care Fraud Prevention and Enforcement Action Team, 421–422

cabling, network, 199

CAC (Common Access Card), DoD physical safeguards, 698–700

CAHIMS (Certified Associate in Healthcare Information and Management Systems)

    defined, 4

    healthcare information credentials/training/education, 12

    project management training, 267

Calico (Google-owned), 627

cancer

    BRCA Challenge project for breast, 622

    genetic testing for susceptibility to, 619

    precision medicine research on, 397, 618

cancer care hospitals, as specialty hospitals, 24

Cancer Moonshot program, 10

cancer registry, public health department, 76

CAPEX (capital expenditures), in budget planning process, 492

CAPM (Certified Associate in Project Management), 267

cardiology

    acute care in emergency department for, 27–28

    heart hospitals for, 24

CareGroup, 655

Carrier Sense Multiple Access with Collision Avoidance (CSMA/CA), 189

Carrier Sense Multiple Access with Collision Detection (CSMA/CD), 182

CART (Classification And Regression Tree) algorithm, applying data mining, 160

case law

    common law vs., 424

    judiciary responsible for, 423–424

    structure/function of U.S court system, 424

case scenarios, training evaluation via, 549

case sensitivity

    C language, 116

    C++ language, 116

    HTML tags, 120

categories

    health data standards, 326–331

    Structured Query Language, 136

CD optical disks, 96

CDA (Clinical Document Architecture), using LOINC coding system, 77

CDC (Centers for Disease Control and Prevention), 72

CDHPs (Consumer-Directed Health Plans), 53–54

CDISC (Clinical Data Interchange Standards Consortium), 330

CDRH (Center for Devices and Radiological Health), 785

CDSSs (clinical decision support systems)

    connection with quality measurement, 565–566

    content and structure standards, 330